GOOD GUIDE TO
DOG
FRIENDLY
PUBS, HOTELS
AND B&Bs 2007/8

1 3 5 7 9 10 8 6 4 2

Published in 2007 by Ebury Press, an imprint of Ebury Publishing

Ebury Publishing is a division of the Random House Group

Copyright © Alisdair Aird and Fiona Stapley 2007

Alisdair Aird and Fiona Stapley have asserted their right to be identified as authors of this work under the Copyright, Designs and Patents Act 1988

The Random House Group Limited Reg. No. 954009

Addresses for companies within the Random House Group can be found at www.randomhouse.co.uk

A CIP catalogue record for this book is available from the British Library

The Random House Group Limited makes every effort to ensure that the papers used in our books are made from trees that have been legally sourced from well-managed and credibly certified forests. Our paper procurement policy can be found on www.randomhouse.co.uk

Printed and bound in Great Britain by Cox and Wyman Ltd

ISBN 9780091909239

GOOD GUIDE TO
DOG
FRIENDLY
PUBS, HOTELS
AND B&Bs 2007/8

EDITED BY ALISDAIR AIRD AND FIONA STAPLEY
MANAGING EDITOR KAREN FICK
WALKS CONSULTANT TIM LOCKE
ADDITIONAL RESEARCH FIONA WRIGHT

EBURY PRESS

Contents

Introduction

Most of the staff who put this guide together own dogs and like going away with them. So we're rather well placed to know what places suit dog owners best – but we could never have put this book together without the help of the many thousands of reports we have had over the years from readers of our companion guides.

We have chosen just under 1,000 places with a real welcome for dogs and their owners. These are all places that we would have no hesitation in including in a 'non-dog' guide book – indeed, many of them are distinguished entries in one of our sister publications. They span a tremendous range of styles, from simple B&Bs or farmhouses through cheerful pubs and venerable inns to luxurious hotels. We have put particular effort into tracking down places with plenty of good walks nearby.

Information in this Guide was correct when it was researched towards the end of 2006. Unfortunately, over the years, we have found that establishments can change their policy on welcoming dogs. One bad experience with a dog guest can be enough to cause a place to completely rescind their dog welcome. It is therefore possible that by the time you come to making a reservation, a handful of places included in the Guide will no longer welcome dogs.

Do please help us by telling us about places you have visited with your dog. Simply send an e-mail to dogs@goodguides.com, write to Dogs, FREEPOST TN1569, WADHURST, TN5 7BR – no stamp needed if you post in the UK – or use the pre-printed forms at the back of the book.

Ten tips for top dog holidays

Making sure your dog enjoys a break as much as you do boils down mainly to common sense and a little forethought. And do think of other people – a little consideration for staff and other visitors goes a long way.

1. Always phone the establishment to discuss with the owners or manager what their rules are regarding dogs BEFORE you book a room. If you turn up with two large rottweilers without pre-booking, you might not get the warm reception you were hoping for. Many places set aside bedrooms that are particularly suitable for dogs, such as ground floor rooms or rooms with access to the outside. And often, there is a small charge for dogs – confirm this when booking.

2. Check your pet insurance to see that it covers personal liability – knocking over furniture, tripping up people, and so forth.

3. Check which areas your dog is allowed into, as some places will only allow them in bedrooms.

4. Most establishments will not allow dogs to be left alone in bedrooms as they could become unhappy, anxious or bored and then might howl endlessly or even end up chewing the room to pieces.

5. Make sure to take your dog's own bedding, a towel for drying muddy paws, and any favourite toys. Some places do provide bowls and food but often it's best to stick to regular mealtimes and the food they are used to.

6. Hairy dogs need a really thorough brushing beforehand, to minimise errant hairs.

7. Obviously, you wouldn't want to take a really unsociable dog away. Many proprietors have dogs and other animals of their own (and children of course), and therefore will not want a visiting pet that is difficult with them – or with other guests.

8. Do remember to keep your dog under control all the time – we find that it's more relaxing to keep even the best-behaved dogs on leads.

9. Make sure when you leave that there is no evidence that your dog has been there – either inside or out.

10. If you are hoping to explore the area, most proprietors will be able to point you in the direction of good nearby walks, and some attractions have facilities where you can leave your dog in special kennels; it is worth checking this beforehand.

In the countryside with your dog

Many dogs appreciate the countryside as much as their owners do. Whether your dog likes the hills, open heaths or coastal landscapes, there is plenty of choice across Britain. However, there's by no means unlimited access, and the law requires you to keep your dog under control and put it on a lead when crossing fields with livestock in. A farmer actually has the right to shoot dogs that are worrying his farm animals: though this is not a common occurrence, it does happen from time to time.

Places you can generally walk your dog in England and Wales are:

Public roads, though they're obviously not always ideal.

Most **beaches**. Some popular beaches ban dogs in the summer, and – even more than anywhere else – it is always considerate to clean up after your dog on beaches (as it is anywhere else).

Paths and tracks on **National Trust land** (apart from National Trust gardens and house estates, where you need a ticket to get in, though some of these welcome dogs on leads) that are dedicated as public land and have free access: these include areas of coast, woodlands and open land.

Canal towpaths unless there's a sign to the contrary.

Paths and tracks in areas of forest owned by the **Forestry Commission**, though these may be temporarily closed during felling operations.

Areas designated as **country parks**. Many of these are owned by local authorities, and you are allowed to wander where you like within them.

Anywhere along a **public footpath**, **public bridleway** or **public byway** (the three together are also known generically as **public rights of way**). Bridleways are also open to horse-riders and cyclists, and byways are open to all traffic, so unless these have a paved surface they can be a lot more muddy in wet weather. Public rights of way are normally signposted from roads, and once you're on them there may be **waymark arrows** (red for byways, blue for bridleways and yellow for footpaths). There are also paths where the landowner allows access as 'permissive paths' or 'licensed paths' but which aren't formally public rights of way; here the landowner has the right to close the path at any time.

Access land in uncultivated countryside, where you have a 'right to roam' under recent legislation (the Countryside and Rights of Way Act) that is now in effect across England and Wales.

Scotland has a quite different law about access to the countryside. There are some legal rights of way, but not many, and they aren't shown as such on OS maps. Generally things get by on an informal basis: there's a general tolerance towards walkers, who can effectively go anywhere on moorland and mountains outside the grouse-shooting and deer-stalking seasons. Dogs may not be welcome on moorland because of nesting game birds; look out for notices, or check locally at tourist information centres.

What the right to roam means

The new law on right to roam in four million acres of uncultivated land is the most radical change to countryside access for more than half a century. The new law was phased in during 2004 and 2005, and allows access on foot only to many areas of moors, mountains, downland, heaths and registered commons that have been designated as **access land**. Here you have the right to walk freely and don't have to stick to paths, although in places vegetation and the lie of the land won't make it universally possible to go absolutely everywhere. Not all uncultivated land is access land – just the bits that have been designated and mapped (some of it may have been open informally for years). And it doesn't cover farmland, woods, coast or parkland; even in areas of open-looking hills such as the South Downs, the access areas are quite confined.

A large number of new gates and stiles have been erected to allow you to get in to access land, though once you are inside the access area there may only be one exit. In many places special brown and white signs are placed at the entrance points to access land. These show a pictogram of a walker wandering through countryside. The latest OS Explorer 1:25,000 scale maps (see below) show where these access areas are.

Do note the restrictions: you must keep dogs on a lead if near livestock, and at all times during March to July; dogs may also, at any time, be banned temporarily or permanently from some areas of land such as places where birds tend to nest. You also aren't allowed to ride a horse, cycle, light fires, camp or feed livestock; if you do, you lose your right to roam for 72 hours. There may also be local restrictions on night-time access.

Getting information

OS maps Wherever you are in England and Wales, the first point of reference is the local Ordnance Survey (OS) map: both the purple-covered Landranger series (at a scale of 1:50,000, or about one and a quarter inches to the mile) and the orange-covered Explorer series (at a scale of 1:25,000, or about two and a half inches to the mile) show rights of way (green crosses for byways, long green dashes for bridleways and short green dashes for footpaths; sometimes these are partly overprinted with green diamonds denoting long-distance routes like the Cotswold Way); on Landranger maps it's the same set of symbols, but with red instead of green. Access land is shown with a yellow wash and a dark orange border, on Explorer maps only; they also show with an *i* in an orange circle the points of 'primary access', where there's an information board and a way in to the access land; but other gates and stiles giving you access on to the land aren't shown. Areas of other land that are always open as access land (National Trust, National Trust for Scotland and Forestry Commission) are shown on Explorer and Landranger maps with purple boundaries.

Dog stiles and gates Bridleways and byways use gates rather than stiles, which makes things much easier for dog walking, as some stiles are baffling for dogs. But you usually need local knowledge to find out whether a particular public footpath is going to be suitable for your dog in its provision of stiles and gates. Some councils and landowners are increasingly installing easily climbed stiles, or gates rather than stiles, or excellent stiles with dog gates built into them – and there's now a legal requirement for councils to take into account the needs of the less mobile when stiles or gates are installed. In the meantime, finding out if a certain path has dog-friendly stiles or gates isn't straightforward. Some local tourist information centres stock leaflets showing stile-free walks suitable for dogs.

Dogs on trains are carried free of charge. Obviously you need to have the dog on a lead. For journey planners: rail see www.nationalrail.co.uk. For buses see www.traveline.org.uk.

Guided walks are run by all sorts of organisations. The largest of these is the Ramblers' Association, which has local clubs across the entire country. Leaders may or may not allow dogs, so it's always worth checking first. For details of group walks and other events, as well as a wide array of information about where to walk, rights of access and walking gear, see www.ramblers.org. You can try a walk for free, but are expected to join the Ramblers' Association if you go on several. There's also the splendid Butcher's Great North Dog Walk (*www.cooksondogwalk.co.uk*), held each June in north-east England. A major fund-raising event, it has made it into the Guinness Book of Records as the largest dog walk ever held, with numbers each time now well in excess of 6,000 dogs.

Finally, although it's not really connected to dog walking, if you're into cycling and want to take your dog along with you, there are **dog cycle trailers** that hitch on to the back of your bike, allowing your dog to enjoy the ride. A search on www.google.co.uk for dog + "cycle trailers" comes up with plenty of results.

Factual Details

Each chapter is divided into two sections – Dog Friendly Pubs, followed by Dog Friendly Hotels, B&Bs and Farms. The explanation below tells you about the factual information we have included in each section.

Dog Friendly Pubs

We show opening hours for pubs and note any days that places are closed altogether, whether they have a restaurant, and if they offer bar food.

Standard food service times in pubs are 12–2, 7–9 Monday to Saturday (food service often stops a bit earlier on Sundays). If food times are significantly different to this, we list the times. We note days when we know pubs do not do food, but suggest you check first before planning an expedition that depends on getting a meal there.

Pubs that are out of the way may cut down on cooking times if they're quiet, which they tend to be except at holiday times.

Bedroom prices normally include full english breakfasts (if these are available, which they usually are), VAT and any automatic service charge that we know about. If we give just one price, it is the total price for two people sharing a double or twin-bedded room for one night. Otherwise, prices before the / are for single occupancy, prices after it for double. A capital B against the price means that it includes a private bathroom, a capital S a private shower.

Dog Friendly Hotels, B&Bs and Farms

The first price we give in each entry in this section of the Guide is the total for two people sharing a double or twin-bedded room with its own bathroom for one night in high season. It includes a full english breakfast, VAT and any automatic service charge that we know about.

We say if dinner is included in this total price, which it may be for some of the more remote places.

A price at the end of an entry tells you how much a place charges for your dog to stay.

Many hotels have very good value short break prices, especially out of season, so it's always worth asking.

If we know that the back rooms are the quietest or the front ones have the best views or the ones in the new extension are more spacious, then we say so.

We always mention a restaurant if we know there is one and we commend food if we have information supporting a positive recommendation. Many B&Bs will recommend nearby pubs for evening meals if they do not offer dinner.

Dog Quiz

Here is a fun quiz for you to try in the car on the way to your dog friendly destination. The answers are on page 342.

1. What's the name of the german shepherd which has been said to own luxury mansions (including a former home of Madonna) in several countries?
2. Who said 'You're the man now, dog!'?
3. Can you name any of the Queen's corgis?
4. Which breed is famous for rescuing people from drowning?
5. What was Laika famous for, and when?
6. Which is the biggest breed of dog?
7. Which is the smallest breed of dog?
8. How long ago did domestic dogs evolve from their ancestor the wolf?
9. What was the name of the dog featured in the named portrait of it in the 2006/7 David Hockney exhibition at the National Portrait Gallery?
10. Which can hear distant sounds best, dogs or humans?
11. What was the name of Stanley Ipkiss's dog in the film *The Mask*?
12. Which mythical three-headed dog guarded the gate to Hades, the lower world?
13. Which surprising breed of dog might turn up in whose wheelbarrow?
14. Huckleberry Hound resides in which national park?
15. In which language is the sound of a dog barking represented as 'wun, wun, wun'?
16. Brian was the snail, Ermintrude the cow. But who was the dog?
17. Which early Shakespeare play has Launce saying, 'I think Crab my dog be the sourest-natured dog that lives'?
18. The Hounds of the Baskervilles appeared in which area that is now a National Park?
19. What was the name of the dog whose biography was written by a sort of wolf?
20. What is the proper word for a dog's 'knee'?
21. What was Rod Steiger's dog called in *Across the Bridge*?
22. Which of these terriers is the odd man out: wire-haired fox, yorkshire, jack russell, bedlington, norfolk, cairn?
23. Name the dog in the title of Kent Lavoie's song 'Me and You and a Dog Named ...'.

24. What is Sharon Osbourne's pomeranian called?
25. Which dog was awarded the 'dog VC', the Dickin Medal, for making 20 parachute jumps with the SAS – but in fact didn't?
26. Who wrote that his dog would always come through even if his lover faded – in a 60s song hit?
27. When did the expression 'It's raining cats and dogs' become popular?
28. Who was Jock's mother, in *Jock of the Bushveld*?
29. When was the Dog Licence abolished in England, Wales and Scotland?
30. Can dogs blush?
31. On Independence Day, how many hot dogs will Americans eat: (a) 3 million, (b) 6 million, (c) 150 million?
32. How many vertebrae are there in a typical dog's undocked tail?
33. Dalmatians are born white all over – true or false?
34. What was the name of the little dog which helped Beethoven get out of the travelling cage in the film *Beethoven*?
35. Where is hound trailing a popular traditional sport?
36. What were the names of the dog hero and heroine of the Disney film *The Lady Is A Tramp*?
37. How tall is a typical parson jack russell?

Calendar of Dog Events

All the events listed here include some sort of doggy attraction – anything from working dog displays to a waggiest tail competition. Organisers of the events listed here have told us that well behaved dogs are welcome on a lead. As the Guide is biennial we have only given the month, so please ring to confirm the date before you set out, and it's worth checking that the dog welcome policy hasn't changed since we researched this information.

BEDFORDSHIRE
July
Old Warden
Bedfordshire County Show at the English School of Falconry with dog shows and working dog displays (01767) 627527
September
Old Warden
Bedfordshire Steam and Country Fair at the Shuttleworth Collection: working dog demonstrations, steam tractors, heavy horses, working crafts, motor show (01462) 851711

BERKSHIRE
May
Riseley
Animal Fun Day (0118) 932 6444
July
Riseley
Puppy Dog Picnic: lakeside show and displays (0118) 932 6444

CAMBRIDGESHIRE
July
Peterborough
Championship Dog Show inc dog agility at the East of England Showground (01733) 234451
October
Peterborough
Autumn Show: trade stands, heavy horses, pony club and have-a-go dog agility at the East of England Showground (01733) 234451

CHESHIRE
June
Tabley
Cheshire County Show: livestock, dog shows (over 100 classes), horses, flowers, food hall with live demonstrations, crafts, country pursuits, trade stands and main ring events (01565) 722050

August
Knutsford
Country Show at Tatton Park: gundog display, have-a-go fun scurry, sheepdog handling, lurcher and terrier shows, flyball racing, scurry driving, country trade, craft village (01283) 820548
Knutsford
Fun Dog Show at Tatton Park: turn up and take part – ten novelty classes including saddest eyes, waggiest tail and scruffiest dog, and fun agility course (01625) 534400

September
Cholmondeley
Game and Country Show at Cholmondeley Castle: gundog display, have-a-go fun scurry, flyball racing, sheepdog handling, lurcher and terrier shows, scurry driving, country trade, craft village (01283) 820548

CORNWALL
June
Wadebridge
Royal Cornwall Show: huge show with main arena, motor and steam fair, lots of animals and major dog show (01208) 812183

CUMBRIA
July
Carlisle
Cumberland County Show: main arena, lots of animals, countryside area, food hall and dog show at Rickerby Park (01697) 747397

August
Patterdale
Dog Day: sheepdog trials, foxhound and terrier shows, children's pet dog show, gun dog show, sheep, adults and children's fell race, trail hound races with bookmaker, crafts tent, tradestands, beer tent and refreshments (017684) 83407
Threlkeld
Sheepdog Trials (017687) 79032

September
Crooklands
Westmorland County Show at the Westmorland County Showfield: over 200 trade stands, dog shows and terrier racing (015395) 67804

DERBYSHIRE
August
Hope
Show and Sheepdog Trials at The Showground with vintage tractors and engines, classic cars and gundogs (01433) 620507
Ashbourne
Sheepdog Trials with a few stalls (07989) 150889
September
Chatsworth
Country Fair: dog agility, terrier racing and show, fun dog show, lurcher racing, sheepdog and gundog trials, grand ring, hot air balloons, trade and craft stands (01328) 701133
Hayfield
Sheepdog Trials and Country Show at Spray House Farm (01663) 746653/733644

DEVON
May
Clyst St Mary
County Show at Westpoint Arena, lots to see inc Dog Show daily (01392) 446000
July
Totnes
Totnes and District Show: terrier racing, possibly sheepdog display, livestock, donkeys, rabbits, craft tent, over 100 trade stands, show jumping and main ring entertainment (01548) 821070

DORSET
May
Sherborne
Country Fair at Sherborne Castle: dog scurries, dog show, dog agility displays, gundogs and retriever event. Also falconry, craft stalls and demonstrations of country crafts and skills, main ring attractions, rural and leisure pursuits demonstrations and heavy horses and rare breeds show (01935) 813182

ESSEX
September
Billericay
Essex Country Show: monster trucks, animal displays, steam engines, vintage cars, food hall and dog demonstrations (01268) 290229/532253

HAMPSHIRE
May
Highclere
Country Fair at Highclere Castle: sheepdogs, gun dogs, terriers and lurchers, shooting, trade shows, main arena demonstrations – till 31 May (01889) 563232/0845 2305175

Romsey
Hampshire Country Show at Broadlands: gundog display, have-a-go fun scurry, sheepdog handling, lurcher and terrier shows, scurry driving, country trade, craft village, reptile marquee (01283) 820548

July
Fordingbridge
Fordingbridge Show: gundog display, have-a-go fun scurry, sheepdog handling, lurcher and terrier shows, scurry driving, country trade, craft village (01283) 820548
Brockenhurst
New Forest and County Show: large agricultural and equestrian event with international showjumping, terrier racing, working hounds, horses, cattle, sheep, goats, flower show, crafts, forestry, ring dislays and 450 display stands (01590) 622400

HERTFORDSHIRE
May
Knebworth
Game and Country Show: gundog display, have-a-go fun scurry, sheepdog handling, lurcher and terrier shows, scurry driving, country trade, craft village (01438) 812661

ISLE OF WIGHT
April
Binstead
Canine Show at Brickfields Horse Country (01983) 566801

KENT
April
Tunbridge Wells
South Eastern Game and Country Show at Eridge Park: gundog display, have-a-go fun scurry, sheepdog handling, lurcher and terrier shows, scurry driving, country trade, craft village (01283) 820548

July
Detling
Kent Show: agricultural show with food, wine, rural crafts, game fair, terrier racing, sheepdogs, police dogs, gun dogs (01622) 630975

LANCASHIRE
July
Ribchester
Royal Lancashire Show: agricultural show with livestock, trade stands, sheepdogs and good companion dog show at Salesbury Hall Farm (01254) 813769

August
Garstang
Agricultural Show: cattle, sheep and horse competitions, vintage machinery displays, dog show, sheepdog display and parade of vintage and modern tractors (01253) 799119

LEICESTERSHIRE
August
Lutterworth
Country Fair at Stanford Hall: sheepdogs, gun dogs, terriers and lurchers, shooting, trade shows, main arena demonstrations (01889) 563232/0845 230 5175
October
Belvoir
Game and Country Show: gundog display, have-a-go fun scurry, sheepdog handling, lurcher and terrier shows, scurry driving, country trade, craft village (01283) 820548

NORFOLK
June
Norwich
Royal Norfolk Show: livestock, dog shows, trade stands, arena displays, gardening show, arts and crafts (01603) 748931
July
Holkham
Biennial Country Fair at Holkham Hall: dog agility, terrier racing and show, fun dog show, lurcher racing, sheepdog and gundog trials, grand ring, hot air balloons, trade and craft stands (01328) 701133
Snetterton
Summer Show: arena displays, trade stands, dog show, agility and flyball (0870) 366 6924
September
Sandringham
Game and Country Show at Sandringham House: gundog display, have-a-go fun scurry, sheepdog handling, lurcher and terrier shows, scurry driving, country trade, craft village, steam engines (01283) 820548

NORTHAMPTONSHIRE
April
Kelmarsh
Country Fair at Kelmarsh Hall: working dogs, terriers and lurchers, main arena demonstrations, crafts (01889) 563232/0845 2305175

NOTTINGHAMSHIRE
May
Newark
Newark and Nottinghamshire County Show inc gun dog display at Newark Showground (01636) 702627

OXFORDSHIRE
April
Thame
Thame Country Show: gundog display, have-a-go fun scurry, sheepdog handling, lurcher and terrier shows, scurry driving, country trade (01283) 820548

SOMERSET
July
Shepton Mallet
West Country Game Fair at the Royal Bath and West Showground: equine events, gun dog training, game cookery theatre, lurcher display team, racing terriers, turn up and enter dog shows (01884) 250230

STAFFORDSHIRE
September
Weston-under-Lizard
Midland Game and Country Fair: sheepdogs, gun dogs, terriers and lurchers, shooting, trade shows, main arena demonstrations (01889) 563232

SUFFOLK
March
Ipswich
Eastern Counties Country Show at Suffolk Showground: gundog display, have-a-go fun scurry, sheepdog handling, lurcher and terrier shows, craft village, scurry driving, country trade (01283) 820548

SUSSEX
June
Pulborough
Sussex Steam and Country Fair at Parham House: sheepdogs, gun dogs, terriers and lurchers, shooting, trade shows, main arena demonstrations (01889) 563232/0845 230 5175

WARWICKSHIRE
August
Stoneleigh
Town and Country Festival at Stoneleigh Park: top dog ring events, fun dog shows, canine makeovers, discover breeds, dog scurry (test your dog's speed against the clock) and international flyball (024) 7669 6969

WILTSHIRE
August
Calne
Wiltshire Game and Country Show at Bowood House: gundog display, have-a-go fun scurry, sheepdog handling, lurcher and terrier shows, scurry driving, country trade, craft village (01283) 820548

SCOTLAND
January
Aviemore
Sled Dog Rally in Glenmore Forest Park, the biggest event in the British husky calendar (0871) 277 6783

June
Ingliston
Royal Highland Show inc terrier racing, gundogs or sheepdogs (0131) 335 6200

WALES
August
Monmouth
Monmouthshire Show at Vauxhall Fields: biggest one day agricultural show in Wales with a variety of main and countryside ring attractions, horses, livestock, big dog show (over 1000 dogs), craft marquee, shopping mall, food hall and trade stands (01291) 691160

Bedfordshire

Dog Friendly Pubs

BIDDENHAM

Three Tuns *Village signposted from A428 just W of Bedford; MK40 4BD*

'Wonderfully ordinary' is the gentle commendation from one reader about this pleasantly straightforward thatched village pub. The low-beamed lounge has wheelback chairs round dark wood tables, window seats and pews on a red turkey carpet, and country paintings. The green-carpeted oak panelled public bar (readers have found it a bit smoky in here) has photographs of local sports teams, also darts, skittles, board games and dominoes. The dining area and lounge bar are no smoking; piped music. Standard but enjoyable food is served in generous helpings. On handpump, Greene King Abbot is kept under light blanket pressure alongside a guest such as Everards. There are seats in the attractively sheltered spacious garden, and a big decked terrace has lots of picnic-sets. The very good children's play area has swings and a climbing frame.

Greene King ~ Tenant Kevin Bolwell ~ Real ale ~ Bar food (not Sun evening) ~ Restaurant ~ (01234) 354847 ~ Children in dining room ~ Dogs allowed in bar ~ Open 11.30-2.30, 6-11; 12-3, 7-10.30 Sun

BROOM

Cock *High Street; from A1 opposite northernmost Biggleswade turn-off follow Old Warden 3, Aerodrome 2 signpost, and take first left signposted Broom; SG18 9NA*

Readers love the sense they get that little has changed over three centuries at this simple village green pub. There's no bar counter, so the very well kept Greene King IPA, Abbot and Ruddles County are tapped straight from casks by the cellar steps off a central corridor. Original latch doors lead from one cosy little room to the next (four in all), inside which you'll find warming winter open fires, low ochre ceilings, stripped panelling, and farmhouse tables and chairs on antique tiles. Straightforward but well liked bar food. The restaurant is no smoking; piped (perhaps classical) music, darts and board games. There are picnic-sets and flower tubs on the terrace by the back lawn, and caravanning and camping facilities are available.

Greene King ~ Tenants Gerry and Jean Lant ~ Real ale ~ Bar food (12-2.30,

7-9; not Sun evening) ~ Restaurant ~ (01767) 314411 ~ Children welcome ~
Dogs allowed in bar ~ Open 12-3(4 Sat), 6-11; 12-4, 7-10.30 Sun

HOUGHTON CONQUEST

Knife & Cleaver *Between B530 (old A418) and A6, S of Bedford; MK45*
3LA

You may well have to book at this nice-looking 17th-c dining pub, and do
be aware that they may not serve bar meals if the restaurant is full on
Saturday evenings and Sunday lunchtimes. With emphasis on good quality
ingredients, the food here is very well prepared. A nicely balanced bar
menu changes seasonally. Batemans XB and a beer from Potton are well
kept on handpump alongside Stowford Press farm cider, around 30 good
wines by the glass, and over 20 well aged malt whiskies. The rather lovely
dark panelling in the comfortably civilised bar is reputed to have come
from nearby ruined Houghton House. Maps, drawings and old documents
on the walls, as well as lamps, comfy seating and a blazing winter fire add a
cosy feel. The airy white-walled no smoking conservatory restaurant has
rugs on the tiled floor and lots of hanging plants. There's also a family
room, and tables on a terrace alongside a neatly kept attractive garden;
unobtrusive piped music.

Free house ~ Licensees David and Pauline Loom ~ Real ale ~ Bar food (12-2.30(2
Sat), 7-9.30; not Sun evening; see note in text about weekends) ~ Restaurant ~
(01234) 740387 ~ Children welcome ~ Dogs allowed in bedrooms ~ Open 12-
2.30(2 Sat, 3 Sun), 7-11; closed Sun evening, 27-30 Dec ~ Bedrooms:
£59B/£74B

NORTHILL

Crown *Ickwell Road; village signposted from B658 W of Biggleswade; SG18*
9AA

This jolly nice black and white pub stands just across from the church in a
green and peaceful village, with picnic-sets under cocktail parasols out in
front looking over the village pond. The smallish bar has a big open fire,
flagstones and low heavy beams, comfortable bow window seats, and well
kept Greene King IPA and Abbot and Old Speckled Hen and a guest such
as Brains Reverend James on handpump from the copper-topped counter.
On the left is a small dining area while on the right, the airy main no
smoking dining room has elegantly laid tables on bare boards, with steps up
to a smaller more intimate side room. The atmosphere throughout is warm
and relaxed with fairly unobtrusive piped music. Bar food includes
lunchtime sandwiches and daily specials. A sheltered side terrace has more
picnic-sets, and opens into a very large garden with a few widely spaced
canopied tables, plenty of trees and shrubs, a good play area, and masses of
room for children to run around.

Greene King ~ Tenant Kevin Blois ~ Real ale ~ Bar food (12-2.30(3 Sun),
6.30-9.30; not Sun evening) ~ Restaurant ~ (01767) 627337 ~ Children
welcome away from main bar ~ Dogs allowed in bar ~ Open 11.30-3, 6-11;
11.30-12 Sat; 11.30-11 Sun; 11.30-3.30, 6-11 Sat; 11-4 Sun, d Sun evening
in winter

OLD WARDEN

Hare & Hounds *Village signposted off A600 S of Bedford and B658 W of Biggleswade; SG18 9HQ*

Readers are full of praise for the splendid food served at this beautifully kept and rather elegant pub. Breads and ice-cream are home-made, and where possible they use local ingredients such as pork from the Shuttleworth estate. Service from well-turned-out staff remains attentive and friendly throughout the session. Rambling around a central servery, in cosy reds and creams, the four beamed rooms (now completely no smoking) have dark standing timbers, comfortable upholstered armchairs and sofas on stripped flooring, light wood tables and coffee tables, a woodburning stove in an inglenook fireplace and fresh flowers on the bar. Prints and photographs depict the historic aircraft in the Shuttleworth Collection just up the road. Although the accent is firmly on dining, you can pop in for just a drink. Charles Wells Eagle and Bombardier and a guest such as Greene King Old Speckled Hen are well kept on handpump, with eight or so wines by the glass including some from a local vineyard; piped music. The village itself is part of the Shuttleworth estate and was built about 200 years ago in a swiss style. The glorious sloping garden (with tables on a terrace) which stretches up to pine woods behind the pub, dates back to the same period and style, and there are some substantial walks nearby. Though there's an ample car park you may need to use the village hall parking as an overflow.

Charles Wells ~ Lease Jane Hasler ~ Real ale ~ Bar food (12-2(3 Sun), 6.30-9.30; not Sun evening, not Mon) ~ (01767) 627225 ~ Children welcome away from bars ~ Dogs allowed in bar ~ Open 12-3, 6-11; 12-10.30 Sun; closed Mon except bank hols; 26 Dec-1 Jan

RISELEY

Fox & Hounds *High Street; village signposted off A6 and B660 N of Bedford; MK44 1DT*

The speciality at this cheery bustling pub is their steaks: you choose your own piece and pay by weight – say, £11.60 for 8oz rump, £12.60 for 8oz of sirloin and £14.20 for 8oz of fillet – and watch it cooked on an open grill. Other good food is listed on blackboards. Even if you don't see anything you fancy, it's worth asking: they're very obliging here, and will try to cope with particular food requests. Service is normally very attentive and friendly, but it does get busy, and as they don't take bookings on Saturday night you may have to wait for your table and food. A relaxing lounge area, with comfortable leather chesterfields, lower tables and wing chairs, contrasts with the more traditional pub furniture spread among timber uprights under the heavy low beams; unobtrusive piped classical or big band piped music. Charles Wells Eagle and Bombardier are kept well on handpump alongside a decent collection of other drinks including bin-end wines and a range of malts and cognacs. An attractively decked terrace with wooden tables and chairs has outside heating, and the pleasant garden has shrubs and a pergola.

Charles Wells ~ Managers Jan and Lynne Zielinski ~ Real ale ~ Bar food (11.30-

1.45, 6.30-9.30 (12-2, 7-9 Sun)) ~ Restaurant ~ (01234) 708240 ~ Children welcome ~ Dogs allowed in bar ~ Open 11.30-2.30, 6.30-11; 12-3, 7-10.30 Sun

Dog Friendly Hotels, B&Bs and Farms

ASPLEY GUISE

Moore Place *The Square, Aspley Guise, Milton Keynes, Buckinghamshire MK17 8DW (01908) 282000* £75, plus special breaks; 63 well equipped, pretty rms. Elegantly restored Georgian house in attractive gardens, with cocktail bar and lounge, enjoyable food and nice breakfasts in light and airy Victorian-style conservatory restaurant, and friendly, helpful staff; 5 mins from Woburn Abbey and Safari Park; disabled access; dogs in bedrooms, reception and lounge; plenty of nearby walks

FLITWICK

Flitwick Manor *Church Rd, Flitwick, Bedford, Bedfordshire MK45 1AE (01525) 712242* £175, plus special breaks; 18 thoughtfully decorated rms with antiques and period pieces. 17th-c country house surrounded by acres of rolling gardens and wooded parkland; log fire in entrance hall, comfortable, tranquil lounge and library, and smart restaurant with fine french wines and imaginative food using home-grown and local produce; tennis, putting, croquet; dogs in downstairs bdrms

MARSTON MORETEYNE

White Cottage *Marston Hill, Marston Moreteyne, Cranfield, Bedfordshire MK43 0QJ (01234) 751766* £50; 6 comfortable rms. Neatly kept, white painted no smoking cottage with fine views across the gardens and countryside, residents` lounge, super breakfasts in attractive dining room (good evening meals weekdays only), and a friendly, relaxed atmosphere; nearby country walks; dogs in annexe rooms only

SANDY

Highfield Farm *Tempsford Rd, Sandy, Bedfordshire SG19 2AQ (01767) 682332* (off A1 S-bound carriageway just S of Tempsford flyover) £75; 8 well equipped rms with hospitality trays and home-made biscuits. Neatly kept no smoking whitewashed house and beautifully converted barns set well away from A1 with walks on own grounds (dogs must be on leads) and surrounded by attractive arable farmland; warmly friendly, helpful owner, open fire in comfortable sitting room, and breakfasts in very attractive light and airy dining room; farm cats (not allowed inside); disabled access; dogs in bedrooms and sitting room, £15 (£10 subsequent nights)

Berkshire

Dog Friendly Pubs

ALDWORTH
Bell *A329 Reading—Wallingford; left on to B4009 at Streatley; RG8 9SE*
A favourite with many readers, this warmly friendly 14th-c country pub is a very special place. It's quite unspoilt and unchanging and has been run by the same family for over 200 years who make sure that mobile phones, piped music and games machines are banned. With a good mix of customers, it's at its quietest on weekday lunchtimes, and the rooms have benches around the panelled walls, an ancient one-handed clock, beams in the shiny ochre ceiling, and a woodburning stove – and rather than a bar counter for service, there's a glass-panelled hatch. Well priced Arkells BBB and Kingsdown are superbly kept alongside Old Tyler, Dark Mild and a monthly guest on handpump from the local West Berkshire Brewery; Upton farm cider; no draught lager. They also serve good house wines and winter mulled wine. Excellent value bar food is limited to filled hot crusty rolls and a variety of ploughman's, and in winter they also do home-made soup. Darts, shove-ha'penny, and dominoes. The quiet, old-fashioned cottagey garden is by the village cricket ground, and behind the pub there's a paddock with farm animals. In summer there may be occasional morris dancers, while at Christmas local mummers perform in the road by the ancient well-head (the shaft is sunk 365 feet through the chalk). It tends to get very busy at weekends; dogs must be kept on leads.
Free house ~ Licensee H E Macaulay ~ Real ale ~ Bar food (11-2.30, 6-10.30; 12-2.30, 7-10 Sun; not Mon) ~ No credit cards ~ (01635) 578272 ~ Children in Tap Room ~ Dogs welcome ~ Open 11-3, 6-11; 12-3, 7-10.30 Sun; closed Mon

EAST ILSLEY
Crown & Horns *Just off A34, about 5 miles N of M4 junction 13; Compton Road; RG20 7LH*
Right in the heart of horse-training country, this bustling pub has lots of interesting racing prints and photographs on the walls, and the side bar may have locals (including stable lads) poring over the day's races. The rambling set of snug beamed rooms is relaxed and unpretentious, with soft lighting, a

blazing log fire, and tables tucked into intimate corners. There's also a separate no smoking snug (ideal for a small party), and an oak panelled dining room, as well as two more formal dining rooms. Bar food ranges from fairly straightforward to quite elaborate. They have Adnams Regatta, Brakspears, and Timothy Taylors Landlord on handpump, and over 150 whiskies from all over the world (some of the bottles have clearly been there for ages). Piped music, TV and games machine. Under two chestnut trees, there is a paved courtyard with comfortable new furniture; the surrounding countryside is laced with tracks and walks.

Free house ~ Licensee Sally Allsop ~ Real ale ~ Bar food (12-2.30, 6-9.30) ~ Restaurant ~ (01635) 281545 ~ Children welcome ~ Dogs allowed in bar and bedrooms ~ Open 11-11; 12-10.30 Sun ~ Bedrooms: £60S/£70B

INKPEN

Crown & Garter *Inkpen signposted with Kintbury off A4; in Kintbury turn left into Inkpen Road, then keep on into Inkpen Common; RG17 9QR*

Run by friendly people, this 16th-c brick pub has a lovely long side garden with picnic-sets and a play area, and there are plenty of good downland walks nearby. It is surprisingly substantial for somewhere so remote-feeling, and has an appealing low-ceilinged bar with a few black beams and a relaxed central bar serving well kept West Berkshire Mr Chubbs Lunchtime Bitter and Good Old Boy plus a guest such as Fullers London Pride or Timothy Taylors Landlord on handpump; decent wines by the glass and several malt whiskies. Three areas radiate from here; our pick is the parquet-floored part by the raised log fire, which has a couple of substantial old tables, a huge old-fashioned slightly curved settle, and a neat little porter's chair decorated in commemoration of the Battle of Corunna (the cats' favourite seat – they've two). Other parts are slate and wood, with a good mix of well spaced tables and chairs, and nice lighting. A good range of bar food includes quite a few thai curries. In a separate single-storey building, the well equipped bedrooms form an L around a pretty garden. James II is reputed to have used the pub on his way to visit his mistress locally.

Free house ~ Licensee Gill Hern ~ Real ale ~ Bar food (not Mon-Tues lunchtime) ~ Restaurant ~ (01488) 668325 ~ Children welcome ~ Dogs allowed in bar ~ Open 12-3, 5.30-11; 12-5, 7-10.30 Sun; closed Mon and Tues lunchtime ~ Bedrooms: £55B/£80B

REMENHAM

Little Angel *A4130, just over bridge E of Henley; RG9 2LS*

This attractive pub is all very roomy and relaxed. Several areas link openly together so you feel part of what's going on, yet each has its own distinct individual feel. There are well spaced seats and tables on the bare boards or ochre tiles, and furnishings are mainly in pale fabrics or soft suede, running from comfortable bar seats through tub chairs to deep sofas, with just a few prints on walls painted mainly in gentle seaside pastels. In one corner a case of art books and the like helps to set the tone. Imaginative cooking is modern international in style. The no smoking conservatory has unusual patterned tablecloths and grey Lloyd Loom wicker seating. The attractive curved bar counter has a good choice of a dozen wines by the glass (plus champagne), and Brakspears Bitter and Special on handpump; board games, unobtrusive piped music, and tv; live music Wednesday evenings. Service is friendly, helpful and unhurried – mildly continental in style. A sheltered floodlit back terrace has tables under cocktail parasols, looking over to the local cricket ground.

Brakspears ~ Lease Douglas Green ~ Real ale ~ Bar food (12-3, 7-9.30; 12-4, 7-9 Sun) ~ Restaurant ~ (01491) 411008 ~ Children allowed but must be well behaved and must be over 10 in evening ~ Dogs allowed in bar ~ Live music Weds ~ Open 11-11; 12-10.30 Sun

RUSCOMBE

Royal Oak *Ruscombe Lane (B3024 just E of Twyford); RG10 9JN*

The majority of customers come to this smartened up village pub to enjoy the wide choice of popular food. Throughout, it's open plan and carpeted (not the cheerful side garden room), and well laid out so that each bit is fairly snug, yet keeps the overall feel of a lot of people enjoying themselves. A good variety of furniture runs from dark oak tables to big chunky pine ones, with mixed seating to match – the two sofas facing one another are popular. Contrasting with the exposed ceiling joists, mostly unframed modern paintings and prints decorate the walls, mainly dark terracotta over a panelled dado; one back area has a big bright fruity cocktail mural. Bar food includes reasonably priced lunchtime snacks, tasty meals and set-course menus; friendly staff. Well kept Brakspears Bitter, Fullers London Pride, and a guest beer on handpump, and half a dozen nicely chosen wines in two glass sizes; the restaurant and conservatory are no smoking. Picnic-sets are ranged around a venerable central hawthorn in the garden behind (where there are ducks and chickens); summer barbecues, spit roasts and morris dancing. Please note, they no longer offer bedrooms.

Enterprise ~ Lease Jenny and Stefano Buratta ~ Real ale ~ Bar food (12-2.30, 7-9.30; 12-4 Sun; not Sun or Mon evenings) ~ Restaurant ~ (0118) 934 5190 ~ Children welcome ~ Dogs allowed in bar ~ Open 12-3, 6-11; 12-4 Sun; closed Sun and Mon evenings

SHINFIELD

Magpie & Parrot *2.6 miles from M4 junction 11, via B3270; A327 just SE of Shinfield – heading out on Arborfield Road, keep eyes skinned for small hand-painted green Nursery sign on left, and Fullers 'bar open' blackboard; RG2 9EA*

Unless you already knew, you'd never guess that this little brick roadside cottage contained a genuine pub (as indeed it has done since the 17th c). Go in through the lobby (with its antiquated telephone equipment), and you find a cosy and inviting high-raftered room with a handful of small polished tables – each with a bowl of peanuts (they don't do any food) – and a comfortable mix of individualistic seats from Georgian oak thrones to a red velveteen sofa, not to mention the armchair with the paw-printed cushion reserved for Spencer the dog. It's a charming and relaxed place to while away an hour or so in the afternoon beside the warm open fire!

Everything is spick and span, from the brightly patterned carpet to the plethora of interesting bric-a-brac covering the walls: miniature and historic bottles, dozens of model cars, veteran AA badges and automotive instruments, and mementoes of a pranged Spitfire (ask about its story – they love to chat here). Well kept Fullers London Pride and a changing guest on handpump from the small corner counter, a good range of malt whiskies and of soft drinks; very hospitable landlady. There are teak tables on the back terrace, and an immaculate lawn beyond. There are hog roasts and morris men at various summer events, and an annual beer festival in May with twenty-two real ales; Aunt Sally. Note the unusual opening hours; no children inside.

Free house ~ Licensee Mrs Carole Headland ~ Real ale ~ No credit cards ~ (0118) 988 4130 ~ Dogs allowed in bar ~ Open 12-7; 12-3 Sun; closed Sun evening

STANFORD DINGLEY

Bull *Off A340 via Bradfield, coming from A4 just W of M4 junction 12; RG7 6LS*

The half-panelled lounge bar of this attractive 15th-c brick pub reflects the motorsport and classic car interests of the licensees, and on Saturdays between April and October, owners of classic cars and motorcycles gather in the grounds. The main part of the building has an old brick fireplace, cushioned seats carved out of barrels, a window settle, wheelback chairs on the red quarry tiles, and an old station clock; a carpeted section has an exposed wattle and daub wall. The beamed tap room is firmly divided into two by standing timbers hung with horsebrasses. Well kept Bass, Brakspears Bitter, Greene King Morlands Original, and West Berkshire Good Old Boy and Skiff (exclusive to the pub) on handpump, and up to eight wines by the glass. Fairly traditional bar food includes lunchtime sandwiches and filled baguettes and they do Sunday roast. The dining room (which has waitress service at weekends only) and saloon bar are both no smoking; dominoes, ring-the-bull and piped music. In front of the building are some big rustic tables and benches, and to the side the big garden has plenty of seats. Morris men visit in August, and on St George's Day and New Year's Day.

Free house ~ Licensees Robert and Kate Archard ~ Real ale ~ Bar food (12-2.30, 6.30-9.30; not winter Sun evenings) ~ (0118) 974 4409 ~ Children in saloon bar and dining room ~ Dogs allowed in bar ~ Folk/blues 2nd Weds of month ~ Open 12-3, 6-11; 12-3, 7-10.30 Sun ~ Bedrooms: £68S/£85S

Old Boot *Off A340 via Bradfield, coming from A4 just W of M4 junction 12; RG7 6LT*

In warm weather you can sit in the quiet sloping back garden or on the terrace here and enjoy the pleasant rural views; there are more tables out in front. It's a stylish, 18th-c pub and very neatly kept inside, and the beamed bar has two welcoming fires (one in an inglenook), fine old pews, settles, old country chairs and well polished tables. The fabrics for the old-fashioned wooden-ring curtains are attractive, and there are some striking pictures and hunting prints, boot ornaments in various sizes, and fresh flowers. The well liked bar food is fairly straightforward. The dining conservatory is no smoking. Well kept West Berkshire Good Old Boy, Youngs Bitter, and a guest on handpump, and ten wines by the glass.

Free house ~ Licensees John and Jeannie Haley ~ Real ale ~ Bar food ~ Restaurant ~ (0118) 974 4292 ~ Children welcome ~ Dogs allowed in bar ~ Open 11-3, 6-11

WINTERBOURNE

Winterbourne Arms *3.7 miles from M4 junction 13; A34 S, then cutting across to B4494 Newbury—Wantage from first major slip-road (bearing left in Chieveley towards North Heath when the main road bends round to the right), and follow Winterbourne signs; RG20 8BB*

Charming both inside and out, this bustling country pub is run by friendly people. The bars have a collection of old irons around the fireplace, early prints and old photographs of the village, and a log fire; piped music. The peaceful view over the rolling fields from the big bar windows cleverly avoids the quiet road, which is sunken between the pub's two lawns. There's a good wine list with 16 by the glass (served in elegant glasses and including sparkling and sweet wines), and well kept Fullers London Pride, Ramsbury Gold, Wadworths 6X, and West Berkshire Good Old Boy on handpump. As well as a traditional lunchtime bar menu there are more imaginative daily specials, and they do a Sunday brunch. A large landscaped garden has been created this year to the side of the building and the furniture has been refurbished; pretty flowering tubs and hanging baskets. The surrounding countryside here is lovely and there are nearby walks to Snelsmore Common and Donnington.

Free house ~ Licensee Frank Adams ~ Real ale ~ Bar food (12-2.30, 6-10; all day Sun and bank hols) ~ Restaurant ~ (01635) 248200 ~ Children in restaurant ~ Dogs allowed in bar ~ Open 12-3, 6-11; 12-10.30 Sun

Dog Friendly Hotels, B&Bs and Farms

HUNGERFORD

Bear Hotel *41 Charnham St, Hungerford, Berkshire RG17 0EL (01488) 682512* £**105**, plus special breaks; 41 stylish, well equipped rms, some with views over the river. Civilised and carefully restored 13th-c hotel with open fires, a contemporary new cocktail bar, cosy and relaxing snug, good food in attractive beamed restaurant, and courtyard and riverside terrace; dog biscuits and maybe treats and doggy stockings at christmas; walks by canal or on common 2 mins away; dogs welcome in bedrooms

MAIDENHEAD

Sheephouse Manor *Sheephouse Rd, Maidenhead, Berkshire SL6 8HJ (01628) 776902* £**75**; 8 individually decorated no smoking rms. 16th-c former farmhouse with original beams, timber floors and antique pine doors, open fireplaces, english breakfasts, and two acres of gardens with children's playground; river path and footpaths nearby for walks; plenty of pubs and restaurants nearby for evening meals; self-catering also; disabled access; dogs in cottages only; bedding available; £5

STREATLEY
Swan at Streatley *High St, Streatley, Reading, Berkshire RG8 9HR (01491) 878800* **£150**, plus special breaks; 45 attractive rms, many overlooking the water. Well run, friendly riverside hotel with comfortable, relaxed lounges and bars, consistently good food in attractive restaurant, popular spa with indoor pool, restored Magdalen College Barge, and flower-filled gardens where dogs may walk – other walks nearby; disabled access; dogs in bedrooms and most public areas (not dining room); £13

Buckinghamshire

Dog Friendly Pubs

BOVINGDON GREEN
Royal Oak *¼ mile N of Marlow, on back road to Frieth signposted off West Street (A4155) in centre; SL7 2JF*

For those who enjoy their pudding wines, this friendly and rather civilised whitewashed pub is just the place to come to – they have a fantastic range of ten by two sizes of glass. There are 17 other wines by the glass, too, plus Brakspears, Fullers London Pride, and the local Rebellion IPA on handpump. Several attractively decorated areas open off the central bar, the half-panelled walls variously painted in pale blue, green or cream: the cosiest part is the low-beamed room closest to the car park, with three small tables, a woodburner in an exposed brick fireplace, and a big pile of logs. Throughout there's a mix of church chairs, stripped wooden tables and chunky wall seats, with rugs on the partly wooden, partly flagstoned floors, co-ordinated cushions and curtains, and a very bright, airy feel; thoughtful extra touches set the tone, with a big, square bowl of olives on the bar, smart soaps and toiletries in the lavatories, and carefully laid out newspapers – most tables have fresh flowers or candles. The raised dining area is no smoking. Using as much local produce as possible, the popular food is a contemporary blend of imaginative world cooking. A good few tables may have reserved signs (it's worth booking ahead, especially on Sundays); quick, helpful service, and piped music. A terrace with good solid tables leads to an appealing garden with plenty more, and there's a smaller garden at the side as well.

Salisbury Pubs ~ Lease Trasna Rice Giff ~ Real ale ~ Bar food (12-2.30(4 Sun), 7-10) ~ Restaurant ~ (01628) 488611 ~ Children welcome ~ Dogs allowed in bar ~ Open 11-11; 12-10.30 Sun; closed 25-26 Dec

CHALFONT ST GILES
White Hart *Three Households (main street, W); HP8 4LP*

The civilised bar here has been refurbished this year with chocolate leather seats and sofas and modern artwork on the mushroom coloured walls. There's quite an emphasis on the food, and the extended, spreading no smoking dining room (similarly furnished to the bar) is mainly bare boards

– the bright acoustics make for a lively medley of chatter – sometimes rather on the noisy side when it's busy. As well as lunchtime sandwiches, the menu includes some traditional dishes alongside good modern food. Greene King IPA, Abbot and Morlands Original on handpump, and several wines by the glass; broadsheet daily papers, piped music, and neatly dressed young staff. A sheltered back terrace has squarish picnic-sets under cocktail parasols, with more beyond in the garden, which has a neat play area. Please note, no under 21s (but see below for children).

Greene King ~ Lease Scott MacRae ~ Real ale ~ Bar food ~ Restaurant ~ (01494) 872441 ~ Children allowed if with an adult ~ Dogs allowed in bar ~ Open 11.30-2.30, 6-11; 12-10.30 Sun; closed evening 25 Dec, 26 Dec ~ Bedrooms: £77.50S/£97.50S

CHENIES

Red Lion *2 miles from M25 junction 18; A404 towards Amersham, then village signposted on right; Chesham Road; WD3 6ED*

The long-standing and friendly licensees here are determined in their goal to keep this well run place as a traditional pub serving a wide range of good British home-made food rather than a restaurant serving beer. The bustling, unpretentious L-shaped bar has comfortable built-in wall benches by the front windows, other traditional seats and tables, and original photographs of the village and traction engines; there's also a small back snug and a no smoking dining room (where, for the first time in 20 years they now take bookings). Very well kept Rebellion Lion Pride (brewed for the pub), Vale Best Bitter, Wadworths 6X, and a guest beer on handpump, and at least 10 wines by the glass. The hanging baskets and window boxes are pretty in summer, and there are picnic-sets on a small side terrace. No children, games machines or piped music.

Free house ~ Licensee Mike Norris ~ Real ale ~ Bar food (12-2, 7-10(9.30 Sun)) ~ (01923) 282722 ~ Dogs allowed in bar ~ Open 11-2.30, 5.30-11; 12-3, 6.30-10.30 Sun; closed 25 Dec

DENHAM

Swan *¼ mile from M40 junction 1 or M25 junction 16; follow Denham Village signs; UB9 5BH*

With particularly good interesting food and friendly, helpful staff, this civilised dining pub is, not surprisingly, very popular and it's best to book a table in advance. The rooms are stylishly furnished with a nice mix of antique and old-fashioned chairs and solid tables, individually chosen pictures on the cream and warm green walls, rich heavily draped curtains, inviting open fires (usually lit), newspapers to read, and fresh flowers; the dining room is no smoking. A smashing choice of 17 wines plus 10 pudding wines by two sizes of glass, and Courage Best, Rebellion IPA and Wadworths 6X on handpump; piped music. The extensive garden is floodlit at night, and leads from a sheltered terrace with tables to a more spacious lawn. It can get busy at weekends, and parking may be difficult. The wisteria is very pretty in May.

Salisbury Pubs ~ Lease Mark Littlewood ~ Real ale ~ Bar food (12-2.30(4 Sun),

7-10) ~ Restaurant ~ (01895) 832085 ~ Children welcome ~ Dogs allowed in bar ~ Open 11-11; 12-10.30 Sun; closed 25 and 26 Dec

DORNEY
Pineapple *2.4 miles from M4 junction 7; turn left on to A4, then left on B3026 (or take first left off A4 at traffic lights, into Huntercombe Lane S, then left at T-junction on main road – shorter but slower); Lake End Road; SL4 6QS*

It's the sandwiches which come in for highest praise at this nicely old-fashioned and unpretentious pub – a choice of five different fresh breads, good generous fillings, and at £5.95 quite a bargain as they come with your choice of hearty vegetable soup, salad or chips. Up to 1,000 varieties run from cream cheese with beetroot, smoked salmon and cream cheese to chicken, avocado, crispy bacon and lettuce with a honey and mustard dressing; Sunday roasts. China pineapples join the decorations on a set of shelves in one of three cottagey carpeted linked rooms, all no smoking, on the left. It's bare boards on the right, where the bar counter has Greene King IPA, Fullers London Pride and Hook Norton Old Hooky on handpump, good wines by the glass, and good coffee. Throughout there are low shiny Anaglypta ceilings, black-panelled dadoes and sturdy country tables – one very long, another in a big bow window. There is a woodburning stove at one end, a pretty little fireplace in another room; half the pub is no smoking. Plenty of young staff, a quietly friendly black labrador; the piped pop music is fairly unobtrusive; disabled access and facilities. A roadside verandah has some rustic tables, and there are plenty of round picnic-sets out in the garden, some on fairy-lit decking under an oak tree; the nearby motorway makes itself heard out here.

Punch ~ Lease Stuart Jones ~ Real ale ~ Bar food (12-9) ~ (01628) 662353 ~ Children welcome ~ Dogs welcome ~ Open 11-11; 11-10.30 Sun

HAWRIDGE COMMON
Full Moon *Hawridge Common; left fork off A416 N of Chesham, then follow for 3.5 miles towards Cholesbury; HP5 2UH*

This is a pretty setting, best enjoyed in summer when you can sit out on the terrace (which has an awning and outside heaters for cooler evenings), and gaze over the windmill nestling behind; plenty of walks over the common, too. The six real ales on handpump are quite a draw, too: Adnams, Bass, Brakspears Special, Fullers London Pride and Original, and Greene King Ruddles County. The low-beamed rambling bar is the heart of the building, with oak built-in floor-to-ceiling settles, ancient flagstones and flooring tiles, hunting prints and an inglenook fireplace. The pubby lunchtime menu, which runs from sandwiches up to stews and curries, is rounded out by fairly imaginative daily specials and more robust evening dishes; Sunday roast. They hold supper evenings with films or sports events shown on a 50-inch plasma screen, and there are eight wines by the glass; good service, cribbage, and piped music. Both the restaurants and one bar area are no smoking.

Enterprise ~ Lease Peter and Annie Alberto ~ Real ale ~ Bar food ~ Restaurant ~ (01494) 758959 ~ Children welcome ~ Dogs allowed in bar ~ Open 12-11; 12-10.30 Sun; closed 25 Dec

HEDGERLEY

White Horse *2.4 miles from M40 junction 2; at exit roundabout take Slough turnoff then take Hedgerley Lane (immediate left) following alongside M40; after 1.5 miles turn right at T-junction into Village Lane; SL2 3UY*

It's a very pleasant surprise to come across an old-fashioned drinkers' pub such as this in the Gerrards Cross commuter belt. There's a good mix of customers and a fine range of seven real ales all tapped from the cask in a room behind the tiny hatch counter: Greene King IPA and Rebellion IPA are well kept alongside five daily changing guests from anywhere in the country, with good farm cider and perry, and belgian beers too; their regular ale festivals are very popular. The cottagey main bar has plenty of character, with lots of beams, brasses and exposed brickwork, low wooden tables, some standing timbers, jugs, ballcocks and other bric-a-brac, a log fire, and a good few leaflets and notices about future village events. There is a little flagstoned public bar on the left; darts. On the way out to the garden, which has tables and occasional barbecues, they have a canopy extension to help during busy periods. The atmosphere is jolly with warmly friendly service from the cheerful staff. At lunchtimes they do bar food such as sandwiches, ploughman's, cold meats and quiches, and changing straightforward hot dishes. In front are lots of hanging baskets and a couple more tables overlooking the quiet road. There are good walks nearby, and the pub is handy for the Church Wood RSPB reserve. It can get crowded at weekends.

Free house ~ Licensees Doris Hobbs and Kevin Brooker ~ Real ale ~ Bar food (lunchtime only) ~ (01753) 643225 ~ Children in canopy extension area ~ Dogs allowed in bar ~ Open 11-2.30, 5-11; 11-11 Sat; 12-10.30 Sun

MENTMORE

Stag *Village signposted off B488 S of Leighton Buzzard; The Green; LU7 0QF*

All the 50 wines on the list in this pretty village pub are available by the glass; they offer champagne cocktails, too. If it's just a drink you are after, you must go to the bustling public bar where they serve Charles Wells Bombardier and Eagle IPA and maybe St Austell Tribute on handpump; board games. There's a small, civilised no smoking lounge bar with a relaxed atmosphere, low oak tables, attractive fresh flower arrangements and an open fire, though this tends to be used by customers heading for the restaurant. Bar food is fairly straightforward; no smoking restaurant. There are seats out on the pleasant flower-filled front terrace looking across towards Mentmore House, and a charming, well tended, sloping garden.

Charles Wells ~ Lease Jenny and Mike Tuckwood ~ Real ale ~ Bar food ~ Restaurant ~ (01296) 668423 ~ Children in eating areas but not in restaurant on weekend evenings ~ Dogs allowed in bar ~ Open 12-11(10.30 Sun); may be shorter opening hours in winter

PRESTWOOD

Polecat *170 Wycombe Road (A4128 N of High Wycombe); HP16 0HJ*

There's a good mix of chatty customers in this friendly and rather civilised pub – and an especially loyal local following. Opening off the low-ceilinged bar are several smallish rooms with an assortment of tables and chairs, various stuffed birds as well as the stuffed white polecats in one big cabinet, small country pictures, rugs on bare boards or red tiles, and a couple of antique housekeeper's chairs by a good open fire; the Gallery room and Drover Bar are no smoking. Enjoyable food from sandwiches up to more imaginative dishes is popular and fairly priced. Well kept Brakspears Bitter, Flowers IPA, Greene King Old Speckled Hen and Marstons Pedigree on handpump, quite a few wines by the glass, and 20 malt whiskies; piped music. The attractive garden has lots of bulbs in spring, and colourful hanging baskets, tubs, and herbaceous plants; quite a few picnic-sets under parasols on neat grass out in front beneath a big fairy-lit pear tree, with more on a big well kept back lawn.

Free house ~ Licensee John Gamble ~ Real ale ~ Bar food (not Sun evening) ~ No credit cards ~ (01494) 862253 ~ Children in Gallery Room and Drovers Bar ~ Dogs welcome ~ Open 11.30-2.30, 6-11; 12-3 Sun; closed Sun evening, evenings 25 and 31 Dec, all day 26 Dec and 1 Jan

SKIRMETT

Frog *From A4155 NE of Henley take Hambleden turn and keep on; or from B482 Stokenchurch—Marlow take Turville turn and keep on; RG9 6TG*

Our readers enjoy this bustling and friendly country pub – as somewhere to drop into for a pint after a walk along one of the many hiking routes, to enjoy a leisurely meal or stay overnight. The neatly kept beamed bar area has a mix of comfortable furnishings, a striking hooded fireplace with a bench around the edge (and a pile of logs sitting beside it), big rugs on the wooden floors, and sporting and local prints around the salmon painted walls. The function room leading off is sometimes used as a dining overflow. Although brightly modernised, there is still something of a local feel with leaflets and posters near the door advertising raffles and so forth. Modern imaginative food, and they also offer a good value weekday two and three-course set menu; you must book to be sure of a table. All the food areas are no smoking; piped music. Well kept Adnams, Rebellion IPA and Sharps Doom Bar on handpump, 15 wines by the glass (including champagne), and 20 malt whiskies. A side gate leads to a lovely garden with a large tree in the middle, and the unusual five-sided tables are well placed for attractive valley views. Henley is close by, and just down the road is the delightful Ibstone windmill.

Free house ~ Licensees Jim Crowe and Noelle Greene ~ Real ale ~ Bar food (12-2.30, 6.30-9.30; not winter Sun evening) ~ Restaurant ~ (01491) 638996 ~ Children welcome ~ Dogs allowed in bar ~ Open 11-3, 6-11; 11-11 Sun; 11-4 Sun in winter; closed Sun evening Oct-May ~ Bedrooms: £55B/£70B

STOKE MANDEVILLE

Woolpack *Risborough Road (A4010 S of Aylesbury); HP22 5UP*

The contemporary furnishings inside this partly thatched old pub are a triumphant blend of the traditional with the trendy. It's all very stylish, and original stripped beams, timbers and a massive inglenook log fireplace comfortably jostle for attention with gleaming round copper-topped tables, low leather armchairs and rich purple walls. In the comfortable, knocked-through front areas by the bar it's the wood and low beams that make the deepest impression, but there are also substantial candles artfully arranged around the fireplace, and illuminated Mouton Rothschild wine labels (designed by top artists) on the walls. Beyond here is a big, busily chatty dining room with chunky wooden tables, a dividing wall made up of logs of wood, thick columns with ornate woodcarvings, and a real mix of customers; it's no smoking in here. The good modern food includes rustic bread wood-fired pizzas and other imaginative dishes; prompt obliging service from uniformed young staff. Fullers London Pride and a changing guest on handpump, decent wines, and various coffees; piped music. Tables in the neatly landscaped back garden and on the new front terrace where there are outside heaters; large car park.

Mitchells & Butlers ~ Manager Abby Selby ~ Real ale ~ Bar food (12-2.30, 6-9.30; Sun 12-7.30) ~ Restaurant ~ (01296) 615970 ~ Children allowed but must be quiet and well behaved ~ Dogs allowed in bar ~ Open 12-11; 12-10 Sun

TURVILLE
Bull & Butcher *Off A4155 Henley—Marlow via Hambleden and Skirmett; RG9 6QU*

There are plenty of walks in the lovely Chilterns valley around this black and white timbered pub – which is handily open all day; no muddy boots inside. There are two low-ceilinged, oak-beamed rooms both with inglenook fireplaces (the Windmill lounge is no smoking), and the bar has a 50ft well incorporated into a glass-topped table, with tiled floor and cushioned wall settles. Brakspears Bitter, Special, and a seasonal guest, and Hook Norton Hooky Dark on handpump, and a good choice of wines by the glass; piped music. The imaginative bar food is popular, and they may serve cream teas and light bar snacks through the day during the summer months. There are seats on the lawn by fruit trees in the attractive garden and a children's play area. The village is popular with television and film companies; *The Vicar of Dibley*, *Midsomer Murders* and *Chitty Chitty Bang Bang* were all filmed here. The pub does get crowded at weekends.

Brakspears ~ Tenant Lydia Botha ~ Real ale ~ Bar food (12-2.30, 6.30-9.30; 12-4, 7-9.30 Sun and bank hol Mon) ~ Restaurant ~ (01491) 638283 ~ Children in eating area of bar and restaurant ~ Dogs allowed in bar ~ Open 12-11; 12-10.30 Sun

Dog Friendly Hotels, B&Bs and Farms

AYLESBURY
Hartwell House *Oxford Rd, Aylesbury, Buckinghamshire HP17 8NL (01296) 747444 (1.4 miles from A41, via A418 Oxford Rd)*, **£290**, plus special breaks; 46 rms, some large and well equipped, others with four-posters and fine panelling, inc 10 secluded suites in restored 18th-c stables

with private garden and statues. Elegant Grade I listed building with Jacobean and Georgian façades, wonderful decorative plasterwork and panelling, fine paintings and antiques, a marvellous Gothic central staircase, splendid morning room, and library; exceptional service, fine wines, and excellent food in no smoking dining rooms; 90 acres of parkland with ruined church, lake and statues and spa with indoor swimming pool, saunas, gym and beauty rooms, and informal buttery and bar; tennis, croquet and fishing; dogs walking in grounds and on nearby footpaths; children over 6; good disabled access; dogs in Hartwell Court

MARLOW

Compleat Angler *Bisham Rd, Marlow, Buckinghamshire SL7 1RG (01628) 484444* **£240**, plus special breaks; 64 pretty, stylish rms named after fishing flies and overlooking garden or river. Famous Thames-side hotel with oak-panelled, 400-year-old cocktail bar, comfortable lounge, spacious beamed restaurant and conservatory-style brasserie with riverside terrace, imaginative food, and prompt service; tennis, croquet, coarse fishing and two boats for hire; disabled access; dogs in bedrooms; £10

TAPLOW

Cliveden *Taplow, Maidenhead, Berkshire SL6 0JF (01628) 668561* **£265** (plus £7 each paid to National Trust), plus special breaks; 39 superb, luxurious rms. Superb Grade I listed stately home with gracious, comfortable public rooms, fine paintings, tapestries and armour, and a surprisingly unstuffy atmosphere; lovely views over the magnificent NT Thames-side parkland and formal gardens (open to the public); imaginative food in the two no smoking restaurants with lighter meals in the conservatory, super buffet breakfasts, and impeccable staff; Pavilion Spa with swimming pool, gym, etc.; tennis, squash, croquet, and boats for river trips; dogs can walk in most parts of the grounds; disabled access; dogs everywhere indoors except dining rooms and Spa; dog menu and dog sitting

WESTBURY

Mill Farmhouse *Westbury, Brackley, Northamptonshire NN13 5JS (01280) 704843* **£60**; 2 pretty rms. Carefully restored miller`s house on large farm with colourful big garden with swimming pool; plenty of original features and open fire in comfortable sitting/dining room, oak furniture and plenty of hunting prints; charming owners and good light suppers if ordered; two self-contained flats, too; resident dog and cat; footpaths and bridleways to walk along; disabled access; dogs in bedrooms by arrangement

WINSLOW

Bell *Market Sq, Winslow, Buckingham, Buckinghamshire MK18 3AB (01296) 714091* **£72**; 43 rms. Carefully furnished and elegant black and white timbered inn overlooking the market square, with beams and open fires, plush hotel bar, all-day coffee lounge, enjoyable bar food, and good lunchtime and evening carvery in restaurant; disabled access; dogs welcome in bedrooms

Cambridgeshire

Dog Friendly Pubs

CAMBRIDGE
Cambridge Blue *85 Gwydir Street; CB1 2LG*
The two peaceful rooms and attractive little conservatory at this friendly back street pub (which is completely no smoking) are simply decorated with old-fashioned bare-boards style furnishings, candles on the tables, and a big collection of oars; there's also the bow section of the Cambridge boat that famously rammed a barge and sank before the start of the 1984 boat race, and such a nice selection of rowing photographs you feel you're browsing through someone's family snaps; cribbage and dominoes. The interesting range of seven well kept real ales on handpump includes Adnams Bitter, Elgoods Black Dog, Woodfordes Wherry and changing guests from brewers such as Cottage, Hadrian & Border, Oakham and Old Cannon; they also have Aspall's farm cider, malt whiskies and fresh orange juice. Straightforward bar food and Sunday roast. Children like the surprisingly rural feeling and large back garden.
Free house ~ Licensees Chris and Debbie Lloyd ~ Real ale ~ Bar food (12-2.30, 6-9.30) ~ (01223) 505110 ~ Children welcome in conservatory ~ Dogs welcome ~ Open 12-2.30(3 Sat), 5.30-11; 12-3, 6-10.30 Sun

Free Press *Prospect Row; CB1 1DU*
This unspoilt little pub has a homely tucked-away atmosphere, and is completely no smoking. In winter you can sit peacefully reading a newspaper by the log fire (no piped music, mobile phones or games machines), and in summer the sheltered paved garden at the back is quite a suntrap. In a nod to the building's history as home to a local newspaper, the walls of its characterful bare-board rooms are hung with old newspaper pages and printing memorabilia, as well as old printing trays that local customers are encouraged to top up with little items. Well kept Greene King IPA, Abbot and Mild and a guest or two such as Caledonian 80/- and Titanic White Star on handpump, around 20 malt whiskies, and winter mulled wine; TV and quite a few assorted board games. Good value tasty bar food is served in generous helpings.
Greene King ~ Tenant Donna Thornton ~ Real ale ~ Bar food (12-2, 6-8.30;

not Sun evening) ~ (01223) 368337 ~ Children welcome till 8pm ~ Dogs allowed
in bar ~ Open 12-2.30(3 Sat, Sun), 6-11(7-10.30 Sun)

Live & Let Live *40 Mawson Road; off Mill Road SE of centre; CB1 2EA*
The landlord at this down-to-earth but popular old local is a real ale
enthusiast so there's usually an interesting selection of seven very well kept
beers from thoughtfully sourced brewers such as Cropton, Dark Star,
Fenland or Tring, plus around 20 belgian beers, and a dozen malt whiskies.
The atmosphere is relaxed and friendly, and the heavily timbered
brickwork rooms have sturdy varnished pine tables with pale wood chairs
on bare boards, and real gas lighting. An assortment of collectables takes in
lots of interesting old country bric-a-brac and some steam railway and
brewery memorabilia, and posters advertise local forthcoming events;
cribbage and dominoes. The eating area of the bar with simple but good
value home-made food is no smoking until 9pm; all day breakfast on
Saturday and roast lunch on Sunday.
Burlison Inns ~ Lease Peter Wiffin ~ Real ale ~ Bar food (12-2, 6(7 Sun)-9) ~
(01223) 460261 ~ Children in eating area of bar ~ Dogs welcome ~ Open
11.30-2.30, 5.30(6 Sat)-11; 12-2.30, 7-11 Sun

ELTON
Black Horse *B671 off A605 W of Peterborough and A1(M); Overend; PE8*
6RU
This well run dining pub has all you'd expect of a country inn from its
welcoming atmosphere and roaring fires to hop-strung beams, a homely and
comfortable mix of furniture (no two tables and chairs seem the same),
antique prints, and lots of ornaments and bric-a-brac including an intriguing
ancient radio set. Dining areas at each end of the partly no smoking bar have
parquet flooring and tiles, and the stripped stone back lounge towards the
restaurant has an interesting fireplace. Consider booking, especially on
Sunday, as the emphasis is very much on the good (though not cheap) food.
They may ask you to leave your credit card behind the bar, or pay on
ordering. As well as a good choice of 15 wines by the glass, the four real ales
on handpump such as Barnwell (brewed locally), Bass, Everards Tiger or
Nethergate Suffolk County do attract the odd local for a pint at the bar. The
big garden has super views across to Elton Hall park and the village church,
there are seats on the terrace, some tables shaded by horse chestnut trees, and
a couple of acres of grass for children to play.
Free house ~ Licensee John Clennell ~ Real ale ~ Bar food (12-2(3 Sun), 6-9; not
Sun evening) ~ Restaurant ~ (01832) 280240 ~ Children welcome ~ Dogs allowed
in bar ~ Open 12-11(12 Sat, 8 Sun); closed Sun evening

ELY
Fountain *Corner of Barton Square and Silver Street; CB7 4JF*
This simple yet genteel 19th-c corner pub, despite being very close to the
cathedral, manages to escape the tourists and maintain a local following.
Old cartoons, local photographs, regional maps and mementoes of the
neighbouring King's School punctuate the elegant dark pink walls, and

neatly tied-back curtains hang from gold colour rails above the big windows. Above one fireplace is a stuffed pike in a case, and there are a few antlers dotted about – not to mention a duck at one end of the bar. A recent extension at the back provides much needed additional seating. Everything is very clean and tidy, and there's no music, fruit machines or even food. Well kept Adnams Bitter and Broadside, Fullers London Pride and a changing guest such as Timothy Taylors Landlord on handpump. Note the limited opening times below.

Free house ~ Licensees John and Judith Borland ~ Real ale ~ No credit cards ~ (01353) 663122 ~ Children welcome away from bar until 8pm ~ Dogs welcome ~ Open 5-11(cl weekday lunchtimes); 12-2, 6-11.30 Sat; 12-2, 7-10.30 Sun

FEN DITTON
Ancient Shepherds *Off B1047 at Green End, The River signpost, just NE of Cambridge; CB5 8ST*

The nicest room at this solidly beamed old pub (now completely no smoking) is the softly lit central lounge, where you can't fail to be comfortable on one of the big fat dark red button-back leather settees or armchairs which are grouped round low dark wood tables. The warm coal fire, and heavy drapes around the window seat with its big scatter cushions, add to the cosiness. Above a black dado the walls (and ceiling) are dark pink, and decorated with comic fox and policeman prints and little steeplechasing and equestrian ones. On the right the smallish more pubby bar, with its coal fire, serves Adnams and Greene King IPA, while on the left is a pleasant restaurant (piped music in here). Generously served bar food is fairly priced. The licensee's west highland terrier, Billie, might be around outside food service times.

Punch ~ Tenant J M Harrington ~ Real ale ~ Bar food (12-2(2.30 Sun), 6.30-9) ~ Restaurant ~ (01223) 293280 ~ Children welcome with restrictions ~ Dogs allowed in bar ~ Open 12-2.30, 6-11; 12-5 Sun; closed Sun evening

HELPSTON
Blue Bell *Woodgate; off B1443; PE6 7ED*

Cheery service and reasonably priced food, including a senior citizens' two-course lunch, draws a happy crowd at this friendly bustling pub. Comfortable cushioned chairs and settles, plenty of pictures, ornaments, mementoes and cart-wheel displays, and piped music give a homely atmosphere to the lounge, smoking parlour and snug. The dining extension is light and airy with a sloping glass roof; no smoking except in the bar. Adnams Southwold, Everards Tiger and Old Original and a couple of guests from brewers such as Batemans and Greene King Abbot are served from handpumps, and there may be jam and marmalade for sale; darts, pool and board games; wheelchair access. A sheltered terrace has plastic garden tables under outdoor heaters.

Free house ~ Licensee Aubrey Sinclair Ball ~ Real ale ~ Bar food (not Sun evenings) ~ Restaurant ~ (01733) 252394 ~ Children welcome in dining areas ~ Dogs allowed in bar ~ Open 11.30-2.30, 5-11; 11.30-3, 6-12 Sat; 11-3.30, 6.30-11 Sun

HEYDON
King William IV *Off A505 W of M11 junction 10; SG8 7RY*
A charming assortment of rustic jumble fills the rambling rooms at this neatly kept dining pub. Its beamed nooks and crannies (warmed in winter by a log fire) are filled with ploughshares, yokes and iron tools, cowbells, beer steins, samovars, brass or black wrought-iron lamps, copper-bound casks and milk ewers, harness, horsebrasses, and smith's bellows – as well as decorative plates, cut-glass and china ornaments; piped music. Adnams Best, Fullers London Pride, Greene King IPA and Timothy Taylors Landlord are well kept on handpump. The tempting menu includes more vegetarian dishes than at most pubs. The restaurant and snug areas are no smoking; you will need to book at weekends. A wooden deck has teak furniture and outdoor heaters, and there are more seats in the pretty garden.
Free house ~ Licensee Elizabeth Nicholls ~ Real ale ~ Bar food (12-2, 6.30-9.30) ~ Restaurant ~ (01763) 838773 ~ Children welcome with restrictions ~ Dogs allowed in bar ~ Open 12-2.30(3 Sat), 6-11; 12-3, 7-10.30 Sun

HINXTON
Red Lion *2 miles off M11 junction 9 northbound; take first exit off A11, A1301 N, then left turn into village – High Street; a little further from junction 10, via A505 E and A1301 S; CB10 1QY*
The calmly quiet atmosphere at this carefully extended pink-washed 16th-c inn makes a restful break from the nearby M11, and it's not far from the Imperial War Museum at Duxford. Its dusky, mainly open-plan beamed bar has leather chesterfields on wooden floors, Adnams Best, Greene King IPA, Woodfordes Wherry and a guest such as City of Cambridge Hobson's Choice on handpump, ten wines by the glass, and Aspall's cider. Off here there are high-backed upholstered settles in an informal dining area (no smoking on Sundays), and the smart no smoking restaurant is filled with mirrors, pictures and assorted clocks. Fairly straightforward bar food is served by friendly helpful staff. It's peaceful too in the neatly kept big garden which has a pleasant terrace with picnic-sets, a dovecote and views of the village church.
Free house ~ Licensee Alex Clarke ~ Real ale ~ Bar food (12-2, 6.45-9(9.30 Fri, Sat); 12-2.30, 7-9 Sun) ~ Restaurant ~ (01799) 530601 ~ Well behaved children welcome ~ Dogs allowed in bar ~ Open 11-3, 6-11; 12-4, 7-10.30 Sun

KEYSTON
Pheasant *Just off A14 SE of Thrapston; village loop road, off B663; PE28 0RE*
The highly thought-of robustly flavoured modern cooking is the focus at this long low thatched inn. Although they do keep real ales, and its look is quite pubby, this is essentially a restaurant (now completely no smoking). Imaginative food (not cheap) is beautifully prepared using carefully sourced ingredients. Service is cheerful and efficient. The immaculately kept spacious oak-beamed bar has a comfortably civilised atmosphere, open fires, simple wooden tables and chairs on deep coloured carpets, guns on pale pink walls, and country paintings. An excellent range of drinks

includes a fine wine list with an interesting choice of reasonably priced bottles and 16 wines by the glass (plus eight sweet wines and two champagnes), fine port and sherry, freshly squeezed or locally pressed juices and Adnams Bitter and a couple of changing guests such as Oakham JHB and Potton Village Bike on handpump. There are seats out in front of the building (which has been owned by the Hoskins family for over 40 years).
Huntsbridge ~ Licensees Johnny Dargue and John Hoskins ~ Real ale ~ Bar food (12-2(2.30 Sun), 6-9.30) ~ Restaurant ~ (01832) 710241 ~ Children welcome ~ Dogs allowed in bar ~ Open 12-3, 6-11(10.30 Sun)

PETERBOROUGH
Brewery Tap *Opposite Queensgate car park; PE1 2AA*
An impressive range of 12 real ales is served at this enormous brewpub. Nine guests come from a plethora of thoughtfully sourced countrywide brewers, and the three Oakham beers (Bishops Farewell, JHB and White Dwarf) are produced here. They also keep a good number of bottled belgian beers, and a fun wine list with quite a few by the glass. The first thing that will probably grab your attention at this striking modern conversion of an old labour exchange is the vast two-storey-high glass wall that divides the bar and brewery, giving fascinating views of the massive copper-banded stainless brewing vessels. There's an easy going relaxed feel to the open-plan contemporary interior, with an expanse of light wood and stone floors for drinkers, blue-painted iron pillars holding up a steel-corded no smoking mezzanine level, and hugely enlarged newspaper cuttings on light orange or burnt red walls. It's stylishly lit by a giant suspended steel ring with bulbs running around the rim, and steel-meshed wall lights. A band of chequered floor tiles traces the path of the long sculpted light wood bar counter, which is boldly backed by an impressive display of bottles in a ceiling-high wall of wooden cubes. A sofa seating area downstairs provides a comfortable corner for a surprisingly mixed bunch of customers from young to old; there's a big screen TV for sporting events, piped music and games machines and DJs or live bands at the weekends. It gets very busy in the evening. They serve a comprehensive range of very tasty thai food.
Own brew ~ Licensees Stuart Wright, Jessica Loock, Paul Hook ~ Real ale ~ Bar food (12-2.30, 6-9.30; 12-10.30 Fri, Sat) ~ Restaurant ~ (01733) 358500 ~ Children welcome during food service times ~ Dogs allowed in bar ~ DJs or live bands weekends ~ Open 12-11; 12-10.30 Sun

REACH
Dyke's End *From B1102 E of A14/A1103 junction, follow signpost to Swaffham Prior and Upware – keep on through Swaffham Prior (Reach signposted from there); Fair Green; CB5 0JD*
Peaceful and cosy, this 17th-c farmhouse is in a charming village-green setting next to the church, with picnic-sets under big green canvas parasols out in front on the grass. Inside, a high-backed winged settle screens off the door, and the simply decorated ochre-walled bar has stripped heavy pine tables and pale kitchen chairs on dark boards with one or two rugs, a few rather smarter dining tables on parquet flooring in a panelled section on the

left, and on the right a step down to a red-carpeted bit with the small red-walled servery, and sensibly placed darts at the back. All the tables have lit candles in earthenware bottles, and there may be a big bowl of lilies to brighten up the serving counter. Adnams Bitter and a couple of guests from breweries such as Archers or Youngs are well kept on handpump alongside a good wine list, and Old Rosie cider. Bar food is enjoyable, and ranges from traditional to a little more adventurous. The entire pub is no smoking except for a small area by the bar.

Free house ~ Licensee Simon Owers ~ Real ale ~ Bar food (not Sun evening or Mon lunchtime) ~ Restaurant ~ (01638) 743816 ~ Children welcome with restrictions ~ Dogs allowed in bar ~ Open 12-3, 6-11(7-10.30 Sun); closed Mon lunchtime

Dog Friendly Hotels, B&Bs and Farms

ELY
Lamb *2 Lynn Rd, Ely, Cambridgeshire CB7 4EJ (01353) 663574* (Lynn Rd) *£95*; 32 comfortable rms. Pleasant, neatly kept 15th-c coaching inn near cathedral, with crackling log fire in reception room, two smart bars, enjoyable food in an attractive restaurant, very friendly staff, and limited car parking; dogs in bedrooms, £10

HUNTINGDON
Old Bridge *1 High St, Huntingdon, Cambridgeshire PE29 3TQ (01480) 451591* (just off A14; High St (ring rd just off B1044 entering from easternmost Huntingdon slip rd)) *£150*, plus wknd breaks; 24 excellent rms with CD stereos and power showers. Creeper-covered Georgian hotel with pretty lounge, log fire in panelled bar, imaginative british cooking and extensive wine list in the light, lively and informal no smoking restaurant; there's also a very smart and formal weekend evening restaurant; quick courteous service, riverside gardens where well behaved dogs are allowed, and walks behind the hotel; partial disabled access; dogs in bedrooms, bar, and lounge

SIX MILE BOTTOM
Swynford Paddocks *Six Mile Bottom, Newmarket, Cambridgeshire CB8 0UE (01638) 570234* (1 mile from A11, via A1304) *£135*; 15 individually furnished rms with good bthrms. Gabled country house in neat grounds overlooking stud paddocks; carefully furnished rooms with fresh flowers and log fires, bar decorated with Brigadier memorabilia (a tribute to the great racehorse who is buried in the hotel grounds), good food in no smoking conservatory Garden Room and restaurant, a relaxed atmosphere, and friendly service; tennis, putting and croquet; two resident bernese mountain dogs who live at the Gatehouse; dog walking in closeby recreation ground and surrounding fields or on Newmarket heath and gallops (after midday); disabled access; dogs in bedrooms and conservatory; £5

WANSFORD
Haycock *London Rd, Wansford, Peterborough, Cambridgeshire PE8 6JA*
(01780) 782223 (just off A1, highly visible just S of A47) £119, plus
special breaks; 48 individually decorated rms. 16th-c golden stone inn –
mainly no smoking – with relaxed, comfortable and carefully furnished
lounges and pubby bar; pretty lunchtime café, smart restaurant with good
food, excellent wines and efficient friendly service; garden with boules,
fishing and cricket; dogs can walk in the grounds and there are lots of
nearby country walks too; disabled access. The little village it dominates is
attractive, with a fine bridge over the Nene, and a good antiques shop; dogs
in some bedrooms

Cheshire

Dog Friendly Pubs

ALDFORD
Grosvenor Arms *B5130 Chester—Wrexham; CH3 6HJ*
As this bustling place is so popular and never disappoints it's worth visiting just outside peak times as they do serve food all day, otherwise it's best to book. A buoyantly chatty atmosphere fills its spacious open–plan interior, with good solid pieces of traditional furniture, plenty of interesting pictures, and attractive lighting adding a personal feel. The huge no smoking panelled library area has tall book shelves lining one wall, and lots of substantial tables well spaced on the handsomely boarded floor. Lovely on summer evenings, the airy terracotta-floored no smoking conservatory has lots of gigantic low hanging flowering baskets and chunky pale wood garden furniture. This opens on to a large elegant suntrap terrace (delightful for a summer evening drink), and a neat lawn with picnic-sets, young trees and a tractor. A particularly comprehensive range of drinks includes around 16 wines (largely new world and all served by the glass) a tempting range of whiskies (including 100 malts, 30 bourbons, and 30 irish whiskeys) as well as Flowers IPA, Caledonian Deuchars IPA, Weetwood and a couple of guests from brewers such as Beartown and St Austell. The menu is not ridiculously elaborate, it's sensibly imaginative, well balanced and fairly priced with something for everyone. Service is friendly, attentive and reliable. They keep a good selection of board games.
Brunning & Price ~ Managers Gary Kidd and Jeremy Brunning ~ Real ale ~ Bar food (12-10(9 Sun and bank hols)) ~ (01244) 620228 ~ Children welcome till 7pm, no prams or pushchairs ~ Dogs allowed in bar ~ Open 11.30-11; 12-10.30 Sun

ASTON
Bhurtpore *Off A530 SW of Nantwich; in village follow Wrenbury signpost; CW5 8DQ*
You're bound to feel completely spoilt for choice when it comes to ordering a drink at this enthusiastically run red brick free house. Each year, over 1,000 different superbly kept real ales – anything from Moorhouses to Wentworth – pass through the 11 handpumps. They also stock dozens of

unusual bottled beers and fruit beers, a great many bottled ciders and perries, over 100 different whiskies, carefully selected soft drinks and have a good wine list. If you're a very keen real ale enthusiast it's worth going during their summer beer festival. The pub takes its unusual name from the town in India, where a local landowner, Lord Combermere, won a battle, and in the carpeted lounge bar a collection of exotic artefacts has an indian influence, with one turbaned statue behind the counter proudly sporting any sunglasses left behind by customers; also good local period photographs, and some attractive furniture. Tables in the comfortable public bar are reserved for people not eating, several no smoking areas; darts, dominoes, cribbage, pool, TV and fruit machine. At lunchtime and early weekday evenings the atmosphere is cosy and civilised, and on weekends, when it gets packed, the cheery staff cope superbly. The enjoyable menu includes snacks (not Friday or Saturday night), five different tasty curries, traditional dishes and daily changing specials.

Free house ~ Licensee Simon George ~ Real ale ~ Bar food (12-9) ~ Restaurant ~ (01270) 780917 ~ Children welcome in dining room till 8pm ~ Dogs allowed in bar ~ Folk session third Thurs ~ Open 12-2.30(3 Sat), 6.30-11.30(12 Fri, Sat); 12-11 Sun

BARTHOMLEY

White Lion *A mile from M6 junction 16; from exit roundabout take B5078 N towards Alsager, then Barthomley signposted on left; CW2 5PG*

We're hoping that a tidy up at this lovely old 17th-c black and white thatched place won't detract from the unpretentious charm of the place. Up till now the main bar has kept a lovely timeless feel, with its blazing open fire, heavy low oak beams dating back to Stuart times, attractively moulded black panelling, cheshire watercolours and prints on the walls, latticed windows, and thick wobbly old tables. Up some steps, a second room has another welcoming open fire, more oak panelling, a high-backed winged settle, a paraffin lamp hinged to the wall, and shove-ha'penny, cribbage and dominoes; local societies make good use of a third room. Outside, seats and picnic-sets on the cobbles have a charming view of the attractive village, and the early 15th-c red sandstone church of St Bertiline across the road is well worth a visit. It's best to arrive early on weekends to be sure of a table if you are after their very good value lunchtime food. Well kept real ales on handpump include Marstons Bitter and Pedigree, Mansfield and a couple of guests such as Everards Tiger and Jennings Snecklifter.

Union Pub Company ~ Tenant Laura Cowdliffe ~ Real ale ~ Bar food (lunchtime only) ~ (01270) 882242 ~ Children welcome with restrictions ~ Dogs welcome ~ Open 11.30-11; 12-10.30 Sun

BUNBURY

Dysart Arms *Bowes Gate Road; village signposted off A51 NW of Nantwich; and from A49 S of Tarporley – coming this way, coming in on northernmost village access road, bear left in village centre; CW6 9PH*

This civilised dining pub is just the place for a relaxed chatty meal. An immaculately kept series of well laid out knocked-through cream-walled rooms rambles around the pleasantly lit central bar, and is furnished with an attractive variety of well spaced sturdy wooden tables and chairs, a couple of tall filled bookcases, a small amount of carefully chosen bric-a-brac, properly lit pictures, and good winter fires. Under deep venetian red ceilings, some areas have red and black tiles, some stripped boards and some carpet. They've lowered the ceiling in the more restauranty end room (with its book-lined back wall), and there are lots of plants on the window sills. Service is efficient and friendly, and most of the pub is no smoking. Food from a changing menu is tasty, just imaginative enough, attractively presented and fairly priced. Thwaites and Weetwood and a couple of guests such as Humpty Dumpty and Phoenix Arizona are very well kept on handpump, alongside a good selection of ten wines by the glass, around 20 malts and fresh apple juice. Sturdy wooden tables on the terrace and picnic sets on the lawn in the neatly kept slightly elevated garden are lovely in summer, with views of the splendid church at the end of the pretty village, and the distant Peckforton Hills beyond.

Brunning & Price ~ Managers Darren and Elizabeth Snell ~ Real ale ~ Bar food (12-9.30(9 Sun)) ~ (01829) 260183 ~ No children under 10 after 6pm ~ Dogs allowed in bar ~ Open 11.30-11; 12-10.30 Sun

CHESTER
Albion *Park Street; CH1 1RQ*

With a layout that's little changed since Victorian times, this strongly traditional pub is tucked away on a quiet street corner just below the Roman Wall, and has been leased by the same landlord for some 35 years. Most unusually, it's the officially listed site of four war memorials and attracts a handful of War veterans during commemorative events. Throughout the peacefully quiet rooms (no games machines or children here) you'll find an absorbing collection of World War I memorabilia, from big engravings of men leaving for war, and similarly moving prints of wounded veterans, to flags, advertisements and so on. Even the ancient pub cat is called Kitchener. The post-Edwardian décor is appealingly muted, with dark floral William Morris wallpaper (designed on the first day of WWI, a cast-iron fireplace, appropriate lamps, leatherette and hoop-backed chairs, a period piano and cast-iron-framed tables; there's an attractive side dining room too. Service is friendly, though this is a firmly run place: groups of race-goers are discouraged (opening times may be limited during meets), and they don't like people rushing in just before closing time. Three or four well kept real ales on handpump might be from brewers such as Batemans, Black Sheep and St Peters, with over 25 malt whiskies, new world wines, and fresh orange juice. The wholesome good value bar food is served in generous helpings. The eating area is no smoking in the evening. It can get very busy at lunchtime. If you stay here please tell us about the bedrooms.

Punch ~ Lease Michael Edward Mercer ~ Real ale ~ Bar food (12-2, 5(6 Sat)-8; 12-4 Sun, not Sun evening) ~ No credit cards ~ (01244) 340345 ~ Dogs allowed in bar ~ Open 12-3, 5(6 Sat)-11; 12-11 Fri; 12-3, 7-10.30 Sun ~ Bedrooms: £60B/£70B

EATON
Plough *A536 Congleton—Macclesfield; CW12 2NH*
The neatly converted bar at this attractive 17th-c village pub has plenty of beams and exposed brickwork, a couple of snug little alcoves, comfortable armchairs and cushioned wooden wall seats on red patterned carpets, long red curtains, mullioned windows and a big stone fireplace. Moved here piece by piece from its original home in Wales, the heavily raftered barn at the back is a striking restaurant. The entire pub is no smoking. The big tree-filled garden is attractive, with good views of nearby hills, and there are picnic-sets on the lawn and a smaller terrace. Local ingredients are used where possible in the very good home-made bar food and handful of interesting daily specials. Changing beers might include Copper Dragon, Hydes Bitter (very reasonably priced) and Moorhouses on handpump, and there's a decent wine list (ten by the glass). Service is friendly and attentive, and spare a few words for Thunder, the resident black labrador; piped music, TV. The appealingly designed bedrooms are in a converted stable block.
Free house ~ Licensee Mujdat Karatas ~ Real ale ~ Bar food (12-2.30, 6-8.30; 12-8 Sun) ~ Restaurant ~ (01260) 280207 ~ Children welcome ~ Dogs allowed in bedrooms ~ Open 11.30-11.30; 12 noon-1am Sat; 12-11 Sun ~ Bedrooms: £55B/£70B

HIGHER BURWARDSLEY
Pheasant *Burwardsley signposted from Tattenhall (which itself is signposted off A41 S of Chester) and from Harthill (reached by turning off A534 Nantwich—Holt at the Copper Mine); follow pub's signpost on up hill from Post Office; OS Sheet 117 map reference 523566; CH3 9PF*
Readers love the fantastic views from this half-timbered and sandstone 17th-c pub. On a clear day the telescope on the terrace (with nice hard wood furniture) lets you make out the pier head and cathedrals in Liverpool, while from inside you can see right across the Cheshire plain. A big side lawn has picnic-sets. The nicely timbered interior has an airy modern feel, with wooden floors and well spaced furniture including comfy leather armchairs and nice old chairs. They say the see-through fireplace houses the largest log fire in the county, and there's a pleasant no smoking restaurant. Four local Weetwood beers are well kept on handpump alongside a guest from a brewer such as Mallard, a selection of bottled beers, nine wines by the glass and around 20 malts; piped music, daily newspapers. Bar food is straightforward and pubby, and on summer weekends they sometimes have barbecues. Popular with walkers, the pub is well placed for the Sandstone Trail along the Peckforton Hills.
Free house ~ Licensee Andrew Nelson ~ Real ale ~ Bar food (12-3, 6-9.30 Mon; 12-9.30 (10 Fri/Sat, 8.30 Sun)) ~ (01829) 770434 ~ Children welcome till 6pm ~ Dogs allowed in bar and bedrooms ~ Open 12-11(12 Sat) ~ Bedrooms: £65B/£80B

PEOVER HEATH

Dog *Off A50 N of Holmes Chapel at the Whipping Stocks, keep on past Parkgate into Wellbank Lane; OS Sheet 118 map reference 794735; note that this village is called Peover Heath on the OS map and shown under that name on many road maps, but the pub is often listed under Over Peover instead; WA16 8UP*

A cheery welcome and tasty food are the principal attractions at this pleasant dining pub. It's pleasing however to be able to say that their remarkably well priced and rather interesting range of very well kept real ales (Copper Dragon Scotts 1816, Hydes, Moorhouses Black Cat and Weetwood Best) has earned them a new beer award this year. They also have Addlestone's cider, 35 different malt whiskies and eight wines by the glass. It can be busy here, so it's worth arriving early to try for a seat in the slightly more spacious feeling main bar. This is comfortably furnished with easy chairs and wall seats (including one built into a snug alcove around an oak table), and two wood-backed seats built in at either side of a coal fire, opposite which logs burn in an old-fashioned black grate. You may have a short wait for the generous helpings of traditional bar food. The dining room is no smoking; games machine, darts, pool, dominoes, TV and piped music. There are picnic-sets beneath colourful hanging baskets on the peaceful lane, and more out in a pretty back garden. It's a pleasant walk from here to the Jodrell Bank Centre and Arboretum.

Free house ~ Licensee Steven Wrigley ~ Real ale ~ Bar food (12-2.30, 6-9; 12-8.30 Sun) ~ Restaurant ~ (01625) 861421 ~ Children welcome ~ Dogs allowed in bar ~ Live music monthly Fri ~ Open 11.30-3, 4.30-11; 11.30-11 Sat; 12-11 Sun ~ Bedrooms: £55B/£75B

WINCLE

Ship *Village signposted off A54 Congleton—Buxton; SK11 0QE*

The two simple little tap rooms at this attractive 16th-c pub have an enjoyably welcoming atmosphere, thick stone walls and a coal fire. It's in an area of lovely countryside so can get very busy at weekends with walkers (they sell their own book of local walks, £3) and tourists so you may need to book. Tasty bar food, which is several notches up from straightforward pubby, is served by efficient young staff. A couple of thoughtfully sourced guest beers from brewers such as Titanic and Thornbridge are well kept alongside Fullers London Pride and Lancaster Duchy, belgian beers, Weston's farm cider and fruit wines; no smoking area. A small garden has wooden tables.

Free house ~ Licensee Giles Henry Meadows ~ Real ale ~ Bar food (12-2.30, 6.30-9.30; 12-3, 6.30-9.30(5.30-8 Sun) Sat; not Mon) ~ Restaurant ~ (01260) 227217 ~ Children in family room ~ Dogs allowed in bar ~ Open 12-3, 6.30-11; 12-11 Sat; 12-10.30 Sun; closed Mon

WRENBURY

Dusty Miller *Village signposted from A530 Nantwich—Whitchurch; CW5 8HG*

This substantial brick building, right next to the Shropshire Union Canal, is a neatly converted 19th-c corn mill – you can still see the old lift hoist up under the rafters. The River Weaver runs in an aqueduct under the canal at this point, and it was the river that once powered the millrace. These days a constant stream of boats slipping through the striking counter-weighted canal drawbridge, just outside here, provides entertainment if you're sitting at picnic-sets among rose bushes on the gravel terrace or at one of the tables inside by the series of tall glazed arches. The atmosphere is low-key restauranty, with some emphasis on the generously served monthly changing and gently imaginative menu, though drinkers are welcome, and in summer the balance may even tip. The spacious modern main bar area is comfortably welcoming, including long low-hung hunting prints on green walls, and a mixture of seats flanking the rustic tables that includes tapestried banquettes, oak settles and wheelback chairs. Further in, a quarry-tiled part by the bar counter has an oak settle and refectory table. All the dining areas are no smoking. Friendly staff serve three well kept Robinsons beers on handpump; eclectic piped music and dominoes.

Robinsons ~ Tenant Mark Sumner ~ Real ale ~ Bar food (12-2, 6.30-9.30; not Mon in winter) ~ Restaurant ~ (01270) 780537 ~ Children in dining area ~ Dogs allowed in bar ~ Open 11.30-3, 6.30-11; 11.30-11 Sat; 12-11 Sun; 11.30-3, 6.30-11 Sat and 12-3, 7-11 Sun winter; closed Mon lunchtime in winter

Dog Friendly Hotels, B&Bs and Farms

BEESTON
Wild Boar Hotel *Whitchurch Rd, Beeston, Tarporley, Cheshire CW6 9NW* (01829) 260309 £105.75, plus special breaks; 37 rms with appealing touches such as fresh fruit. Striking timbered 17th-c former hunting lodge, much extended over the years, with relaxed and comfortable bars and lounges, enjoyable bar meals and formal beamed restaurant, and friendly, professional service; lots of nearby walks; disabled access; dogs in ground-floor bedrooms only; £5

BICKLEY MOSS
Cholmondeley Arms *Cholmondeley, Malpas, Cheshire SY14 8HN* (01829) 720300 £70, plus special breaks; 6 rms. Airy converted Victorian schoolhouse close to castle and gardens (famously, Cholmondeley is pronounced 'Chumley'), with lots of atmosphere, very friendly staff, interesting furnishings, open fire, imaginative bar food, and very good choice of wines; disabled access; dogs in bedrooms (bring his own blanket)

FULLERS MOOR
Frogg Manor *Nantwich Rd, Broxton, Chester, Cheshire CH3 9JH* (01829) 782629 (A534 just E of A41 junction) £99, plus special breaks; 7 lavishly decorated rms with thoughtful extras. Enjoyably eccentric Georgian manor house full of ornamental frogs and antique furniture, open fires and ornate

dried-flower arrangements, a restful upstairs sitting room, cosy little bar, a large collection of 30s/40s records, and good English cooking in elegant dining room which leads to conservatory overlooking the gardens; disabled access; dogs in one bedroom only

HOOLE

Hoole Hall *Warrington Rd, Hoole, Chester, Cheshire CH2 3PD (01244) 408800* (just off M53 junction 12; off A56 towards Chester) £**87.50**, plus special breaks; 97 well equipped rms. Extended and attractively refurbished no smoking 18th-c hall with five acres of gardens where dogs may walk, good food in two restaurants, and friendly service; good disabled access; dogs in downstairs bedrooms with doors to terrace

KNUTSFORD

Longview *51-55 Manchester Rd, Knutsford, Cheshire WA16 0LX (01565) 632119* £**103**, plus special breaks; 32 individually decorated rms. Friendly family-run Victorian hotel with attractive period and reproduction furnishings, open fires in original fireplaces, cosy cellar bar, no smoking period-style restaurant, and good well presented food; cl Christmas and New Year; dogs can walk on the heath directly opposite hotel; disabled access; dogs in bedrooms; £10

MACCLESFIELD

Sutton Hall Hotel *Bullocks Lane, Sutton, Macclesfield, Cheshire SK11 0HE (01260) 253211* £**94.95**; 9 marvellous rms. Welcoming and secluded historic baronial hall, full of character, with stylish rooms, high black beams, stone fireplaces, suits of armour and so forth, friendly service, and good food in no smoking restaurant; resident dog; dogs can walk in grounds and along canal closeby; can arrange clay shooting/golf/fishing; partial disabled access; dogs in bedrooms only; £5

MOBBERLEY

Laburnum Cottage *Knutsford Rd, Mobberley, Knutsford, Cheshire WA16 7PU (01565) 872464* £**61**; 5 pretty rms. Neatly kept and friendly no smoking country guest house in an acre of landscaped garden; relaxed atmosphere in comfortable residents' lounge with books, a sunny conservatory, and very good food; resident cat, ducks and chickens; dogs can walk in the grounds and in nearby fields; dogs by arrangement in annexe; £5

POT SHRIGLEY   .

Shrigley Hall *Shrigley Park, Pott Shrigley, Macclesfield, Cheshire SK10 5SB (01625) 575757* (2.5 miles off A523, in Adlington just N of Macclesfield) £**118**, plus special breaks; 145 smart well equipped rms, some with country views. In over 260 acres of parkland, this impressive country house has a splendid entrance hall with several elegant rooms leading off, enjoyable food in the conservatory-style Courtyard Bar and restaurant, and good service from friendly staff; championship golf course, fishing, tennis, and leisure centre in former church building; resident cat; dogs can walk in grounds and in Lyme Park; plenty to do nearby; disabled access; dogs in bedrooms and restaurant; £15

TARPORLEY
Swan *50 High St, Tarporley, Cheshire CW6 0AG (01829) 733838* **£87.50**, plus special breaks; 16 rms. Well managed Georgian inn with a good mix of individual tables and chairs in attractive bar, well kept real ales, decent wines, and quite a few malt whiskies, good food from extensive menu, nice breakfasts, and friendly staff; limited disabled access; dogs in coach house annexe bedrooms

WORLESTON
Rookery Hall *Main Rd, Worleston, Nantwich, Cheshire CW5 6DQ (01270) 610016* (1.5 miles off A51/A500 roundabout N of Nantwich, via B5074) **£190**, plus special breaks; 46 individually decorated rms. Fine early 19th-c hotel in 38 acres of lovely parkland, with ornamental ceilings and polished mahogany panelling, elegant lounges, log fires, intimate restaurant with enjoyable food, and friendly service; disabled access; dogs in some bedrooms that include bowl, treats and bedding; £25

Cornwall

Dog Friendly Pubs

ALTARNUN
Rising Sun *Village signposted off A39 just W of A395 junction; pub itself NW of village, so if coming instead from A30 keep on towards Camelford; PL15 7SN*
Very popular with cheery locals (and their dogs), this is a pretty straightforward inn on the edge of Bodmin Moor. The low-beamed L-shaped main bar has plain traditional furnishings, bare boards and polished delabole slate flagstones, some stripped stone, guns on the wall, and a couple of coal fires. The central bar has well kept Bass, Cotleigh Golden Eagle and Tawny, Flowers Original, Greene King IPA, and Sharps Doom Bar on handpump, and decent house wines. Home-made bar food is hearty and traditional. A small back area has darts, games machine, juke box and a pool table, with a second pool table in the carpeted room beyond (no dogs allowed in that one); cribbage and dominoes. The main bar can get a bit smoky sometimes. There are tables outside; the field opposite has space for caravans, though screened off by high evergreens. The village itself (with its altarless church – hence the name) is well worth a look.
Free house ~ Licensee Jim Manson ~ Real ale ~ Bar food ~ No credit cards ~ (01566) 86636 ~ Children in family room only ~ Dogs allowed in bar ~ Open 11-3, 5.30-11; 11-11 Sat; 12-10.30 Sun ~ Bedrooms: £22/£40

BLISLAND
Blisland Inn *Village signposted off A30 and B3266 NE of Bodmin; PL30 4JF*
The present licensees of this welcoming local have offered over 2,000 guest beers during their time here. They keep up to eight at any one time tapped from the cask or on handpump and from all over the country, too: two are named for the pub (brewed by Sharps), as well as Cottage Normans Conquest, Itchen Valley Fagins, Larkins Best, Thwaites Mild, St Austell Black Prince and one from Uncle Stuarts. Every inch of the beams and ceiling is covered with beer badges (or their particularly wide-ranging collection of mugs), and the walls are similarly filled with beer-related posters and memorabilia. They also have a changing farm cider, fruit wines, and real apple juice. Above the fireplace a blackboard has the choice of

enjoyable, hearty home-made food; service is cheerful and friendly. The carpeted no smoking lounge has a number of barometers on the walls, a rack of daily newspapers for sale, a few standing timbers, and a good chatty atmosphere. The family room has pool, table skittles, euchre, cribbage and dominoes; piped music. Plenty of picnic-sets outside. The popular Camel Trail cycle path is close by – though the hill up to Blisland is pretty steep. As with many pubs in this area, it's hard to approach without negotiating several single-track roads.

Free house ~ Licensees Gary and Margaret Marshall ~ Real ale ~ Bar food (12-2.30(2 Sun), 6.30-9.30; may not do Sun evening food Jan/Feb) ~ (01208) 850739 ~ Children in family room only ~ Dogs welcome ~ Live music Sat evening ~ Open 11.30-11; 12-10.30 Sun

CADGWITH

Cadgwith Cove Inn *Down very narrow lane off A3083 S of Helston; no nearby parking; TR12 7JX*

Before – or after – a visit to this old-fashioned, bustling local you could enjoy one of the superb coastal walks in either direction. The two snugly dark front rooms have plain pub furnishings on their mainly parquet flooring, a log fire in one stripped stone end wall, lots of local photographs including gig races, cases of naval hat ribands and of fancy knot-work, and a couple of compass binnacles. Some of the dark beams have ship's shields and others have spliced blue rope hand-holds. Well kept Flowers IPA, Greene King Abbot, Sharps Doom Bar and maybe a guest on handpump. A plusher pink back room has a huge and colourful fish mural. One room and the area by the bar counter are no smoking. The home-made bar food is traditional, and it's best to check food times in winter. The left-hand room has darts, euchre and maybe piped music. A good-sized front terrace has green-painted picnic-sets, some under a fairy-lit awning, looking down to the fish sheds by the bay. The pub is set at the bottom of a steep working fishing cove; you can park at the top and walk down but it's quite a hike back up again.

Punch ~ Lease David and Lynda Trivett ~ Real ale ~ Bar food ~ (01326) 290513 ~ Children welcome away from main bar ~ Dogs welcome ~ Live music frequently in summer ~ Open 12-11(midnight Sat); 12-10.30 Sun; 12-3, 7-11 weekdays in winter (but open all day Fri then) ~ Bedrooms: £27.50/£55(£75S)

DULOE

Olde Plough House *B3254 N of Looe; PL14 4PN*

There's quite an emphasis on the popular food which is served by friendly, efficient staff in this neatly kept, well run pub. The small more modern restaurant is no smoking; piped music. Butcombe Bitter and Sharps Doom Bar on handpump and eight wines by the glass; local cider. The three communicating rooms have lovely dark polished delabole slate floors, some turkey rugs, a mix of pews, modern high-backed settles and smaller chairs, foreign banknotes on the beams, and three woodburning stoves. The décor is restrained – prints of waterfowl and country scenes, and a few copper jugs and a fat wooden pig perched on window sill. There are a few picnic-sets out by the road. The friendly jack russell is called Jack, and the two cats, Amy and Tia.

Free house ~ Licensees Gary and Alison Toms ~ Real ale ~ Bar food ~ Restaurant ~ (01503) 262050 ~ Children welcome away from main bar ~ Dogs allowed in bar ~ Open 12-2.30, 6.30-11; 12-2.30, 7-10.30 Sun; closed 25 Dec, evening 26 Dec

LANLIVERY
Crown *Signposted off A390 Lostwithiel—St Austell (tricky to find from other directions); PL30 5BT*

This is a proper old-fashioned pub (now no smoking) with a lovely chatty-buzzy atmosphere and a genuinely warm welcome from the licensees and their staff. The small, dimly lit public bar has heavy beams, a slate floor and built-in wall settles, and an attractive alcove of seats in the dark former chimney. A much lighter room leads off, with beams in the white boarded ceiling, cushioned black settles, and a little fireplace with an old-fashioned fire; there's also another similar small room. Bar food includes some local fish. Well kept Sharps Doom Bar and Eden Ale, and Skinners Betty Stogs and Cornish Knocker on handpump, seven wines by the glass, and local cider; board games. The slate-floored porch room has lots of succulents and a few cacti, and wood-and-stone seats, and at the far end of the restaurant is a sun room, full of more plants, with tables and benches. There's a sheltered garden with granite faced seats, white cast-iron furniture, and several solid wooden tables. The Eden Project is only ten minutes away.

Wagtail Inns ~ Licensee Andrew Brotheridge ~ Real ale ~ Bar food (12-2.30, 6-9.30) ~ Restaurant ~ (01208) 872707 ~ Children welcome but must be away from bar ~ Dogs allowed in bar ~ Live music Sun lunchtime ~ Open 12-11; 12-10.30 Sun; 12-3, 6.30-11 in winter ~ Bedrooms: £39.95S/£69.95S

MITHIAN
Miners Arms *Just off B3285 E of St Agnes; TR5 0QF*

A new garden area has been opened here and there are also seats on the back terrace, with more on the sheltered front cobbled forecourt. Inside, several cosy little rooms and passages are warmed by winter open fires, and the small back bar has an irregular beam and plank ceiling, a wood block floor, and bulging squint walls (one with a fine old wall painting of Elizabeth I); another small room has a decorative low ceiling, lots of books and quite a few interesting ornaments. The menu includes some interesting dishes, and the restaurant areas are no smoking. Served by helpful, friendly staff the good bar food uses only fresh local produce. Well kept Adnams Broadside, Bass, and Sharps Doom Bar on handpump, and several wines by the glass.

Punch ~ Lease Dyanne Hull and Chris Mitchell ~ Real ale ~ Bar food ~ (01872) 552375 ~ Children allowed until 9pm ~ Dogs allowed in bar ~ Open 12-midnight; 12-11.30 Sun

MYLOR BRIDGE

Pandora *Restronguet Passage: from A39 in Penryn, take turning signposted Mylor Church, Mylor Bridge, Flushing and go straight through Mylor Bridge following Restronguet Passage signs; or from A39 further N, at or near Perranarworthal, take turning signposted Mylor, Restronguet, then follow Restronguet Weir signs, but turn left down hill at Restronguet Passage sign; TR11 5ST*

As well as driving to this idyllically placed pub, you can reach it by walking along the estuary amongst avenues of wild flowers or arrive (as do quite a few customers) by boat; in fine weather you can sit with your drink on the long floating pontoon and watch children crabbing. Inside, the several rambling, interconnecting rooms have low wooden ceilings (mind your head on some of the beams), beautifully polished big flagstones, cosy alcoves with leatherette benches built into the walls, old race posters, and three large log fires in high hearths (to protect them against tidal floods); part of the bar area is no smoking – as is the restaurant. The lunch menu includes some pubby dishes, while the evening menu is more modern and imaginative; afternoon teas, too. Well kept St Austell HSD, Tinners and Tribute, a guest beer on handpump, and a dozen wines by the glass. It does get very crowded and parking is difficult at peak times.

St Austell ~ Tenant John Milan ~ Real ale ~ Bar food (all day) ~ Restaurant ~ (01326) 372678 ~ Children welcome away from bar area ~ Dogs allowed in bar ~ Jazz Fri evenings in winter ~ Open 10-midnight; 10.30-11pm in winter

PERRANWELL

Royal Oak *Village signposted off A393 Redruth—Falmouth and A39 Falmouth—Truro; TR3 7PX*

Although drinkers do get a look in, most emphasis in this pretty and quietly set stone-built village pub is on the very good food. The roomy, carpeted bar is welcoming and relaxed, with a buoyant, gently upmarket atmosphere, horsebrasses and pewter and china mugs on its black beams and joists, plates and country pictures on its cream-painted stone walls, and cosy wall and other seats around its candlelit tables. It rambles around beyond a big stone fireplace (with a good log fire in winter) into a snug little nook of a room behind, with just a couple more tables. Well kept Bass, Flowers IPA, and Sharps Special on handpump from the small serving counter and good wines by the glass (the wine list is well balanced and not over-long); prompt, friendly service and a particularly helpful landlord. Well presented, the interesting bar food includes super tapas and lots of fish dishes. The restaurant area is no smoking; piped music, table football and shove-ha'penny. There are tables out in front and in a secluded canopied garden.

Free house ~ Licensee Richard Rudland ~ Real ale ~ Bar food (12-2.30, 7-9.30) ~ Restaurant ~ (01872) 863175 ~ Children in dining areas only ~ Dogs allowed in bar ~ Open 11-3, 6-midnight; 12-3.30, 6-11 Sun

PHILLEIGH

Roseland *Between A3078 and B3289, NE of St Mawes just E of King Harry Ferry; TR2 5NB*

With a father and son now at the helm, this busy little pub has a good mix of customers enjoying the friendly atmosphere. The two bar rooms (one with flagstones and the other carpeted) have wheelback chairs and built-in red-cushioned seats, open fires, old photographs, and some giant beetles and butterflies in glasses. The small lower back bar is liked by locals. Good food is imaginatively pubby at lunchtime, with more elaborate evening dishes. Adnams Best, Sharps Doom Bar and Skinners Betty Stogs on handpump, and a dozen wines (plus champagne) by the glass. The pretty paved front courtyard is a very pleasant place on a sunny day, and the pub is handy for Trelissick Gardens and the King Harry ferry.

Free house ~ Licensees Douglas and William Richards ~ Real ale ~ Bar food (12-2.30, 5.30-9.30; 12-3, 6-9 Sun) ~ Restaurant ~ No credit cards ~ (01872) 580254 ~ Children in restaurant ~ Dogs allowed in bar ~ Open 11.30-3, 5.30-11; 12-3, 6-10.30 Sun

PORTHLEVEN

Ship *Village on B3304 SW of Helston; pub perched on edge of harbour; TR13 9JS*

This friendly old fisherman's pub is actually built into the base of the steep cliffs. So from seats inside you can watch the sea surging against the harbour wall only yards from the window. There are tables out in the terraced garden that make the most of the view too, and at night the harbour is interestingly floodlit. The knocked-through bar has log fires in big stone fireplaces and some genuine individuality. The no smoking family room is a conversion of an old smithy with logs burning in a huge open fireplace; piped music, games machine, cribbage and dominoes. Well liked bar food is traditionally pubby; the candlelit dining room also looks over the sea. Well kept Courage Best, and Sharps Atlantic, Doom Bar and Eden Ale on handpump.

Free house ~ Licensee Colin Oakden ~ Real ale ~ Bar food ~ (01326) 564204 ~ Children in family room only ~ Dogs allowed in bar ~ Open 11.30-11; 12-10.30 Sun

PORTHTOWAN

Blue *Beach Road, East Cliff; use the car park (fee in season), not the slippy sand; TR4 8AW*

All sorts of customers of any age enjoy this bustling bar – by no means a traditional pub. It's right by a fantastic beach and huge picture windows look across the terrace to the huge expanse of sand and sea. Very light and airy, there are built-in pine seats in the front bays, chrome and wicker chairs around plain wooden tables on the stripped wood floor, quite a few high-legged chrome and wooden bar stools, and plenty of standing space around the bar counter; powder blue painted walls, ceiling fans, some big ferny plants, two large TVs showing silent surfing videos, and fairly quiet piped music; pool table. Perky, busy young staff and a chatty informal atmosphere. Good modern bar food includes all-day breakfasts at weekends with the newspapers. Quite a few wines by the glass, cocktails and shots, and giant cups of coffee.

Free house ~ Licensees Tara Roberts, Luke Morris and Alexandra George ~ Bar food (12(10 weekends)-3, 6-9; some food served all afternoon weekdays) ~

Restaurant ~ (01209) 890329 ~ Children welcome away from bar ~ Dogs welcome ~ djs Fri evening, live bands Sat evening ~ Open 11-11; 10-midnight Sat; 11-10.30 Sun; closed first 3 weeks Jan

PORTMELLON COVE
Rising Sun *Just S of Mevagissey; PL26 6PL*

This spotless and appealing black-shuttered seaside pub combines plenty of atmosphere in its properly pubby main bar with real quality on the food side (dishes are home made and imaginative). They have well kept Adnams Bitter and Broadside, and a changing guest beer such as Sharps Doom Bar on handpump, and a dozen wines from a good choice and strong in new world ones. The helpful landlord is backed by friendly efficient staff. The bar has black beams (some with small bits of ropework), an unusual log fire at the far end, lots of small old local photographs along with a former local boatbuilder's sign and a variety of nautical hardware on the ochre walls above its dark panelled dado, and nice pub tables on the sealed crazy paving; piped music. Windows looking over the quiet shore road to the sea have a few house plants and musical instruments such as a saxophone and melodion. The attractive no smoking side restaurant, with a rewarding evening menu, has proper tablecloths and so on, and there's also a big upper family/games room (bar billiards and board games) and charming well shaded plant-filled conservatory. There are a few good solid tables and seats (and a water bowl for dogs) out by the side entrance steps, which are flanked by good tubs of flowers, and some more modern tables on the small front terrace. This sandy rock cove is much quieter than nearby Mevagissey even in summer, and very peaceful indeed out of season; some of the bedrooms overlook the water. The sea is safe for swimming and boating, with an August regatta; the pub has tide-time dials outside.

Free house ~ Licensees Clive and Christopher Walker and Daniel Tregonning ~ Real ale ~ Bar food (12-3(4 Sun), 6.30-9) ~ Restaurant ~ (01726) 843235 ~ Children welcome till 6pm (teens then allowed in snug bar and restaurant) ~ Dogs allowed in bar and bedrooms ~ Live music every second Fri evening ~ Open 12-11.30(midnight Fri and Sat); closed Nov-end Feb ~ Bedrooms: £42.50B/£55B

SENNEN COVE
Old Success *Off A30 Land's End road; TR19 7DG*

The view over Whitesands Bay, either from seats inside this old-fashioned seaside hotel or from the terraced garden, are super; Land's End is a pleasant walk away. The unpretentious beamed and timbered bar has plenty of lifeboat memorabilia, including an RNLI flag hanging on the ceiling; elsewhere are ship's lanterns, black and white photographs, dark wood tables and chairs, and a big ship's wheel that doubles as a coat stand. Bar food is straightforward. Well kept Sharps Doom Bar, Skinners Heligan Honey, and a guest beer on handpump. The upper bar and restaurant are no smoking; piped music, TV and darts. Bedrooms are basic but comfortable, enjoying the sound of the sea, and they have four self-catering suites. It does get crowded at peak times.

Free house ~ Licensee Martin Brooks ~ Real ale ~ Bar food (12-2.30, 6-9.30; all day August) ~ Restaurant ~ (01736) 871232 ~ Children welcome ~ Dogs allowed in bar ~ Live music Sat and Thurs ~ Open 11-11(midnight Sat); 12-11(10.30 in winter) Sun ~ Bedrooms: £35(£44B)/£88B

ST ANNS CHAPEL
Rifle Volunteer *A390; PL18 9HL*
The two front bars here have a pleasantly pubby feel. The main one on the left has a log fire in its big stone fireplace, cushioned pews and country kitchen chairs, a turkey rug on its parquet floor, and a relaxed ochre and green décor; on the right, the Chapel Bar has similar furnishings on its dark boards, another open fire, and motorcycle prints on its cream walls. Well kept Sharps Cornish Coaster and Doom Bar and Wadworths 6X are tapped from the cask, there are over 70 whiskies, local farm cider, and decent wines by the glass; pool, TV, and skittle alley. Well liked home-made bar food is fairly traditional. The modern back dining room has picture windows to take advantage of a very wide view that stretches down to the Tamar estuary and Plymouth. An elevated Astroturf deck beside it has some tables, with more in the garden which slopes away below.
Free house ~ Licensees Frank and Lynda Hilldrup ~ Real ale ~ Bar food ~ Restaurant ~ (01822) 832508 ~ Children in restaurant ~ Dogs allowed in bar ~ Open 12-2.30, 6-11 ~ Bedrooms: £35S/£50B

ZENNOR
Tinners Arms *B3306 W of St Ives; TR26 3BY*
Originally built in 1271 to house the masons building the church next door, this is a friendly pub with a good mix of customers. The new licensees have gently refurbished the place but don't plan any major changes to the bar. There are wooden ceilings, newly cushioned settles, benches, and a mix of chairs around wooden tables, antique prints on the stripped plank panelling, and a log fire in cool weather. Tasty bar food is fairly traditional at lunchtime, with a few extra dishes in the evening. The dining room is no smoking. Sharps Doom Bar and a beer named for the pub, and St Austell Tinners on handpump. You can sit on benches in the sheltered front courtyard, or at tables on a bigger side terrace.
Free house ~ Licensee Grahame Edwards ~ Real ale ~ Bar food (12-2.30, 6.30-9) ~ (01736) 796927 ~ Children not allowed in main bar ~ Dogs allowed in bar ~ Open 11-11; 12-10.30 Sun; 11-3, 6.30-11 Mon-Sat in winter

Dog Friendly Hotels, B&Bs and Farms

BODINNICK
Old Ferry *Bodinnick, Fowey, Cornwall PL23 1LX (01726) 870237* **£70**; 12 comfortable and spacious rms, most with own bthrm and river views. 400-year-old inn in lovely situation overlooking Fowey estuary; back flagstoned bar partly cut into the rock, real ales, comfortable residents' lounge with

french windows opening onto a terrace, and decent food in both bar and no smoking little evening restaurant; quiet out of season; a dog and two resident cats; walks nearby; cl 25 Dec; dogs everywhere except restaurant; £3

CARNE BEACH
Nare Hotel *Carne Beach, Veryan, Truro, Cornwall TR2 5PF (01872) 501279* **£240**, plus special breaks; 36 lovely rms to suit all tastes – some stylish ones overlook garden and out to sea. Attractively decorated and furnished hotel in magnificent clifftop position with secluded gardens, outdoor and indoor swimming pools, tennis, sailboarding and fishing; antiques, fresh flowers and log fires in the airy, spacious day rooms, very good food in two restaurants (one with a more relaxed atmosphere), wonderful breakfasts, and run by staff who really care; ideal for quiet family hols, with safe sandy beach below; disabled access; dogs welcome from £12 inc daily meal

CONSTANTINE BAY
Treglos Hotel *Constantine Bay, Padstow, Cornwall PL28 8JH (01841) 520727* **£162**; 42 light rms, some with dramatic coastal views. Quiet and relaxed hotel close to good sandy beach, and in the same family for over 30 years; comfortable traditional furnishings in light and airy lounges and bar, open fires, good food in attractive restaurant, friendly helpful staff, sheltered garden plus playground and adventure equipment, indoor swimming pool, table tennis, table football and pool table, and children's playroom with electronic games; self-catering apartments; lovely surrounding walks; cl Dec-Feb; children over 7 in evening restaurant; disabled access; dogs in bedrooms by arrangement; £7

CRANTOCK
Crantock Bay Hotel *West Pentire, Crantock, Newquay, Cornwall TR8 5SE (01637) 830229* **£138**, plus special breaks; 31 comfortable rms, most with fine sea views. In a lovely setting on the West Pentire headland, facing the Atlantic and a huge sheltered sandy beach, this relaxed and informal hotel has been run by the same friendly family for over 50 years; four acres of grounds, an indoor swimming pool, toddlers' pool, new Spa, sauna and exercise room, all-weather tennis court, a putting course and children's play area; two lounges (one is no smoking), bar, and no smoking restaurant, enjoyable food using local produce, and nice afternoon teas; wonderful surrounding walks; cl Dec-Feb; families most welcome; lots to do nearby; disabled access and facilities; dogs in bedrooms; can also provide meals if wanted; £5

FALMOUTH
Penmere Manor *Mongleath Rd, Falmouth, Cornwall TR11 4PN (01326) 211411* **£162**, plus special breaks; 37 spacious rms. Run by the same owners for over 30 years, this quietly set Georgian manor has five acres of subtropical gardens and woodland, heated outdoor swimming pool, giant

chess, croquet, and leisure centre with indoor swimming pool, gym, and sauna; particularly helpful friendly staff, a convivial and informal bar, and enjoyable food using local produce in smart restaurant; disabled access; dogs in some bedrooms only; £7.50

FOWEY

Fowey Hall *Fowey, Cornwall PL23 1ET (01726) 833866* **£230** inc dinner; 36 rms inc 12 suites many with estuary views. Fine Gothic-style mansion in five acres of grounds overlooking the harbour and run as a luxury family hotel; marble fireplaces, baroque plasterwork, panelling, antiques, big potted plants, deeply comfortable lounge with open log fire, two enjoyable restaurants, a no smoking library, marvellous facilities for children inc supervised nursery, and covered swimming pool, croquet and badminton; plenty of fine walks in grounds, surrounding coastline and beach (dogs are not allowed on beaches during the summer); dogs welcome away from dining areas if on lead; £7

Marina Villa Hotel *17 Esplanade, Fowey, Cornwall PL23 1HY (01726) 833315* **£154**, plus special breaks; 18 rms, several with lovely views (some with balcony). Friendly no smoking Georgian hotel in fine position overlooking Fowey River and open sea (private access from secluded walled garden); comfortable lounge/reading room, contemporary stylish bar area, light and airy attractive dining room overlooking the water, very good food (super fresh fish and shellfish), and helpful service; nearby beach for walks; dogs in bedrooms

LOOE

Talland Bay Hotel *Porthallow, Looe, Cornwall PL13 2JB (01503) 272667* **£130**, plus special breaks; 23 charming rms with sea or country views. Down a little lane between Looe and Polperro, this restful partly 16th-c country house has lovely subtropical gardens just above the sea; comfortable drawing room with log fire, smaller lounge with library, fresh flowers, courteous service, good food in pretty oak-panelled dining room, and pleasant afternoon teas; heated outdoor swimming pool, putting, croquet; children over 5 in evening restaurant (high tea for younger ones); resident dog; coastal walks and guide for countryside walks provided; limited disabled access; dogs in some bedrooms with dog towels, mats and bowls; £7.50

MAWNAN SMITH

Meudon Hotel *Mawnan Smith, Falmouth, Cornwall TR11 5HT (01326) 250541* **£240** inc dinner, plus special breaks; 29 well equipped comfortable rms in modern wing. Run by the same caring family for over 40 years, this is an old stone mansion with a newer wing set in beautiful subtropical gardens laid out 200 years ago by R W Fox; fine views from the no smoking dining room, comfortable lounge with log fire and fresh flowers, good english cooking, and old-fashioned standards of service; resident cat; walks in own grounds and along coastal footpath at bottom of garden; hotel yacht available for skippered charter and free golf at 6 clubs; cl Jan; disabled access; dogs in bedrooms; £7.50

MITHIAN

Rose-in-Vale Country House Hotel *Mithian, St Agnes, Cornwall TR5 0QD (01872) 552202* (3.5 miles from A30: A3075, then left on B3284, bearing left to village) **£140**, plus special breaks; 18 pretty rms inc 2 suites. Secluded and quietly set Georgian house in four acres of neatly kept gardens, with comfortable spacious day rooms, a friendly atmosphere, helpful, long-standing local staff, and good food in enlarged dining room; ducks on ponds, a trout stream, outdoor swimming pool, badminton and croquet, plus a sauna and solarium; children over 7 in evening in public rooms and restaurant (high tea for smaller ones); cl Jan; dogs in bedrooms; £4.95

MULLION

Caunce Head *Predannack, Mullion, Cornwall TR12 7HA (01326) 240128* **£70**; 3 restful rms with farmland and sea views. Handsome no smoking 17th-c stone house set back from Mullion Cliffs in lovely countryside with a peaceful atmosphere, comfortable sitting room with antiques, log fire, and plants, fine Aga-cooked breakfasts in farmhouse kitchen, and wonderful walks from the door; two resident dogs (bitches); children over 12; dogs anywhere but must be on leads in public rooms

Polurrian Hotel *Mullion, Helston, Cornwall TR12 7EN (01326) 240421* **£156**; 39 rms, some with memorable sea view. White clifftop hotel, mainly no smoking, in lovely gardens with path down to sheltered private cove below; a restful atmosphere in the comfortable lounges and bright cocktail bar, good food using fresh local ingredients in all day restaurant (stunning sea views), and enjoyable breakfasts; leisure club with heated swimming pool, and outdoor pool, tennis, mini-golf and squash; coastal path runs through hotel grounds; particularly good for families; cl Jan; limited disabled access; dogs in bedrooms; £8

PADSTOW

St Petroc's Hotel & Bistro *4 New St, Padstow, Cornwall PL28 8EA (01841) 532700* **£120**; 10 comfortable little rms. Attractive little hotel (under the same ownership as the Seafood Restaurant) with a stylish lounge, a quiet reading room, an airy no smoking dining room, good quickly served food from a short bistro-type menu (plenty of fish), a sensible wine list, and friendly atmosphere; dogs in bedrooms; bedding and bowls offered; £15

PENRYN

Prospect House *1 Church Road, Falmouth, Cornwall TR10 8DA (01326) 373198* **£65**; 3 lovely rms named after sailing ships, and little kitchenette for teas, coffee and biscuits. Built for a local packet-ship captain, this Georgian house is set on the Penryn River in a walled garden; original features such as panelled mahogany doors and painted cornices, a comfortable elegant guest lounge with an open fireplace, good traditional english breakfasts, and a restful atmosphere; resident cat; riverside walks nearby; dogs in bedrooms; £5

PENZANCE
Abbey Hotel *Abbey St, Penzance, Cornwall TR18 4AR (01736) 366906* **£120**; 9 charming rms. Stylish little 17th-c house close to harbour with marvellous views, a relaxed atmosphere in comfortable drawing room full of flowers, fine paintings and antiques, a good set menu in small Abbey Restaurant next door and pretty garden; cl Jan; children over 7 in dining room; park nearby for walks and beaches (out of season); dogs welcome in bedrooms

PORT ISAAC
Port Gaverne Hotel *Port Gaverne, Port Isaac, Cornwall PL29 3SQ (01208) 880244* **£100**, plus special breaks; 15 comfortable rms. Lovely place to stay and an excellent base for area (dramatic coves, super clifftop walks and lots of birds); big log fires in well kept bars, relaxed lounges, decent bar food and good meals in no smoking restaurant, and fine wines; also, restored 18th-c self-catering cottages; cl Christmas; children over 7 in restaurant; dogs welcome away from dining room; dog treats in bar; £3.50

PORTSCATHO
Rosevine *Porthcurnick Beach, Portscatho, Cornwall TR2 5EW (01872) 580206* **£200**, plus special breaks; 17 rms, 6 in courtyard annexe. Imposing house set above a fine beach with an attractive, semi-tropical garden, traditionally decorated lounges (one has views of the garden and sea) and bar, enjoyable food including lots of fish and local produce in smart no smoking restaurant, and genuinely friendly staff; indoor swimming pool, games room and children's playroom; resident dog and two cats; walks in grounds and on coastal paths, country lanes, and beach (no summer ban); cl Jan; limited disabled access; dogs in bedrooms; bowls and treats

SENNEN
Lands End Hotel *Sennen, Penzance, Cornwall TR19 7AA (01736) 871844* **£140**, plus special breaks; 33 elegant airy rms named after local landscape features and many with splendid sea views. Comfortable hotel right on the clifftop with fine sea views, good food in attractive conservatory-style restaurant, elegant seating areas, informal bar with lots of malt whiskies, and helpful staff; lots to do nearby; dogs welcome away from bar and restaurant, £10

ST MAWES
Rising Sun *The Square, St Mawes, Truro, Cornwall TR2 5DJ (01326) 270233* **£160**; 8 rms. Small, attractive old hotel in popular picturesque waterside village, with harbour views, large comfortable and airy lounge with bustling bar area, elegant no smoking conservatory restaurant, very

good food majoring on local fish, super breakfasts, and charming terrace; beach and coastal walks; dogs in bedrooms and bar

TREVAUNANCE COVE
Driftwood Spars *Trevaunance Cove, St Agnes, Cornwall TR5 0RT (01872) 552428* £82; 15 attractive, comfortable rms, some with sea view, 8 in separate building. Friendly family-owned hotel dating from the 17th c and just up the road from the beach and dramatic cove; woodburner in comfortable lounge, main bar with large open fire, upstairs no smoking gallery, beamed ceilings, helpful staff and enjoyable food; live music wknds; coastal footpath passes the door, 3 rms have own garden and 5 rms have access to cliff garden; several resident dogs (heard but not seen); cl 25 Dec; dogs everywhere except seafood restaurant; £3

Isles of Scilly

Dog Friendly Hotels, B&Bs and Farms

BRYHER
Hell Bay *Bryher, Isles of Scilly TR23 0PR (01720) 422947* £310 inc dinner; 24 rms and suites, many with stunning sea views. Relaxed and peaceful hotel on the western tip of the island's rugged coastline and in extensive private grounds with outdoor heated swimming pool, golf, boules and croquet; light, airy contemporary décor and original sculptures and paintings from the owners' private collections, residents' lounge, and sea-view restaurant with plenty of local fish and shellfish; boat trips, fishing, diving and water sports; cl Jan/Feb; disabled access; dogs welcome in bedrooms

ST AGNES
Coastguards *St Agnes, Isles of Scilly TR22 0PL (01720) 422373* £88 inc dinner; 2 rms with views of the sea. Peacefully set former coastguard cottages with open fire, interesting artefacts, and sea views in the sitting room, enjoyable homely dinners and breakfasts, friendly, helpful owners, and big garden; no smoking; cl Nov-Mar; children over 12; dogs in bedrooms only

ST MARTIN'S
St Martin's on the Isle *Lower Town, St Martin's, Isles of Scilly TR25 0QW (01720) 422092* £300 inc dinner, plus special breaks; 30 attractively decorated rms, most with fine sea views. Welcomed by the manager as you step off the boat, you find this stone-built hotel set idyllically on a white sand beach, with stunning sunsets; comfortable, light and airy split-level bar-lounge with doors opening onto the terrace, lovely flower

arrangements, genuinely friendly professional staff, sophisticated food in main restaurant (lighter lunches in the bar), and a fine wine list; they are particularly kind to children, with buckets and spades to borrow, videos, and high tea (they must be over 9 in evening restaurant); fine walks (the island is car free), launch trips to other islands, and good bird-watching; small swimming pool; cl Nov–end Feb; disabled access; dogs in bedrooms; £15

Cumbria

Dog Friendly Pubs

AMBLESIDE

Golden Rule *Smithy Brow; follow Kirkstone Pass signpost from A591 on N side of town; LA22 9AS*

The main bar with its warm log fire and cosy atmosphere is the place to head for in this no frills town local. There are lots of local country pictures decorating the butter-coloured walls, horsebrasses on the black beams, built-in wall seats, and cast-iron-framed tables. Also, a no smoking back room with TV (not much used), a left-hand room with darts and a fruit machine, and a further room down a few steps on the right with lots of seats. Robinsons Hatters Dark, Hartleys XB, Cumbrian Way, Old Stockport, Unicorn and Double Hop on handpump. Snacks include pies, scotch eggs and filled rolls. The back yard has some benches and especially colourful window boxes. The golden rule referred to in its name is a brass measuring yard mounted over the bar counter.

Robinsons ~ Tenant John Lockley ~ Real ale ~ Bar food ~ No credit cards ~ (015394) 32257 ~ Children welcome until 9pm ~ Dogs welcome ~ Open 11-midnight

APPLEBY

Royal Oak *B6542/Bongate is E of the main bridge over the River Eden; CA16 6UN*

With new licensees, this old-fashioned coaching inn is still a friendly place with a good mix of customers. As we went to press, some refurbishments were taking place but the oak-panelled public bar still has a relaxed and chatty atmosphere with a good open fire, and the beamed lounge has old pictures on the timbered walls, some armchairs and a carved settle, and a panelling-and-glass snug enclosing the bar counter. Bar food is well liked and the restaurant is no smoking. Black Sheep Bitter, Jennings Cumberland and John Smiths on handpump; piped music, board games, dominoes (very popular), and TV. There are seats on the front terrace, and attractive flowering tubs, troughs and hanging baskets. You can get here on the scenic Leeds/Settle/Carlisle railway (best to check times and any possible delays to avoid missing lunch).

Enterprise ~ Tenants Kyle Macrae and Janice Hunter ~ Real ale ~ Bar food (11.45-2.30, 5.30-9.30; all day Sun) ~ Restaurant ~ (01768) 351463 ~ Children welcome ~ Dogs allowed in bar ~ Open 11-midnight; 11-midnight Sun ~ Bedrooms: £35S/£69B

ARMATHWAITE
Dukes Head *off A6 S of Carlisle; CA4 9PB*

Every couple of months they hold tasting nights here with samples of local food and interesting drinks – Hot & Spicy, Fish Feast or Food from France. At other times the good popular bar food includes interesting daily specials. The civilised, no smoking lounge bar has oak settles and little armchairs among more upright seats, oak and mahogany tables, antique hunting and other prints, and some brass and copper powder-flasks above the open fire. The restaurant is no smoking. Black Sheep and Jennings Cumberland on handpump, home-made lemonade and ginger cordial and blackcurrant liqueur; dominoes, and a separate public bar with darts and table skittles. This year, there's a new heated and lit up outside seating area with more seats on the lawn behind; boules. Day tickets for fishing are available.

Punch ~ Tenant Henry Lynch ~ Real ale ~ Bar food ~ Restaurant ~ (016974) 72226 ~ Children welcome ~ Dogs allowed in bar and bedrooms ~ Open 11.30-11.30(midnight Sat) ~ Bedrooms: £38.50B/£58.50B

BOUTH
White Hart *Village signposted off A590 near Haverthwaite; LA12 8JB*

Much enjoyed by our readers, this is a well run and cheerful place with a thoroughly authentic lakeland feel. No smoking throughout, the sloping ceilings and floors show the building's age, and there are lots of old local photographs and bric-a-brac – farm tools, stuffed animals, a collection of long-stemmed clay pipes – and two woodburning stoves. Good bar food is thoughtfully traditional and they have a good children's menu. Well kept Black Sheep, Jennings Cumberland, Tetleys and guests like Copper Dragon Black Gold, Hawkshead Gold and York Stonewall on handpump; 30 malt whiskies, and Weston's cider. The games room (where dogs are allowed) has darts, pool, dominoes, fruit machine, TV and juke box; piped music. There are some seats outside and fine surrounding walks.

Free house ~ Licensees Nigel and Peter Barton ~ Real ale ~ Bar food (12-2, 6-8.45; not Mon or Tues lunchtime except bank hols) ~ (01229) 861229 ~ Children in eating area of bar and restaurant ~ Dogs allowed in bedrooms ~ Open 12-2, 6-11; 12-11 Sat; 12-10.30 Sun; closed Mon and Tues lunchtimes (except bank hols) ~ Bedrooms: £47.50S(£37.50B)/£80S(£60B)

BROUGHTON MILLS
Blacksmiths Arms *Off A593 N of Broughton-in-Furness; LA20 6AX*

After enjoying one of the fine nearby walks, this charming little pub is a smashing place to relax. Three of the four simply but attractively decorated small rooms have open fires, ancient slate floors, and Dent Aviator, Hawkshead Bitter and Jennings Cumberland on handpump, and summer farm cider. Using local produce, the good bar food is sensibly imaginative.

There are three smallish dining rooms (the back one is no smoking). Darts, dominoes, and cards. Pretty summer hanging baskets and tubs of flowers in front of the building.

Free house ~ Licensees Mike and Sophie Lane ~ Real ale ~ Bar food (12-2, 6-9; not Mon lunchtime) ~ Restaurant ~ (01229) 716824 ~ Children welcome ~ Dogs allowed in bar ~ Open 12-11; 12-10.30 Sun; 5-11 Mon (cl winter Mon), 12-2.30, 5-11 Tues-Fri in winter

CARTMEL
Kings Arms *The Square; LA11 6QB*

In fine weather, the seats outside this rather grand little black and white pub make the most of the lovely square. Inside, the rambling bar has small antique prints on the walls, a mixture of seats including old country chairs, settles and wall banquettes, and tankards hanging over the bar counter. Bar food includes some interesting dishes. The snug and restaurant are no smoking. Black Sheep, Coniston Bluebird, Hawkshead Bitter and maybe a couple of guest beers on handpump, and several wines by the glass; piped music. This ancient village has a grand priory church, and close to the pub is a fine medieval stone gatehouse; the race track is 200 yards away.

Enterprise ~ Lease Richard Grimmer ~ Real ale ~ Bar food (12-2.30, 5.30-8.45; 12-8.45 weekends) ~ Restaurant ~ (01539) 536220 ~ Children welcome ~ Dogs allowed in bar ~ Open 11-11; 11-10.30 Sun; 11-3, 5-11 in winter; closed 25 Dec

CHAPEL STILE
Wainwrights *B5343; LA22 9JH*

The position here is lovely with fells rising directly behind this white-rendered lakeland house, and you can enjoy the views from the picnic-table sets out on the terrace; good surrounding walks. Inside, the characterful slate-floored bar has plenty of room, and it is here that walkers and their dogs are welcomed. There's a relaxed and friendly atmosphere, an old kitchen range, cushioned settles, and well kept Jennings Cumberland Ale and Sneck Lifter, and up to four changing guests on handpump or tapped from the cask; eight wines by the glass and summer fruit smoothies. Bar food is heartily traditional. The family dining area is no smoking; piped music, darts, dominoes and TV.

Free house ~ Licensees Mrs C Darbyshire and B Clarke ~ Real ale ~ Bar food (12-2(2.30 Sun), 6-9) ~ 015394 38088 ~ Children in family dining area ~ Dogs allowed in bar ~ Open 11.30-11; 11.30-11 Sat; 12-10.30 Sun; 11.30-3, 6-11 in winter

CROSTHWAITE
Punch Bowl *Village signposted off A5074 SE of Windermere; LA8 8HR*

Given a stylish and sympathetic up-to-date makeover, this is an appealing no smoking dining pub with good food, yet with no pressure to eat if you just drop in for a drink. Reopened late in 2005 by the owners of the Drunken Duck near Hawkshead, it has an enlarged raftered and hop-hung bar with a couple of eye-catching rugs on its flagstones, and bar stools by the slate-topped counter, which has Barngates Cat Nap and Tag Lag (brewed at their sister pub) and a guest beer on handpump, and a good range of wines by the glass. This opens on the right into two linked carpeted and beamed rooms with well spaced country pine furnishings of varying sizes, including a big refectory table. The walls, painted in restrained neutral tones, have an attractive assortment of prints, with some copper objects, and there's a dresser with china and glass. There's a winter log fire, they have daily papers, and service by young staff is prompt, friendly and attentive. On the left is the wooden-floored restaurant area, also attractive, with comfortable leather seating. Throughout, the pub feels relaxing and nicely uncluttered. For most people, it will be the wide choice of traditionally imaginative food which is the main attraction. There are some tables on a terrace stepped into the hillside, overlooking the lovely Lythe Valley.

Free house ~ Licensee Stephen Carruthers ~ Real ale ~ Bar food (12-3, 6-9) ~ Restaurant ~ (015395) 68237 ~ Children welcome ~ Dogs allowed in bar ~ Open 12-11 ~ Bedrooms: £75B/£100B

GREAT SALKELD

Highland Drove *B6412, off A686 NE of Penrith; CA11 9NA*

This is a smashing place and deservedly popular with both the cheerful locals enjoying a chat and a pint and visitors keen to sample the particularly good food. A new downstairs eating area (they use the best local produce) has been opened up with cushioned dining chairs around wooden tables on the pale wooden floorboards; brick walls and ceiling joists, and a two-way fire in a raised brick fireplace that separates this room from the new no smoking coffee lounge with its comfortable leather chairs and sofas. The convivial main bar has sandstone flooring, brick walls, cushioned wheelback chairs around a mix of tables, an open fire in a raised stone fireplace, and John Smiths, Theakstons Black Bull and Timothy Taylors Landlord on handpump; a good choice of wines and 25 malt whiskies. Piped music, TV, juke box, darts, pool, games machine and dominoes. The eating areas are no smoking. There are lovely views over the Eden Valley and the Pennines – best enjoyed from seats on the upstairs verandah.

Free house ~ Licensees Donald and Paul Newton ~ Real ale ~ Bar food (12-2, 6.30-8.45; not Mon lunchtime, 25 Dec, 1 Jan) ~ Restaurant ~ (01768) 898349 ~ Children welcome ~ Dogs allowed in bar ~ Open 12-2.30(3 Sun), 6-midnight; 12-midnight Sat; closed Mon lunchtime ~ Bedrooms: £32.50B/£60B

HAWKSHEAD

Drunken Duck *Barngates; the hamlet is signposted from B5286 Hawkshead— Ambleside, opposite the Outgate Inn; or it may be quicker to take the first right from B5286, after the wooded caravan site; OS Sheet 90 map reference 350013; LA22 0NG*

Tag Lag and Westmorland Gold plus local microbrewery ales on handpump; belgian and german draught beers, 20 wines by the glass, and several malt whiskies. There are beams and oak floorboards, leather-topped bar stools by the slate-topped bar counter, leather club chairs, photographs, coaching prints and hunting pictures, and some kentish hop bines. The only nod to bar food comes in the form of pre-made sandwiches wrapped in greaseproof paper. The imaginative à la carte menu is about much more serious dining. Rustic seating on the grass bank opposite the building offers spectacular views across the fells, and there are thousands of spring and summer bulbs.

Own brew ~ Licensee Steph Barton ~ Real ale ~ Restaurant ~ (015394) 36347 ~ Children welcome ~ Dogs allowed in bar ~ Open 11.30-11; 12-10.30 Sun; closed 25 Dec except between 12 and 2 ~ Bedrooms: £71.25B/£95B

Kings Arms *The Square; LA22 0NZ*

You can sit on the terrace outside this 16th-c inn and look over the central square of this lovely Elizabethan village. There are some fine original features, traditional pubby furnishings, and an open log fire: Black Sheep, Coniston Bluebird, and Hawkshead Bitter and Red on handpump, 33 malt whiskies, a decent wine list, and organic soft drinks. Piped music, games machine, TV and board games. Decent bar food and no smoking restaurant. As well as bedrooms, they offer self-catering cottages. There are free fishing permits for residents.

Free house ~ Licensees Rosalie and Edward Johnson ~ Real ale ~ Bar food (12-2.30, 6-9.30) ~ Restaurant ~ (015394) 36372 ~ Children in eating area of bar and restaurant ~ Dogs allowed in bar and bedrooms ~ Live music last Thurs in month ~ Open 11-11(midnight Sat); closed evening 25 Dec ~ Bedrooms: £45S/£80S

INGS

Watermill *Just off A591 E of Windermere; LA8 9PY*

'This is the one pub I will come to every time I visit the Lake District,' said one happy reader who regularly walks in this area. It's a particularly well run and very popular pub run by an enthusiastic and hard-working landlord. They keep a fantastic range of 16 real ales on handpump with regulars such as Black Sheep Bitter and Special, Coniston Bluebird, Hawkshead Bitter, Moorhouses Black Cat, and Theakstons Best and Old Peculier, guests like Batemans XB, Brakspears Bee Sting, Cotleigh Tawny Owl, Fyne Highlander, Harviestoun Navigator, Jennings Cumberland, Loddon Flight of Fancy, Wadworths 6X and Yates Fever Pitch, and their own-brewed A Bit of Ruff, Collie Wobbles and Ruff Nite. 60 foreign bottled beers and over 50 whiskies. The building is cleverly converted from a wood mill and joiner's shop, and the partly no smoking bars have a friendly, bustling atmosphere, a happy mix of chairs, padded benches and solid oak tables, bar counters made from old church wood, open fires, and interesting photographs and amusing cartoons by a local artist. The spacious no smoking lounge bar, in much the same traditional style as the other rooms, has rocking chairs and a big open fire; two areas are no smoking. Using locally sourced produce, the well liked, mostly traditional bar food comes in generous helpings. Darts and board games. Seats in the gardens, and lots to do nearby.

Free house ~ Licensee Brian Coulthwaite ~ Real ale ~ Bar food (12-4.30, 5-9) ~ (01539) 821309 ~ Children in lounge area ~ Dogs allowed in bar and bedrooms

~ Storytelling first Tues of month ~ Open 12-11(10.30 Sun); closed 25 Dec ~
Bedrooms: £35S/£68B

LEVENS
Strickland Arms *4 miles from M6 junction 36, via A590; just off A590, by Sizergh Castle gates; LA8 8DZ*
Closed since the late 1990s, this has now been reopened after sympathetic refurbishment by the owner of the Eagle & Child down at Bispham Green (see Lancashire main entries), who has leased it from its owners, the National Trust. It's now a no smoking dining pub, and word has quickly got around locally about its friendly service and atmosphere, and good food and drink. Largely open plan, it has oriental rugs on the flagstones of the bar on the right, which has a log fire and serves Thwaites Original and Lancaster Bomber from handpump, with two local guest beers such as Coniston Bluebird or Hawkshead Gold, 25 malt whiskies, and good wines by the glass. On the left are polished boards, and another log fire (they have central heating, too), and throughout there's a nice mix of sturdy country furniture, with candles on tables, hunting scenes and other old prints on the walls, heavy fabric for the curtains, and some staffordshire china ornaments. There is a further dining room upstairs. The good interesting food relies strongly on fresh produce from local farms and estates, Service is friendly and personal, they have disabled access and facilities, and there are tables out in front on a new flagstone terrace. The Castle, in fact a lovely partly medieval house with beautiful gardens, is open in the afternoon (not Friday/Saturday) from April to October.
Free house ~ Licensees Emma Bigland and Martin Ainscough ~ Real ale ~ Bar food (12-2, 6-9; all day weekends) ~ (015395) 61010 ~ Children welcome ~ Dogs welcome ~ Open 12-3, 5.30-11; 12-midnight(11pm Sun) Sat

LITTLE LANGDALE
Three Shires *From A593 3 miles W of Ambleside take small road signposted The Langdales, Wrynose Pass; then bear left at first fork; LA22 9NZ*
Readers enjoy their visits to this pleasantly placed stone-built inn – totally no smoking now. There are lovely views over the valley to the partly wooded hills below Tilberthwaite Fells from seats on the terrace, with more seats on a well kept lawn behind the car park, backed by a small oak wood. Inside, the comfortably extended back bar has stripped timbers and a beam-and-joist stripped ceiling, antique oak carved settles, country kitchen chairs and stools on its big dark slate flagstones, and lakeland photographs; there's a warm winter fire in the modern stone fireplace. An arch leads through to a small, additional area. Good lunchtime bar food is imaginative.Well kept Jennings Bitter and Cumberland, and maybe Hawkshead Red or Theakstons Black Bull on handpump, over 30 malt whiskies, and a decent wine list; darts and board games. The three shires are the historical counties Cumberland, Westmorland and Lancashire, which meet at the top of the nearby Wrynose Pass. The summer hanging baskets are very pretty.
Free house ~ Licensee Ian Stephenson ~ Real ale ~ Bar food (12-2, 6-8.45; no

evening meals Dec and Jan) ~ Restaurant ~ (015394) 37215 ~ Children welcome ~ Dogs allowed in bar ~ Open 11-10.30(11 Sat); 12-10.30 Sun; 11-3, 8-10.30 Dec and Jan winter ~ Bedrooms: /£80S(£78B)

LOWESWATER
Kirkstile Inn *From B5289 follow signs to Loweswater Lake; OS Sheet 89 map reference 140210; CA13 0RU*
In a glorious spot between Loweswater and Crummock Water, this popular little no smoking country inn is surrounded by arresting peaks and fells. The bustling bar is low-beamed and carpeted, with a good mix of customers, a roaring log fire, comfortably cushioned small settles and pews, and partly stripped stone walls; slate shove-ha'penny board. Enjoyable food is pubby at lunchtime with more imaginative evening dishes. They serve their own-brewed and well kept Loweswater Grasmoor Dark and Melbreak Bitter plus Coniston Bluebird, and Yates Bitter on handpump. You can enjoy the view from picnic-sets on the lawn, from the very attractive covered verandah in front of the building, and from the bow windows in one of the rooms off the bar.
Own brew ~ Licensee Roger Humphreys ~ Real ale ~ Bar food (12-2, 6-9) ~ Restaurant ~ (01900) 85219 ~ Children welcome ~ Dogs allowed in bar ~ Open 11-11; 12-10.30 Sun; closed 25 Dec ~ Bedrooms: £55B/£78B

NEAR SAWREY
Tower Bank Arms *B5285 towards the Windermere ferry; LA22 0LF*
A new licensee has taken over this no smoking little country inn and has freshened up the décor to give a much brighter feel. The low-beamed main bar has plenty of rustic charm, settles and other seats on the rough slate floor, game and fowl pictures and postcards of Beatrix Potter, a grandfather clock, an open fire and fresh flowers. Many illustrations in the Beatrix Potter books can be traced back to their origins in this village, including this pub which features in *The Tale of Jemima Puddleduck*. Well kept Barngates Cat Nap, Dent Bitter, Hawkshead Bitter and Theakstons Old Peculier on handpump. Bar food is pubby at lunchtime and a little more imaginative in the evening. Cards and dominoes. Seats outside have pleasant views of the wooded Claife Heights.
Free house ~ Licensee Anthony Hutton ~ Real ale ~ Bar food (12-2, 6-9; snacks served all day) ~ Restaurant ~ (015394) 36334 ~ Children welcome until 9pm ~ Dogs welcome ~ Open 10-11(all day); 12-10.30 Sun; 10-3, 6-11 Nov-Jan winter ~ Bedrooms: £45B/£70B

SANDFORD
Sandford Arms *Village and pub signposted just off A66 W of Brough; CA16 6NR*
A former farmhouse, this is a neat little inn tucked away in a very small village by the River Eden. The compact and comfortable no smoking dining area is on a slightly raised balustraded platform at one end of the L-shaped carpeted main bar, which has stripped beams and stonework, Black Sheep and a guest from Hesket Newmarket on handpump, and a

good range of malt whiskies. The two sons cook the pubby food. There's also a more formal separate dining room (open if pre-booked), and a second bar area with broad flagstones, charming heavy-horse prints, an end log fire, and darts, dominoes, board games and piped music. The eating areas are no smoking. Some picnic-sets outside. Please note the restricted opening times; they may open longer at weekend lunchtimes if there are enough customers.

Free house ~ Licensee Susan Stokes ~ Real ale ~ Bar food (12-1.45, 6.30-8.30; not weekday lunchtimes) ~ Restaurant ~ (017683) 51121 ~ Children welcome ~ Dogs allowed in bar ~ Open 6.30-11; 12-1.45, 6.30-11 Sat; 12-2, 7-10.30 Sun; closed Tues and weekday lunchtimes; 3-12 June ~ Bedrooms: £50B/£60B

SANTON BRIDGE
Bridge Inn *Off A595 at Holmrook or Gosforth; CA19 1UX*
With cheerful, helpful staff and a friendly atmosphere, this busy little black and white hotel is popular with our readers. The turkey-carpeted bar has stripped beams, joists and standing timbers, a coal and log fire, and three rather unusual timbered booths around big stripped tables along its outer wall, with small painted school chairs and tables elsewhere. Bar stools line the long concave bar counter, which has well kept Jennings Bitter, Cocker Hoop, Cumberland, and Sneck Lifter, and a guest such as Golden Host on handpump; good big pots of tea, speciality coffees, and eight wines by the glass. Piped music, pool, games machine, TV and board games. Well liked bar food includes several pub standards. The italian-style bistro is no smoking (children must be over 10 in here), the small reception hall has a rack of daily papers, and there's a comfortable more hotelish lounge on the left. There are fell views and seats out in front by the quiet road, and plenty of surrounding walks.

Jennings (W & D) ~ Lease John Morrow and Lesley Rhodes ~ Real ale ~ Bar food (12-2.30, 6-9.30) ~ Restaurant ~ (01946) 726221 ~ Children allowed in bar and Esk Room but must be over 10 in bistro ~ Dogs allowed in bar and bedrooms ~ Open 10-midnight ~ Bedrooms: £50(£58S)/£60(£70B)

SEATHWAITE
Newfield Inn *Duddon Valley, near Ulpha (ie not Seathwaite in Borrowdale); LA20 6ED*
As food is served all day in this cottagey and friendly 16th-c inn, there's nearly always a good bustling atmosphere; it is particularly popular with walkers and climbers at weekends. The slate-floored bar has a genuinely local and informal atmosphere, wooden tables and chairs, some interesting pictures, well kept, Caledonian Deuchars IPA, Jennings Cumberland and Theakstons Old Peculier on handpump, and half a dozen wines by the glass. There's a comfortable side room and a games room with shove-ha'penny and board games; piped music. Good value pubby bar food uses only local meat from named butchers. The dining room and one bar are no smoking. Tables outside in the nice garden have good hill views. The pub owns and lets the next-door self-catering flats, and there are fine walks from the doorstep.

Free house ~ Licensee Paul Batten ~ Real ale ~ Bar food (12-9) ~ (01229)
716208 ~ Children welcome ~ Dogs allowed in bar ~ Open 11-11; 11-10.30
Sun; closed lunchtimes 25 and 26 Dec

TROUTBECK
Queens Head *A592 N of Windermere; LA23 1PW*
Very well run and extremely popular, this rather civilised old inn remains a
smashing place for either a drink, a good meal or somewhere to spend a
few days. The big rambling original U-shaped bar (partly no smoking) has
beams and flagstones, a very nice mix of old cushioned settles and mate's
chairs around some sizeable tables (especially the one to the left of the
door), and a log fire in the raised stone fireplace with horse harness and so
forth on either side of it; there's another log fire, some trumpets, cornets
and saxophones on one wall with country pictures on others, stuffed
pheasants in a big glass case, and a stag's head with a tie around his neck. A
massive Elizabethan four-poster bed is the basis of the finely carved counter
where they serve around five or six real ales well kept on handpump such
as Black Sheep Bitter, Boddingtons Bitter, Coniston Bluebird, Hawkshead
Red, Jennings Bitter and Tirril Academy Ale. Bar food is interesting and
enjoyable. The newer dining rooms (where you can also drop in for just a
drink) are similarly decorated to the main bar, with oak beams and stone
walls, settles along big tables, and an open fire. Piped music. Seats outside
have a fine view over the Trout valley to Applethwaite moors.
Free house ~ Licensees Mark Stewardson and Joanne Sherratt ~ Real ale ~ Bar food
~ Restaurant ~ (015394) 32174 ~ Children welcome ~ Dogs allowed in bar ~
Open 11-11; 12-10.30 Sun; closed 25 Dec ~ Bedrooms: /£105B

ULVERSTON
Bay Horse *Canal Foot signposted off A590 and then you wend your way past*
the huge Glaxo factory; LA12 9EL
Once a staging post for coaches crossing the sands of Morecambe Bay to
Lancaster, this is a smart and civilised hotel on the water's edge of the
Leven Estuary; the views of both the lancashire and cumbrian fells are
lovely. It's at its most informal at lunchtime, and the bar, notable for its
huge stone horse's head, has a relaxed atmosphere despite its smart
furnishings: attractive wooden armchairs, some pale green plush built-in
wall banquettes, glossy hardwood traditional tables, blue plates on a delft
shelf, and black beams and props with lots of horsebrasses. Magazines are
dotted about, there's an open fire in the handsomely marbled green granite
fireplace, and decently reproduced piped music; board games. Imaginative
bar food and good breakfasts. Well kept Coach House Rabbits Punch,
Marstons Double Drop and Moorhouses Pendle Witches Brew on
handpump, and a dozen wines by the glass (champagne, too) from a
carefully chosen and interesting wine list. The no smoking conservatory
restaurant has fine views over Morecambe Bay (as do the bedrooms) and
there are some seats out on the terrace.
Free house ~ Licensee Robert Lyons ~ Real ale ~ Bar food (12-2(4 weekends);
only restaurant food at night) ~ Restaurant ~ (01229) 583972 ~ Children in

eating area of bar but must be over 10 in restaurant at night ~ Dogs allowed in bar and bedrooms ~ Open 11-11; 12-10.30 Sun ~ Bedrooms: £80B/£95B

Dog Friendly Hotels, B&Bs and Farms

ALSTON
Lovelady Shield Country House *Nenthead Rd, Alston, Cumbria CA9 3LF (01434) 381203* £**210** inc dinner, plus special breaks; 13 rms. In a lovely setting with River Nent running along bottom of garden (tennis and croquet), this handsome country house has a tranquil atmosphere, courteous staff, log fires in comfortable rooms (no smoking in sitting room or restaurant), and very good food inc fine breakfasts; children over 7 in evening restaurant; dogs in bedrooms only; £5

BARBON
Barbon Inn *Barbon, Carnforth, Cumbria LA6 2LJ (015242) 76233* £**70**; 9 simple but comfortable rms, some with own bthrm. Small friendly 17th-c village inn in quiet spot below fells, with relaxing bar, traditional lounge, good meals in candlelit dining room, and helpful service; lots of good tracks and paths all around; dogs in bedrooms

BASSENTHWAITE LAKE
Armathwaite Hall Hotel *Bassenthwaite Lake, Keswick, Cumbria CA12 4RE (017687) 76551* £**210**, plus special offers; 42 rms. Turreted 17th-c mansion in 400 acres of deerpark and woodland; handsome public rooms (several are no smoking) with lovely fireplaces, fine panelling, antiques, paintings and fresh flowers, good french and english cooking using local seasonal produce, a super wine list, and helpful staff; snooker room, croquet, pitch-and-putt, tennis court, indoor swimming pool, gym and beauty salon, fishing, archery and clay pigeon shooting, jogging and mountain-bike tracks, and free children's club; three resident dogs; disabled access; dogs in bedroom; £10

BASSENTHWAITE LAKE
Pheasant *Bassenthwaite Lake, Cockermouth, Cumbria CA13 9YE (017687) 76234* (just off A66, signed on loop rd just E of B5291); dogs in bar and in Garden Lodge bedrooms

BRAMPTON
Farlam Hall *Hallbankgate, Brampton, Cumbria CA8 2NG (016977) 46234* (1.8 miles off A69, via A689) £**305** inc dinner, plus special breaks; 12 smart and comfortable rms. Very civilised, mainly 19th-c country house with log fires in ornately Victorian lounges, excellent attentive service, good 4-course dinner using fine china and silver in friendly but formal restaurant, marvellous breakfasts, and peaceful, spacious grounds with croquet lawn

and small pretty lake; plenty of fine nearby walks; cl 25-30 Dec; children over 5; dogs welcome but not to be left alone at any time

CARTMEL
Uplands *Haggs Lane, Cartmel, Grange-over-sands, Cumbria LA11 6HD (01539) 536248* £**178** inc dinner, plus special breaks; 5 pretty rms. Comfortable Edwardian house in two acres of grounds (plenty of wildlife) with views over to Morecambe Bay; large, attractively decorated lounge, welcoming owners, an informal atmosphere, very good modern food in the no smoking restaurant cooked by the owner, and super breakfasts; cl Mon, Jan-Feb; children over 8; walks from the front door; dogs welcome away from public rooms

CROOK
Wild Boar *Crook, Windermere, Cumbria LA23 3NF (015394) 45225* £**106**, plus special offers; 36 rms. Comfortable well run, extended hotel with period furnishings and log fires in its ancient core, attentive service, and good food in no smoking dining room; free access to nearby leisure club and discounts on watersports; children's club at sister hotel, The Lowwood; dogs in bedrooms; £15

CROSBY ON EDEN
Crosby Lodge *High Crosby, Crosby on Eden, Carlisle, Cumbria CA6 4QZ (01228) 573618* (4.7 miles from M6 junction 44 (A7/A74 terminal roundabout), via A689 eastbound; High Crosby) £**140**, plus special breaks; 11 spacious rms (2 in stable conversion). Imposing and carefully converted country house in attractive mature grounds, with comfortable and appealing individual furnishings, enjoyable home-made food using local produce in no smoking restaurant, friendly long-established owners, and nice surrounding countryside – plenty of walks in grounds; resident donkey and horse; cl 26 Dec-mid Jan; limited disabled access; dogs in courtyard bedrooms; £5

DERWENT WATER
Lodore Falls *Borrowdale, Keswick, Cumbria CA12 5UX (017687) 77285* £**128**, plus special breaks; 71 newly refurbished rms with lakeside or fell views. Long-standing, imposing hotel set in 40 acres of lakeside gardens and woodlands with comfortable day rooms, good modern cooking in elegant restaurant and lounge bar, indoor swimming pool, gym and leisure suite with new health and beauty salon; tennis and squash, outdoor swimming pool, children's play area, and games room; plenty of children's faciliites; self-catering house too; marvellous walks all round; dogs in bedrooms; £7.50

ELTERWATER
Britannia Inn *Elterwater, Ambleside, Cumbria LA22 9HP (015394) 37210* £**96**, plus special breaks; 9 rms. Simple charmingly traditional pub in fine surroundings opposite village green, with a happy friendly atmosphere (it does get very busy at peak times), hearty home cooking inc superb

breakfast, coal fires in the small, cosy bars, a comfortable no smoking residents' lounge, and real ales; fine walks all around; cl 25 Dec; dogs welcome away from residents' lounge and dining room

ENNERDALE BRIDGE
Shepherds Arms *Ennerdale, Cleator, Cumbria CA23 3AR (01946) 861249* £**77**; 8 rms. Set on the popular Coast-to-Coast path and with wonderful surrounding walks, this welcoming inn has a convivial bar, a woodburning stove, carpeted main bar with coal fire and a homely variety of comfortable seats, and a no smoking conservatory; cheerful and obliging service, substantial bar food using local fresh produce, well kept real ales, and a good choice of wines by the glass; resident dog; walks around Ennerdale Lake a mile away; dogs in bedrooms and bar; £5

FAR SAWREY
Sawrey *Far Sawrey, Ambleside, Cumbria LA22 0LQ (015394) 43425* £**70**, plus special breaks; 19 rms. Friendly hotel well placed at the foot of Claife Heights, with simple pubby and smarter bars, friendly staff, good straightforward food, and seats on pleasant lawn; resident dog; cl Christmas; kind to children; partial disabled access; dogs in bedrooms as long as not left alone; £2.50

GRASMERE
Swan *Keswick Rd, Grasmere, Ambleside, Cumbria LA22 9RF (015394) 35551* £**139**, plus special breaks; 38 rms, most with fine views. Smart and friendly 17th-c hotel in beautiful fell-foot surroundings, with beams and winter log fires in inglenooks, several comfortable lounges, a walkers' bar and drying room for walkers, elegant no smoking dining room, enjoyable food, and attractive sheltered garden; lovely walks; partial disabled access; dogs in some bedrooms; £15

IREBY
Overwater Hall *Ireby, Carlisle, Cumbria CA5 1HH (017687) 76566* £**150**, plus special breaks; 12 individually decorated rms. Relaxed and friendly family-run hotel, partly castellated, in 18 acres of gardens and woodland (there's a new boardwalk); log fire in traditionally furnished, comfortable drawing room, good imaginative food in cosy dining room, hearty breakfasts, and lots of walks; two resident dogs and a cat; cl 2 wks early Jan; children over 5 in restaurant (high tea 5pm); partial disabled access; dogs in bedrooms, bar and one lounge

KENDAL
Low Jock Scar *Selside, Kendal, Cumbria LA8 9LE (01539) 823259* £**68**; 5 rms, most with own bthrm. Small no smoking country guesthouse in six acres of garden and woodland, with a relaxed and friendly atmosphere, a residents' lounge, and good home cooking (picnic lunches on request); two resident cats; walks in grounds and surrounding countryside; cl Nov-late Mar; children over 12; dogs welcome in bedrooms

LANGDALE

Old Dungeon Ghyll *Great Langdale, Ambleside, Cumbria LA22 9JY* *(015394) 37272* £**100**, plus special breaks; 13 rms, some with shared bthrm. Friendly, simple and cosy walkers' and climbers' inn dramatically surrounded by fells, wonderful views and terrific walks straight from the front door; cosy residents' lounge and popular food in no smoking dining room – best to book for dinner if not a resident; cl Christmas; dogs in bedrooms and other areas but not in dining room

MUNGRISDALE

Mill Hotel *Mungrisdale, Penrith, Cumbria CA11 0XR (017687) 79659* £**178** inc dinner, plus special breaks; 9 rms, most with own bthrm. Very friendly small streamside no smoking hotel, beautifully placed in lovely valley hamlet hidden away below Blencathra; open fire in cosy and comfortable sitting room, a tiny library, imaginative and delicious 5-course evening meals, a small carefully chosen wine list, and super breakfasts; resident dog; cl Nov-beginning Mar; they are kind to children; disabled access; dogs in bedrooms; bowls and treats offered

RYDAL WATER

White Moss House *White Moss, Ambleside, Cumbria LA22 9SE (015394)* *35295* £**118**, plus special breaks; 6 thoughtfully furnished and comfortable little rms in main house plus separate cottage let as one unit with 2 rms. Bought by Wordsworth for his son, this attractive stripped-stone country house – set in charming mature grounds overlooking the lake – is a marvellously relaxing place to stay, with owners who have been there for over 20 years, a comfortable lounge, excellent fixed-price 5-course meals in pretty no smoking dining room, a fine wine list, and exemplary service; free fishing and free use of local leisure club; cl Dec-Jan; no toddlers; dogs in cottage

SCALES

Scales Farm *Scales, Threlkeld, Cumbria CA12 4SY (01768) 779660* £**56**; 6 comfortable, well equipped rms, 3 with ground-floor access. Converted 17th-c no smoking farmhouse with wide stretching views, a friendly welcome, woodburning stove and wide screen TV in homely beamed lounge, traditional english breakfasts in large dining room (good pub next door for evening meals), and packed lunches on request; fine walks all around; 3 resident dogs and 1 cat; disabled access; dogs in bedrooms and lounge; £3

SEATOLLER

Seatoller House *Borrowdale, Keswick, Cumbria CA12 5XN (017687)* *77218* £**110** inc dinner; 10 spotless, comfortable rms. Friendly house-party atmosphere in 17th-c house that has been a guesthouse for over 100 years, with self-service drinks and board games in comfortable lounges (no TV), and good no-choice fixed-time hearty dinner (not Tues) served at two big oak tables; packed lunches; two acres of grounds and many walks from doorstep (house is at the foot of Honister Pass); cl Dec-Mar; children over 5 in dining room; dogs welcome in bedrooms

TIRRIL
Queens Head *Tirril, Penrith, Cumbria CA10 2JF (01768) 863219* £**70**, plus special breaks; 7 lovely rms. Bustling inn with flagstones and bare boards in the bar, spacious back no smoking restaurant, low beams, black panelling, inglenook fireplace and old-fashioned settles in older part, good interesting food inc snacks and OAP specials, and well kept real ales (inc their own brews); nearby walks; children below 3 and over 13; dogs in bedrooms and bars; £5

WASDALE HEAD
Wasdale Head Hotel *Wasdale Head, Seascale, Cumbria CA20 1EX (019467) 26229* £**108**, plus special breaks; 9 simple but warmly comfortable pine-clad rms, with 3 more luxurious ones in farmhouse annexe. Old flagstoned and gabled walkers' and climbers' inn in magnificent setting surrounded by steep fells and wonderful walks; micro-brewery (tours welcome), civilised day rooms, resident lounge with books and games, popular home cooking, good wine list, huge breakfasts, and cheerfully busy public bar; steam room; self-catering cottages; partial disabled access; dogs in bedrooms; £5

WATERMILLOCK
Rampsbeck Country House *Watermillock, Penrith, Cumbria CA11 0LP (017684) 86442* £**120**, plus special breaks; 19 attractive, traditional rms, many with stunning views. Fine Victorian hotel in wonderful lakeside setting with 18 acres of formal gardens and parkland; open fire in the cosy sitting room, french windows into the garden from the plush, comfortable lounge, friendly attentive staff, and carefully prepared food in the attractive dining room; croquet; lots to do nearby; cl Jan; no children in evening dining room; dogs welcome in bedrooms

WINDERMERE
Langdale Chase Hotel *Windermere, Cumbria LA23 1LW (015394) 32201* (on A591 N towards Ambleside) £**140**, plus special breaks; 27 rms, many with marvellous lake view. Welcoming family-run hotel in lovely position on the edge of Lake Windermere with bathing from the hotel jetty; croquet, putting, afternoon tea on the terraces, gracious oak-panelled rooms with antiques, paintings, fresh flowers, open fires, very good food (huge breakfasts, too), and friendly service; two resident dogs; dogs may walk in grounds on a lead but plenty of good walks all around; disabled access; dogs in bedrooms, and in bar and lounges at management discretion

Derbyshire

Dog Friendly Pubs

ALDERWASLEY
Bear *Village signposted with Breanfield off B5035 E of Wirksworth at Malt Shovel; inn ½ mile SW of village, on Ambergate—Wirksworth high back road; DE56 2RD*

Charmingly unspoilt and extremely popular, this busy village pub has a good mix of both locals and visitors. The dark, low-beamed rooms have a cheerful miscellany of antique furniture including high-backed settles and locally made antique oak chairs with derbyshire motifs, and there are staffordshire china ornaments, old paintings and engravings, and a trio of grandfather clocks; the warm open fires in stone fireplaces are welcoming on a cold, dull day. One little room is filled right to its built-in wall seats by a single vast table. It's all very easy going with dominoes players clattering about beside canaries trilling in a huge Edwardian-style white cage (elsewhere look out for the budgerigars and talkative cockatoos). There's a large choice of particularly good often imaginative food. Service is friendly and helpful, and the restaurant is no smoking. You must book to be sure of a table. Well kept Bass, Black Sheep, Greene King Old Speckled Hen, Marstons Pedigree and Whim Hartington Bitter on handpump, and quite a few wines by the glass; darts and board games. Well spaced picnic-sets out on the side grass with peaceful country views. There's no obvious front door – you get in through the plain back entrance by the car park.

Free house ~ Licensee Nicky Fletcher-Musgrave ~ Real ale ~ Bar food (12-9.30) ~ Restaurant ~ (01629) 822585 ~ Children welcome away from bar areas ~ Dogs welcome ~ Open 12-midnight ~ Bedrooms: £45S/£70S

BRASSINGTON
Olde Gate *Village signposted off B5056 and B5035 NE of Ashbourne; DE4 4HJ*

Just a five-minute drive from Carsington Water, this cosy ivy-clad inn is popular with walkers. The traditionally furnished public bar is prettily candlelit at night and has a fine ancient wall clock, rush-seated old chairs, antique settles, including one ancient black solid oak one, and roaring log

fires. Gleaming copper pots sit on a 17th-c kitchen range, pewter mugs
hang from a beam, and a side shelf boasts a collection of embossed Doulton
stoneware flagons. To the left of a small hatch-served lobby, another cosy
beamed room has stripped panelled settles, scrubbed-top tables, and a
blazing fire under a huge mantelbeam. Bar food, from a regularly changing
menu, is mostly home-made (some with a new england influence: the
landlady, Evie, is from Connecticut). The panelled room and bar area are
no smoking. Well kept Marstons Pedigree and a guest such as Wychwood
Wychcraft on handpump, and a good selection of malt whiskies; board
games. Stone-mullioned windows look out across lots of tables in the
pleasant garden to small silvery-walled pastures, and there are some benches
in the small front yard. Maybe Sunday evening boules in summer and
Friday evening bell-ringers. Although the date etched on the building reads
1874, it was originally built in 1616, from magnesian limestone and timbers
salvaged from armada wrecks, bought in exchange for locally mined lead.
*Marstons (W & D) ~ Lease Paul Burlinson ~ Real ale ~ Bar food (12-1.45,
7-8.45; not Mon) ~ (01629) 540448 ~ Children over 10 only ~ Dogs welcome
~ Open 12-2.30(3 Sat and Sun), 7-11; closed Mon except bank hols*

DERBY
Brunswick *Railway Terrace; close to Derby Midland station; DE1 2RU*
Up to 16 real ales on handpump or tapped from the cask are well kept in
this former railwaymen's hostelry. Seven are brewed here (Father Mikes
Dark Rich Ruby, Old Accidental, Second Brew Usual, Mild, Pilsner,
Triple Hop and Triple Gold), with regularly changing guests like
Batemans, Everards Tiger, Holdens Golden Glow, Marstons Pedigree, and
Timothy Taylors Landlord. You can tour the brewery – £7.50 including a
meal and a pint. Weston's Old Rosie farm cider is tapped from the cask.
The welcoming high-ceilinged bar has heavy well padded leather seats,
whisky-water jugs above the dado, and a dark blue ceiling and upper wall,
with squared dark panelling below. The no smoking room is decorated
with little old-fashioned prints and swan's neck lamps, and has a high-
backed wall settle and a coal fire; behind a curved glazed partition wall is a
chatty family parlour (also no smoking) narrowing to the apex of the
triangular building. Informative wall displays tell you about the history and
restoration of the building, and there are interesting old train photographs.
Lunchtime bar food consists of a handful of basic pubby dishes. There are
two outdoor seating areas, including a terrace behind. They'll gladly give
dogs a bowl of water.
*Everards ~ Licensee Graham Yates ~ Real ale ~ Bar food (11.30-2.30 Mon-
Thurs; 11.30-5 Fri and Sat) ~ No credit cards ~ (01332) 290677 ~ Children in
family room ~ Dogs welcome ~ Blues Mon evenings, jazz Thurs evenings ~ Open
11-11; 12-10.30 Sun*

FOOLOW
Bulls Head *Village signposted off A623 Baslow—Tideswell; S32 5QR*
This village pub, close to a small green with a duck pond, has a simply
furnished flagstoned bar plus a couple of quieter areas for eating. A step or

two takes you down into what may once have been a stables with its high ceiling joists, stripped stone, and woodburning stove. On the other side, a smart no smoking dining room has more polished tables set in cosy stalls. Interesting photographs include a good collection of Edwardian naughties. Straightforward bar food includes lunchtime snacks. Adnams, Black Sheep, Shepherd Neame Spitfire and a guest beer on handpump; piped music and darts. The jack russells are called Honey and Jack. Picnic-sets at the side have nice views, and from here you can follow paths out over rolling pasture enclosed by dry-stone walls.

Free house ~ Licensee William Leslie Bond ~ Real ale ~ Bar food (12-2, 6.30-9; 12-2, 5-8 Sun) ~ Restaurant ~ (01433) 630873 ~ Children welcome ~ Dogs allowed in bar ~ Live folk Fri evening and Sun ~ Open 12-3, 6.30-11; 12-10.30 Sun; closed Mon ~ Bedrooms: £50S/£70S

HOLBROOK
Dead Poets *Village signposted off A6 S of Belper; Chapel Street; DE56 0TQ*
There's a thoroughly good mix of customers of all ages in this old-fashioned place – most are keen to enjoy one of the eight well kept real ales on handpump or served in a jug from the cellar: Bass, Greene King Abbot and Marstons Pedigree with guests from breweries such as Church End, Everards, Exmoor and Ossetts. Farm cider and country wines. It's quite a dark interior with low black beams in the ochre ceiling, stripped stone walls, and broad flagstones. There are candles on scrubbed tables, a big log fire in the end stone fireplace, high-backed winged settles forming snug cubicles along one wall, and pews and a variety of chairs in other intimate corners and hideaways. The décor makes a few nods to the pub's present name (it used to be the Cross Keys) including a photo of W B Yeats and a poem dedicated to the pub by Les Baynton, and adds some old prints of Derby. Alongside cobs (from £2, nothing else on Sundays), bar food is limited to a few good value hearty dishes; piped music. Behind is a sort of verandah room with lanterns, fairy lights and a few plants, and more seats out in the yard with outdoor heaters.

Everards ~ Tenant William Holmes ~ Real ale ~ Bar food (lunchtime only) ~ No credit cards ~ (01332) 780301 ~ Children in family room ~ Dogs welcome ~ Open 12-3, 5-11; 12-11 Fri-Sat; 12-10.30 Sun

HOPE
Cheshire Cheese *Off A6187, towards Edale; S33 6ZF*
In an attractive village, this 16th-c pub is close to the Pennine Way and well placed for a walk in the lovely Edale Valley. The friendly chatty landlord will make you feel welcome, and the three very snug oak-beamed rooms all have their own coal fires. As well as lunchtime snacks food includes some traditional pub dishes. The restaurant is no smoking. Well kept Black Sheep Bitter and Whim Hartington plus guests like Coach House Coachmans Best Bitter, Greene King IPA and Salamander Cloud Nine on handpump, and a good range of spirits; piped music. When it's busy, parking can be a problem.

Free house ~ Licensee David Helliwell ~ Real ale ~ Bar food (12-2(2.30 Sat),

6.30-9; all day Sun) ~ Restaurant ~ (01433) 620381 ~ Children in eating area till 9pm ~ Dogs allowed in bar ~ Open 12-3, 6.30-midnight; 12-midnight Sat; 12-10.30 Sun ~ Bedrooms: £50S/£65S(£75B)

KIRK IRETON
Barley Mow *Village signed off B5023 S of Wirksworth; DE6 3JP*
In a pretty hilltop village and surrounded by good walks, this is an unspoilt and unchanging rural inn that has been welcoming travellers since 1750. The dimly lit passageways and narrow stairwells have a timeless atmosphere, helped along by traditional furnishings and civilised old-fashioned service. It's a place to sit and chat and there's a good mix of customers of all ages. The small main bar has a relaxed pubby feel, with antique settles on the tiled floor or built into the panelling, a roaring coal fire, four slate-topped tables, and shuttered mullioned windows. Another room has built-in cushioned pews on oak parquet and a small woodburning stove, and a third room has more pews, a tiled floor, beams and joists, and big landscape prints. One room is no smoking. In casks behind a modest wooden counter are five or six well kept (and reasonably priced) real ales: Archers, Burton Bridge, Cottage, Eccleshall Slaters, Hook Norton Old Hooky, Storm and Whim Hartington IPA; Thatcher's farm cider too. Lunchtime filled rolls are the only food; the decent evening meals are reserved for residents staying in the comfortable rooms. There's a decent-sized garden, and a couple of benches out in front, and a post office in what used to be the pub stables. Handy for Carsington Water.
Free house ~ Licensee Mary Short ~ Real ale ~ No credit cards ~ (01335) 370306 ~ Children in side rooms lunchtime only ~ Dogs allowed in bar and bedrooms ~ Open 12-2, 7-11(10.30 Sun); closed 25 Dec and 1 Jan ~ Bedrooms: £35S/£55B

LADYBOWER RESERVOIR
Yorkshire Bridge *A6013 N of Bamford; S33 0AZ*
Just a short stroll away from the Ladybower Dam and close to the Derwent and Howden reservoirs, this is a friendly and pleasantly old-fashioned hotel. One area has a country cottage feel with floral wallpaper, sturdy cushioned wall settles, staffordshire dogs and toby jugs above a big stone fireplace, china on delft shelves, and a panelled dado. Another extensive area, also with a fire, is lighter and more airy with pale wooden furniture, good big black and white photographs and lots of polished brass and decorative plates on the walls. The Bridge Room (with yet another coal-effect fire) has oak tables and chairs, and the Garden Room gives views across a valley to steep larch woods. Two areas are no smoking. Well liked bar food is traditional. Black Sheep, Copper Dragon Best Bitter, Fullers London Pride, Theakstons Old Peculier on handpump; darts, games machine, board games and piped music; disabled lavatories.
Free house ~ Licensees Trevelyan and John Illingworth ~ Real ale ~ Bar food (12-2, 6-9(9.30 Fri, Sat); 12-8.30 Sun) ~ Restaurant ~ (01433) 651361 ~ Children in dining areas only ~ Dogs allowed in bedrooms ~ Open 10am-11pm ~ Bedrooms: £50B/£68B

LITTON

Red Lion *Village signposted off A623, between B6465 and B6049 junctions; also signposted off B6049; SK17 8QU*

You can be sure of a warm welcome at this 17th-c stone-built village pub, popular with locals and walkers. The two inviting homely linked front rooms have low beams and some panelling, and blazing log fires. There's a bigger back room (no smoking during food service) with an amusing collection of pigs, good-sized tables, and large antique prints on its stripped stone walls. The small bar counter has well kept Barnsley real ale on handpump, plus three guests that usually include Black Sheep, Timothy Taylors and another often from a small brewery such as Kelham Island, with decent wines and several malt whiskies; darts and board games; tasty bar food. A particularly rewarding time to visit is during the annual village well-dressing carnival (usually the last weekend in June), when villagers create a picture from flower petals, moss and other natural materials, and at Christmas a brass band plays carols. It's such a small pub that it's not ideal for children.

Free house ~ Licensees Terry and Michele Vernon ~ Real ale ~ Bar food (12-2, 6-8 (not Sun evening)) ~ (01298) 871458 ~ No children under 6 ~ Dogs welcome ~ Open 11.30-midnight ~ Bedrooms: /£65S(£60B)

OVER HADDON

Lathkil *Village and inn signposted from B5055 just SW of Bakewell; DE45 1JE*

Particularly at lunchtime, there's a chatty, cheerful atmosphere as the many socked customers discuss their walk through Lathkill Dale, a gorgeously secretive limestone valley; dogs are welcome, too, though muddy boots are not and must be left in the lobby. The walled garden is a good place to sit and soak in the views. The licensees have been running this much loved inn for 25 years now and readers continue to sing its praises. The airy room on the right as you go in has a nice fire in the attractively carved fireplace, old-fashioned settles with upholstered cushions and chairs, black beams, a delft shelf of blue and white plates, original prints and photographs, and big windows. On the left, the spacious and sunny no smoking dining area doubles as an evening restaurant. Well kept Charles Wells Bombardier and Whim Hartington Bitter plus guests like Adnams Explorer, Everards Tiger and Thornbridge Lord Marples on handpump, a few unusual malt whiskies, and decent range of wines. The buffet style lunch menu with pubby staples is popular, also daily specials and more elaborate restaurant food in the evening. Piped music, darts, bar billiards, shove-ha'penny, and card and board games.

Free house ~ Licensee Robert Grigor-Taylor ~ Real ale ~ Bar food (lunchtime) ~ Restaurant ~ (01629) 812501 ~ Children allowed away from bar ~ Dogs allowed in bar ~ Open 11.30-11; 12-10.30 Sun; 11.30-3, 6.30-11 in winter ~ Bedrooms: £40B/£65S(£80B)

SHELDON

Cock & Pullet *Village signposted off A6 just W of Ashford; DE45 1QS*

It's quite a surprise to discover that this family-run place was only converted into a pub around 10 years ago – the bar with its flagstones and cheerful assembly of deliberately mismatched furnishings makes it feel much older. As well as low beams, exposed stonework, scrubbed oak tables and pews, and an open fire, the small, cosy rooms have 24 fully working clocks (one for every hour of the day). Black Sheep, Timothy Taylors Landlord and a guest such as Thornbridge Lord Marples on handpump. Bar food is straightforward and reasonably priced. A fireplace is filled with flowers in summer, and around it are various representations of poultry, including some stuffed. A plainer room has pool and a TV; there's also a no smoking snug, and darts and dominoes. At the back is a pleasant little terrace with tables and a water feature. The pub is a year-round favourite with walkers (it can be busy at weekends); the pretty village is just off the Limestone Way.

Free house ~ Licensees David and Kath Melland ~ Real ale ~ Bar food (12-2.30, 6-9) ~ No credit cards ~ (01629) 814292 ~ Children allowed until 8.30 ~ Dogs allowed in bar ~ Open 11-11; 12-10.30 Sun ~ Bedrooms: /£60B

WARDLOW

Three Stags Heads *Wardlow Mires; A623 by junction with B6465; SK17 8RW*
Genuinely traditional, this is a real find if you like your pubs basic and full of character, and enjoy a chat with the locals at the bar. It's situated in a natural sink, so don't be surprised to find the floors muddied by boots in wet weather (and the dogs even muddier). Warmed right through by a cast-iron kitchen range, the tiny flagstoned parlour bar has old leathercloth seats, a couple of antique settles with flowery cushions, two high-backed windsor armchairs and simple oak tables (look out for the petrified cat in a glass case). Abbeydale Absolution, Black Lurcher (brewed for the pub at a hefty 8% ABV), Brimstone and Matins on handpump, and lots of bottled continental and english beers. Hearty home-made food is served on hardy plates that are made in the barn which is a pottery workshop. The front terrace looks across the main road to the distant hills. Please note the opening times.

Free house ~ Licensees Geoff and Pat Fuller ~ Real ale ~ Bar food (12.30-3.30, 7-9 when open) ~ No credit cards ~ (01298) 872268 ~ No toddlers; children allowed away from bar room ~ Dogs welcome ~ Folk music most Sat evenings and alternate Fri ~ Open 7pm-11 Fri; 12-11 Sat, Sun and bank hols; closed Mon-Thurs and Fri lunchtime

WOOLLEY MOOR

White Horse *Badger Lane, off B6014 Matlock—Clay Cross; DE55 6FG*
New licensees have done some refurbishment in this attractive old pub but the tap room is still very much in its original state and has a chatty, pleasant atmosphere. Black Sheep, St Austell Tribute and Timothy Taylors Landlord on handpump, and piped music in the lounge and conservatory (great views of the Ogston reservoir from here). Bar food includes one or two imaginative dishes. The pub looks over the Amber valley, there are picnic-sets in the garden, and a good children's play area.

Musketeers ~ Manager John Parsons ~ Real ale ~ Bar food (12-2, 5-9; not Sun evening) ~ Restaurant ~ (01246) 590319 ~ Children welcome away from tap room ~ Dogs allowed in bar ~ Open 12-3, 5-11; 12-10.30 Sun

Dog Friendly Hotels, B&Bs and Farms

ASHBOURNE
Callow Hall *Mappleton Rd, Ashbourne, Derbyshire DE6 2AA (01335) 300900* (0.5 miles off A515; Mappleton Rd, off B5035 (Union St)) **£140**, plus special breaks; 16 lovely well furnished rms, excellent bthrms. Quietly smart and friendly Victorian mansion up a long drive through grounds with fine trees and surrounded by marvellous countryside with walks; comfortable drawing room with open fire, fresh flowers and plants, and period furniture, very good traditional food using home-grown produce in warmly decorated dining room, excellent breakfasts, and kind hosts; good private fishing; cl 25-26 Dec; disabled access; dogs in bedrooms only

BAKEWELL
Hassop Hall *Hassop, Bakewell, Derbyshire DE45 1NS (01629) 640488* (2.7 miles from A6 in Bakewell via A619 and B6001) **£180.90**, plus winter breaks; 13 gracious rms. Mentioned in the Domesday Book and in lovely parkland surrounded by fine scenery, this handsome no smoking hotel has antiques and oil paintings, an elegant drawing room, oak-panelled bar, good food and friendly service; tennis; no accommodation 3 nights over Christmas; partial disabled access; dogs in bedrooms only

BIGGIN-BY-HARTINGTON
Biggin Hall *Biggin-by-Hartington, Buxton, Derbyshire SK17 0DH (01298) 84451* (0.8 miles off A515, just S of Hartington) **£80**, plus special breaks; 20 spacious rms with antiques, some in converted 18th-c stone building and in bothy. Cheerfully run, no smoking 17th-c house in 8 acres of quiet grounds with a very relaxed atmosphere, two comfortable sitting rooms, one with a library, the other with a woodburning stove in inglenook fireplace, and attractive dining room serving traditional country house home-cooking using local and free range wholefoods; plenty of trails and dales to walk; resident cat, geese and horses; children 12 and over; limited disabled access; dogs in annexe bedrooms only

BIRCH VALE
Waltzing Weasel *New Mills Rd, Birch Vale, High Peak, Derbyshire SK22 1BT (01663) 743402* (2.7 miles off A6, via A6015 New Mills rd) **£75**; 8 lovely rms. Attractive traditional inn with open fire, some handsome furnishings, daily papers and plants in quiet civilised bar, very good food using the best seasonal produce in charming no smoking back restaurant (fine views), and obliging service; walks nearby; no children in evening restaurant; disabled access; dogs in bedrooms and bar

DOVE DALE
Peveril of the Peak *Thorpe, Ashbourne, Derbyshire DE6 2AW (08704) 008109* £**130**, plus special breaks; 45 rms, many with lovely views. Relaxing hotel in pretty village amidst some of the finest scenery in the Peak District and with 11 acres of grounds; comfortable sofas and log fire in spacious lounge bar, friendly staff, and good english cooking in attractive restaurant overlooking the garden; wonderful walking nearby; dogs welcome away from restaurant; £15

GRINDLEFORD
Maynard Arms *Main Rd, Nether Padley, Grindleford, Hope Valley, Derbyshire S32 2HE (01433) 630321* (2 miles off A623, via B6001; Nether Padley) £**85**, plus special breaks; 10 rms. Comfortable hotel with log fire and good Peak District views from the first-floor lounge, smart welcoming bar, good choice of food, popular evening restaurant, and particularly attentive service; good walks in garden and nearby; disabled access; dogs in bedrooms only

HOPE
Underleigh House *Edale Rd, Hope, Castleton, Derbyshire S33 6RF (01433) 621372* £**75**, plus special breaks; 6 thoughtfully decorated rms. In unspoilt countryside, this spotlessly kept, no smoking converted barn has fine views from the comfortable sitting room, hearty breakfasts with good home-made preserves enjoyed around communal table in flagstoned dining room, friendly cheerful owners, and attractive gardens; packed lunches can be arranged; terrific walks on the doorstep; resident dog and cat; cl Christmas, New Year, and Jan; children over 12; partial disabled access; dogs in ground floor bedrooms only (not in any public areas) and by prior arrangement

KIRK IRETON
Barley Mow *Kirk Ireton, Ashbourne, Derbyshire DE6 3JP (01335) 370306* £**55**; 5 rms. Tall, Jacobean, walkers' inn with lots of woodwork in series of interconnecting bar rooms, a solid-fuel stove in beamed residents' sitting room, and well kept real ales; close to Carsington Reservoir so lots of walks; cl Christmas and New Year; dogs in one ground-floor bedroom and in bar

MATLOCK
Riber Hall *Matlock, Derbyshire DE4 5JU (01629) 582795*, £**140**, plus special breaks; 14 lovely beamed rms. Elizabethan manor house in pretty grounds surrounded by peaceful countryside, with antique-filled heavily beamed rooms (one lounge is no smoking and one has a log fire), fresh flowers, an elegant no smoking restaurant with enjoyable food and fine wines, and tennis and croquet; walks in grounds and nearby fields; dogs in bedrooms only; £5

MONSAL HEAD

Monsal Head Hotel *Monsal Head, Buxton, Derbyshire DE45 1NL (01629)*
640250 (1.6 miles off A6 in Ashford, via B6465) **£50**, plus special breaks;
7 very good rms, some with outstanding views. Comfortable and enjoyable
small hotel in marvellous setting high above the River Wye, with horsey
theme in bar (converted from old stables), freshly prepared enjoyable food
using seasonal produce in no smoking restaurant, well kept real ales, and
good service; resident dog; lots of trails and walks from the hotel; cl 25
Dec.; dogs in bedrooms and much of pub but not dining room; £5

ROWSLEY

Peacock *Rowsley, Matlock, Derbyshire DE4 2EB (01629) 733518* (on A6)
£165, plus special breaks; 16 comfortable rms. Smart 17th-c country house
hotel by River Derwent (private fishing in season), with well kept gardens,
friendly staff, interesting and pleasant old-fashioned inner bar, spacious and
comfortable lounge, and very popular restaurant; it's a lovely place just to
stop for coffee (with excellent shortbread), too; dogs may walk in garden,
on moors and at Chatsworth Park; dogs in bedrooms; £10

Devon

Dog Friendly Pubs

ASHPRINGTON
Durant Arms *Village signposted off A381 S of Totnes; OS Sheet 202 map reference 819571; TQ9 7UP*
It would be stretching the imagination a bit to describe this attractive Victorian gabled place as a pub, but readers continue to enjoy their visits here. It's more of a small country hotel with a busy dining side and attached bar but they still stock St Austell Dartmoor Best and Tribute on handpump. The charming and helpful licensees keep the three linked areas spotlessly clean, and there are turkey carpets throughout, comfortably upholstered red dining chairs around clothed tables, and a small corner bar counter in one area with a couple of bar stools in front; piped music. The food is popular so it's best to book if you want to be sure of a table. Good, attentive service. The no smoking dining room has lots of oil and water-colours by local artists on the walls. The flagged back courtyard has teak furniture, and the bedrooms are carefully decorated and comfortable.
Free house ~ Licensees Graham and Eileen Ellis ~ Real ale ~ Bar food ~ Restaurant ~ (01803) 732240 ~ Children welcome with restrictions ~ Dogs allowed in bar ~ Open 11.30-2.30, 6.30-11; 12-2.30, 7-10.30 Sun ~ Bedrooms: £45B/£75B

BRANSCOMBE
Masons Arms *Main Street; signed off A3052 Sidmouth—Seaton, then bear left into village; EX12 3DJ*
This pretty 14th-c longhouse is in a village surrounded by little wooded hills and close to the sea. At the heart of the building is the rambling low-beamed main bar with a massive central hearth in front of the roaring log fire (winter spit roasts), windsor chairs and settles, slate floors, ancient ships' beams, and a good bustling atmosphere. The no smoking Old Worthies bar also has a slate floor, a fireplace with a two-sided woodburning stove, and woodwork that has been stripped back to the original pine. There's also the original no smoking restaurant (warmed by one side of the woodburning stove), and a new beamed restaurant that has been opened above the main bar. Good bar food starts with sandwiches and works up to some very

imaginative dishes. Well kept Branscombe Vale Branoc, Otter Bitter, St Austell Tribute, Wolf Coyote Bitter and a beer named for the pub on handpump, 14 wines by the glass, and 33 malt whiskies; darts, shove-ha'penny, cribbage and dominoes. Outside, the quiet flower-filled front terrace has tables with little thatched roofs, extending into a side garden. They may insist that you leave your credit card behind the bar.

Free house ~ Licensees Colin and Carol Slaney ~ Real ale ~ Bar food ~ Restaurant ~ (01297) 680300 ~ Children in bar with parents but not in restaurant ~ Dogs allowed in bar ~ Open 11-11; 12-10.30 Sun; 11-3, 6-11 weekdays in winter ~ Bedrooms: £40(£55S)(£70B)/£60(£75S)(£90B)

BROADHEMBURY
Drewe Arms *Signposted off A373 Cullompton—Honiton; EX14 3NF*

Even if you drop into this civilised place for just a drink or a sandwich, you will be made just as welcome as those here to enjoy one of the delicious fish dishes. It's a consistently well run place and the small bar has neatly carved beams in its high ceiling and handsome stone-mullioned windows (one with a small carved roundabout horse). On the left, a high-backed stripped settle separates off a little room with flowers on the three sturdy country tables, plank-panelled walls painted brown below and yellow above with attractive engravings and prints, and a big black-painted fireplace with bric-a-brac on a high mantelpiece; some wood carvings, walking sticks and framed watercolours for sale. The flagstoned entry has a narrow corridor of a room by the servery with a couple of tables, and the cellar bar has simple pews on the stone floor. By the time this book is published, all rooms will be no smoking. It's best to book to be sure of a table for the unfailingly good (if not cheap) food, which includes quite a few imaginatively prepared fish dishes. Well kept Otter Bitter, Ale and Bright, plus O'Hanlon's Yellowhammer tapped from the cask, and a very good wine list laid out extremely helpfully – including around half a dozen by the glass. There are picnic-sets in the lovely garden which has a lawn stretching back under the shadow of chestnut trees towards a church with its singularly melodious hour-bell. Thatched and very pretty, the 15th-c pub is in a charming village of similar cream-coloured cottages.

Free house ~ Licensees Kerstin and Nigel Burge ~ Real ale ~ Bar food (not Sun evening) ~ Restaurant ~ (01404) 841267 ~ Children in eating area of bar, restaurant and family room ~ Dogs allowed in bar ~ Open 11-3, 6-11; 12-5 Sun; closed Sun evening

BUCKFAST
Abbey Inn *Just off A38 at A384 junction; take B3380 towards Buckfastleigh, but turn right into Buckfast Road immediately after bridge; TQ11 0EA*

On a fine day, try to bag one of the tables on the terrace overlooking the River Dart here. The pub is a sizeable, pleasant place and the bar has partly panelled walls with some ships' crests there and over the gantry (Mr Davison was in the Royal Navy for many years), two chequered green and beige wooden-armed settees, a mix of high-backed chairs and captain's chairs around a few circular tables, and a woodburning stove in an ornate fireplace. The big no smoking dining room also has a woodburning stove, as well as more panelling and river views. There's quite an emphasis on the well liked pubby bar food. Well kept St Austell Dartmoor Best, HSD and Tribute on handpump, 13 wines by the glass and local cider; piped music and board games. The pub is reached down a steep little drive from the car park.

St Austell ~ Tenants Terence and Elizabeth Davison ~ Real ale ~ Bar food ~ Restaurant ~ (01364) 642343 ~ Children welcome ~ Dogs allowed in bar and bedrooms ~ Open 11-midnight(11pm Sun); 11-2.30, 6-11 Mon-Thurs in winter; closed 26 Dec ~ Bedrooms: £50S/£80S

BUCKLAND BREWER
Coach & Horses *Village signposted off A388 S of Monkleigh; OS Sheet 190 map reference 423206; EX39 5LU*

This is an enjoyable and friendly old village pub with a good mix of regulars and visitors. The heavily beamed bar has comfortable seats (including a handsome antique settle) and a woodburning stove in the inglenook – there's also a good log fire in the big stone inglenook of the cosy lounge. A small back room has darts and pool. Well liked bar food is pubby with a couple of more imaginative specials. The restaurant and lounge bar are no smoking. Well kept Cotleigh Golden Eagle, Fullers London Pride and Shepherd Neame Spitfire on handpump, and around six wines by the glass; games machine, skittle alley (that doubles as a function room), piped music and occasional TV for sports. Tables on a terrace in front and in the side garden, and a self-contained flat above the pub to rent out. Nearby moorland walks and the beaches of Westward Ho! are close by.

Free house ~ Licensees Oliver Wolfe and Nicola Barrass ~ Real ale ~ Bar food (not 25 Dec) ~ Restaurant ~ (01237) 451395 ~ Children welcome ~ Dogs allowed in bar ~ Open 12-3, 6(7 Sun)-11.30

BUCKLAND MONACHORUM
Drake Manor *Off A386 via Crapstone, just S of Yelverton roundabout; PL20 7NA*

The friendly landlady has now been running this charming little pub for 17 years. The heavily beamed public bar on the left has plenty of local customers as well as those from Tavistock and Plymouth, brocade-cushioned wall seats, prints of the village from 1905 onwards, some horse tack and a few ship badges on the wall, and a really big stone fireplace with a woodburning stove; a small door leads to a low-beamed cubbyhole. The snug Drakes Bar has beams hung with tiny cups and big brass keys, a woodburning stove in an old stone fireplace, horsebrasses and stirrups, a fine stripped pine high-backed settle with a partly covered hood, and a mix of other seats around just four tables (the oval one is rather nice). On the right is a small, beamed no smoking dining room with settles and tables on the flagstoned floor. Shove-ha'penny, darts and fruit machine. Well liked bar food is gently imaginative. Well kept Courage Best, Greene King Abbot and Sharps Doom Bar on handpump, around 40 malt whiskies and eight wines by the glass. The sheltered back garden – where there are picnic-sets

– is prettily planted, and the floral displays in front are very attractive all year round.

Punch ~ Lease Mandy Robinson ~ Real ale ~ Bar food (12-2, 7-10(9.30 Sun)) ~ (01822) 853892 ~ Children in restaurant and cellar bar ~ Dogs allowed in bar ~ Open 11.30-2.30(3 Sat), 6.30-11; 12-10.30 Sun

CHERITON BISHOP
Old Thatch Inn *Village signposted from A30; EX6 6JH*
Several of our readers now time their journeys to Cornwall to fit in with a lunchtime stop at this friendly and old-fashioned 16th-c pub. You can be sure of a warm welcome from the landlord, and the lounge and the rambling beamed bar are separated by a large open stone fireplace (lit in the cooler months): Otter Ale, Sharps Doom Bar and a guest like O'Hanlons Yellowhammer or Princetown Jail Ale on handpump, and 10 wines by two sizes of glass. As well as sandwiches and other bar snacks, they offer good, interesting daily specials. The sheltered garden has lots of pretty flowering baskets and tubs.

Free house ~ Licensees David and Serena London ~ Real ale ~ Bar food ~ Restaurant ~ (01647) 24204 ~ Children welcome away from bar area ~ Dogs allowed in bar ~ Open 11.30-3, 6-11; 12-3, 6.30-10.30 Sun; closed winter Sun evenings ~ Bedrooms: £45B/£60B

CLAYHIDON
Merry Harriers *3 miles from M5 junction 26: head towards Wellington; turn left at first roundabout signposted Ford Street and Hemyock, then after a mile turn left signposted Ford Street; at hilltop T-junction, turn left towards Chard – pub is 1½ miles on right; EX15 3TR*
New licensees for this charmingly laid out dining pub, and readers have been quick to voice their enthusiasm. There's a bustling, convivial atmosphere in the several small linked green-carpeted areas, comfortably cushioned pews and farmhouse chairs, lit candles in bottles, a woodburning stove with a sofa beside it, and plenty of horsey and hunting prints and local wildlife pictures. Two dining areas have a brighter feel with quarry tiles and lightly timbered white walls; the restaurant is no smoking. Using local produce, the food is very good and imaginative. Well kept Blackdown Devons Pride, Exmoor Hound Dog and Otter Head on handpump, 14 wines by the glass, local cider and juice, and 25 malt whiskies. Picnic-sets on a small terrace, with more in a sizeable garden sheltered by shrubs and the old skittle alley; this is a good walking area.

Free house ~ Licensees Peter and Angela Gatling ~ Real ale ~ Bar food (not Sun evening or Mon (except bank hol lunchtime)) ~ Restaurant ~ (01823) 421270 ~ Children allowed away from bar but no under 6s Fri or Sat evening ~ Dogs allowed in bar ~ Open 12-3, 6-11; 12-3 Sun; closed Sun evening, Mon (but open lunchtime bank hols)

COCKWOOD
Anchor *Off, but visible from, A379 Exeter—Torbay; EX6 8RA*
Even in mid-winter, this former ex-seaman's mission – totally no smoking

now – remains immensely popular, and you must arrive early to be sure of a table (and even a parking space). There's often a queue to get in but they do two sittings in the restaurant on winter weekends and every evening in summer to cope with the crowds. They are still hoping to build a large extension. As well as the usual dishes, a good range of fish dishes includes 30 different ways of serving mussels, 13 ways of serving scallops and five ways of serving oysters. But despite the emphasis on food, there's still a pubby atmosphere, and they keep six real ales on handpump or tapped from the cask: Bass, Fullers London Pride, Greene King Abbot and Old Speckled Hen, Otter Ale and Timothy Taylors Landlord. Also, a fine wine list of 300 (bin ends and reserves and 12 by the glass), 20 brandies and 20 ports, and 130 malt whiskies. The small, low-ceilinged, rambling rooms have black panelling, good-sized tables in various alcoves, and a cheerful winter coal fire in the snug. Darts, dominoes, cards, fruit machine and piped music. From the tables on the sheltered verandah you can look across the road to the bobbing yachts and crabbing boats in the harbour.

Heavitree ~ Tenants Mr Morgan and Miss Sanders ~ Real ale ~ Bar food (all day) ~ Restaurant ~ (01626) 890203 ~ Children in snug ~ Dogs allowed in bar ~ Open 11-11; 12-10.30 Sun; closed evening 25 Dec

COLEFORD
New Inn *Just off A377 Crediton—Barnstaple; EX17 5BZ*
In an attractive hamlet of thatched cottages, this 13th-c inn strikes a good balance between a proper pub and restaurant. It's an L-shaped building with the servery in the 'angle', and interestingly furnished areas leading off it: ancient and modern settles, spindleback chairs, plush-cushioned stone wall seats, some character tables – a pheasant worked into the grain of one – and carved dressers and chests; also, paraffin lamps, antique prints and old guns on the white walls, and landscape plates on one of the beams, with pewter tankards on another. The chatty resident parrot Captain is most chatty when it's quieter. Bar food ranges from snacks to gently imaginative pub standards. The end-of-the-month pig roasts are popular; good, cheerful service. The restaurant is no smoking. Well kept Badger Best, Otter Ale and Sharps Doom Bar on handpump; piped music and darts. There are chairs, tables and umbrellas on decking under the willow tree along the stream, and more on the terrace.

Free house ~ Licensees Simon and Melissa Renshaw ~ Real ale ~ Bar food ~ Restaurant ~ (01363) 84242 ~ Children welcome ~ Dogs allowed in bar ~ Open 12-3, 6-11; 12-3, 7-10.30 Sun; closed 25 and 26 Dec ~ Bedrooms: £55B/£70B

CULMSTOCK
Culm Valley *B3391, off A38 E of M5 junction 27; EX15 3JJ*
Idiosyncratic and far from smart, this isn't an obvious dining out place. So that makes the good enjoyably imaginative food all the more appreciated by those who like a really unfussy country atmosphere. The salmon-coloured bar has a hotch-potch of modern and unrenovated furnishings, a big fireplace with some china above it, newspapers, and a long stripped

wooden bar counter; further along is a dining room with a chalkboard menu, a small front conservatory, and leading off here, a little oak-floored room with views into the kitchen. You may smoke in the bar but nowhere else. Board games and maybe TV for major sporting events. The landlord and his brother import wines from smaller french vineyards, so you can count on a few of those (they offer 50 wines by the glass), as well as some unusual french fruit liqueurs, somerset cider brandies, vintage rum, good sherries and madeira, local ciders and around six well kept real ales tapped from the cask: Branscombe Vale Branoc, Dark Star American Pale Ale, Dorset Weymouth Harbour Master, O'Hanlons Firefly and Royal Oak, Otter Bitter and Woodfordes Great Eastern. They may hold a May bank holiday weekend beer festival. Outside, tables are very attractively positioned overlooking the bridge and the River Culm. The gents' are in an outside yard.

Free house ~ Licensee Richard Hartley ~ Real ale ~ Bar food (not Sun evening) ~ Restaurant ~ No credit cards ~ (01884) 840354 ~ Children allowed away from main bar ~ Dogs welcome ~ Occasional impromptu piano and irish music ~ Open 12-3, 7-11 (may open all day in good weather); 12-11(10.30 Sun) Sat ~ Bedrooms: £30B/£55B

EAST BUDLEIGH
Sir Walter Raleigh *High Street; EX9 7ED*

This is a nice bustling little local in a pretty thatch-and-cob village. There's a lively local atmosphere, pleasant staff, a low-beamed bar with lots of books on shelves, and well kept Adnams Broadside and Explorer, and Otter Bitter on handpump. The attractive restaurant down a step from the bar is no smoking. Imaginative bar food is very good and changes every couple of months. They are hoping to re-do the garden. There's a fine church with a unique collection of carved oak bench ends, and the pub is handy for Bicton Park gardens. Raleigh himself was born at nearby Hayes Barton, and educated in a farmhouse 300 yards away. Parking is about 100 yards away. No children.

Enterprise ~ Lease Lindsay Mason ~ Real ale ~ Bar food ~ Restaurant ~ (01395) 442510 ~ Dogs allowed in bar ~ Open 11.45-2.30, 6-11; 12-2.30, 7-10.30 Sun

EXMINSTER
Turf Hotel *Follow the signs to the Swan's Nest, signposted from A379 S of village, then continue to end of track, by gates; park, and walk right along canal towpath – nearly a mile; there's a fine seaview out to the mudflats at low tide; EX6 8EE*

The friendly licensees of this very popular pub have now been here for 17 years and have opened a new outside bar with six beers tapped from the cask: Otter Bitter and Ale, O'Hanlons Yellowhammer, Princetown Dartmoor IPA, Skinners Betty Stogs and Topsham & Exminster Ferryman. Also, local Green Valley cider, local juices, local rosé wine and jugs of Pimms. The main outdoor barbecue area is much used in good weather (there are smaller barbecues, too) and there are plenty of picnic-sets spread around the big garden and a children's play area built using a lifeboat from a liner that sank off the Scilly Isles around 100 years ago. Inside, the end room has a slate floor, pine walls, built-in seats, lots of photographs of the pub and a woodburning stove; along a corridor (with an eating room to one side) is a simply furnished room with wood-plank seats around tables on the stripped wooden floor. The tables in the bay windows are much prized so get there early if you want to bag one. Two rooms are no smoking. As well as lunchtime snacks, the imaginative bar food is very good indeed, though there may be quite a wait at peak times. To get to the pub you must either walk (which takes about 20 minutes along the ship canal) or cycle, and there's a 60-seater boat which brings people down the Exe estuary from Topsham quay (15-minute trip, adult £3, child £2); there's also a canal boat from Countess Wear Swing Bridge every lunchtime. Best to phone the pub for all sailing times. For those arriving in their own boat there is a large pontoon as well as several moorings. Although the pub and garden do get packed in good weather and there are inevitable queues, the staff remain friendly and efficient.

Free house ~ Licensees Clive and Ginny Redfern ~ Real ale ~ Bar food (12-2.30(3 weekends), 7-9(9.30 Fri and Sat); not Sun evening) ~ (01392) 833128 ~ Children welcome ~ Dogs welcome ~ Open 11.30-11; 11.30-10.30 Sun; closed Nov-Feb but open weekends in March

HOLNE

Church House *Signed off B3357 W of Ashburton; TQ13 7SJ*
After a walk on Dartmoor, this medieval inn is a welcome place to drop in to and you'll find a friendly welcome from the licensees; there are fine moorland views from the pillared porch (where regulars tend to gather). The lower bar has stripped pine panelling and an 18th-c curved elm settle, and is separated from the lounge bar by a 16th-c heavy oak partition; open log fires in both rooms. Bar food runs from lunchtime snacks to more elaborate choices in the evening. Only one bar is for smoking. Well kept Butcombe Bitter and Teignworthy Reel Ale on handpump, several wines by the glass, and organic cider, apple juice and ginger beer; darts. Morris men and clog dancers in the summer. Charles Kingsley (of *Water Babies* fame) was born in the village.

Free house ~ Licensee J Silk ~ Real ale ~ Bar food (not Sun evening or Mon in winter) ~ Restaurant ~ (01364) 631208 ~ Children in eating area of bar and restaurant ~ Dogs allowed in bar and bedrooms ~ Open 12-2.30(3 Sat and Sun), 7-11; closed Sun evening and Mon in winter ~ Bedrooms: £33S/£55(£66B)

HORNDON

Elephants Nest *If coming from Okehampton on A386 turn left at Mary Tavy Inn, then left after about ½ mile; pub signposted beside Mary Tavy Inn, then Horndon signposted; on the Ordnance Survey Outdoor Leisure Map it's named as the New Inn; PL19 9NQ*
From benches on the spacious lawn in front of this isolated 16th-c inn you can look over dry-stone walls to the pastures and the rougher moorland above; plenty of surrounding walks. Inside, the bar has original stone walls,

flagstones, three woodburning stoves and a beam-and-board ceiling; there's a no smoking dining room and garden room. Well kept Otter Bright, Palmers IPA and Copper Ale, and a guest such as Princetown Jail Ale on handpump, farm cider and a few wines by the glass; piped music. Bar food includes pub staples with a handful of more imaginative dishes. New bedrooms have been added this year.

Free house ~ Licensee Hugh Cook ~ Real ale ~ Bar food (12-2.15, 6.30-9) ~ (01822) 810273 ~ Children allowed but with restrictions ~ Dogs welcome ~ Jazz 2nd Weds of month ~ Open 12-3, 6.30-11(10.30 Sun) ~ Bedrooms: /£65B

IDDESLEIGH
Duke of York *B3217 Exbourne—Dolton; EX19 8BG*

Bustling and unspoilt, full of chatty, friendly regulars (and their dogs), this pub is a throwback to old-fashioned hospitality. The enjoyably unfussy bar has a lot of homely character: rocking chairs by the roaring log fire, cushioned wall benches built into the wall's black-painted wooden dado, stripped tables, and other simple country furnishings. Well kept Adnams Broadside, Cotleigh Tawny, and Sharps Doom Bar tapped from the cask, and quite a few wines by the glass. Good bar food is honestly traditional. It does get pretty cramped at peak times. Darts. Through a small coach arch is a little back garden with some picnic-sets. Fishing nearby. The bedrooms are quirky and in some cases very far from smart, so their appeal is very much to people who enjoy taking the rough with the smooth.

Free house ~ Licensees Jamie Stuart and Pippa Hutchinson ~ Real ale ~ Bar food (all day) ~ Restaurant ~ (01837) 810253 ~ Children welcome ~ Dogs welcome ~ Open 11-11(11.30 Sat); 12-11 Sun; closed evening 25 Dec ~ Bedrooms: £30B/£60B

LOWER ASHTON
Manor Inn *Ashton signposted off B3193 N of Chudleigh; EX6 7QL*

This is a friendly creeper-covered pub with a good, bustling atmosphere and welcoming licensees. Locals tend to head for the left-hand room with beer mats and brewery advertisements on the walls, whereas on the right, two rather more discreet rooms have a wider appeal. Well kept Princetown Jail Ale, RCH Pitchfork and Teignworthy Reel Ale with a couple of guests such as O'Hanlons Yellowhammer and Teignworthy Martha's Mild; Gray's farm cider, several wines by the glass, and local organic fruit juice and ginger beer. Well liked food is home-made. The garden has lots of picnic-sets under cocktail parasols (and a fine tall scots pine), and pretty hanging baskets. No children inside.

Free house ~ Licensee Mark Quilter ~ Real ale ~ Bar food (12-1.30, 7-9; not Mon except bank hols) ~ (01647) 252304 ~ Dogs welcome ~ Open 12-2(2.30 Sat), 6.30-11; 12-2.30, 7-10.30 Sun; closed Mon

LUSTLEIGH
Cleave *Village signposted off A382 Bovey Tracey—Moretonhampstead; TQ13 9TJ*

As this charming thatched no smoking pub is popular with walkers, it's best to get here early. The low-ceilinged lounge bar has attractive antique high-backed settles, cushioned wall seats, and wheelback chairs around the tables on its patterned carpet, granite walls and a roaring log fire. A second bar has similar furnishings, a large dresser, harmonium, an HMV gramophone and prints, and there's a family room with toys for children. Bar food is well presented. Otter Ale, Timothy Taylors Landlord and Wadworths 6X on handpump kept under light blanket pressure, quite a few malt whiskies, several wines by the glass and local organic soft drinks. In summer, you can sit in the sheltered garden – the hanging baskets and flower beds are lovely. Until the car parking field in the village is opened during the summer, parking can be very difficult.

Heavitree ~ Tenant A Perring ~ Real ale ~ Bar food (not Mon) ~ (01647) 277223 ~ Children in family room ~ Dogs welcome ~ Open 11.30-3, 6-11; 11-11 Sat; 12-10.30 Sun; closed Mon

LYDFORD
Castle Inn *Off A386 Okehampton—Tavistock; EX20 4BH*
There's plenty of character and charm in this bustling pink-washed Tudor inn – probably helped by its position next to the daunting, ruined 12th-c castle. The twin-roomed bar has country kitchen chairs, high-backed winged settles and old captain's chairs around mahogany tripod tables on big slate flagstones. One room has low lamp-lit beams, a sizeable open fire, masses of brightly decorated plates, some Hogarth prints and, near the serving counter, seven Lydford pennies hammered out in the old Saxon mint in the reign of Ethelred the Unready, in the 11th c. The bar area has a bowed ceiling with low beams, a polished slate flagstone floor, and a stained-glass door with the famous Three Hares; there's also a snug with high-backed settles. Bar food includes some imaginative dishes.The snug, restaurant and lounge are no smoking. Fullers London Pride, Greene King IPA and Otter Ale on handpump, and 10 wines by the glass; darts, board games, and Wednesday quiz night. You can walk in the beautiful nearby river gorge (owned by the National Trust; closed November-Easter).

Heavitree ~ Tenant Richard Davies ~ Real ale ~ Bar food ~ Restaurant ~ (01822) 820241 ~ Children allowed in snug, restaurant and lounge ~ Dogs allowed in bar and bedrooms ~ Open 11.30-11; 12-10.30 Sun ~ Bedrooms: £45B/£65B

MARLDON
Church House *Just off A380 NW of Paignton; TQ3 1SL*
The spreading bar in this attractive no smoking inn has several different areas that radiate off the big semicircular bar counter. The main part has interesting windows, some beams, dark pine chairs around solid tables on the turkey carpet, and yellow leather bar chairs; leading off here is a cosy little candlelit room with just four tables on the bare-board floor, a dark wood dado and stone fireplace; next to this is the restaurant with a large stone fireplace. At the other end of the building, a similarly interesting room is split into two parts with a stone floor in one bit and a wooden floor in another (which has a big woodburning stove). Bar food is well liked and interesting. Bass, Fullers London Pride, Otter Ale and St Austell Dartmoor

Best on handpump, and 12 wines by the glass; piped music. There are three grassy terraces with picnic-sets behind.

Enterprise ~ Lease Julian Cook ~ Real ale ~ Bar food (12-2, 6.30-9.30) ~ Restaurant ~ (01803) 558279 ~ Children welcome ~ Dogs allowed in bar ~ Open 11.30-2.30, 5-11(11.30 Sat); 12-3, 5.30-10.30 Sun

MOLLAND
London *Village signposted off B3227 E of South Molton, down narrow lanes; EX36 3NG*

Tucked away down narrow lanes, this is a proper Exmoor inn and much enjoyed by those who don't like uniformity. It's a bit quirky and very much huntin', shootin' and fishin', with a water-bowl by the good log fire for the working dogs that come in with their keepers, a Crufts working-dog rosette won by one of the regulars sitting proudly on a shelf, and a really good mix of customers (Princess Anne dropped in for lunch just before we went to press). You can be sure of a genuinely warm welcome from the licensees, and they keep proper farm cider as well as Cotleigh Tawny and Exmoor Ale tapped from casks. The two small linked rooms by the old-fashioned central servery have lots of local stag-hunting pictures, tough carpeting or rugs on flagstones, cushioned benches and plain chairs around rough stripped trestle tables, a table of shooting and other country magazines, ancient stag and otter trophies, and darts, table skittles and dominoes. On the left an attractive beamed room has accounts of the rescued stag which lived a long life at the pub some 50 years ago, and on the right, a panelled dining room with a great curved settle by its fireplace has particularly good hunting and gamebird prints, including ones by McPhail and Hester Lloyd. Honest bar food is traditional at lunchtime and includes some more imaginative evening dishes. The dining room and lower bar are no smoking. A small hall with stuffed birds and animals and lots of overhead baskets has a box of toys, and there are good country views from a few picnic-sets out in front. The low-ceilinged lavatories are worth a look, with their Victorian mahogany and tiling (and in the gents' a testament to the prodigious thirst of the village cricket team). And don't miss the next-door church, with its untouched early 18th-c box pews – and a spring carpet of tenby daffodils in the graveyard. Readers in tune with the down-to-earth style of the pub have enjoyed staying here.

Free house ~ Licensees Mike and Linda Short ~ Real ale ~ Bar food (not Sun evening) ~ Restaurant ~ No credit cards ~ (01769) 550269 ~ Children welcome ~ Dogs allowed in bar and bedrooms ~ Open 11.30-2.30, 6-11.30; 12-2.30, 7-10.30 Sun ~ Bedrooms: /£50B

NEWTON FERRERS
Dolphin *Riverside Road East – follow Harbour dead end signs; PL8 1AE*

By day, the two terraces across the lane from this friendly 18th-c pub have a grandstand view of the boating action on the busy tidal River Yealm below the cottages on these steep hillsides, and at night the floodlit church over in Noss Mayo makes a lovely focal point. Inside, the L-shaped bar has a few low black beams, slate floors, some white-painted plank panelling, and simple pub furnishings including cushioned wall benches and small winged settles; chatty and relaxed out of season, it can get packed in summer. Well liked food is traditional. Sharps Doom Bar, a beer from Skinners named after the pub, and a guest beer on handpump, Heron Valley cider, and eight wines by the glass; darts, a popular quiz night on winter Wednesdays, local card games on Monday evenings, and lots of coastal watercolours. The carpeted no smoking dining room is up a few steps at the back. Parking by the pub is very limited, with more chance of a space either below or above.

Free house ~ Licensee Sandra Dunbar Rees ~ Bar food ~ (01752) 872007 ~ Children in dining room until 9pm; no children in bar ~ Dogs allowed in bar ~ Open 12-3(2.30 in winter), 6-11; 12-3, 7-10.30 Sun; opens 12.30 in winter

NOMANSLAND
Mount Pleasant *B3137 Tiverton—South Molton; EX16 8NN*

As we went to press, we heard that the long-standing licensees were thinking of selling this friendly pub, so we'd be grateful for any news on the forthcoming new people. The long bar here is divided into three with huge fireplaces each end, one with a woodburning stove under a low dark ochre black-beamed ceiling, the other with a big log fire, and there are tables in a sizeable bay window extension. A nice mix of furniture on the patterned carpet includes an old sofa with a colourful throw, old-fashioned leather dining chairs, pale country kitchen chairs and wall pews, and tables all with candles in attractive metal holders; country prints and local photographs including shooting parties. The bar, with plenty of bar stools, has Cotleigh Tawny, Greene King IPA and Sharps Doom Bar on handpump, and nine wines by the glass. Bar food is well liked. On the left, a high-beamed stripped stone no smoking dining room was once a smithy and still has the raised forge fireplace. Piped music, darts and board games; picnic-sets under smart parasols in the neat back garden.

Free house ~ Licensees Anne, Karen and Sarah Butler ~ Real ale ~ Bar food (all day) ~ Restaurant ~ (01884) 860271 ~ Children welcome ~ Dogs allowed in bar ~ Open 11.30-11.30; 12-10.30 Sun; closed evening 25 Dec, 1 Jan

NOSS MAYO
Ship *Off A379 via B3186, E of Plymouth; PL8 1EW*

Almost as soon as this bustling pub opens, all the seats are taken. The front terrace is extremely popular in fine weather – you can sit at the octagonal wooden tables under parasols and look over the inlet, and visiting boats can tie up alongside (with prior permission); there are outdoor heaters for cooler evenings. Inside it's all no smoking, and the two thick-walled bars have a happy mix of dining chairs and tables on the wooden floors, log fires, bookcases, dozens of local pictures, newspapers and magazines to read and a friendly, chatty atmosphere; board games. Changing daily, the popular food takes an interesting twist on traditional dishes. Well kept Butcombe Blonde, Princetown Jail Ale, St Austell Tribute and Summerskills Tamar on handpump, lots of malt whiskies, and 10 wines by the glass. Parking is restricted at high tide. They also own the Turtley Corn Mill at Avonwick.

*Free house ~ Licensees Lesley and Bruce Brunning ~ Real ale ~ Bar food (all day)
~ (01752) 872387 ~ Children allowed before 7pm unless eating ~ Dogs allowed
in bar ~ Open 11.30-11; 12-10.30 Sun*

PETER TAVY
Peter Tavy Inn *Off A386 near Mary Tavy, N of Tavistock; PL19 9NN*
New licensees have taken over this attractive old stone pub but have kept on
the chef and quite a few of the senior staff. The low-beamed bar has high-
backed settles on the black flagstones by the big stone fireplace (a fine log fire
on cold days), smaller settles in stone-mullioned windows, and a good bustling
atmosphere; there's also a snug, no smoking dining area and restaurant. Good
food is imaginative. Blackawton Original Bitter, Princetown Jail Ale, Sharps
Doom Bar and a guest like St Austell HSD on handpump, kept under light
blanket pressure; local farm cider, 20 malt whiskies and 10 wines by the glass;
piped music. From the picnic-sets in the pretty garden, there are peaceful
views of the moor rising above nearby pastures.
*Free house ~ Licensees Chris and Joan Wordingham ~ Real ale ~ Bar food ~
Restaurant ~ (01822) 810348 ~ Children welcome ~ Dogs welcome ~ Open
12-3(4 Sat and Sun), 6-11(10.30 Sun)*

POSTBRIDGE
Warren House *B3212 ¼ mile NE of Postbridge; PL20 6TA*
This no-frills place is handy for a drink after a damp hike on Dartmoor.
The cosy bar has a fireplace at either end (one is said to have been kept
almost continuously alight since 1845), and is simply furnished with easy
chairs and settles under a beamed ochre ceiling, wild animal pictures on the
partly panelled stone walls, and dim lighting (fuelled by the pub's own
generator); there's a no smoking family room. Standard bar food and
Badger Tanglefoot, Otter Ale and Ringwood Old Thumper on
handpump, local farm cider, and malt whiskies. Darts, board games, and
piped music. There are picnic-sets on both sides of the road that enjoy the
moorland views.
*Free house ~ Licensee Peter Parsons ~ Real ale ~ Bar food (all day summer and all
day Thurs-Sun in winter; 12-4 Mon-Weds in winter) ~ (01822) 880208 ~
Children in family room ~ Dogs allowed in bar ~ Open 11-11; 12-10.30 Sun;
11-5 Mon-Weds in winter*

POUNDSGATE
Tavistock Inn *B3357 continuation; TQ13 7NY*
After enjoying one of the many moorland hikes, walkers (and their boots
and dogs on leads) are made welcome in this picturesque old pub. Some
original features include a narrow-stepped granite spiral staircase, original
flagstones, ancient log fireplaces, and beams, and there's a friendly
atmosphere and a good mix of locals and visitors; one small room is no
smoking. Brakspears, Courage Best, Greene King Old Speckled Hen and
Wychwood Hobgoblin Best on handpump, decent wines, and a few malt
whiskies. Traditional bar food and summer afternoon teas. Tables on the
front terrace and pretty flowers in stone troughs, hanging baskets and

window boxes, and more seats (and ducks) in the quiet back garden; lovely scenery. Sir Arthur Conan-Doyle wrote *The Hound of the Baskervilles* while staying here.

InnSpired ~ Lease Peter and Jean Hamill ~ Real ale ~ Bar food (all day in summer) ~ Restaurant ~ (01364) 631251 ~ Children in eating area of bar ~ Dogs allowed in bar ~ Open 11-3, 6-11; 11-11 Sat; 12-10.30 Sun

RATTERY

Church House *Village signposted from A385 W of Totnes, and A38 S of Buckfastleigh; TQ10 9LD*

Dating back to 1028, this is one of Britain's oldest pubs, and the spiral stone steps behind a little stone doorway on your left as you come in date back to that time. The original building here probably housed the craftsmen who built the Norman church, and may then have served as a hostel for passing monks. There are massive oak beams and standing timbers in the homely open-plan bar, large fireplaces (one with a little cosy nook partitioned off around it), windsor armchairs, comfortable seats and window seats, and prints on the plain white walls; the dining room is separated from this room by heavy curtains, and there's also a no smoking lounge area. Bar food is traditional. Well kept Greene King Abbot, Otter Ale, Princetown Jail Ale and St Austell Dartmoor Best on handpump, several malt whiskies, and eight wines by the glass; obliging service. The garden has picnic benches on the large hedged-in lawn, and peaceful views of the partly wooded surrounding hills.

Free house ~ Licensee Ray Hardy ~ Real ale ~ Bar food ~ Restaurant ~ (01364) 642220 ~ Children welcome ~ Dogs allowed in bar ~ Open 11-2.30, 6-11; 12-2.30, 6-10.30 Sun

SANDY PARK

Sandy Park Inn *A382 Whiddon Down—Moretonhampstead; TQ13 8JW*

There's a super mix of customers and a terrific bustling atmosphere in this little thatched inn – all helped along by the friendly and enthusiastic young landlord. The small bar on the right has rugs on the black-painted composition floor, black beams in the cream ceiling, varnished built-in wall settles forming separate areas around nice tables, and bar stools by the chatty bar with Otter Bitter and St Austell Tribute, and perhaps a couple of guests like Exe Valley Dobs Best or O'Hanlons Yellowhammer on handpump, local cider, and a decent choice of wines by the glass; big blow-ups of old golfing pictures and some smaller interestingly annotated Dartmoor photographs. The back snug has one big table that a dozen people could just squeeze around, stripped stone walls and a cream-painted bright-cushioned built-in wall bench. On the left is a small dining room with golfing and other prints on the red walls and just a few tables, and an inner private no smoking dining room with lots of prints and one big table. Enjoyable food includes some traditional and some more imaginative dishes. Board games. There's a large garden with fine views. This is a nice place to stay and the decent breakfasts are cooked by the landlord. They may have preferential fishing rates on the River Teign.

Free house ~ Licensee Simon Saunders ~ Real ale ~ Bar food (12-2.30, 6-9) ~ Restaurant ~ (01647) 433267 ~ Children in snug or dining room ~ Dogs allowed in bar and bedrooms ~ Open 12-11.30; 12-11 Sun ~ Bedrooms: /£80B

SIDBURY
Hare & Hounds *3 miles N of Sidbury, at Putts Corner; A375 towards Honiton, crossroads with B3174; EX10 0QQ*
Extremely popular, this very well run roadside pub is so much bigger inside than you could have guessed from outside. There are two good log fires (and rather unusual wood-framed leather sofas complete with pouffes), heavy beams and fresh flowers throughout, some oak panelling, plenty of tables with red leatherette or red plush-cushioned dining chairs, window seats and well used bar stools too; it's mostly carpeted, with bare boards and stripped stone walls at one softly lit end. At the opposite end of the pub, on the left, another big dining area has huge windows looking out over the garden. The two dining areas are no smoking. The much enjoyed daily carvery counter has a choice of joints and enough turnover to keep up a continuous supply of fresh vegetables. Other food is fairly traditional. Well kept Branscombe, O'Hanlons Yellowhammer and Otter Ale and Bitter tapped from the cask; a side room has a big-screen sports TV. The big garden, giving good valley views, has picnic-sets, a new children's play area, and a new marquee; maybe a small strolling flock of peafowl.
Free house ~ Licensee Peter Cairns ~ Real ale ~ Bar food (all day) ~ Restaurant ~ (01404) 41760 ~ Children welcome with restrictions ~ Dogs allowed in bar ~ Live music Sun lunchtimes in marquee ~ Open 10-11.30; 11.30-11.30 Sun

SLAPTON
Tower *Signposted off A379 Dartmouth—Kingsbridge; TQ7 2PN*
Although many customers come to this atmospheric old place to enjoy the interesting food, they do keep Badger Tanglefoot, Butcombe Bitter and St Austell Tribute on handpump and plenty of our readers drop in with their dogs after a walk. The low-ceilinged beamed bar has armchairs, low-backed settles and scrubbed oak tables on the flagstones or bare boards, open log fires, and farm ciders and several wines by the glass; piped music and board games. The picnic-sets on the neatly kept lawn in the pretty back garden are overlooked by the ivy-covered ruin of a 14th-c chantry – lovely in summer. The lane up to the pub is very narrow and parking is difficult.
Free house ~ Licensees Annette and Andrew Hammett ~ Real ale ~ Bar food ~ Restaurant ~ (01548) 580216 ~ Children not allowed in bar ~ Dogs allowed in bar ~ Open 12-2.30(3 Sat), 6-11; 12-3, 7-10.30 Sun; closed Sun evening and Mon in winter ~ Bedrooms: £50S/£70S

STRETE
Kings Arms *A379 SW of Dartmouth – car park is S of pub; TQ6 0RW*
With its wrought-iron work and canopied upper balcony, this family run pub is very pretty, and there's a back terrace and garden with views over Start Bay. Inside, the L-shaped bar has country kitchen chairs and tables, some comfortable brocaded dining chairs, very nice fish prints on the dark

salmon pink walls, and bar stools by the attractively carved oak bar counter where the chatty locals gather. Well kept Adnams Best, Fullers London Pride and Otter Ale on handpump, 15 wines by the glass (including sweet ones) from a carefully chosen list, a dozen malt whiskies and local Heron Valley cider; board games. Up some stairs is the little no smoking restaurant decorated in cool blue/green colours with dark green padded plush and pale wood chairs around wooden tables. Using local and regional produce and baking their own breads, brioche, oatcakes and biscuits, the main menu is the same throughout, and includes lots of imaginatively prepared fish dishes. The pub is on the South West Coastal Path.

Heavitree ~ Tenant Rob Dawson ~ Real ale ~ Bar food (12-2 (3 Sun), 6.30-9.30) ~ Restaurant ~ (01803) 770377 ~ Children welcome ~ Dogs allowed in bar ~ Open 11.30-2.30(3 Sat), 6.30(6 Sat)-11; 12-4, 7-10.30 Sun; Sun evening and all day Mon in winter

TORBRYAN

Old Church House *Most easily reached from A381 Newton Abbot—Totnes via Ipplepen; TQ12 5UR*

Quietly set next to the part-Saxon church with its battlemented Norman tower, this Grade II★ listed 13th-c inn is doing very well at the moment. The particularly attractive bar on the right of the door is neatly kept and bustling, and has benches built into the fine old panelling as well as a cushioned high-backed settle and leather-backed small seats around its big log fire. On the left there are a series of comfortable and discreetly lit lounges, one with a splendid deep Tudor inglenook fireplace with a side bread oven. The restaurant is no smoking, and the traditional bar food is enjoyable; piped music. Well kept Skinners Betty Stogs and Cornish Knocker and maybe a guest beer on handpump, 25 malt whiskies and quite a few wines; friendly service. Plenty of nearby walks.

Free house ~ Licensees Kane and Carolynne Clarke ~ Real ale ~ Bar food ~ Restaurant ~ (01803) 812372 ~ Children welcome but with restrictions ~ Dogs allowed in bar ~ Accoustic guitar Thurs evening, open music night Sun ~ Open 11-11; 12-10.30 Sun ~ Bedrooms: £54B/£69B

TUCKENHAY

Maltsters Arms *Take Ashprington road out of Totnes (signed left off A381 on outskirts), keeping on past Watermans Arms; TQ9 7EQ*

This is a lovely spot by a peaceful wooded creek with tables by the water, and in summer there are barbecues and regular live music concerts on the quayside. Inside, the long, narrow bar links two other rooms – a little snug one with an open fire and plenty of bric-a-brac, and another with red-painted vertical seats and kitchen chairs on the wooden floor; there are nautical charts and attractive local photographs on the walls. Well kept Princetown Dartmoor IPA, Sharps Atlantic, South Hams Devon Pride and Teignworthy Springtide on handpump, 19 wines by the glass, a dozen malt whiskies, local farm cider and summer Pimms and cocktails. As well as nice bar nibbles, the bar food is enjoyably imaginative and includes several healthy children's dishes. The restaurant is no smoking. Darts, board games, and TV for sports.

Free house ~ Licensees Denise and Quentin Thwaites ~ Real ale ~ Bar food (12-3, 7-9.30; all day summer weekends) ~ Restaurant ~ (01803) 732350 ~ Children welcome away from bar and must be over 12 in main restaurant ~ Dogs welcome ~ Live music 1st and 3rd Fri of month; outside events in summer ~ Open 11-11; closed evening 25 Dec ~ Bedrooms: /£85S

WINKLEIGH

Kings Arms *Village signposted off B3220 Crediton—Torrington; Fore Street; EX19 8HQ*

There's a welcome for all from the friendly licensees here – children and dogs included. The attractive beamed main bar has some old-fashioned built-in wall settles, scrubbed pine tables and benches on the flagstones, and a woodburning stove in a cavernous fireplace; another woodburning stove separates the bar from the no smoking dining rooms (one has military memorabilia and a mine shaft). Popular bar food is mostly traditional. Well kept Butcombe Bitter, and Sharps Cornish Coaster and Doom Bar on handpump, local cider and decent wines; darts, board games, shut-the-box and Jenga. There are seats out in the garden.

Enterprise ~ Lease Chris Guy and Julia Franklin ~ Real ale ~ Bar food (all day) ~ Restaurant ~ (01837) 83384 ~ Children welcome ~ Dogs allowed in bar ~ Open 11-11; 12-10.30 Sun

WONSON

Northmore Arms *A30 at Merrymeet roundabout, take first left on old A30, through Whiddon Down; new roundabout and take left on to A382; then right down lane signposted Throwleigh/Gidleigh. Continue down lane over hump-back bridge; turn left to Wonson; OS Sheet 191 map reference 674903; EX20 2JA*

Tucked away down narrow lanes, this secluded cottage is perhaps nicest on a sunny day when you can sit out in the sloping rustic and peaceful garden. The two small connected beamed rooms – modest and informal – have wall settles, up to three tables in each room, and an open fire and woodburning stove; the granite walls are hung with some attractive photographs. Well kept Adnams Broadside, Cotleigh Tawny and Exe Valley Dobs tapped from the cask, and good house wines; darts and board games. A small range of bar food is traditional and simple. The ladies' lavatory is up steep steps. Excellent walking from the pub (or to it, perhaps from Chagford or Gidleigh Park). Castle Drogo is close by. Although the pub is open all day, readers have occasionally found it shut, so it might be best to phone before setting out.

Free house ~ Licensee Mrs Mo Miles ~ Real ale ~ Bar food (all day Mon-Sat; 12-2.30, 7-9 Sun) ~ (01647) 231428 ~ Children allowed away from bar ~ Dogs allowed in bar ~ Open 11-11; 12-10.30 Sun ~ Bedrooms: /£40

WOODLAND

Rising Sun *Village signposted off A38 just NE of Ashburton – then keep eyes peeled for Rising Sun signposts (which may be hidden in the hedges); pub N of village itself, near Combe Cross; TQ13 7JT*

Friendly new licensees have taken over this bustling pub but happily not much seems to have changed. There's an expanse of softly lit red plush button-back banquettes and matching studded chairs, partly divided by wooden banister rails, masonry pillars and the odd high-backed settle. A forest of beams is hung with thousands of old doorkeys, and a nice part by the log fire has shelves of plates and books, and old pictures above the fireplace. Princetown Jail Ale and a local guest beer on handpump, 10 wines by the glass and Luscombe cider. The family area has various toys. Bar food includes some interesting dishes. You may smoke only in the bar area. There are some picnic-sets in the spacious garden which has a play area including a redundant tractor.

Free house ~ Licensees Simon and Hazel Towle ~ Real ale ~ Bar food (12-2.15(3 Sun), 6(7 Sun)-9.15; not Mon) ~ Restaurant ~ (01364) 652544 ~ Children welcome ~ Dogs allowed in bar ~ Open 12-3, 6-11; 12-3, 7-10.30 Sun; closed Mon ~ Bedrooms: £38B/£65B

YEALMPTON
Rose & Crown *A379 Kingsbridge—Plymouth; PL8 2EB*
An offshoot of the Dartmoor Union over at Holbeton, this newly reopened pub is now a stylish place for a drink or an imaginatively prepared meal, satisfyingly civilised without being at all formal or overbearing. The big central bar counter, all dark wood and heavy brass with good solid leather-seated bar stools, has a splendid range of wines by the glass, Courage Best and Sharps Doom Bar on handpump, a fine choice of other drinks, and Burts crisps. Service by neatly aproned black-dressed staff is quick and friendly. There's an attractive mix of tables and old dining chairs, with good lighting, and some leather sofas down on the left. With its stripped wood floor and absence of curtains and other soft furnishings, the open-plan bar's acoustics are lively; beige carpeting keeps the two dining areas on the right rather quieter, and here smart leather high-backed dining chairs, flowers on the tablecloths and framed 1930s high-life posters take you a notch or two upscale.They also have an attractive adjacent seafood restaurant with super big fishing photographs, lobster pots and nets on decking, and high-backed powder blue cushioned dining chairs around white clothed tables.

Free house ~ Licensee Simon Warner ~ Real ale ~ Bar food (12-2, 6.30-9.30; 12-3.30, 6.30-9 Sun) ~ Restaurant ~ (01752) 880223 ~ Children welcome ~ Dogs allowed in bar ~ Open 12-11(10.30 Sun)

Dog Friendly Hotels, B&Bs and Farms

ALLERFORD
West Lynch Farm *West Lynch, Allerford, Somerset TA24 8HJ (01643) 862816 £55*; 3 rms. Listed 15th-c no smoking National Trust farmhouse in six acres of landscaped gardens and paddocks on the edge of Exmoor; lots of original features, antiques and persian rugs, homely lounge with

woodburning stove, super breakfasts with their own honey and home-made marmalade, and lots of animals; falconry tuition and hawking all year, a collection of owls and birds of prey, clay pigeon shooting, and riding; children over 5; no walking in the grounds but lots in surrounding countryside; 6 resident dogs; dogs welcome by arrangement; £5

ASHBURTON

Holne Chase *Ashburton, Newton Abbot, Devon TQ13 7NS (01364) 631471* **£160**, plus winter breaks; 16 comfortable and individually furnished rms, many with views over the Dart Valley, and some split-level suites in converted stables. Marvellously peaceful ex-hunting lodge of Buckfast Abbey, in 70 acres with sweeping lawns and plenty of woodland walks, two miles of Dart fishing, shooting and riding on Dartmoor; cheerful welcoming owners, comfortable public rooms with log fires, very good modern english cooking using home-grown vegetables in no smoking restaurant, and enjoyable breakfasts and afternoon teas (home-made breads and so forth); resident dog; children over 10 in evening restaurant; dogs welcome away from restaurant; bed, towels, own menu, spa; £7.50

Roborough House *85 East Street, Ashburton, Devon TQ13 7AL (01364) 654614* **£60**; 3 individually furnished rms. Handsome listed townhouse with welcoming staff, a relaxed, informal atmosphere and particularly good west country breakfasts using as much organic produce as possible; large romantic garden with small Victorian knot maze, large lawned area and safe children's garden with bouncy castle; lots of places in village for evening meals; dogs in bedrooms

BAMPTON

Bark House *Oakford Bridge, Bampton, Devon EX16 9HZ (01398) 351236* **£90**; 5 cottagey rms. Charming no smoking hotel with lovely rural views, garden with croquet and plenty of surrounding walks; caring, hospitable owners, open fires and low beams in comfortable homely sitting and dining rooms, delicious food using local produce, a thoughtful wine list, and super breakfasts; resident cat; dogs in bedrooms; £3.50

BIGBURY-ON-SEA

Henley *Folly Hill, Bigbury-on-sea, Kingsbridge, Devon TQ7 4AR (01548) 810240* **£100**; 6 compact rms. Renovated no smoking Edwardian cottage with fine views of the Avon estuary, Burgh Island, and beyond; lounge and conservatory dining room with magnificent sea views, deep wicker chairs and polished furniture, binoculars and books, good, enjoyable food from a small menu, super breakfasts, and steep, private path down the cliff to a sandy bay where dogs may walk; cl Nov-Mar; dogs in bedrooms only; £3

BISHOP'S TAWTON

Halmpstone Manor *Bishop's Tawton, Barnstaple, Devon EX32 0EA (01271) 830321* (3.6 miles off A39; A377 for 2 miles, then turn left just before crossing railway and river) **£100**; 4 pretty rms. Quietly relaxing small country house with log fire in comfortable sitting room, enjoyable food in panelled dining room by arrangement, good breakfasts, caring service, an attractive garden, and nice views; field walks all round for dogs and plenty to do nearby; resident dog; cl Christmas and New Year; dogs welcome away from restaurant

BOLBERRY
Port Light *Bolberry, Salcombe, Devon TQ7 3DY (01548) 561384* £**108**; 6 pleasant rms with lovely views. Clifftop former RAF radar station (an easy walk from Hope Cove) with a warmly friendly welcome, good home-made food (super fresh fish) in attractive bar and restaurant, woodburner, and good outdoor children's play area; 20 acre NT field borders the garden; dogs welcome

BOVEY TRACEY
Edgemoor Hotel *Haytor Rd, Bovey Tracey, Newton Abbot, Devon TQ13 9LE (01626) 832466* (3.3 miles off A38; B3344 from Chudleigh Knighton, then keep on into B3387) £**135**, plus special breaks; 16 charming rms.No smoking ivy-covered country house in neatly kept gardens on the edge of Dartmoor, with comfortable lounge and bar, log fires, good modern english cooking in elegant restaurant; two resident dogs; walks in grounds and on Dartmoor; cl 27 Dec-12 Jan; no children; limited disabled access; dogs in Woodland Wing bedrooms with back door leading to private patio

BRADWORTHY
Lake Villa *Bradworthy, Devon EX22 7SQ (01409) 241962* £**52**; 2 rms with garden or country views. 300-year-old farmhouse offering a warm welcome from the friendly owners to well-behaved pets (and their owners); gardens, tennis court and barbecue equipment, and nearby common for dog exercise; walking holidays arranged, and self-catering also; dogs in bedrooms

BRATTON FLEMING
Bracken House Hotel *Bratton Fleming, Barnstaple, Devon EX31 4TG (01598) 710320* £**134** inc dinner; 8 rms. Peacefully set little no smoking hotel, once a rectory, on the edge of Exmoor in eight acres of gardens and woodland with plenty of wildlife and walks – they also care for injured owls; a genuine welcome from the friendly owners, comfortable drawing room with a small bar, library with books on the area, plenty of owl ornaments and house plants, open fires, hearty breakfasts, and enjoyable Aga-cooked evening meals using local produce; children over 13; chickens and ducks; self-catering cottage, too; cl Christmas and New Year; disabled access; dogs welcome away from dining room; bowls, towels, bedding and blankets available

CHAGFORD
Easton Court *Sandy Park, Chagford, Newton Abbot, Devon TQ13 8JN (01647) 433469* £**72**; 5 comfortable rms. Extended Tudor thatched

longhouse (no smoking now) in four acres of gardens and paddocks, with a relaxed and informal atmosphere, hearty breakfasts in guest lounge/breakfast room, helpful, friendly owners, and lots to do nearby; resident dog; plenty of surrounding pubs and restaurants; children over 10; partial disabled access; dogs in some bedrooms; £2.50

Gidleigh Park *Chagford, Newton Abbot, Devon TQ13 8HH (01647) 432367* £440 inc dinner, plus winter breaks; 24 opulent and individual rms with fruit and flowers. Exceptional and luxurious Dartmoor-edge mock Tudor hotel – no smoking throughout – with deeply comfortable panelled drawing room, wonderful flowers, conservatory overlooking the fine grounds (45 acres, with walks straight up on to the moor), log fires, particularly fine cooking and a marvellous wine list, and caring staff; children over 7 in restaurant; disabled access; dogs in bedrooms only

CLAWTON
Court Barn Hotel *Clawton, Holsworthy, Devon EX22 6PS (01409) 271219* £80, plus special breaks; 7 individually furnished rms. Charming country house in three acres of pretty gardens with croquet, 9-hole putting green, small chip-and-putt course, and tennis and badminton courts; comfortable lounges, log fires, library/TV room, a bar (the only place you may smoke), good service, imaginative food and super wines (and teas), and a quiet relaxed atmosphere; walks in grounds and surrounding country lanes; they are kind to families; dogs in bedrooms only with bowls and treats; £3

DARTMOUTH
Royal Castle *11 The Quay, Dartmouth, Devon TQ6 9PS (01803) 833033* £165, plus special breaks; 25 individually furnished, charming rms. Well restored and partly no smoking mainly Georgian hotel (part 16th c) overlooking the inner harbour – great views from most rooms; lively and interesting public bar with open fires and beams, quiet library/lounge with antiques, drawing room overlooking the quayside, winter spit-roasts in lounge bar, elegant upstairs river view restaurant, decent bar food, and friendly staff; walks in nearby park and more nearby; dogs in some bedrooms

EXETER
Barcelona Hotel *Magdalen St, Exeter, Devon EX2 4HY (01392) 281000* £105, plus special breaks; 46 beautifully furnished rms with CD-player and video, and lovely bthrms. Stylishly modern, converted Victorian eye hospital filled with bright posters and paintings, a bar with 1950s-style furniture and fashionable cocktails, a smart but informal no smoking restaurant overlooking the big walled garden, good contemporary food, a nightclub, and very helpful staff; walks in nearby park; disabled access; dogs in bedrooms; £15

Edwardian Hotel *30-32 Heavitree Rd, Exeter, Devon EX1 2LQ (01392) 276102* £**66**, plus special breaks; 12 individually furnished rms, 3 with four-posters. Popular no smoking guesthouse close to cathedral and city centre, with pretty lounge, enjoyable breakfasts in attractive dining rooms, and warmly friendly and knowledgeable resident owners; plenty of places nearby for evening meals; park opposite for dog walking; partial disabled access; dogs in bedrooms and lounge; must be well behaved; £10

EXFORD

Crown *Exford, Minehead, Devon TA24 7PP (01643) 831554* £**99**; 17 rms. Comfortably upmarket no smoking coaching inn on the village green in Exmoor National Park with a delightful back water garden – a lovely summer spot with trout stream, gently sloping lawns, tall trees and plenty of tables; brightly furnished lounge with very relaxed feel, hunting prints on cream walls, old photographs of the area, and smart cushioned benches; real ales, a good wine list, and enjoyable modern cooking in candlelit dining room with simpler meals in the bar; a good base for walking; resident dog; children must be over 12 in restaurant; dogs in bedrooms; £5

GALMPTON

Burton Farm *Galmpton, Kingsbridge, Devon TQ7 3EY (01548) 561210* £**77.50**; 14 pretty rms. Welcoming working farm in lovely countryside with dairy herd and pedigree sheep (guests can enjoy farm activities) and traditional farmhouse cooking using home-produced ingredients; own tea time and play area for children; no smoking throughout; kennels available; coastal walks; cl Christmas and New Year; dogs in cottage; £5

GITTISHAM

Combe House *Gittisham, Honiton, Devon EX14 3AD (01404) 540400* (2 miles off A30 at W end of Honiton bypass) £**170**, plus winter breaks; 16 individually decorated pretty rms with lovely views. Peaceful, Grade I listed, Elizabethan country hotel in gardens with 400-year-old cedar of Lebanon, and walks around the 3,500-acre estate; elegant sitting rooms with fine panelling, antiques, portraits and fresh flowers, a happy relaxed atmosphere, very good food in no smoking restaurant and faithfully restored Georgian kitchen, and fine wines; resident cat; cl 2 wks end Jan; dogs in some bedrooms and public rooms (not restaurant); £6

HAWKCHURCH

Fairwater Head Country House *Hawkchurch, Axminster, Devon EX13 5TX (01297) 678349* £**140**; 20 rms most with country views. Edwardian hotel in quiet, flower-filled gardens with genuinely friendly, attentive owners and staff, open fire in comfortable lounge hall, a well stocked bar and wine cellar, and enjoyable food in no smoking restaurant; croquet; resident dog; cl Jan; disabled access; dogs in bedrooms

HAYTOR VALE

Rock Inn *Haytor Vale, Newton Abbot, Devon TQ13 9XP (01364) 661305*
£**86.95**, plus special breaks; 9 individual rms. Civilised and no smoking old
coaching inn on the edge of Dartmoor National Park, with very good
lunchtime and evening food, a nice mix of visitors and locals in the two
rooms of the panelled bar, open fires, courteous service, and big garden;
walking on the moor and fishing, riding and golf nearby; cl 25 Dec; dogs in
some bedrooms; £5

HEXWORTHY

Forest Inn *Hexworthy, Princetown, Yelverton, Devon PL20 6SD (01364)*
631211 £**70**; 10 cosy, comfortable rms. Country inn in fine Dartmoor
setting, popular with walkers and anglers; varied menu in both bar and no
smoking restaurant, local ales, good choice of wines, and welcoming staff;
two resident pets; cl 25 Dec; dogs welcome with treats

ILFRACOMBE

Strathmore Hotel *57 St Brannock's Road, Ilfracombe, Devon EX34 8EQ*
(01271) 862248 £**60**; 8 pretty rms. Victorian hotel close to the town
centre and beach with a comfortable and well stocked lounge bar, hearty
breakfasts in attractive dining room, welcoming owners and staff, and a
terraced garden; resident dog; plenty of nearby walks; dogs in bedrooms;
own personal letter and big breakfasts; £5

LEWDOWN

Lewtrenchard Manor *Lewdown, Okehampton, Devon EX20 4PN (01566)*
783256 £**155**, plus special breaks; 14 well equipped rms with fresh flowers
and period furniture. Lovely Elizabethan manor house in garden with fine
dovecot and surrounded by peaceful estate with shooting, fishing and
croquet – and walks; dark panelling, ornate ceilings, antiques, fresh flowers,
and log fires, a friendly welcome, relaxed atmosphere, and candlelit no
smoking restaurant with very good imaginative food; resident cat; children
over 8 in evening restaurant; partial disabled access; dogs in bedrooms
(must not be left alone); £10

LIFTON

Arundell Arms *Fore St, Lifton, Devon PL16 0AA (01566) 784666* (a mile
off A30, at A388 turn–off) £**160**, plus special breaks; 21 well equipped rms.
Carefully renovated old coaching inn with 20 miles of its own waters –
salmon and trout fishing and a long-established fly-fishing school;
comfortable sitting room, log fires, super food in both bar and elegant no
smoking restaurant, carefully chosen wines, and kind service from local
staff; attractive terraced garden (where dogs may walk) and walks in nearby
playing fields; cl 3 nights over Christmas; dogs welcome away from
restaurant; bowls and food on request; £6

MALBOROUGH
Soar Mill Cove Hotel *Malborough, Salcombe, Devon TQ7 3DS (01548)*
561566 £**200** inc dinner, plus special breaks; 22 comfortable rms that open
on to garden. Neatly kept single-storey no smoking hotel in idyllic spot by
peaceful and very beautiful cove on NT coast (excellent walks; they also
have a dog walk map), with lovely views, extensive private grounds,
tennis/putting, and warm indoor pool; outstanding service, very good food
(marvellous fish) in restaurant and coffee shop, and they are particularly
kind to children of all ages: microwave, fridge and so forth, for little ones,
own high tea or smaller helpings of most meals, fully equipped laundry, a
play room, table tennis and snooker, and swings; resident dog; cl Jan;
disabled access; dogs in bedrooms and coffee shop

MEMBURY
Lea Hill *Membury, Axminster, Devon EX13 7AQ (01404) 881881* £**70**,
plus winter breaks; 4 individually furnished rms. Thatched, no smoking
14th-c longhouse in 8 acres of secluded grounds and lovely views;
comfortable and cosy guest lounge with books and helpful information,
beamed dining room with woodburning stove, relaxed and friendly
owners, good breakfasts, and light suppers by arrangement; resident dog
and cat; self-catering, too; footpaths from the grounds for walks; dogs in
bedrooms and guest lounge (if other guests are agreeable)

MORETONHAMPSTEAD
Great Sloncombe Farm *Moretonhampstead, Newton Abbot, Devon TQ13
8QF (01647) 440595* £**60**; 3 rms – the big double is the favourite. Lovely
no smoking 13th-c farmhouse on a working stock farm, with friendly
owners, carefully polished old-fashioned furniture in oak-beamed lounge
with woodburning stove in inglenook and games and books, hearty
breakfasts, a relaxed atmosphere, and good nearby walking and bird-
watching; three resident dogs and outside farm cats; children over 8; dogs
welcome in bedrooms

NORTHAM
Yeoldon House *Durrant Lane, Northam, Bideford, Devon EX39 2RL
(01237) 474400* £**105**, plus special breaks; 10 individually decorated rms.
Quietly set hotel in two acres of grounds by the River Torridge, with a
warmly friendly and relaxed atmosphere, a comfortable lounge (the only
place you may smoke), good food using local produce in the attractive
dining room, and helpful service; two resident dogs; plenty of walks; lots to
do nearby; cl Christmas; dogs in bedrooms and lounge; £5

NORTH BOVEY
Gate House *North Bovey, Newton Abbot, Devon TQ13 8RB (01647)
440479* £**70**, plus special breaks; 3 charming rms. 15th-c thatched cottage
in picturesque village, with huge granite fireplace in attractive beamed
sitting room, breakfasts and candlelit evening meals in beamed dining
room, tea with home-made cakes, friendly owners, and outdoor swimming

pool in peaceful garden; plenty to do nearby and walks down to the river; cl Christmas; no children; dogs in bedrooms only; must be fed outside

PARKHAM

Penhaven *Rectory Lane, Parkham, Bideford, Devon EX39 5PL (01237) 451711* £140; 12 spacious rms inc suites in cottages. No smoking former rectory – under new ownership – in ten acres of lovely grounds with plenty of wildlife – the local badgers come onto the lawn at night; friendly, peaceful atmosphere, big fire in the lounge, and good seasonal food using local produce in the dining room that overlooks the wood and garden; walks in grounds; cl Jan; children over 10; dogs in bedrooms only; £7

PORLOCK

Andrews on the Weir *Porlock Weir, Minehead, Somerset TA24 8PB (01643) 863300* £130; 5 rms, some with sea view. Victorian villa housing a restaurant-with-rooms overlooking the harbour; country house-style décor, imaginative modern british cooking using first-class local produce (Exmoor hill lamb, fish freshly landed on the nearby quay, and west country cheeses are excellent), lovely puddings, and a well chosen wine list; cl Mon and Tues and all Jan; children over 12; dogs welcome in bedrooms

Seapoint *Redway, Porlock, Minehead, Somerset TA24 8QE (01643) 862289* £60, plus winter breaks; 1 rm plus two apartments. Surrounded by the Exmoor hills and with views of Porlock Bay (plenty of fine walks), this no smoking Edwardian guesthouse has a comfortable sitting room with winter log fire, a friendly and relaxing atmosphere, enjoyable home-made food in candlelit dining room, and fine breakfasts; cl Dec/Jan; they are kind to children; dogs in bedrooms

POSTBRIDGE

Lydgate House *Postbridge, Yelverton, Devon PL20 6TJ (01822) 880209* £120; 7 rms. Friendly and relaxed no smoking Victorian country house in a secluded wild Dartmoor valley spot (lots of wildlife), with a log fire in the comfortable sitting room, good, simple modern cooking in candlelit conservatory dining room, and fine breakfasts (light lunches and picnics are available); good walks from the door; resident dogs and cats; no children; dogs in bedrooms and guest lounge; £5

SALCOMBE

Tides Reach *Cliff Rd, South Sands, Salcombe, Devon TQ8 8LJ (01548) 843466* £212 inc dinner, plus special breaks; 35 rms, many with estuary views. Unusually individual resort hotel run by long-serving owners in pretty wooded cove by the sea, with airy luxury day rooms, big sea aquarium in cocktail bar, good restaurant food using fresh local produce, friendly efficient service, and squash, snooker, leisure complex, health area, and big heated pool; windsurfing etc, beach over lane, and lots of coast walks; cl Dec-Jan; children over 8; dogs in bedrooms; £8.50

SANDY PARK

Mill End *Sandy Park, Chagford, Newton Abbot, Devon TQ13 8JN (01647) 432282* (3.5 miles off A30, via A382) **£150**, plus special breaks; 15 attractive rms with fine bthrms and views. Quietly set no smoking former flour mill with waterwheel in neatly kept grounds below Dartmoor with 600 yards of private salmon and trout fishing, access to miles of game fishing and still-water fishing on local lakes; comfortable lounges, carefully prepared interesting food, fine breakfasts, cream teas on the lawn, and good service; two resident dogs and one cat; plenty of surrounding walks; cl 2 wks Jan; children over 12; partial disabled access; dogs in bedrooms; towels, leads, bowls and so forth; £10

SELWORTHY

Hindon Farm *Selworthy, Minehead, Somerset TA24 8SH (01643) 705244* **£70**; 3 rms. Organic and no smoking Exmoor hill farm of 500 acres with sheep, pigs, cattle, donkeys and ducks; lovely walks from the door to the heather moors (must be on a lead on the farm until away from stock animals); fine breakfasts using their own organic bacon, sausages, eggs and fresh baked bread; self-catering cottage with free organic produce hamper on arrival; own organic farm shop; several resident dogs; no B&B Christmas and New Year; dogs in bedrooms if well house trained, £5

SHEEPWASH

Half Moon *Sheepwash, Beaworthy, Devon EX21 5NE (01409) 231376* **£90**, plus special breaks; 14 rms inc some in converted stables. Civilised and no smoking heart-of-Devon hideaway in colourful village square with 10 miles of private salmon, sea trout and brown trout fishing on the Torridge and plenty of walks; a neatly kept friendly bar, solid old furnishings and big log fire, good wines, lovely evening restaurant (not Sun), and lunchtime bar snacks; three resident dogs; cl 20-27 Dec; limited disabled access; dogs welcome away from dining room; £5

SIDFORD

Salty Monk *Church St, Sidford, Exeter, Devon EX10 9QP (01395) 513174* **£100**; 5 cottagey rms, some with spa baths. 16th-c, no smoking former salt house (where monks trading in salt stayed on their way to Exeter) with leather armchairs in comfortable lounge, good food using local produce cooked by the owners, and quiet garden; two resident dogs; nearby walks; cl 3 wks Jan, 3 wks Nov; dogs in bedrooms with outside door; bedding, bowls and meals; £3

SOUTH ZEAL

Oxenham Arms *South Zeal, Okehampton, Devon EX20 2JT (01837) 840244* **£80**; 8 rms. Grandly atmospheric old inn dating back to 12th c and first licensed in 1477 (a neolithic standing stone still forms part of the wall in the back bar); elegant beamed and panelled bar with chatty relaxed atmosphere and open fire, no smoking restaurant, and charming ex-monastery small garden; walks nearby; dogs welcome away from dining room

STAVERTON
Sea Trout *Staverton, Totnes, Devon TQ9 6PA (01803) 762274* (1.9 miles off A384; village signed from just W of Dartington) £80; 10 cottagey rms. Comfortable pub in quiet hamlet near River Dart with two relaxed beamed bars (you may smoke only in the locals' one), log fires, popular food in lounge and airy dining conservatory, and terraced garden with marquee for outside eating; resident dog; plenty of surrounding walks; cl Christmas; disabled access; dogs away from restaurant; treats at the bar

STOCKLAND
Kings Arms *Stockland, Honiton, Devon EX14 9BS (01404) 881361* (2.4 miles off A30 in Yarcombe; village signposted) £70; 3 rms. Cream-faced thatched pub with elegant rooms, open fires, first-class food in no smoking bar and evening restaurant (esp fish), and interesting wine list; skittle alley; two resident dogs; plenty of walks from front door; cl 25 Dec; dogs in bedrooms

THURLESTONE
Thurlestone Hotel *Thurlestone, Kingsbridge, Devon TQ7 3NN (01548) 560382* £98; 64 comfortable rms, many with sea or country views. Owned by the same family since 1896, this well run hotel is in lovely grounds with marvellous views over the coast, and tennis and squash courts, badminton court, swimming pool, golf course, and super play area for children; stylish and spacious public rooms, relaxing cocktail bar, imaginative food in attractive no smoking restaurant, and courteous helpful staff; lots for families; marvellous nearby beaches and walks, and fishing, riding, and sailing on request; cl 9 days after New Year; disabled access; dogs in bedrooms; £6

TWO BRIDGES
Prince Hall *Two Bridges, Yelverton, Devon PL20 6SA (01822) 890403* £150, plus special breaks; 8 attractive spacious rms. Surrounded by Dartmoor National Park, this tranquil 18th-c country house is run by caring friendly owners and their helpful staff; lovely views from convivial bar (the only place you may smoke), comfortable sitting room, and cosy dining room, open fires, very good evening meals and enjoyable breakfasts, and lots of fine walks; resident dog; cl Jan; children over 10; dogs welcome away from restaurant; treats from reception

Dorset

Dog Friendly Pubs

CERNE ABBAS
Royal Oak *Long Street; DT2 7JG*
This cheery Tudor inn focuses on dining, with a range of changing food that is sourced locally and changes within the seasons. The son of the licensees does the cooking, and sometimes catches the fish himself (all the fish is wild). The three flagstoned communicating rooms have sturdy oak beams, lots of shiny black panelling, an inglenook with an oven, and warm winter log fires. Stone walls and the ceilings are packed with all sorts of small ornaments from local photographs to antique china, brasses and farm tools; candles on tables, fresh flowers; occasional piped music. Four Badger beers are served from handpumps on the uncommonly long bar counter. From an extensive wine list, they do 16 wines by the glass. The enclosed back garden is very pleasant, with comfortable chairs and tables under cocktail parasols, and outdoor heaters on purbeck stone terracing and cedarwood decking. On sunny summer afternoons they sometimes serve drinks and snacks out here. Parking can be a problem at busy times.
Badger ~ Tenants Maurice and Sandra Ridley ~ Real ale ~ Bar food (12-3, 7-9) ~ (01300) 341797 ~ Children welcome ~ Dogs welcome ~ Open 11-11; 11-3, 6.30-11 in winter

EAST CHALDON
Sailors Return *Village signposted from A352 Wareham—Dorchester; from village green, follow Dorchester, Weymouth signpost; note that the village is also known as Chaldon Herring; OS sheet 194 map reference 790834; DT2 8DN*
This extended rural thatched pub is a pleasant place to stop for a drink, perhaps as part of a walk over the downs to join the coast path above the cliffs between Ringstead Bay and Durdle Door. The flagstoned bar still keeps much of its original country-tavern character, while the newer part has unfussy furnishings, old notices for decoration, and open beams showing the roof. Half a dozen well kept real ales include Hampshire Strongs Best and Ringwood Best, alongside guests such as Dorset Durdle Door and Palmers Dorset Gold, and they also have country wines and several malt whiskies. Straightforward bar food includes a handful of daily

specials. The no smoking restaurant has solid old tables in nooks and corners; darts, TV and piped music. Picnic-sets, benches and log seats on the grass in front of the pub look down over fields to the village. Although fairly isolated, it gets very busy at weekends, especially in fine weather.

Free house ~ Licensees Mike Pollard and Claire Kelly ~ Real ale ~ Bar food (12-2, 6-9(9.30 weekends); 12-9.30 weekends in summer) ~ Restaurant ~ (01305) 853847 ~ Children in restaurant ~ Dogs allowed in bar ~ Open 11-11; 12-10.30 Sun

EAST MORDEN
Cock & Bottle *B3075 between A35 and A31 W of Poole; BH20 7DL*

Originally a longhouse, this popular dining pub has plenty to suggest its rustic origins. There's a pubby wood-floored bar (fruit machine, and sensibly placed darts alcove), while the rest of the interior comprises two dining areas, with heavy rough beams, some stripped ceiling boards, squared panelling, a mix of old furnishings in various sizes and degrees of antiquity, small Victorian prints and some engaging bric-a-brac, some reflecting the landlord's passion for vintage cars and motorcycles (the pub hosts meetings for such vehicles in summer). There's a roaring log fire, and comfortably intimate corners, each with just a couple of tables. The imaginative changing bar menu uses local produce where possible, and booking is advisable. The restaurant areas are no smoking. Badger Best, King and Barnes and Tanglefoot are on handpump, and they have several wines by the glass; helpful service from the pleasant staff. There are a few picnic-sets outside, a garden area, and an adjoining field with a nice pastoral outlook.

Badger ~ Tenant Peter Meadley ~ Real ale ~ Bar food (12-2, 6(7 Sun)-9) ~ Restaurant ~ (01929) 459238 ~ Children in restaurant ~ Dogs welcome ~ Open 11-2.30, 6-11; 12-3, 7-10.30 Sun

MIDDLEMARSH
Hunters Moon *A352 Sherborne—Dorchester; DT9 5QN*

West country ales feature large at this peaceful and delightfully attired village pub, with typically Sharps Doom Bar, St Austell Tribute and Tinners, and Otter on handpump. The comfortably welcoming interior rambles around in several linked areas, with a great variety of tables and chairs, plenty of bric-a-brac from decorative teacups, china ornaments and glasses through horse tack and brassware, to quite a collection of spirits miniatures. Beams, some panelling, soft lighting from converted oil lamps, three log fires (one in a capacious inglenook), and the way that some attractively cushioned settles form booths all combine to give a cosy relaxed feel. Food is good and reasonably priced, and includes a bargain range of 'smaller appetite meals'. Also decent wines by the glass, proper coffee, and a good range of spirits and soft drinks; faint piped music. A neat lawn has circular picnic-sets as well as the more usual ones, and the bedrooms are in what was formerly a skittle alley and stable block.

Free house ~ Licensee Brendan Malone ~ Real ale ~ Bar food (6-9.30) ~ Restaurant ~ (01963) 210966 ~ Children welcome ~ Dogs allowed in bar ~ Open 11-3, 6-11.30; 12-10.30 Sun ~ Bedrooms: £48S/£60S

MUDEFORD
Ship in Distress *Stanpit; off B3059 at roundabout; BH23 3NA*
Unassuming from outside, this cheerful cottagey place is full of entertaining
bits and pieces, with nautical bric-a-brac from rope fancywork and
brassware through lanterns, oars and ceiling nets and ensigns, to an
aquarium, boat models (we particularly liked the Mississippi steamboat),
and the odd piratical figure. Besides a good few boat pictures, the room on
the right has masses of snapshots of locals caught up in various waterside
japes, under its glass tabletops. The wide choice of carefully cooked fresh
local fish and seafood is good and imaginative, as are other dishes. Service is
friendly, and they have Adnams, Bass, Ringwood and a guest such as
Shepherd Neame Spitfire on handpump, and good wines by the glass; darts,
fruit machine, a couple of TV sets – the dated piped pop music seems to fit
in rather well; they also have live jazz on Sundays. A spreading two-room
no smoking restaurant area, as cheerful in its way as the bar, has a light-
hearted mural sketching out the impression of a window open on a sunny
boating scene, and another covering its dividing wall with vines. There are
tables out on the back terrace; look out for the two springer spaniels.
*Punch ~ Tenants Sally Canning, Colin Pond, Ed Blanchard ~ Real ale ~ Bar food
(12-2.30, 7-9.30) ~ Restaurant ~ (01202) 485123 ~ Children welcome until
9pm ~ Dogs allowed in bar ~ Live jazz on Sun ~ Open 11-11*

NETTLECOMBE
Marquis of Lorne *Off A3066 Bridport—Beaminster, via W Milton; DT6 3SY*
In deep and unspoilt country within strolling distance of Eggardon Hill, one of
Dorset's most evocative iron-age hillfort sites, this pub has recently been giving
a lot of pleasure with its locally sourced food and very well kept beer, and also
has good bedrooms. The comfortable bustling main bar has a log fire,
mahogany panelling, and old prints and photographs around its neatly
matching chairs and tables; two dining areas lead off, the smaller of which has
another log fire. The wooden-floored snug has cribbage, dominoes, board
games and table skittles; gentle piped music. Food is gently imaginative and
tasty, and they may also have locally-made chutneys and marmalade for sale.
Four real ales from Palmers are on handpump, with Copper, IPA and 200
alongside Gold in summer or Tally Ho in winter, and Thatcher's Gold cider or
perhaps a cloudy farm cider; a good wine list with about a dozen by the glass,
and several malt whiskies. The maturing big garden is full of pretty herbaceous
borders, and has a rustic-style play area among the picnic-sets under its apple
trees. It is all no smoking apart from one bar (to which dogs are also allowed).
*Palmers ~ Tenants David and Julie Woodroffe ~ Real ale ~ Bar food (12-2.30,
7-9.30(9 winter)) ~ Restaurant ~ (01308) 485236 ~ Children in eating area of
bar and restaurant ~ Dogs allowed in bar ~ Open 11.30(12 in winter)-2.30,
6.30(7 Sun in winter)-11 ~ Bedrooms: £45S/£80S*

PAMPHILL
Vine *Off B3082 on NW edge of Wimborne: turn on to Cowgrove Hill at
Cowgrove signpost, then turn right up Vine Hill; BH21 4EE*
The atmosphere is really special in this enchantingly unchanged and simple

pub, run by the same family for three generations (although it's now owned by the National Trust as part of the Kingston Lacy estate). Its two tiny bars have that well cared-for feel and friendly service that make little places like this feel so special. One, with a warm coal-effect gas fire, has only three tables, the other just half a dozen or so seats on its lino floor, some of them huddling under the stairs that lead up via narrow wooden steps to an upstairs games room; darts; no smoking throughout. Local photographs (look out for the one of the regular with his giant pumpkin) and notices decorate the painted panelling. On our weekday inspection visit, piped Classic FM mingled quietly with a blackbird's song drifting in through the french window, though at weekends and in summer it can get very busy. One beer from Fullers London Pride, Hidden or Archers Best on handpump together with a guest such as Archers Golden from the cask, real cider, and good fresh sandwiches and ploughman's are on offer. There are picnic-sets and benches out on a sheltered gravel terrace, and more share a fairy-lit, heated verandah with a grapevine. Round the back a patch of grass has a climbing frame; outside lavatories. The National Trust estate includes Kingston Lacy house and the huge Badbury Rings iron-age hill fort (itself good for wild flowers), and there are many paths. They don't accept credit cards or cheques.

Free house ~ Licensee Mrs Sweatland ~ Real ale ~ Bar food (11(12 Sun)-2) ~ No credit cards ~ (01202) 882259 ~ Well behaved children welcome, except in bar ~ Dogs welcome ~ Open 11-3, 7-10.30(11 Fri, Sat)

SHAVE CROSS

Shave Cross Inn *On back lane Bridport—Marshwood, signposted locally; OS Sheet 193 map reference 415980; DT6 6HW*

There's a distinctively caribbean slant to several aspects of this historic flint and thatch inn, which dates back to the 14th c. The building is traditionally english: the original timbered bar is a lovely flagstoned room, surprisingly roomy and full of character, with country antiques, two armchairs either side of a warming fire in an enormous inglenook fireplace and hops round the bar – a scene little altered from the last century. The origins of the chef show in some of the caribbean seasonings, spices and recipes of the tasty home-made food. Bar food features a few international dishes with nicely english puddings. They also have a more elaborate evening restaurant menu. They serve Branscombe Vale Branoc and their own-label 4Ms and Dorset Marshwood Vale on handpump, alongside half a dozen wines by the glass, Thatcher's and Old Rosie farm cider, several vintage rums and a caribbean beer; piped music (jazz or caribbean). The refurbished skittle alley has pool, darts and a juke box, and the dining area and restaurant have table cloths, and caribbean pictures (for sale). Lovingly tended, the sheltered flower-filled garden with its thatched wishing-well, carp pool and children's play area is very pretty. Bedrooms are planned for 2007.

Free house ~ Licensee Mel Warburton ~ Real ale ~ Bar food (11-3, 6-7; not Sun evenings) ~ Restaurant (7-9.30) ~ (01308) 868358 ~ Children in restaurant and skittle alley ~ Dogs allowed in bar ~ Jazz and discos some nights ~ Open 11-3, 6-11.30; 12-3, 7-11.30 Sun; closed Mon except bank hols

SHERBORNE

Digby Tap *Cooks Lane; park in Digby Road and walk round corner; DT9 3NS*

A couple of minutes' walk from the famous abbey and now open all day, this is a delightfully unpretentious alehouse that serves an interesting range of beer. Its simple flagstoned bar is full of character, with a good mix of chatty customers. The beers are quite cheap and change regularly, with four pumps serving around 20 to 25 different ones a week, and might include Cottage, Hopback, Slaters or Youngs. A little games room has pool and a quiz machine, and there's a TV room. Straightforward bar food comes in large reasonably priced helpings. They don't do puddings apart from ice-cream. There are some seats outside.

Free house ~ Licensees Oliver Wilson and Nick Whigham ~ Real ale ~ Bar food (12-1.45, not Sun) ~ No credit cards ~ (01935) 813148 ~ Children welcome lunchtimes only ~ Dogs welcome ~ Open 11-11; 12-3, 7-11 Sun

SYDLING ST NICHOLAS

Greyhound *Off A37 N of Dorchester; High Street; DT2 9PD*

The new owners of this attractively kept village inn won a great many friends among our readers, at their last place the West Bay. Here, you get an instant sense of welcome, with everyone from the adept barmen to the cheerful kitchen and serving staff obviously keen to give you a good time. That can be practically guaranteed if you're eating, with good attractively presented, seasonally changing and locally sourced food . They have Palmers Copper, Wadworths 6X and a monthly guest such as Youngs St George on handpump at the long brick bar counter, and a good range of fairly priced wines by the glass; this beamed and flagstoned serving area is airy and alluring, with its big bowl of lemons and limes, backdrop of gleaming bottles and copper pans, and plenty of bar stools, with more opposite ranging against a drinking shelf. On one side a turkey-carpeted area with a warm coal fire in a handsome portland stone fireplace has a comfortable mix of straightforward tables and chairs and country decorations such as a stuffed fox eyeing a collection of china chickens and a few farm tools. There may be fairly unobtrusive piped music; board games. At the other end, a cosy separate dining room with smart white table linen has some books and a glass-covered well set into its floor. Apart from the small bar area the pub is no smoking. A garden room with succulents and other plants on its sills has simple modern café furniture, and the small front garden has a wooden climber and slide alongside its picnic-sets. The new bedrooms are in a separate block; this is a quiet and very pretty streamside village.

Free house ~ Licensees John Ford and Karen Trimby ~ Real ale ~ Bar food (12-2(2.30 Sun), 6.30-9(9.30 Sat)) ~ Restaurant ~ (01300) 341303 ~ Children welcome ~ Dogs allowed in bar ~ Open 11-2.30, 6-11; 12-3 Sun; closed Sun evening ~ Bedrooms: /£65S(£75B)

TARRANT MONKTON
Langton Arms *Village signposted from A354, then head for church; DT11 8RX*
This 17th-c thatched dining pub has been refreshed with cream walls and has more of an airy, contemporary look than you might expect from outside. It's now all no smoking apart from one bar, and the light oak beamed bar has flagstone floors, a light oak counter with recessed lighting, and fresh flowers on light wood furniture; paintings for sale (by a local artist) are displayed on the walls. There is one guest beer such as Hampshire Lionheart on handpump alongside brews from Hop Back, Hidden and Ringwood. The public bar has a juke box, darts, pool and TV. The bistro restaurant is in an attractively reworked barn, and the skittle alley doubles as a family room during the day; piped music. Bar food is fairly traditional. Tarrant Monkton is a charming village (with a ford that can flow quite fast in wet weather), and is well located for local walks and exploring the area. There's a very good wood-chip children's play area in the garden, and the comfortable ensuite bedrooms are in a modern block at the back; good breakfasts. They are licensed for weddings; service can be erratic at times.
Free house ~ Licensees Barbara and James Cossins ~ Real ale ~ Bar food (11.30-2.30, 6-9.30; all day Sat, Sun) ~ Restaurant ~ (01258) 830225 ~ Children welcome ~ Dogs allowed in bedrooms ~ Open 11.30(12 Sun)-12 ~ Bedrooms: £60B/£80B

WEST BAY
West Bay *Station Road; DT6 4EW*
New tenants have taken over this popular seaside dining pub, with their son Mike running the kitchen – which is still on good form. As well as a short snack and lunchtime menu it continues to specialise in fish. The pub is largely set out for eating. An island servery separates the fairly simple bare-boards front part, with its coal-effect gas fire and mix of sea and nostalgic prints, from a cosier carpeted no smoking dining area with more of a country kitchen feel; piped music. Though its spaciousness means it never feels crowded, booking is virtually essential in season. Palmers IPA, Copper and 200 are served on handpump alongside good house wines (with seven by the glass) and Thatcher's farm cider. A local team meets to play in the skittles alley. There are tables outside on a dining terrace, with more in a large garden; plenty of parking. The bedrooms, quiet and comfortable, have recently been refurbished.
Palmers ~ Tenants Richard and Lorraine Barnard ~ Real ale ~ Bar food (12-2(3 Sun); 6.30-9.30) ~ Restaurant ~ (01308) 422157 ~ Children allowed in restaurant if well behaved ~ Dogs allowed in bar ~ Open 11.30-3, 6-11; 12-3, 6-10 Sun ~ Bedrooms: £65B/£70B

Dog Friendly Hotels, B&Bs and Farms

BEAMINSTER

Bridge House *3 Prout Bridge, Beaminster, Dorset DT8 3AY (01308)
862200* £**142**; 15 rms, more spacious in main house. 13th-c priest`s house,
family owned and no smoking, with open fire in sitting room, cosy bar,
breakfast room overlooking the attractive walled garden (where dogs may
walk), good food using local produce in Georgian dining room, friendly
service, and an informal, relaxed atmosphere; disabled access; dogs in coach
house bedrooms

BOURNEMOUTH

Langtry Manor *26 Derby Rd, Eastcliff, Bournemouth, Dorset BH1 3QB
(01202) 290550* £**99**, plus special breaks; 25 pretty rms, some in the
manor, some in the lodge. Built by Edward VII for Lillie Langtry and with
lots of memorabilia, this popular hotel has relaxed public rooms, helpful
friendly staff, and good food inc Edwardian banquet every Sat evening;
walks for dogs in grounds and some fine walks in the area; disabled access;
dogs in bedrooms

White Topps *Southbourne, Bournemouth, Dorset BH6 4BB (01202) 428868*
£**69**; 6 rms, shared bthrms. Edwardian house that is 100% dog oriented and
all guests bring at least one dog; two lounges, one with a bar and one with
a fridge for guests (used for storing dog food), traditional meals (and
vegetarian choices) in no smoking dining room, and lots of doggy pictures
and ornaments; several resident pets; walks on nearby beach; cl Nov-Mar;
no children; dogs welcome everywhere and ground floor rms for elderly or
disabled dogs

BRIDPORT

Britmead House *West Bay Rd, Bridport, Dorset DT6 4EG (01308)
422941* (0.5 miles off A35; take West Bar Rd from B3157 roundabout)
£**70**, plus special breaks; 8 rms. Extended no smoking Victorian hotel with
lots to do nearby, comfortable lounge overlooking garden, attractive dining
room, good breakfasts, and kind helpful service; fields at back of grounds to
walk dogs and nearby beach; disabled access; dogs in bedrooms (must not
be unattended)

DORCHESTER

Maiden Castle Farm *Dorchester, Dorset DT2 9PR (01305) 262356* (0.5
miles off A35; first turn right off A354) £**65**; 4 rms. Victorian farmhouse in
2 acres of gardens in the heart of Hardy country and set beneath the
prehistoric earthworks from which the farm takes its name; views of the hill
fort and countryside, nice breakfasts, afternoon tea with home-made cakes,
and comfortable traditionally furnished sitting room which overlooks the
garden (where dogs may walk); resident dog; dogs in bedrooms; £5

EAST KNIGHTON

Countryman *East Knighton, Dorchester, Dorset DT2 8LL (01305) 852666*
£78; 6 rms. Attractively converted and much liked pair of old cottages
with open fires and plenty of character in the main bar which opens into
several smaller areas; no smoking family room, half a dozen real ales,
imaginative, generously served food inc nice breakfasts and a hot carvery in
large no smoking restaurant, and courteous staff; resident dog and cat; walks
in garden and nearby; cl 25 Dec; dogs in bedrooms

EVERSHOT

Summer Lodge *Evershot, Dorchester, Dorset DT2 0JR (01935) 83424*
£185, plus special breaks; 24 big, individually decorated rms. Beautifully
kept, peacefully set former dower house with lovely flowers in the
comfortable and elegantly furnished day rooms, excellent food using the
best local produce in most attractive restaurant overlooking pretty garden,
delicious breakfasts and afternoon tea, and personal caring service; indoor
swimming pool, tennis and croquet; dogs on lead in garden, walks nearby;
children over 7 in evening restaurant; partial disabled access; dogs in
bedrooms away from main house with dog bed, bowls, biscuits; £10

FARNHAM

Museum Inn *Farnham, Blandford Forum, Dorset DT11 8DE (01725)*
516261 (1.5 miles off A354) **£95**; 8 rms. Odd-looking thatched building
with various civilised areas such as a flagstoned bar with big inglenook
fireplace, light beams and good comfortably cushioned furnishings, a dining
room with a cosy hunt theme, and what feels rather like a contemporary
version of a baronial hall, soaring up to a high glass ceiling, with dozens of
antlers and a stag's head looking down on to a long wooden table and
church-style pews; excellent food, three real ales, a fine choice of wines,
and very good attentive service; walks in surrounding fields; two resident
dogs; cl 25 Dec; children over 5; dogs welcome away from restaurant;
doggie treats

KINGSTON

Kingston Country Courtyard *West St, Kingston, Corfe Castle, Wareham,*
Dorset BH20 5LH (01929) 481066 **£70**; 10 rms in most attractive farm
building conversion. A collection of stylish suites and apartments in
beautifully decorated houses keeping much original character and charm,
and with wonderful views over Corfe Castle, Arne peninsula, and the Isle
of Wight; enjoyable full english or continental breakfasts in Old Cart Shed
dining room; self-catering too; two resident dogs; plenty of surrounding
walks and lots to do nearby; cl Dec/Jan; good disabled access; dogs in
bedrooms (not to be left unattended); £10

LOWER BOCKHAMPTON

Yalbury Cottage *Lower Bockhampton, Dorchester, Dorset DT2 8PZ (01305)*
262382 (1.3 miles off A35, E of Dorchester) **£103**, plus special breaks; 8
rms overlooking garden or fields. Very attractive family-run 16th-c

thatched house with a relaxed friendly atmosphere, and low beams and inglenook fireplaces in comfortable lounge and dining room; carefully cooked often imaginative food, good wines, and attractive mature garden; cl 2 wks Jan; partial disabled access; dogs in bedrooms; £6

SHIPTON GORGE
Innsacre Farmhouse *Shipton Lane, Shipton Gorge, Bridport, Dorset DT6 4LJ (01308) 456137* **£85**; 4 rms. 17th-c no smoking farmhouse in 24 acres of lawns, woodland and nature trails and tucked away in a little valley; french country-style furnishings, a simple and comfortable lounge with a woodburning stove in big inglenook fireplace, good, interesting no-choice evening meals (by arrangement) in a dinner party atmosphere in the beamed dining room, and nice breakfasts that include brioche, pastries and pancakes as well as a traditional english choice; packed lunches for walkers, an informal, friendly atmosphere, and three resident dogs, two cats and a parrot; cl Christmas and New Year; children over 10; dogs in bedrooms (must not be left unattended), bar and sitting room; £10

STUDLAND
Knoll House *Studland, Swanage, Dorset BH19 3AH (01929) 450450* **£290** inc lunch and dinner; 80 comfortable rms. Spacious, very well run hotel owned by the same family for over 45 years and set in 100 acres with marvellous views of Studland Bay and direct access to the fine 3-mile beach; relaxed friendly atmosphere, particularly helpful staff, super food in no smoking dining room overlooking the gardens, cocktail bar, TV lounge, and excellent facilities for families; table tennis, pool and table football, heated outdoor pool and health spa, tennis courts, small private golf course, marvellous adventure playground, and nearby sea fishing, riding, walking, sailing and windsurfing; three resident dogs; cl end Nov-Mar; disabled access; dogs welcome away from dining rooms, pool and spa; £5 inc food

STURMINSTER NEWTON
Plumber Manor *Hazelbury Bryan Rd, Plumber, Sturminster Newton, Dorset DT10 2AF (01258) 472507* **£135**, plus special breaks; 16 very comfortable rms, some in nearby period buildings and many in the house itself that overlook the peaceful, pretty garden and down the stream with herons and even maybe egrets. Handsome 17th-c, family-run house in quiet countryside, with warm fires, a convivial well stocked bar, attractive writing room/lounge, good interesting food in three dining rooms, nice breakfasts, a relaxed atmosphere, and exceptionally friendly helpful service; tennis; cl Feb; disabled access; dogs welcome in bedrooms

Essex

Dog Friendly Pubs

CHAPPEL
Swan *Wakes Colne; pub visible just off A1124 Colchester—Halstead; CO6 2DD*
The low-beamed rambling bar at this spacious old pub has standing oak
timbers dividing off side areas, plenty of dark wood chairs around lots of
dark tables for diners, a couple of swan pictures and plates on the white and
partly panelled walls, and a few attractive tiles above the very big fireplace.
The central bar area keeps a pubbier atmosphere, with regulars dropping in
for a drink; fruit machine, cribbage, dominoes and piped music. The
restaurant and one of the lounge bars are no smoking. As well as just under
two dozen malt whiskies they keep Greene King IPA and Abbot and a
guest on handpump. The menu features a good range of fresh fish, served
in generous helpings. The River Colne runs through the garden from
where you can see a splendid Victorian viaduct. Flower tubs and french
street signs lend the suntrap cobbled courtyard a continental feel, and gas
heaters mean that even on cooler evenings, you can sit outside. The
Railway Centre (a must for train buffs) is only a few minutes' walk away.
*Free house ~ Licensee Terence Martin ~ Real ale ~ Bar food (12-2.30, 6.30-10;
12-3, 6.30-9.30 Sun) ~ Restaurant ~ (01787) 222353 ~ Children welcome
away from bar ~ Dogs allowed in bar ~ Open 11-3, 6-11; 11-11 Sat; 12-10.30
Sun*

DEDHAM
Sun *High Street (B2109); CO7 6DF*
Stylishly simple décor allows the structure of this handsome Tudor inn to
speak for itself – indeed carefully observed quality rather than elaboration
seems to be the thing here, throughout. The main draw is probably the
robustly flavoured daily changing menu, which focuses on top notch
locally sourced ingredients rather than complicated cooking; children's
helpings are available, and young staff offer friendly relaxed but efficient
service. Adnams Broadside and Crouch Vale Brewers Gold are well kept
on handpump alongside a couple of guests from brewers such as Oakham
and Phoenix, and they've a very good selection of more than 60 wines (30
by the glass) and some interesting soft drinks. A window seat in the bar

looks across to the church which is at least glimpsed in several of Constable's paintings. Elsewhere you'll find high carved beams, squared panelling, wall timbers and big log fires in splendid fireplaces. A variety of seats takes in high settles and easy chairs. The entire pub is no smoking apart from the Oak Room; maybe piped music, cribbage, dominoes and board games. On the way out to picnic-sets on the quiet and attractive back lawn, notice the unusual covered back staircase, with what used to be a dovecot on top. If you have time, beautiful walks into the heart of Constable country lead out of the village, over water meadows towards Flatford Mill. The panelled bedrooms are nicely done and have abundant character.
Free house ~ Licensee Piers Baker ~ Real ale ~ Bar food (12-2.30(3 Sat and Sun), 6.30-9.30) ~ Restaurant ~ (01206) 323351 ~ Children welcome ~ Dogs allowed in bar ~ Open 12-11(6 Sun) ~ Bedrooms: £60B/£120B

FINGRINGHOE
Whalebone *Follow Rowhedge, Fingringhoe signpost off A134, the part that's just S of Colchester centre; or Fingringhoe signposted off B1025 S of Colchester; CO5 7BG*
Attractively redecorated since the last edition, the three airily opened together rooms here have cream walls above aubergine dado, some timber studding, and leather dining chairs and oak and cream painted tables on oak floors. Served by friendly staff, the tasty bar food includes quite a few interesting dishes. Caledonian Deuchars and Greene King IPA are well kept alongside a couple of guests from brewers such as Archers or Mersea Island, and there are decent house wines; piped music. The rather lovely back garden, with gravel paths winding through the grass around a sizeable old larch tree, has picnic-sets with a peaceful valley view, and the newly finished front terrace has bistro style tables and chairs with gingham parasols. The pub is no smoking throughout.
Free house ~ Licensees Sam and Victoria Burroughes ~ Real ale ~ Bar food (10-2.30, 7-9.30(9 Sun, Mon)) ~ Restaurant ~ (01206) 729307 ~ Children welcome with restrictions ~ Dogs allowed in bar ~ Open 11-3, 5.30-11; 12-11 Sat; 12-10.30 Sun

GOSFIELD
Green Man *3 miles N of Braintree; CO9 1TP*
The help-yourself cold buffet table (lunchtimes March-December) makes a change at this traditional dining pub. Other dishes are served in big helpings from a mostly traditional english menu. A happy relaxed atmosphere is generated by friendly staff and licensees, and the two little oak beamed bars (one has an inglenook fireplace) feel warmly welcoming. Many of the decent nicely priced wines are available by the glass, and they've very well kept Greene King IPA and Abbot on handpump. The main bar and restaurant are no smoking; piped music; garden.
Greene King ~ Tenants Debbie With and Tony Bowen ~ Real ale ~ Bar food ~ Restaurant ~ (01787) 472746 ~ Children welcome with restrictions ~ Dogs allowed in bar ~ Open 11-3, 6-11; 12-4.40 Sun; closed Sun evening and Mon evening in winter

HORNDON-ON-THE-HILL

Bell *M25 junction 30 into A13, then left into B1007 after 7 miles, village signposted from here; SS17 8LD*

The heavily beamed bar at this ancient pub maintains a strongly pubby appearance with some antique high-backed settles and benches, rugs on the flagstones or highly polished oak floorboards, and a curious collection of ossified hot cross buns hanging from a beam. They also keep a very good range of drinks, including Greene King IPA and Bass and five guests from brewers such as Archers, Crouch Vale, Shepherd Neame and Youngs (the pub holds occasional beer festivals) and over a hundred well chosen wines from all over the world, including 16 by the glass. However it's here that the pubbiness ends as the frequently changing menu (the same in the bar and restaurant) is fairly elaborate and not especially cheap, and you will need to book. Note the accommodation is a couple of hundred yards away from the pub itself.

Free house ~ Licensee John Vereker ~ Real ale ~ Bar food (12-2, 6.30(7 Sun)-9.45; not bank hol Mon) ~ Restaurant ~ (01375) 642463 ~ Children in eating area of bar and restaurant ~ Dogs allowed in bar and bedrooms ~ Open 11-2.30(3 Sat), 5.30(6 Sat)-11; 12-4, 7-10.30 Sun ~ Bedrooms: /£64B

LITTLE BRAXTED

Green Man *Kelvedon Road; village signposted off B1389 by NE end of A12 Witham bypass – keep on patiently; OS Sheet 168 map reference 848133; CM8 3LB*

The traditional little lounge at this pretty brick house has an interesting collection of bric-a-brac, including 200 horsebrasses, some harness, mugs hanging from a beam, and a lovely copper urn; it's especially cosy in winter when you'll really feel the benefit of the open fire. The tiled public bar has books, darts, cribbage and dominoes; the saloon bar is no smoking till 9.30. Welcoming staff serve two Greene King beers and a guest such as Titanic White Star. Reasonably priced bar food is pubby and straightforward; picnic sets in pleasant sheltered garden.

Greene King ~ Tenant Neil Pharaoh ~ Real ale ~ Bar food ~ (01621) 891659 ~ Dogs allowed in bar ~ Open 11.30-3, 6-11; 12-4, 7-10.30 Sun

LITTLE WALDEN

Crown *B1052 N of Saffron Walden; CB10 1XA*

In winter months the cosy low-beamed bar at this friendly white 18th-c country cottage is cosily welcoming with two blazing log fires in brick fireplaces. Bookroom-red walls, flowery curtains and a mix of bare boards and navy carpeting add to the homely snugness. Seats ranging from high-backed pews to little cushioned armchairs are spaced around a good variety of closely arranged tables, mostly big, some stripped. The small red-tiled room on the right has two little tables; piped local radio. City of Cambridge Boathouse, Greene King IPA and possibly a guest are tapped straight from casks racked up behind the bar. Hearty bar food is popular, so you may need to book at weekends. There is a no smoking restaurant, and in summer you can eat outside at tables on the patio, whilst taking in the tranquil countryside.

Free house ~ Licensee Colin Hayling ~ Real ale ~ Bar food (not Sun or Mon evening)
~ Restaurant ~ (01799) 522475 ~ Children welcome with restrictions ~ Dogs
allowed in bar ~ Trad jazz Weds evening ~ Open 11.30-3, 6-11; 12-10.30 Sun

STOW MARIES
Prince of Wales *B1012 between S Woodham Ferrers and Cold Norton Posters;*
CM3 6SA
The chatty low-ceilinged rooms at this appealingly laid-back pub appear
unchanged since the turn of the last century. Few have space for more than
one or two tables or wall benches on their tiled or bare-boards floors,
though the room in the middle squeezes in quite a jumble of chairs and
stools. As well as five interesting, frequently changing real ales on
handpump from brewers such as Dark Star, Deuchars and Hopback, you'll
also find bottled and draught belgian beers, several bottled fruit beers and
farm cider too. Bar food (with good fish specials) is enjoyable and served in
generous helpings; the restaurant and part of the bar area are no smoking.
On Thursday evenings in winter they fire up the old bread oven to make
pizzas in the room that used to be the village bakery, and on some summer
Sundays, they barbecue steaks and unusual fish. There are seats and tables in
the back garden, and between the picket fence and the pub's white
weatherboarded frontage is a terrace, with herbs in Victorian chimneypots,
sheltered by a huge umbrella. There are live bands on most bank holidays
and some Sundays.
Free house ~ Licensee Rob Walster ~ Real ale ~ Bar food (12-2.30, 6.30-9.30,
12-9.30 Sat, Sun) ~ Restaurant ~ No credit cards ~ (01621) 828971 ~ Children
in family room ~ Dogs allowed in bar ~ Occasional live music ~ Open 11-11;
12-10.30 Sun

Dog Friendly Hotels, B&Bs and Farms

BURNHAM-ON-CROUCH
White Harte *The Quay, Burnham-on-crouch, Essex CM0 8AS (01621)*
782106 £85; 19 rms, 11 with own bthrm. Old-fashioned 17th-c yachting
inn on quay overlooking the River Crouch with its own jetty; high
ceilings, oak tables on polished parquet flooring, sea pictures, panelling,
residents' lounge, and decent food in bar and restaurant; resident dog; walks
by the river; dogs welcome; £3

GREAT CHESTERFORD
Crown House *Great Chesterford, Saffron Walden, Essex CB10 1NY*
(01799) 530515 £84.50; 16 rms, 10 in restored stable block. Carefully
restored, imposing Georgian coach house in lovely gardens with plenty of
original features, an open fire and brown leather chairs in attractive lounge
bar, an airy conservatory with avocado tree, good, interesting food in no
smoking panelled restaurant, and pleasant, efficient staff; dogs in bedrooms

Gloucestershire

Dog Friendly Pubs

ALMONDSBURY
Bowl *1¼ miles from M5, junction 16 (and therefore quite handy for M4, junction 20); from A38 towards Thornbury, turn left signposted Lower Almondsbury, then first right down Sundays Hill, then at bottom right again into Church Road; BS32 4DT*

Even though a new licensee has taken over this very popular pub, little seems to have changed. It remains well run and cheerful with plenty of chatty customers and is much favoured by travellers on the M5. The long beamed no smoking bar is neatly kept, with terracotta plush-patterned modern settles, dark green cushioned stools and mate's chairs around elm tables, horsebrasses on stripped bare stone walls, and big winter log fire at one end, with a woodburning stove at the other. Up to seven real ales are well kept on handpump: Bass, Butcombe Bitter, Courage Best, Moles Best and Rucking Mole, and a couple of changing guests; piped music. Reasonably priced bar food includes good pub standards; efficient service even when stretched, but it's a shame they still ask to keep your credit card behind the bar. This is a pretty setting with the church next door and lovely flowering tubs, hanging baskets and window boxes.

Free house ~ Licensee Mrs J Stephenson ~ Real ale ~ Bar food (all day Sun) ~ Restaurant ~ (01454) 612757 ~ Children welcome ~ Dogs allowed in bar and bedrooms ~ Open 11.30-3, 5-11; 12-10.30 Sun; closed 25 Dec ~ Bedrooms: £48.50S/£76S

BARNSLEY
Village Pub *B4425 Cirencester—Burford; GL7 5EF*

There's a good mix of customers in this smart and rather civilised pub – those popping in for a pint and a chat (with their dogs) and others looking forward to a special meal out. The low-ceilinged communicating rooms have oil paintings, plush chairs, stools and window settles around polished candlelit tables, and country magazines and newspapers to read. Using mainly local and organic produce, food is enjoyable. Adnams, Hook Norton Bitter and Wadworths 6X on handpump, and an extensive wine list with over a dozen by the glass. The sheltered back courtyard has plenty of good solid wooden furniture under umbrellas, outdoor heaters and its own outside servery.

Free house ~ Licensees Tim Haigh and Rupert Pendered ~ Real ale ~ Bar food (12-2.30(3 Fri-Sun), 7-9.30(10 Fri and Sat)) ~ Restaurant ~ (01285) 740421 ~ Children welcome ~ Dogs allowed in bar ~ Open 11-3, 6-11; 11-11 Sat; 11-11 Sun ~ Bedrooms: £75S/£105S(£115B)

BLAISDON
Red Hart *Village signposted off A4136 just SW of junction with A40 W of Gloucester; OS Sheet 162 map reference 703169; GL17 0AH*

Readers very much enjoy their visits to this bustling and friendly pub. The flagstoned main bar has cushioned wall and window seats, traditional pub tables, a big sailing-ship painting above the log fire, and a thoroughly relaxing atmosphere – helped along by well reproduced piped bluesy music and maybe Spotty the perky jack russell (who is now ten). On the right, there's an attractive beamed two-room no smoking dining area with some interesting prints and bric-a-brac, and on the left, you'll find additional dining space for families. Well kept Bath Ales SPA, Butcombe Bitter, Hook Norton Best, RCH Pitchfork and Tetleys on handpump (three of these change regularly), and a decent wine list; board games and table skittles. Good bar food extends to a few interesting dishes. There are some picnic-sets in the garden and a children's play area, and at the back of the building is a terrace for barbecues. The little church above the village is worth a visit.

Free house ~ Licensee Guy Wilkins ~ Real ale ~ Bar food ~ Restaurant ~ (01452) 830477 ~ Children allowed but must be well behaved ~ Dogs allowed in bar ~ Open 12-2.30, 6-11(11.30 Sat); 12-3.30, 7-10.30 Sun

BLEDINGTON
Kings Head *B4450; OX7 6XQ*

Originally a cider house, this rather smart 500-year-old inn is set back from the village green where there are usually ducks pottering about. The main bar is full of ancient beams and other atmospheric furnishings (high-backed wooden settles, gateleg or pedestal tables), and there's a warming log fire in the stone inglenook where a big black kettle hangs. To the left of the bar a drinking space for locals (popular with a younger crowd in the evening) has benches on the wooden floor, a woodburning stove, and darts. Well kept Hook Norton Best and guests like Goffs Jouster, Slaters Original and Vale Best Bitter on handpump, an excellent wine list with 10 by the glass, 20 malt whiskies, interesting bottled ciders. Using as much free range, organic and local produce as possible bar food is interesting. The restaurant is no smoking; piped music. There are seats in the back garden.

Free house ~ Licensees Nicola and Archie Orr-Ewing ~ Real ale ~ Bar food ~ Restaurant ~ (01608) 658365 ~ Children allowed in restaurant and back bar only ~ Dogs allowed in bar ~ Open 11.30-3, 6-11; 11.30-11 Sat; 12-11 Sun; 12-3, 6.30-11 Sun in winter; closed 25 and 26 Dec ~ Bedrooms: £55B/ £70S(£125B)

BOX

Halfway House *Edge of Minchinhampton Common; from A46 S of Stroud follow Amberley signpost, then after Amberley Inn turn right towards Box, then left along common edge as you reach Box; OS Sheet 162 map reference 856003; can also be reached from Brimscombe on A419 SE of Stroud; GL6 9AE*

The new licensees in this tall 300-year-old house have created a downstairs no smoking restaurant which will have booths where customers can adjust the lighting or volume of music to suit themselves; there will be a disabled lavatory, a lift and new terrace, too. Upstairs, the light and airy open-plan bars wrap themselves around the central serving bar, and there are simple rush seated sturdy blond wooden chairs around good wooden tables, a built-in wall seat and long pew, a woodburning stove, and stripped wood floors. The bar has yellowy cream walls and ceiling, the dining area is mainly a warm terracotta, there are windows with views to the common, and an unusual pitched-roof area. Using only local produce (apart from fish from Cornwall), food is totally home-made and interesting. Well kept Nailsworth Artists Ale, Otter Bitter, Timothy Taylors Landlord, Wickwar BOB and Wychwood Englands Ale on handpump, and decent wines; piped music. There are seats in the landscaped garden.

Free house ~ Licensee Dawn Winchester ~ Real ale ~ Bar food (no restaurant food Mon) ~ Restaurant ~ (01453) 832631 ~ Children welcome ~ Dogs allowed in bar ~ Open 11-11; 12-11 Sun

BRIMPSFIELD

Golden Heart *Nettleton Bottom (not shown on road maps, so we list the pub instead under the name of the nearby village); on A417 N of the Brimpsfield turning northbound; GL4 8LA*

This is an enjoyable roadside pub of some genuine character and run by a friendly hands-on landlord. The main low-ceilinged bar is divided into five cosily distinct areas; there's a roaring log fire in the huge stone inglenook fireplace in one, traditional built-in settles and other old-fashioned furnishings throughout, and quite a few brass items, typewriters, exposed stone and wood panelling; newspapers to read. A comfortable parlour on the right has another decorative fireplace, and leads into a further room that opens onto the terrace; three areas are no smoking. A fair choice of bar food includes lots of pubby staples. Well kept Archers Best Bitter, Marstons Pedigree, Timothy Taylors Golden Best and Wickwar BOB on handpump, and quite a few wines by the glass. From the rustic cask-supported tables on the suntrap terrace, there are pleasant views down over a valley; nearby walks. If you are thinking of staying here, bear in mind that the nearby road is a busy all-night link between the M4 and M5.

Free house ~ Licensee Catherine Stevens ~ Real ale ~ Bar food (12-3, 6-10; all day Sun) ~ (01242) 870261 ~ Children welcome ~ Dogs welcome ~ Open 11-3, 5.30-11; 11-11 Sat; 12-10.30 Sun; closed 25 Dec ~ Bedrooms: £35S/£55S

CHEDWORTH

Seven Tuns *Village signposted off A429 NE of Cirencester; then take second signposted right turn and bear left towards church; GL54 4AE*

Run by genuinely friendly people, this little 17th-c pub is handy for the

famous nearby Roman villa, and there are nice walks through the valley. The snug little no smoking lounge on the right has comfortable seats and decent tables, sizeable antique prints, tankards hanging from the beam over the serving bar, a partly boarded ceiling, and a good winter log fire in a big stone fireplace. Down a couple of steps, the public bar on the left has an open fire, and this opens into a no smoking dining room with another open fire. Well kept Youngs Special and two seasonal guests on handpump, 12 wines by the glass, and 18 malt whiskies; darts, TV, skittle alley and piped music. Well liked bar food includes some interesting choices. One sunny terrace has a boules pitch and across the road there's another little walled raised terrace with a waterwheel and a stream; plenty of tables and seats.
Youngs ~ Tenant Mr Davenport-Jones ~ Real ale ~ Bar food (12-2.30(3 Sun), 6.30-9.30(10 Sat, 9 Sun)) ~ (01285) 720242 ~ Children welcome ~ Dogs allowed in bar ~ Open 11.30-midnight; 12-2am Fri and Sat; 12-10.30 Sun; 11.30-3, 6-midnight Mon-Fri in winter; closed 25 Dec

CHIPPING CAMPDEN
Eight Bells *Church Street (which is one way – entrance off B4035); GL55 6JG*
Neatly kept and handsome, this old inn is a pleasant place with heavy oak beams, massive timber supports, and stripped stone walls. It's totally no smoking now, and there are cushioned pews and solid dark wood furniture on the broad flagstones, daily papers, and log fires in up to three restored stone fireplaces. Part of the floor in the dining room has a glass inlet showing part of the passage from the church by which Roman Catholic priests could escape from the Roundheads. There's quite an emphasis on the gently imaginative food with menus on most tables. Well kept Goffs Jouster, Hook Norton Best and Old Hooky and Wickwar Cotswold Way on handpump from the fine oak bar counter, quite a few wines, Old Rosie cider, and country wines. Piped music, darts and board games. There's a large terraced garden with plenty of seats, and striking views of the almshouses and church. The pub is handy for the Cotswold Way walk to Bath.
Free house ~ Licensee Neil Hargreaves ~ Real ale ~ Bar food (12-2(2.30 Fri and Sat), 6.30-9(9.30 Fri and Sat); 12-2.30, 7-9 Sun) ~ Restaurant ~ (01386) 840371 ~ Children welcome until 9pm ~ Dogs allowed in bar ~ Open 12-11(10.30 Sun); closed 25 Dec ~ Bedrooms: £50S/£95S(£85B)

COWLEY
Green Dragon *Off A435 S of Cheltenham at Elkstone, Cockleford signpost; OS Sheet 163 map reference 970142; GL53 9NW*
The two bars in this attractive stone-fronted dining pub have a cosy and genuinely old-fashioned feel: big flagstones and wooden boards, beams, two stone fireplaces (welcoming fires in winter), candlelit tables and a woodburning stove. The furniture and the bar itself in the upper Mouse Bar were made by Robert Thompson, whose little hand-carved mice run over the chairs, tables and mantelpiece; the larger Lower Bar (and upstairs restaurant) are no smoking. Under the new licensees bar food can be imaginative; piped music. Terraces outside overlook Cowley Lake and the River Churn, and the pub is a good centre for the local walks.

Buccaneer Holdings ~ Managers Simon and Nicky Haly ~ Real ale ~ Bar food (12-2.30(3 Sat, 3.30 Sun), 6-10(9.30 Sun)) ~ Restaurant ~ (01242) 870271 ~ Children welcome ~ Dogs allowed in bar and bedrooms ~ Open 11-11; 12-10.30 Sun ~ Bedrooms: £57B/£75B

DUNTISBOURNE ABBOTS

Five Mile House *Off A417 at Duntisbourne Abbots exit sign; then, coming from Gloucester, pass filling station and keep on parallel to main road; coming from Cirencester, take Duntisbourne Abbots services sign, then immediate right and take underpass below main road, then turn right at T junction; GL7 7JR*

A favourite with many of our readers and somewhere they meet up with friends to enjoy 'the larky atmosphere', good beer and food, and friendly welcome. It's an imposing stone building with plenty of original character and a super mix of customers, and the front room has a companionable bare-boards drinking bar on the right (plenty of convivial banter from the locals), with wall seats around the big table in its bow window and just one other table. On the left is a flagstoned hallway tap room snug formed from two ancient high-backed settles by a woodburning stove in a tall carefully exposed old fireplace; newspapers to read. There's a small cellar bar, a back restaurant down steps, and a family room on the far side; darts. The eating areas are no smoking. Cooked by the landlord, food is enjoyably homely. Well kept Donningtons BB, Timothy Taylors Landlord and Youngs Bitter with maybe a local guest from Cottage on handpump (the cellar is temperature-controlled), and an interesting wine list (strong on new world ones). The gardens have nice country views; the country lane was once Ermine Street, the main Roman road from Wales to London.

Free house ~ Licensees Jo and Jon Carrier ~ Real ale ~ Bar food (12-2.30, 6-9.30; 12-2.30, 7-9 Sun) ~ Restaurant ~ (01285) 821432 ~ Children welcome if well behaved ~ Dogs allowed in bar ~ Open 12-3, 6-11; 12-3, 7-11 Sun

EWEN

Wild Duck *Village signposted from A429 S of Cirencester; GL7 6BY*

Attractively civilised and usually very busy, this 16th-c inn is on the edge of a peaceful village – though handy for Cirencester. The high-beamed main bar has a nice mix of comfortable armchairs and other seats, paintings on the red walls, crimson drapes, a winter open fire, and maybe candles on tables. The residents' lounge, which overlooks the garden, has a handsome Elizabethan fireplace and antique furnishings. Besides Duckpond Bitter (brewed especially for the pub), you'll find well kept Archers Golden, Theakstons Old Peculier and a guest on handpump, 28 wines by the glass, and several malt whiskies; piped music and shove-ha'penny. Bar food includes some interesting dishes. Pleasant in summer, the neatly kept and sheltered garden has wooden tables and seats. You will be asked to leave your credit card behind the bar.

Free house ~ Licensees Tina and Dino Mussell ~ Real ale ~ Bar food (12-2, 7-10; all day weekends) ~ Restaurant ~ (01285) 770310 ~ Children welcome ~ Dogs allowed in bar and bedrooms ~ Open 11-11(midnight Sat); 12-11 Sun ~ Bedrooms: £70B/£95B

FAIRFORD

Bull *Market Place; GL7 4AA*

The sizeable main bar in this rather smart and civilised old hotel – redecorated this year – is popular locally and has a thriving, chatty atmosphere. It's nicely laid out, with beams and timbers, comfortably old-fashioned pubby furnishings including dark pews and settles (try to sit at the big table in the bow window overlooking the little market square), and on its ochre walls, aircraft pictures and photographs of actors and actresses who have stayed here. The coal-effect gas fire is rather realistic. The long bar has well kept Arkells 2B, 3B and Kingsdown on handpump, and service is friendly. Up a few stone steps a nice little residents' lounge has some attractive soft leather sofas and armchairs around its big stone fireplace, and fishing prints and plates. The no smoking restaurant, in former stables, is charming, and there's quite a choice of reasonably priced bar food. Disabled lavatories have been installed. The village is charming, and the church just along the street has Britain's only intact set of medieval stained glass windows.

Arkells ~ Tenants Judy and Mark Dudley ~ Real ale ~ Bar food (12-2, 6-9) ~ Restaurant ~ (01285) 712535 ~ Children welcome ~ Dogs allowed in bar and bedrooms ~ Open 10am-11pm; 12-10.30 Sun; closed evening 25 Dec ~ Bedrooms: £39.50(£49.50B)/£79.50B

GUITING POWER

Hollow Bottom *Village signposted off B4068 SW of Stow-on-the-Wold (still called A436 on many maps); GL54 5UX*

On the edge of an unspoilt village, this friendly 17th-c inn is extremely popular. The comfortable beamed bar has lots of racing memorabilia including racing silks, tunics and photographs (it's owned by a small syndicate that includes Peter Scudamore and Nigel Twiston-Davies), and a winter log fire in an unusual pillar-supported stone fireplace. The public bar has flagstones and stripped stone masonry and racing on TV; newspapers to read, darts, board games and piped music. Well kept Fullers London Pride, Wye Valley O'er the Sticks, and a beer named for the pub (from Badger) on handpump, 15 malt whiskies, and seven wines (including champagne) by the glass; the staff are friendly and obliging. Bar food runs to some interesting daily specials. The restaurant is no smoking. From the pleasant garden behind are views towards the peaceful sloping fields, and there are decent walks nearby.

Free house ~ Licensees Hugh Kelly and Charles Pettigrew ~ Real ale ~ Bar food (all day) ~ Restaurant ~ (01451) 850392 ~ Children welcome ~ Dogs allowed in bar and bedrooms ~ Open 10am-12.30pm ~ Bedrooms: £45B/£70B

LITTLE BARRINGTON

Inn For All Seasons *On the A40 3 miles W of Burford; OX18 4TN*

This is a handsome and well run old inn with quite an emphasis on the popular food. The attractively decorated, mellow lounge bar has low beams, stripped stone and flagstones, old prints, leather-upholstered wing armchairs and other comfortable seats, country magazines to read, and a big log fire. From a particularly good wine list, there are 20 wines by the glass (from a 120 bin list), 60 malt whiskies, and Sharps Own and Wadworths 6X on handpump with maybe a guest like Fullers London Pride on handpump; friendly, kind service. Quite a choice of fish is the speciality here, alongside other interesting dishes. The restaurant and conservatory are no smoking. Cribbage, board games and piped music. The pleasant garden has tables, a play area and aunt sally, and there are walks straight from the inn. It gets very busy during Cheltenham Gold Cup Week.

Free house ~ Licensees Matthew and Heather Sharp ~ Real ale ~ Bar food (12-2.30, 6-9.30; 12-2 Sun; not Sun evening) ~ Restaurant ~ (01451) 844324 ~ Children welcome ~ Dogs allowed in bar and bedrooms ~ Open 10.30-2.30, 6-10.30(11 Sat); 12-2.30, 7-10.30 Sun ~ Bedrooms: £59B/£102B

LOWER ODDINGTON

Fox *Signposted off A436 between Stow and Chipping Norton; GL56 0UR*
There's no doubt that most people come to this smart, busy inn to enjoy the food but they do serve Greene King Abbot, Hook Norton and a beer from Wickwar on handpump, and there are some bar stools. The simply furnished rooms have fresh flowers and flagstones, hunting scene figures above the mantelpiece, a display cabinet with pewter mugs and stone bottles, daily newspapers, and an inglenook fireplace. Well presented imaginative food is served by neat, uniformed staff . There's a good wine list with quite a few by the glass. The terrace has a custom-built awning and outdoor heaters, and the cottagey garden is pretty. A good eight-mile walk starts from here (though a stroll around the pretty village might be less taxing).

Free house ~ Licensees James Cathcart and Ian MacKenzie ~ Real ale ~ Bar food (12-2(3 Sun), 6.30-10(7-9.30 Sun)) ~ Restaurant ~ (01451) 870555 ~ Children welcome ~ Dogs allowed in bar ~ Open 12-11(midnight Fri and Sat); 12-10.30 Sun; closed 25 Dec ~ Bedrooms: /£68S(£95B)

MISERDEN

Carpenters Arms *Village signposted off B4070 NE of Stroud; also a pleasant drive off A417 via the Duntisbournes, or off A419 via Sapperton and Edgeworth; OS Sheet 163 map reference 936089; GL6 7JA*
With new owners and a new licensee, this attractively placed pub remains the only building in this idyllic Cotswold estate village that is not owned by the Misarden Estate. The two open-plan bar areas have low beams, nice old wooden tables and some cushioned settles and spindlebacks on the bare boards; stripped stone walls, some interesting bric-a-brac and two big log fires. The small dining room is no smoking. Bar food includes plenty of pub standards. Greene King IPA, Wadworths 6X and a guest on handpump. There are seats out in the garden; the nearby gardens of Misarden Park are well worth visiting.

Esteemed Pubs Ltd ~ Lease Miss M Barrett ~ Real ale ~ Bar food ~ Restaurant ~ (01285) 821283 ~ Children welcome ~ Dogs allowed in bar ~ Open 11.30-3, 6.30(6 Sat)-midnight(1am Sat); 12-midnight Sun

NAILSWORTH
Weighbridge *B4014 towards Tetbury; GL6 9AL*

The 2 in 1 pies at this busy pub remain a great favourite with customers. They come in a large bowl, and half the bowl contains the filling of your choice while the other is full of home-made cauliflower cheese (or broccoli mornay or root vegetables), and topped with pastry. Other dishes on the menu are traditional. Most of the pub is now no smoking, and the relaxed bar has three cosily old-fashioned rooms with stripped stone walls, antique settles and country chairs, and window seats. The black beamed ceiling of the lounge bar is thickly festooned with black ironware – sheepshears, gin traps, lamps and a large collection of keys, many from the old Longfords Mill opposite the pub. Upstairs is a raftered hayloft with an engaging mix of rustic tables. No noisy games machines or piped music. Well kept Uley Old Spot and Laurie Lee and Wadworths 6X on handpump, 16 wines (and champagne) by the glass, Weston's cider, and 10 malt whiskies; fast, friendly service. Behind the building is a sheltered landscaped garden with picnic-sets under umbrellas. Good disabled access and facilities.
Free house ~ Licensee Howard Parker ~ Real ale ~ Bar food (12-9.30) ~ (01453) 832520 ~ Children allowed away from the bars until 9pm ~ Dogs welcome ~ Open 12-11; 12-10.30 Sun; closed 25 and 31 Dec; 10 days Jan

OLDBURY-ON-SEVERN
Anchor *Village signposted from B4061; BS35 1QA*

Well priced for the area and kept on handpump in very good condition, the real ales here might include Bass, Butcombe Bitter, Otter Bitter, Theakstons Old Peculier and a guest such as Bath Ales Gem Bitter; also, 27 malt whiskies and a dozen wines by the glass. The neatly kept lounge has modern beams and stone, a mix of tables including an attractive oval oak gateleg, cushioned window seats, winged seats against the wall, oil paintings by a local artist, and a big winter log fire. Diners can eat in the lounge or bar area or in the no smoking dining room at the back of the building (good for larger groups) and the menu is the same in all rooms. Using local produce where possible, bar food includes one or two twists on the fairly traditional. In summer, you can eat in the pretty garden – the hanging baskets and window boxes are lovely then; boules. They have wheelchair access and a disabled lavatory. Plenty of walks to the River Severn and along the many footpaths and bridleways, and St Arilda's church nearby is interesting, on its odd little knoll with wild flowers among the gravestones (the primroses and daffodils in spring are lovely).
Free house ~ Licensees Michael Dowdeswell and Mark Sorrell ~ Real ale ~ Bar food (12-2(2.30 Sat and bank hols), 6.30(6 Sat and bank hols)-9.30; 12-3, 6-9 Sun) ~ Restaurant ~ (01454) 413331 ~ Children in dining room only ~ Dogs allowed in bar ~ Open 11.30-2.45, 6.30-11; 11.30-11 Sat; 12-10.30 Sun

SAPPERTON
Bell *Village signposted from A419 Stroud—Cirencester; OS Sheet 163 map reference 948033; GL7 6LE*

Being at the heart of lots of attractions and outdoor pursuits means this well

run place has quite a mix of customers – summed up for us by a party of our readers sitting quite happily in their walking gear next to a table of smartly dressed lunchers out for a celebration meal. There are three separate, cosy rooms (all no smoking now) with stripped beams, a nice mix of wooden tables and chairs, country prints and modern art on stripped stone walls, one or two attractive rugs on the flagstones, and roaring log fires and woodburning stoves; fresh flowers and newspapers. Food is good and imaginative. They use traceable meat and fish, and local seasonal vegetables; and make their own bread and puddings. Four well kept ales from small local brewers like Bath, Butcombe, Uley and Wickwar, sixteen wines by two sizes of glass from a large and diverse wine list with very helpful notes, Long Ashton cider, some interesting aperitifs, 20 malt whiskies and several armagnacs and cognacs. Harry the springer spaniel is very sociable but must not be fed for health reasons. There are tables out on a small front lawn and in a partly covered and very pretty courtyard, for eating outside. Horses have their own tethering rail (and bucket of water).
Free house ~ Licensees Paul Davidson and Pat Le Jeune ~ Real ale ~ Bar food ~ Restaurant ~ (01285) 760298 ~ Children allowed but not under 10 in evenings ~ Dogs welcome ~ Open 11-2.30, 6.30-11; 12-3, 7-10.30 Sun; closed 3-10 Jan

TETBURY

Snooty Fox *Market Place; small residents' car park, nearby pay & display; free car park some way down hill; GL8 8DD*
Although this is more a hotel than pub, the high-ceilinged main bar on the left does score rather well with its bustling unstuffy atmosphere and three real ales on handpump: Bath Ales Barnstormer, Butcombe Bitter and Moles Best. Also, 20 wines by the glass (including rosé champagne as well as 'ordinary'), a fine collection of armagnac, cognac, calvados and port, and an espresso machine; good service from neat young staff and unobtrusive piped jazz. This front room – stripped stone, like much of the rest of the ground floor – has comfortable sturdy leather-armed chairs round the cast-iron tripod tables on its carpet, a big log fireplace flanked by an imposing pair of brass flambeaux, brass ceiling fans, and Ronald Searle pony-club cartoons. Behind is a similar room, with a colourful rug on bare boards and a leather sofa among other seats; the no smoking restaurant is beyond. On the right a smaller quieter room has leather wing armchairs and sofas, and a couple of imposing portraits. Well liked bar food is a good mix of traditional and imaginative dishes. Outside, a sheltered entryway has teak tables and chairs facing the ancient central covered market.
Free house ~ Licensee Marc Gibbons ~ Real ale ~ Bar food (12-2, 6-9; 12-8 Sun) ~ Restaurant ~ (01666) 502436 ~ Children welcome ~ Dogs allowed in bar and bedrooms ~ Open 11-11; 12-10.30 Sun ~ Bedrooms: £73B/£95B

Trouble House *A433 towards Cirencester, near Cherington turn; GL8 8SG*
Popular with the country set, this smart and friendly pub places firm emphasis on its good, interesting food. Furnishings are mainly close-set stripped pine or oak tables with chapel chairs, some wheelback chairs and

the odd library chair, and there are attractive mainly modern country prints on the cream or butter-coloured walls. The rush-matting room on the right is no smoking, and on the left there's a parquet-floored room with a chesterfield by the big stone fireplace, a hop-girt mantelpiece, and more hops hung from one of its two big black beams. In the small saggy-beamed middle room you can commandeer one of the bar stools, where they have well kept Wadworths IPA and 6X on handpump, and a good wine list with helpful notes and 14 wines by the glass; piped music. Food from the (not cheap) menu is ambitious and good, and service attentive. You can also sit out at picnic-sets on the gravel courtyard behind.

Wadworths ~ Tenants Michael and Sarah Bedford ~ Real ale ~ Bar food (not Sun evening or Mon) ~ Restaurant ~ (01666) 502206 ~ Children in restaurant only ~ Dogs welcome ~ Open 11-3, 6.30(7 winter)-11; 12-3 Sun; closed Sun evening, all day Mon; Christmas and New Year period

Dog Friendly Hotels, B&Bs and Farms

BIBURY
Bibury Court *Bibury, Cirencester, Gloucestershire GL7 5NT (01285) 740337* £**145**, plus special breaks; 18 individual rms, some overlooking garden. Lovely peaceful mansion dating from Tudor times set in seven acres of beautiful gardens (where dogs may walk), with an informal friendly atmosphere, panelled rooms, antiques, huge log fires, conservatory, a fine choice of breakfasts, and good interesting food in no smoking dining room; partial disabled access; dogs in bedrooms – but not to be left unattended; £5

Swan *Bibury, Cirencester, Gloucestershire GL7 5NW (01285) 740695* £**140**, plus special breaks; 18 very pretty individually decorated rms. Handsome creeper-covered hotel on the River Coln, with private fishing and attractive formal garden (where dogs may walk); lovely flowers and log fires in carefully furnished comfortable lounges, a cosy no smoking parlour, good food in opulent dining room, stylish modern brasserie/bar, nice breakfasts, and attentive staff; disabled access; dogs in bedrooms; £5

CHELTENHAM
Alias Hotel Kandinsky *Bayshill Rd, Cheltenham, Gloucestershire GL50 3AS (01242) 527788 (3.5 miles off M5 junction 11; A40 into town; turn left into Montpellier St, bearing left into Parabola Rd; turn right into Bayshill Rd)* £**126**; 48 large, stylish and well equipped rms. White-painted Regency hotel with an interesting mix of old and new furnishings, antiques and modern paintings, big pot plants, lots of mirrors, unusual collections on walls, log fire in comfortable drawing room, and a relaxed, informal atmosphere; enjoyable modern food in bustling Café Paradiso, popular afternoon tea, friendly bar, willing young staff, downstairs cocktail bar, and

seats out on decked terrace; they are kind to families; disabled access; dogs in bedrooms; if cleaning is needed, £15

CHIPPING CAMPDEN

Cotswold House *The Square, Chipping Campden, Gloucestershire GL55 6AN (01386) 840330* £225; 20 italian-style, comfortable rms. Imposing Regency house in lovely town and run by warmly friendly `hands-on` owners; beautiful central staircase, relaxing drawing room with log fire, good modern cooking in brasserie or restaurant, a cosseting atmosphere, sunny terraces, and formal garden; plenty to see nearby; disabled access; dogs welcome in bedrooms

CLEARWELL

Tudor Farmhouse *Clearwell, Coleford, Gloucestershire GL16 8JS (01594) 833046* £80, plus special breaks; 22 cottagey, well equipped rms. Carefully restored Tudor farmhouse and stone cottages with landscaped gardens and surrounding fields (walks for dogs); lots of beams and panelling, oak doors and sloping floors, inglenook fireplaces, enjoyable food in no smoking candlelit restaurant, and friendly staff; cl Christmas; disabled access; dogs in bedrooms

CORSE LAWN

Corse Lawn House *Corse Lawn, Gloucester, Gloucestershire GL19 4LZ (01452) 780771* £145, plus special breaks; 19 pretty, individually furnished rms. Handsome Queen Anne building with comfortable and attractive day rooms, a distinguished restaurant with imaginative, refined food plus lighter meals in a brightly decorated bistro, excellent wines, warmly friendly staff, and a relaxed atmosphere; indoor swimming pool, tennis court, croquet, and horses in 12 acres of surrounding gardens and fields, and plenty of walks in grounds and nearby common and forest; two resident dogs; cl 3 days over Christmas; disabled access; dogs welcome away from restaurant

GUITING POWER

Guiting Guest House *Post Office Lane, Guiting Power, Cheltenham, Gloucestershire GL54 5TZ (01451) 850470* £77; 7 pretty rms with thoughtful extras. 16th-c Cotswold stone guesthouse with inglenook fireplaces, beams, and rugs on flagstones, two sitting rooms, enjoyable evening meals by candlelight, attentive owners and a very relaxed atmosphere; dogs in bedrooms

LOWER SLAUGHTER

Washbourne Court *Lower Slaughter, Cheltenham, Gloucestershire GL54 2HS (01451) 822143* £140; 28 individually decorated rms, some in cottage suites. Honey-coloured stone hotel by the river Eye in 4 acres of neat grounds where dogs may walk (nearby local walks, too); comfortable and charming lounges, beams, open fires and persian rugs on polished parquet floors, stone mullioned windows, and delicious modern cooking in light airy no smoking restaurant; children must be over 12 in restaurant; disabled access; dogs in bedrooms; £10

NORTH CERNEY
Bathurst Arms *North Cerney, Cirencester, Gloucestershire GL7 7BZ (01285) 831281* (2.6 miles off A417, exit at NW end of Cirencester bypass heading N of main rd and across to turn left on to A435) £75; 6 pleasant rms. Civilised and handsome old inn with lots of atmosphere, a nice mix of polished old furniture and a fireplace at each end of the beamed and panelled bar, small no smoking dining room, imaginative food, quite a few well chosen wines by the glass, well kept real ales, and an attractive garden running down to the River Churn; lots of surrounding walks; dogs welcome in bedrooms

PAINSWICK
Painswick Hotel *Kemps Lane, Painswick, Stroud, Gloucestershire GL6 6YB (01452) 812160* £145, plus special breaks; 19 individually furnished and comfortable newly refurbished rms with views of the village or countryside. 18th-c Palladian mansion – once a grand rectory – with fine views, antiques and paintings in the elegant rooms, open fires, good food using the best local produce, a thoughtful wine list, and a relaxed, friendly atmosphere; garden with croquet lawn; dogs in newly refurbished garden rms; £10

PARKEND
Edale House *Folly Rd, Parkend, Lydney, Gloucestershire GL15 4JF (01594) 562835* £66, plus special breaks; 6 rms, most with own bthrm. No smoking Georgian house opposite cricket green and backing on to Nagshead Nature Reserve; comfortable, homely sitting room, honesty bar, very good food in attractive dining room, and a relaxed atmosphere; resident cat; walks nearby; children over 12; disabled access; dogs in bedrooms and lounge; £3

STOW-ON-THE-WOLD
Grapevine *Sheep St, Stow-on-the-wold, Cheltenham, Gloucestershire GL54 1AU (01451) 830344* (0.2 miles off A429; Sheep St (A436)) £140, plus special breaks; 22 individually decorated, attractive, no smoking rms. Warm, friendly and very well run hotel with antiques, comfortable chairs and a relaxed atmosphere in the lounge, a beamed bar, and imaginative food in the attractive, sunny restaurant with its 70-year-old trailing vine; partial disabled access; dogs in bedrooms (if small and well behaved)

Old Stocks *The Square, Stow-on-the-wold, Cheltenham, Gloucestershire GL54 1AF (01451) 830666* (0.1 mile off A429; Market Sq, best entered from N end of town) £90, plus special breaks; 18 rms. Well run 16th/17th-c cotswold stone hotel overlooking the Market Square with cosy welcoming small bar, old beams and open fire, comfortable residents' lounge, good food in no smoking restaurant, friendly staff, and sheltered garden; cl

Christmas; disabled access; dogs in bedrooms and some public rooms but not restaurant; £5

THORNBURY
Thornbury Castle *Castle St, Thornbury, Bristol BS35 1HH (01454) 281182* **£180**; 25 opulent rms, some with big Tudor fireplaces or fine oriel windows. Impressive and luxuriously renovated early 16th-c castle with antiques, tapestries, huge fireplaces and mullioned windows in the baronial public rooms, three dining rooms (one in the base of a tower), fine cooking, extensive wine list (inc wine from their own vineyard), thoughtful friendly service, and vast grounds inc the oldest Tudor gardens in England; partial disabled access; dogs at manager's discretion; £10

Hampshire

Dog Friendly Pubs

BENTWORTH
Sun *Sun Hill; from the A339 coming from Alton the first turning takes you there direct; or in village follow Shalden 2¼, Alton 4¼ signpost; GU34 5JT*
Readers have been unanimous in praise for this charming 17th-c country pub – its welcoming landlady, the well kept beer she serves and the food too. There's a fine choice of eight changing real ales, some coming from local brewers; these might include Badger Fursty Ferret, Butcombe Best, Flower Pots, Fullers London Pride, Ringwood Best and Old Thumper, Stonehenge Pigswill and Timothy Taylors Landlord on handpump; several malt whiskies. Another strength at this delightful place is the promptly served good home-made bar food. Popular with both locals and visitors, the two little traditional communicating rooms have high-backed antique settles, pews and schoolroom chairs, olde-worlde prints and blacksmith's tools on the walls, and bare boards and scrubbed deal tables on the left; big fireplaces (one with a winter fire) and candles make it especially snug in winter; an arch leads to a brick-floored room with another open fire. There are seats out in front and in the back garden, and pleasant nearby walks.
Free house ~ Licensee Mary Holmes ~ Real ale ~ Bar food (12-2, 7-9.30) ~ (01420) 562338 ~ Children welcome (with restrictions) ~ Dogs allowed in bar ~ Open 12-3, 6-11; 12-10.30 Sun

BRAISHFIELD
Wheatsheaf *Village signposted off A3090 on NW edge of Romsey, pub just S of village on Braishfield Road; SO51 0QE*
In addition to using eggs from their own cotswold legbar chickens, the friendly owners of this nicely idiosyncratic pub have made this a charming place to eat, drink and chat: they source ingredients carefully and make good use of their own serious and sizeable herb garden (eggs come from their own chickens), and you may be in luck to visit when their soft fruit cage is cropping. The décor is eclectic, with a miscellany of tables from elegant little oak ovals through handsome Regency-style drum tables to sturdy more rustic ones, with a similarly wide variety of chairs, and on the stripped brick or deep pink-painted walls a profusion of things to look at,

from Spy caricatures and antique prints through staffordshire dogs and other decorative china to a leg in a fishnet stocking kicking out from the wall and a jokey 'Malteser grader' (a giant copper skimmer). It sounds a bit of a mish-mash, but in fact works well, making for an attractive and relaxed atmosphere – helped along by the way the efficient young staff clearly enjoy their work. Two of the dining areas are no smoking. In addition to lots of snacks, food is enjoyable and interesting; on Wednesdays they have burger evenings, where you customise your own burger, and they sell chocolates and sweets. Hook Norton Old Hooky, Ringwood Best, Timothy Taylors Landlord and a couple of guests such as Caledonian Deuchars IPA and Charles Wells Bombardier are on handpump, and they have 16 wines by the glass, speciality belgian beers and good coffee; daily papers and several reference books; piped music, TV; disabled access and facilities. Unusually, the chairs, tables and picnic-sets out on the terrace are painted in greek blue. There are woodland walks nearby, and the pub is handy for the Sir Harold Hillier Arboretum.

Enterprise ~ Lease Peter and Jenny Jones ~ Real ale ~ Bar food (11-9.30; 12-9 Sun) ~ Restaurant ~ (01794) 368372 ~ Children welcome ~ Dogs allowed in bar ~ Open 11-midnight

CHAWTON
Greyfriar *Signposted off A31/A32 roundabout just S of Alton; Winchester Road; GU34 1SB*

In a quiet and attractive bypassed village straight opposite Jane Austen's house, this spotlessly kept open-plan pub is justly popular for its imaginative food. They bake their own bread, steaks are prime aberdeen angus, and in winter they have local game. The black-beamed bar part on the left has neat seating around sturdy varnished pub tables on its carpet, with a couple of pine farmhouse tables in recesses – one with a shelf of foodie books and guides. By the brick counter is a timber support studded with hundreds of coins – and a goodly row of comfortably backed bar chairs. Besides three Fullers beers there might be a guest such as Gales Festival Mild on handpump and decent wines by the glass; they do good coffees. There's a relaxed atmosphere, with quick helpful service by pleasant staff, and quite a few older midweek lunchers. The partly no smoking restaurant part on the right has more of the pine farmhouse furnishings, and a menu blackboard. There may be unobtrusive piped music. Behind is a small garden with terrace tables and a barbecue; there are good nearby walks.

Fullers ~ Lease Peter and Fran Whitehead ~ Real ale ~ Bar food (12-2, 7-9.30; 12-3, 6-8 Sun) ~ Restaurant ~ (01420) 83841 ~ Children welcome ~ Dogs allowed in bar ~ Open 12-11(10.30 Sun)

EASTON
Chestnut Horse *3.6 miles from M3 junction 9: A33 towards Kings Worthy, then B3047 towards Itchen Abbas; Easton then signposted on right – bear left in village; SO21 1EG*

The open-plan interior manages to have a pleasantly rustic and intimate feel, with a series of cosily separate areas, making this upmarket country dining pub a cheering experience from the moment you walk in. Its really snug décor takes in candles and fresh flowers on the tables, log fires in cottagey fireplaces, comfortable furnishings, black beams and joists hung with all sorts of jugs, mugs and chamber-pots, and lots of attractive pictures of wildlife and the local area. Served by efficient and friendly staff, food is good but by no means cheap. A much more reasonably priced two-course menu is good value, and a favourite with readers: Mon-Sat lunchtime and Mon-Thurs evenings 6-7.30pm. Courage Best and Chestnut Horse (brewed for the pub by Itchen Valley) along with one or two guests from brewers like Itchen Valley or Ringwood on handpump, several wines by the glass, and around 60 malt whiskies; piped music. There are good tables out on a smallish sheltered decked area, with colourful flower tubs and baskets, and plenty of walks in the Itchen Valley from here.

Free house ~ Licensees John and Jocelyn Holland ~ Real ale ~ Bar food (12-2.30, 6-9.30; 12-8.30(4 winter) Sun) ~ Restaurant ~ (01962) 779257 ~ Children welcome ~ Dogs allowed in bar ~ Open 12-3.30, 5.30-12; 12-10.30 Sun; closed Sun evenings in winter

FRITHAM

Royal Oak *Village signed from exit roundabout, M27 junction 1; quickest via B3078, then left and straight through village; head for Eyeworth Pond; SO43 7HJ*
It's surprising how many walkers and cyclists find their way to this remote thatched pub, in a delightfully rural location in the New Forest. It is part of a working farm so there are ponies and pigs out on the green, and plenty of livestock nearby. Locals (needless to say it still has a strong local following) and visitors alike are greeted with genuine warmth. Three neatly kept black beamed rooms (one is no smoking) are very simple but full of proper traditional character, with prints and pictures involving local characters on the white walls, restored panelling, antique wheelback, spindleback and other old chairs and stools with colourful seats around solid tables on new oak flooring, and two roaring log fires. The back bar has quite a few books. Seven well kept ales are tapped from the cask, with Flower Pots, Ringwood Best and Fortyniner, and Hop Back Summer Lightning along with guests from brewers such as Archers and RCH; also a dozen wines by the glass (mulled wine in winter), and they hold a beer festival in September. Simple lunchtime food is limited to home-made soup, sausage ring, home-cooked pork pie or ploughman's. Summer barbecues are put on in the neatly kept big garden, which has a marquee for poor weather; darts, board games and pétanque.

Free house ~ Licensees Neil and Pauline McCulloch ~ Real ale ~ Bar food (lunchtime only) ~ No credit cards ~ (023) 8081 2606 ~ Children welcome if well behaved ~ Dogs welcome ~ Open 11-11; 12-10.30 Sun; 11-3 weekdays in winter

HAWKLEY

Hawkley Inn *Take first right turn off B3006, heading towards Liss ¼ mile from its junction with A3; then after nearly 2 miles take first left turn into Hawkley village – Pococks Lane; OS Sheet 186 map reference 746292; GU33 6NE*
'Welcoming enough so that you could feel comfortable going in on your

own; wish it was our local, enthuses one reader of this friendly pub, where the good real ale selection features usually seven constantly changing beers, and often from small local breweries such as Ballards, Flower Pots, Kings and Ringwood, as well as a couple of local ciders. The opened-up bar and back dining room have a simple and unassuming rather than smart décor – big pine tables, dried flowers, and prints on the mellowing walls. The snug can get a bit smoky when it's busy, but there is a no smoking area to the right of the bar – both sides now have a real fire; piped music, backgammon. Bar food includes hearty traditional dishes; friendly service; several malt whiskies and wines by the glass. The pub is on the Hangers Way Path, and at weekends there are plenty of walkers; tables in the pleasant garden. As we went to press a new kitchen was being built and new bedrooms were about to be completed; we would welcome reports from readers who stay here.

Free house ~ Licensee Nick Troth ~ Real ale ~ Bar food (12-2(4 Sat, Sun), 7-9.30) ~ (01730) 827205 ~ Children welcome until 8pm ~ Dogs allowed in bar ~ Live music Sat nights in winter ~ Open 12-3(5 Sat), 5.30-11; 12-5, 7-10.30 Sun ~ Bedrooms: /£69S

LITTLETON
Running Horse *Village signposted off B3049 just NW of Winchester; Main Road; SO22 6QS*

This crisply furnished dining pub, now in the hands of the expert publicans who run the Plough at Sparsholt so well, is now completely no smoking, offers bed and breakfast, and has widened its menu to include simple lunchtime bar food as well as gourmet options. The food is inventive and very rewarding, and they bake their own bread and use local produce where possible. The stylishly decorated bar has some deep leather chairs as well as ochre-cushioned metal and wicker ones around matching modern tables on its polished boards, up-to-date lighting, good colour photographs of hampshire landscapes and townscapes, a potted palm as well as a log fire, and venetian blinds in its bow windows. The neat modern marble and hardwood bar counter (with swish leather, wood and brass bar stools) has Itchen Valley Winchester Ale and Ringwood Best on handpump, ten wines by the glass, and an espresso machine. Linking openly from here, the back no smoking restaurant area has the same sort of elegant modern furniture, on flagstones. Good disabled access and facilities; there may be piped pop music. There are green metal tables and chairs out on terraces front and back, with picnic-sets on the back grass by a spreading sycamore.

Free house ~ Licensee Catherine Crawford ~ Real ale ~ Bar food (12-2, 6.30-9.30; 12-4.30 Sun) ~ Restaurant ~ (01962) 880218 ~ Children in eating area of bar and restaurant ~ Dogs allowed in bar ~ Open 11-3, 5.30-11; 11-11 Sat; 12-9.30 Sun ~ Bedrooms: /£65B

LONGSTOCK
Peat Spade *Village signposted off A30 on W edge of Stockbridge, and off A3057 Stockbridge—Andover; SO20 6DR*

Right by the River Test, this is a popular haunt for anglers, and the fishing and shooting theme extends to the pictures on the walls, together with stuffed fish by the bar, and there's even a little fishing shop at the end of the garden for anyone who needs angling gear. The new owners here have made several changes, extending the terrace into the garden (to which they were about to add a gas pit – an open-air gas fire – just as we went to press), adding six letting rooms and creating a locals' bar. Residents and diners can also use the lounge upstairs, which has board games, cards, dominoes and chess. Local and seasonal produce feature significantly on the imaginative menu (best to book a table in advance). All the food apart from the bread and chips is home-made. The roomy and attractive squarish main bar is airy and high-ceilinged, with pretty windows, well chosen furnishings and a nice show of toby jugs and beer mats around its fireplace. A rather elegant no smoking dining room leads off, and there are doors to the patio. Ringwood Best and Fortyniner together with a changing guest also from Ringwood on handpump, and eight wines by the glass from a carefully chosen list. There are plenty of surrounding walks, along the Test Way at the end of the road and in the water meadows around Stockbridge, and Longstock Water Gardens at the end of village.

Free house ~ Licensees Andrew Clark and Lucy Townsend ~ Real ale ~ Bar food (12-2, 7-9.30) ~ Restaurant ~ (01264) 810612 ~ Children welcome if eating in restaurant; no children under 10 in bedrooms ~ Dogs allowed in bar ~ Open 11-3, 6.30-11 ~ Bedrooms: /£110B

LOWER WIELD

Yew Tree *Turn off A339 NW of Alton at Medstead, Bentworth 1 signpost, then follow village signposts; or off B3046 S of Basingstoke, signposted from Preston Candover; SO24 9RX*

In winter the crackling fire is a welcoming sight as you enter this beautifully placed and relaxed tile-hung pub, while in summer you might see cricket in progress across the road. The atmosphere is nicely informal: a small flagstoned bar area on the left has a few military prints above its stripped brick dado, a steadily ticking clock and a log fire. Around to the right of the serving counter – which has a couple of stylish wrought-iron bar chairs – it's carpeted, with a few attractive flower pictures, and throughout there is a mix of tables, including some quite small ones for two, and miscellaneous chairs; piped music. Using fresh local ingredients, good bar food is gently imaginative. Vegetables are tasty and seasonal, and nice breads come with good properly served butter; no smoking dining area. The well chosen wine list, with a dozen or more by the glass, is reasonably priced, and may include Louis Jadot burgundies from a shipper based just along the lane; they generally have local beers, with Flower Pots and a guest from one of 17 breweries such as Itchen Valley, Suthwyk or White Star on handpump. Service is friendly and helpful, with a real personal touch – however busy he is in the kitchen, the enthusiastic landlord always seems to find time to come out and say hello. There are solid tables and chunky seats out on the front terrace, with picnic-sets in a sizeable side garden and pleasant views. Nearby walks include one around lovely Rushmoor Pond.

Free house ~ Licensees Tim Manktelow-Gray and Penny Appel-Billsberry ~ Real ale ~ Bar food (12-2, 6.30-9(8.30 Sun)) ~ (01256) 389224 ~ Children welcome ~ Dogs allowed in bar ~ Open 12-3, 6-11; 12-10.30 Sun; 12-3, 6-10.30 Sun in winter; closed Mon

LYMINGTON

Kings Head *Quay Hill; pedestrian alley at bottom of High Street, can park down on quay and walk up from Quay Street; SO41 3AR*

Tankards hang from great rough beams in this rambling, candlelit 17th-c pub, and they serve Fullers London Pride, Gales HSB, Greene King Old Speckled Hen and two guests from brewers such as Adnams and Ringwood on handpump, with several wines by the glass. Up and down steps and through timber dividers, mainly bare-boarded rooms with a rug or two contain a nice old-fashioned variety of seating at a great mix of tables from an elegant gateleg to a huge chunk of elm, and the local pictures include good classic yacht photographs. A cosy upper corner past the serving counter has a good log fire in a big fireplace, its mantelpiece a shrine to all sorts of drinking paraphernalia from beer tankards to port and champagne cases. Enjoyable food is tasty and gently imaginative. A wall rack holds daily papers; piped pop music; no smoking area.

Inn Partnership (Pubmaster) ~ Lease Paul Stratton ~ Real ale ~ Bar food (11-2.30(3 Fri-Sun), 6-10) ~ (01590) 672709 ~ Children welcome ~ Dogs welcome ~ Open 11-3, 6-12; 11-1am Sat; 12-11 Sun

OVINGTON

Bush *Village signposted from A31 on Winchester side of Alresford; SO24 0RE*

The back garden runs down to the River Itchen, making this family-run pub a popular place to sit out on a sunny day. Inside it's delightfully cottagey, with a marked absence of piped music, fruit machines or similar intrusions. A low-ceilinged bar is furnished with cushioned high-backed settles, elm tables with pews and kitchen chairs, masses of old pictures in heavy gilt frames on the walls, and a roaring fire on one side with an antique solid fuel stove opposite. Three rooms are no smoking. Though not cheap the food is of high quality and imaginative (note there's a minimum charge at Sunday lunchtime), where possible using local ingredients Three to five real ales on handpump such as Archers Bitter, JCB, Wadworths Henrys IPA, 6X or Summersault, with several country wines, 13 wines by the glass and malt whiskies; board games. Look out for the sociable scottish springer spaniel, Paddy. Please note that if you want to bring children it's best to book, as there are only a few tables set aside for families.

Wadworths ~ Managers Nick and Cathy Young ~ Real ale ~ Bar food (not Sun evening) ~ (01962) 732764 ~ No children in lower room, new room or bar ~ Dogs welcome ~ Open 11-3, 6-11; 12-3, 7-10.30 Sun

PETERSFIELD

Trooper *From B2070 in Petersfield follow Steep signposts past station, but keep on up past Steep, on old coach road; OS Sheet 186 map reference 726273; GU32 1BD*

For its rural setting, welcoming landlord, comfortable accommodation (with good breakfasts) and satisfying food, this country dining inn receives very high praise. It's best to book to be sure of a table (particularly on Friday and Saturday evenings). Kept on handpump, the three or four beers change frequently but tend to be from local or fairly local brewers such as Flower Pots, Hogs Back, Hop Back and Itchen Valley, and they have decent house wines. There's an island bar, blond chairs and a mix of tripod tables on bare boards or red tiles, tall stools by a broad ledge facing big windows that look across to rolling downland fields, old film star photos and paintings by local artists for sale, little persian knick-knacks here and there, quite a few ogival mirrors, big baskets of dried flowers, lit candles all around, fresh flowers, a well tended log fire in the stone fireplace, and carefully chosen piped music; newspapers and magazines to read. The attractive raftered restaurant has french windows to a partly covered sunken terrace, and there are lots of picnic-sets on an upper lawn; the dining areas are no smoking. The horse rail in the car park ('horses and camels only before 8pm') does get used, though probably not often for camels.

Free house ~ Licensee Hassan Matini ~ Real ale ~ Bar food (12-2(2.30 Sun), 6-9(9.30 Fri, Sat)) ~ Restaurant ~ (01730) 827293 ~ Children welcome ~ Dogs allowed in bar ~ Open 12-3, 5-11; 12-3.30 Sun; closed Sun evening and all day Mon ~ Bedrooms: £69B/£89B

ROWLAND'S CASTLE

Castle Inn *Village signposted off B2148/B2149 N of Havant; Finchdean Road, by junction with Redhill Road and Woodberry Lane; PO9 6DA*

Now no smoking throughout, this friendly pub sets a cheerful mood from the moment you walk in, and the food is generously served and consistently good value. There are two appealing little eating rooms on the left. The front one has rather nice simple mahogany chairs around sturdy scrubbed pine tables, one quite long, rugs on flagstones, a big fireplace, and quite a lot of old local photographs on its ochre walls. The back one is similar, but with bare boards and local watercolour landscapes by Bob Payne for sale. There is a small separate public bar on the right with a good fire and Fullers London Pride, Gales Butser and HSB and a guest such as Fullers Discovery on handpump. Served by smartly dressed staff, the lunchtime menu includes traditional items. Dishes are only a little pricier in the evening, and on Mondays they do a tex-mex buffet. The publicans' own ponies are in view from the largish garden, which is equipped with picnic-sets and a couple of swings; disabled access and facilities are good.

Gales (Fullers) ~ Tenants Jan and Roger Burrell ~ Real ale ~ Bar food (12-9; not after 2pm on winter Sun) ~ Restaurant ~ (023) 9241 2494 ~ Children in eating area of bar ~ Dogs allowed in bar ~ Open 11-11(12 Fri, Sat)

SPARSHOLT

Plough *Village signposted off B3049 (Winchester—Stockbridge), a little W of Winchester; SO21 2NW*

'There were happy noises from all areas' and 'prices reasonable for the very high standard of food' are typical comments from readers in praise of this deservedly popular dining pub; it does get very busy, and booking is strongly recommended (you might have a wait for your food at peak times). Everything is neatly kept, and the main bar has an interesting mix of wooden tables and chairs, with farm tools, scythes and pitchforks attached to the ceiling; most of the pub is no smoking. The very good interesting bar food is listed on daily changing blackboards. Wadworths IPA, 6X and Summersault together with St Austell Tribute on handpump, and an extensive wine list with a good selection by the glass, including champagne and pudding wine. Disabled access and facilities; there's a children's play fort, and plenty of seats on the terrace and lawn.

Wadworths ~ Tenants Richard and Kathryn Crawford ~ Real ale ~ Bar food (12-2, 6-9(8.30 Mon, Sun; 9.30 Fri, Sat)) ~ (01962) 776353 ~ Children welcome except in main bar area ~ Dogs welcome ~ Open 11-3, 6-11

STOCKBRIDGE
Grosvenor *High Street; SO20 6EU*
Well divided into separate room areas (all no smoking apart from the bar), this comfortably old-fashioned Georgian coaching inn has a relaxing, high-ceilinged main bar with a good log fire. The restrained décor is entirely in keeping with the distinction of the building itself. Greene King IPA and Abbot are on handpump, alongside a dozen enjoyable wines by the glass, and decent coffee; piped music. As we went to press they were unable to give us specific information about the bar food as the menu was about to be completely changed. The impressive oak-panelled restaurant has some hand-etched panels of horses done 200 years ago with a poker from the fire. A back conservatory has more tables. A couple of pavement tables stand out beside the imposing front portico, with more tables in the good-sized back garden, prettily laid out with attractive plantings. This is an appealing little town, with good antiques shops, the National Trust Common Marsh along the River Test, and downland walks all around. Please tell us about the bedrooms if you stay here.

Greene King ~ Managers David and Margo Fyfe ~ Real ale ~ Bar food (12-2.30, 6.30-9.30(8.30 Sun)) ~ Restaurant ~ (01264) 810606 ~ Children welcome ~ Dogs allowed in bar and bedrooms ~ Open 11-11; 12-10.30 Sun ~ Bedrooms: £85B/£99.50B

TICHBORNE
Tichborne Arms *Village signed off B3047; SO24 0NA*
You can expect to find quite a few walkers at this delightfully unspoilt country pub during the day, as the Wayfarers Walk and Itchen Way pass close by, and the countryside around is attractively rolling. The comfortable square-panelled room on the right has wheelback chairs and settles (one very long), a stone fireplace, and latticed windows. On the left is a larger, livelier, partly panelled room used for eating. Pictures and documents on the walls recall the bizarre Tichborne Case, in which a mystery man from Australia claimed fraudulently to be the heir to this estate. Home-made bar food is mostly traditional. Ringwood Best, Wadworths 6X and a couple of local guests are tapped from the cask, alongside a decent choice of wines by the glass, country wines and farm

cider; sensibly placed darts, bar billiards, shove-ha'penny, cribbage and piped music; the long-haired german shepherd is called Dylan. Picnic-sets outside in the big well kept garden. No children inside.

Free house ~ Licensees Nigel and Sarah Burt ~ Real ale ~ Bar food ~ (01962) 733760 ~ Children welcome except in bars ~ Dogs allowed in bar ~ Open 11.30-2.30, 6-11; 12-3, 7-11 Sun; closed Mon evening in winter

WHERWELL
Mayfly *Testcombe (over by Fullerton, and not in Wherwell itself); A3057 SE of Andover, between B3420 turn-off and Leckford where road crosses River Test; OS Sheet 185 map reference 382390; SO20 6AX*

The tables on the decking and the conservatory overlooking the duck-populated and trout-filled River Test make this scenically placed pub a delightful place to while away a summer afternoon. Inside, the spacious, beamed and carpeted bar has fishing pictures on the cream walls, rustic pub furnishings, and a woodburning stove, and most of the pub is no smoking; piped music. Efficient staff serve six real ales on handpump, with Greene King Abbot, Ringwood Best, Wadworths 6X and Wychwood Hobgoblin together with a couple of guests such as Gales HSB and Ringwood Fortyniner; piped music. Handily available all day, tasty bar food comes from a buffet-style servery: they do a choice of hot and cold meats, pies and quiches, salads and a great selection of cheeses. The blackboard menu features some traditional dishes.

Enterprise ~ Manager Barry Lane ~ Real ale ~ Bar food (11.30-9) ~ (01264) 860283 ~ Children welcome ~ Dogs welcome ~ Open 10am-11pm

Dog Friendly Hotels, B&Bs and Farms

BROCKENHURST
Cloud Hotel *Meerut Rd, Brockenhurst, Hampshire SO42 7TD (01590) 622165* **£136**; 18 pretty rms. Neatly kept and friendly hotel with New Forest views, several cosy lounges, log fires and fresh flowers, an intimate little bar, dancing memorabilia highlighting the career of the owner, good food in attractive no smoking restaurant, popular cream teas, and an attractive garden; children over 8; partial disabled access; dogs in bedrooms; £10

CHERITON
Flower Pots *Cheriton, Alresford, Hampshire SO24 0QQ (01962) 771318* (0.7 miles off A272; pub signed left off B3046 in village) **£65**; 4 no smoking rms. Unspoilt and quietly comfortable village local run by very friendly family, with two pleasant little bars, log fire, decent bar food (not Sun evening), super own-brew beers, and old-fashioned seats on the pretty lawns; no credit cards; no accommodation Christmas and New Year; two resident dogs; lots of walks nearby; no children; dogs in bedrooms and bars if well behaved and on a lead

HURSTBOURNE TARRANT

Esseborne Manor *Hurstbourne Tarrant, Andover, Hampshire SP11 0ER* *(01264) 736444* **£150**, plus special breaks; 20 individually decorated rms. Small stylish Victorian manor with a relaxed, friendly atmosphere, comfortable lounge and snug little bar, good modern cooking and log fires in elegant no smoking dining room, and courteous staff; three acres of neat gardens (where dogs may walk) with tennis and croquet; special arrangement with local golf club and health and leisure centre; disabled access; dogs welcome in bedrooms

LYMINGTON

Efford Cottage *Milford Rd, Everton, Lymington, Hampshire SO41 0JD* *(01590) 642315* **£60**, plus winter breaks; 3 comfortable rms. Spacious Georgian cottage in an acre of garden which has a special doggy area marked out; marvellous breakfasts with home-baked bread, home-made preserves and honey from their own bees served in charming dining room, and friendly, helpful owners; resident dog; good parking; walks on nearby beach, footpaths and New Forest; no children; dogs in bedrooms but must not be left unattended; special sitting service; £2

Stanwell House *High St, Lymington, Hampshire SO41 9AA (01590) 677123* **£110**, plus special breaks; 29 pretty rms. Handsome no smoking town house with comfortable attractively furnished lounge, newly refurbished, cosy little bar, good bistro-style food using local produce in candlelit dining room, and pretty walled back garden; New Forest nearby for walks; dogs in bedrooms; bowl and treats; £5

MILFORD ON SEA

Westover Hall *Park Lane, Milford-on-sea, Lymington, Hampshire SO41 0PT* *(01590) 643044* **£220**, plus winter breaks; 12 individually furnished rms, 6 with sea views. Victorian mansion in marvellous spot near peaceful beach, views of Christchurch Bay, Isle of Wight and the Needles rocks; impressive original features including dramatic stained glass, magnificent oak panelling, and ornate ceilings, very good food using the best local produce in grand (but not stuffy) no smoking candlelit restaurant overlooking garden and sea, lighter lunches in lounge bar also with water views, sunny terrace, and helpful friendly staff; resident cat; plenty of fine nearby walks; dogs in bedrooms and maybe lounge bar (if on a lead); £10

OWER

Ranvilles Farm House *Pauncefoot Hill, Romsey, Hampshire SO51 6AA* *(023) 80814481* (3.3 miles off M27 exit 2; after just under 2 miles on A31 towards Romsey, turn back into southbound carriageway – Ranvilles is next on left) **£60**; 4 attractively decorated rms with antique furniture. Dating from the 13th c when Richard de Ranville came from Normandy and settled with his family, this Grade II★ listed house is in five quiet acres of gardens and paddock, with warmly friendly owners and enjoyable breakfasts; no evening meals; two resident dogs; walks in the grounds and in the New Forest; disabled access; dogs in bedrooms

SPARSHOLT
Lainston House *Sparsholt, Winchester, Hampshire SO21 2LT (01962) 863588* £**135**, plus wknd breaks; 50 spacious, individually decorated rms. Close to Winchester, this elegant William and Mary hotel stands in 63 acres of fine parkland, with tennis court, croquet, fishing, archery and clay pigeon shooting; fresh flowers and paintings in relaxing and elegant no smoking lounge, panelled bar and no smoking restaurant, a fine wine list, and modern english cooking; gym; disabled access; dogs in bedrooms; special dog menu inc vegetarian and walking service avail; £10

WINCHESTER
Wykeham Arms *75 Kingsgate St, Winchester, Hampshire SO23 9PE (01962) 853834* £**105**; 14 well equipped attractive no smoking rms. Very well run, smart old town inn, close to cathedral, with interestingly furnished bustling bars, two small no smoking dining rooms serving delicious daily changing food (very good breakfasts, too), fine wines (lots by the glass), and prompt friendly service; walks along water meadows and more close by; resident dog; cl 25 and 31 Dec; dogs in one bedroom and in bar; bonios given; £7.50

Herefordshire

Dog Friendly Pubs

AYMESTREY
Riverside Inn *A4110, at N end of village, W of Leominster; HR6 9ST*
In beautiful semi-wooded scenery, this is a lovely spot to stay, and the
position by a double-arched bridge over the River Lugg is much enjoyed
by readers – picnic-sets make the most of the view, and rustic tables and
benches up above in a steep tree-sheltered garden. The rambling beamed
bar has several cosy areas and the décor is drawn from a pleasant mix of
periods and styles, with fine antique oak tables and chairs, stripped pine
country kitchen tables, fresh flowers, hops strung from a ceiling wagon-
wheel, horse tack and nice pictures; the eating areas are no smoking. Warm
log fires in winter, while in summer big overflowing flower pots frame the
entrances; fairly quiet piped pop music. Three beers from Woods and Wye
Valley on handpump, two local farm ciders and more than 20 malt
whiskies. The landlord likes to talk to his customers and service is good.
Many of the ingredients used in the enjoyable food are locally sourced. It
does get busy at weekends, so booking would be wise. Residents can try
fly-fishing on the river.
Free house ~ Licensees Richard and Liz Gresko ~ Real ale ~ Bar food (12-2.15,
7-9 Mon-Sat; 12-2.30, 6.30-8.30 Sun) ~ Restaurant ~ (01568) 708440 ~
Children welcome ~ Dogs welcome ~ Open 11-4, 6-11; 11-4, 6.30-10.30 Sun;
closed Sun evening and Mon in winter ~ Bedrooms: £40B/£65B

BRIMFIELD
Roebuck Inn *Village signposted just off A49 Shrewsbury—Leominster; SY8*
4NE
You might find locals drinking and playing dominoes and cribbage by an
impressive inglenook fireplace in the opened-out front bar of this smart
dining pub (which has comfortable bedrooms). This bar merges into a
light, contemporary-looking area, done in beige, green and cream colours,
with a big bay window; TV, piped music. Pale oak panelling in the 15th-c
no smoking lounge bar makes for a quietly relaxed atmosphere. There's
also a brightly decorated cane-furnished dining room (also no smoking). As
well as lunchtime snacks and platters with assorted cheeses, there's a more

elaborate menu. Banks's and one or two guests such as Black Sheep or Marstons are on handpump. Seats are placed out on the enclosed terrace. As we went to press the lease of this was about to be offered to a new landlord.

Union Pub Company ~ Lease Steve O'Donoghue ~ Real ale ~ Bar food (12-2.30(2 Sun), 6.9.30; not Sun evening) ~ Restaurant ~ (01584) 711230 ~ Children in eating area of bar and restaurant ~ Dogs allowed in bar and bedrooms ~ Open 11.30-3, 6.30-11; 12-3, 7-10.30 Sun ~ Bedrooms: £50B/£80B

HOARWITHY

New Harp *Village signposted off A49 Hereford—Ross-on-Wye; HR2 6QH*

Reopened after being closed for some years, this is now a delightful country pub, beautifully placed in a quiet village. Bow windows look up the hill to a remarkable italianate Victorian church with a tall tower, and the little stream which runs through the pretty tree-sheltered garden soon meets the nearby River Wye. There are plenty of picnic-sets, some on decking in a sort of arbour, and in summer they have barbecues. It's right on the new Herefordshire Trail (good walking, with a campsite close by). Inside, it's been completely reworked in a refreshing contemporary style, with brown leather tub armchairs in front of a woodburning stove, a mix of comfortable dining chairs around individual tables, stone floor tiling and stripped masonry in one wall, but mainly crisp off-white paintwork with nicely lit modern artwork, including cartoons and caricatures. The bar angles round to a cosy dining room, and the atmosphere is relaxed and welcoming throughout, with nicely informal service. The good blackboard food, carefully cooked and attractively presented, uses as much Herefordshire produce as possible, including organic vegetables from nearby Carey. They cure their own ham and make their own chutneys, and have fresh fish from Brixham on Tuesday evenings. They have three or four changing real ales on handpump such as Bath Gem, Hop Back Summer Lightning and St Austell Tribute, a growing collecting of unusual bottled beers, good Broome Farm ciders and perhaps perries, an interesting range of sensibly priced wines, and an enterprising choice of soft drinks, and you can get bowls of nuts and other nibbles. Muddy boots are no problem, and they stock bones for visiting dogs; Foxy the pub labrador is an indulgent host. There is a beer festival around the August bank holiday; unobtrusive piped music.

Badger ~ Tenants Fleur and Andrew Cooper ~ Real ale ~ Bar food (12-2.30, 6-9.30(9 Sun)) ~ (01432) 840900 ~ Children welcome ~ Dogs allowed in bar ~ Open 12-3, 6(5 Fri)-11; 12-11(10.30 Sun) Sat

SELLACK

Lough Pool *Back road Hoarwithy—Ross-on-Wye; HR9 6LX*

As well as producing good food using local and seasonal produce (including local meat, game, cream and fruit from Herefordshire and the welsh borders), this unspoilt timber-framed country pub is still somewhere you can feel at ease if you just want to enjoy a drink. The beamed central room has kitchen chairs and cushioned window seats around wooden tables on the mainly flagstoned floor, sporting prints, bunches of dried flowers and fresh hop bines, and a log fire at one end with a woodburner at the other. Other rooms lead off, gently brightened up with attractive individual furnishings and nice touches like the dresser of patterned plates; the bar area is no smoking; newspapers are left out for customers. The same contemporary interesting menu – which changes daily – is available in the chatty bar as well as the no smoking restaurant. They also have a lighter lunchtime menu (not Sunday). Adnams Explorer and Wye Valley Bitter and Butty Bach plus a guest such as Greene King Old Speckled Hen or Theakstons XB on handpump, several malt whiskies, local farm ciders, perries and apple juices, and a well chosen reasonably priced wine list with ten by the glass. Service is good. There are plenty of picnic-sets on its neat front lawned area, and pretty hanging baskets; plenty of bridleways and surrounding walks.

Free house ~ Licensees David and Janice Birch ~ Real ale ~ Bar food ~ Restaurant ~ (01989) 730236 ~ Children welcome ~ Dogs allowed in bar ~ Open 11.30-3, 6.30-11; 12-3, 6.30-10.30 Sun; Sun evening, all day Mon in winter

TITLEY
Stagg *B4355 N of Kington; HR5 3RL*
With imaginative and skilful use of local and organic ingredients, the landlord/chef here creates wonderful results with the food and readers leave well satisfied with both the food and the warm welcome. There's a pubby blackboard menu (not available Saturday evening or Sunday lunchtime) and a more elaborate restaurant menu (which can also be eaten in the bar). A nice touch is the choice of around 21 british cheeses, mostly from Herefordshire and Wales. The extensive dining rooms are no smoking. A carefully chosen wine list features ten wines and champagne by the glass, as well as ports and pudding wines; Black Sheep and Hobsons Town Crier are served on handpump, and they have local cider perry and apple juice and a dozen malt whiskies. The bar, though comfortable and hospitable, is not large, and the atmosphere is civilised rather than lively. They also have guest accommodation in three double ensuite rooms above the pub and in a Georgian vicarage four minutes away. while the two-acre garden has a croquet lawn, chairs and tables on the terrace, and a vegetable and herb garden for the kitchen.

Free house ~ Licensees Steve and Nicola Reynolds ~ Real ale ~ Bar food (12-2, 6.30-9.30) ~ Restaurant ~ (01544) 230221 ~ Children welcome ~ Dogs allowed in bar ~ Open 12-3, 6.30-11; closed Sun evening and Mon (exc bank hol weekends other than May Day bank hol), Tues after bank hol weekends (exc May Day), 1 Jan, first 2 weeks of Nov, 25 and 26 Dec ~ Bedrooms: £60B/£80B

WOOLHOPE
Butchers Arms *Signposted from B4224 in Fownhope; carry straight on past Woolhope village; HR1 4RF*
They have five beers on handpump at this pleasantly 14th-c rural pub: Hook Norton Old Hooky, Shepherd Neame Spitfire, Wye Valley Butty Bach and a couple of guests such as Charles Wells Bombardier and a

seasonal Wye Valley ale; also a good selection of malt whiskies. One of the spacious and welcoming bars has very low beams decorated with hops, old-fashioned well worn built-in seats with brocaded cushions, high-backed chairs and stools around wooden tables, and a brick fireplace filled with fresh flowers when it is not in use. Broadly similar though with fewer beams, the other bar has a large built-in settle and another log fire. Tables have fresh flowers; darts, board games and unobtrusive background music; the restaurant and part of the bar are no smoking. Bar food is traditional, and at quieter times of year they run occasional food nights. There's a relaxing beer garden with picnic-sets and cheerful flowering tubs and borders looking on to a tiny willow-lined brook. To enjoy some of the best of the surroundings, turn left as you come out and take the tiny left-hand road at the end of the car park; this turns into a track and then into a path, and the view from the top of the hill is quite something.

Free house ~ Licensees Cheryl and Martin Baker ~ Real ale ~ Bar food ~ Restaurant ~ (01432) 860281 ~ Children welcome until 8.30pm ~ Dogs allowed in bedrooms ~ Jazz and discos some evenings ~ Open 12-3, 6.30-11(12 Sat); 12-3, 7-11.30 Sun; closed Mon lunchtime in winter ~ Bedrooms: £35/£50

Dog Friendly Hotels, B&Bs and Farms

GLEWSTONE
Glewstone Court *Glewstone, Ross-on-wye, Herefordshire HR9 6AW (01989) 770367* £**115**; 8 well equipped rms. Elegant, partly Georgian and partly Victorian country house set in neat grounds with a fine cedar of Lebanon and views over Ross-on-Wye; long-standing, warmly welcoming owners and staff, comfortable and relaxing public rooms, and good food in antique-filled, no smoking dining room; croquet; three resident dogs and two cats; walks in the grounds and in surrounding countryside; cl 24–27 Dec; dogs in bedrooms, bar and lounge; bedding, bowls and clean towels; £10

HEREFORD
Castle House *Castle St, Hereford, Herefordshire HR1 2NW (01432) 356321* £**210**; 15 rms. Stylish and elegant Georgian hotel near the cathedral with views of the garden and quiet castle moat; a restful lounge and bar, beautifully presented elaborate food using first-class ingredients in smart restaurant, and impeccable service; disabled access; dogs in bedrooms (must be small dogs)

LEDBURY
Feathers *25 High St, Ledbury, Herefordshire HR8 1DS (01531) 635266* (just off A449; High St) £**110**, plus special breaks; 19 carefully decorated rms making the most of the old beams and timbers. Very striking, mainly 16th-c, black and white hotel with a relaxed atmosphere, log fires, comfortable

lounge hall with country antiques, beams and timbers, particularly enjoyable food and friendly service in hop-decked Fuggles bar, a good wine list, and a fine mix of locals and visitors; health and leisure spa with indoor swimming pool; dogs in bedrooms if small and well behaved

PUDLESTON

Ford Abbey *Pudleston, Leominster, Herefordshire HR6 0RZ (01568) 760700* **£125**; 6 luxury suites, one with own sitting room. Former Benedictine Abbey dating in part back to the 12th c and surrounded by 320 acres of farmland; elegant and comfortable drawing room with inglenook fireplaces, cosy study, a restful atmosphere, friendly staff, and good food using the best local produce (and some from their own farm); indoor heated swimming pool, fitness centre and self-catering lodges; plenty of walks but must be on lead in gardens as they have chickens; good disabled access; dogs in bedrooms

Hertfordshire

Dog Friendly Pubs

ALDBURY

Greyhound *Stocks Road; village signposted from A4251 Tring—Berkhamsted, and from B4506; HP23 5RT*

This spacious dining pub can draw quite a bustling crowd these days, though friendly staff stay on top of things well. The beamed interior shows some signs of considerable age (around the copper-hooded inglenook, for example), with plenty of tables in the two traditionally furnished rooms off either side of the drinks and food serving areas. Badger Best, Tanglefoot and a Badger seasonal beer are well kept on handpump; smoking in the public bar only, piped music and games machine. An airy oak floored restaurant at the back overlooks a suntrap gravel courtyard, and it's also well worth a winter visit, when the lovely warm fire and subtle lighting make it really cosy inside. Popular quickly served bar food is gently imaginative. Benches outside face a picturesque village green complete with stocks and lively duckpond.

Badger ~ Manager Tim O'Gorman ~ Real ale ~ Bar food (12-2.30(4 Sun), 6.30-9.30; not Sun evening) ~ Restaurant ~ (01442) 851228 ~ Children welcome ~ Dogs allowed in bar ~ Open 11-11; 12-10.30 Sun ~ Bedrooms: £65S/£75B

ASHWELL

Three Tuns *Off A505 NE of Baldock; High Street; SG7 5NL*

Relaxing chairs, big family tables, lots of pictures, stuffed pheasants and fish, and antiques lend an air of Victorian opulence to the cosy lounge at this flower-decked 18th-c inn; piped light classical music. The simpler more modern public bar has pool, darts, cribbage, dominoes, a fruit machine and Sky TV. Served by friendly efficient staff, the tasty bar food comes in generous helpings; no smoking dining room. There's a good choice of wines, as well as Greene King IPA, Abbot and a guest on handpump. A big terrace has metal tables and chairs, and the substantial shaded garden has boules, and picnic-sets under apple trees. The charming village is full of pleasant corners and is popular with walkers at summer weekends, as the landscape around rolls enough to be rewarding.

Greene King ~ Tenants Claire and Darrell Stanley ~ Real ale ~ Bar food (12-2.30, 6.30-9.30; all day Fri-Sun) ~ Restaurant ~ (01462) 742107 ~ Children welcome with restrictions ~ Dogs allowed in bar ~ Open 11-11; 12-10.30 Sun ~ Bedrooms: £39/£49(£59B)

BATFORD
Gibraltar Castle *Lower Luton Road; B653, S of B652 junction; AL5 5AH*
Still pleasantly traditional, this neatly kept little roadside pub is stashed with an impressive collection of militaria including rifles, swords, medals, uniforms and bullets (with plenty of captions to read), and pictures depicting its island namesake, and various moments in its history. The long carpeted bar has a pleasant old fireplace, comfortably cushioned wall benches and a couple of snugly intimate window alcoves, one with a fine old clock; in one area the low beams give way to soaring rafters; several board games are piled on top of the piano, and they've piped music. Fullers Discovery, ESB, London Pride and an occasional guest beer are served on handpump, and they keep a good range of malt whiskies, and a thoughtful choice of wines by the glass. The tasty traditional bar food is reasonably priced. The pub is completely no smoking at lunchtime, with a few no smoking tables in the evening. There are tables and chairs on a decked back terrace, a few more in front by the road, and hanging baskets and tubs dotted around.
Fullers ~ Lease Hamish Miller ~ Real ale ~ Bar food (12-2.30(4 Sun), 7-9; not Sun evening) ~ Restaurant ~ (01582) 460005 ~ Children welcome at lunchtime only ~ Dogs welcome ~ Open 11.30-11; 12-10.30 Sun

CHAPMORE END
Woodman *Off B158 Wadesmill—Bengeo; 300 yards W of A602 roundabout keep eyes skinned for discreet green sign to pub pointing up otherwise unmarked narrow lane; OS Sheet 166, map reference 328164; SG12 0HF*
Tucked away near the duck pond in a small hamlet, this peaceful early Victorian local takes you back through time. Two straightforward little linked rooms have plain seats around stripped pub tables, flooring tiles or broad bare boards, log fires in period fireplaces, cheerful pictures for sale, lots of local notices, and darts on one side, with a piano (and a couple of squeeze boxes) on the other. There's a refreshing lack of piped music and gimmicks, leaving you at peace to enjoy a game of boules, chess, backgammon, darts, shove ha'penny or cribbage. The lounge bar is no smoking. They have well kept Greene King IPA, Abbot and usually a guest such as Ridleys Prospect tapped from the cask, as well as several malt whiskies. Served by cheerful staff, the very short lunchtime menu includes snacky items. Thursday evening their very small kitchen might conjure up a themed evening, or a couple of main courses such as mixed grill or lamb tagine. In summer they have regular barbecues and tasty hog roasts. There are picnic-sets out in front under a couple of walnut trees, and a bigger garden behind has a good fenced play area (there are often toys left around by the publicans' daughters, who generally don't mind other children playing with them). The car park has little room but there is usually plenty of on-street parking.

Greene King ~ Tenant Dr Danny Davis ~ Real ale ~ Bar food (lunchtime (not Mon) and Thurs evening) ~ No credit cards ~ (01920) 463143 ~ Children welcome in lounge bar till 8pm ~ Dogs welcome ~ Open acoustic night second Weds ~ Open 12-2.30, 5.30-11; 12-11 Sat, Sun; cl Mon lunchtime

FRITHSDEN
Alford Arms *From Berkhamsted take unmarked road towards Potten End, pass Potten End turn on right, then take next left towards Ashridge College; HP1 3DD* It's worth booking to be sure of a table at this very popular dining pub, and as parking can be a problem we suggest getting there early. The fashionably elegant but understated interior has simple prints on pale cream walls, with blocks picked out in rich Victorian green or dark red, and an appealing mix of good antique furniture from Georgian chairs to old commode stands on bare boards and patterned quarry tiles. It's all pulled together by luxurious opulently patterned curtains, and piped jazz. The welcoming staff are thoughtful and conscientious, though a couple of readers found service slowed down at busy times. Where possible dishes are made from fresh local produce, and the seasonally changing menu is temptingly imaginative. The dining room is no smoking. A good wine list features 10 good pudding wines and 15 other wines by the glass, and they've well kept Brakspears, Flowers Original, Marstons Pedigree and Rebellion on handpump. The pub stands by a village green, surrounded by lovely National Trust woodland, and there are plenty of tables out in front.
Salisbury Pubs ~ Lease Richard Coletta ~ Real ale ~ Bar food (12-2.30(4 Sun), 7-10) ~ Restaurant ~ (01442) 864480 ~ Children welcome ~ Dogs allowed in bar ~ Open 11-11; 12-10.30 Sun

Dog Friendly Hotels, B&Bs and Farms

KNEBWORTH
Homewood *Park Lane, Old Knebworth, Knebworth, Hertfordshire SG3 6PP (01438) 812105* (3 miles off A1(M) junction 7; B187 right off A602, then on N edge of Knebworth (not before) turn right towards Knebworth House) £80; 2 rms. Lovely Lutyens-designed house in six beautiful acres; elegant rooms with antiques and tapestries and interestingly decorated by the owner, good breakfasts, nearby places for evening meals, and five resident cats and a friendly dog; walks in the grounds and nearby woods; cl 20 Dec-5 Jan; dogs welcome in bedrooms

Isle of Wight

Dog Friendly Pubs

BEMBRIDGE

Crab & Lobster *Foreland Fields Road, off Howgate Road (which is off B3395 via Hillgate Road); PO35 5TR*

Picnic sets on the terrace outside this well positioned inn, which is perched on low cliffs within yards of the shore and prettily adorned with flower baskets in summer, take in great views over the Solent. The dining area and some of the bedrooms share the same views. Inside it's roomier than you might expect, and it's done out in a civilised, almost parlourish style, with lots of yachting memorabilia and old local photographs, and a blazing fire in winter months; darts, dominoes and cribbage. They serve a very good choice of fresh local seafood specials every day, as well as other very well prepared traditional dishes; the restaurant is no smoking. Flowers Original, Goddards Fuggle-Dee-Dum and Greene King IPA are on handpump, with decent house wines, about 20 malt whiskies, farm cider and good coffee; piped music (even in the lavatories).

Enterprise ~ Lease Richard, Adrian and Pauline Allan ~ Real ale ~ Bar food (12-2.30, 6-10) ~ Restaurant ~ (01983) 872244 ~ Children welcome ~ Dogs allowed in bar ~ Open 11-11(12 Sat); 12-10.30 Sun ~ Bedrooms: £40B/£80B

BONCHURCH

Bonchurch Inn *Bonchurch Shute; from A3055 E of Ventnor turn down to Old Bonchurch opposite Leconfield Hotel; PO38 1NU*

The bar, no smoking restaurant, rooms and kitchens of this curious little place are spread around a tucked away cobbled courtyard, and all snuggled below a steep, rocky slope. Tables, a fountain and pergola out here are nicely enclosed, giving the courtyard a slightly continental feel on warm summer days. The layout makes more sense when you remember that before it gained its licence in the 1840s it was the stables for the nearby manor house. The furniture-packed Victorian bar has a good chatty local atmosphere, and conjures up images of salvaged shipwrecks, with its floor of narrow-planked ship's decking, and seats like the ones that old-fashioned steamers used to have. A separate entrance leads to the very simple no smoking family room (a bit cut off from the congenial atmosphere of the public bar). As well as Scottish Courage Directors and Best tapped from the cask, there are italian wines by the glass, a few bottled french wines, darts, shove-ha'penny, dominoes and cribbage. The welcoming landlord is Italian, and the traditional menu reflects this; there is a £1 charge for credit cards.

Free house ~ Licensees Ulisse and Gillian Besozzi ~ Real ale ~ Bar food ~ Restaurant ~ (01983) 852611 ~ Children in family room ~ Dogs allowed in bar ~ Open 11-3, 6.30-11; 12-3, 7-10.30 Sun ~ Bedrooms: /£80B

FRESHWATER
Red Lion *Church Place; from A3055 at E end of village by Freshwater Garage mini-roundabout follow Yarmouth signpost, then take first real right turn signed to Parish Church; PO40 9BP*

The grown up atmosphere at this bustling pub tends to be appreciated by visitors without smaller children (unusually these days smoking is permitted throughout). Indeed it's so popular that if you want to eat it's a good idea to book ahead. Though the food is a big draw, chatting locals who fill the stools along the counter keep a pubby feel. The not over done yet comfortably furnished open-plan bar has open fires, low grey sofas and sturdy country-kitchen style furnishings on mainly flagstoned floors, with bare boards at one end. The well executed paintings (between photographs and china platters) hung round the walls are by the licensee's brother and are well worth a look in themselves. The very enjoyable food is listed on blackboards behind the bar. Flowers Original, Fullers London Pride, Goddards and Wadworths 6X are kept under light blanket pressure, and the good choice of wines includes 16 by the glass. Fines on mobile phone users go to charity (they collect a lot for the RNLI); there's a games machine but no music. There are tables on a carefully tended grass and gravel area at the back (some under cover), beside which is the kitchen's herb garden, and a couple of picnic-sets in a quiet square at the front, overlooked by the church. The pub is virtually on the Freshwater Way footpath that connects Yarmouth with the southern coast at Freshwater Bay.

Enterprise ~ Lease Michael Mence ~ Real ale ~ Bar food (12-2, 6.30-9) ~ (01983) 754925 ~ Children over 10 ~ Dogs allowed in bar ~ Open 11.30-3, 5.30-11; 11.30-4, 6-11 Sat; 12-3, 7-10.30 Sun

HULVERSTONE
Sun *B3399; PO30 4EH*

This thatched whitewashed country pub has a captivating position, with a view down from the charming secluded cottagey garden (which has a terrace and several picnic-sets) to a wild stretch of coast. It's very well positioned for some splendid walks along the cliffs, and up Mottistone Down to the prehistoric Long Stone. The bar (smoking in here only) is full of friendly chatter (with no piped music or games machines) and is unpretentiously traditional and low-ceilinged, with a fire blazing at one end and horsebrasses and ironwork hung around the fireplace, a nice mix of old furniture on flagstones and floorboards, and stone and brick walls; piped music, darts and board games. Leading off from one end is the more modern dining area, with large windows making the most of the view. Home-made bar food is fairly traditional, and they do an 'all you can eat' curry night on Thursdays. The four quickly changing real ales are quite a feature here. Last year they got through 287 different ones from brewers such as Bass, Shepherd Neame, Timothy Taylors and Wadworths. Staff are helpful and friendly.

Enterprise ~ Lease Chris and Kate Cole ~ Real ale ~ Bar food (12-9) ~ (01983) 741124 ~ Children welcome ~ Dogs allowed in bar ~ Open 11-11; 12-10.30 Sun

SHALFLEET
New Inn *A3054 Newport—Yarmouth; PO30 4NS*
A good set of enthusiastic reader reports makes this buzzing 18th-c fisherman's haunt, which is just a short stroll from the marshy inlets of the yacht-studded Newtown estuary, a pleasure to write about. Its strengths lie equally in its cheery welcome, great food and good beer. They're well known for their crab salad and up to 12 different types of fresh fish a day. Other dishes on the changing menu are mostly quite traditional. You will need to book, and there may be double sittings in summer. The partly panelled flagstoned public bar has yachting photographs and pictures, a boarded ceiling, scrubbed pine tables and a roaring log fire in the big stone hearth, and the carpeted beamed lounge bar has boating pictures and a coal fire. The snug and gallery have slate floors, bric-a-brac and more scrubbed pine tables. Bass, Goddards, Greene King IPA and Ventnor Golden are kept under a light blanket pressure, and they stock around 60 wines; piped music.

Enterprise ~ Lease Mr Bullock and Mr McDonald ~ Real ale ~ Bar food (12-2.30, 6-9.30) ~ Restaurant ~ (01983) 531314 ~ Children welcome ~ Dogs welcome ~ Open 12-3, 6-11(10.30 Sun)

VENTNOR
Spyglass *Esplanade, SW end; road down very steep and twisty, and parking nearby can be difficult – best to use the pay-and-display (free in winter) about 100 yards up the road; PO38 1JX*
There seems to be something that appeals to nearly everyone at this cheerfully popular pub. It's in a super position, perched on the sea wall just above the beach – tables outside on a terrace have lovely views over the water. A fascinating jumble of seafaring memorabilia fills the snug quarry-tiled interior, with anything from wrecked rudders, ships' wheels, old local advertisements and rope-makers' tools to stuffed seagulls, an Admiral Benbow barometer and an old brass telescope; two no smoking areas, games machine and piped music. Generous helpings of very tasty quite traditional bar food are promptly served. Half a dozen well kept hand-pulled real ales include a couple from Badger and Ventnor, alongside three guests such as Badger Fursty Ferret, Goddards Fuggle-Dee-Dum and Ventnor Molly Downer. There are strolls westwards from here along the

coast towards the Botanic Garden as well as heftier hikes up on to St Boniface Down and towards the eerie shell of Appuldurcombe House, and the pub owners don't mind muddy boots.

Free house ~ Licensees Neil and Stephanie Gibbs ~ Real ale ~ Bar food (12-9.30) ~ (01983) 855338 ~ Children welcome away from main bar area ~ Dogs allowed in bar ~ Live entertainment every night except Mon ~ Open 10.30-11 ~ Bedrooms: /£60B

Dog Friendly Hotels, B&Bs and Farms

BONCHURCH
Lake Hotel *Bonchurch, Ventnor, Isle of Wight PO38 1RF (01983) 852613* **£80**, plus special breaks; 20 rms. Early 19th-c country house in two acres of pretty gardens, 400 metres from beach; lots of flowers and plants in three light and airy lounges (one is an attractive conservatory), a well stocked bar (the only place you may smoke), and good food in comfortable restaurant; walks in part of the grounds and on the beach; cl Nov-Feb; children over 3; partial disabled access; dogs in bedrooms and one lounge area; £5

SEAVIEW
Priory Bay Hotel *Priory Croft, Priory Rd, Seaview, Isle of Wight PO34 5BU (01983) 613146* **£170**, plus special breaks; 18 individually furnished rms with 10 more in cottages. Former Tudor farmhouse with Georgian and more recent additions in grounds leading to a fine sandy private beach with a beach bar (good for lunch); lovely day rooms with comfortable sofas, books and magazines on coffee tables, pretty flower arrangements, imaginative food in no smoking restaurants with charming Georgian murals and elaborate plasterwork, and an informal, relaxed atmosphere; outdoor swimming pool, tennis, croquet and a nine-hole par three golf course; resident dog; plenty of walks; disabled access; dogs in cottages in grounds; £10

Seaview Hotel *High St, Seaview, Isle of Wight PO34 5EX (01983) 612711* **£115**, plus special breaks; 17 attractively decorated rms, some with sea views and private drawing rooms. Small, friendly and spotlessly kept hotel with fine ship photographs in the chatty and relaxed front dining bar, an interesting old-fashioned back bar, and good imaginative food; cl 3 days over Christmas; proper high tea for children (must be over 5 in evening restaurant); partial disabled access; dogs welcome away from restaurant; bring their own bedding

TOTLAND
Sentry Mead Hotel *Totland Bay, Isle of Wight PO39 0BJ (01983) 753212* **£100**; 14 pretty rms. Victorian country house hotel in flower-filled gardens overlooking the Solent and 100 yards from the beach; traditionally

furnished rooms, open fire in lounge, a bar area and airy conservatory, caring, attentive staff, and good food in stylish restaurant; dogs welcome by arrangement, if well behaved; £3

YARMOUTH

George Hotel *Quay St, Yarmouth, Isle of Wight PO41 0PE (01983) 760331* **£180**; 17 comfortable rms. 17th-c house by the harbour, with gardens leading to little private beach; a fine flagstoned hall, fresh flowers and open fires, a convivial bar and attractive residents' sitting room with marvellously relaxing atmosphere, imaginative enjoyable food in informal brasserie and smart restaurant, hearty breakfasts, and prompt courteous service; motor yacht for hire; dogs in bedrooms; £10

Kent

Dog Friendly Pubs

BIDDENDEN
Three Chimneys *A262, 1 mile W of village; TN27 8LW*

After a visit to nearby Sissinghurst Gardens, this busy pub is just the place to head for. It's best to arrive early or book in advance to be sure of a table and the imaginative food is extremely good. Feeling quite pubby, with Adnams Best, Harveys Best and a guest like Fullers Discovery tapped straight from casks racked behind the counter, the series of low-beamed, very traditional little rooms have plain wooden furniture and old settles on flagstones and coir matting, some harness and sporting prints on the stripped brick walls, and good log fires. The simple public bar has darts, dominoes and cribbage. French windows in the civilised candlelit bare-boards restaurant open on to the garden (ploughman's only out here) with picnic-sets in dappled shade, and the smart terrace area has tables and outdoor heaters. They've a good wine list, with several by the glass, local Biddenden cider and several malt whiskies.

Free house ~ Licensee Craig Smith ~ Real ale ~ Bar food (12-2, 6.30-9.30; 12-2.30, 7-9 Sun) ~ Restaurant ~ (01580) 291472 ~ Children in eating area of bar and restaurant ~ Dogs welcome ~ Open 11.30-3, 6-11; 12-3,30, 7-10.30 Sun

BOUGH BEECH
Wheatsheaf *B2027, S of reservoir; TN8 7NU*

The older part of this very popular pub is thought to have been a hunting lodge belonging to Henry V and the place is full of history with masses of interesting things to look at. The neat central bar and the long front bar (with an attractive old settle carved with wheatsheaves) have unusually high ceilings with lofty oak timbers, a screen of standing timbers and a revealed king post; dominoes and board games. Divided from the central bar by two more rows of standing timbers – one formerly an outside wall to the building – are the snug, and another bar. Other similarly aged features include a piece of 1607 graffiti, 'Foxy Holamby', thought to have been a whimsical local squire. There are quite a few horns and heads, as well as a sword from Fiji, crocodiles, stuffed birds, swordfish spears and a matapee on the walls and above the massive stone fireplaces. Thoughtful touches include piles of smart magazines, tasty nibbles and chestnuts to roast. It's appealing outside too, with plenty of seats, flowerbeds and fruit trees in the sheltered side and back gardens. Shrubs help divide the garden into various areas, so it doesn't feel too crowded even when it's full. Well kept Greene King Old Speckled Hen, Harveys Sussex Best, Shepherd Neame Master Brew, and from a village just three miles away, Westerham Brewery Grasshopper on handpump; three farm ciders (including a local one), a decent wine list, several malt whiskies, summer Pimms and winter mulled wine. Served in generous helpings, bar food includes traditional dishes and a few gently imaginative options.

Enterprise ~ Lease Liz and David Currie ~ Real ale ~ Bar food (12-10) ~ (01732) 700254 ~ Children welcome with restrictions ~ Dogs welcome ~ Open 11am-11.30pm

BOYDEN GATE

Gate Inn *Off A299 Herne Bay—Ramsgate – follow Chislet, Upstreet signpost opposite Roman Gallery; Chislet also signposted off A28 Canterbury—Margate at Upstreet – after turning right into Chislet main street keep right on to Boyden; the pub gives its address as Marshside, though Boyden Gate seems more usual on maps; CT3 4EB*

The long-time tenant of this traditional and unchanging village pub (now no smoking) has a wonderful knack of making all his customers, locals or visitors, feel genuinely welcome and at home. The comfortably worn interior is properly pubby with an inglenook log fire serving both the well worn quarry-tiled rooms, flowery-cushioned pews around tables of considerable character, hop bines hanging from the beams and attractively etched windows. Well kept Shepherd Neame Bishops Finger, Master Brew, Spitfire and a seasonal ale are tapped from the cask and you can also get interesting bottled beers, half a dozen wines by the glass, and country wines; board games. Tasty bar food includes lots of different sandwiches and other pubby dishes. The sheltered hollyhock flowered garden is bounded by two streams with tame ducks and geese (they sell bags of food, 10p), and on fine summer evenings you can hear the contented quacking of a multitude of ducks and geese, coots and moorhens out on the marshes.

Shepherd Neame ~ Tenant Christopher Smith ~ Real ale ~ Bar food ~ No credit cards ~ (01227) 860498 ~ Well behaved children in eating area of bar and family room ~ Dogs welcome ~ Open 11-3, 6-11; 10-3, 7-10.30 Sun

BROOKLAND

Woolpack *On A259 from Rye, about 1 mile before Brookland, take the first right turn signposted Midley where the main road bends sharp left, just after the expanse of Walland Marsh; OS Sheet 189 map reference 977244; TN29 9TJ*

Bustling and friendly and very popular locally – though there's a warm welcome for visitors, too – this pretty 15th-c white cottage has plenty of marshland character. The ancient entrance lobby has an uneven brick floor and black-painted pine-panelled walls. To the right, the simple quarry tiled main bar has basic cushioned plank seats in the massive inglenook fireplace (with a lovely log fire on chilly days), a painted wood-effect bar counter hung with lots of water jugs, some very early ships' timbers (maybe 12th-c) in the low-beamed ceiling, a long elm table with shove-ha'penny carved into one end, other old and newer wall benches, chairs at mixed tables with flowers and candles, and photographs of locals on the walls. To the left of the lobby is a sparsely furnished little room, and an open-plan, no smoking family room; piped music.Well kept Shepherd Neame Master Brew, Spitfire and a seasonal brew on handpump; look out for the two pub cats Liquorice and Charlie Girl. Traditional food is served in generous helpings. The big garden has plenty of picnic-sets, well developed shrubs, and pretty hanging baskets; it's all nicely lit up in the evenings.

Shepherd Neame ~ Tenant Barry Morgan ~ Real ale ~ Bar food (12-2, 6-9; all day in summer and all day winter weekends) ~ (01797) 344321 ~ Children in family room ~ Dogs welcome ~ Open 11-11; 11-11 Sat; 12-10.30 Sun

CHIDDINGSTONE

Castle Inn *Village signposted from B2027 Tonbridge—Edenbridge; TN8 7AH*
Just around the corner from the castle and in a pretty National Trust village, this rambling old place can get busy at peak times. The handsome, carefully modernised beamed bar has well made settles forming booths around the tables, cushioned sturdy wall benches, an attractive mullioned window seat in one small alcove, and latticed windows (a couple of areas are no smoking); darts, shove-ha'penny, dominoes and cribbage. There are tables in front of the building facing the church, with more in the pretty secluded vine-hung garden. Larkins Traditional and winter Porter (both brewed in the village) and Harveys Best on handpump, an impressive wine list and quite a few malt whiskies. Priced in euros and sterling, food is imaginative (particularly in the evening) and not cheap, though they do offer a slightly more reasonably priced set menu (not Sunday). The licensees publish three circular walks from the village.

Free house ~ Licensee Nigel Lucas ~ Real ale ~ Bar food (12-6, 7-9.30) ~ Restaurant ~ (01892) 870247 ~ Children welcome away from public bar ~ Dogs welcome ~ Open 11-11; 12-11 Sun

DARGATE

Dove *Village signposted from A299; ME13 9HB*
Even though this well run dining pub is tucked away down a network of narrow lanes in a quiet hamlet, it's pretty essential to book a table in advance. The very friendly landlady ensures a relaxed welcoming atmosphere in the charmingly unspoilt airy rambling rooms, which have flowers on stripped wood tables, photographs of the pub and its licensees throughout the past century on the walls, a good winter log fire, and plenty of seats on the bare boards; piped classical music. There are some lunchtime snacks such but it's the exceptionally good restaurant-style food that most customers are here to enjoy. Well kept Shepherd Neame Master Brew and Special on handpump. Lovely in fine weather, the sheltered garden has roses, lilacs, peonies and many other flowers, picnic-table sets under pear trees, a dovecote with white doves, a rockery and pool, and a swing. A

bridlepath leads up from the pub (along the quaintly named Plumpudding Lane) into Blean Wood.

Shepherd Neame ~ Tenants Nigel and Bridget Morris ~ Real ale ~ Bar food (not Mon and maybe not Sun or Tues evenings) ~ Restaurant ~ (01227) 751360 ~ Children welcome ~ Dogs allowed in bar ~ Live music first Sun of month ~ Open 12-3.30, 6-11.30; 12-4, 7-11 Sun; closed Mon (but open bank hol Mon, when they then close Tues instead)

GROOMBRIDGE
Crown *B2110; TN3 9QH*

This tile-hung pub is prettily positioned at the end of a horseshoe-shaped row of comely cottages, and there are picnic-sets out in front on a wonky but sunny brick terrace that looks down over the steep village green. Inside is a snug left-hand room with old tables on worn flagstones and a big brick inglenook with a cosy winter log fire – arrive early for a table in here. The low beamed rooms have roughly plastered walls, some squared panelling and timbering, and a quite a bit of bric-a-brac, from old teapots and pewter tankards to antique bottles. Walls are decorated with small topographical, game and sporting prints, and a circular large-scale map with the pub at its centre. The no smoking end room (normally for eaters) has fairly close-spaced tables with a variety of good solid chairs, and a log-effect gas fire in a big fireplace. Greene King Abbot and IPA, Harveys and Larkins on handpump, and 10 wines by the glass. Bar food is traditional and reasonably priced. There's a back car park and pub garden. A public footpath across the road beside the small chapel leads through a field to Groombridge Place Gardens.

Free house ~ Licensee Peter Kilshaw ~ Real ale ~ Bar food (12-3(4 Sun), 7-9; not Sun evening) ~ Restaurant ~ (01892) 864742 ~ Children welcome ~ Dogs allowed in bar ~ Open 11-3, 5-11; 11-11 Sat; 12-10.30 Sun; 11-3, 6-11 Sat and closed Sun evening in winter ~ Bedrooms: £40/£45(£60S)

LANGTON GREEN
Hare *A264 W of Tunbridge Wells; TN3 0JA*

There's a good choice of drinks in this no smoking Edwardian roadside pub: Greene King IPA and Abbot with guests such as Belhaven Six Nations and Greene King Old Speckled Hen on handpump, over 50 malt whiskies, quite a few wines by the glass, and freshly squeezed juices. The front bar (piped music here) tends to be where drinkers gather, and the knocked-through interior has big windows and high ceilings giving a spacious feel. Décor, more or less in period with the building, runs from dark-painted dados below light walls, 1930s oak furniture, and turkey carpets on stained wooden floors to old romantic pastels, and a huge collection of chamber-pots hanging from one beam. Interesting old books, pictures and two huge mahogany mirror-backed display cabinets crowd the walls of the big room at the back, which has lots of large tables (one big enough for at least a dozen) on a light brown carpet; from here french windows open onto picnic-sets on a big terrace, and pretty views of the tree-ringed village green; shove-ha'penny, draughts and backgammon. The blackboard menu features imaginative takes on traditional dishes. Parking is limited.

Brunning & Price ~ Tenant Christopher Little ~ Real ale ~ Bar food (12-9.30(9 Sun)) ~ (01892) 862419 ~ Children in eating area till 7pm ~ Dogs allowed in bar ~ Open 11-11; 12-10.30 Sun

OARE
Shipwrights Arms *S shore of Oare Creek, E of village; coming from Faversham on the Oare road, turn right into Ham Road opposite Davington School; or off A2 on B2045, go into Oare village, then turn right towards Faversham, and then left into Ham Road opposite Davington School; OS Sheet 178 map reference 016635; ME13 7TU*

You can reach this unspoilt old place on foot from the village, by boat or by car. It's in the middle of marshland with lots of bird life and is actually 3ft below sea level. Three simple little bars are dark and cosy, and separated by standing timbers and wood part-partitions or narrow door arches. A medley of seats runs from tapestry cushioned stools and chairs to black wood-panelled built-in settles forming little booths, and there are pewter tankards over the bar counter, boating jumble and pictures, pottery boating figures, flags or boating pennants on the ceilings, several brick fireplaces, and a good woodburning stove. Look out for the electronic wind gauge above the main door, which takes its reading from the chimney. Well kept ales from Goachers, Hopdaemon and Whitstable Oyster Brewery Company, and a maybe a couple of other kentish guests tapped from the cask, too; piped local radio. Bar food is very straightforward, and the eating area is no smoking. Parking can be difficult at busy times.

Free house ~ Licensees Derek and Ruth Cole ~ Real ale ~ Bar food (not Sun or Mon evening) ~ Restaurant ~ (01795) 590088 ~ Children welcome if seated ~ Dogs allowed in bar ~ Open 11-3(4 summer Sat), 6-11; 12(11 in winter)-4, 6-11 Sun; closed Mon in winter

PENSHURST
Bottle House *Coldharbour Lane, Smarts Hill; leaving Penshurst SW on B2188 turn right at Smarts Hill signpost, then bear right towards Chiddingstone and Cowden; keep straight on; TN11 8ET*

This is a tile-hung old house standing alone in quiet countryside. The low-beamed and neatly kept front bar has a well worn brick floor that extends behind the polished copper-topped bar counter and big windows that look on to a terrace with climbing plants, hanging baskets, and picnic-sets under cocktail parasols. The simply decorated red-carpeted main bar has massive hop-covered supporting beams, two large stone pillars with a small brick fireplace (with a stuffed turtle to one side), and old paintings and photographs on mainly plastered walls; quite a collection of china pot lids, with more in the no smoking low-ceilinged dining room. Several cosy little areas lead off the main bar – one is covered in sporting pictures right up to the ceiling and another has pictures of dogs. Very well liked food is served by efficient staff. Well kept Courage Directors, Harveys and Larkins on handpump and several wines by the glass; piped music. Good surrounding walks.

Free house ~ Licensees Gordon and Val Meer ~ Real ale ~ Bar food (12(11.30

Sun)-9.30) ~ Restaurant ~ (01892) 870306 ~ Children welcome ~ Dogs allowed in bar ~ Open 11-11; 12-10.30 Sun; closed 25 Dec, evenings 26 and 31 Dec and 1 Jan

PLUCKLEY
Dering Arms *Pluckley Station, which is signposted from B2077; The Grove; TN27 0RR*
This striking old building was originally built as a hunting lodge on the Dering estate. The stylishly plain high-ceilinged main bar has a solid country feel, with a variety of good wooden furniture on stone floors, a roaring log fire in the great fireplace, country prints and some fishing rods. The smaller half-panelled back bar has similar dark wood furnishings, and an extension to this area has a woodburning stove, comfortable armchairs and sofas, and a grand piano; board games. The imaginative menu includes quite a few fish dishes. Goachers Gold Star, Old Ale and a beer named for the pub on handpump, a good wine list, home-made lemonade, local cider and over 25 malt whiskies. The big simple bedrooms have old ad hoc furnishings and breakfasts are good. Classic car (the long-standing landlord has a couple) meetings are held here on the second Sunday of the month.
Free house ~ Licensee James Buss ~ Real ale ~ Bar food (not Sun evening, not Mon) ~ Restaurant ~ (01233) 840371 ~ Children welcome ~ Dogs allowed in bar ~ Open 11.30(11 Sat)-3, 6-11; 12-3 Sun; closed Sun evening, all day Mon, 25-27 Dec, 1 Jan ~ Bedrooms: £35/£45

Mundy Bois *Mundy Bois – spelled Monday Boys on some maps – off Smarden Road SW of village centre; TN27 0ST*
Now renamed the Mundy Bois (it was the Rose & Crown), this quietly set pub has also had some refurbishment. The relaxed Village Bar is friendly and welcoming, with a massive inglenook fireplace (favourite spot of Ted the pub labrador) and chesterfield sofas. This leads on to a little pool room; TV and piped music. Using local produce and meats from traditional breeds, the enjoyable bar food is good value. You can also eat from the pricier and more elaborate restaurant menu in the bar. Shepherd Neame Master Brew, Wadworths 6X and a guest beer on handpump, and nine wines by the glass. There are seats in the rather nice garden, which has a good children's play area, and dining facilities on the terrace.
Free house ~ Licensees Peter and Helen Teare ~ Real ale ~ Bar food (all day Sun) ~ Restaurant ~ (01233) 840048 ~ Children welcome ~ Dogs allowed in bar ~ Open 11.30-11; 10am-11pm Sat; closed 25 Dec

SELLING
Rose & Crown *Signposted from exit roundabout of M2 junction 7: keep right on through village and follow Perry Wood signposts; or from A252 just W of junction with A28 at Chilham follow Shottenden signpost, then right turn signposted Selling, then right signposted Perry Wood; ME13 9RY*
New licensees have taken over this popular pub and as we went to press were hoping to open all day in summer and serve food all day then, too. Décor is in keeping with the age of the building – hop bines strung from

the beams, interesting corn-dolly decorations amongst hand-made tapestries, winter log fires in two inglenook fireplaces, fresh flowers, and comfortably cushioned seats. Steps lead down to the timbered no smoking restaurant. Adnams Southwold, Goachers Mild, Harveys Sussex Best, and Roosters Leghorn on handpump; piped music, cribbage, dominoes, and board games. The bar menu includes many pub staples. The cottagey garden behind is charmingly planted with climbers, ramblers and colourful plants, there's a fairy lit pergola, plenty of picnic-sets, a neatly kept children's play area, bat and trap and a small aviary. The flowering tubs and hanging baskets in front are pretty too, and the terrace has outdoor heaters. The pub is surrounded by natural woodland, with good walking; hitching rail for horses and drinking bowls for dogs.

Free house ~ Licensees Tim Robinson and Vanessa Grove ~ Real ale ~ Bar food (they hope to serve food all day in summer; 12-2, 7-9.30 winter; not Sun or Mon evenings) ~ Restaurant ~ (01227) 752214 ~ Children welcome ~ Dogs allowed in bar ~ Open 11-11(10.30 Sun); 11-3, 6.30-11 winter Mon-Sat; 12-3, 7-10.30 Sun in winter

SHIPBOURNE

Chaser *Stumble Hill (A227 N of Tonbridge); TN11 9PE*

Bustling and rather smart, this attractively placed stone and tile-hung pub has several open-plan areas that meander into each other, all converging on a large central island bar counter. There are stripped wood floors and the décor is comfortably relaxed, with frame-to-frame pictures on deepest red and cream walls, stripped pine wainscoting, an eclectic mix of solid old wood tables (with candles) and chairs, shelves of books, and open fires. A striking school chapel-like restaurant, right at the back, has dark wood panelling and a high timber vaulted ceiling. French windows open on to a covered and heated central courtyard with teak furniture and big green parasols, and a side garden, with the pretty church rising behind, is nicely enclosed by hedges and shrubs. Good, popular bar food is served in generous helpings. No smoking except in bar area. Well kept Greene King IPA and Abbot and perhaps Black Country Fireside or Ridleys Prospect on handpump, and 15 wines by the glass; piped music. There is a small car park at the back, or you can park in the lane opposite by a delightful green; farmer's market Thursday morning.

Whiting & Hammond ~ Tenant Darren Somerton ~ Real ale ~ Bar food (12-9.30(9 Sun)) ~ (01732) 810360 ~ Very well behaved children welcome ~ Dogs welcome ~ Open 12-11(midnight Sat); 12-10.30 Sun

STAPLEHURST

Lord Raglan *About 1fi miles from town centre towards Maidstone, turn right off A229 into Chart Hill Road opposite Chart Cars; OS Sheet 188 map reference 785472; TN12 0DE*

Although unpretentious, this friendly country pub has a relaxed and rather civilised atmosphere. The interior is cosy but compact, with a narrow bar – you walk in almost on top of the counter and chatting locals – widening slightly at one end to a small area with a big log fire in winter. In the other

direction it works its way round to an intimate area at the back, with lots of
wine bottles lined up on a low shelf. Low beams are covered with masses of
hops, and the mixed collection of comfortably worn dark wood furniture
on quite well used dark brown carpet tiles and nice old parquet flooring, is
mostly 1930s. Goachers Light, Harveys Best and a guest like Westerham
Brewery British Bulldog on handpump, a good wine list and local farm
cider. There is a reasonably priced pub snack menu, and a pricier more
imaginative main menu. Small french windows lead out to an enticing little
high-hedged terrace area with green plastic tables and chairs, and there are
wooden picnic-sets in the side orchard; reasonable wheelchair access.
*Free house ~ Licensees Andrew and Annie Hutchison ~ Real ale ~ Bar food
(12-2.30, 7-10; not Sun) ~ (01622) 843747 ~ Children welcome ~ Dogs
welcome ~ Open 12-3, 6.30(6 Sat)-11; closed Sun*

STOWTING
Tiger *3.7 miles from M20 junction 11; B2068 N, then left at Stowting signpost,
straight across crossroads, then fork left after ¼ mile and pub is on right; coming from
N, follow Brabourne, Wye, Ashford signpost to right at fork, then turn left towards
Posting and Lyminge at T-junction; TN25 6BA*
Deep in the heart of some lovely countryside, this is a peaceful old pub
with friendly, welcoming staff. It's traditionally furnished and decorated,
with plain chairs and dark pews built in against the walls, candles stuck into
bottles, faded rugs on the dark floorboards, and some floor-to-ceiling plank
panelling; there's an open fire at each end of the main bar, paintings for
sale, and books meant to be opened, rather than left as shelf decoration.
Well kept Adnams, Fullers London Pride, Harveys Sussex Best and
Shepherd Neame Early Bird, Master Brew and Spitfire on handpump, 50
malt whiskies and local cider. Bar food is enjoyable. Seats out on the front
terrace.
*Free house ~ Licensee Emma Oliver ~ Real ale ~ Bar food (12-2.30, 6-9; all day
Fri-Sun) ~ Restaurant ~ (01303) 862130 ~ Children welcome ~ Dogs allowed in
bar ~ Jazz Mon evenings ~ Open 12-11.30(10.30 Sun)*

Dog Friendly Hotels, B&Bs and Farms

BOUGHTON LEES
Eastwell Manor *Eastwell Park, Boughton Lees, Ashford, Kent TN25 4HR
(01233) 219955* (4.4 miles off M20 junction 9, via A28 towards
Canterbury, forking left on A251) **£215**, plus special breaks; 62 prettily
decorated rms in hotel and 19 courtyard cottages (some cottages have their
own garden and can also be booked on self-catering basis). Fine Jacobean-
style manor (actually rebuilt in the 1920s) in 62 acres with croquet lawn,
tennis court, two boules pitches and putting green; grand oak-panelled
rooms, open fires, comfortable leather seating, antiques and fresh flowers,
courteous helpful service, and extremely good food; health and fitness spa

with 20-metre indoor pool and 15 treatment rooms; walks on the estate; disabled access; dogs in mews cottages only

CANTERBURY

Cathedral Gate *36 Burgate, Canterbury, Kent CT1 2HA (01227) 464381* £90, plus special breaks; 27 rms, 12 with own bthrm and some overlooking cathedral. 15th-c hotel that predates the adjoining sculpted cathedral gateway; bow windows, massive oak beams, sloping floors, antiques and fresh flowers; continental breakfast in little dining room or your own room, and a restful atmosphere; three resident cats; municipal car parks a few minutes away; dogs in bedrooms

DOVER

Hubert House *9 Castle Hill Road, Dover, Kent CT16 1QW (01304) 202253* £45; 8 pleasant rms. Fine, no smoking Georgian building just beneath the castle and close to the beach and ferry; enjoyable breakfasts and home-baked croissants in smart coffee house (open all day) and friendly owners; resident dog; walking area nearby; forecourt parking; dogs in bedrooms if well behaved and by arrangement

TENTERDEN

White Lion 57 High Street, Tenterden, Kent TN30 6BD (01580) 765077 £84; 15 comfortable rms. 16th-c inn with beams and timbers, masses of pictures, china and books, a big log fire, cheerful and helpful young staff, a wide choice of generous popular food and good breakfasts, real ales, a smart no smoking panelled back restaurant, and a relaxed and friendly atmosphere; tables on heated terrace overlooking street; exercise area nearby; dogs in bedrooms

Lancashire

Dog Friendly Pubs

BISPHAM GREEN
Eagle & Child *Maltkiln Lane (Parbold—Croston road, off B5246); L40 3SG*
Well liked for its food and drink, and free from piped music and similar
intrusions, this friendly pub has an interesting range of five changing beers
typically including ales such as Eccleshall Slaters Top Totty, Moorhouses
Black Cat, Phoenix Arizona, Southport Natterjack Premium Bitter,
Thwaites Original and Timothy Taylors Landlord, and they also have
changing farm cider, decent wines, some country wines and around 30
malt whiskies. The pub holds a popular beer festival in May over the first
bank holiday weekend. Well divided by stubs of walls, the largely open-
plan bar is appealingly simple and civilised. Attractively understated old
furnishings include a mix of small oak chairs around tables in corners, an
oak coffer, several handsomely carved antique oak settles (the finest
apparently made partly from a 16th-c wedding bed-head), and old hunting
prints and engravings. There's coir matting in the snug, and oriental rugs
on flagstones in front of the fine old stone fireplaces; two areas of the pub
are no smoking. There's quite an emphasis on the well cooked lunchtime
snacks and more elaborate specials, which are served by helpful staff. The
handsome side barn was being converted into a deli, with an antiques shop
above, as we went to press. A nice wild garden has crested newts and
nesting moorhens; the pub's dogs are called Harry and Doris. You can try
your hand at bowls or croquet on the neat green outside this brick pub, but
beware that the crowns deceive even the most experienced players.
*Free house ~ Licensees Monica Evans and David Anderson ~ Real ale ~ Bar food
(12-2, 5.30-8.30(9 Fri, Sat); 12-8.30 Sun) ~ (01257) 462297 ~ Children
welcome except in bar area ~ Dogs welcome ~ Open 12-3, 5.30-11; 12-10.30
Sun*

GREAT MITTON
Three Fishes *Mitton Road (B6246, off A59 NW of Whalley); BB7 9PQ*
Smartly renovated by the people behind renowned restaurant with rooms
Northcote Manor, this 16th-c dining pub has since it reopened quickly
become one of the county's stand-out places to eat, thanks to its very good

regional cooking. The emphasis is on traditional Lancastrian dishes with a modern twist, with all ingredients carefully sourced from small local suppliers – many of whom are listed on the back of the menu, or immortalised in black and white photographs on the walls. They've already won various awards and accolades (particularly for the way they look after children, who have their own good menu), and readers have very much enjoyed coming here over the last few months, praising not only the food, but also the décor, the range of drinks, and the efficient service and organisation. They don't take bookings, but write your name on a blackboard when you arrive, and find you when a table becomes free; it works rather well, even at the busiest times, and the polite staff are rather good at remembering the names of people waiting. Completely no smoking, the pub stretches back much further than you'd initially expect; the areas closest to the bar are elegantly traditional with a couple of big stone fireplaces, rugs on polished floors, newly upholstered stools, and a good chatty feel, then there's a series of individually furnished and painted rooms with exposed stone walls and floors, careful spotlighting, and wooden slatted blinds, ending with another impressive fireplace. You order at various food points dotted around, and there's lots of space, but they do get busy (the big car park is sometimes overflowing). The long bar counter has elaborate floral displays and three real ales, usually including one or two from Thwaites, and guests like the local Three Bs Bobbins; also various cocktails, a good choice of wines by the glass, and unusual soft drinks. The lavatories are smart, and they have facilities for the disabled and parents with young children. Overlooking the Ribble Valley, the garden has tables and perhaps its own menu in summer.

Free house ~ Licensees Nigel Haworth, Andy Morris ~ Real ale ~ Bar food (12-2, 6-9; 12-8.30 Sun) ~ Restaurant ~ (01254) 826888 ~ Children welcome ~ Dogs allowed in bar ~ Open 12-11(10.30 Sun); closed 25 Dec

LITTLE ECCLESTON

Cartford *Cartford Lane, off A586 Garstang—Blackpool, by toll bridge; PR3 0YP*

Readers enjoy the range of real ales at this pub, and the tranquil setting by a toll bridge over the River Wyre is very attractive; there are tables out in a garden (not by the water), with a play area. Aside from a couple from Hart (from the pub's own good microbrewery behind the building, with brewery tours by arrangement), you'll find Fullers London Pride and up to six changing ales mostly from smaller brewers such as Bank Top, Bradfield, Greenfield, Moorhouses and Roosters; also decent house wines and several malt whiskies. The rambling interior has oak beams, dried flowers, a log fire and an unusual layout on four different levels, with uncoordinated seating areas; pool, darts, games machine, small TV and piped music. Two levels are largely set for dining. There may be a wait at busy times for the straightforward low-priced bar food. The pub has fishing rights along 1½ miles of the river.

Own brew ~ Licensee Andrew Mellodew ~ Real ale ~ Bar food (12-2, 6.30-9.30; 12-9 Sun) ~ (01995) 670166 ~ Children welcome ~ Dogs welcome ~ Open

12-3, 6.30-11; 11.30-3, 6.30-11.45 Sat; 12-10.30 Sun ~ Bedrooms: £36.95B/£48.95B

MELLOR
Oddfellows Arms *Heading out of Marple on the A626 towards Glossop, Mellor is the next road after the B6102, signposted off on the right at Marple Bridge; keep on for nearly 2 miles up Longhurst Lane and into Moor End Road; SK6 5PT*
Warmed by open fires, the pleasant low-ceilinged flagstoned bar at this pub makes a civilised place for a meal and there's no piped music; there's also a small no smoking restaurant upstairs. The menu and specials board feature a wide choice of dishes. Adnams Southwold, Marstons Best, Phoenix Arizona and a weekly changing guest such as Cottage Best are on handpump. There are a few tables out by the road. It can be tricky to secure a parking space when they're busy; get here early to be sure of a table.
Free house ~ Licensee Olivier Berton ~ Real ale ~ Bar food (12-2, 6.30-9.30; not Sun evening) ~ Restaurant ~ (0161) 449 7826 ~ Children welcome ~ Dogs allowed in bar ~ Open 12-3, 5.30-11; 12-7 Sun; closed Sun evening and Mon

WHEELTON
Dressers Arms *2.1 miles from M61 junction 8; Briers Brow, off A674 Blackburn rd from Wheelton bypass (towards Brinscall); 3.6 miles from M65 junction 3, also via A674; PR6 8HD*
Nicely atmospheric with a series of cottagey low-beamed rooms, this enticingly snug place has very good-value bar food as well as an interesting choice of beer. It's much bigger than it looks from the outside, and the rooms are full of old oak and traditional features, including a handsome old woodburning stove in the flagstoned main bar. Candles on tables add to the welcoming feel, and there are newspapers and magazines; two areas are no smoking (including one side of the bar); piped music, juke box, pool table and games machine. They usually keep eight real ales on at once, such as their own Big Franks (now brewed off the site) as well as the more familiar Boddingtons, Tetleys and Timothy Taylors Landlord, plus five guests such as Barnlsey Bitter, St Austell Tribute, Three Rivers Suitably Irish and Northumberland Whitley Wobbler; also around 20 malt whiskies and some well chosen wines. Served all day at weekends, the good locally sourced bar food is very traditional, though there is a cantonese restaurant on the first floor. Lots of picnic-sets on a terrace in front of the pub, as well as a large umbrella with lighting and heaters; they have a very big car park, across the road. The licensees are great pet-lovers and welcome dogs.
Own brew ~ Licensees Steve and Trudie Turner ~ Real ale ~ Bar food (12-2.30, 5-9; 12-9 weekends and bank hols) ~ (01254) 830041 ~ Children welcome, except in bar after 9pm ~ Dogs welcome ~ Open 11-12.30am(1am Sat)

YEALAND CONYERS
New Inn *3 miles from M6 junction 35; village signposted off A6; LA5 9SJ*
This ivy-covered 17th-c village pub has excellent food served all day, and

makes a handy stopping place from the nearby M6 or if you're exploring the area's wonderfully varied walks up Warton Crag and through Leighton Moss RSPB reserve. Inside, the simply furnished little beamed bar on the left has a cosy village atmosphere, with its log fire in the big stone fireplace. On the right, two communicating no smoking cottagey dining rooms have dark blue furniture, shiny beams and an attractive kitchen range. Robinsons Hartleys XB, one of their seasonal ales and perhaps another such as Unicorn on handpump and around 30 malt whiskies; piped music. The same menu runs through the dining rooms and bar, and includes some good vegetarian. A sheltered lawn at the side has picnic-sets among roses and flowering shrubs.

Robinsons ~ Tenants Bill Tully and Charlotte Pinder ~ Real ale ~ Bar food (11.30(12 Sun)-9.30) ~ Restaurant ~ (01524) 732938 ~ Children welcome ~ Dogs allowed in bar ~ Open 11.30-11; 12-10.30 Sun

Dog Friendly Hotels, B&Bs and Farms

ASHWORTH VALLEY
Leaches Farm *Ashworth Rd, Rochdale, Lancashire OL11 5UN (01706) 41117* £**44**; 3 rms, shared bthrm. Creeper-clad 17th-c hill farm with really wonderful views, massive stone walls, beams and log fires, and nice breakfasts in no smoking dining room; self-catering too; walks on farm but must be on lead (especially at lambing time) plus unrestricted walking on nearby moorland; farm cats; cl 22 Dec-2 Jan; children over 8; dogs in bedrooms by arrangement

BLACKPOOL
Imperial Hotel *North Promenade, Blackpool, Lancashire FY1 2HB (01253) 623971* £**99**, plus special breaks; 180 well equipped rms, many with sea views. Fine Victorian hotel overlooking the sea, with spacious and comfortable day rooms, lots of period features, enjoyable food and fine wines, and a full health and leisure club with indoor swimming pool, gym, sauna and so forth; children's club during summer, Christmas and Easter; lots to do nearby; disabled access; dogs in bedrooms; £15

BROMLEY CROSS
Last Drop Village Hotel *Hospital Rd, Bromley Cross, Bolton, Lancashire BL7 9PZ (01204) 591131* (2.5 miles off A58, via A676 and B6472) £**105**; 128 rms, most with views over the moor or peaceful courtyard. Big well equipped hotel complex cleverly integrated into olde-worlde pastiche village complete with stone-and-cobbles street of gift and teashops, bakery, etc, even a spacious creeper-covered pub with lots of beamery and timbering, popular buffet, and heavy tables out on attractive flagstoned terrace; disabled access; dogs in bedrooms; £10

CHIPPING
Gibbon Bridge Hotel *Green Lane, Chipping, Preston, Lancashire PR3 2TQ* *(01995) 61456* £**120**, plus special breaks; 29 spacious individual rms, inc 22 split-level suites, most with views of the Bowland Hills. Country hotel on the edge of the Forest of Bowland, with beautiful landscaped gardens and old-fashioned values of quality and personal service; attractively presented food using home-grown produce in airy restaurant and adjoining conservatory, a quiet relaxing atmosphere, and fine wines; health and gym area; tennis court; a fine base for walking and short driving trips; good disabled access; dogs in two restricted bedrooms

COWAN BRIDGE
Hipping Hall *Cowan Bridge, Kirkby Lonsdale, Carnforth, Lancashire LA6 2JJ* *(01524) 271187* £**180**, plus special breaks; 7 pretty rms, 5 in main hotel, 2 cottage suites across courtyard (with self-catering facilities). Relaxed country-house atmosphere and elaborate modern british food in handsome and sensitively refurbished small hotel, an open fire, a lovely beamed Great Hall with minstrels' gallery, and four acres of walled gardens; fine walks from front door; cl Christmas and New Year; children over 12; dogs in one bedroom only

HURST GREEN
Shireburn Arms *Whalley Rd, Hurst Green, Clitheroe, Lancashire BB7 9QJ* *(01254) 826518* £**80**, plus special breaks; 18 rms. Lovely 17th-c country hotel with a refined but friendly atmosphere, an airy modernised bar, comfortable lounge, open fires, well presented enjoyable food, good service, and fine view of the Ribble Valley from the conservatory; disabled access; dogs in bedrooms if well behaved; £10

MANCHESTER
Malmaison *Piccadilly, Manchester M1 3AQ (0161) 278 1000* £**165.50**; 167 chic rms with CD player, in-house movies, smart bthrms, and really good beds. Stylishly modern hotel with comfortable contemporary furniture, exotic flower arrangements, bright paintings, very efficient service, french brasserie, generous breakfasts, and free gym; good disabled access; dogs in bedrooms; £10

Rossetti *107 Piccadilly, Manchester M1 2DB (0161) 247 7744* £**135**; 61 well equipped modern rms with eclectic décor and 5 suites – each floor offers 50s-style diners with help-yourself tea, coffee, croissants, fruit and cereals. Formerly the headquarters of the Horrocks cotton dynasty, this impressive hotel has stylish rooms with lots of mirrors, old tiling, parquet floors, huge gold-painted ironwork columns, and lots of artwork; good mediterranean cooking in no smoking café (brazilian jazz all day), enjoyable breakfasts, basement cocktail bar, and cheerful informal service; dogs welcome in bedrooms

WHITEWELL
Inn at Whitewell *Whitewell, Clitheroe, Lancashire BB7 3AT (01200) 448222 £96*; 23 rms, some with open peat fires. Civilised Forest of Bowland stone inn on the River Hodder, with seven miles of trout, salmon and sea trout fishing, and six acres of grounds with views down the valley; old-fashioned pubby main bar with sonorous clocks, antique furniture, roaring log fires, newspapers and magazines to read, well kept real ales, an exceptionally good wine list, particularly good food in no smoking bar and dining room, and courteous, friendly staff; lots of fine walks from the door; dogs in bedrooms and other areas but away from kitchen

Leicestershire and Rutland

Dog Friendly Pubs

CLIPSHAM
Olive Branch *Take B668/Stretton exit off A1 N of Stamford; Clipsham signposted E from exit roundabout; LE15 7SH*
Everything is done to the highest possible standard at this very well run pub. It scores high on all fronts, leaving you to enjoy a comfortably civilised, relaxing visit. There's quite an emphasis on the beautifully prepared and presented food (served by friendly attentive staff) from an imaginative changing menu so it's worth booking in advance. A great range of drinks includes well kept Grainstore Olive Oil and a guest or two such as Holts on handpump, an enticing wine list (with about 18 by the glass), a fine choice of malt whiskies, armagnacs and cognacs, and 14 different british and continental bottled beers. The various smallish attractive rambling room have dark joists and beams, and there's a cosy log fire in the stone inglenook fireplace, an interesting mix of pictures (some by local artists) and country furniture. Many of the books were bought at antiques fairs by one of the partners, so it's worth asking if you see something you like, as much is for sale. The dining rooms are no smoking; shove-ha'penny and maybe unobtrusive piped music. Outside, there are tables, chairs and big plant pots on a pretty little terrace, with more on the neat lawn, sheltered in the L of its two low buildings. We'd like to hear about their new bedrooms so do please send us a report if you stay.
Free house ~ Licensees Sean Hope and Ben Jones ~ Real ale ~ Bar food (12-2(3 Sun), 7-9.30(9 Sun)) ~ Restaurant ~ (01780) 410355 ~ Children welcome ~ Dogs allowed in bar and bedrooms ~ Open 12-3, 6-11; 12-11(10.30 Sun) Sat ~ Bedrooms: £75S(£85B)/£85S(£95B)

EMPINGHAM
White Horse *Main Street; A606 Stamford—Oakham; LE15 8PS*
This big, well used, old stone-built dining pub is handy if you're visiting Rutland Water. The bustling open-plan carpeted lounge bar has a big log fire below an unusual free-standing chimney-funnel, and lots of fresh flowers. There are some rustic tables among urns of flowers outside. Bar food is fairly traditional, and during the afternoon they serve sandwiches,

baguettes and tea; most of the pub is no smoking; TV, fruit machine and piped music. Well kept Adnams Best and Greene King Abbot and Ruddles Best and possibly a guest such as Grainstore Triple B on handpump, and around eight wines by the glass. Bedrooms are in a converted stable block and they have wheelchair access.

Enterprise ~ Lease Ian and Sarah Sharp ~ Real ale ~ Bar food (12-6, 7-9.30; 12-9 Sun) ~ (01780) 460221 ~ Children welcome away from bar ~ Dogs allowed in bedrooms ~ Open 11-11 ~ Bedrooms: £50B/£65B

EXTON
Fox & Hounds *Signposted off A606 Stamford—Oakham; LE15 8AP*
As the hospitable landlord at this handsome old country coaching inn is Italian, it's not surprising that the menu includes quite a few italian dishes. As well as a vast selection of handmade pizzas (Mon-Sat evenings only), and quite a few pasta and risotto dishes, they also serve british pub favourites. The comfortable high-ceilinged lounge bar is traditionally civilised, with some dark red plush easy chairs, as well as wheelback seats around lots of pine tables, maps and hunting prints on the walls, fresh flowers, a winter log fire in a large stone fireplace, well kept Archers Best Bitter, Grainstore Ten Fifty and Greene King IPA on handpump, and a good range of wines by the glass; the restaurant and lounge are no smoking; darts, dominoes, cribbage and piped music. Seats among large rose beds on the pleasant well kept back lawn look out over paddocks, and the tranquil village green with its tall trees out in front is most attractive.

Free house ~ Licensees Valter and Sandra Floris ~ Real ale ~ Bar food (not Sun evening) ~ Restaurant ~ (01572) 812403 ~ Children welcome ~ Dogs allowed in bar ~ Open 11-3, 6-11; 12-3, 7-10.30 Sun ~ Bedrooms: £45B/£60(£70B)

MEDBOURNE
Nevill Arms *B664 Market Harborough—Uppingham; LE16 8EE*
Readers enjoy the easy-going welcoming atmosphere and good value food at this handsome old inn. You get to it by a footbridge over the little duck-filled River Welland, giving you time to take in its lovely stonework, imposing latticed mullioned windows and large studded oak door. The inviting main bar has a buoyant pubby feel, with a good mix of drinkers and diners, log fires in stone fireplaces at either end, chairs and small wall settles around its tables, and a lofty dark-joisted ceiling; a second smaller room has dark furniture and another open fire; piped music. Much needed at busy times (it's worth getting here early), a spacious back room by the former coachyard has pews around more tables, its own bar, and children's toys. The traditional bar food is popular and served by friendly staff. Well kept Adnams Bitter, Fullers London Pride, Greene King Abbot and two changing guests such as Nethergate on handpump, and about two dozen country wines; darts, shove-ha'penny, cribbage, dominoes and carpet bowls. Look out for Truffles the cat and the inquisitive great dane, Bertie. Seats outside by the dovecote overlook the village green, and the church over the bridge is worth a visit. The bedrooms are in two neighbouring

cottages, and the first-class breakfasts are served in the pub's sunny conservatory.

Free house ~ Licensees Nicholas and Elaine Hall ~ Real ale ~ Bar food (12-2, 7-9.45) ~ (01858) 565288 ~ Children welcome ~ Dogs allowed in bar ~ Open 12-2.30(3 Sat), 6-11; 12-3, 7-10.30 Sun ~ Bedrooms: £50B/£65B

NEWTON BURGOLAND

Belper Arms *Village signposted off B4116 S of Ashby or B586 W of Ibstock; LE67 2SE*

Although the original building has been very opened up, the many ancient interior features, including heavy beams, changing floor levels and varying old floor and wall materials, break this bustling place up into enjoyable little nooks and seating areas. Parts are said to date back to the 13th c, and much of the exposed brickwork certainly looks at least three or four hundred years old. A big freestanding central chimney at the core of the building has a cottagey old black range on one side, and open fire on the other, with chatty groups of nice old captain's chairs. There's plenty to look at, from a suit of old chain mail, to a collection of pewter teapots, some good antique furniture and, framed on the wall, the story of the pub ghost – Five to Four Fred. They hold a beer festival during the August bank holiday, but usually have well kept Marstons Pedigree, and three or four guests from brewers such as Archers, Batemans and Wadworths on handpump, with ten wines by the glass; piped music and dominoes. Bar food is tasty and they do a three-course Sunday lunch. The restaurant is very big, and service can slow down when they get busy. A rambling garden has boules, cricket nets and a children's play area, and works its way round the pub to teak tables and chairs on a terrace, and a steam-engine-shaped barbecue; there's a good caravan site here too.

Mercury Taverns ~ Manager Paul Jarvis ~ Real ale ~ Bar food (12-2.30, 7-9.30; 12-9.30 Fri-Sun) ~ Restaurant ~ (01530) 270530 ~ Children welcome ~ Dogs allowed in bar ~ Open 12-12(1 Fri, Sat)

OAKHAM

Grainstore *Station Road, off A606; LE15 6RE*

This somewhat masculine conversion of a three-storey Victorian grain station warehouse is particularly popular for its own-brewed beers. Laid back or lively, depending on the time of day, with noises of the brewery workings above, the interior is plain and functional, with wide well worn bare floorboards, bare ceiling boards above massive joists (and noises of the workings above) which are supported by red metal pillars, a long brick-built bar counter with cast-iron bar stools, tall cask tables and simple elm chairs. Their fine ales (they usually serve six of the full complement of nine) are served both traditionally at the left end of the bar counter, and through swan necks with sparklers on the right; the friendly staff are happy to give you samples. Decent pubby food is good value. In summer they pull back the huge glass doors that open on to a terrace with picnic-sets, and often stacked with barrels; sporting events on TV, fruit machine, bar billiards, cribbage, dominoes, darts, giant Jenga and bottle-walking; disabled access.

You can tour the brewery by arrangement, they do take-aways, and hold a real ale festival with over 65 real ales and lots of live music during the August bank holiday weekend.

Own brew ~ Licensee Tony Davis ~ Real ale ~ Bar food (12-2.30; not evenings or Sun) ~ (01572) 770065 ~ Children welcome till 8 pm ~ Dogs allowed in bar ~ Live jazz monthly Sun afternoon and blues and rock monthly Sun evening ~ Open 11-11(12 Sat)

SOMERBY

Stilton Cheese *High Street; off A606 Oakham—Melton Mowbray, via Cold Overton, or Leesthorpe and Pickwell; can also be reached direct from Oakham via Knossington; LE14 2QB*

Readers enjoy the cheery traditional welcome, reasonably priced tasty food and jolly decent range of beers at this bustling 17th-c village pub – even when very busy, the friendly staff make time for a chat. The comfortable hop-strung beamed bar/lounge has dark carpets, lots of country prints on its stripped stone walls, a collection of copper pots, a stuffed badger and plenty of restful seats. Five handpumps serve Grainstore Ten Fifty, Marstons Pedigree, Tetleys and a couple of thoughtfully sourced ales from brewers such as Belvoir and Brewsters, and they've cider on handpump and over 25 malt whiskies; shove-ha'penny, cribbage and dominoes. The wide range of fairly priced changing bar food is gently imaginative and well liked. The Farmers Bar is no smoking. There are seats and outdoor heaters on the terrace.

Free house ~ Licensees Carol and Jeff Evans ~ Real ale ~ Bar food (12-2, 6-9) ~ (01664) 454394 ~ Children welcome ~ Dogs allowed in bedrooms ~ Open 12-3, 6(7 Sun)-11 ~ Bedrooms: £30/£40

STATHERN

Red Lion *Off A52 W of Grantham via the brown-signed Belvoir road (keep on towards Harby – Stathern signposted on left); or off A606 Nottingham—Melton Mowbray via Long Clawson and Harby; LE14 4HS*

Under the same ownership as the Olive Branch in Clipsham, and run along the same rather civilised lines and to the same high standards, this very popular dining pub, though placing much emphasis on the imaginative food does nevertheless offer a splendid range of drinks too. Grainstore Olive Oil and changing guests such as Batemans XB, Greene King Abbot and Shepherd Neame Spitfire are well kept on handpump, alongside draught belgian beer and continental bottled beers, several ciders, a varied wine list with around a dozen by the glass, and winter mulled wine and summer home-made lemonade. As at the Olive Branch, great care goes into the delicious bar food. Ingredients are sourced locally, they smoke their own meats, make their own preserves and pickles, and even have a kitchen shop where you can buy produce and fully prepared dishes. There's a relaxed country pub feel to the yellow room on the right, and a relaxing lounge has sofas, a fireplace, and a big table with books, paper and magazines; it leads off the smaller, more traditional flagstoned bar, with terracotta walls, another fireplace with a pile of logs beside it, and lots of beams and hops. Dotted around are various oddities picked up by one of the licensees on visits to Newark Antiques Fair: some unusual lambing chairs for example, and a collection of wooden spoons. A little room with tables set for eating leads to the long, narrow main dining room in what was once the pub's skittle alley, and out to a nicely arranged suntrap garden, with good hardwood furnishings spread over its lawn and terrace, and an unusually big play area behind the car park, with swings, climbing frames and so on.

Free house ~ Licensees Sean Hope, Ben Jones, Marcus Welford ~ Real ale ~ Bar food (12-2, 7(6 Sat)-9.30; 12-4 Sun) ~ Restaurant ~ (01949) 860868 ~ Children welcome ~ Dogs allowed in bar ~ Open 12-3, 6-11; 12-11 Fri, Sat; 12-6.30 Sun; closed Sun evening

Dog Friendly Hotels, B&Bs and Farms

EMPINGHAM
White Horse *Main St, Empingham, Oakham, Rutland LE15 8PR (01780) 460221* (0.3 miles off A606; Main St) £65, plus special breaks; 13 pretty rms, some in a delightfully converted stable block. Attractive, bustling old inn, handy for Rutland Water (plenty of walks); a relaxed and comfortable atmosphere, a big log fire and fresh flowers in open-plan lounge, big helpings of very enjoyable food inc fine breakfasts, coffee and croissants from 8am, and cream teas all year; attractive no smoking restaurant, well kept real ales, and efficient friendly service; cl 25 Dec; good disabled access; dogs in bedrooms; £5

MELTON MOWBRAY
Sysonby Knoll *Asfordby Rd, Melton Mowbray, Leicestershire LE13 0HP (01664) 563563* (0.6 miles off A606/A607 junction; A6006 Asfordby Rd) £78; 30 rms, most facing a central courtyard, and 6 in annexe. Family-run and mainly no smoking Edwardian brick house on the edge of a bustling market town; reception and lounge areas furnished in period style, winter open fire, friendly owners and excellent service, generous helpings of imaginative food inc lots of puddings in airy restaurant, and five acres of gardens (where dogs may walk) leading down to the river Eye where guests can fish; footpaths from the door; resident dog; cl Christmas–New Year; disabled access; dogs welcome away from restaurant

STAPLEFORD
Stapleford Park *Stapleford, Melton Mowbray, Leicestershire LE14 2EF (01572) 787522* £250; 55 individually designed rms inc cottages. Luxurious country house, extravagantly restored, in lovely large grounds with riding and stabling, tennis, croquet, putting green, 18-hole championship golf course, trout fishing, falconry and clay pigeon shooting; lots of opulent furnishings, fine oil paintings and an impressive library,

delicious food in no smoking restaurants, enthusiastic owner, and warmly welcoming staff; health spa and indoor swimming pool; walks around the grounds and in nearby Rutland Park; disabled access; dogs in bedrooms (not to be left unattended) and most public areas; welcome pack; £15

STRETTON
Ram Jam Inn *Great North Rd, Stretton, Oakham, Rutland LE15 7QX (01780) 410776* (0.2 miles off A1; just off B668 towards Oakham) **£62**; 7 comfortable and well equipped rms. Handily placed on the A1, this civilised inn has a comfortable airily modern lounge bar, a café bar and bistro, good interesting food quickly served all day from open-plan kitchen, and useful small wine list; large garden and orchard; cl 25 Dec; dogs welcome in bedrooms

UPPINGHAM
Lake Isle *16 High St East, Uppingham, Oakham, Rutland LE15 9PZ (01572) 822951* (just off A6003; High St E) **£75**, plus special breaks; 12 rms with home-made biscuits, sherry and fresh fruit, and three cottage suites. In a charming market town, this 18th-c, no smoking restaurant-with-rooms has an open fire in the attractive lounge, a comfortable bar, good imaginative food and enjoyable breakfasts, a carefully chosen wine list, and a small and pretty garden; dogs in bedrooms if well behaved

Lincolnshire

Dog Friendly Pubs

SOUTH WITHAM
Blue Cow *Village signposted just off A1 Stamford—Grantham (with brown sign for pub); NG33 5QB*

Happily, the new landlord at this old stone-walled country pub plans to continue brewing the reasonably priced Blue Cow Best and Witham Wobbler. There's a nice pubby atmosphere in its two appealing rooms, which are completely separated by a big central open-plan counter. One dark-beamed room has bentwood chairs at big indonesian hardwood tables, wickerwork and panelling, and prettily curtained windows, and the second room has big black standing timbers and beams, partly stripped stone walls, shiny flagstones and a dark blue flowery carpet; piped music and darts. Bar food is basic but tasty. The garden has tables on a pleasant terrace.

Own brew ~ Licensee Simon Crathore ~ Real ale ~ Bar food (12-2.30, 6-9.30) ~ Restaurant ~ (01572) 768432 ~ Children welcome ~ Dogs welcome ~ Open 12-11(10.30 Sun) ~ Bedrooms: £45S/£55B

WOOLSTHORPE
Chequers *The one near Belvoir, signposted off A52 or A607 W of Grantham; NG32 1LU*

With a good range of dishes, running from the fairly pubby to more imaginative, the food at this 17th-c coaching inn is very tasty. There's a good value three course evening menu, and two course Sunday lunch. The heavy-beamed main bar has two big tables (one a massive oak construction) a comfortable mix of seating including some handsome leather chairs and leather banquettes, and a huge boar's head above a good log fire in the big brick fireplace. Among cartoons on the wall are some of the illustrated claret bottle labels from the series commissioned from famous artists, initiated by the late Baron Philippe de Rothschild. The lounge on the right has a deep red colour scheme, leather sofas and big plasma TV, and on the left there are more leather seats in a dining area housed in what was once the village bakery; piped music. A corridor leads off to the light and airy main restaurant with contemporary pictures, and a second bar; smoking in the bar only. A good range of drinks includes well kept

Brewsters Marquis and a guest such as Black Sheep on handpump, a selection of belgian beers, local fruit pressés, over 35 wines by the glass, over 20 champagnes, and 50 malt whiskies. There are nice teak tables, chairs and benches outside, and beyond some picnic-sets on the edge of the pub's cricket field; boules too, and views of Belvoir Castle.
Free house ~ Licensee Justin Chad ~ Real ale ~ Bar food (12-2.30, 6-9.30; 12-4, 6-8.30) ~ Restaurant ~ (01476) 870701 ~ Children welcome ~ Dogs allowed in bar and bedrooms ~ Open 12-3.30, 5.30-12; 12-1am Sat; 12-11 Sun ~ Bedrooms: £55B/£69B

Dog Friendly Hotels, B&Bs and Farms

STAMFORD
George *71 St Martins, Stamford, Lincolnshire PE9 2LB (01780) 750700* (1.7 miles off A1 via B1081 from S end of Stamford bypass; St Martins, just S of bridge) **£140**, plus special breaks; 47 individually decorated rms. Ancient former coaching inn with a quietly civilised atmosphere, sturdy timbers, broad flagstones, heavy beams and massive stonework, and open log fires; good food in Garden Lounge, restaurant and summer courtyard, an excellent range of drinks inc very good value italian wines, and welcoming staff; well kept walled garden and sunken croquet lawn, and an area where dogs may walk; two resident cats; children over 8 in evening restaurant; disabled access; dogs in bedrooms and some other areas (not the restaurant)

WINTERINGHAM
Winteringham Fields *1 Silver St, Winteringham, Scunthorpe, Lincolnshire DN15 9ND (01724) 733096* **£120**; 10 pretty rms (3 off courtyard). Thoughtfully run restaurant-with-rooms in 16th-c manor house with comfortable and very attractive Victorian furnishings, beams and open fires, really excellent, inventive and beautifully presented food (inc a marvellous cheeseboard) in no smoking dining room, fine breakfasts, exemplary service, and an admirable wine list; two resident dogs; miles of walks directly from door; cl 2 wks Christmas, 2 wks summer, 1 wk April; disabled access; babes in arms and children over 8; dogs in bedrooms (not to be left unattended); welcome pack; £10

WOODHALL SPA
Petwood *Stixwould Road, Woodhall Spa, Lincolnshire LN10 6QF (01526) 352411* **£136**; 53 pleasant rms. Sizeable Edwardian house in 30 acres of mature woodland, lawns and gardens; many original features inc panelling and a fine main staircase, spacious public rooms decorated and furnished in keeping with the style of the hotel, smart restaurant, and snooker table, putting green and croquet lawn; dogs in bedrooms; £5

Norfolk

Dog Friendly Pubs

BLAKENEY
Kings Arms *West Gate Street; NR25 7NQ*

This attractive white inn does get pretty crowded at peak times as it's just a stroll from the harbour. The three simply furnished, knocked-through pubby rooms have a good mix of locals and visitors, low ceilings, some interesting photographs of the licensees' theatrical careers, other pictures including work by local artists, and what must be the smallest cartoon gallery in England – in a former telephone kiosk. Look out for the brass plaque on the wall that marks a flood level. Two small rooms are no smoking, as is the airy garden room; darts, games machine, bar billiards, table skittles and board games. Adnams, Greene King Old Speckled Hen, Marstons Pedigree and Woodfordes Wherry on handpump, and quite a few wines by the glass. Reasonably priced bar food includes hearty traditional dishes. Lots of tables and chairs in the large garden; good nearby walks.

Free house ~ Licensees John Howard, Marjorie Davies and Nick Davies ~ Real ale ~ Bar food (12-9.30(9 Sun)) ~ (01263) 740341 ~ Children welcome ~ Dogs welcome ~ Open 11(11.30 Sun)-midnight; closed evening 25 Dec ~ Bedrooms: /£65S

BRANCASTER STAITHE
Jolly Sailors *Main Road (A149); PE31 8BJ*

This is prime bird-watching territory and the pub is set on the edge of thousands of acres of National Trust dunes and salt flats; walkers are welcome. It's unpretentious and simply furnished with three cosy rooms, a log fire and a good mix of seats. Good bar food includes oysters and mussels from the harbour just across the road, and other pubby dishes. Both restaurants are no smoking. From their on-site microbrewery they produce Brancaster Staithe Brewery Old Les and IPA and keep a guest like Woodfordes Great Eastern on handpump. There's a sizeable garden and covered terrace, both with tables, and a children's play area.

Free house ~ Licensee Mr Boughton ~ Real ale ~ Bar food (all day) ~ Restaurant ~ (01485) 210314 ~ Children welcome ~ Dogs allowed in bar ~ Open 11-11; 12-10.30 Sun; closed 25 Dec

White Horse *A149 E of Hunstanton; PE31 8BY*

Many customers come to this well run place to enjoy the very good imaginative food, but the bar remains popular (particularly with locals) for a pint and a chat or a light lunchtime meal. It's all more or less open-plan, and you must book to be sure of a table. The front bar has good local photographs on the left, with bar billiards and maybe piped music, and on the right is a quieter group of cushioned wicker armchairs and sofas by a table with daily papers and local landscapes for sale. This runs into the no smoking back restaurant with well spaced furnishings in unvarnished country-style wood, and some light-hearted seasidey decorations; through the big glass windows you can look over the sun deck to the wide views of the tidal marshes and Scolt Head Island beyond. Well kept Adnams, Fullers London Pride, Woodfordes Wherry and a guest like Archers Swindon on handpump from the handsome counter, 15 malt whiskies and about a dozen wines by the glass from an extensive and thoughtful wine list. The coast path runs along the bottom of the garden.

Free house ~ Licensees Cliff Nye and Kevin Nobes ~ Real ale ~ Bar food ~ Restaurant ~ (01485) 210262 ~ Children welcome but must be supervised ~ Dogs allowed in bar ~ Open 11-11; 12-10.30 Sun ~ Bedrooms: £75B/£120B

BURNHAM THORPE

Lord Nelson *Village signposted from B1155 and B1355, near Burnham Market; PE31 8HL*

With much character and a fine relaxing atmosphere, this friendly 17th-c pub is much enjoyed by our readers. There are plenty of pictures and memorabilia of Nelson (who was born in this sleepy village), and the little bar has well waxed antique settles on the worn red flooring tiles and smoke ovens in the original fireplace. An eating room has flagstones, an open fire, and more pictures of Nelson, and there are two no smoking rooms. Well kept Greene King IPA and Abbot, Woodfordes Nelsons Revenge and Wherry, and a guest such as Fox Nelsons Blood Bitter tapped from the cask, and 13 wines by the glass. They also have secret rum-based recipes called Nelson's Blood and Lady Hamilton's Nip; Nelson's Blood was first concocted in the 18th c and is passed down from landlord to landlord by word of mouth. Bar food is imaginative and tasty. The eating areas are no smoking. Cribbage, dominoes, chess, bar skittles and board games. There's a good-sized play area in the very big garden.

Greene King ~ Lease David Thorley ~ Real ale ~ Bar food (12-2(2.30 weekends), 6-9(9.30 Fri-Sun); not Sun evening or Mon in winter) ~ Restaurant ~ (01328) 738241 ~ Children welcome ~ Dogs allowed in bar ~ Live bands Thurs Sept-June ~ Open 11-3, 6(5 Fri)-11; 12-3, 6.30-10.30 Sun; 12-2.30, 6-11 weekdays in winter; closed Mon Sept-June (except school hols and bank hol Mon)

HOLKHAM

Victoria *A149 near Holkham Hall; NR23 1RG*

This charmingly furnished small hotel cleverly doubles as an all-day pub. Virtually the whole of the ground floor is opened up into linked but quite individual areas. The main bar room, decorated in cool shades of green, has an eclectic mix of furnishings including deep low sofas with a colourful scatter of cushions, a big log fire, a dozen or so fat lighted candles in heavy sticks and many more tea lights, and some decorations conjuring up India (such as the attractive Rajasthan cotton blinds for a triple bow window). This is quite up market, but very informally so: young women tucking their stockinged feet up into the cushions, people almost nodding off over the daily papers, good-natured young staff chatting to customers or among themselves – though this never delays the prompt service. Round at the back are smaller rooms, with more of a local feel in one bare-boards bar-propping area. The island servery has a decent range of wines by the glass as well as four well kept ales on handpump such as Adnams, Caledonian 80/-, Everards Tiger and Woodfordes Wherry, and good coffees and hot chocolate; there may be unobtrusive piped music. Two linked dining rooms continue the mood of faintly anglo-indian casual elegance. The good imaginative food includes produce from the owners' Holkham estate, with a 'wild' shoot – no artificially reared birds – so the game is excellent. The local seafood is also top-notch. Several separate areas outside with plenty of tables and picnic-sets include a sheltered courtyard with a high retractable awning and regular summer barbecues, and an orchard with a small play area. Just across the road is a walk down past nature-reserve salt marshes, alive with many thousands of geese and duck in winter, to seemingly endless broad beaches. As we went to press, the manager was leaving, but we are sure that with the Cokes (who own it as well as Holkham Hall itself) keeping an eye on things, all should continue to go well.

Free house ~ Licensee Tom Coke ~ Real ale ~ Bar food ~ Restaurant ~ (01328) 711008 ~ Children welcome ~ Dogs allowed in bar ~ Open 11-11 ~ Bedrooms: £95S(£120B)/£115S(£150B)

ITTERINGHAM

Walpole Arms *Village signposted off B1354 NW of Aylsham; NR11 7AR*
Rather civilised, the biggish open-plan bar in this popular dining pub has exposed beams, stripped brick walls, little windows, a mix of dining tables, and quietly chatty atmosphere. Well kept Adnams Bitter and Broadside and a beer named for the pub brewed for them by Wolf on handpump, 15 wines by the glass, Aspel's cider, and local apple juice. There's an imaginative snack menu, and other modern ambitious dishes. Service can be stretched at peak times. The attractive restaurant is no smoking; piped music. Behind the pub is a two-acre landscaped garden and there are seats on the vine-covered terrace.

Free house ~ Licensee Richard Bryan ~ Real ale ~ Bar food (not Sun evening) ~ Restaurant ~ (01263) 587258 ~ Children welcome ~ Dogs allowed in bar ~ Occasional live music Sun evenings ~ Open 12-3, 6-11; 12-3, 7-10.30 Sun

MORSTON

Anchor *A149 Salthouse—Stiffkey; The Street; NR25 7AA*
While the bar here has a snug and cheerily traditional feel, an airy new no smoking extension on the left is quite contemporary. So you can choose

the latter's groups of deep leather sofas around low tables, with grey-painted country dining furniture, fresh flowers and fish pictures beyond; or turn right for three small rooms with pubby seating and tables on shiny black floors, coal fires, local 1950s beach photographs, lots of prints and bric-a-brac. The coffee lounge and second bar are no smoking. Whichever way you go, there's well kept Greene King Old Speckled Hen and local Winters Gold on handpump, decent wines by the glass, oyster shots (a local oyster in vodka) and daily papers. A very useful menu includes plenty of fish and local seafood, and food is enjoyable and generously served. Service is pleasant and efficient. There are tables and benches out in front, with more tables on a side lawn. You can book seal-spotting trips here.

Free house ~ Licensee N J Handley ~ Real ale ~ Bar food (12-2.30, 6-9(9.30 Sat); 12-8 Sun) ~ Restaurant ~ (01263) 741392 ~ Children welcome ~ Dogs allowed in bar ~ Open 11-11(midnight Sat); 12-10.30 Sun

SNETTISHAM

Rose & Crown *Village signposted from A149 King's Lynn—Hunstanton just N of Sandringham; coming in on the B1440 from the roundabout just N of village, take first left turn into Old Church Road; PE31 7LX*

The improvements continue at this pretty white cottage. The friendly licensees are thrilled with their new, very well equipped bedrooms (and hope to start refurbishment on the older ones soon), the Garden Room should be finished by the time this book is published (inviting wicker based wooden chairs, new tables and careful lighting). The front restaurant has a lovely oiled wooden floor, goldy green walls, new tables and chairs, and antique brass stable lamps. The garden has been re-landscaped, the terrace improved and wheelchair ramps installed; it's the car park's turn next! There are two bars (the only places you can smoke), each with a separate character: an old-fashioned beamed front bar with black settles on its tiled floor and a big log fire, and a back bar with another large log fire and the landlord's sporting trophies and old sports equipment. Good imaginative food is prepared using local seasonal produce where possible, and is served by courteous staff. Well kept Adnams Bitter, Bass, Fullers London Pride and Greene King IPA on handpump, 20 wines by the glass, organic fruit juices and farm cider. Stylish café-style aluminium and blue chairs with matching blue tables under cream parasols on the terrace, and an outdoor heater. Disabled lavatories.

Free house ~ Licensee Anthony Goodrich ~ Real ale ~ Bar food (12-2.30, 6.30-9.30) ~ Restaurant ~ (01485) 541382 ~ Children welcome ~ Dogs allowed in bar and bedrooms ~ Open 11-11; 12-10.30 Sun ~ Bedrooms: £60B/£90B

STIFFKEY

Red Lion *A149 Wells—Blakeney; NR23 1AJ*

On a cold evening with torrential rain, one reader found this was an outpost of warmth and cheer. There's a bustling atmosphere, plenty of customers, and the oldest parts of the simple bars have a few beams, aged flooring tiles or bare floorboards, and big open fires; there's also a mix of pews, small settles and a couple of stripped high-backed settles, a nice old long deal table among quite a few others, and oil-type or lantern wall lamps. Well kept Woodfordes Nelsons Revenge and Wherry and a couple of guests on handpump, quite a few wines by the glass, and 30 malt whiskies; board games. Bar food is well liked. A back gravel terrace has proper tables and seats, with more on grass further up beyond; there are some pleasant walks nearby.

Free house ~ Licensee Andrew Waddison ~ Real ale ~ Bar food (all day Sun) ~ (01328) 830552 ~ Children welcome ~ Dogs welcome ~ Open 12-midnight(11 Sun); 12-3, 6-11 winter

WELLS-NEXT-THE-SEA
Crown *The Buttlands; NR23 1EX*
Even though this is a smart 16th-c coaching inn, there's now more of a pubby feel than there has been, which has pleased readers very much. The no smoking beamed bar is a friendly place with an informal mix of furnishings on the stripped wooden floor, local photographs on the red walls, a good selection of newspapers to read in front of the open fire, and well kept Adnams Bitter, Woodfordes Wherry and a guest on handpump; 15 wines by the glass. The sunny no smoking conservatory with wicker chairs on the tiled floor, beams and modern art is where families with well behaved children can sit, and there's a pretty restaurant; piped music and board games. The good modern bar food is served by attentive staff. You can sit outside on the sheltered sun deck.

Free house ~ Licensees Chris and Jo Coubrough ~ Real ale ~ Bar food (12-2.30, 6.30-9.30) ~ Restaurant ~ (01328) 710209 ~ Children welcome ~ Dogs allowed in bar ~ Open 11-11 ~ Bedrooms: £100B/£120B

Dog Friendly Hotels, B&Bs and Farms

BLAKENEY
Blakeney Hotel *Blakeney, Holt, Norfolk NR25 7NE (01263) 740797* **£178**, plus special breaks; 64 very comfortable rms, many with views over the salt marshes and some with own little terrace. Overlooking the harbour with fine views, this friendly, mainly no smoking hotel has comfortable and appealing public rooms, good food, very pleasant staff, indoor swimming pool, saunas, spa bath, billiard room and safe garden; very well organised for families, with plenty to do for them nearby; good disabled access; dogs in bedrooms only; £5

BURNHAM MARKET
Hoste Arms *Market Pl, Burnham Market, King's Lynn, Norfolk PE31 8HD* *(01328) 738777* **£117**, plus special breaks; 34 comfortable rms. Handsome inn on green of lovely Georgian village, with a smartly civilised atmosphere, attractive bars, some interesting period features, big log fires, conservatory lounge, stylish food (plus morning coffee and afternoon tea)

in no smoking restaurant, well kept real ales and good wines, and professional friendly staff; big new awning covering a sizeable eating area in the garden; lovely beaches for walking nearby; partial disabled access; dogs in bedrooms, bar and lounge; £7.50

ERPINGHAM

Saracens Head *Wolterton, Norwich, Norfolk NR11 7LZ (01263) 768909* (2.3 miles off A140; keep straight on past Erpingham itself, then through Calthorpe to Wolterton) £85; 6 cottagey rms. Comfortably civilised inn with simple but stylish two-room bar, a nice mix of seats, log fires and fresh flowers, excellent inventive food, very well kept real ales, interesting wines, and a charming old-fashioned gravel stableyard with picnic-sets; cl 25 Dec; limited disabled access; dogs in bedrooms

MORSTON

Morston Hall *The Street, Morston, Holt, Norfolk NR25 7AA (01263) 741041* £270 inc dinner, plus special breaks; 7 comfortable rms with country views. Attractive 17th-c flint-walled house in tidal village, with lovely quiet gardens, two small lounges, one with an antique fireplace, a no smoking conservatory, and hard-working friendly young owners; particularly fine modern english cooking (they also run cookery demonstrations and hold wine and food events), a thoughtful small wine list, and super breakfasts; croquet; resident cat; coastal path for walks right outside; cl Jan; they are kind to families; partial disabled access; dogs in bedrooms; £5

MUNDFORD

Crown *Crown St, Mundford, Thetford, Norfolk IP26 5HQ (01842) 878233* (0.2 miles off A134 roundabout; first fork left off A1065) £69.50; 32 good rms. Friendly no smoking village pub, originally a hunting inn and rebuilt in the 18th c, with an attractive choice of reasonably priced straightforward food, very welcoming staff, a happy atmosphere and well kept real ales; disabled access; dogs in some bedrooms if well behaved; plenty of walks in Thetford Forest; £10

NORTH WALSHAM

Beechwood *Cromer Rd, North Walsham, Norfolk NR28 0HD (01692) 403231* £90 inc dinner; 17 comfortable rms. Creeper-covered and no smoking Georgian house once Agatha Christie`s Norfolk hideaway, with a comfortable lounge and bar, charming owners and super staff, good, imaginative modern cooking in attractive dining room, nice breakfasts, and lovely garden where dogs may walk – there's also a park nearby; two resident dogs; children over 10; dogs in bedrooms; treats in bar; £9

OLD CATTON

Catton Old Hall *Lodge Lane, Old Catton, Norwich, Norfolk NR6 7HG (01603) 419379* £75; 7 comfortable rms. 17th-c former farmhouse with lots of original features such as oak timbers, flint walls and inglenook fireplaces; cosy lounge, huge dresser in beamed no smoking dining room, small honesty bar, hearty breakfasts (evening meals by prior arrangement), and attentive, welcoming owners; plenty of country walks nearby; resident dog; no children; dogs if small, in some bedrooms

SWAFFHAM

Strattons *Ash Close, Swaffham, Norfolk PE37 7NH (01760) 723845* (1.5 miles off A47; Ash Cl, off Lynn St nr centre) £140, plus special breaks; 10 interesting and opulent rms. No smoking and environment-friendly Palladian–style villa near the centre of this old town; individual and comfortably decorated rooms filled with sculptures, ornaments and original paintings, fresh and dried flower arrangements, log fires, imaginative food using local organic produce from a short daily-changing menu, good breakfasts using their own eggs and home-baked bread, and a carefully chosen wine list; two resident cats, one dog and chickens; plenty of nearby walks; disabled access; dogs in bedrooms but must not be left unattended; welcome pack; £6.50

THORNHAM

Lifeboat *Ship Lane, Thornham, Hunstanton, Norfolk PE36 6LT (01485) 512236* £96, plus special breaks; 12 pretty rms, most with sea view. Rambling old white-painted stone pub, well placed by coastal flats, with lots of character in the main bar – open fires, antique oil lamps, low settles and pews around carved oak tables, big oak beams hung with traps and yokes, and masses of guns, swords and antique farm tools; several rooms lead off; enjoyable popular food in bar and elegant no smoking restaurant and well kept real ales; sunny no smoking conservatory with steps up to terrace with seats and playground; marvellous surrounding walks; disabled access; dogs in bedrooms and bars

THORPE MARKET

Elderton Lodge *Cromer Rd, Thorpe Market, Norwich, Norfolk NR11 8TZ (01263) 833547* (3 miles off A140 via A149) £100, plus special breaks; 11 rms. No smoking 18th-c shooting lodge for adjacent Gunton Hall, with lots of original features, fine panelling, a relaxing lounge bar with log fire, an airy conservatory where breakfast and lunch are served, and Langtry Restaurant with good food using fresh fish and game; six acres of mature grounds overlooking herds of deer and lots of walks; dogs in bedrooms and lounge; £5

TITCHWELL

Titchwell Manor Hotel *Main Rd, Titchwell, King's Lynn, Norfolk PE31 8BB (01485) 210221* £108, plus special breaks; 25 light, pretty rms. Comfortable hotel, handy for nearby RSPB reserve, and with lots of walks and footpaths nearby; roaring log fire, magazines and good naturalists' records of the wildlife, a cheerful bar, attractive no smoking brasserie restaurant (lots of seafood) with french windows onto lovely sheltered walled garden, good breakfasts, and particularly helpful licensees and staff;

high tea for younger children; disabled access; dogs in ground-floor bedrooms; towel, bowl, walk map, biscuits; £5

WARHAM
Three Horseshoes *The Street, Warham, Wells-next-the-Sea, Norfolk NR23 1NL (01328) 710547* £**56**; 5 rms, one with own bthrm. Basic but cheerful local with marvellously unspoilt traditional atmosphere in its three friendly gaslit rooms, simple furnishings, a log fire, very tasty generous bar food, decent wines and very well kept real ales; bedrooms are in the Old Post Office adjoining the pub, with lots of beams and a residents' lounge dominated by an inglenook fireplace; resident dog; plenty of surrounding walks; cl 25-26 Dec; no children; dogs in bedrooms

WINTERTON-ON-SEA
Fishermans Return *The Lane, Winterton-on-Sea, Great Yarmouth, Norfolk NR29 4BN (01493) 393305* £**70**; 3 rms reached by a tiny staircase. Traditional 300-year-old pub in quiet village, close to the beach (fine walking), with warmly welcoming and helpful owners, a relaxed lounge bar with well kept real ales, open fire, good home-made food inc fresh fish (fine crabs in season), enjoyable breakfasts, and sheltered garden with children's play equipment; dogs welcome

Northamptonshire

Dog Friendly Pubs

CRICK
Red Lion *1 mile from M1 junction 18; A428; NN6 7TX*
The cosy low-ceilinged bar at this welcoming old stone and thatched pub, though getting a little well worn these days, is nice and traditional, with lots of comfortable seating, some rare old horsebrasses, pictures of the pub in the days before it was surrounded by industrial estates, and a tiny log stove in a big inglenook; no smoking snug. The straightforward lunchtime menu is incredibly good value, making this a great break if you're on the M1, and they do a similarly bargain-price Sunday roast. Prices go up a little in the evening when they offer a wider range of dishes. Four well kept beers on handpump include Charles Wells Bombardier, Greene King Old Speckled Hen, Websters and a guest from a brewer such as Everards. There are a few picnic-sets under cocktail parasols on grass by the car park, and in summer you can eat on the terrace in the old coachyard, which is sheltered by a Perspex roof; lots of pretty hanging baskets.
Wellington ~ Lease Tom and Paul Marks ~ Real ale ~ Bar food (12-2, 6.30-9; not Sun evening) ~ (01788) 822342 ~ Children under 14 welcome lunchtimes only ~ Dogs welcome ~ Open 11-2.30, 6.15-11; 12-3, 7-10.30 Sun

EYDON
Royal Oak *Lime Ave; village signed off A361 Daventry—Banbury, and from B4525; NN11 3PG*
The room on the right at this enjoyable old stone village pub has low beams, cushioned wooden wall benches built into alcoves, seats in a bow window, some cottagey pictures, flagstones and an open fire in an inglenook fireplace. The bar counter, with bar stools, runs down a long central flagstoned corridor room and links several other small idiosyncratic beamed rooms. An attractive covered terrace with hardwood furniture is a lovely place for a meal in fine weather. Served by friendly staff, the very tasty bar food comes in nice substantial helpings. Well kept Fullers London Pride, Greene King IPA and a couple of guests such as Archers Sunchaser and St Austell Tribute on handpump; piped music, darts and table skittles.
Free house ~ Licensee Justin Lefevre ~ Real ale ~ Bar food (12-2, 7-9; not Mon)

~ *Restaurant* ~ *(01327) 263167* ~ *Children welcome* ~ *Dogs allowed in bar* ~
Open 12-2.30, 6-11.30(12 Sat); 12-3, 6-10.30 Sun

FARTHINGSTONE
Kings Arms *Off A5 SE of Daventry; village signposted from Litchborough on
former B4525 (now declassified); NN12 8EZ*
The list of retail food produce on sale at this quirky gargoyle-embellished
stone 18th-c country pub makes very tempting reading indeed. Products
(including cheeses, cured and fresh meat and cured and fresh fish) are
sourced for their originality of style, methods of rearing, smoking or organic
farming methods. Unfortunately the short but good list of bar food is only
served weekend lunchtimes. The timelessly intimate flagstoned bar has
plenty of character, as well as a huge log fire, comfortable homely sofas and
armchairs near the entrance, whisky-water jugs hanging from oak beams,
and lots of pictures and decorative plates on the walls. A games room at the
far end has darts, dominoes, cribbage, table skittles and board games.
Batemans XB and Youngs are well kept on handpump alongside a couple of
guests such as Oakham JHB and St Austell Tribute, the short wine list is
quite decent, and they have a few country wines; the outside gents' has an
interesting newspaper-influenced décor. Some visitors come specially to see
the gardens, where there's always something new and often wacky; in
summer the hanging baskets are at their best, the tranquil terrace is
charmingly decorated with flower and herb pots and plant-filled painted
tractor tyres, and they grow their own salad vegetables and herbs too. The
village is picturesque, and there are good walks including the Knightley
Way. It's worth ringing ahead to check the limited opening and food
serving times noted below as the licensees are sometimes away.
Free house ~ *Licensees Paul and Denise Egerton* ~ *Real ale* ~ *Bar food (12-2 Sat,
Sun lunchtime only)* ~ *No credit cards* ~ *(01327) 361604* ~ *Children welcome* ~
Dogs welcome ~ *Open 7(6.30 Fri)-11; 12-3.30, 7(9 Sun)-11 Sat; closed wkday
lunchtimes and Mon, Weds evenings*

FOTHERINGHAY
Falcon *Village signposted off A605 on Peterborough side of Oundle; PE8 5HZ*
Although the beautifully presented, inventive food at this civilised no
smoking pub will probably be your main reason for visiting here, it does
still have a thriving little local's tap bar (and darts team) if you do just want
a drink. It's the sort of knowledgeably run place where everything is done
at top notch level. A very good range of drinks includes well kept Adnams
and Greene King IPA on handpump alongside a guest, good wines with 20
by the glass, organic cordials and fresh orange juice. Food takes in quite a
few pub favourites and then works its way up to seasonally changing, quite
intensely flavoured and heavily italian influenced specials. The buzz of
contented conversation fills the neatly kept little bar, which has cushioned
slatback armchairs and bucket chairs, good winter log fires in a stone
fireplace, and fresh flower arrangements. The conservatory restaurant is
pretty, and if the weather's nice the attractively planted garden is
particularly enjoyable. The vast church behind is worth a visit, and the

ruins of Fotheringhay Castle, where Mary Queen of Scots was executed, are not far away.

Huntsbridge ~ Licensee John Hoskins ~ Real ale ~ Bar food (12-2.15, 6.15-9.30) ~ Restaurant ~ (01832) 226254 ~ Children welcome ~ Dogs allowed in bar ~ Open 12-3, 6-11(10.30 Sun)

GREAT BRINGTON

Fox & Hounds/Althorp Coaching Inn *Off A428 NW of Northampton, nr Althorp Hall; NN7 4JA*

The ancient bar at this friendly golden stone thatched coaching inn has a lovely relaxed atmosphere with lots of old beams and saggy joists, an attractive mix of country tables (maybe with fresh flowers) and chairs on its broad flagstones and bare boards, plenty of snug alcoves, nooks and crannies, some stripped pine shutters and panelling, two fine log fires, and an eclectic medley of bric-a-brac from farming implements to an old typewriter and country pictures. The superb range of nine real ales (under light blanket pressure) includes Greene King IPA, Abbot and Old Speckled Hen, with up to five guests from a thoughtfully sourced range of brewers such as Archers, Cottage, Elgoods, Highgate and (local to them) Hoggleys, and they've about a dozen wines by the glass and a dozen malt whiskies. Bar food from a nicely varied menu is very tasty; the restaurant is no smoking; friendly service; piped music and TV. A cellarish games room down steps has a view of the casks in the cellar. A coach entry goes through to a lovely little paved courtyard with sheltered tables and tubs of flowers, and there are more, with a play area, in the side garden.

Free house ~ Licensee Jacqui Ellard ~ Real ale ~ Bar food (12-2.30, 6.30-9.30) ~ Restaurant ~ (01604) 770164 ~ Children welcome ~ Dogs allowed in bar ~ Jazz, folk, R&B Tues evening ~ Open 11-11; 12-10.30 Sun

WADENHOE

Kings Head *Church Street; village signposted (in small print) off A605 S of Oundle; PE8 5ST*

This stone-built no smoking 16th-c country inn is in an idyllic setting by a big wooded meadow next to the River Nene, with views of the church, and if you're arriving by boat there's no charge for mooring here if you are using the pub. Picnic-sets among the willows and aspens on the sloping grass make pleasant vantage points, and this is a pretty village of up-and-down lanes and thatched stone cottages. Because of its lovely setting it does get very busy on summer days. There's an uncluttered simplicity to the very welcoming partly stripped-stone main bar, which has pleasant old worn quarry tiles, solid pale pine furniture with a couple of cushioned wall seats, and a leather-upholstered chair by the woodburning stove in the fine inglenook. The bare-boarded public bar has similar furnishings and another fire; steps lead up to a games room with dominoes and table skittles, and there's yet more of the pale pine furniture in an attractive little beamed dining room. As well as Digifield Kings Head and Oakham JHB a couple of interesting guests might be from brewers such as Barnwell and Potbelly, they've belgian fruit beers, and their 18 wines are all available by the glass. Bar food is traditionally pubby.

*Free house ~ Licensee Alex Burgess ~ Real ale ~ Bar food (12-2.30(3 Sun),
6.30-9) ~ Restaurant ~ (01832) 720024 ~ Children welcome ~ Dogs allowed in
bar ~ Open 11-11; 12-10.30 Sun; closed Sun evening*

Dog Friendly Hotels, B&Bs and Farms

BADBY
Windmill *Main St, Badby, Daventry, Northamptonshire NN11 3AN (01327)
702363* £**72.50**, plus special breaks; 10 rms. Carefully modernised and
warmly welcoming thatched stone inn with beams, flagstones and huge
inglenook fireplace in front bar, a cosy comfortable lounge, a relaxed and
civilised atmosphere, good generously served bar and restaurant food, and
decent wines; fine views of the pretty village from car park, and woods to
walk in a mile away; disabled access; dogs welcome away from main restaurant

CRANFORD
Dairy Farm *12 St Andrews Lane, Cranford, Kettering, Northamptonshire
NN14 4AQ (01536) 330273* (1.7 miles off A14 at A510 junction; turn
right off High St into Grafton Rd, then next right into St Andrews Lane)
£**70**; 4 comfortable rms. Charming and no smoking 17th-c manor house
of great character on an arable and sheep farm, with oak beams and
inglenook fireplaces, good homely cooking using home-grown fruit and
vegetables, kind, attentive owners, and garden with charming summer
house and ancient dovecote; walks half a mile away; cl Christmas; partial
disabled access; dogs in annexe bedrooms; £5

DAVENTRY
Fawsley Hall *Fawsley, Daventry, Northamptonshire NN11 3BA (01327)
892000* £**199**; 52 fine rms. Lovely Tudor hotel with Georgian and
Victorian additions set in quiet gardens designed by Capability Brown and
surrounded by 2,000 acres of parkland (where dogs may walk); smart,
beautifully furnished antique-filled reception rooms with impressive décor,
open fires, a Great Hall for afternoon tea, excellent food in the no smoking
restaurant based in the original Tudor kitchens, and health and beauty
treatment rooms; tennis, gym, putting green and croquet; dogs in
bedrooms but not to be left unattended

OLD
Wold Farm *Harrington Rd, Old, Northampton, Northamptonshire NN6 9RJ
(01604) 781258* (3.1 miles off A43 via Walgrave; handy too for A508 via
Lamport; Harrington Rd) £**60**; 5 rms. No smoking 18th-c farmhouse in a
quiet village, with spacious interesting rooms, antiques and fine china, an
open log fire, hearty breakfasts in the beamed dining room, attentive
welcoming owners, snooker table, and two pretty gardens where dogs may
walk; resident dog; dogs in bedrooms; £2

Northumbria

Dog Friendly Pubs

BLANCHLAND
Lord Crewe Arms *B6306 S of Hexham; DH8 9SP*
You are immersed in history as you enter this remarkable building, originally a guest-house built 1235 for the neighbouring Premonstratensian monastery, in a picturesque village built robustly enough to resist most border raiding parties, and the lovely walled garden was formerly the cloisters. Still separated from the rest of the world by several miles of moors, rabbits and sheep, the building became home to several distinguished families after the dissolution in 1536. An ancient-feeling bar is housed in an unusual long and narrow stone barrel-vaulted crypt, its curving walls being up to eight feet thick in some places. Plush stools are lined along the bar counter on ancient flagstones, and next to a narrow drinks shelf down the opposite wall; TV. Upstairs, the Derwent Room has low beams, old settles, and sepia photographs on its walls, and the Hilyard Room has a massive 13th-c fireplace once used as a hiding place by the Jacobite Tom Forster (part of the family who had owned the building before it was sold in 1704 to the formidable Lord Crewe, Bishop of Durham). Apart from the bar and some bedrooms, the whole of the hotel is no smoking. Bar food is fairly straightforward. Black Sheep is on handpump alongside a summer guest ale.
Free house ~ Licensees A Todd, Peter Gingell and Ian Press, Lindsey Sands ~ Real ale ~ Bar food ~ Restaurant ~ (01434) 675251 ~ Children welcome in no smoking areas ~ Dogs allowed in bar and bedrooms ~ Open 11-11 ~ Bedrooms: £80B/£120B

CARTERWAY HEADS
Manor House Inn *A68 just N of B6278, near Derwent Reservoir; DH8 9LX*
Continuing to be a strong all-rounder for excellent food, well kept beer and well chosen wine this popular and welcoming inn has sweeping views towards the Derwent valley and reservoir. Highly praised food, using local ingredients where possible, is served in generous helpings. The locals' bar has an original boarded ceiling, pine tables, chairs and stools, old oak pews and a mahogany counter. Picture windows in the comfortable lounge bar (with woodburning stove) and from the partly no smoking restaurant give

fine views over moorland pastures, and rustic tables in the garden have the same views; darts, dominoes, TV and piped music (only in the bar). They've around 70 malt whiskies, farm cider and decent wines (with about dozen by the glass), along with Charles Wells Bombardier, Courage Directors, Theakstons Best and a guest from a local brewer such as Greene King on handpump. You can buy local produce, as well as chutneys, puddings and ice-cream made in the kitchens from their own little deli.

Free house ~ Licensees Moira and Chris Brown ~ Real ale ~ Bar food (12-9.30(9 Sun)) ~ Restaurant ~ (01207) 255268 ~ Well behaved children welcome away from bar ~ Dogs welcome ~ Open 11(12 Sun)-11 ~ Bedrooms: £38S/£60S

LUCKER
Apple *Village (and pub) well signposted off A1 N of Morpeth; NE70 7JH*
Cheerful service and good food have generated strong reports for this village pub on the Duke of Northumberland's estate. The welcoming bar area has some walls stripped to show massive neatly dressed blocks of masonry, others painted a restful ochre, and some sturdy padded seats-for-two among other more usual pubby furnishings such as dark country-kitchen chairs and padded banquettes. The large brick-and-stone fireplace has a woodburning stove. Decoration is restrained, and the overall impression is of spacious civilised relaxation. The roomy and big-windowed side dining area on the left is fresh and airy, with flowers on the tables. The enjoyable bar food is given an uplift by quite a few individual touches, and vegetables are carefully cooked. The no smoking restaurant menu includes more ambitious dishes (evenings only). The short well chosen wine list is sensibly priced, with decent wines by the glass; it would be nice if they installed a cask-conditioned ale; piped music, darts, dominoes and board games. The campsite behind the pub is completely separate.

Free house ~ Licensees Jane and Bob Graham ~ Bar food (12-2, 6.30-8.45; 12-8.45 Sun) ~ Restaurant ~ (01668) 213450 ~ Children welcome ~ Dogs allowed in bar ~ Open 12-3, 6.30-11; 12-10.30 Sun; closed Mon

NEWTON-BY-THE-SEA
Ship *Village signposted off B1339 N of Alnwick; Low Newton – paid parking 200 metres up road on right, just before village (none in village); NE66 3EL*
You'll need to book in the evening to eat at this popular pub, which has an enchanting coastal setting, in a row of converted fishermen's cottages, and looking across a sloping village green to a sandy beach just beyond. We recommend a phone call before your visit anyway as the opening times can vary, particularly in winter (but they are open every lunchtime except Christmas Day). Brilliantly simple cooking lets the marvellous quality of the fresh local, and quite often organic, ingredients shine through; service can be slow at times. There's a short lunchtime menu (when it's likely you'll be in the company of local walkers and their dogs), but in the evening, the atmosphere gently shifts a gear. The plainly furnished bare-boards bar on the right has nautical charts on its dark pink walls, beams and hop bines. Another simple room on the left has some bright modern

pictures on stripped-stone walls, and a woodburning stove in its stone fireplace; darts, dominoes. It's very quiet here in winter when they have just one or two local real ales. By contrast, they really only just cope when queues build up on hot summer days, and the beer range extends to up to four from mostly local brewers such as Hadrian & Border and Wylam; also decent wines, an espresso machine (colourful coffee cups, good hot chocolate), several malt whiskies and good soft drinks. Out in the corner of the square are some tables among pots of flowers, with picnic-sets over on the grass. There's no nearby parking, but there's a car park up the hill.
Free house ~ Licensee Christine Forsyth ~ Real ale ~ Bar food (12-2.30, 7-8 Tues in school hols and Wed-Sat) ~ No credit cards ~ (01665) 576262 ~ Children welcome ~ Dogs welcome ~ Live bands during some weekends and bank hols ~ Open 11-11 in school holidays (phone for other periods)

WARK

Battlesteads *B6320 N of Hexham; NE48 3LS*
This stone-built inn is flourishing under new licensees, and makes a splendid stop on this scenic North Tynedale alternative to the A68 route north. It's warmly welcoming, with a relaxed unhurried atmosphere (no piped music), and good changing local ales such as Black Sheep, Durham Magus and Wylam Gold Tankard from handpumps on the heavily carved dark oak bar counter. The nicely restored carpeted bar has a log fire, with horsebrasses around the fireplace and on the low beams, comfortable seats including some dark blue wall banquettes, floral wallpaper above its dark dado, and double doors to a no smoking panelled inner snug. The good value food uses prime local ingredients, including game, lamb from their own sheep, and aberdeen angus beef. The puddings are particularly good, and sensibly they don't do 'children's dishes' but are happy to serve children with smaller helpings off the normal menu. You can eat in the bar, or a restaurant beyond the snug. They do good coffee (and a great breakfast if you're staying), and service is cheerful. Some of the bedrooms are on the ground floor (with disabled access). There are picnic-sets on a terrace in the walled garden, and fine walks nearby.
Free house ~ Licensees Richard and Dee Slade ~ Real ale ~ Bar food (12-3, 7-10) ~ Restaurant ~ (01434) 230209 ~ Children welcome ~ Dogs allowed in bar and bedrooms ~ Open 10(11 Sun)-11; 12-3, 6-11 in winter ~ Bedrooms: £45S/£80B

WELDON BRIDGE

Anglers Arms *B6344, just off A697; village signposted with Rothbury off A1 N of Morpeth; NE65 8AX*
Attached to this hotel is a former railway dining car that now functions as a light, airy no smoking restaurant, with crisp white linen and a pink carpet. Whether you dine in there or in the less formal surroundings of the bar, you'll need a very healthy appetite to eat your way through the massive helpings of fairly pubby food. Nicely lit and comfortable, the traditional turkey-carpeted bar is divided into two parts: cream walls on the right, and oak panelling and some shiny black beams hung with copper pans on the

left, with a grandfather clock and sofa by the coal fire, staffordshire cats and other antique ornaments on its mantelpiece, old fishing and other country prints, some in heavy gilt frames, a profusion of other fishing memorabilia, and some taxidermy. Some of the tables are lower than you'd expect for eating, but their chairs have short legs to match – different, and rather engaging. Timothy Taylors Landlord is on handpump alongside a couple of guests such as Black Sheep and Greene King Old Speckled Hen; also decent wines and an espresso machine. There are tables in the attractive garden with a good play area that includes an assault course; they have rights to fishing on a mile of the River Coquet just across the road.

Free house ~ Licensee John Young ~ Real ale ~ Bar food (12-9.30) ~ Restaurant ~ (01665) 570271 ~ Children welcome ~ Dogs allowed in bedrooms ~ Open 11-11; 12-10.30 Sun ~ Bedrooms: £37.50S/£60S

Dog Friendly Hotels, B&Bs and Farms

CORNHILL-ON-TWEED
Tillmouth Park *Cornhill-on-tweed, Northumberland TD12 4UU (01890) 882255* (3 miles off A697 via A698 towards Berwick) **£120**, plus special breaks; 14 spacious, pretty rms with period furniture. Solid stone-built country house in 15 acres of parkland (where dogs may walk), with comfortable relaxing lounges, open fires, a galleried hall, good food in bistro or restaurant, and a carefully chosen wine list; two resident dogs; nearby golf, and shooting; lots to do nearby; dogs in bedrooms and ground floor bar

CROOKHAM
Coach House *Crookham, Cornhill-on-Tweed, Northumberland TD12 4TD (01890) 820293* (A697 S of Cornhill) **£78**; 10 individual rms with fresh flowers and nice views, 8 with own bthrm. 17th-c farm buildings around a sunny courtyard, with helpful and friendly staff, an airy beamed lounge with comfortable sofas and big arched windows, good breakfasts with home-made preserves (which you can also take home), afternoon tea, and enjoyable dinners using local vegetables; resident cat; paddocks for walking; lots to do nearby; cl Christmas; good disabled access; dogs in bedrooms; £5

GRETA BRIDGE
Morritt Arms *Greta Bridge, Barnard Castle, County Durham DL12 9SE (01833) 627232* (just off A66 on village loop) **£99**, plus special breaks; 27 rms. Smart, old-fashioned coaching inn where Dickens stayed in 1838 to research for *Nicholas Nickleby* – one of the interesting bars has a colourful Dickensian mural; comfortable no smoking lounges, fresh flowers, good open fires, and pleasant garden; lots of surrounding walks; coarse fishing; disabled access; dogs in some bedrooms; £5

HEADLAM

Headlam Hall *Headlam, Darlington, County Durham DL2 3HA (01325)*
730238 £110, plus special breaks; 41pretty rms, in the main house and
adjacent coach house. Peaceful, no smoking Jacobean mansion in four acres
of carefully kept gardens with a little trout lake, tennis court and croquet
lawn; elegant rooms, a fine carved oak fireplace in the main hall, stylish
food in the four individually decorated rooms of the restaurant, and
courteous staff; new spa with swimming pool, sauna, gym and treatment
rooms; 9-hole golf course, driving range and shop; walks in grounds and
surrounding footpaths; cl 25 and 26 Dec; disabled access; dogs in mews
bedrooms

LONGFRAMLINGTON

Embleton Hall *Longframlington, Morpeth, Northumberland NE65 8DT*
(01665) 570249 (on A697) £105; 13 comfortable, pretty and individually
decorated rms. Charming hotel in lovely grounds surrounded by fine
countryside, with a particularly friendly relaxed atmosphere and courteous
staff; neat little bar, elegant no smoking lounge, log fires, excellent value
bar meals, and very good food in the attractive no smoking dining room;
resident dog; disabled access; dogs welcome in bedrooms

LONGHORSLEY

Linden Hall *Longhorsley, Morpeth, Northumberland NE65 8XF (01670)*
516611 (just off A697 N of Morpeth) £140, plus special breaks; 50
individually decorated rms. Georgian hotel in 450 acres of landscaped park
with clay pigeon shooting, mountain biking (bike hire available), 18-hole
golf course, pitch and putt, croquet, lots of leisure facilities inc a swimming
pool, and health and beauty treatments; pubby bar, elegant drawing room,
and good food in attractive restaurant; children in main restaurant early
evening only; disabled access; dogs in two bedrooms only; £10

NEWCASTLE UPON TYNE

Malmaison *Quayside, Newcastle upon Tyne, Tyne & Wear NE1 3DX (0191)*
245 5000 £155; 122 individually decorated and well equipped rms. In a
former Co-op warehouse and overlooking the river, this stylish hotel is
boldly decorated throughout, with contemporary furniture and artwork,
genuinely friendly staff, modern cooking in fashionable no smoking
brasserie, and decent breakfasts; disabled access; dogs in bedrooms; bedding
and bowls offered; £10

ROMALDKIRK

Rose & Crown *Romaldkirk, Barnard Castle, County Durham DL12 9EB*
(01833) 650213 £126, plus special breaks; 12 rms – those in the main
house have lots of character. Smart and interesting old coaching inn by
green of delightful Teesdale village, with Jacobean oak settle, log fire, old
black and white photographs, and lots of brass in the beamed traditional
bar; cosy residents' lounge, very good imaginative food in bar and fine oak-
panelled restaurant, and well kept real ales and wines; walks along old

railway line nearby; cl Christmas; disabled access; dogs welcome in bedrooms

ROTHBURY

Tosson Tower Farm *Great Tosson, Morpeth, Northumberland NE65 7NW (01669) 620228* (3.5 miles off A697 via B6341) *£70*; 3 pretty rms. Traditional farmhouse on 170 acres of sheep pasture set in the Northumberland national park, with friendly owners, log fire, TV and plenty of books in comfortable and relaxing lounge, good farmhouse breakfasts in spacious dining room (plenty of eating places in Rothbury), lots of walks from the door, free fishing (salmon, sea trout and brown trout), and cycling; self catering, too; dogs welcome in bedrooms

Nottinghamshire

Dog Friendly Pubs

CAUNTON
Caunton Beck *Main Street; village signposted off A616 Newark—Ollerton; NG23 6AB*

You can get something to eat at most times of the day at this delightfully civilised dining pub, starting with a hearty english breakfast first thing, then later going on to delicious sandwiches and a fairly elaborate quarterly changing menu (with a handful of daily specials); no smoking restaurant. The lovely building itself is almost new, but as it was reconstructed using original timbers and reclaimed oak, around the skeleton of the old Hole Arms, it seems old. Scrubbed pine tables, clever lighting, an open fire and country-kitchen chairs, low beams and rag-finished paintwork in a spacious interior make for a relaxed atmosphere. With lots of flowers and plants in summer, the terrace is a nice place to sit when the weather is fine. About half the wines (around 35) on the very good wine list are available by the glass, and they've well kept Batemans XB and Black Sheep and a guest such as Milestone Loxley on handpump; also espresso coffee. Service is pleasant and attentive; daily papers and magazines, no music.

Free house ~ Licensee Julie Allwood ~ Real ale ~ Bar food (8am-11pm) ~ Restaurant ~ (01636) 636793 ~ Children welcome ~ Dogs allowed in bar ~ Open 8am-11pm

LAXTON
Dovecote *Signposted off A6075 E of Ollerton; NG22 0NU*

This very welcoming red-brick free house manages to maintain a pubby atmosphere, despite the popularity of the food (you may need to book). Served by very friendly and courteous staff, fairly priced traditional dishes come in big helpings, and puddings are made by Aunty Mary, the landlord's aunt, who lives in the village. The central lounge has dark wheelback chairs and tables on wooden floors, and a coal-effect gas fire. This opens through a small bay (the former entrance) into a carpeted dining area. Around the other side, another little lounge leads through to a pool room (smoking in here only) with darts, fruit machine, pool, dominoes and piped music. Three changing beers on handpump might be from brewers such as Batemans, Charles Wells and Marstons, and they've around ten wines by the glass. There are wooden tables and chairs on a small front terrace by a sloping garden, which has a disused white dovecote. It's handy for the A1, and as well as the two bedrooms, they have a site and facilities for six caravans. The pub stands next to three huge medieval open fields as Laxton is one of the few places in the country still farmed using the traditional open field system. Every year in the third week of June the grass is auctioned for haymaking, and anyone who lives in the parish is entitled to a bid – and a drink. You can find out more at the visitor centre behind the pub.

Free house ~ Licensees Lisa and Betty Shepherd ~ Real ale ~ Bar food (12-2, 6.30-9) ~ Restaurant ~ (01777) 871586 ~ Children welcome in restaurant ~ Dogs allowed in bar ~ Open 11-3, 6.30(6 Sat)-11(10.30 Sun) ~ Bedrooms: £35B/£50B

NOTTINGHAM
Cock & Hoop *Lace Market Hotel, High Pavement; NG1 1HF*
Civilised and completely no smoking, this carefully restored pub is in the heart of the Lace Market, opposite the former courthouse and jail, and is a welcome alternative to the somewhat louder bars that at weekends characterise this area of town. It's part of Nottingham's nicest hotel, but feels quite separate, with its own entrance, leading into a tiny front bar. There are a few tables and comfortable armchairs in here, as well as a small pewter-topped counter serving Caledonian Deuchars IPA, Fullers London Pride, and three guests like Charles Wells Bombardier, Morlands Old Speckled Hen and Nottingham Rock; cheery service. A corridor and stairs lead off to the most distinctive part of the pub – the big downstairs cellar bar, a long, windowless stone-flagged room with part panelled and part exposed brick walls, leatherette sofas and upholstered chairs and stools, and, on one side, several tiny alcoves each with a single table squeezed in. The wall lights have unusual cone-shaped shades; piped music. Bar food is tasty, and it can get busy at lunchtimes. Bedrooms are smart and comfortably upmarket (the ones overlooking the street can be noisy at weekends); breakfasts are good.

Free house ~ Licensee Mark Cox ~ Real ale ~ Bar food (12-7 Mon-Sat, 12-9 Sun) ~ Restaurant ~ (0115) 852 3231 ~ Children allowed in cellar bar till 7 if eating ~ Dogs allowed in bar and bedrooms ~ Open 12-11; 12-2am Sat; 12-10.30 Sun; closed 25/26 Dec, 1 Jan ~ Bedrooms: £90S/£119B

Dog Friendly Hotels, B&Bs and Farms

LANGAR
Langar Hall *Church Lane, Langar, Nottingham, Nottinghamshire NG13 9HG (01949) 860559 (3.5 miles off A52; heading E, 1st right turn into Tithby Rd, keeping straight on into Bingham Rd; in Langar, 1st right into*

Barnstone Rd then Church Lane) £150, plus special breaks; 12 lovely, nicely old-fashioned rms, some in wing and courtyard as well. Fine, no smoking country house in spacious grounds with family portraits in the hall and up the stairs, a friendly homely drawing room, library, small modern bar, pillared dining hall; antiques and fresh flowers, a relaxed informal atmosphere, lively, helpful owner and willing young staff, and very good food; resident cats; 30 acres of surrounding fields for walks; dogs in some bedrooms, if small; £20

NOTTINGHAM

Harts *Standard Hill, Park Row, Nottingham, Nottinghamshire NG1 6FN (0115) 988 1900* £135; 27 well appointed quiet rms with fine views. Adjacent to the well known restaurant of the same name, this is a smart and stylish purpose-built hotel in a traffic-free cul-de-sac on the site of the city's medieval castle; charming, friendly staff, lounge and snack bar, small exercise room, and private gardens (no dogs here but can go to park next door); disabled access; dogs in bedrooms; £5

Lace Market *29-31 High Pavement, Nottingham, Nottinghamshire NG1 1HE (0115) 852 3232,* £149, plus special breaks; 42 modern, comfortable rms. Next to a lovely church, this Georgian town house has a relaxed atmosphere, friendly young staff, a convivial bar with daily papers, wood-strip floors and strong but subtle colours, good brasserie-style food in contemporary restaurant, and enjoyable breakfasts; dogs in bedrooms, if small; £15

SOUTHWELL

Old Forge *Burgage Lane, Southwell, Nottinghamshire NG25 0ER (01636) 812809* (1.7 miles off A617 from Hockerton via Hockerton Rd, keeping straight on through Normanton into Burgage Lane) £75; 4 rms. In a quiet but central spot with its own parking, this no smoking 200-year-old former blacksmith's house has a welcoming owner, interesting furnishings, super breakfasts in conservatory overlooking the Minster, and pretty terrace; three resident dogs; Southwell Trail half a mile away for walks; cl 25 Dec; limited disabled access; dogs in bedrooms but must be well behaved; £5

Oxfordshire

Dog Friendly Pubs

COLESHILL
Radnor Arms *B4019 Faringdon—Highworth; village signposted off A417 in Faringdon and A361 in Highworth; SN6 7PR*
This pub, like the attractive village itself, is owned by the National Trust, and for the last months has been blossoming under splendid new management – the new tenants have previously made the Trout at nearby Tadpole Bridge very popular with readers. They take great care in tracking down prime ingredients for their tasty imaginative food, often local and sometimes even from Mr Green's father's farm. Service is friendly and quick. Despite the quality of the food, this remains very much a pub in atmosphere. The small welcoming carpeted bar has Goffs Galahad and Youngs tapped from casks behind the counter, which like as not has a couple of locals chatting over their pints; a good range of wines by the glass is fairly priced, they make good coffees, and in summer they do a fine Pimms, and elderflower pressé. This room has a couple of cushioned settles as well as its comfortable plush carver chairs, and a woodburning stove; a back alcove has a few more tables. Steps take you down into the main no smoking dining area, once a blacksmith's forge: with a lofty beamed ceiling, this has kept its brick chimney stack angling up (with a log fire now), and its canary walls are decorated with dozens of forged tools and smith's gear. A small garden up behind, with a big yew tree, has picnic-sets under cocktail parasols; there is plenty of good walking nearby.
Free house ~ Licensees Chris Green and Shelley Crowhurst ~ Real ale ~ Bar food (no food Sun evening) ~ Restaurant ~ (01793) 861575 ~ Children welcome ~ Dogs welcome ~ Open 11.30-3, 6-11; 12-3, 7-10.30 Sun; closed Mon

FIFIELD
Merrymouth *A424 Burford—Stow; OX7 6HR*
Readers enjoy staying in the quaint, well cared for bedrooms here. It's a family run place dating back to the 13th c and the Domesday Book mentions an inn on this site (its name comes from the Murimuth family who once owned the village). The simple but comfortably furnished L-shaped bar has nice bay-window seats, flagstones, horsebrasses and

antique bottles hanging from low beams, some walls stripped back to the old masonry, and an open fire in winter. Except for five tables in the bar, the pub is no smoking; piped classical music. Popular bar food includes light lunches and a varied range of daily specials. Well kept Timothy Taylors Landlord and Wychwood Hobgoblin on handpump, and decent wines. There are tables on a terrace and in the back garden (there may be a little noise from fast traffic on the road).

Free house ~ Licensees Andrew and Timothy Flaherty ~ Real ale ~ Bar food (12-2, 6.30-9; not winter Sun evenings) ~ Restaurant ~ (01993) 831652 ~ Children welcome ~ Dogs allowed in bar and bedrooms ~ Open 11-3, 6-11(7-10.30 Sun); closed Sun evening in winter ~ Bedrooms: £45S/£65B

HOOK NORTON

Gate Hangs High *Banbury Road; a mile N of village towards Sibford, at Banbury—Rollright crossroads; OX15 5DF*

This is a friendly place with efficient staff and is popular for both its real ales and food. The bar has joists in the long, low ceiling, a brick bar counter, stools and assorted chairs on the carpet, baby oil lamps on each table, a gleaming copper hood over the hearth in the inglenook fireplace, and hops over the bar counter. Well kept Hook Norton Best, Old Hooky and a monthly guest on handpump, bottled beers and decent wines. Food is particularly nice and they offer set weekday menus; you'll need to book for Saturday evening and Sunday lunch in the slightly chintzy no smoking side dining extension. Piped music, dominoes and cards. There's a pretty courtyard garden and seats on a broad lawn behind, with holly and apple trees and fine views; the flower tubs and wall baskets are very colourful.

Hook Norton ~ Tenant Stephen Coots-Williams ~ Real ale ~ Bar food (12-2.30, 6-11; all day Sat and Sun) ~ Restaurant ~ (01608) 737387 ~ Children welcome ~ Dogs allowed in bar ~ Open 11.30-3, 6-11; 11.30-11 Sat; 12-11 Sun; closed evening 25 Dec ~ Bedrooms: £40B/£60B

KELMSCOTT

Plough *NW of Faringdon, off B4449 between A417 and A4095; GL7 3HG*

This pretty pub is in a lovely spot in a peaceful hamlet by the upper Thames. The small traditional beamed front bar has ancient flagstones and stripped stone walls, along with a good log fire and the relaxed chatty feel of a real village pub. Most of the bar food is served in a choice of small and large helpings, from a menu that takes in a good choice of substantial sandwiches. The pleasant no smoking dining area has attractively plain and solid furnishings. Archers Best, Hook Norton Best, Timothy Taylors Landlord and Wychwood Hobgoblin on handpump, and Black Rat farm cider; piped music, pool, TV and darts. The garden is pretty, with seats among plantings of unusual flowers and aunt sally, and there are picnic-sets under cocktail parasols out in front. The Oxfordshire Cycleway runs close by.

Free house ~ Licensee Martin Platt ~ Real ale ~ Bar food (12-2.30, 7-9; all day weekends) ~ Restaurant ~ (01367) 253543 ~ Children welcome ~ Dogs allowed in bar and bedrooms ~ Live entertainment Sat evening ~ Open 11-midnight(2am Sat) ~ Bedrooms: £45S/£75B

LANGFORD
Bell *Village signposted off A361 N of Lechlade, then pub signed; GL7 3LF*
Tucked away near the church in a quiet and charming village, this little
country dining pub is a really relaxing and civilised spot for a leisurely
lunch. The simple low-key furnishings and décor add to the appeal: the
main bar has just five sanded and sealed mixed tables on grass matting, a
variety of chairs, three nice cushioned window seats, am attractive carved
oak settle, polished broad flagstones by a big stone inglenook fireplace with
a good log fire, low beams and butter-coloured walls with two or three
antique engravings. A second even smaller room on the right is similar in
character and is no smoking. The small back servery has Hook Norton
Hooky, Timothy Taylors Landlord and Charles Wells Bombardier on
handpump, with a good interesting range of wines by the bottle, and good
coffees; daily papers on a little corner table back here. The good food is
unquestionably the main thing and takes ih half a dozen or so daily
changing fresh fish dishes; service is friendly and efficient. There may be
inoffensive piped music. There are two or three picnic-sets out in a small
garden with a play house. They hope to open bedrooms this year. Dogs
must be on a lead.
*Free house ~ Licensees Paul and Jackie Wynne ~ Real ale ~ Bar food ~ Restaurant
~ (01367) 860249 ~ Children welcome ~ Dogs welcome ~ Open 12-3, 7-11;
closed Sun evening, all day Mon*

LEWKNOR
Olde Leathern Bottel *Under a mile from M40 junction 6; just off B4009
towards Watlington; OX49 5TW*
Happily unchanging, this is a pleasant country pub with a cheery welcome
and good service. There are heavy beams and low ceilings in the two bar
rooms (both no smoking), as well as rustic furnishings, open fires and an
understated décor of old beer taps and the like; the family room is separated
only by standing timbers, so you won't feel segregated from the rest of the
pub. Bar food is tasty and reasonably priced. Well kept Brakspears Bitter
and Special on handpump, and all their wines are available by the glass. The
attractive sizeable garden has plenty of picnic-sets under parasols, and a
children's play area.
*Brakspears ~ Tenant L S Gordon ~ Real ale ~ Bar food (12-2, 7-9.30) ~
(01844) 351482 ~ Children in restaurant and family room ~ Dogs allowed in bar
~ Open 10.30-2.30(3 Sat), 6-11; 12-3, 7-10.30 Sun*

LONGWORTH
Blue Boar *Off A420/A415; Tucks Lane; OX13 5ET*
Even in rotten weather this 17th-c thatched stone local is likely to be full of
chatty customers. The three low-beamed, characterful little rooms are
warmly traditional with well worn fixtures and furnishings and two blazing
log fires, one beside a fine old settle. Brasses, hops and assorted knick-
knacks like skis and an old clocking-in machine line the ceilings and walls,
there are fresh flowers on the bar and scrubbed wooden tables, and faded
rugs on the tiled floor; benches are firmly wooden rather than upholstered.

The main eating area is the no smoking red-painted room at the end and this year they've added a no smoking restaurant extension. Plenty of blackboards list standard dishes, a good range of vegetarian meals, and more interesting changing weekend specials, which are promptly served, in good-sized helpings. Brakspears, Greene King Ruddles Best and Timothy Taylors Landlord on handpump, 25 malt whiskies and a wide choice of wines, several by the glass. The licensee has been here for 28 years, though his friendly young team are generally more in evidence. There are tables in front, and the Thames is a short walk away.

Free house ~ Licensee Paul Dailey ~ Real ale ~ Bar food (12-2(2.30 Sat, 3 Sun), 7-10(9 Sun)) ~ Restaurant ~ (01865) 820494 ~ Children welcome ~ Dogs allowed in bar ~ Open 12-midnight(1am Sat); 12-11 Sun; closed 25 Dec, 1 Jan

SHIPLAKE
Baskerville Arms *Station Road, Lower Shiplake (off A4155 just S of Henley); RG9 3NY*

The hardworking, professional and friendly licensees who run this neat brick house are no strangers to the pages in this Guide. They ran another Oxfordshire pub for many years, culminating in that pub becoming the county's Dining Pub of the Year – so their recent award for the Baskerville Arms is a case of history repeating itself, but a bit more quickly this time around. There's a nice, partly no smoking bar with blue armchairs, darts and piles of magazines where locals gather for a chat and a pint of well kept Fullers London Pride, Loddon Hoppit or Timothy Taylors Landlord on handpump – but mostly, it's laid out for eating with much space given over to the restaurant; a couple of other comfortable areas, too. Apart from the wooden flooring around the light, modern bar counter, it's all carpeted and there are a few beams, pale wooden furnishings (lit candles on all the tables), plush red banquettes around the windows, and a brick fireplace with plenty of logs next to it. A fair amount of sporting memorabilia and pictures, especially old rowing photos (the pub is very close to Henley), plus some maps of the Thames are hung on the red walls, and there are flowers and large houseplants dotted about. It all feels quite homely, but in a smart way, with some chintzy touches such as a shelf of china dogs. The delicious range of bar food (from sausages to much more elaborate dishes) is extremely good, and absolutely everything is made on the premises: The pretty garden has a proper covered barbecue area and smart teak furniture under huge parasols.

Enterprise ~ Lease Graham and Mary Cromack ~ Real ale ~ Bar food ~ Restaurant ~ (0118) 940 3332 ~ Children welcome but with restrictions ~ Dogs allowed in bar ~ Open 11.30-2.30, 6-11; 12-4.30, 7-10.30 Sun ~ Bedrooms: £45S/£75S

STANTON ST JOHN
Star *Pub signposted off B4027, in Middle Lane; village is signposted off A40 heading E of Oxford (heading W, you have to go to the Oxford ring-road roundabout and take unclassified road signposted to Stanton St John, Forest Hill etc); OX33 1EX*

Not easy to find, this pleasant old place is popular locally and run by a friendly landlord. It is appealingly arranged over two levels, with the oldest parts two characterful little low-beamed rooms, one with ancient brick flooring tiles, and the other quite close-set tables. Up some stairs is an attractive extension on a level with the car park, with old-fashioned dining chairs, an interesting mix of dark oak and elm tables, rugs on flagstones, bookshelves on each side of an attractive inglenook fireplace (good blazing fires in winter), shelves of good pewter, terracotta-coloured walls with a portrait in oils, and a stuffed ermine. Bar food is decent. Well kept Wadworths IPA and 6X on handpump. The rather straightforward family room and conservatory are no smoking; piped music, darts, shove-ha'penny, cribbage, chess, and draughts. The walled garden has seats among the rockeries and children's play equipment.

Wadworths ~ Tenant Michael Urwin ~ Real ale ~ Bar food (not Sun evening) ~ (01865) 351277 ~ Children in family room and lower bar area only ~ Dogs welcome ~ Open 11-2.30, 6.30-11; 12-2.30, 7-10.30 Sun

TADPOLE BRIDGE
Trout *Back road Bampton—Buckland, 4 miles NE of Faringdon; SN7 8RF*
Just as we went to press, we heard that this comfortably upmarket inn was about to change hands. But as this is a lovely spot and we know the new people have a country house hotel background, we're hoping that things here will not change too much. The L-shaped bar has plenty of seats and some rugs on flagstones, a modern wooden bar counter with terracotta wall behind, some stripped stone, a woodburning stove and a large stuffed trout; the restaurant is no smoking, and it's all appealingly candlelit in the evenings. Food has been extremely good and real ales have included Butts Traditional, Ramsbury Bitter and Youngs Bitter on handpump; maybe a dozen wines by the glass. The well kept garden is a lovely place to sit in summer, with small fruit trees, attractive hanging baskets, and flower troughs. They sell day tickets for fishing on a two-mile stretch.

Free house ~ Licensees Gareth and Helen Pugh ~ Real ale ~ Bar food (not Sun evening) ~ Restaurant ~ (01367) 870382 ~ Children welcome ~ Dogs welcome ~ Open 12-3, 6-11; 12-3 Sun ~ Bedrooms: £55B/£80B

Dog Friendly Hotels, B&Bs and Farms

BURFORD
Lamb *Sheep St, Burford, Oxfordshire OX18 4LR (01993) 823155* (0.4 miles off A40, via A361; Sheep St, left off High St) **£145**, plus special breaks; 15 rms. Very attractive, no smoking 500-year-old Cotswold inn with lovely restful atmosphere, spacious beamed, flagstoned and elegantly furnished lounge, and classic civilised public bar; bunches of flowers on good oak and elm tables, three winter log fires, antiques, modern british food in lovely restaurant, and pretty little walled garden; disabled access; dogs in ground floor bedrooms

CHOLSEY
Well Cottage *Caps Lane, Cholsey, Wallingford, Oxfordshire OX10 9HQ* *(01491) 651959* £60; 2 neatly kept, lemon–yellow rms in garden flat overlooking courtyard. Extended old workman`s cottage with pretty rose-filled garden, open fire in homely sitting room, bird prints and paintings in dining room where breakfast is taken around one big table, and plenty of places nearby for evening meals; three resident dogs; horse riding is available as the owners have four horses; walks along the Thames, down quiet lane and in paddocks; disabled access; dogs in bedrooms but must be well behaved; £10

CLIFTON
Duke of Cumberlands Head *Clifton, Banbury, Oxfordshire OX15 0PE* *(01869) 338534* £75; 6 rms in sympathetic extension. Pretty thatched 17th-c stone inn with a friendly atmosphere, very good food in bar and no smoking back restaurant, enjoyable breakfasts, log fire, well kept beers and wines, and helpful service; tables in garden (where dogs are allowed; towpath and bridle paths nearby); dogs in bedrooms and bar

KINGHAM
Mill House *Station Rd, Kingham, Chipping Norton, Oxfordshire OX7 6UH* *(01608) 658188* £120, plus special breaks; 23 good rms with country views. Carefully renovated 17th-c flour mill in ten acres with trout stream; comfortable spacious lounge with books and magazines, open fire in lounge bar, open log fire in lounge bar, original features such as two bread ovens, a cosy and popular no smoking restaurant, and very good interesting food; resident dog; disabled access; dogs welcome in bedrooms

KINGSTON BAGPUIZE
Fallowfields *Southmoor, Kingston Bagpuize, Abingdon, Oxfordshire OX13 5BH (01865) 820416* (0.9 miles off A420; A415 S, then 1st right on to Faringdon Rd; Southmoor) £160, plus special breaks; 10 rms. Delightful and beautifully kept Gothic-style manor house with elegant, relaxing sitting rooms, open fires, imaginative food using home-grown produce in attractive no smoking conservatory dining room, courteous helpful service, and 12 acres of pretty gardens and paddocks (where dogs may walk – countryside all around for longer walks); two resident cats; lots to see nearby and plenty for children; cl 22 Dec-10 Jan; dogs in bedrooms and lounge; £5

OXFORD
Old Parsonage *1 Banbury Rd, Oxford OX2 6NN (01865) 310210* £165; 30 lovely rms. Handsome and civilised 17th-c parsonage, fairly central, with very courteous staff, good breakfasts and excellent light meals in cosy bar/restaurant; small lounge, open fires and fine paintings, and pretty little garden; they provide picnics; walks in nearby parks; dogs welcome away from restaurant; bowls, basket and meals on request

SHILLINGFORD

Shillingford Bridge Hotel *Shillingford Rd, Shillingford, Wallingford, Oxfordshire OX10 8LZ (01865) 858567* £**125**, plus special breaks; 40 rms. Riverside hotel with own river frontage, terraced gardens, fishing and moorings; spacious comfortable bars and attractive airy restaurant (all with fine views), squash, outdoor heated swimming pool, and Sat dinner-dance; walks along the Thames; disabled access; dogs welcome away from restaurant; £7.50

SHIPTON-UNDER-WYCHWOOD

Shaven Crown *High St, Shipton-under-Wychwood, Chipping Norton, Oxfordshire OX7 6BA (01993) 830330* £**85**, plus special breaks; 8 comfortable rms. Densely beamed, ancient stone hospice built around striking medieval courtyard with seating by lily pool and roses; impressive medieval hall with a magnificent lofty ceiling, sweeping stairway and old stone walls, log fire in comfortable bar, no smoking residents' lounge, intimate candlelit no smoking restaurant, well chosen wine list, good friendly service, warm relaxed atmosphere, and bowling green; lots of walks not far away; partial disabled access; dogs welcome away from restaurant

WOODSTOCK

Feathers *Market St, Woodstock, Oxfordshire OX20 1SX (01993) 812291* £**165**, plus special breaks; 20 individually decorated rms. Lovely old building with a fine relaxing drawing room and study, open fires, first-class friendly staff, a gentle atmosphere, daily changing imaginative food inc lovely puddings in no smoking restaurant, and a sunny courtyard with attractive tables and chairs; resident parrot; walks nearby; dogs in some bedrooms; £10

Shropshire

Dog Friendly Pubs

BRIDGES
Horseshoe *Near Ratlinghope, below the W flank of the Long Mynd; SY5 0ST*
You will need to get here early as quite a crowd (often including walking groups) manages to find its way to this remote pub, which is in splendid country in the Shropshire hills. The interior has light oak beams, log burners and lots of rustic bygones, and the down-to-earth yet comfortable bar has interesting windows, lots of farm implements, pub mirrors and musical instruments, and well kept Six Bells Big Nev, Cloud Nine and Wood Quaff on handpump, and they've also Old Rosie farm cider. A small no smoking dining room leads off from here; cribbage, darts and dominoes, Scrabble (Monday evenings) and occasional, discreet piped music. Home-made bar food is nicely pubby, and on Wednesday evenings they have a 'feast for a fiver', with themed food such as curry or mexican for just £5. Tables are placed out by the little River Onny; the Long Mynd rises up behind.
Free house ~ Licensees Bob and Maureen Macauley ~ Real ale ~ Bar food (12-2.45, 6-8.45; 12-8.45 Sat; 12-4 Sun) ~ No credit cards ~ (01588) 650260 ~ Children welcome till 8.45 ~ Dogs welcome ~ Open 12(4 Mon)-12

BURLTON
Burlton Inn *A528 Shrewsbury—Ellesmere, near junction with B4397; SY4 5TB*
Attention to detail is the watch-word at this extremely welcoming and attractively refurbished old pub, where everything seems meticulously arranged and well cared for, from the pretty flower displays in the brick fireplace or beside the neatly curtained windows, to the piles of interior design magazines in the corner. There are a few sporting prints, spurs and brasses on the walls, open fires in winter and dominoes and cribbage. Service is just as thoughtful, and kind, and the imaginative food here continues to deserve high praise; there may be two set-time evening sittings in the restaurant, part of which is no smoking. French windows lead from the garden dining room to the pleasant terrace, with its smart wooden furniture; the snug has comfortable seats, great for sinking into with a drink

– maybe one of their dozen wines by the glass, or a pint of Banks's, which is well kept alongside three continually changing guests from brewers such as Burton Bridge, Greene King and Salopian. They have facilities for the disabled. There are tables on a small lawn behind, with more on a strip of grass beyond the car park.

Free house ~ Licensee Gerald Bean ~ Real ale ~ Bar food (12-2, 6.30-9.45(7-9.30 Sun)) ~ Restaurant ~ (01939) 270284 ~ Well behaved children welcome ~ Dogs welcome ~ Open 11-3, 6-11; 12-3.30, 7-10.30 Sun; closed bank hol Mon lunchtimes ~ Bedrooms: £50B/£80B

CHETWYND ASTON

Fox *Village signposted off A41 and A518 just S of Newport; TF10 9LQ*

This roomy extended 1920s building, previously the Three Fishes, has now been handsomely reworked as a thriving dining pub by the small Brunning & Price group. As usual, they've used good materials, and the style will be familiar to anyone who has tried their other pubs, though in a good way – not at all mass-produced. A series of linked semi-separate areas, mainly no smoking and one with a broad arched ceiling, have plenty of tables in all shapes and sizes, some quite elegant, and a vaguely matching diversity of comfortable chairs, all laid out in a way that's fine for eating but serves equally well for just drinking and chatting. There are masses of attractive prints, three open fires, a few oriental rugs on parquet or boards, some floor tiling; big windows and careful lighting help towards the relaxed and effortless atmosphere (though no doubt the easy-going nature of people from nearby Harper Adams agricultural college and the Lilleshall Sport England centre helps too). With something for most tastes, the good range of food is gently imaginative. The handsome bar counter, with a decent complement of bar stools, serves an excellent changing range of about a dozen wines by the glass, and has Thwaites Original, Timothy Taylors Landlord, Shropshire Gold and three guests from brewers such as Cottage, Oakham and Phoenix on handpump. The staff, mainly young, are well trained, cheerful and attentive. Disabled access and facilities are good (no push chairs or baby buggies, though). There are picnic-sets out in a good-sized garden with quiet country views from the sunny terrace, or shade from some mature trees.

Brunning & Price ~ Manager Sam Cornwall-Jones ~ Real ale ~ Bar food (12-10.30(9.30 Sun)) ~ (01952) 815940 ~ Children welcome till 7pm ~ Dogs allowed in bar ~ Open 12-11(10.30 Sun)

GRINSHILL

Inn at Grinshill *Off A49 N of Shrewsbury; SY4 3BL*

The civilised 19th-c bar at the front of this attractively refurbished and well cared for completely no smoking early Georgian inn takes its name from the pub's former name: the Elephant and Castle. Greene King Ruddles, Hanbys Drawell and Theakstons XB, plus a guest from a brewer such as Batemans are well kept on handpump; TV, piped music, dominoes, and an evening pianist on Friday. The spacious contemporary styled main restaurant has a view straight into the kitchen, and doors into the rear garden, which is laid out with tables and chairs. Prepared with care, food is imaginative and very good. At lunchtime and before 7.30 during weekdays you can take advantage of the 'lunchtime and early bird menu', with three courses for £9.95. Though not at all high, the nearby hill of Grinshill has an astonishingly far-ranging view.

Free house ~ Licensees Kevin and Victoria Brazier ~ Real ale ~ Bar food (12-2.30, 6.30-9.30; not Sun evening) ~ Restaurant ~ (01939) 220410 ~ Children welcome ~ Dogs allowed in bar ~ Open 11-3, 6-11; 12-4 Sun; closed Sun evening ~ Bedrooms: £60S/£120B

LITTLE STRETTON

Ragleth *Village signposted off A49 S of Church Stretton; Ludlow Road; SY6 6RB*

This completely no smoking family friendly pub has been nicely opened up and refurbished by very friendly new licensees. The bay-windowed front bar, with a warming fire in winter, is now lighter and airier with fresh plaster and an eclectic mix of light wood old tables and chairs, and some of the original wall brick and timber work has been exposed. The heavily beamed brick-and-tile-floored public bar has a huge inglenook; darts and juke box; piped music. Courage Directors, Hobsons Best and an Archers guest are well kept on handpump. Served by friendly young staff, bar food is good, and sensibly priced. Tables on the lawn (where there's a tulip tree) look across to a thatched and timbered church that looks ancient, but was actually built this century, and there's a good play area.

Free house ~ Licensees Chris and Wendy Davis ~ Real ale ~ Bar food (12-2.30, 6.30-9.30(9 Sun)) ~ Restaurant ~ (01694) 722711 ~ Children welcome ~ Dogs allowed in bar ~ Open 12-3, 6.30-11; 12-11 Sat; 12-10.30 Sun; 12-3, 6.30-10.30 Sun in winter

PICKLESCOTT

Bottle & Glass *Village signposted off A49 N of Church Stretton; SY6 6NR*

The jovial character of the whimsical bow-tied landlord ensures a cheery welcoming atmosphere at this really lovely old 16th-c pub. He works hard to make sure everyone is happy, easily running the bar and striking up conversations with customers – ask him to tell you about the antics of the resident ghost of the former landlord, Victor. Much to the delight surely of the two resident cats, Hello and Cookie, the fire rarely goes out in the small low beamed and quarry-tiled cosy candlelit no smoking bar. The lounge, dining area and library area (for dining or sitting in), each have their own open fire too. Hobsons, Woods Shropshire Lad and a changing guest beer such as Fullers London Pride are well kept on handpump. The very good home-made bar food is promptly served, in hearty helpings, and the puddings are tasty; unobtrusive piped music. There are picnic-sets in front and the pub has a lovely position 1,000 feet above sea level and near the Long Mynd.

Free house ~ Licensees Paul and Jo Stretton-Downes ~ Real ale ~ Bar food ~ Restaurant ~ (01694) 751345 ~ Children welcome with restrictions ~ Dogs allowed in bar ~ Open 12-3.30, 6-12; closed Sun evening, Mon

Dog Friendly Hotels, B&Bs and Farms

BISHOP'S CASTLE

Castle Hotel *Market Sq, Bishop's Castle, Shropshire SY9 5BN (01588) 638403* £**80**, plus special breaks; 6 spacious rms with fine views. On the site of the old castle keep, this enjoyable 17th/18th-c hotel has good fires, a relaxed and friendly atmosphere, lovely home-made food, well kept beers, and welcoming owners; crown bowling green at top of garden (available for residents); dogs in bedrooms but must be well behaved

CLUN

New House Farm *Clun, Craven Arms, Shropshire SY7 8NJ (01588) 638314* £**65**; 2 rms. Remote 18th-c farmhouse near the Welsh border with plenty of surrounding hillside walks; no smoking homely rooms, packed lunches, good breakfasts, plenty of books, a country garden and peaceful farmland (which includes an Iron Age hill fort), and helpful friendly owner; two resident cats; cl end Oct-Easter; children over 10; dogs in bedrooms if well behaved; bring own bed, must be towelled down if wet; £5

HOPTON WAFERS

Crown *Hopton Wafers, Kidderminster, Worcestershire DY14 0NB (01299) 270372* £**95**, plus special breaks; 18 charming rms. Attractive creeper-covered stone inn in pleasant countryside, with interestingly furnished bar, beams, stonework, and an inglenook fireplace, enjoyable food, decent house wines and well kept real ales, friendly efficient service, and streamside garden; nearby walks; dogs in bedrooms; £10

KNOCKIN

Top Farmhouse *Knockin, Oswestry, Shropshire SY10 8HN (01691) 682582* (2 miles W off A5 via B4396/B4397; turn left in village) £**60**; 3 pretty rms. Most attractive Grade I listed black and white timbered house dating back to the 16th c, with friendly owners, lots of timbers and beams, a log fire in the restful comfortable drawing room, good breakfasts in the large no smoking dining room, and an appealing garden; nearby walks; children over 12; dogs in bedrooms

LONGVILLE

Longville Arms *Longville, Much Wenlock, Shropshire TF13 6DT (01694) 771206* £**60**; 5 comfortable rms in converted stables, with showers. Warmly friendly inn with two spacious bars, well kept real ales, a wide range of enjoyable food in the no smoking restaurant or lounge bar, superb breakfasts, and a large terrace overlooking the big children's play area; fine surrounding walks; disabled access; dogs in bedrooms

LUDLOW

Dinham Hall *Dinham, Ludlow, Shropshire SY8 1EJ (01584) 876464* (1.7 miles off A49; Dinham, which is rd to the Teme bridge below the Castle) **£140**; 13 individually decorated rms, 2 in cottage. Late 18th-c manor house in quiet walled gardens opposite the ruins of Ludlow Castle, with restful lounges, open fires and period furnishings, friendly, helpful staff, and modern british cooking in the elegant no smoking restaurant; dogs in cottage bedrooms only; £20

NORTON

Hundred House *Bridgnorth Rd, Norton, Shifnal, Shropshire TF11 9EE (01952) 730353* (on A442 S of Telford), **£125** plus special breaks; 10 cottagey rms with lavender-scented sheets. Carefully refurbished mainly Georgian inn with quite a sophisticated feel, neatly kept bar with old quarry-tiled floors, beamed ceilings, oak panelling and handsome fireplaces, elaborate evening meals using inn's own herbs in no smoking restaurant, friendly service, good bar food, and excellent breakfasts; delightful garden (dogs allowed here under owner's control) and walks at Ironbridge Gorge and the Severn Walking Trail; cl 25-27 Dec; dogs in bedrooms if well behaved; £10

RHYDYCROESAU

Pen-y-Dyffryn Hall *Rhydycroesau, Oswestry, Shropshire SY10 7JD (01691) 653700* **£106**, plus special breaks; 12 rms with really helpful information packs about where to go. No smoking, handsome Georgian stone-built rectory in five acres with lovely views of the Shropshire and Welsh hills, and trout fishing, hill-walking and riding (shooting can be arranged); log fires in both comfortable lounges, good food using the best local ingredients, helpful staff, and a relaxed friendly atmosphere; two resident dogs; lovely nearby woodland for walks; children over 3; disabled access; dogs welcome away from restaurant

STREFFORD

Strefford Hall Farm *Strefford, Craven Arms, Shropshire SY7 8DE (01588) 672383* (0.2 miles off A49; minor rd E, just under a mile N of A489 junction – farm is then on right) **£60**; 3 rms. No smoking Victorian stone-built farmhouse surrounded by 360 acres of working farm; woodburner in sitting room, good breakfasts in sunny dining room with home-made preserves and local honey (pubs and restaurants nearby for evening meals), and lots of walks; three resident dogs and several cats; self-catering and farm shop, too; cl Dec and Jan; dogs welcome in bedrooms

WORFIELD

Old Vicarage *Hallon, Worfield, Bridgnorth, Shropshire WV15 5JZ (01746) 716497* (1.5 miles off A442, from Lower Alscot) **£140**, plus special breaks; 14 pretty rms. Restful and carefully restored no smoking Edwardian rectory in two acres; two airy conservatory-style lounges, very good interesting food in no smoking restaurant, a fine wine list, a cosseting atmosphere, and

warmly friendly, helpful service; two resident dogs; cl Christmas; good
disabled access; dogs in bedrooms; £10

WREKIN
Buckatree Hall *Wrekin, Telford, Shropshire TF6 5AL (01952) 641821* (1.4
miles off M54 junction 7; S on minor rd towards The Wrekin, then 1st left)
£85; 62 neatly decorated rms, several with own balconies and many with
lake views. Comfortable former hunting lodge dating from 1820, in large
wooded estate at the foot of the Wrekin; extended and modernised with
comfortable day rooms, enjoyable food in the Terrace Restaurant, and
helpful attentive service; dogs welcome in bedrooms

WROCKWARDINE
Church Farm *Wrockwardine, Telford, Shropshire TF6 5DG (01952)
244917* (1.7 miles off M54 junction 7, via Drummery Lane (1st right,
heading W on B5061 from exit)) £58, plus special breaks; 5 individual well
equipped rms, most with own bthrm. Friendly Georgian farmhouse on
very ancient site overlooking the attractive garden and church; a relaxed
atmosphere, particularly good caring service, beams and log fire in lounge,
and good daily changing food in traditionally furnished no smoking dining
room; two resident dogs; walking in surrounding footpaths; children over
10; dogs in certain bedrooms; £5

Somerset

Dog Friendly Pubs

ASHILL
Square & Compass *Windmill Hill; off A358 between Ilminster and Taunton; up Wood Road for 1 mile behind Stewley Cross service station; OS Sheet 193 map reference 310166; TA19 9NX*
The well worn edges of this nicely remote simple pub are very much part of the appeal. It's an impressive spot, with sweeping views over the rolling pastures around Neroche Forest from the upholstered window seats in the little bar; there are other seats and an open winter fire – and perhaps the pub cats Daisy and Lilly. Butcombe, Exmoor Ale, Flowers IPA and St Austell HSD on handpump; skittle alley. Very generously served bar food is very traditional. The piped music is often classical. There's a garden with picnic-sets, and regular live music in their Barn.
Free house ~ Licensees Chris, Janet and Beth Slow ~ Real ale ~ Bar food (not Tues, Weds or Thurs lunchtimes) ~ (01823) 480467 ~ Children welcome ~ Dogs welcome ~ Monthly live music in separate barn ~ Open 12-2.30, 6.30-11; 12-2.30, 7-10.30 Sun; closed Tues, Weds and Thurs lunchtimes; 25/26 Dec

BATCOMBE
Three Horseshoes *Village signposted off A359 Bruton—Frome; BA4 6HE*
Very much a dining pub, with a wide range of thoughtfully prepared food, this well placed and attractive honey-coloured stone house now has bedrooms – we look forward to reports on these from readers. Smartly traditional, the longish narrow main room has beams, local pictures on the lightly ragged dark pink walls, built-in cushioned window seats and solid chairs around a nice mix of old tables, a woodburning stove at one end, and a big open fire at the other; at the back on the left, the snug has dark panelled walls, tiled floors, and old pictures. They plan to introduce duck spit roasts by the time this edition hits the shops. The no smoking, stripped stone dining room is pretty (no mobile phones allowed). They recommend booking at weekends, and you may otherwise find all the tables reserved. Butcombe Bitter and Bats in the Belfry (brewed for the pub) and Wadworths 6X on handpump, and ten wines by two sizes of glass. The back terrace has picnic-sets, with more on the grass, outdoor heaters, and a

pond with koi carp. The pub is on a quiet village lane by the church which has a very striking tower.

Free house ~ Licensees Bob Wood and Shirley Greaves ~ Real ale ~ Bar food (not Mon) ~ Restaurant ~ (01749) 850359 ~ Children in eating area of bar and restaurant lunchtimes only; must be over 12 evenings ~ Dogs allowed in bar ~ Guitarist/singer Thurs night ~ Open 12-3, 6.30-11; 12-3, 7-10.30 Sun; closed all day Mon; evening 25 Dec ~ Bedrooms: £50B/£75B

BATH

King William *Thomas Street, corner with A4 London Road – may be no nearby parking; BA1 5NN*

This little corner pub has good food (and drink), and seems all the better for being not at all smart. Its two plain rooms have simple seating and just three chunky old tables each on dark bare boards, and big windows looking out on the busy street; at night heavy curtains can keep out the lights of the traffic. It's certainly a place where people are comfortable just dropping in for a drink or a chat. They have Blindmans Golden Spring, Otter and Palmers Copper on handpump, and a fine choice of good wines in two glass sizes, including good sherries and ports. However, the special draw here is the good individual food, much of which is good and hearty. Helpful informal service by nice young staff, daily papers, a few lighted church candles, and perhaps a big bunch of lilies on the counter. Steep stairs go up to a simple and attractive dining room, used mainly on Wednesday to Saturday evenings, decorated with Jane Grigson *British Cooking* prints.

Free house ~ Licensees Charlie and Amanda Digney ~ Real ale ~ Bar food (12-2.30, 6-10; not Sun evening) ~ Restaurant ~ (01225) 428096 ~ Children welcome ~ Dogs allowed in bar ~ Open 12-3, 5-11(12 Fri); 12-12 Sat; 12-11 Sun

Star *23 Vineyards; The Paragon (A4), junction with Guinea Lane; BA1 5NA*

On a street of undeniably handsome if well worn stone terraces, this honest old town pub has a historic interior that hasn't changed for years. It's the brewery tap for Abbey Ales, so among the three or four well kept real ales you'll always find Abbey Bellringer – and Bass tapped stright from the cask. Not smart, the four (well, more like three and a half) small linked rooms are served from a single bar, separated by sombre panelling with glass inserts. They are furnished with traditional leatherette wall benches and the like – even one hard bench that the regulars call Death Row – and the lighting's dim, and not rudely interrupted by too much daylight. With no machines or music, chat's the thing here – or perhaps cribbage, dominoes and shove-ha'penny. Food is limited to filled rolls only (served throughout opening hours during the week) – though they have rather unusual bar nibbles Sunday lunchtime and Thursday evening; friendly staff and customers. The pub can get busy at weekends.

Punch ~ Lease Paul Waters and Alan Morgan ~ Real ale ~ Bar food (see text) ~ (01225) 425072 ~ Dogs allowed in bar ~ Open 12-2.30, 5.30-12; 12-12 Sat; 12-10.30 Sun

CHURCHILL

Crown *The Batch; in village, turn off A368 into Skinners Lane at Nelson Arms, then bear right; BS25 5PP*

Unspoilt and characterful, this bustling little cottage is a real favourite with some readers, particularly those who like their pubs simple and unpretentious rather than pristine and modern. For some the atmosphere is the main draw, but others come for the excellent range of well kept real ales, with up to ten tapped from the cask, usually including Bass, Bath Spa, Cotleigh Batch, Hop Back GFB, Palmers IPA, RCH Hewish and PG Steam, and two changing guests; also farm ciders. Especially busy at weekends, the small and rather local-feeling stone-floored and cross-beamed room on the right has a wooden window seat, an unusually sturdy settle, and built-in wall benches; the left-hand room has a slate floor, and some steps past the big log fire in a big stone fireplace lead to more sitting space. No noise from music or games (except perhaps dominoes), just a steady murmur of happy chat. Straightforward lunchtime bar food. Outside lavatories. There are garden tables on the front and a smallish back lawn, and hill views; the Mendip Morris Men come in summer. Good walks nearby.

Free house ~ Licensee Tim Rogers ~ Real ale ~ Bar food (12-2.30; not evenings) ~ No credit cards ~ (01934) 852995 ~ Children welcome away from bar ~ Dogs welcome ~ Open 11-11; 12-11 Sun

COMPTON MARTIN

Ring o' Bells *A368 Bath—Weston; BS40 6JE*

Overlooked by the Mendip Hills, this bustling family-friendly country pub is in an attractive position, and there's a friendly welcome from the landlord and his staff. The cosy, traditional front part of the bar has rugs on the flagstones and inglenook seats right by the log fire, and up a step is a spacious carpeted back part with largely stripped stone walls and pine tables. Well kept Butcombe Bitter, Blond, and Gold and a guest like Bath Gem on handpump, and bar food is fairly straightforward; darts, cribbage and dominoes in the public bar. The lounge and eating areas are no smoking; a family room has blackboards and chalks, a Brio track, and a rocking horse. The big garden has swings, a slide and a climbing frame. Blagdon Lake and Chew Valley Lake are not far away.

Butcombe ~ Real ale ~ Bar food ~ Restaurant ~ (01761) 221284 ~ Children in family room ~ Dogs allowed in bar ~ Open 11.30-3, 6-11; 12-3, 6.30-10.30 Sun

CONGRESBURY

White Hart *Wrington Road, which is off A370 Bristol—Weston just E of village – keep on; BS49 5AN*

The L-shaped main bar of this pleasant country dining pub has a few heavy black beams in the bowed ceiling of its longer leg, along with country-kitchen chairs around good-sized tables, and a big stone inglenook fireplace at each end, with woodburning stoves and lots of copper pans. The short leg of the L is more cottagey, with wooden games and other bric-a-brac above yet another fireplace and on a delft shelf, lace and old-gold brocaded curtains, and brocaded wall seats. A roomy family Parlour Bar, open to the main bar, is similar in mood, though with lighter-coloured country-style furniture, some stripped stone and shiny black panelling, and big bright airy conservatory windows on one side; the restaurant is no smoking. The home-made traditional bar food is promptly served; decent children's menu, and they're happy to help with dietary requirements such as gluten or dairy free dishes. Badger Fursty Ferret, Gold and Tanglefoot on handpump; shove-ha'penny, cribbage, dominoes and table skittles. There are picnic-sets under an arbour on the terrace behind, and in the big landscaped garden (fom which, beyond the tall trees, you may see the Mendips).

Badger ~ Tenants Paul Merrick and Rebecca North ~ Real ale ~ Bar food (12-2, 6-9.30(9 Sun); maybe longer in summer) ~ Restaurant ~ (01934) 833303 ~ Children allowed away from bar, but not late at night ~ Dogs welcome ~ Open 11.30-2.30, 6-11; 12-3, 6-10.30 Sun; closed 25 Dec

CROWCOMBE
Carew Arms *Village (and pub) signposted just off A358 Taunton—Minehead; TA4 4AD*

A nicely located 17th-c beamed inn, with a genuinely friendly welcome from the family in charge. The front bar has long benches and a couple of old long deal tables on its dark flagstones, a high-backed antique settle by the woodburning stove in its huge brick inglenook fireplace, and a thoroughly non-PC collection of hunting trophies to remind you that this is the Quantocks. (Another reminder is the freedom dogs enjoy throughout the pub.) A back room behind the bar is a carpeted and gently updated version of the front one, and on the right is a library, and residents' lounge. The smart no smoking dining room has doors to one side leading to an outside terrace where you can eat in fine weather. Exmoor Ale and either Fox, Gold or Hart on handpump, along with a changing beer from the Cottage Brewery, eight wines by the glass, Lane's strong farm cider, and a dozen malt whiskies. Dominoes, cribbage, darts, skittle alley, fruit machine and piped music (only in the Garden Room); several dogs. The sensibly imaginative bar food is particularly enjoyable, though some dishes may run out at busy times, and the informal service can seem erratic at times – some readers find this all part of the charm, but a few do not. Though the jazz is usually monthly, it may be more frequent in summer. Picnic-sets out on the back grass look over rolling wooded pasture, and the attractive village at the foot of the hills has a fine old church and church house.

Free house ~ Licensees Simon and Reg Ambrose ~ Real ale ~ Bar food (not winter Sun evenings) ~ Restaurant ~ (01984) 618631 ~ Children in restaurant ~ Dogs welcome ~ Live jazz monthly, Sun lunchtime ~ Open 11-3.30, 5-12; 11-1am Sat; 11-midnight Sun; closed weekend afternoons in winter ~ Bedrooms: £49B/£79B

DOULTING
Waggon & Horses *Doulting Beacon, 2 miles N of Doulting; eastwards turn off A37 on Mendip ridge N of Shepton Mallet, just S of A367 junction; pub is also signed from A37 at Beacon Hill crossroads and from the A361 at Doulting and Cranmore crossroads; BA4 4LA*

The big walled garden at this bustling pub is very enjoyable on a fine day, with tables and chairs on a terrace, picnic-sets out on the grass, and perennials and flowering shrubs interspersed in a pretty and pleasantly informal way. There's a wildlife pond, several rabbits, and a climber for children. Inside, the rambling bar has studded red leatherette seats and other chairs, a homely mix of tables including antiques, Butcombe Bitter, Greene King IPA and Wadworths 6X on handpump, and quite a few wines by the glass. Half the pub is no smoking. Bar food tends to be fairly traditional. The new licensees appear to be settling in well, and they still have music nights organised by the previous landlord.

InnSpired ~ Lease Simon Cooke and Clare Wilson ~ Real ale ~ Bar food (11.30-2.30, 6.30-9.30) ~ Restaurant ~ (01749) 880302 ~ Children tolerated but must be well-behaved and quiet ~ Dogs allowed in bar ~ Jazz 1st Fri of month ~ Open 11.30-3, 6-11; 12-3, 7-11 Sun

DULVERTON
Woods *Bank Square; TA22 9BU*

Originally a baker's and café known some decades ago as Woods Refreshment and Chocolate House, this was reopened in 2004 after rebuilding as a comfortable bar with some emphasis on good interesting food. They take particular care with their puddings, and the evening menu is rather more elaborate than the lunchtime menu. The atmosphere is comfortably relaxed, mildly upmarket in a country way, and very Exmoor – plenty of good sporting prints on the salmon pink walls, some antlers, other hunting trophies and stuffed birds, a couple of salmon rods. There are bare boards on the left by the bar counter, which has four changing local ales from brewers such as Exmoor, Otter, St Austell and O'Hanlons on handpump, and Cheddar Valley farm cider. You can order any of the 400 or so wines from the amazing wine list by the glass, and the landlord also keeps an unlisted collection of about 500 old new world wines which he will happily chat about; they have daily papers. Its tables partly separated by stable-style timbering and masonry dividers, the bit on the right is carpeted and has a woodburning stove in the big fireplace set into its end wall, which has varnished plank panelling. There may be unobjectionable piped music. Big windows keep you in touch with what's going on out in the quiet town centre (or you can sit out on the pavement at a couple of metal tables). A small suntrap back courtyard has a few picnic-sets.

Free house ~ Licensee Patrick Groves ~ Real ale ~ Bar food (12-2, 6-9.45(7-9.30 Sun)) ~ Restaurant ~ (01398) 324007 ~ Children welcome ~ Dogs allowed in bar ~ Open 11-3, 6-12(1 Sat); 12-3, 7-10.30 Sun

EXFORD
White Horse *B3224; TA24 7PY*

The hands-on licensee and helpful staff have both been praised by readers visiting this substantial creeper-covered coaching inn in recent months. It's a pretty spot in summer, with the River Exe running past; there are tables outside to enjoy the view. The more or less open-plan bar has windsor and other country kitchen chairs, a high-backed antique settle, scrubbed deal tables, hunting prints, photographs above the stripped pine dado and a good winter log fire; it can get very busy. Up to five real ales on handpump (less in winter), usually Exmoor Ale, Fox and Gold, Fullers London Pride and Greene King Old Speckled Hen, and a fine collection of malt whiskies, currently standing at around 150, but aiming for 200 by 2007. Bar food is straightforward but very good value, and they do cream teas all day. The restaurant and eating area of the bar are no smoking. They run daily Landrover 'safaris' of Exmoor's wildlife. Note the price we quote for bedrooms is their standard rate – they often have cheaper rooms so it's worth checking. Though the old coach road climbs from here up over Exmoor, the attractive village itself is sheltered; the village green with children's play equipment is next to the pub.

Free house ~ Licensees Peter and Linda Hendrie ~ Real ale ~ Bar food (12-2.30, 6-9.30) ~ Restaurant ~ (01643) 831229 ~ Children welcome ~ Dogs allowed in bar and bedrooms ~ Open 11-11(12 Sat) ~ Bedrooms: £63B/£126B

HUISH EPISCOPI
Rose & Crown *Off A372 E of Langport; TA10 9QT*
Known locally as 'Eli's' after the friendly landlady's father, this very unspoilt thatched pub has been in the same family for well over 140 years. It's a real step back in time, with a determinedly unpretentious atmosphere and character: there's no bar as such – to get a drink, you just walk into the central flagstoned still room and choose from the casks of Teignworthy Reel Ale and guests such as Hopback GFB and Sharps Doombar. Also offering several farm ciders (and local cider brandy), this servery is the only thoroughfare between the casual little front parlours with their unusual pointed-arch windows – and genuinely friendly locals. Food is home-made, simple and cheap and uses local produce (and some home-grown fruit and vegetables): good helpful service. Shove-ha'penny, dominoes and cribbage, and a much more orthodox big back extension family room has pool, darts, fruit machine and juke box; skittle alley and popular quiz nights. One room is no smoking. There are tables in a garden, and a second enclosed garden with a children's play area. The welsh collie is called Bonny. Summer morris men, good nearby walks, and the site of the Battle of Langport (1645) is close by.

Free house ~ Licensee Mrs Eileen Pittard ~ Real ale ~ Bar food (12-2, 5.30-7.30; not Sun evening) ~ No credit cards ~ (01458) 250494 ~ Children welcome ~ Dogs welcome ~ Folk singers every 3rd Sat and irish night 4th Thurs in month Sept-May ~ Open 11.30-2.30, 5.30-11; 11.30-11 Fri and Sat; 12-10.30 Sun; closed evening 25 Dec

LOVINGTON
Pilgrims Rest *B3153 Castle Cary—Keinton Mandeville; BA7 7PT*
With the emphasis very much on the top quality imaginative food cooked by the landlord (using local produce and daily fresh fish), this quietly placed and civilised country bar/bistro is rather upmarket, but not in a stuffy way: there's a relaxed, chatty atmosphere, and a nice unhurried feel – even on busy nights they won't rush you with your food. They do smaller helpings of most things, including their two-course Sunday lunch.Totally no

smoking, the bar has a few stools by a corner counter, a rack of daily papers, nice wines by the glass and Cottage Champflower on handpump, from the nearby brewery. A cosy little dark green inner area has sunny modern country and city prints, a couple of shelves of books and china, a cushioned pew, a couple of settees and an old leather easy chair by the big fireplace. With flagstones throughout, this runs into the compact eating area, with candles on tables and some stripped stone; piped music. There's also a separate, more formal carpeted dining room. The landlady's service is efficient and friendly. The enclosed garden has tables, chairs and umbrellas on a decked terrace. The car park exit has its own traffic lights – on your way out line your car up carefully or you may wait for ever for them to change.

Free house ~ Licensees Sally and Jools Mitchison ~ Real ale ~ Bar food (see opening hours) ~ Restaurant ~ (01963) 240597 ~ Children welcome ~ Dogs allowed in bar ~ Open 12-2.30, 7-11; closed Sun evening, all day Mon and Tues, plus first week of May and first two weeks of October

LUXBOROUGH
Royal Oak *Kingsbridge; S of Dunster on minor roads into Brendon Hills – OS Sheet 181 map reference 983378; TA23 0SH*

In the heart of Exmoor, this is a fine place to stay in, with temptingly enjoyable and imaginative food and a particularly warm welcome from staff who go out of their way to make visits special. Recently sensitively refurbished, the bar rooms date back to the 14th c, and have beams and inglenooks, good log fires, flagstones in the front public bar, a fishing theme in one room, and a real medley of furniture; the three dining rooms are no smoking. Well kept Cotleigh Tawny, Exmoor Gold and Palmers IPA and 200 on handpump, local farm ciders, and a good range of malt whiskies. No music or machines; darts, dominoes and board games. If you're staying, expect comfortable bedrooms and good, generous breakfasts. Tables out in the charming back courtyard, and lots of surrounding walks, notably the recently opened Coleridge Way.

Free house ~ Licensees James and Sian Waller and Sue Hinds ~ Real ale ~ Bar food ~ Restaurant ~ (01984) 640319 ~ Children in dining rooms and bedrooms only ~ Dogs allowed in bar and bedrooms ~ Open 12-2.30, 6 (7 Sun)-11; closed 25 Dec ~ Bedrooms: £55B/£60(£65B)

MONKSILVER
Notley Arms *B3188; TA4 4JB*

The good, generously served food at this bustling nicely set pub has a real emphasis on fresh, local produce, and the menu lists the suppliers of everything from their meats, fish and cheese to the ice-cream, potatoes and eggs. Good service from the friendly staff and attentive landlord. They can get busy, even midweek and out of season. The beamed and L-shaped bar has small settles and kitchen chairs around the plain country wooden and candlelit tables, original paintings on the ochre-coloured walls fresh flowers, and a couple of woodburning stoves. Bath Ale, Exmoor Ale and Wadworths 6X on handpump, and farm ciders; cribbage, dominoes and alley skittles. There's a bright no smoking little family room (an area near the food servery is no smoking too). The immaculate garden has plenty of tables, and runs down to a swift clear stream. This is a lovely village.

Unique (Enterprise) ~ Lease Russell and Jane Deary ~ Real ale ~ Bar food ~ (01984) 656217 ~ Children in family room if well behaved ~ Dogs welcome ~ Open 12-2.30, 6.30-11; 12-2.30, 7-10.30 Sun; closed Mon lunchtime (all day Mon in winter)

NORTON ST PHILIP
George *A366; BA2 7LH*
The building itself is the main draw here; a pub for nearly 600 years, it's a remarkable old place, very impressive as you approach, and no less interesting inside. The central Norton Room, which was the original bar, has really heavy beams, an oak panelled settle and solid dining chairs on the narrow strip wooden floor, a variety of 18th-c pictures, an open fire in the handsome stone fireplace, and a low wooden bar counter. Wadworths IPA, 6X, and perhaps a seasonal guest on handpump, and pleasant service. As you enter the building, there's a room on the right with high dark beams, squared dark half-panelling, a broad carved stone fireplace with an old iron fireback and pewter plates on the mantelpiece, a big mullioned window with leaded lights, and a round oak 17th-c table reputed to have been used by the Duke of Monmouth who stayed here before the Battle of Sedgemoor – after their defeat, his men were imprisoned in what is now the Monmouth Bar. The Charterhouse Bar is mostly used by those enjoying a drink before a meal: a wonderful pitched ceiling with trusses and timbering, heraldic shields and standards, jousting lances and swords on the walls, a fine old stone fireplace, high backed cushioned heraldic-fabric dining chairs on the big rug over the wood plank floor, and an oak dresser with some pewter. Bar food usually lives up to the surroundings. The no smoking dining room (a restored barn with original oak ceiling beams, a pleasant if haphazard mix of early 19th-c portraits and hunting prints, and the same mix of vaguely old-looking furnishings) has a good relaxing, chatty atmosphere. The bedrooms are very atmospheric and comfortable – some reached by an external Norman stone stair-turret, and some across the cobbled and flagstoned courtyard and up into a fine half-timbered upper gallery (where there's a lovely 18th-c carved oak settle). A stroll over the meadow behind the pub (past the picnic-sets on the narrow grass pub garden) leads to an attractive churchyard around the medieval church whose bells struck Pepys (here on 12 June 1668) as 'mighty tuneable'.

Wadworths ~ Managers David and Tania Satchell ~ Real ale ~ Bar food ~ Restaurant ~ (01373) 834224 ~ Well behaved children welcome ~ Dogs allowed in bar ~ Open 11.30-2.30, 5.30-11; 11-11 Sat; 12-10.30 Sun; closed evenings 25 Dec and 1 Jan ~ Bedrooms: £60B/£80B

PITNEY
Halfway House *Just off B3153 W of Somerton; TA10 9AB*
A warmly friendly, traditional village local, this busy place has an excellent range of changing real ales, with between eight and ten on at any one time;

regular beers tapped from the cask include Branscombe Vale Branoc, Butcombe Bitter, Hop Back Crop Circle and Summer Lightning, and Teignworthy Reel Ale, with guests like Archers Golden, Bath Spa and Otter Bright. They also have 20 or so continental bottled beers, Wilkins's farm cider, and a dozen malt whiskies; cribbage, dominoes and board games. There's a good mix of people chatting at communal tables in the three old-fashioned rooms, all with roaring log fires and a homely feel underlined by a profusion of books, maps and newspapers; it can get a bit smoky. The traditional bar food is good, simple and filling, and in the evening they do about half a dozen home-made curries. There are tables outside.

Free house ~ Licensee Julian Lichfield ~ Real ale ~ Bar food (not Sun) ~ (01458) 252513 ~ Children welcome ~ Dogs allowed in bar ~ Open 11.30-3, 5.30-11(12 Sat); 12-3, 7-11 Sun; closed 25 Dec

SHEPTON MONTAGUE

Montague Inn *Village signposted just off A359 Bruton—Castle Cary; BA9 8JW*

This busy little country pub is doing well under its newish licensees, who readers have particularly praised for their friendly welcome and helpful service. Recently redecorated, the rooms are simply but tastefully furnished with stripped wooden tables and kitchen chairs, and a log fire in the attractive inglenook fireplace; the restaurant has french windows overlooking the pretty back terrace and gardens, now tidied up with clearer views. Using regional and often organic ingredients, the mostly traditional bar food is made fresh every day – they don't have a freezer. Butcombe, Greene King IPA and a local guest like Hidden Brewery Hidden Quest tapped from the cask, local cider, and a big varied wine list with a good choice by the glass.

Free house ~ Licensee Sean O'Callaghan ~ Bar food (not Sun evening, Mon) ~ Restaurant ~ (01749) 813213 ~ Children welcome ~ Dogs allowed in bar ~ Open 12-3, 6-11; closed evening Sun and all day Mon ~ Bedrooms: /£75S

STOKE ST GREGORY

Rose & Crown *Woodhill; follow North Curry signpost off A378 by junction with A358 – keep on to Stoke, bearing right in centre, passing church and follow lane for ½ mile; TA3 6EW*

A thriving family business, this bustling country pub has a cheerful, friendly feel, and is well liked for its food. Not smart (even some of its staunchest supporters this year felt a tidying-up was probably in order), the cosy bar is decorated in a pleasant stable theme: dark wooden loose-box partitions for some of the interestingly angled nooks and alcoves, lots of brasses and bits on the low beams and joists, stripped stonework, a wonky floor, and appropriate pictures including a highland pony carrying a stag. Many of the wildlife paintings on the walls are the work of the landlady, and there's an 18th-c glass-covered well in one corner. The two rooms of the dining rarea lead off here with lots of country prints and paintings of hunting scenes, animals and birds on the walls, more horsebrasses, jugs and mugs hanging from the ceiling joists, and candles in bottles on all tables. Bar food is very pubby at lunchtime with slightly more imaginative evening dishes; helpful, polite service. The restaurants are no smoking. Butcombe, Exmoor Ale and Otter on handpump, and decent wines; piped music and fruit machine. Under cocktail parasols by an apple tree on the sheltered front terrace are some picnic-sets. Readers who've stayed in the modest bedrooms don't rate them as highly as they do the food or atmosphere. The pub is in an interesting Somerset Levels village with willow beds still supplying the two basket works.

Free house ~ Licensees Stephen, Sally, Richard and Leonie Browning ~ Real ale ~ Bar food ~ Restaurant ~ (01823) 490296 ~ Children welcome ~ Dogs allowed in bar ~ Open 11-3, 6.30-11; 12-3, 7-10.30 Sun; closed evening 25 Dec ~ Bedrooms: £36.50(£46.50B)/£53(£73B)

TARR

Tarr Farm *Tarr Steps – rather narrow road off B3223 N of Dulverton, very little nearby parking (paying car park quarter-mile up road); OS Sheet 181 map reference 868322 – as the inn is on the E bank, don't be tempted to approach by car from the W unless you can cope with a deep ford; TA22 9PY*

The setting is glorious, an Exmoor hillside looking down on Tarr Steps just below – that much-photographed clapper bridge of massive granite slabs for medieval packhorses crossing the River Barle as it winds through this lightly wooded coombe. Given the site, the inn does get very busy even out of season, but they work hard here to keep their customers happy. The pub part consists of a line of compact and unpretentious rooms, with plenty of good views, slabby rustic tables, stall seating, wall seats and pub chairs, a woodburning stove at one end, salmon pink walls, nice game bird pictures and a pair of stuffed pheasants. The serving bar up a step or two has Exmoor Ale and St Austell on handpump, eight wines by the glass and a good choice of other drinks. They do a wide range of food, and popular cream teas. The residents' end has a smart little evening restaurant, and a pleasant log-fire lounge with dark leather armchairs and sofas. Outside lots of chaffinches hop around between slate-topped stone tables above the steep lawn.

Free house ~ Licensees Richard Benn and Judy Carless ~ Real ale ~ Bar food (12-3; cream teas 11-5) ~ Restaurant ~ (01643) 851507 ~ Children over 10 in bedrooms and evenings ~ Dogs allowed in bar and bedrooms ~ Open 11-11; closed one week beg. Feb ~ Bedrooms: £80B/£130B

WITHYPOOL

Royal Oak *Village signposted off B3233; TA24 7QP*

Tucked down below some of the most attractive parts of Exmoor, this country local has a nicely old-fashioned beamed interior and a particularly welcoming atmosphere. There's a fine raised log fireplace in the lounge, as well as comfortably cushioned wall seating and slat-backed chairs, sporting trophies and paintings, and various copper and brass ornaments on its walls. The locals' bar has some old oak tables, and plenty of character. Exmoor Ale and a guest like Courage Best or Exmoor Gold on handpump, and several wines by the glass. Not cheap bar food, and no smoking dining room.   R D Blackmore stayed in this country village inn while writing *Lorna Doone*. There are wooden benches on the terrace, and just up the road some grand views from Winsford Hill. The River Barle runs through the village itself, with pretty bridleways following it through a wooded combe further upstream.

Coast & Country Inns ~ Managers Helga Tarttaglione and James Allen ~ Real ale ~ Bar food (12-2, 6.30-9) ~ (01643) 831506 ~ Children in eating area of bar and restaurant ~ Dogs allowed in bar and bedrooms ~ Open 11-11; 12-10.30 Sun; closed 25 Dec ~ Bedrooms: £65B/£110B

Dog Friendly Hotels, B&Bs and Farms

BABINGTON

Babington House *Babington, Frome, Somerset BA11 3RW* (01373) 812266 £225; 28 individually decorated, well equipped contemporary rms, 12 in coach house, 5 in stable block, 3 in lodge. Georgian mansion in lovely grounds with cricket and football pitches, indoor and outdoor swimming pools, walled garden, tennis courts and croquet; interestingly decorated lounges, comfortable sofas and an open fire in bar; library, pool room; a wide range of good food in both contemporary Log Room restaurant and light and air House Kitchen, a particularly relaxed, informal atmosphere, and helpful and welcoming young staff; free cinema with films five days a week, and lots for children to do; gym, sauna, steam and aroma rooms, and treatment cabins; disabled access; dogs in some ground floor bedrooms

BARWICK

Little Barwick House *Barwick, Yeovil, Somerset BA22 9TD* (01935) 423902 (0.4 miles off A37 Keyford roundabout, via Church Lane E) £140, plus special breaks; 6 attractive rms. Carefully run listed Georgian dower house in 3½ acres 2m S of Yeovil, and thought of as a restaurant-with-rooms; lovely relaxed atmosphere, log fire in cosy lounge, excellent food using local produce in no smoking dining room, a thoughtful wine list, super breakfasts, nice afternoon tea, and particularly good service; two resident dogs; walks in grounds and nearby; cl 2 wks from Christmas; children over 5; dogs in bedrooms; £5

BATHFORD

Eagle House *23 Church St, Bathford, Bath BA1 7RS* (01225) 859946 £82, plus winter breaks; 8 rms, 2 in cottage with sitting room and kitchen. Friendly and relaxed B&B in Georgian house with homely furnishings and family mementoes, winter log fires, elegant drawing room, nice continental breakfasts in no smoking breakfast room (full english is extra), and two-acre gardens with tennis, croquet, treehouse and swings (dogs may walk here but public footpaths close by, too); resident dog and cat; plenty to do nearby; cl 12 Dec–8 Jan; dogs in bedrooms and public rooms by arrangement; £3.50

BRUTON
Bruton House *2-4 High Street, Bruton, Somerset BA1 0AA (01749) 813395* **£85**; 3 recently refurbished rms. Beautifully restored Georgian building housing a restaurant-with-rooms; residents' sitting room and bar, good breakfasts with daily newspapers, and super, locally sourced food in small, intimate restaurant; terrace with lovely views over to the Dovecote and St Mary's church; dogs in bedrooms if well behaved; dog bed, bowl and goodie bag

HATCH BEAUCHAMP
Farthings *Hatch Beauchamp, Taunton, Somerset TA3 6SG (01823) 480664* (0.5 miles off A358 SE of Taunton) **£110**, plus special breaks; 9 pretty rms with thoughtful extras. Charming no smoking Georgian house in two acres of gardens; open fires in comfortable lounge, convivial bar, and good varied food using fresh local produce in two elegant dining rooms; plenty of open countryside for walks; dogs in some bedrooms; must be well behaved

HOLFORD
Combe House *Holford, Bridgwater, Somerset TA5 1RZ (01278) 741382* **£125**, plus special breaks; 15 rms. Warmly friendly and no smoking former tannery (still has waterwheel) in a pretty spot, with comfortable rooms, log fires, good home-made food and a relaxed atmosphere; heated indoor swimming pool and tennis court; two resident dogs and two cats; walks on the Quantock Hills; dogs in bedrooms and bar; £3

HUNSTRETE
Hunstrete House *Hunstrete, Pensford, Bristol BS39 4NS (01761) 490490* (1.5 miles off A37 from Chelwood via A368 E) **£215.25**, plus special breaks; 25 individually decorated rms. Classically handsome, mainly 18th-c country-house hotel on the edge of the Mendips, in 92 acres inc lovely Victorian walled garden and deer park (plenty of walks); comfortable and elegantly furnished day rooms with antiques, paintings, log fires, fresh garden flowers, a tranquil atmosphere, excellent service, and very good food using home-grown produce when possible; croquet lawn, heated outdoor swimming pool, all-weather tennis court, and nearby riding; limited disabled access; dogs in bedrooms; £10

LANGFORD BUDVILLE
Bindon Country House *Langford Budville, Wellington, Somerset TA21 0RU (01823) 400070* **£115**; 12 stylish rms. Tranquil 17th-c house designed as a bavarian hunting lodge and set in seven acres of formal and woodland gardens; comfortable, elegant drawing room, panelled bar, and intimate no smoking restaurant all decorated with Duke of Wellington memorabilia, enjoyable modern cooking and a thoughtful wine list; outdoor swimming pool, tennis and croquet; dogs in some bedrooms

LUXBOROUGH
Royal Oak *Luxborough, Watchet, Somerset TA23 0SH (01984) 640319*
£65; 12 rms. Unspoilt and interesting old pub in idyllic spot, marvellous
for exploring Exmoor; bar rooms with log fires in inglenook fireplaces,
beams, flagstones, character furnishings and a thriving feel, four distinctive
no smoking dining rooms, and good food and real ales; dogs in bedrooms
and bar area

NETHER STOWEY
Old Cider House *25 Castle St, Nether Stowey, Bridgwater, Somerset TA5
1LN (01278) 732228* **£60**, plus special breaks; 5 individually decorated
rms. Carefully restored Edwardian house (previously used to produce cider)
in secluded garden, with big comfortable lounge, log fire, delicious
breakfasts (their own bread and preserves) and imaginative, candlelit
evening meals using home-grown and local produce, and a small carefully
chosen wine list; plenty of walks and dog friendly beaches nearby; dogs if
well behaved are welcome; £3.50

SHEPTON MALLET
Charlton House and Mulberry Restaurant *Charlton Rd, Shepton
Mallet, Somerset BA4 4PR (01749) 342008* (0.5 miles off A37; A361 E)
£180, plus special breaks; 25 attractive and stylish rooms with nice extras,
and large bthrms. Substantial Georgian hotel in landscaped grounds (dogs
must be kept on a lead); bare-boarded rooms with oriental rugs, dark red
walls with lots of old photographs and posters, and showcasing the owners'
Mulberry style of informal furnishings; smart dining room and three-bay
conservatory, restored 18th-c orangery dining room, exceptionally good
modern cooking, interesting wines, and helpful, efficient uniformed staff;
seats on the back terrace overlooking a big lawn, and croquet; health spa;
they are kind to children; disabled access; dogs in the lodge and public
areas; £10

SOMERTON
Lynch Country House *4 Behind Berry, Somerton, Somerset TA11 7PD
(01458) 272316* **£60**; 8 prettily decorated rms, plus 3 extra in summer
cottage. Carefully restored and homely Georgian house, with books in
comfortable lounge, and good breakfasts (no evening meals) in airy room
overlooking tranquil grounds and lake with black swans and exotic ducks;
self-catering, too; cl Christmas and New Year; disabled access; dogs
welcome in bedrooms

STON EASTON
Ston Easton Park *Ston Easton, Bath BA3 4DF (01761) 241631* (off A37
just S of A39 junction) **£180**; 22 really lovely rms. Majestic Palladian
mansion of bath stone with beautifully landscaped 18th-c gardens and 26
acres of parkland; elegant day rooms with antiques and flowers, an
attractive no smoking restaurant with good food (much grown in the
kitchen garden), fine afternoon teas, library and billiard room, and

extremely helpful, friendly and unstuffy service; two resident dogs; children over 7 in the dining room; walks in the grounds and lovely surrounding countryside; some disabled access; dogs in bedrooms and some other areas; £10

TAUNTON

Castle *Castle Green, Taunton, Somerset TA1 1NF (01823) 272671* **£220**, plus special breaks; 44 lovely rms. Appealingly modernised partly Norman castle with english cooking in no smoking restaurant and brasserie, good breakfasts, a range of good value wines from a thoughtful list, and efficient friendly service; pretty garden; walks in nearby park; disabled access; dogs in bedrooms, if small; £10

WELLS

Infield House *36 Portway, Wells, Somerset BA5 2BN (01749) 670989* **£52**; 3 comfortable rms (best view from back one). Carefully restored no smoking Victorian town house with period furnishings and family portraits, elegant lounge (with lots of local guidebooks), good breakfasts in dining room with Adam-style fireplace, evening meals by arrangement, and friendly personal service; walks on nearby playing fields; resident dog; cl two wks beg Nov and beg Feb; children over 12; dogs in bedrooms but must not be left unattended

Staffordshire

Dog Friendly Pubs

BURTON UPON TRENT
Burton Bridge Inn *Bridge Street (A50); DE14 1SY*
Gloriously unchanged from one year to the next, this straightforward bustling old brick local is as genuinely friendly and cheerily down-to-earth as ever. It's the tap for Burton Bridge Brewery (out in the long old-fashioned yard at the back) which produces the Bitter, Festival, Golden Delicious, Gold Medal and Porter that are well kept and served on handpump here, alongside a guest such as Timothy Taylors Landlord. They also keep around 25 whiskies and over a dozen country wines. The simple little front area leads into an adjacent bar, separated from a no smoking oak-panelled lounge by the serving counter. The bar has wooden pews, plain walls hung with notices, awards and brewery memorabilia, and the lounge has oak beams, a flame-effect fire and old oak tables and chairs. The few bar snacks on offer are hearty and simple; the panelled upstairs dining room is open only at lunchtime. A blue-brick patio overlooks the brewery.
Own brew ~ Licensees Kevin and Jan McDonald ~ Real ale ~ Bar food (lunchtime only, not Sun) ~ No credit cards ~ (01283) 536596 ~ Dogs welcome ~ Open 11.30-2.15, 5-11; 12-2, 7-10.30 Sun; closed bank hol Mon lunchtime

ENVILLE
Cat *A458 W of Stourbridge (Bridgnorth Road); DY7 5HA*
The nicest part of this pub is the bar closest to the road, where its 17th-c origins seem clearest. Here, two linked carpeted rooms with a slight step between have heavy black beams, ancient timbers showing in the walling, a log fire in a small brick fireplace, cast-iron framed and other pub tables, and brocaded wall seats with comfortable matching oak carver chairs – the tabby cat may have its eye on one, but the quiet collie wouldn't dare. The bar counter has changing Enville real ales on handpump, brewed on the other side of the estate, using honey, to add to their distinctive tastes: typically Ale, White, Ginger or Phoenix on handpump. It also has three or four guests from brewers such as Hop Back, Kinver and Wye Vallley; the landlord can help with your choice. He does mulled wine in winter, and keeps a range of country wines; darts, piped music, games machine. A

speciality here is the sausage mix and mash menu. The sausages are made for the pub by a local butcher, and you get to choose from a list of ten. Then there's a list of eight mashes and eight gravies, in any combination you want. A comfortable back family area has plush wall banquettes and dark tables, and there is a restaurant upstairs, both no smoking. If you don't want sausages there's a traditional menu, and some more imaginative specials. You come into the pub through a splendidly old-fashioned paved yard alongside the monumentally tall and massive estate wall, and back here there are picnic-sets on a gravel terrace. The estate has attractive lakeside grounds, and the pub is also on the Staffordshire Way, so popular with walkers. Until 2004 Sunday walkers went dry here because it was only in that year that the estate lifted a 300-year ban on Sunday drinking.

Free house ~ Licensee Guy Ayres ~ Real ale ~ Bar food (12-2(2.30 Fri, 3 Sun)), 7-9.30; not Sun evening or Mon) ~ Restaurant ~ (01384) 872209 ~ Children in family room and main lounge ~ Dogs allowed in bar ~ Open 12-2.30(3 Sat), 7(6.30 Fri, Sat)-11; 12-5.30 Sun; closed Sun evening

KIDSGROVE
Blue Bell *25 Hardings Wood; off A50 NW edge of town; ST7 1EG*
They take beer very seriously at this simple little pub, converted from two cottages at the junction of the Trent & Mersey and Macclesfield canals. The constantly changing range of six real ales is carefully selected from smaller, often very unsual brewers, typically including Acorn, Crouch Vale, Oakham, Townhouse and Whim. More than two thousand brews have passed through the pumps over the last eight years; current and forthcoming choices are listed on the pub's website, www.bluebellkidsgrove.co.uk. They don't stock beers from the bigger producers, and lagers are restricted to czech or belgian brews; there's also usually a draught continental beer, at least one farm cider, a good range of bottled beers, and various teas, coffees and soft drinks. Service is friendly and knowledgeable. The four small, carpeted rooms are unfussy and straightforward, with only a few tables in each, and blue upholstered benches running around the the white-painted walls; there's a coal fire, and maybe soft piped music. In fine weather there are tables in front, and more on a tiny back lawn. Bar food is limited to filled rolls, at weekends only. Note the limited opening hours, and they may not always open on time: on our sping evening visit quite a crowd was patiently waiting before the doors finally opened.

Free house ~ Licensees Dave and Kay Washbrook ~ Real ale ~ No credit cards ~ (01782) 774052 ~ Well behaved children until 9 ~ Dogs welcome ~ Impromptu folk Sun eves ~ Open evenings only on wkdys, 7.30-11; 1-4, 7-11 Sat; 12-10.30 Sun; closed Mon

Dog Friendly Hotels, B&Bs and Farms

BETLEY
Adderley Green Farm *Heighley Castle Lane, Betley, Crewe, Cheshire CW3 9BA (01270) 820203* £**56**, plus special breaks; 3 rms. Georgian farmhouse on big dairy farm, with good breakfasts in homely dining room, and large garden; cl Christmas and New Year; children over 5; dogs in bedrooms by arrangement; £1

HOPWAS
Oak Tree Farm *Hints Rd, Hopwas, Tamworth, Staffordshire B78 3AA (01827) 56807* (just off A51 W of Tamworth; Hints Rd) £**75**; 8 comfortable, spacious and pretty rms. Carefully restored no smoking farmhouse with elegant little lounge, fresh flowers, an attractive breakfast room, a friendly atmosphere and owners, enjoyable breakfasts, gardens overlooking the River Tame, indoor swimming pool and steam room; cl Christmas–New Year; no children; dogs welcome in bedrooms

ROLLESTON ON DOVE
Brookhouse Hotel *Station Rd, Rolleston on Dove, Burton upon Trent, Staffordshire DE13 9AA (01283) 814188* (1.7 miles N off A38 from A5121 junction E of Stretton, via Claymills Rd and Dovecliff Rd, leading into Station Rd) £**115**, plus wknd breaks; 19 comfortable rms with Victorian brass or four-poster beds. Handsome ivy-covered William & Mary brick building in five acres of lovely gardens with comfortable antiques-filled rooms, and good food using seasonal local produce in elegant little no smoking dining room; resident cat; walks on open farmland; children over 12; disabled access; dogs in ground floor bedrooms only

STOKE-ON-TRENT
Haydon House *Haydon Street, Basford, Stoke-on-Trent, Staffordshire ST4 6JD (01782) 711311* £**55**; 23 rms, some in annexe. Family-run Victorian house with a relaxed, friendly atmosphere, attractive and comfortable cocktail lounge and conservatory, good food (popular locally) in no smoking restaurant, and an extensive wine list; dogs in bedrooms and public areas

TAMWORTH
Old Rectory *Churchside, Harlaston, Tamworth, Staffs B79 9HE (01827) 383583* £**45**; 4 attractive rms overlooking open countryside. Former Victorian rectory in large grounds in award-winning village; spacious sunny kitchen opening onto the garden with enjoyable breakfasts that include home-made preserves and local specialities; resident dog; walks all round; dogs in bedrooms; £2

Suffolk

Dog Friendly Pubs

BUXHALL

Crown *Village signposted off B1115 W of Stowmarket; fork right by post office at Gt Finborough, turn left at Buxhall village sign, then second right into Mill Road, then right at T-junction; IP14 3DW*

This 17th-c timber framed pub is tucked away near a windmill down a quiet country lane. It's now totally no smoking, and the intimate little bar on the left has an open fire in a big inglenook, a couple of small round tables on a tiled floor, and low hop-hung beams. Standing timbers separate it from another area with pews and candles, and flowers in summer on beech tables with leather chairs, and there's a further light and airy room which they call the Mill Restaurant. As well as Cox & Holbrook Old Mill (brewed just two minutes away), they have Greene King IPA, Tindalls Best and Woodfordes Wherry on handpump, and 25 whiskies. Bar food includes some imaginative options and is generally well liked. Plenty of seats and solid wood tables under parasols on the heated terrace, and they've a pretty garden, with nice views over gently rolling countryside. A large enclosed side garden has wooden decking and raised flowerbeds.

Greene King ~ Lease Trevor Golton ~ Real ale ~ Bar food (not Sun evening or Mon) ~ Restaurant ~ (01449) 736521 ~ Children welcome if well behaved ~ Dogs allowed in bar ~ Open 12-3.30, 6.30-11.30; 12-3.30 Sun; closed Sun evening, Mon, 25 and 26 Dec

EARL SOHAM

Victoria *A1120 Yoxford—Stowmarket; IP13 7RL*

It's certainly worth coming to this unpretentious place to enjoy the three Earl Soham beers from the brewery right across the road: Albert, Victoria and Sir Rogers Porter on handpump; farm cider too. There's an easy-going local atmosphere in the well worn bar, which is fairly basic and sparsely furnished, with stripped panelling, kitchen chairs and pews, plank-topped trestle sewing-machine tables and other simple scrubbed pine country tables, tiled or board floors, an interesting range of pictures of Queen Victoria and her reign, and open fires. The short choice of traditional bar food is fairly priced. There are seats on the raised back lawn, with more out in front. The pub is quite close to a wild fritillary meadow at Framlingham, and a working windmill at Saxtead.

Free house ~ Licensee Paul Hooper ~ Real ale ~ Bar food (12-2, 7-10) ~ (01728) 685758 ~ Children welcome ~ Dogs allowed in bar ~ Open 11.30-3, 6-11; 12-3, 7-10.30 Sun

GREAT GLEMHAM

Crown   *Between   A12   Wickham   Market—Saxmundham   and   B1119 Saxmundham—Framlingham; IP17 2DA*

As we went to press we heard that this immaculately kept pub was on the market, so by the time this book is published, there might be new people at the helm. There's a big entrance hall with sofas on rush matting, and an open-plan beamed lounge with wooden pews and captain's chairs around stripped and waxed kitchen tables, local photographs and interesting paintings on cream walls, fresh flowers, and some brass ornaments; log fires in two big fireplaces. They offer a fair choice of good pubby food. Adnams Bitter and Broadside are served from old brass handpumps, and they've seven wines by the glass. A tidy, flower-fringed lawn, raised above the corner of the quiet village lane by a retaining wall, has some seats and tables under cocktail parasols; disabled access. The pub is in a particularly pretty village.

Free house ~ Licensees Barry and Susie Coote ~ Real ale ~ Bar food (not Mon) ~ (01728) 663693 ~ Children welcome ~ Dogs allowed in bar ~ Open 11.30-3, 6.30-11; 12-3, 7-10.30 Sun; closed Mon except bank hols, maybe 2 weeks Oct

LONG MELFORD

Black Lion *Church Walk; CO10 9DN*

Comfortable and civilised, this 400-year-old hotel faces the village green and there are seats and tables under terracotta parasols on the terrace that make the most of the view; more, too in the appealing Victorian walled garden. Inside, one side of the oak serving counter is decorated in ochre, and, besides bar stools, has deeply cushioned sofas, leather wing armchairs and antique fireside settles, while the other, in shades of terracotta, has leather dining chairs around handsome tables set for the good modern food. The modern menu includes some interesting dishes. The restaurant is no smoking. Big windows with swagged-back curtains have a pleasant outlook over the green, and there are large portraits, of racehorses and of people. Service by neatly uniformed staff is friendly and efficient; piped music. Adnams Best and Broadside tapped from the cask, 10 wines by the glass (and local ones), and 20 malt whiskies.

Ravenwood Group ~ Manager Yvonne Howland ~ Real ale ~ Bar food (till 10pm Fri and Sat) ~ Restaurant ~ (01787) 312356 ~ Children welcome ~ Dogs allowed in bar and bedrooms ~ Open 9am-midnight ~ Bedrooms: £87.50B/£120B

ORFORD

Jolly Sailor *Quay Street; IP12 2NU*

Some time during this year, the straight-talking (but very much liked by our readers) landlord and his charming wife will be retiring, so we're obviously hoping that the brewery won't change too much. It's an unspoilt 17th-c brick pub, built mainly from wrecked ships' timbers; the several snugly traditional rooms have lots of exposed brickwork and are served from counters and hatches in an old-fashioned central cubicle. There's an unusual spiral staircase in the corner of the flagstoned main bar – which also has 13 brass door knockers and other brassware, local photographs, two cushioned pews, a long antique stripped deal table, and an open woodburning stove in the big brick fireplace (with nice horsebrasses above it); a small room is popular with the dominoes and cribbage players. Well kept Adnams Bitter and Broadside on handpump. The short choice of tasty straightforward food is served in generous helpings. The dining room and some tables in the bar are no smoking. There are lovely surrounding coastal walks and plenty of outside pursuits; several picnic-sets on grass at the back have views over the marshes.

Adnams ~ Tenant Philip Attwood ~ Real ale ~ Bar food (not Mon evening, nor Mon-Thurs evenings Nov-Mar) ~ No credit cards ~ (01394) 450243 ~ Dogs allowed in bar ~ Open 11.30-2.30, 7-11; 12-2.45, 7-10.30 Sun ~ Bedrooms: /£50

ROUGHAM
Ravenwood Hall *Just off A14 E of Bury St Edmunds; IP30 9JA*
A peaceful and civilised escape from the nearby trunk road, this country house hotel has a thoroughly welcoming all-day bar which does a pub's job better than any of the pubs that are handy for this stretch of the A14. Basically two fairly compact rooms, it has tall ceilings, gently patterned wallpaper, and heavily draped curtains for big windows overlooking a sweeping lawn with a stately cedar. The part by the back serving counter is set for food, its nice furnishings including well upholstered settles and dining chairs, sporting prints and a log fire. They smoke their own meats and fish, make their own preserves, and use as much local produce as possible. Well kept Adnams Bitter and Broadside on handpump, good wines by the glass, mulled wine around Christmas, and freshly squeezed orange juice; neat unobtrusive staff give good service. The other end of the bar has horse pictures, several sofas and armchairs with lots of plump cushions, one or two attractively moulded beams, and a good-sized fragment of early Tudor wall decoration above its big inglenook log fire. There may be piped local radio. They have a more formal quite separate restaurant. Outside, teak tables and chairs, some under a wooden shelter, stand around a swimming pool, and out in the wooded grounds big enclosures by the car park hold geese and pygmy goats.

Free house ~ Licensee Craig Jarvis ~ Real ale ~ Bar food (till 10pm Fri and Sat) ~ Restaurant ~ (01359) 270345 ~ Children welcome ~ Dogs allowed in bar and bedrooms ~ Open 9am-midnight ~ Bedrooms: £98.50B/£135B

SOUTHWOLD
Lord Nelson *East Street, off High Street (A1095); IP18 6EJ*
With a friendly, ever-present licensee and chatty locals, this lively seaside pub does get extremely busy at peak times, but it is so well run that there's

never any sense of strain, and the good-natured service is always quick and attentive. The partly panelled bar and its two small side rooms are kept spotless, with a small but extremely hot coal fire, light wood furniture on the tiled floor, lamps in nice nooks and corners, and some interesting Nelson memorabilia, including attractive nautical prints and a fine model of HMS *Victory*. Well kept Adnams Bitter, Broadside, Explorer and maybe Oyster Stout on handpump, and good wines by the glass. Straightforward bar food is tasty. Daily papers but no piped music or games machines. There are nice seats out in front with a sidelong view down to the sea and more in a sheltered back garden, with the brewery in sight (and often the appetising fragrance of brewing in progress). The seafront is just moments away. Disabled access is not perfect but is possible, and they help.

Adnams ~ Tenant John Illston ~ Real ale ~ Bar food ~ No credit cards ~ (01502) 722079 ~ Children in family room and snug ~ Dogs welcome ~ Open 10.30(12 Sun)-11

STOKE-BY-NAYLAND

Angel *B1068 Sudbury—East Bergholt; also signposted via Nayland off A134 Colchester—Sudbury; CO6 4SA*

We are always heartened to come across a place – such as this elegant inn – that manages to appeal to a wide cross-section of customers. It's not an easy thing to do but it's clear that visitors hoping for a delicious meal and locals in for a chat and a pint, are all made extremely welcome. The comfortable main bar area has handsome Elizabethan beams, some stripped brickwork and timbers, a mixture of furnishings including wing armchairs, mahogany dining chairs, and pale library chairs, local watercolours, modern paintings and older prints, attractive table lamps and a huge log fire. Round the corner is a little tiled-floor stand-and-chat bar. Neatly uniformed smiling staff serve well kept Greene King IPA, Abbot and a guest on handpump and ten wines by the glass. Another room has a low sofa and wing armchairs around its woodburning stove, and mustard-coloured walls. From a changing menu, the extremely good food is temptingly imaginative. People may smoke in the village bar only. There are seats and tables on a sheltered terrace.

Horizon Inns ~ Manager Neil Bishop ~ Real ale ~ Bar food (12-2, 6-9.30; all day Sun) ~ Restaurant ~ (01206) 263245 ~ Children welcome ~ Dogs allowed in bar ~ Open 11-11(10.30 Sun) ~ Bedrooms: £70B/£85B

Crown *Park Street (B1068); CO6 4SE*

An unusual feature in this rather smart dining pub is the glass-walled wine 'cellar' in one corner. From around 200 wines on their list, you can choose from two dozen by the glass plus champagne; they also sell wines by the half-case to take away. Most of the pub is open to the three-sided bar servery, yet it's well divided, and with two or three more tucked-away areas too. The main area, with a big woodburning stove, has quite a lot of fairly closely spaced tables, in a variety of shapes, styles and sizes. Elsewhere, several smaller areas each have just three or four tables. Seating varies from deep armchairs and sofas to elegant dining chairs and comfortable high-backed woven rush seats – and there are plenty of bar stools. This all gives a good choice between conviviality and varying degrees of cosiness and privacy. With a subtle colour scheme of several gentle toning colours, cheerful wildlife and landscape paintings, quite a lot of attractive table lamps and carefully placed gentle spotlighting, low ceilings (some with a good deal of stripped old beams), and floors varying from old tiles through broad boards or dark new flagstones to beige carpet, the overall feel is of relaxation. There is a table of daily papers. Adnams Bitter and Greene King IPA and a couple of guests on handpump, and nicely served coffee. Food is well liked and imaginative. Half the pub is no smoking (the division is the wall and fireplace); good service. A sheltered (and heated) back terrace with cushioned teak chairs and tables under big canvas parasols, looks out over a neat lawn to a landscaped shrubbery that includes a small romantic ruined-abbey folly. There are many more picnic-sets out on the front terrace. Disabled access is good, and the car park is big.

Free house ~ Licensee Richard Sunderland ~ Real ale ~ Bar food (12-2.30, 6-9.30 (10 Fri, Sat); 12-9 Sun) ~ (01206) 262001 ~ Children allowed away from bar ~ Dogs allowed in bar ~ Open 11-11; 12-10.30 Sun; closed 25 and 26 Dec, 1 Jan

WALBERSWICK

Anchor *Village signposted off A12; The Street (B1387); IP18 6UA*

Stylishly reworked by the couple who have made such a success of the White Horse on Parsons Green in West London, this brings out to the Suffolk coast that pub's civilised atmosphere, warmly welcoming service and clever coupling of a fine range of drinks with good individual food. A short menu using fresh local seafood and other local supplies suggests a particular wine and beer to go with each dish. They do good coffee, attractively served, and have daily papers. The big-windowed comfortable front bar has heavy stripped tables on its dark blue carpet, sturdy built-in wall seats cushioned in green leather, nicely framed black and white photographs of local fishermen and their boats on the varnished plank panelling, and log fires in the chimney breast which divides it into two snug halves. They have loads of bottled beers from all over the world and a remarkable range of interesting wines by the glass (sensibly served in 125ml glasses) including two sweet ones, as well as well kept Adnams Bitter, Broadside and another Adnams beer such as Flagship on handpump. Quite an extensive no smoking dining area stretching back from a more modern-feeling small lounge on the left is furnished much like the bar, with a gentle blue-grey décor, and looks out on a good-sized sheltered and nicely planted garden. The pub is right by the coast path, and there's a pleasant walk across to Southwold – in season you can also cross by a pedestrian ferry.

Adnams ~ Lease Mark and Sophie Dorber ~ Real ale ~ Bar food (12-3, 6-9) ~ Restaurant ~ (01502) 722112 ~ Children welcome with restrictions ~ Dogs allowed in bar and bedrooms ~ Open 11(12 Sun)-4, 6-11 ~ Bedrooms: /£90B

Dog Friendly Hotels, B&Bs and Farms

ALDEBURGH
Wentworth *Wentworth Rd, Aldeburgh, Suffolk IP15 5BD (01728) 452312*
£138, plus special breaks; 35 rms, 7 in annexe which are more spacious.
Comfortable and traditional hotel that has been in the same family for over
80 years and overlooks fishing huts and boats; plenty of comfortable seats,
lounges (one of which is no smoking) with log fires, antiques and books, a
convivial bar, cheerful long-standing staff, good enjoyable food in no
smoking restaurant, nice breakfasts, and sunny terrace for light lunches;
walks on the beach (restricted during high season); may cl 2 wks Christmas;
partial disabled access; dogs in bedrooms and lounges; £2

BILDESTON
Crown *High St, Bildeston, Ipswich, Suffolk IP7 7EB (01449) 740510* £110;
10 pretty, individually furnished rms. Lovely, newly refurbished timber-
framed Tudor inn with log fires and stripped wooden floors in the spacious
and convivial beamed bar, comfortable, heavily beamed lounge and elegant
no smoking restaurant, enjoyable modern cooking, well kept real ales, and
welcoming courteous service; seats in the central courtyard and on the
heated terrace; disabled access; dogs welcome; £10

BURY ST EDMUNDS
Angel *3 Angel Hill, Bury St Edmunds, Suffolk IP33 1LT (01284) 714000* (1
mile off A14/A143/A134 junction, following town centre signs; Angel
Hill) £137, plus special breaks; 74 individually decorated rms. Thriving
15th-c country-town hotel with particularly friendly staff, comfortable
lounge and relaxed bar, log fires and fresh flowers, and good food in elegant
restaurant and downstairs medieval vaulted room (Mr Pickwick enjoyed a
roast dinner here); gardens to walk in 50 metres away; disabled access; dogs
welcome in bedrooms

CAMPSEY ASH
Old Rectory *Station Rd, Campsey Ash, Woodbridge, Suffolk IP13 0PU
(01728) 746524* (1.4 miles off A12 via B1078 E) £85; 7 comfortable,
pretty rms. Very relaxed and welcoming no smoking Georgian house by
church, with charming owner and staff, log fire in comfortable and restful
drawing room, quite a few Victorian prints, first-class food from a set menu
in summer conservatory or two other dining rooms with more log fires, a
good honesty bar, a sensational wine list with very modest mark-ups on its
finest wines, and sizeable homely gardens; cl Christmas-New Year; dogs in
bedrooms

HADLEIGH
Edgehall *2 High St, Hadleigh, Ipswich, Suffolk IP7 5AP (01473) 822458*
£75, plus special breaks; 8 pretty rms. Friendly family-run no smoking
Tudor house with Georgian façade and attractive walled garden where you

can have afternoon tea or play croquet; comfortable, elegant lounge, personal service, and traditional english cooking using home-grown produce and good breakfasts in stately dining room; self-catering also; dogs in certain rooms; £5

HINTLESHAM
Hintlesham Hall *Hintlesham, Ipswich, Suffolk IP8 3NS (01473) 652334* **£195**, plus special breaks; 33 lovely rms. Magnificent mansion, mainly Georgian but dating from Elizabethan times, in 175 acres with big walled gardens, 18-hole golf course, outdoor heated swimming pool, croquet and tennis; restful and comfortable day rooms with books, antiques and open fires, fine modern cooking in three restaurants, a marvellous wine list and exemplary service; snooker, sauna, steam room, gym and beauty salon; well behaved children over 10 in evening restaurant; disabled access; dogs welcome by prior arrangement, away from public areas

HORRINGER
Ickworth *Horringer, Bury St Edmunds, Suffolk IP29 5QE (01284) 735350* **£185**, plus special breaks; 27 rms, 11 in apartments. Lovely 18th-c house in marvellous parkland on an 1800 acre National Trust estate (formerly owned by the Marquess of Bristol), the east wing of which is a luxury hotel; elegant and traditional décor mixes with more contemporary touches, the atmosphere is relaxed and informal, and staff are friendly and helpful; excellent modern cooking in dining conservatory and more formal restaurant; creches and clubs for children, games room with TV and computer games, wellies, bikes and adventure playground, riding, tennis and indoor swimming pool; holistic beauty treatments; two resident dogs; lots of surrounding walks; disabled access; dogs in bedrooms; canine massage and spinal therapy; £7.00

LAVENHAM
Angel *Market Pl, Lavenham, Sudbury, Suffolk CO10 9QZ (01787) 247388* **£80**, plus special breaks; 8 comfortable rms. No smoking, 15th-c inn with original cellar and pargeted ceiling in attractive residents' lounge, several Tudor features such as a rare shuttered shop window front, civilised atmosphere, good food in bar and restaurant, lots of decent wines, several malt whiskies, well kept real ales and thoughtful friendly service; cl 25-26 Dec; disabled access; dogs in one ground-floor room only; £10

Swan *High St, Lavenham, Sudbury, Suffolk CO10 9QA (01787) 247477* **£99**; 51 smart rms. Handsome and comfortable Elizabethan hotel that incorporates several fine half-timbered buildings inc an Elizabethan house and the former wool hall; lots of cosy seating areas, interesting historic prints and alcoves with beams, timbers, armchairs and settees, good food in lavishly timbered no smoking restaurant with a minstrels` gallery (actually built only in 1965), afternoon teas, intriguing little bar, and friendly helpful staff; dogs in bedrooms; £7.50

LONG MELFORD

Bull *Hall St, Long Melford, Sudbury, Suffolk CO10 9JG (01787) 378494*
£120, plus special breaks; 25 rms, ancient or comfortably modern. An inn
since 1580, this fine black and white hotel was originally a medieval
manorial hall, and has handsome and interesting carved woodwork and
timbering, and an old weavers' gallery overlooking the courtyard; a large
log fire, old-fashioned and antique furnishings, enjoyable food, and friendly
service; dogs (if small) in bedrooms; £5

ORFORD

Crown & Castle *Orford, Woodbridge, Suffolk IP12 2LJ (01394) 450205*
£135, plus special breaks; 18 well designed, stylish rms, 10 in garden with
own terrace. Red brick and high gabled no smoking Victorian hotel by the
Norman castle in this seaside village; a lovely relaxed informal atmosphere,
cosy, deeply comfortable lounge, bar, exceptionally good modern british
cooking with european and far eastern influences, super wine list with 20
by the glass (first class children`s menu), light lunches on terrace in summer,
and excellent breakfasts; two resident dogs; can walk in garden and lots of
walks nearby; cl 25 and 26 Dec; children must be over 9 in evening
restaurant; dogs in garden rooms and bar; welcome pack inc treats and
towels; £10

ROUGHAM

Ravenwood Hall *Rougham, Bury St Edmunds, Suffolk IP30 9JA (01359)
270345* (3 miles off A14 from Beyton exit, via old Bury Rd E towards
Blackthorpe) £113.50, plus special breaks; 14 comfortable rms with
antiques, some rms in mews. Tranquil, no smoking Tudor country house
in seven acres of carefully tended gardens and woodland; log fire in
comfortable lounge, cosy bar, good food in timbered restaurant with big
inglenook fireplace (home-preserved fruits and veg, home-smoked meats
and fish), a good wine list, and helpful service; croquet and heated
swimming pool; they are kind to children and have themed occasions for
them and lots of animals; resident dog; dogs may walk in grounds; disabled
access; dogs welcome away from restaurant

SOUTHWOLD

Swan *Market Pl, Southwold, Suffolk IP18 6EG (01502) 722186* £160, plus
winter breaks; 42 well appointed rms, some overlooking the market square.
No smoking, 17th-c hotel with comfortable drawing room, a convivial bar,
interesting enjoyable food in elegant no smoking dining room, fine wines,
well kept real ales (the hotel backs onto Adnams Brewery), and polite
helpful staff; children must be over 5 in evening dining room; dogs in
garden bedrooms; £5

WESTLETON

Crown *The Street, Westleton, Saxmundham, Suffolk IP17 3AD (01728)
648777* £110; 25 quiet, comfortable rms. Smart, recently refurbished
country inn in lovely setting with good nearby walks; comfortable bar, no

smoking dining conservatory, more formal restaurant, a wide range of enjoyable attractively presented food (nice breakfasts, too), log fires, several well kept real ales, decent wines, and a pretty garden with outside heaters; resident dog; cl 25-26 Dec; disabled access; dogs in some bedrooms; bowl and treats; £5

WOODBRIDGE
Seckford Hall *Seckford Hall Rd, Great Bealings, Woodbridge, Suffolk IP13 6NU (01394) 385678* **£135**, plus special breaks; 32 comfortable rms. Handsome red brick Tudor mansion in 32 acres of gardens and parkland with carp-filled lake, putting, and leisure club with indoor heated pool, beauty salon, and gym in lovely tithe barn; fine linenfold panelling, huge fireplaces, heavy beams, plush furnishings and antiques in comfortable day rooms, good food (inc lovely teas with home-made cakes), and helpful service; resident cat; cl 25 Dec; dogs in bedrooms; £7.50

Surrey

Dog Friendly Pubs

BETCHWORTH
Dolphin *Turn off A25 W of Reigate opposite B2032 at roundabout, and keep on into The Street; opposite the church; RH3 7DW*
Now open all day and under new licencees, this 16th-c village pub is a character-laden stopping point if you're walking the Greensand Way, and on Tuesdays you can hear the bell-ringers practising in the church opposite. The neat and homely front bar has kitchen chairs, gas lights over the inglenook and plain tables on the 400-year-old scrubbed flagstones, as does the carpeted smaller bar. The candlelit, no smoking restaurant bar has oak panelling, a blazing fire and a chiming grandfather clock. Youngs Bitter, Special and maybe a seasonal guest are on handpump; decent wines, with several by the glass. It's best to arrive early, or book a table beforehand if you want to enjoy the pubby home-made food. There are some seats in the small west-facing front courtyard, and picnic-sets in the rear garden. Morris men dance one weekend a month here from May to September. Parking can be difficult in the small car park, but there's space along the lanes or perhaps in the car park behind the church.
Youngs ~ Managers Chris and Melanie Gowers ~ Real ale ~ Bar food (12-2.30, 6-9.30; 12-6 Sun) ~ (01737) 842288 ~ Children in restaurant ~ Dogs allowed in bar ~ Open 11-11; 12-10.30 Sun

BLACKBROOK
Plough *On by-road E of A24, parallel to it, between Dorking and Newdigate, just N of the turn E to Leigh; RH5 4DS*
The licensees have recently celebrated 25 years at this neatly kept white-fronted pub, which is nicely placed by oak woods. The no smoking red saloon bar has fresh flowers on its tables and on the window sills of its large windows (which have new green and gold curtains). Down some steps, the public bar has brass-topped treadle tables, old saws on the ceiling, and bottles and flat irons; shove-ha'penny, cribbage and dominoes. Bar food includes lunchtime snacks and blackboard specials (some available in smaller portions). They now do a Sunday roast too, and may be serving food on Sunday evenings, as well as summer cream teas on Sunday afternoons in

summer. Badger Best, K&B Sussex and Tanglefoot, and a guest such as Gribble Fursty Ferret on handpump and 18 wines by the glass, with hot toddies in winter, as well as speciality teas and freshly ground coffees. The outside is prettily adorned with hanging baskets and window boxes; there are tables and chairs outside on the terrace and a little swiss playhouse furnished with little tables and chairs in the secluded garden.

Badger ~ Tenants Chris and Robin Squire ~ Real ale ~ Bar food (12-2, 7-9; Sun 12-4; not Sun or Mon evenings) ~ (01306) 886603 ~ Children welcome until 9pm ~ Dogs allowed in bar ~ Open 11-3, 6-11; 12-10 Sun; closed 1 Jan, 25-26 Dec

CHARLESHILL

Donkey *B3001 Milford—Farnham near Tilford; coming from Elstead, turn left as soon as you see pub sign; GU10 2AU*

On the edge of woodlands, this beamed, cottagey 18th-c place has been a pub since 1850 and takes its name from donkeys that were once kept to transport loads up the hill opposite: even today you might meet two friendly donkeys here, called Pip and Dusty. The pub puts a firm accent on food, using locally sourced ingredients wherever possible, and with a good fish selection. Friendly staff serve fairly pubby food. The bright saloon has lots of polished stirrups, lamps and watering cans on the walls, and prettily cushioned built-in wall benches, while the lounge has a fine high-backed settle, and highly polished horsebrasses and swords on the walls and beams; the dining areas are no smoking. All their wines (including champagne) are available by the glass, and you'll also find any three of Greene King IPA, Abbot, Triumph and Old Speckled Hen on handpump; piped music. There's a wendy house; the attractive garden also has a terrace and plenty of seats. Attractive local walking areas through heathlands include Thursford Common, and there are paths into the woods around the pub.

Greene King ~ Lease Lee and Helen Francis ~ Real ale ~ Bar food (12-2.30(4 Sun), 6-9.30(8.30 Sun)) ~ Restaurant ~ (01252) 702124 ~ Children welcome ~ Dogs allowed in bar ~ Open 11-3, 6-12; 11am-12 midnight Sat; 12-10.30 Sun; 12-3, 6-10.30 Sat and Sun in winter

COBHAM

Plough *3.2 miles from M25 junction 10; A3, then right on A245 at roundabout; in Cobham, right at Downside signpost into Downside Bridge Road; Plough Lane; KT11 3LT*

This is a cheerful and civilised country local, brought new life by the french bistro at one end. The thriving low-beamed bar has a relaxed atmosphere, with Courage Best (just as when we last drank here, more than 20 years ago), Fullers London Pride, Hogs Back TEA and a guest such as Wadworths 6X on handpump, a fine choice of wines by the glass including champagne, and good coffee – served with hot milk. A separate servery takes orders for the good value pubby food. Service is swift and good-natured; the lavatories are stylishly modern, and there are disabled access and facilities. Round on the right is a cosy parquet-floored snug with cushioned seats built into nice stripped pine panelling, and horse-racing prints. The main part is carpeted, with a mix of pubby furnishings, and past some standing timbers a few softly padded banquettes around good-sized tables by a log fire in the ancient stone fireplace. The restaurant part rambles around behind this – pews, bare boards, white table linen. Behind the pretty brick house, which is thought to date back some 500 years, a terrace has picnic-sets sheltering beside a very high garden wall.

Free house ~ Licensee Joe Worley ~ Real ale ~ Bar food (12-2.30, 7-9.30(not Fri/Sat evening)) ~ Restaurant ~ (01932) 589790 ~ Children welcome ~ Dogs allowed in bar ~ Open 11-11; 12-10.30 Sun

COLDHARBOUR

Plough *Village signposted in the network of small roads around Leith Hill; RH5 6HD*

The excellent own-brew ale makes this scenically placed inn a popular destination for walkers: it's high up in a peaceful hamlet in the Surrey hills, and there's some of the best walking in the county around there, with paths up to the tower and viewpoint on Leith Hill and further afield to Friday Street and Abinger Common. From the pub's own Leith Hill Brewery, they serve well kept Crooked Furrow, Hoppily Ever After and Tallywhacker on handpump, along with a couple of guests such as Ringwood Fortyniner and Shepherd Neame Spitfire; also Biddenden farm cider and several wines by the glass; at busy times it may be hard to find somewhere to sit if you're not dining. The two bars (each with a lovely open fire) have stripped light beams and timbering in the warm-coloured dark ochre walls, with quite unusual little chairs around the tables in the snug red-carpeted games room on the left (with darts, board games and cards), and little decorative plates on the walls; the one on the right leads through to the no smoking candlelit restaurant. Bar food is straightforward. The front and the terraced gardens have picnic-sets, tubs of flowers and a fish pond full of water-lilies.

Own brew ~ Licensees Richard and Anna Abrehart ~ Real ale ~ Bar food (12-2.30(3 Sun), 6-9.30(9 Sun)) ~ Restaurant ~ (01306) 711793 ~ Small children not allowed in restaurant ~ Dogs allowed in bar ~ Open 11(12 Sun)-12 midnight(1am Sat); closed 25-26 Dec evenings, 1 Jan evening ~ Bedrooms: £59.50S/£69.50S(£95B)

EASHING

Stag *Lower Eashing; Eashing signposted off A3 southbound, S of Hurtmore turn-off; or pub signposted off A283 just SE of exit roundabout at N end of A3 Milford bypass; GU7 2QG*

Readers enjoy sitting out in the riverside garden here, under mature trees and by a millstream; picnic-sets and tables under cocktail parasols are set out on a terrace and in a lantern-lit arbour. The pub (also known as the Stag on the River) is older than its Georgian brick façade suggests and dates back in part to the 15th c: inside you'll find an attractively opened-up interior with a charming old-fashioned locals' bar on the right with red and black flooring tiles by the counter. They serve Courage Best, Fullers London Pride and Shepherd Neame Spitfire on handpump, and about 14 wines by the glass. A cosy gently lit room beyond has a low white plank ceiling, a big stag print and stag's head on the dark-wallpapered walls, some cookery books on shelves by the log fire, and sturdy cushioned housekeeper's chairs grouped around dark tables on the brick floor. An extensive blue-carpeted area rambles around on the left, with similar comfortable dark furniture, some smaller country prints and decorative plates on pink Anaglypta walls, and round towards the back is a big woodburning stove in a capacious fireplace under a long mantelbeam. It's all rather smart yet cosily traditional; there is a table of conservative daily papers, and they are kind to visiting dogs. At lunchtime they serve bar snacks as well as some imaginative blackboard specials. Prices on the evening menu (available in the bar or restaurant) are more expensive; no smoking restaurant.

Punch ~ Lease Marilyn Lackey ~ Real ale ~ Bar food (12-2.30(3 Sun), 6-9.30; not Sun, Mon evenings) ~ Restaurant ~ (01483) 421568 ~ Children welcome ~ Dogs allowed in bar ~ Open 11-11; 12-10.30 Sun

ESHER

Marneys *Alma Road (one way only), Weston Green; heading N on A309 from A307 roundabout, after Lamb & Star pub turn left into Lime Tree Avenue (signposted to All Saints Parish Church), then left at T junction into Chestnut Avenue; KT10 8JN*

This cottagey place is a pleasant surprise, by a nicely rural-feeling common and near a duck pond. The owner is Norwegian, and proudly displays his country's flags and even national anthem inside, and the chatty low-beamed and black and white plank-panelled bar has shelves of hens and ducks and other ornaments, small blue-curtained windows, and perhaps horse racing on the unobtrusive corner TV; piped music; no smoking at the bar. On the left, past a little cast-iron woodburning stove, a dining area (somewhat roomier but still small) has big pine tables, pews and pale country kitchen chairs, with attractive goose pictures; this leads on to a recently added decking area with seating and large tables. A sensibly small choice of well liked food tends towards the scandinavian style, though they do serve other dishes, and are happy to provide children's portions. Courage Best, Fullers London Pride and a guest such as Charles Wells Bombardier on handpump, 11 wines and pink champagne by the glass, enterprising soft drinks, norwegian schnapps and good coffee. Service by friendly uniformed staff is quick and efficient; and they have daily papers on sticks. The pleasantly planted sheltered garden has a bar, black picnic-sets and tables under green and blue canvas parasols, and occasionally a Spanish guitarist playing under the willow tree; the front terrace has dark blue cast-iron tables and chairs under matching parasols, with some more black tables too, with table lighting.

Free house ~ Licensee Henrik Platou ~ Real ale ~ Bar food (12-(12.30 Sun)- 2.30; 12-2.30, 6-9 Thurs-Sat) ~ (020) 8398 4444 ~ Children welcome (not after 9pm in bar) ~ Dogs welcome ~ Open 11-11; 12-10.30 Sun

FOREST GREEN

Parrot *B2127 just W of junction with B2126, SW of Dorking; RH5 5RZ*

The owners of this quaint, rambling pub have their own farm not far away at Coldharbour, and the pork and lamb that appears on the menu are their own. Comfortably civilised, the pub has a particularly attractive bar, with its profusion of heavy beams, timbers and flagstones, and huge inglenook fireplace. There's plenty of space, with a couple of cosy areas hidden away behind the fireplace, and some more spread out tables opposite the long brick bar counter, which has a few unusual wooden chairs in front. Five or six real ales include Ringwood Best and Youngs, and guests from brewers such as Greene King, Ringwood, St Georges and Shepherd Neame on handpump; freshly squeezed orange juice, and 14 wines (including champagne) by the glass; newspapers are laid out for customers. A brass parrot sits beside a brick fireplace with a stove, then beyond here is a big, no smoking restaurant, less distinctive than the bar (part of which is also no smoking), but with the same enjoyably relaxed atmosphere. You can eat anywhere, from a frequently changing menu; a choice of good, popular Sunday roasts. Outside there's lots of room, with tables in front and among several attractive gardens, one with apple trees and rose beds; they plan to turn the rather run-down play area into a vegetable garden. The pub faces the village cricket field and is handy for the good woodland walks in the hills around Abinger.

Free house ~ Licensee Charles Gotto ~ Real ale ~ Bar food (12-3(4 Sun), 6-9(10 Fri, Sat); no food Sun evening) ~ Restaurant ~ (01306) 621339 ~ Children welcome, with restrictions ~ Dogs allowed in bar ~ Open 11(12 Sun)-11

FRIDAY STREET
Stephan Langton *Village signposted off B2126, or from A25 Westcott— Guildford; RH5 6JR*

With a growing reputation for imaginative food, this prettily placed pub in deeply rural woodlands and a few steps away from a much-frequented lake has more of a restauranty feel in the evening, but by day it's very much a pub, with very good bar food (booking is strongly advised at weekends when it gets extremely busy). The lounge bar has tobacco-coloured walls and is hung with gilded antique mirrors and framed classic menus, and there's a sunflower print above the fireplace; no piped music or games machines. Available at lunchtime only, bar food is all home-made (even the bread, ice-cream, chutney and pasta); in the evening there is a more elaborate menu for the no smoking restaurant. Adnams Best, Fullers London Pride and Hogs Back TEA are on handpump, and they have a well chosen selection of wines, with about ten by the glass; Weston's Old Rosie farm cider. There are plenty of tables in a front courtyard, with more on a back tree-surrounded stream-side terrace. It's surrounded by good walks – Leith Hill is particularly rewarding, and the tiny village is so unspoilt they prefer you to leave your car in a free car park just outside, but if you don't fancy the lovely stroll there are a few spaces in front of the pub itself.

Free house ~ Licensee Cynthia Coomb ~ Real ale ~ Bar food (12.30-2.45) ~ Restaurant (7-10) ~ (01306) 730775 ~ Children until 8pm ~ Dogs allowed in bar ~ Open 11-3, 5.30-11; 11-11 Sat; 11-9 Sun; closed Mon lunchtime

MICKLEHAM
Running Horses *Old London Road (B2209); RH5 6DU*
An elegant place for a meal, this upmarket inn maintains very high standards for its food and professional service, but is still somewhere you would feel perfectly at ease if you just wanted to enjoy a drink. It has two calmly relaxing bar rooms, neatly kept and spaciously open-plan, with fresh flowers (in summer) in an inglenook at one end, lots of race tickets hanging from a beam, some really good racing cartoons, hunting pictures and Hogarth prints, dark carpets, cushioned wall settles and other dining chairs around straightforward pubby tables and bar stools. Brakspears, Fullers London Pride, Greene King Abbot and Youngs are on handpump alongside good, if pricy, wines by the glass, from a serious list; piped music. There is a tempting choice of bar food, and for a special meal out you would probably be more interested in the more elaborate and more expensive restaurant menu. You can eat from this menu in the pubby bar part, but might prefer the extensive no smoking restaurant area. This leads straight out of the bar and, although it is set out quite formally with crisp white cloths and candles on each table, it shares the thriving atmosphere of the bar. There are picnic-sets on a terrace in front by lovely flowering tubs and hanging baskets, with a peaceful view of the old church with its strange stubby steeple.
Punch ~ Lease Steve and Josie Slayford ~ Real ale ~ Bar food (12-2.30(3 Sat, Sun), 7-9.30(9 Sun)) ~ Restaurant ~ (01372) 372279 ~ Children allowed in part of restaurant area ~ Dogs allowed in bar ~ Open 11.30-11; 12-10.30 Sun ~ Bedrooms: £85(£85S)(£95B)/£95(£95S)(£130B)

REIGATE HEATH
Skimmington Castle *3 miles from M25 junction 8: through Reigate take A25 towards Dorking, then on edge of Reigate turn left past Black Horse into Flanchford Road; after ¼ mile turn left into Bonny's Road (unmade, very bumpy track); after crossing golf course fork right up hill; RH2 8RL*
Popular with walkers and horse riders (there's a hitching rail for horses at the front), this prettily situated rural pub has plenty of sitting space outside for enjoying the view in fine weather. The bright main front bar leads off a small room with a central serving counter, with dark simple panelling and lots and lots of keys hanging from the beams. There's a miscellany of chairs and tables, shiny brown plank panelling, a brown plank ceiling; Adnams, Greene King Old Speckled Hen and Harveys Sussex Best, with a guest ale such as Hop Back Summer Lightning, are on handpump, with 17 wines by the glass, Addlestone's farm cider and even some organic spirits. The cosy back rooms are partly panelled too, with old-fashioned settles and windsor chairs; one has a big brick fireplace with its bread-oven still beside it – the chimney is said to have been used as a highwayman's look-out. Steps take you down to just three tables in a small but pleasant no smoking room at the back; ring-the-bull and piped music. The quickly served bar food is good and popular, so you need to get here early for a table as they don't take bookings. There's a crazy-paved front terrace and tables on the grass by lilac bushes. More tables at the back overlook the meadows and the

hillocks (though you may find the views blocked by trees in summer). No
children.

*Punch ~ Tenants Anthony Pugh and John Davidson ~ Real ale ~ Bar food
(12-2(2.30 Sun), 7-9.30(9 Sun)) ~ (01737) 243100 ~ Dogs welcome ~ Open
11-3, 5.30(6 Sat)-11; 12-10.30 Sun; closed 25 Dec, 26 Dec evening*

Dog Friendly Hotels, B&Bs and Farms

BAGSHOT
Pennyhill Park *College Ride, Bagshot, Surrey GU19 5ET (01276) 471774*
(2.3 miles off M3 junction 3; A322, left on to A30 then right into Church
Rd and College Ride) £250, plus special breaks; 123 individually designed
luxury rms and suites. Impressive Victorian country house in 120 acres of
well kept gardens and parkland inc a 9-hole golf course, tennis courts,
outdoor heated swimming pool, clay pigeon shooting, archery, fishing, and
an international rugby pitch; friendly courteous staff, wood-panelled bar
with resident pianist, comfortable two-level lounge and reading room, very
good imaginative food in two restaurants, jazz Sun lunchtime, and terraces
overlooking the golf course; disabled access; dogs in bedrooms and some
other areas; £50

HASLEMERE
Lythe Hill Hotel & Spa *Petworth Rd, Haslemere, Surrey GU27 3BQ*
(01428) 651251 £160, plus weekend breaks; 41 individually styled rms, a
few in the original house. Lovely partly 15th-c building in 22 acres of
parkland and bluebell woods (adjoining the NT hillside) with floodlit
tennis court, croquet lawn, and jogging track; plush, comfortable and
elegant lounges, a relaxed bar, two no smoking restaurants (one with french
cooking, the other with traditional english), and good attentive service; spa
with swimming pool, sauna, steam and beauty rooms and gym; disabled
access; dogs in some bedrooms; £20

NUTFIELD
Nutfield Priory *Nutfield, Redhill, Surrey RH1 4EL (01737) 824400,*
£185 plus special breaks; 60 lovely rms. Recently renovated and
impressive Victorian Gothick hotel in 40 acres of parkland with lovely
elaborate carvings, stained-glass windows, gracious day rooms, a fine
panelled library, cloistered restaurant, and even an organ in the galleried
grand hall; extensive leisure club with indoor heated swimming pool; dogs
in bedrooms; £25

Sussex

Dog Friendly Pubs

AMBERLEY
Black Horse *Off B2139; BN18 9NL*

After a walk along the South Downs Way, the restful garden of this pretty pub with its fine views is just the place to relax with a drink. The main bar has high-backed settles on flagstones, beams over the serving counter festooned with sheep bells and shepherds' tools (hung by the last shepherd on the Downs), and walls decorated with a mixture of prints and paintings. The lounge bar has many antiques and artefacts collected by the owners on their world travels; there are log fires in both bars and two in the no smoking restaurant. Straightforward pubby bar food. Greene King IPA and Charles Wells Bombardier on handpump; piped music.

Punch ~ Lease Gary Tubb ~ Real ale ~ Bar food (12-3, 6-9.30(10 Sat); all day Sun) ~ Restaurant ~ (01798) 831552 ~ Children allowed but must be well supervised at all times ~ Dogs allowed in bar ~ Open 11-midnight; 12-midnight Sun

CHILGROVE
Royal Oak *Off B2141 Petersfield—Chichester, signed Hooksway down steep single track; PO18 9JZ*

Tucked away down a little wooded track, this isolated and friendly white cottage is in the heart of the Downs and popular with walkers; the South Downs Way is close by. It's simply furnished with plain country-kitchen tables and chairs and there are huge log fires in the two cosy rooms of the partly brick-floored beamed bar. The cottagey dining room and plainer family room are both no smoking. Well liked traditional bar food and Exmoor Beast, Gales HSB, Hampshire Hooksway and a guest such as Arundel ASB or Timothy Taylors Landlord on handpump; piped music. There are plenty of picnic-sets under parasols on the grass of the big, pretty garden.

Free house ~ Licensee Dave Jeffery ~ Real ale ~ Bar food (not Sun evening or Mon) ~ Restaurant ~ (01243) 535257 ~ Children in family room ~ Dogs allowed in bar ~ Live music 2nd Fri evening of the month ~ Open 11.30-2.30, 6-11; 12-3 Sun; closed Sun evening and all day Mon; two weeks Oct

White Horse *B2141 Petersfield—Chichester; PO18 9HX*
Handy for Goodwood, this civilised and quietly upmarket inn is a super
place to stay and enjoy the particularly good food. But there are still plenty
of tables for drinkers at the front, and walkers and their dogs are very
welcome (lots of fine walks nearby). No smoking throughout, there are dark
brown deco leather armchairs and a sofa grouped on dark boards near the
bar counter, and on either side are three or four well spaced good-sized
sturdy tables with good pale spindleback side and elbow chairs on lighter
newer boards. The light and airy feeling is helped by uncluttered cream
walls, clear lighting and a big bow window. The bar counter is made up
from claret, burgundy and other mainly french wooden wine cases, and
good wines by the glass, with an impressive range by the bottle, are a big
plus here – in fact, every dish from the restaurant menu has a recommended
wine to go with it; Ballards on handpump and well reproduced piped music.
Interesting, if pricy, bar food. The bar has a woodburner on one side, and a
log fire on the other. Past here, it opens into a restaurant with comfortable
modern seats and attractively laid tables – as in the bar, generously spaced
out. Outside, one neat lawn has white cast-iron tables and chairs under an
old yew tree, and another has wooden benches, tables and picnic-sets under
a tall flag mast. Comfortable bedrooms in separate annexe and super
continental breakfasts brought to your room in a wicker hamper.
*Free house ~ Licensee Charles Burton ~ Real ale ~ Bar food (not Sun evening or
Mon) ~ Restaurant ~ (01243) 535219 ~ Children welcome ~ Dogs allowed in bar
and bedrooms ~ Piano Sat evening in restaurant ~ Open 10.30-3, 6-11; 12-3
Sun; closed Sun evening, Mon ~ Bedrooms: £65B/£95B*

COOLHAM

George & Dragon *Dragons Green, Dragons Lane; pub signed just off A272,
about 1½ miles E of village; RH13 8GE*
This welcoming old tile-hung cottage has a small snug bar with heavily
timbered walls, a partly woodblock, and partly polished tiled floor,
unusually low and massive black beams (see if you can decide whether the
date cut into one is 1677 or 1577), simple chairs and rustic stools, some
brass, and a big inglenook fireplace with an early 17th-c grate. There's also
a smaller back bar and restaurant, and the bar food is home-made and well
liked. Badger K&B Sussex and summer Fursty Ferret or winter Festive
Feasant on handpump; kind service and a relaxed atmosphere. Stretching
away behind the pub, the big grassy orchard garden is neatly kept with lots
of picnic-sets, shrubs and pretty flowers; the little front garden has a sad
19th-c memorial to the son of a previous innkeeper.
*Badger ~ Tenant Jemma Ford ~ Real ale ~ Bar food ~ Restaurant ~ (01403)
741320 ~ Children welcome ~ Dogs allowed in bar ~ Open 12-3, 6-11; 11-11
Sat; 12-10.30 Sun; open from 6 wkdy evenings in winter*

DITCHLING

Bull *High Street (B2112); BN6 8TA*
This 14th-c place was originally a coaching inn and also served as a local
court. The invitingly cosy main bar on the right is quite large, rambling and

pleasantly traditional with well worn old wooden furniture, beams and floorboards, and a blazing winter fire. To the left, the nicely furnished rooms have a calm, restrained mellow décor and candles, and beyond that there's a snug area with chesterfields around a low table; piped music. Half the pub is no smoking. Harveys Sussex Best and Timothy Taylors Landlord with a couple of guests such as Hogs Back Hair of the Hog and Kings Red River on handpump, and 14 wines by the glass. Bar snacks and lunchtime sandwiches as well as more elaborate daily specials. Picnic-sets in the good-sized pretty downland garden which is gently lit at night look up towards Ditchling Beacon, and there are more tables on a suntrap back terrace; good wheelchair access. The charming old village is a popular base for the South Downs Way and other walks.

Free house ~ Licensee Dominic Worrall ~ Real ale ~ Bar food (12-2.30(4 Sat), 7-9.30; 12-6 Sun) ~ (01273) 843147 ~ Children welcome ~ Dogs allowed in bar ~ Open 11-11; 12-11 Sun ~ Bedrooms: /£80B

EAST ASHLING
Horse & Groom *B2178 NW of Chichester; PO18 9AX*

If you're popping into this bustling country pub for just a drink, the best place to head for is the front part with its old pale flagstones and a woodburning stove in a big inglenook on the right or the carpeted area with its old wireless set, nice scrubbed trestle tables, and bar stools along the counter serving well kept Brewsters Hophead, Harveys Sussex Best, Hop Back Summer Lightning and Youngs on handpump. Several wines by the glass; piped music and board games. A couple of tables share a small light flagstoned middle area with the big blackboard that lists daily changing dishes; there may be Sunday lunchtime nibbles. The restaurant is no smoking. The back part of the pub, angling right round behind the bar servery, with a further extension beyond one set of internal windows, has solid pale country-kitchen furniture on neat bare boards, and a fresh and airy décor, with a little bleached pine panelling and long white curtains. French windows lead out to a garden with picnic-sets under cocktail parasols. The pub gets extremely busy on Goodwood race days.

Free house ~ Licensee Michael Martell ~ Real ale ~ Bar food (12-2(2.30 Sun), 6-9; not Sun evening) ~ Restaurant ~ (01243) 575339 ~ Children welcome but must leave bar by 9pm ~ Dogs allowed in bar and bedrooms ~ Open 11-3, 6-11; 11-6 Sun; closed Sun evening ~ Bedrooms: £40.50B/£60.75B

EAST CHILTINGTON
Jolly Sportsman *2 miles N of B2116; Chapel Lane – follow sign to 13th-c church; BN7 3BA*

This is a top notch place and although very foody, does still have some pubbiness. There are a couple of chairs in the chatty little bar by the fireplace set aside for drinkers, and a mix of furniture on the stripped wood floors. Well kept Dark Star Hophead, Triple fff Altons Pride and a guest tapped from the cask, a remarkably good wine list with nine by the glass, farm cider, over 50 malt whiskies and quite a few cognacs and armagnacs. Most people do head, though, for the smart but informal no smoking restaurant with contemporary light wood furniture, and modern landscapes on green painted walls. Very good, imaginative bar and they do a good value two-course and three-course lunch menu. There are rustic tables and benches under gnarled trees in a pretty cottagey front garden with more on the terrace and the front bricked area, and the large back lawn with a children's play area looks out towards the South Downs; fine walks nearby.

Free house ~ Licensee Bruce Wass ~ Real ale ~ Bar food (till 10 Fri and Sat; 12.15-3 Sun; not Sun evening) ~ Restaurant ~ (01273) 890400 ~ Children welcome ~ Dogs welcome ~ Open 12-2.30, 6-11; 12-11 Sat; 12-4.30 Sun; closed Sun evening, all day Mon (except bank hols), 3 days Christmas

EAST DEAN

Tiger *Pub (with village centre) signposted – not vividly – from A259 Eastbourne—Seaford; note that there's another East Dean in Sussex, over near Chichester BN20 0DA*

In summer particularly, this long, low tiled pub is a lovely place to visit and you can sit outside beside the pretty window boxes and flowering climbers and look over the delightful cottage-lined green. Inside, there are just nine tables in the two smallish rooms (candlelit at night) so space at peak times is very limited; best to arrive early for a table as they don't, in the best pub tradition, take bookings. There are low beams hung with pewter and china, polished rustic tables and distinctive antique settles, and old prints and so forth. Harveys Best with guests such as Adnams Broadside and Kings Horsham Best Bitter on handpump, and a good choice of wines with a dozen by the large glass; board games. They get their fish fresh from Hastings, their lamb from the farm on the hill, all vegetables and eggs from another local farm, and meat from the local butcher. Imaginative food from a sensibly short but ever changing menu. At lunchtimes on hot days and bank holidays they usually have only cold food. The South Downs Way is close by so it's naturally popular with walkers, and the lane leads on down to a fine stretch of coast culminating in Beachy Head. No children inside.

Free house ~ Licensee Nicholas Denyer ~ Real ale ~ Bar food ~ (01323) 423209 ~ Dogs allowed in bar ~ Open 11-3, 6-11; 11-11 Sat; 12-10.30 Sun

EAST HOATHLY

Foresters Arms *Village signposted off A22 Hailsham—Uckfield (take south-easternmost of the two turn-offs); South Street; BN8 6DS*

The new licensees have carried out major refurbishments in this village pub. The small counter between the two small linked rooms has been removed, creating more space, and there are just a handful of tables (one in a bow window) and dark woodwork; the one on the right has a small art nouveau fireplace under a big mirror. Back from here is a bigger room with a new extended carved wooden bar counter and attractive etched glass mirrors. Piped music, TV, darts and board games. Decent, straightforward bar food and the newly carpeted restaurant is no smoking. Harveys Best Bitter, Old and Armada on handpump and up to 15 wines by the glass. The garden has been restructured and there's new furniture under parasols. Full disabled facilities.

Harveys ~ Tenants Ernest and Sandra Wright ~ Real ale ~ Bar food (12-2.30, 6-9.30; not Sun evening) ~ Restaurant ~ (01825) 840208 ~ Children welcome with restrictions ~ Dogs allowed in bar ~ Occasional live music Fri evening ~ Open 11-3, 5-11; 11-11 Sat; 12-10.30 Sun

ELSTED

Three Horseshoes *Village signposted from B2141 Chichester—Petersfield; also reached easily from A272 about 2 miles W of Midhurst, turning left heading W; GU29 0JY*

Now totally no smoking, this 16th-c pub is extremely popular and very well run. Although cosy inside in winter, the garden in summer is lovely with free-roaming bantams, plenty of tables, pretty flowers and stunning views. It's all very friendly and cheerful and the snug little rooms have ancient beams and flooring, antique furnishings, log fires, fresh flowers on the tables, attractive prints and photographs, candlelight, and a very congenial atmosphere. Well liked bar food and changing ales racked on a stillage behind the bar counter might include Archers Swindon, Ballards Best, Hop Back Summer Lightning, and the local Langham Brewery's Halfway to Heaven; summer cider; dominoes.

Free house ~ Licensee Sue Beavis ~ Real ale ~ Bar food ~ (01730) 825746 ~ Well behaved children in eating areas ~ Dogs allowed in bar ~ Open 11-2.30, 6-11; 12-3, 7-10.30 Sun

FITTLEWORTH

Swan *Lower Street; RH20 1EL*

In good weather, this pretty tile-hung inn gets very busy. There's a big back lawn with plenty of well spaced tables and flowering shrubs, and benches in front by the village lane; good nearby walks in beech woods. The beamed main bar is comfortable and relaxed with windsor armchairs and bar stools on the part stripped wood and part carpeted floor, there are wooden truncheons over the big inglenook fireplace (which has good winter log fires), and Fullers London Pride and Youngs on handpump; decent food. The restaurant is no smoking; piped music.

Enterprise ~ Real ale ~ Bar food ~ Restaurant ~ (01798) 865429 ~ Children welcome with restrictions ~ Dogs allowed in bar ~ Open 10.30-3, 5-11; 12-4, 7-10.30 Sun ~ Bedrooms: £50B/£85B

FLETCHING

Griffin *Village signposted off A272 W of Uckfield; TN22 3SS*

This is a gently upmarket and civilised old inn with beamed and quaintly panelled bar rooms: blazing log fires, old photographs and hunting prints, straightforward close-set furniture including some captain's chairs, and china on a delft shelf. There's a small bare-boarded serving area off to one side, and a snug separate bar with sofas and TV; the restaurant is no smoking. Very good modern cooking, well kept Badger Tanglefoot, Harveys Best and Kings Horsham Best Bitter on handpump, and a fine wine list with 14 (including champagne) by the glass; efficient, friendly young service. The two acres of garden behind the pub look across fine rolling countryside towards Sheffield Park, and there are plenty of seats here and on the sandstone terrace with its woodburning oven.

Free house ~ Licensees J Pullan, T Erlam, M W Wright ~ Real ale ~ Bar food (12-2.30, 7-9.30) ~ Restaurant ~ (01825) 722890 ~ Children welcome ~ Dogs allowed in bar ~ Duo Fri evening and Sun lunchtime ~ Open 12-1am(1.30am Fri and Sat); 12-midnight Sun; closed 25 Dec and evening 1 Jan ~ Bedrooms: £60B/£95B

ICKLESHAM
Queens Head *Just off A259 Rye—Hastings; TN36 4BL*
This is an extremely well run place and even when really busy – which it deservedly often is – the staff remain friendly and efficient. The open-plan areas work round a very big serving counter which stands under a vaulted beamed roof, the high beamed walls and ceiling of the easy-going bar are lined with shelves of bottles and covered with farming implements and animal traps, and there are well used pub tables and old pews on the brown patterned carpet. Other areas (two are no smoking and popular with diners) have big inglenook fireplaces, and the back room is decorated with old bicycle and motorbike prints. Well kept Courage Directors, and Greene King IPA and Abbot, with guests like Tring Ridgeway, Westerham British Bulldog and Whitstable Wheat Beer on handpump, Biddenden cider, and a dozen wines by the glass. Reasonably priced, decent home-made bar food; shove-ha'penny, dominoes, cribbage, darts, games machine and piped music. Picnic-sets look out over the vast, gently sloping plain of the Brede Valley from the little garden, and there's an outside children's play area, and boules. Good local walks.

Free house ~ Licensee Ian Mitchell ~ Real ale ~ Bar food (12-2.30, 6-9.30; all day Sat, Sun and bank hols; not 25 or 26 Dec) ~ (01424) 814552 ~ Well behaved children in eating area of bar until 8.30pm ~ Dogs welcome ~ Open 11-11; 12-10.30 Sun; closed 25 and 26 Dec

PETWORTH
Welldiggers Arms *Low Heath; A283 towards Pulborough; GU28 0HG*
Under the eye of the long-serving, hands-on landlord, this remains a well run country pub with an unassuming style and appearance. The smallish L-shaped bar has low beams, a few pictures (Churchill and gun dogs are prominent) on shiny ochre walls above a panelled dado, a couple of very long rustic settles with tables to match, and some other stripped tables (many are laid for eating); a second rather lower side room has a somewhat lighter décor. No music or machines. Youngs on handpump, decent wines, and popular home-made food. Outside, screened from the road by a thick high hedge, are plenty of tables and chairs on pleasant lawns and a terrace, looking back over rolling fields and woodland.

Free house ~ Licensee Ted Whitcomb ~ Real ale ~ Bar food (see opening hours) ~ Restaurant ~ (01798) 342287 ~ Children welcome ~ Dogs welcome ~ Open 11-3.30, 6-11; closed Mon; closed Tues, Weds and Sun evenings

RUSHLAKE GREEN
Horse & Groom *Village signposted off B2096 Heathfield—Battle; TN21 9QE*
Now owned by Shepherd Neame and stocking their beers, this country pub is in an attractive setting by the village green. The little L-shaped bar has low beams (watch your head) and is simply furnished with high bar stools and bar chairs, red plush cushioned wall seats and a few brocaded cushioned stools, and there's a brick fireplace with some brass items on the mantelpiece; horsebrasses, photographs of the pub and local scenes on the walls. A small room down a step has jockeys' colours and jockey photographs and watercolours of the pub. To the right of the entrance is the heavily beamed no smoking restaurant with guns and hunting trophies on the walls, plenty of wheelback chairs around pubby tables, and a log fire. Listed on boards by the entrance to the bar, there's a large choice of popular bar food. Well kept Shepherd Neame Master Brew and Spitfire on handpump, and several wines by the glass; piped music. The cottagey garden has oak seats and tables made by the landlord and pretty country views.
Shepherd Neame ~ Tenants Mike and Sue Chappel ~ Real ale ~ Bar food ~ Restaurant ~ (01435) 830320 ~ Children welcome ~ Dogs welcome ~ Open 11.30-3, 5.30(6 Sat)-11; 12-3, 7-10.30 Sun; closed evening 25 Dec

SALEHURST
Salehurst Halt *Village signposted from Robertsbridge bypass on A21 Tunbridge Wells—Battle Road; TN32 5PH*
Two local families have bought this little pub and have redecorated it and renovated the kitchen. It's now totally no smoking and the L-shaped beamed bar has sofas and chairs by the little open brick fireplace on the right, and to the left are plain wooden tables and chairs on the new oak floor; a half wall leads to the dining area. Decent bar food and well kept Harveys Best and maybe a guest beer on handpump; piped music and board games. The charming and pretty back garden now has an extended terrace giving more space for eating.
Free house ~ Licensee Andrew Augarde ~ Real ale ~ Bar food (not Mon) ~ Restaurant ~ (01580) 880620 ~ Children welcome ~ Dogs allowed in bar ~ Open 12-3, 6.30-11(10.30 Sun); 12-11 Sat; closed Mon

SINGLETON
Partridge *Just off A286 Midhurst—Chichester; heading S into the village, the main road bends sharp right – keep straight ahead instead; if you miss this turn, take the Charlton road, then first left; PO18 0EY*
This pretty black and white pub dates from the 16th c. There are polished wooden floors, flagstones and daily papers, some small rooms with red settles and good winter log fires, and a roomy back dining extension. Much of the pub is no smoking. Home-made bar food, Fullers London Pride, Hepworths Sussex and Ringwood Best on handpump, and decent wines by the glass; piped music. There's a terrace and a big walled garden with colourful flowerbeds and fruit trees. The Weald & Downland Open Air Museum is just down the road, and Goodwood Racecourse is not far away.

Enterprise ~ Lease Tony Simpson ~ Real ale ~ Bar food (all day weekends) ~ Restaurant ~ (01243) 811251 ~ Children welcome but with restrictions ~ Dogs allowed in bar ~ Trad jazz 3rd Tues of month ~ Open 11.30-3, 6-11; 11.30-11 Sat; 12-11 Sun

TROTTON
Keepers Arms *A272 Midhurst—Petersfield; pub tucked up above road, on S side; GU31 5ER*

There's certainly plenty of interest in this individually decorated, no smoking pub. A north african-style room has a cushioned bench around all four walls, a large central table, rare ethnic fabrics and weavings, and a big moroccan lamp. The walls throughout are decorated with some unusual pictures and artefacts that reflect Jenny's previous long years of travelling the world, and the beamed L-shaped bar has timbered walls and some standing timbers, sofas by the big log fire, and ethnic rugs scattered on the oak floor. Elsewhere, there are a couple of unusual adult high chairs at an oak refectory table, two huge Georgian leather high-backed chairs around another table, an interesting medley of old or antique seats, and dining tables decorated with pretty candelabra, and bowls of fruit and chillis. Interesting piped music (which they change according to the customers) ranges from Buddha bar-type music to classical. Decent bar food, Ballards Best, Cheriton Pots Ale and Ringwood Fortyniner on handpump, and decent wines. Plenty of seats on the attractive, almost mediterranean-feeling south facing front terrace. Dogs lunchtime only.

Free house ~ Licensee Jenny Oxley ~ Real ale ~ Bar food (not Sun evening, Mon) ~ Restaurant ~ (01730) 813724 ~ Children welcome ~ Dogs welcome (lunchtime only) ~ Open 12-3, 6.30-11; 12-3 Sun; closed Sun evening, all Mon (except bank hols); 24 Dec; first Tues in Jan

WILMINGTON
Giants Rest *Just off A27; BN26 5SQ*

This comfortable no smoking pub is watched over by the impressive chalk-carved Long Man of Wilmington at the foot of the South Downs; it's a popular place to come after a walk. The long wood-floored bar and adjacent open areas, one with a log fire, are simply furnished with old pews and pine tables – each with its own bar game or wooden puzzle; well kept Harveys Best, Hop Back Summer Lightning and Timothy Taylors Landlord on handpump. Good bar food. Sunday lunchtime is especially busy and there may not be much space for those just wanting a drink as most of the tables are booked by diners; piped music. Plenty of seats in the front garden. Elizabeth David the famous cookery writer is buried in the churchyard at nearby Folkington; her headstone is beautifully carved and features mediterranean vegetables and a casserole.

Free house ~ Licensees Adrian and Rebecca Hillman ~ Real ale ~ Bar food ~ Restaurant ~ (01323) 870207 ~ Children welcome ~ Dogs welcome ~ Open 11-3, 6-11; 11-11 Sat; 12-10.30 Sun

WINEHAM
Royal Oak *Village signposted from A272 and B2116; BN5 9AY*
This welcoming and old-fashioned local has changed little. It's been in the same family for over 50 years, and still has no fruit machines, piped music or even beer pumps. Logs burn in an enormous inglenook fireplace with a cast-iron Royal Oak fireback, and there's a collection of cigarette cards showing old English pubs, a stuffed stoat and crocodile, a collection of jugs, ancient corkscrews decorating the very low beams above the serving counter, and racing plates, tools and a coach horn on the walls; maybe a nice tabby cat, and views of quiet countryside from the back parlour. Well kept Harveys Best with a guest such as Wadworths 6X tapped from the cask in a still room; darts and board games. Limited bar snacks. There are some picnic-sets outside – picturesque if you are facing the pub.
Punch ~ Tenant Tim Peacock ~ Real ale ~ Bar food (served during opening hours) ~ No credit cards ~ (01444) 881252 ~ Children allowed away from main bar ~ Dogs allowed in bar ~ Open 11-2.30, 5.30(6 Sat)-11; 12-3, 7-10.30 Sun

Dog Friendly Hotels, B&Bs and Farms

ALFRISTON
George *High St, Alfriston, Polegate, East Sussex BN26 5SY (01323) 870319* £**100**; 7 fine rms. 14th-c timbered inn opposite the intriguing façade of the Red Lion, with massive low beams hung with hops, appropriately soft lighting, a log fire (or summer flower arrangement) in a huge stone inglenook, lots of copper and brass, plenty of sturdy stripped tables, and a thriving atmosphere; popular home-made food, a cosy candlelit restaurant, nice breakfasts, well kept real ales, and a jovial landlord; seats out in the charming flint-walled garden behind; cl 24–27 Dec; dogs in bedrooms

BATTLE
Little Hemingfold Hotel *189 Hastings Rd, Battle, East Sussex TN33 0TT (01424) 774338* (2.2 miles off A21 just N of Hastings, via A2100 (NB it's S of Battle)) £**95**, plus special breaks; 12 rms, 6 on ground floor in adjoining Coach House. Partly 17th-c, partly early Victorian farmhouse in 43 acres of woodland, with trout lake, tennis, gardens and lots of walks; comfortable sitting rooms (one is no smoking), open fires, restful atmosphere and very good food using home-grown produce in no smoking, candlelit restaurant; two resident dogs; children over 7; cl Jan and Feb; dogs in bedrooms only

Powder Mills *Powdermill Lane, Battle, East Sussex TN33 0SP (01424) 775511* £**125**, plus special breaks; 40 rms, some in annexe. Attractive 18th-c creeper-clad manor house in 150 acres of park and woodland with four lakes and outdoor swimming pool, and next to the 1066 battlefield; country-house atmosphere, log fires and antiques in elegant day rooms, attentive service, and good modern cooking in Orangery restaurant; three resident dogs; children over 10 in evening restaurant; disabled access; dogs welcome away from restaurant

BRIGHTON

Grand *97-99 Kings Rd, Brighton, East Sussex BN1 2FW (01273) 224300* £**275**, plus special breaks; 200 handsome rms, many with sea views. Famous Victorian hotel with marble columns and floors and fine moulded plasterwork in the luxurious and elegant day rooms; good service, very good food and fine wines, popular afternoon tea in sunny conservatory, a bustling nightclub, and health spa with indoor swimming pool; walks for dogs on the beach (not during the summer); disabled access; dogs in bedrooms; £5

CHARLTON

Woodstock House *Charlton, Chichester, East Sussex PO18 0HU (01243) 811666* £**95**, plus special breaks; 13 rms. Mainly no smoking 18th-c country house close to Goodwood with a friendly, relaxed atmosphere, log fire in homely sitting room, cocktail bar, and suntrap inner courtyard garden; nearby inns and restaurants for evening meals; lots to see nearby and plenty of downland walks; disabled access; dogs in ground floor bedrooms and if small by arrangement

CHICHESTER

Suffolk House *East Row, Chichester, West Sussex PO19 1PD (01243) 778899* £**89**, plus winter breaks; 8 rms, some overlooking garden. Friendly Georgian house in centre and close to the cathedral, with homely comfortable lounge bar, traditional cooking in no smoking restaurant, good breakfasts, and small walled garden; park nearby for walks; disabled access; dogs in bedrooms but must not be unattended

West Stoke House *West Stoke, Chichester, W Sussex PO18 9BN (01243) 575226* £**130**; 5 charming rms with countryside views. Fine Georgian restaurant-with-rooms in five acres of grounds on the edge of the Downs; a friendly, relaxed atmosphere, large reception lounge with interesting furnishings, antiques and plenty of art, and excellent modern cooking and delicious breakfasts in blue-walled, no smoking, intimate restaurant (and they provide picnics for race days at Goodwood); resident dog; a few minutes walk from Kingly Vale Nature Reserve and nearby beaches; dogs in bedrooms (must be clean and dry)

CLIMPING

Bailiffscourt *Climping St, Climping, Littlehampton, East Sussex BN17 5RW (01903) 723511* £**195**, plus special breaks; 39 rms, many with four-poster beds, winter log fires and super views. Mock 13th-c manor built only 60 years ago but with tremendous character – fine old iron-studded doors, huge fireplaces, heavy beams and so forth – in 30 acres of coastal pastures and walled gardens: open fires, antiques, tapestries and fresh flowers, elegant furnishings, enjoyable modern english and french food, fine wines, a relaxed atmosphere, and spa with indoor swimming pool, outdoor swimming pool, tennis and croquet; children over 7 in restaurant; disabled access; dogs in bedrooms and lounges; menu and some treats; £10

CUCKFIELD

Ockenden Manor *Ockenden Lane, Cuckfield, Haywards Heath, West Sussex RH17 5LD (01444) 416111* (0.6 miles off A272, from W roundabout via B2036) **£160**, plus special breaks; 22 individually decorated, pretty rms. Dating from 1520, this carefully extended manor house has antiques, fresh flowers and an open fire in the comfortable sitting room, good modern cooking in fine panelled restaurant, cosy bar, and super views of the South Downs from the neatly kept garden (in nine acres); dogs in 4 ground floor bedrooms; £10

EASTBOURNE

Grand *King Edward's Parade, Eastbourne, East Sussex BN21 4EQ (01323) 412345* **£170**, plus special breaks; 152 individually designed rms, many with sea views. Gracious and very well run Victorian hotel, with spacious, comfortable lounges, lots of fine original features, lovely flower arrangements, imaginative food in elegant restaurants, and courteous helpful service; leisure club and outdoor pool and terraces; disabled access; dogs if small and includes a daily meal; £7

FAIRLIGHT

Fairlight Cottage *Warren Rd, Fairlight, Hastings, East Sussex TN35 4AG (01424) 812545* (1.9 miles off A259 via Fairlight Rd; in village, 2nd right and on into Warren Rd) **£70**, plus winter breaks; 3 rms, one with four-poster. Comfortable and very friendly no smoking house in fine countryside with views over Rye Bay and plenty of rural and clifftop walks; big comfortable lounge (nice views), good breakfasts in elegant dining room or on new balcony; three resident dogs; children over 10; dogs in bedrooms

HASTINGS

Beauport Park *Hastings Rd, St Leonards-on-sea, East Sussex TN38 8EA (01424) 851222* (1 mile off A21 just N of Hastings; A2100 towards Battle) **£130**; 25 attractive rms. Georgian house in 38 acres of gardens and woodland with outdoor heated swimming pool, tennis and putting green, and riding next door; log fire and a relaxed friendly atmosphere in the Georgian-style lounge, interesting modern cooking in smart, formal restaurant and more relaxed conservatory, a cocktail bar, and Saturday evening pianist; dogs in bedrooms and bar

LEWES

Shelleys *High St, Lewes, East Sussex BN7 1XS (01273) 472361* (1.3 miles off A27 W roundabout; the A277 takes you straight to it, on the High St) **£190**, plus special breaks; 19 pretty rms. Once owned by relatives of the poet, this stylish and spacious 17th-c town house is warm and friendly, with good food, nice breakfasts and bar lunches in elegant dining room, and seats in the quiet back garden; limited disabled access; dogs in bedrooms if small and well behaved

NEWICK
Newick Park Hotel *Newick, Brighton, East Sussex BN8 4SB* (01825) 723633 £165; 16 individually decorated, spacious rms inc 3 suites in a converted granary. Charming and carefully restored Georgian building in a huge estate of open country and woodland; organic walled kitchen garden, two lakes with fishing, pretty views, tennis, badminton, croquet, outdoor swimming pool, quad bikes and tank driving; comfortable and spacious public rooms include a study, a sitting room, bar/morning room and elegant no smoking restaurant with enjoyable dinner-party food using home-grown produce and local game, and good breakfasts; two resident dogs; disabled access; dogs in one ground floor room

PEASMARSH
Flackley Ash *London Road, Peasmarsh, Rye, East Sussex TN31 6YH* (01797) 230651 £148, plus special breaks; 45 newly refurbished rms. Elegant red-brick Georgian house in five acres of neat gardens, with comfortable no smoking lounge and bar areas, good breakfasts in charming no smoking dining room with inglenook fireplace and conservatory extension, and indoor swimming pool, sauna, gym, and beauty suite; croquet and putting green; walks nearby; dogs in bedrooms, £8.50

RUSHLAKE GREEN
Stone House *Rushlake Green, Heathfield, East Sussex TN21 9QJ* (01435) 830553 £135; 7 rms, some with four-posters. In a thousand acres of pretty countryside (with plenty of walks and country sports) and surrounded by an 18th-c walled garden, this lovely house was built at the end of the 15th c and extended in Georgian times; there are open log fires, antiques and family heirlooms in the drawing room, a quiet library, an antique full-sized table in the mahogany-panelled billiard room, wonderful food in the panelled dining room, fine breakfasts, and a cosseting atmosphere; cl Christmas; children over 9; dogs welcome in bedrooms

RYE
Jeakes House *Mermaid St, Rye, East Sussex TN31 7ET* (01797) 222828 £98, plus special breaks; 11 lovely rms (4 with four-posters) overlooking the rooftops of this medieval town or across the marsh to the sea, 10 with own bthrm. Fine 16th-c building, well run and friendly, with good breakfasts in no smoking dining room, lots of books, comfortable furnishings, swagged curtains, linen and lace, a warm fire, and lovely peaceful atmosphere; two resident cats; fields for walking nearby; children over 11; dogs in bedrooms and bar; £5

SHIPLEY

Goffsland Farm *Shipley Rd, Southwater, Horsham, West Sussex RH13 7BQ (01403) 730434* (1.3 miles off A24, from roundabout at S end of Southwater bypass; Mill Straight towards Southwater, then 2nd left on to Shipley Rd; handy for A272 too) £50; 2 rms inc 1 family rm. 17th-c no smoking Wealden farmhouse on 250-acre family farm with good breakfasts, and a friendly welcome; several resident dogs and cats; horse-riding nearby and plenty of surrounding walks; dogs welcome

Warwickshire

Dog Friendly Pubs

ALDERMINSTER

Bell *A3400 Oxford—Stratford; CV37 8NY*

Neatly kept and popular, this Georgian inn places much emphasis on its good food. The communicating rooms of the bar are spacious and open plan and there are stripped slatback chairs around wooden tables on flagstones and beautifully polished wooden floors, little vases of flowers, a counter fronted with rough timber from wine crates, and a solid fuel stove in a stripped brick inglenook. The green walls are hung with huge modern prints. Greene King IPA and Old Speckled Hen on handpump and a fine range of around 20 wines by the glass. A conservatory and terrace overlook the garden and Stour Valley.

Free house ~ Licensees Keith and Vanessa Brewer ~ Real ale ~ Bar food ~ Restaurant ~ (01789) 450414 ~ Children welcome ~ Dogs allowed in bar and bedrooms ~ Open 11.30-2.30, 6.30-11(10.30 Sun); closed evenings 24-30 Dec ~ Bedrooms: £32(£45S)(£60B)/£48(£55S)(£85B)

ARMSCOTE

Fox & Goose *Off A3400 Stratford—Shipston; CV37 8DD*

Enjoyable and very busy, this stylishly simple blacksmith's forge is an interesting mix of gastro pub and local – and the food is good, if not cheap. The small flagstoned bar has red painted walls, bright crushed velvet cushions plumped up on wooden pews, a big gilt mirror over a log fire, polished floorboards and black and white etchings. In a quirky tableau above the dining room's woodburning stove a stuffed fox stalks a big goose. Hook Norton Best and a guest such as Shepherd Neame Spitfire on handpump, well chosen wines and maybe winter mulled wine and summer Pimms; helpful service from charming young staff. Outside, the garden has an elegant vine-covered deck area overlooking a big lawn with tables, benches and fruit trees, and several of the neighbouring houses boast splendid roses in summer.

Free house ~ Licensee Sarah Watson ~ Real ale ~ Bar food ~ Restaurant ~ (01608) 682293 ~ Children allowed away from bar area ~ Dogs allowed in bar ~ Open 12-2.30, 6-midnight; 12-midnight Sun and Sat; 12-2.30, 6-midnight in winter ~ Bedrooms: £60B/£100B

ASTON CANTLOW

Kings Head *Village signposted just off A3400 NW of Stratford; B95 6HY*

In summer particularly, this lovely old black and white timbered Tudor pub is quite a sight with its colourful hanging baskets and wisteria. It's the sort of place that customers enjoy coming back to again and again for the very good (and very popular) food, gently civilised atmosphere, and welcoming, attentive service. The restaurant is no smoking. The clean and comfortable village bar on the right is a nice mix of rustic surroundings with a subtly upmarket atmosphere, flagstones, low beams, and old-fashioned settles around its massive inglenook log fireplace. The chatty quarry-tiled main room has attractive window seats and oak tables. Greene King Abbot, M&B Brew XI and a guest beer on handpump and decent wines; piped jazz. The garden is lovely, with a big chestnut tree. This is a very pretty village; the pub is not far from Mary Arden's house in Wilmcote, and Shakespeare's parents are said to have married in the church next door.

Enterprise ~ Lease Peter and Louise Sadler ~ Real ale ~ Bar food (11-3, 5.30-11; all day Fri and Sat) ~ Restaurant ~ (01789) 488242 ~ Children welcome ~ Dogs allowed in bar ~ Open 11-3, 5.30-11(midnight in summer); 11-midnight Sat; 12-10.30(maybe 11.30) Sun

EDGE HILL

Castle *Off A422; OX15 6DJ*

This crenellated octagon tower (also known as the Round Tower or Radway Tower) is a folly that was built in 1749 by a Gothic Revival enthusiast to mark the spot where Charles I raised his standard at the start of the Battle of Edge Hill. The big attractive garden has lovely glimpses down through the trees of the battlefield, and it's said that after closing time you can hear ghostly sounds of battle – a phantom cavalry officer has even been seen galloping by in search of his severed hand. Inside, there are arched doorways, and the walls of the lounge bar, which has the same eight sides as the rest of the main tower, is decorated with maps, pictures and a collection of Civil War memorabilia. Good bar food and Hook Norton Best Bitter, Old Hooky and Hooky Dark plus a monthly guest on handpump and 40 malt whiskies; piped music, games machine, TV, darts, pool and aunt sally. Upton House is nearby on the A422, and Compton Wynyates, one of the most beautiful houses in this part of England, is not far beyond.

Hook Norton ~ Lease Tony, Susan and Rory Sheen ~ Real ale ~ Bar food (12-2, 6.30-9; snacks available all day in summer) ~ (01295) 670255 ~ Children welcome ~ Dogs allowed in bar ~ Open 12-3, 6-midnight; 11-midnight Sun and Sat; 12-3, 6-midnight in winter; closed 25 Dec ~ Bedrooms: /£60S

FARNBOROUGH

Inn at Farnborough *Off A423 N of Banbury; OX17 1DZ*

This year, the emphasis on food at this elegant old golden stone house is even more pronounced as they have stopped serving real ale – they tell us this is due to lack of demand. The stylishly refurbished interior is a pleasant mix of the traditional and contemporary, with plenty of exposed stonework, and thoughtful lighting. The beamed and flagstoned bar has neat blinds on its mullioned windows, a chrome hood over a warm log fire in the old stone fireplace, plenty of fresh flowers on the modern counter, candles on wicker tables, and smartly upholstered chairs, window seats and stools. A stable door leads out to chic metal furnishings on a decked terrace. The no smoking dining room has a comfortably roomy seat in a fireplace, nice wooden floors, and a good mix of mismatched tables and chairs. Carefully chosen wines with 19 by the glass. Service is professional and courteous; piped music. The landscaped garden is really delightful with a lovely sloping lawn and plenty of picnic-sets (one under a big old tree).

Free house ~ Licensees Anthony and Jo Robinson ~ Bar food (12-3, 6-10; all day weekends) ~ Restaurant ~ (01295) 690615 ~ Children welcome ~ Dogs allowed in bar ~ Open 12-3.30, 6-11; 12-midnight(11pm Sun) Sat; closed 25 Dec

GREAT WOLFORD

Fox & Hounds *Village signposted on right on A3400 3 miles S of Shipston-on-Stour; CV36 5NQ*

This 16th-c stone inn has a cosy low-beamed bar with a nice collection of chairs and old candlelit tables on spotless flagstones, antique hunting prints, and a roaring log fire in the inglenook fireplace with its fine old bread oven. An old-fashioned little tap room serves Hook Norton and a guest beer on handpump, and over 100 malt whiskies; piped music; popular food. The dining area is no smoking. A terrace has solid wood furniture and a well.

Free house ~ Licensees Gill, Jamie and Sioned ~ Real ale ~ Bar food (not Sun evening or Mon) ~ (01608) 674220 ~ Well behaved children welcome ~ Dogs allowed in bar ~ Open 12-3, 6-midnight; 12-3, 7-10.30 Sun; closed Mon ~ Bedrooms: £45B/£70B

PRESTON BAGOT

Crabmill *B4095 Henley-in-Arden—Warwick; B95 5EE*

A very stylish transformation of an old cider mill, this rambling place has a smart two-level lounge area with a good relaxed feel, soft leather settees and easy chairs, low tables, big table lamps and one or two rugs on bare boards. There's also an elegant and roomy low-beamed dining area (no smoking), with candles and fresh flowers, and a beamed and flagstoned bar area with some stripped pine country tables and chairs, snug corners and a gleaming steel bar serving Greene King Abbot, Tetleys and Wadworths 6X on handpump, and eight wines by the glass. Terrific modern food and well chosen and well reproduced piped music. There are lots of tables, some of them under cover, out in a large attractive garden with a play area.

Enterprise ~ Lease Sarah Robinson ~ Real ale ~ Bar food (12-2.30(3.30 Sun), 6.30-9.30) ~ Restaurant ~ (01926) 843342 ~ Children welcome ~ Dogs allowed in bar ~ Open 11-11; 12-6 Sun; closed Sun evening; 25 Dec

PRIORS MARSTON

Holly Bush *Village signposted from A361 S of Daventry (or take the old Welsh Road) from Southam); from village centre follow Shuckburgh signpost, then take first right turn by phone box; CV47 7RW*

'An unusually good pub' is how one reader describes this golden stone inn, and others agree heartily. It's particularly well run with very good service, enjoyable food and well kept beers. The building has plenty of character, and the main part is divided into small beamed rambling rooms by partly glazed timber dividers, keeping a good-sized bar as well as the main dining area, and there are flagstones, some bare boards, a good deal of stripped stone, and good sturdy tables in varying sizes. A log fire blazes in the big stone hearth at one end, and the central lounge area has a woodburning stove. Beside a second smaller and smarter no smoking dining area is a back snug with temptingly squashy leather sofas and a woodburning stove. Fullers London Pride, Hook Norton Old Hooky and a guest like Wychwood England's Ale on handpump and eight wines by the glass; pool, TV and board games. The sheltered garden behind has tables and chairs on the lawn, and this is an attractive village.

Free house ~ Licensee Richard Saunders ~ Real ale ~ Bar food (12-2.30, 6.30-9.30; 12-3, 7-9 Sun) ~ Restaurant ~ (01327) 260934 ~ Children welcome ~ Dogs allowed in bar and bedrooms ~ Open 12-2.30, 5.30-11(midnight Fri); 12-3, 6-midnight Sat; 12-3, 7-10.30 Sun ~ Bedrooms: £45S/£55B

SHUSTOKE

Griffin *5 miles from M6, junction 4; A446 towards Tamworth, then right on to B4114 and go straight through Coleshill; pub is at Church End, a mile E of village; B46 2LB*

A smashing choice of up to ten real ales is well kept on handpump in this unpretentious country local. Dispensed from a servery under a very low heavy beam, they come from an enterprising range of brewers such as Banks's, Bathams, Everards, Exmoor, Fullers, Holdens, Hook Norton, RCH and Stonehenge. Also lots of english wines, farm cider, and mulled wine and hot punch in winter. Usually busy with a cheery crowd, the low-beamed L-shaped bar has log fires in two stone fireplaces (one's a big inglenook). Besides one nice old-fashioned settle the décor is fairly simple, from cushioned café seats (some quite closely packed) to sturdily elm-topped sewing trestles, lots of old jugs on the beams, beer mats on the ceiling and a games machine. Lunchtime bar food includes daily specials. There are old-fashioned seats and tables outside on the back grass, a play area and a large terrace with plants in raised beds.

Free house ~ Licensee Michael Pugh ~ Real ale ~ Bar food (12-2; not Sun or evenings) ~ No credit cards ~ (01675) 481205 ~ Children in conservatory but must be accompanied by parents ~ Dogs welcome ~ Open 12-2.30, 7-11; 12-2.45, 7-10.30 Sun

Dog Friendly Hotels, B&Bs and Farms

BUBBENHALL
Bubbenhall House *Paget's Lane, Bubbenhall, Coventry, Warwickshire CV8 3BJ (02476) 302409* £**67**; 3 rms. Mainly Edwardian house in five acres of mature woodland with marvellous wildlife (including one of only two Dormouse Sanctuaries in the UK) and once the home of the Mini's designer; beams and a fine Jacobean staircase, TV lounge plus other comfortable ones, hearty breakfasts in elegant dining room, and a friendly, family atmosphere; two resident dogs and one cat; tennis court; dogs in bedrooms; £5

HENLEY-IN-ARDEN
Ashleigh House *Whitley Hill, Henley-in-arden, Solihull, West Midlands B95 5DL (01564) 792315* £**67.50**; 11 homely rms, some in former stable block. No smoking Edwardian house in two acres of neatly kept grounds and with new owners; original features, a comfortable residents' lounge and small bar, hearty breakfasts in spacious dining room, and conservatory overlooking the gardens; dogs in bedrooms; £5

LOXLEY
Loxley Farm *Stratford Rd, Loxley, Warwick, Warwickshire CV35 9JN (01789) 840265* (1.2 miles off A429; 1st rd W S of Wellesbourne, then in village bear left on Stratford Rd) £**75**; 2 suites with their own sitting rooms in attractive barn conversion. Not far from Stratford, this tucked-away, thatched and half-timbered partly 14th-c house has low beams, wonky walls and floors, antiques and dried flowers, open fire, helpful friendly owners, and good Aga-cooked breakfasts; resident dogs and a cat (kept away from the B&B area); peaceful garden (where dogs may walk, plus a field), and fine old village church; cl Christmas and New Year; dogs welcome in bedrooms

PILLERTON HERSEY
Dockers Barn Farm *Oxhill Bridle Rd, Pillerton Hersey, Warwick, Warwickshire CV35 0QB (01926) 640475* £**56**; 2 cosy, beamed rms. Quietly set and carefully converted no smoking 18th-c threshing barn surrounded by fields of sheep and ponies; friendly owners, flagstoned floors, beams, interesting collections, and family portraits, and 21 acres of wildlife-friendly garden and land; can use hot tub in garden; two resident dogs; footpaths for walking; cl Christmas; children over 8; dogs in Granary Suite only

STRATFORD-UPON-AVON
Melita *37 Shipston Rd, Stratford-upon-Avon, Warwickshire CV37 7LN (01789) 292432* £**82**, plus winter breaks; 12 well equipped rms. Family-run, no smoking Victorian hotel with pretty, carefully laid-out garden,

comfortable lounge with open fire, extensive breakfasts; close to town centre and theatre; cl Christmas; disabled access; dogs in bedrooms – but must be left in car while owners are at theatre; £3

Shakespeare *Chapel St, Stratford-upon-Avon, Warwickshire CV37 6ER (0870) 400 8182* **£174**, plus wknd breaks; 74 comfortable well equipped rms. Smart hotel based on handsome, lavishly modernised Tudor merchants' houses, with comfortable bar, good food, quick friendly service, and civilised tea or coffee in peaceful chintzy armchairs by blazing log fires; seats out in back courtyard; three mins' walk from theatre; disabled access; dogs in bedrooms; £10

Wiltshire

Dog Friendly Pubs

AXFORD
Red Lion *Off A4 E of Marlborough; on back road Mildenhall—Ramsbury; SN8 2HA*

There's no doubt that the main emphasis in this pretty and welcoming flint-and-brick pub is placed on the imaginative restaurant-style food but they do offer bar snacks and keep Downton Quadhop, Hook Norton Best and Ramsbury Gold on handpump, 15 wines by the glass and 24 malt whiskies. The beamed and pine-panelled bar has a big inglenook fireplace, and a pleasant mix of comfortable sofas, cask seats and other solid chairs on the parquet floor; the pictures by local artists are for sale. There are lovely views over a valley from good hardwood tables and chairs on the terrace outside the no smoking restaurant, and you get the same views from picture windows in the restaurant and lounge; piped music. The sheltered garden has picnic-sets under parasols.

Free house ~ Licensee Seamus Lecky ~ Real ale ~ Bar food ~ Restaurant ~ (01672) 520271 ~ Children welcome ~ Dogs allowed in bar ~ Open 12-2.30, 6.30-11; 12-3, 7-10.30 Sun; closed 25 Dec

BERWICK ST JAMES
Boot *B3083, between A36 and A303 NW of Salisbury; SP3 4TN*

There's a good mix of customers in this flint and stone pub. The partly carpeted and flagstoned bar has a huge winter log fire in the inglenook fireplace at one end, sporting prints over a small brick fireplace at the other, and houseplants on its wide window sills. A small back dining room has a nice mix of dining chairs around four tables, and deep pink walls with an attractively mounted collection of celebrity boots. Well liked bar food that uses local produce where possible and vegetables may even come from the garden. Wadworths IPA and 6X and maybe a guest such as Archers Best on handpump; piped jazz. The neat sheltered side lawn has pretty flowerbeds and some well spaced picnic-sets.

Wadworths ~ Tenant Kathie Duval ~ Real ale ~ Bar food (12-2.30, 6.30-9.30; not Sun evening or Mon) ~ Restaurant ~ (01722) 790243 ~ Children welcome ~ Dogs welcome ~ Open 12-3, 6-11.30; 12-3, 7-10.30 Sun; closed Mon lunchtime

BERWICK ST JOHN
Talbot *Village signposted from A30 E of Shaftesbury; SP7 0HA*
The unspoilt, heavy-beamed bar in this friendly Ebble Valley pub is simply furnished with cushioned solid wall and window seats, spindleback chairs, a high-backed built-in settle at one end, and a huge inglenook fireplace with a good iron fireback and bread ovens. Reasonably priced lunchtime bar food plus Sunday roasts. Bass, Ringwood Best, Wadworths 6X and a guest such as Wadworths JCB on handpump; darts and cribbage. There are seats outside, and this is a peaceful and pretty village, surrounded by thatched old houses.
Free house ~ Licensees Pete and Marilyn Hawkins ~ Real ale ~ Bar food (not Sun evening, or Mon) ~ (01747) 828222 ~ Children in eating area of bar ~ Dogs allowed in bar ~ Open 12-2.30, 6.30-11; 12-4 Sun; closed Sun evening, Mon

BREMHILL
Dumb Post *Off A4/A3102 just NW of Calne; Hazeland, just SW of village itself, OS Sheet 173 map reference 976727; SN11 9LJ*
This is run by and for people who like their pubs unpretentious and brimming with genuine character – but it may not suit those with fussier tastes. The main lounge is a glorious mix of mismatched, faded furnishings, vivid patterned wallpaper, and stuffed animal heads, its two big windows boasting an unexpectedly fine view down over the surrounding countryside; not huge (it has a half dozen or so tables), it has something of the air of a once-grand hunting lodge. There's a big woodburner in a brick fireplace (not always lit) and a log fire on the opposite side of the room, comfortably-worn armchairs and plush banquettes, a standard lamp, mugs, bread and a sombrero hanging from the beams, and a scaled-down model house between the windows; in a cage is an occasionally vocal parrot, Oscar. The narrow bar leading to the lounge is more dimly lit, but has a few more tables, exposed stonework, and quite a collection of toby jugs around the counter; there's a plainer third room with a pool table, darts, games machine and piped music. Wadworths 6X and a couple of summer guests like Archers Best or Butcombe Gold on handpump, and friendly service. Simple and hearty lunchtime bar food and a no smoking dining room. There are a couple of picnic table sets outside, and some wooden play equipment. A peaceful spot in good walking country. Note the limited lunchtime opening times.
Free house ~ Licensee Mr Pitt ~ Real ale ~ Bar food (12-2) ~ No credit cards ~ (01249) 813192 ~ Children welcome ~ Dogs allowed in bar ~ Open 12-2 (not Mon-Weds), 7-11(1am Sat); 12-3, 7-midnight Sun; closed Mon-Weds lunchtimes

DEVIZES
Bear *Market Place; SN10 1HS*
This old coaching inn is comfortable and pleasant with some proper character and it has provided shelter to distinguished guests as diverse as King George III and Dr Johnson. The big main carpeted bar has log fires, black winged wall settles and muted cloth-upholstered bucket armchairs around oak tripod tables; the classic bar counter has shiny black woodwork

and small panes of glass. Separated from the main bar by some steps, a room named after the portrait painter Thomas Lawrence (his father ran the establishment in the 1770s) has dark oak-panelled walls, a parquet floor, a big open fireplace, shining copper pans, and plates around the walls; it's partly no smoking. Well kept Wadworths IPA, 6X and a seasonal guest on handpump, as well as a good choice of wines (including 16 by the glass), and quite a few malt whiskies. Decent straightforward bar food plus buffet meals as well. A mediterranean-style courtyard with olive trees, hibiscus and bouganvillea has some outside tables. It's only a stone's throw from here to Wadworths brewery, where you can buy beer in splendid old-fashioned half-gallon earthenware jars.

Wadworths ~ Tenant Andrew Maclachlan ~ Real ale ~ Bar food (11.30-2.30, 7-9.30) ~ Restaurant ~ (01380) 722444 ~ Children welcome ~ Dogs allowed in bar ~ Live jazz/blues Fri and Sat in cellar bar ~ Open 10am-11pm(10.30pm Sun); closed 25 and 26 Dec ~ Bedrooms: £70B/£95B

DONHEAD ST ANDREW

Forester *Village signposted off A30 E of Shaftesbury, just E of Ludwell; Lower Street; SP7 9EE*

In a charming village, this 14th-c thatched pub has fine country views from a good-sized terrace where there are plenty of seats. Inside, the appealing bar has a warmly welcoming atmosphere, stripped tables on wooden floors, a log fire in its big inglenook fireplace, and usually a few locals chatting around the servery: Ringwood Best, Wadworths 6X and maybe Sharps Doom Bar on handpump, and 18 wines (including champagne) by the glass. The comfortable main no smoking dining room has country-kitchen tables in varying sizes, nicely laid out with linen napkins, and attractive wrought-iron candlesticks – they sell these, if you like the design; there's also a second smaller and cosier (and also no smoking) dining room. Bar food is good and uses local produce and service is pleasant and helpful; no machines or piped music. Good walks nearby, for example to the old and 'new' Wardour castles. The neighbouring cottage used to be the pub's coach house.

Free house ~ Licensee Martin Hobbs ~ Real ale ~ Bar food (12-2(3 Sun), 7-9(9.30 Fri and Sat)) ~ Restaurant ~ (01747) 828038 ~ Children welcome but must be accompanied by adults at all times11 ~ Dogs allowed in bar ~ Open 11-3(3.30 summer Sat), 6-11; 12-3.30(3 in winter), 7-10.30 Sun ~ Bedrooms: £57.50S/£65S

EAST KNOYLE

Fox Hounds *Village signposted off A350 S of A303; The Green (named on some road atlases), a mile NW at OS Sheet 183 map reference 872313; or follow signpost off B3089, about half-mile E of A303 junction nr Little Chef; SP3 6BN*

It's best to come here on a clear day, not just to navigate the little lanes, but primarily to get the bonus of remarkable views right over into Somerset and Dorset – and you might also enjoy a walk in the nearby woods. The pub itself is a pretty sight, an ancient thatched building dating from the 16th c and facing the green where you get the best views, with picnic-sets outside. Inside has the warmly welcoming feel of a proper long-established pub (rather than a more formal pub/restaurant). It does have a small light-painted conservatory restaurant, and three linked areas on different levels around a central horseshoe-shaped servery, with a big log fire in one cosy area and a log-effect gas fire in another, plentiful oak woodwork and flagstones, comfortably padded dining chairs around big scrubbed tables with vases of flowers, and a couple of leather settees; the furnishings are all very individual and uncluttered. The New Zealand landlord's cooking of carefully sourced often local ingredients is now a big draw here and service is smiling and helpful; Bass, Wessex Golden Delirious, Youngs Bitter and a guest like Butcombe Bitter on handpump, farm cider, and a good choice of wines by the glass, quite a few from New Zealand.

Free house ~ Licensees Murray and Pam Seator ~ Real ale ~ Bar food (12-2.30, 6-9.30) ~ (01747) 830573 ~ Children welcome ~ Dogs welcome ~ Open 12-2.30, 6-11

FONTHILL GIFFORD
Beckford Arms *off B3089 W of Wilton at Fonthill Bishop; SP3 6PX*
On the edge of a fine parkland estate with a lake and sweeping vistas, this country house has an enjoyably civilised atmosphere. The smartly informal rooms are big, light and airy, with stripped bare wood, a parquet floor and a pleasant mix of tables with church candles. In winter, a big log fire burns in the lounge bar, which leads into a light and airy back garden room with a high pitched plank ceiling and picture windows looking on to a terrace. Locals tend to gather in the straightforward games room: darts, games machine, pool, board games and piped music. Good, interesting food and Fullers London Pride, Greene King Abbot, Hidden Fantasy and Timothy Taylors Golden Best on handpump, and several wines by the glass.

Free house ~ Licensees Karen and Eddie Costello ~ Real ale ~ Bar food (not 25 Dec or 1 Jan) ~ (01747) 870385 ~ Well behaved children welcome ~ Dogs welcome ~ Open 12-11; 12-10.30 Sun; closed 25 Dec, evening 1 Jan ~ Bedrooms: £45S/£75B

GREAT HINTON
Linnet *3½ miles E of Trowbridge, village signposted off A361 opposite Lamb at Semington; BA14 6BU*
Such is the reputation for the food in this attractive brick pub, that you have to book a few weeks in advance to be sure of a table. Everything on the menu is home-made, from the bread to the sausages and ice-cream and is served by attentive staff in the little bar or restaurant. The bar to the right of the door has a cream carpet and lots of photographs of the pub and the brewery, and there are bookshelves in a snug end part. The no smoking restaurant is candlelit at night. Wadworths IPA and 6X on electric pump, around two dozen malt whiskies, and several wines by the glass; piped music. In summer, the flowering tubs and window boxes with seats dotted among them are quite a sight.

Wadworth ~ Tenant Jonathan Furby ~ Real ale ~ Bar food (not Mon) ~ Restaurant ~ (01380) 870354 ~ Children welcome ~ Dogs allowed in bar ~ Open 11-2.30, 6-11; 12-3, 7-10.30 Sun; closed Mon; 25 and 26 Dec, 1 Jan

GRITTLETON
Neeld Arms *Off A350 NW of Chippenham; The Street; SN14 6AP*
Friendly, helpful licensees run this cheerful 17th-c black-beamed pub, now
totally no smoking. It's largely open-plan, with a convivial and chatty
atmosphere, some stripped stone, and a log fire in the big inglenook on the
right and a smaller coal-effect fire on the left. Flowers on tables and a
pleasant mix of seating from windsor chairs through scatter-cushioned
window seats to some nice arts and crafts chairs and a traditional settle. The
parquet-floored back dining area has yet another inglenook, with a big
woodburning stove; even back here, you still feel thoroughly part of the
action. Brains SA, Moles Best and Wadworths IPA and 6X on handpump
at the substantial central bar counter, and a good choice of reasonably
priced wines by the glass; piped music, board games, cribbage and
dominoes. Well liked bar food plus Sunday roast beef. There's an outdoor
terrace, with pergola. The golden retriever is called Soaky.
*Free house ~ Licensees Charlie and Boo West ~ Real ale ~ Bar food (12-2(2.30
weekends), 7-9.30) ~ Restaurant ~ (01249) 782470 ~ Children welcome ~ Dogs
welcome ~ Open 12-3(3.30 Sat), 5.30(5 Fri)-midnight; 12-3.30, 7-11 Sun ~
Bedrooms: £40S(£40B)/£60S(£70B)*

HINDON
Lamb *B3089 Wilton—Mere; SP3 6DP*
Perhaps more of a hotel nowadays, this smart and civilised place has a big
welcoming log fire, friendly, polite staff, and four real ales. The two
flagstoned lower sections of the roomy long bar have a very long polished
table with wall benches and chairs, blacksmith's tools set behind a big
inglenook fireplace, high-backed pews and settles, and at one end, a
window seat (overlooking the village church) with a big waxed circular
table. Deep red walls add to the comfortable, relaxed feel. Up some steps a
third, bigger area has lots more tables and chairs – though it can fill up fast
and at busy times you may not be able to find a seat. Enjoyable bar food
and maybe cream teas. From the polished dark wooden counter, pleasant
staff serve Youngs Bitter, Special and a seasonal brew, and maybe Hop
Back Summer Lightning on handpump, and a good choice of wines by the
glass; the extensive range of whiskies includes all the malts from the Isle of
Islay, and they have a wide choice of Havana cigars. There are picnic-sets
across the road (which is a good alternative to the main routes west);
parking is limited.
*Free house ~ Licensee Nick James ~ Real ale ~ Bar food (12-2.30, 6.30(7 Sun)-
9.30(9 Sun)) ~ Restaurant ~ (01747) 820573 ~ Children welcome ~ Dogs
allowed in bar and bedrooms ~ Open 11(12 Sun)-11 ~ Bedrooms: £65B/£90B*

HORTON
Bridge Inn *Signposted off A361 Beckhampton road just inside the Devizes limit;
Horton Road; SN10 2JS*
In 1810, this well run place was extended to include a flour mill and bakery
using flour transported along the Kennet & Avon Canal; the pub now has
its own moorings. Inside, there are old black and whites of brightly dressed

bargee families and their steam barges among other old photographs and country pictures on the red walls above a high panelled dado. In the no smoking carpeted area on the left all the sturdy pale pine tables are set for food and the front area has a log fire. On the right of the bar is a pubbier bit with similar country-kitchen furniture on reconstituted flagstones, and some stripped brickwork, with superbly kept Wadworths IPA, 6X and a seasonal ale tapped straight from the cask, and eight decent wines by the glass. Service by the helpful staff is well organised; disabled lavatories, piped music. The safely fenced garden has picnic-sets, and an aviary with two or three dozen white fantail doves.

Wadworths ~ Tenants Sue Jacobs and Kevin Maul ~ Real ale ~ Bar food ~ Restaurant ~ (01380) 860273 ~ Children under parental guidance all the time and away from bar ~ Dogs allowed in bar ~ Open 11.30-3(2.30 in winter), 6.30-11; 12-3, 6.30-10.30 Sun

LOWER CHUTE

Hatchet *The Chutes well signposted via Appleshaw off A342, 2½ miles W of Andover; SP11 9DX*

This neat and friendly thatched 16th-c house is one of the county's most attractive pubs. The very low-beamed bar has a splendid 17th-c fireback in the huge fireplace (and a roaring winter log fire), a mix of captain's chairs and cushioned wheelbacks around oak tables, and a peaceful local feel. Fullers London Pride, Otter Bitter and Timothy Taylors Landlord on handpump; cards, chess, board games and piped music. Decent bar food and a Thursday curry night. The restaurant and part of the bar are no smoking. There are seats out on a terrace by the front car park, or on the side grass, and there's a children's sandpit.

Free house ~ Licensee Jeremy McKay ~ Real ale ~ Bar food (12-2.15, 7-9.45) ~ Restaurant ~ (01264) 730229 ~ Children in restaurant and end bar only ~ Dogs allowed in bar ~ Open 11.30-3, 6-11; 12-3.30, 7-10.30 Sun ~ Bedrooms: /£60S

NEWTON TONY

Malet Arms *Village signposted off A338 Swindon—Salisbury; SP4 0HF*

This is a proper village pub opposite the playing field and run by a landlord who is mad about cricket (and coaches the local school children). The two low-beamed interconnecting rooms have nice furnishings including a mix of different-sized tables with high winged wall settles, carved pews, chapel and carver chairs, and there are lots of pictures, mainly from imperial days. The main front windows are said to have come from the stern of a ship, and there's a log and coal fire in a huge fireplace. The homely back dining room is no smoking. Good changing food and well kept Archers Special, Butts Barbus Barbus, Stonehenge Heelstone, and maybe one from Butcombe, Palmers or Ramsbury on handpump, farm cider, several malt whiskies, and 10 wines by the glass. There's an african grey parrot called Steerpike. The small front terrace has old-fashioned garden seats and some picnic-sets on the grass there, and there are more in the back garden along with a wendy house. There's also a little aviary, and a horse paddock behind. Getting to the pub takes you through a ford and it may be best to use an alternative route in winter as it can be quite deep.

Free house ~ Licensee Noel Cardew ~ Real ale ~ Bar food (12-2.30, 6.30-10 (7-9.30 Sun)) ~ (01980) 629279 ~ Children allowed but not in bar area ~ Dogs allowed in bar ~ Open 11-3, 6-11; 12-3, 7-10.30 Sun; closed 25 and 26 Dec, 1 Jan

NORTON

Vine Tree *4 miles from M4 junction 17; A429 towards Malmesbury, then left at Hullavington, Sherston signpost, then follow Norton signposts; in village turn right at Foxley signpost, which takes you into Honey Lane; SN16 0JP*

Once it's discovered, customers then tend to become enthusiastic regulars at this civilised dining pub. It's extremely well run and despite the emphasis on the imaginative food, there's a buoyant atmosphere and drinkers do pop in for a drink and a chat. Three beautifully kept little rooms open together: old beams, some old settles and unvarnished wooden tables on the flagstone and oak floors, big cream church altar candles, a woodburning stove at one end of the no smoking restaurant and a large open fireplace in the central bar, limited edition and sporting prints, and a mock-up mounted pig's mask (used for a game that involves knocking coins off its nose and ears); look out for Clementine, the friendly and docile black labrador. One side of the inn is no smoking. Using seasonal and traceable local produce, fish from Brixham and Cornwall, and beef from their next door neighbour's farm, the regularly changing food is very good; best to book to be sure of a table, especially at weekends. Butcombe Bitter, Fullers London Pride and St Austell Tribute on handpump, around 35 wines by the glass from an impressive list (they do monthly tutored tastings), and quite a choice of malt whiskies and armagnacs; helpful, attentive staff. There are picnic-sets and a children's play area in a two-acre garden plus a pretty suntrap terrace with teak furniture under big cream umbrellas, a lion fountain, lots of lavender and box hedging. They have a busy calendar of events, with outdoor music in summer, vintage car rallies and lots going on during the Badminton horse trials. Many things to do and see nearby. That said, it's not the easiest place to find, so it can feel more remote than its proximity to the motorway would suggest.

Free house ~ Licensees Charles Walker and Tiggi Wood ~ Real ale ~ Bar food (12-2(2.30 Sat, 3.30 Sun), 7-9.30(10 Fri/Sat)) ~ Restaurant ~ (01666) 837654 ~ Children welcome ~ Dogs welcome ~ Live jazz and blues once a month but during summer, every Sun ~ Open 12-3(3.30 Sat), 6-midnight; 12-midnight Sun; closed 25 Dec

RAMSBURY

Bell *Signed off B4192 NW of Hungerford, or A4 W; SN8 2PB*

This neatly kept dining pub suffered dreadful fire damage recently but has now been refurbished. The airy bar has exposed beams, cream-washed walls, two woodburning stoves, and a chatty, relaxed atmosphere. Victorian stained-glass panels in one of the two sunny bay windows look out onto the quiet village street. The friendly landlord and staff serve local

Ramsbury Gold and one of their guests such as Bitter, Flint Knapper or
Kennet Valley, and Sharps Doom Bar on handpump; well liked bar food.
There are picnic-sets on the raised lawn; roads lead from this quiet village
into the downland on all sides.
*Free house ~ Licensee Jeremy Wilkins ~ Real ale ~ Bar food (not Sun evening) ~
Restaurant ~ (01672) 520230 ~ Children welcome ~ Dogs allowed in bar ~
Open 12-3, 5.30-11; 12-3, 7-10.30 Sun*

ROWDE
George & Dragon *A342 Devizes—Chippenham; SN10 2PN*
Behind the imposing black front door in this attractive no smoking dining
pub are two low-ceilinged rooms with large wooden tables, antique rugs,
and walls covered with old pictures and portraits; the atmosphere is
pleasantly chatty. Popular bar food (fish and seafood are delivered daily
from Cornwall) plus a three course Sunday lunch. Butcombe Bitter on
handpump and nine wines by the glass; board games. A pretty garden at the
back has tables and chairs; the Kennet & Avon Canal is nearby.
*Free house ~ Licensees Philip and Michelle Hale, Christopher Day ~ Real ale ~
Bar food (12-3, 7-10 Tues-Fri; 12-4, 6.30-10 Sat; 12-4 Sun; not Sun evening,
Mon lunchtime) ~ Restaurant ~ (01380) 723053 ~ Children welcome ~ Dogs
allowed in bar ~ Open 12-3(4 Sat and Sun), 7-11; closed Sun evening, Mon
lunchtime, first week Jan*

Dog Friendly Hotels, B&Bs and Farms

BRADFORD-ON-AVON
Woolley Grange *Woolley Green, Bradford-on-avon, Wiltshire BA15 1TX*
(01225) 864705 £**210**, plus winter breaks; 26 rms, with fruit and home-
made biscuits. Civilised Jacobean manor house with a relaxed informal
atmosphere, lovely flowers, log fires and antiques in comfortable and
beautifully decorated day rooms, and pretty conservatory; delicious food
using local (or home-grown) produce, often organic, inc home-baked
breads and muffins and home-made jams and marmalades for breakfast,
marvellous staff, and swimming pool, tennis, badminton and croquet;
particularly well organised for families, with nannies and plenty of
entertainment; resident dog; disabled access; dogs in bedrooms and some
other areas; £10

CASTLE COMBE
Manor House *Castle Combe, Chippenham, Wiltshire SN14 7HR (01249)*
782206 £**185**, plus special breaks; 48 lovely rms, some in mews cottages
just 50 yds from the house. 14th-c manor house in 360 acres of countryside
with an italian garden and parkland, 18-hole golf course with full range of
practice facilities, croquet, boules and all-weather tennis court; gracious day
rooms with panelling, antiques, log fires and fresh flowers, a convivial bar,

warm and friendly atmosphere, and very good innovative food in smart, no smoking restaurants; resident cat; disabled access; dogs in some bedrooms and lounges; £50

CHICKSGROVE

Compasses *Lower Chicksgrove, Tisbury, Salisbury, Wiltshire SP3 6NB (01722) 714318* £**75**, plus special breaks; 4 rms. Lovely thatched house in delightful hamlet with old bottles and jugs hanging from the beams, good freshly cooked food in no smoking dining room, well kept real ales, and peaceful farm courtyard, garden and play area; plenty of surrounding walks; cl Christmas; dogs welcome in bedrooms

COLLINGBOURNE KINGSTON

Manor Farm *Collingbourne Kingston, Marlborough, Wiltshire SN8 3SD (01264) 850859* £**60**; 3 comfortable, very spacious rms with sofas and dining table, and country views. No smoking, 17th-c farmhouse on working arable farm lived in by the same family since 1885; warmly welcoming owners, excellent hearty Aga-cooked breakfasts (you can collect your eggs from their free range chickens), packed lunches on request and several very good local pubs and restaurants; good walking on 550 acres, in forest and along canal, and cycling and riding directly from the farm; their own private airstrip with aerial adventures on offer; dogs in bedrooms; £2.50

CRUDWELL

Old Rectory Country House Hotel *Crudwell, Malmesbury, Wiltshire SN16 9EP (01666) 577194* (just off A429 in village) £**95**, plus special breaks; 12 big homely rms. Elegant, welcoming country-house hotel, formerly the rectory to the Saxon church next door; three acres of lovely landscaped Victorian gardens, an airy drawing room, interesting and enjoyable food in panelled no smoking restaurant, a relaxed atmosphere and unpretentious service; dogs welcome in bedrooms

EASTON GREY

Whatley Manor *Easton Grey, Malmesbury, Wiltshire SN16 0RB (01666) 822888* £**280**, plus special breaks; 15 sumptuous rms and 8 suites. Very stylish Cotswold manor house in 12 acres of gardens, meadows and woodland; spacious and rather fine oak-panelled lounge, italian furniture, silk rugs and limestone floors, a cosseting atmosphere, knowledgeable staff, classical french cooking with contemporary touches in two restaurants, and well stocked wine cellars; cinema and Spa Aquarias with thermal pools, gym, and hydrotherapy pool that extends outside with lovely valley views; children over 12; disabled access; dogs in bedrooms; £25

LACOCK

At the Sign of the Angel *Church St, Lacock, Chippenham, Wiltshire SN15 2LB (01249) 730230* (0.5 miles off A350; Church St) £**105**, plus special breaks; 11 charmingly old rooms with antiques. This fine 15th-c house in a lovely NT village is full of character, with heavy oak furniture, beams and big fireplaces, a restful oak-panelled lounge, and good english cooking in three candlelit restaurants; resident dog and cat; cl Christmas period; dogs welcome in bedrooms

MALMESBURY
Old Bell *Abbey Row, Malmesbury, Wiltshire SN16 0BW (01666) 822344* (0.7 miles off A429; Abbey Row, just off B4014 through town) **£125**, plus special breaks; 31 attractive rms. With some claim to being one of England's oldest hotels and standing in the shadow of the Norman abbey, this fine wisteria-clad building has traditionally furnished rooms with Edwardian pictures, an early 13th-c hooded stone fireplace, two good fires and plenty of comfortable sofas, magazines and newspapers; cheerful helpful service, very good food, and attractively old-fashioned garden; disabled access; dogs in bedrooms; £10

PURTON
Pear Tree *Church End, Purton, Swindon, Wiltshire SN5 4ED (01793) 772100* **£110**, plus special breaks; 17 very comfortable, pretty rms. Impeccably run former vicarage with elegant comfortable day rooms, fresh flowers, fine no smoking conservatory restaurant with good modern english cooking using home-grown herbs, helpful caring staff, and 7½ acres inc a traditional Victorian garden; resident dog; cl 26-30 Dec; disabled access; dogs in bedrooms (but must not be left unattended)

SALISBURY
Rose & Crown *Harnham Rd, Harnham, Salisbury, Wiltshire SP2 8JQ (01722) 399955* (0.3 miles off A338/A354 roundabout, via A3094; handy too for A36) **£130**; 28 rms in the original building or smart modern extension. It's almost worth a visit just for the view – well nigh identical to that in the most famous Constable painting of Salisbury Cathedral; elegantly restored inn with friendly beamed and timbered bar, log fire, good bar and restaurant food, and charming Avonside garden; disabled access; dogs in bedrooms

TEFFONT EVIAS
Howards House *Teffont Evias, Salisbury, Wiltshire SP3 5RJ (01722) 716392* **£155**, plus special breaks; 9 rms. Partly 17th-c house in two acres of pretty gardens with ancient box hedges, croquet, and kitchen gardens; fresh flowers, beams and open fire in restful sitting room, delicious modern cooking in no smoking restaurant, fine breakfasts, and attentive, helpful staff; walks all round; two resident dogs; cl Christmas; dogs in bedrooms; £7

WARMINSTER
Bishopstrow House *Bishopstrow, Warminster, Wiltshire BA12 9HH (01985) 212312* (1.5 miles off A36 from Heytesbury roundabout at E end of bypass; B3414) **£199**, plus special breaks; 32 sumptuous rms, some with

jacuzzi. Charming ivy-clad Georgian house in 27 acres with heated indoor and outdoor swimming pools, indoor and outdoor tennis courts, fitness centre and beauty treatment rooms, and own fishing on River Wylye; very relaxed friendly atmosphere, log fires, lovely fresh flowers, antiques and fine paintings in boldly decorated day rooms, and really impressive food in no smoking restaurants; walks in grounds and nearby; disabled access; dogs welcome away from restaurants; £10

Worcestershire

Dog Friendly Pubs

BERROW GREEN
Admiral Rodney *B4197, off A44 W of Worcester; WR6 6PL*
Welcoming licensees run this enjoyable country inn with forethought and attention to detail. Pleasantly light and roomy throughout, the bare-boards entrance bar is still a place you can just enjoy a drink; with high beams and a sunny bow window, it has big stripped kitchen tables and cushioned chairs, a traditional winged settle, and a woodburning stove in a fireplace that opens through to the comfortable no smoking lounge area. This has some carpet on its slate flagstones, dark red settees, a table of magazines and rack of broadsheet newspapers, quite a few board games, and prints of the Battle of the Saints, where Lord Rodney obliterated the french fleet in the Caribbean. A separate skittle alley has pool; also darts and board games. Very good bar food from a nicely balanced menu and there's a rebuilt barn stepping down through three levels that forms a charming end restaurant with a more elaborate menu. Alongside well kept Wye Valley Bitter, they've three changing guests from brewers such as Beartown, Goffs and Youngs and you'll find a tempting choice of wines and malt whiskies, and local perry and apple juice. A terrace has outdoor heating and a retractable canopy, and neat green, solid tables and chairs look over the Lower Teme valley; good walking.
Free house ~ Licensees Gillian and Kenneth Green ~ Real ale ~ Bar food (12-2(2.30 Sun), 6.30-9(9.30 Sat)) ~ Restaurant ~ (01886) 821375 ~ Children welcome ~ Dogs allowed in bar and bedrooms ~ Folk night first Weds of month ~ Open 11-3, 5-11; 11-11 Sat; 12-10.30 Sun; closed Mon lunchtime ~ Bedrooms: /£65B

BIRTSMORTON
Farmers Arms *Birts Street, off B4208 W; WR13 6AP*
Little changes from year to year at this peacefully old-fashioned and fairly straightforward half-timbered village local. Quietly free of piped music or games machines, the neatly kept big room on the right (with no smoking area), rambles away under very low dark beams, with some standing timbers, and flowery-panelled cushioned settles as well as spindleback

chairs; on the left an even lower-beamed room seems even cosier, and in both the white walls have black timbering; the local cribbage and darts teams play here, and you can also play shove-ha'penny or dominoes. Sociable locals gather at the bar for Hook Norton Hooky and Old Hooky, which are well kept on handpump, alongside a changing guest from a brewer such as Wye Valley. Good value simple bar food. You'll find seats out on the large lawn (though one reader thought they were getting a bit rickety), and the pub is surrounded by plenty of walks. Please treat the opening hours we give below as approximate – they may vary according to how busy or quiet things are.

Free house ~ Licensees Jill and Julie Moore ~ Real ale ~ Bar food (12-2, 6.30(7 Sun)-9.30) ~ No credit cards ~ (01684) 833308 ~ Children welcome ~ Dogs welcome ~ Open 11-4, 6-11; 12-4, 7-10.30 Sun

HANLEY SWAN
Swan *B4209 Malvern—Upton; WR8 0EA*

This prettily set pub has two main areas – the extended back part laid out for dining with french windows looking out over the picnic-sets on the good-sized side lawn and its play area, and the front part that is more of a conventional bar; each area has its own servery. Good sturdy dining tables have comfortably high-backed chairs, and one part of the bar has dark leather bucket armchairs and sofas brightened up by scatter cushions. It's all been given a fresh and up-to-date country look, with cream paintwork, some attractive new oak panelling contrasting with older rough timbering, well chosen prints, some stripped masonry and bare boards, a log fire, and stylishly rustic lamps. They have three changing real ales on handpump, typically Adnams, Charles Wells Bombardier and Shepherd Neame Spitfire. Bar food includes a good choice of sandwiches and a help yourself baked potato counter as well as a popular Sunday lunch. The young staff are cheerful, attentive and helpful; disabled access and facilities. The five bedrooms are new. This is charming countryside, and the inn, handy for the Malvern show ground and set well back from the road, faces a classic green complete with duck pond and massive oak tree.

Punch ~ Lease Michelle Steggles and Adrian Bowden ~ Real ale ~ Bar food (12-2.30, 6.30-9) ~ Restaurant ~ (01684) 311870 ~ Children in restaurant ~ Dogs allowed in bedrooms ~ Open 11-3, 6-11(10.30 Sun), all day summer weekends ~ Bedrooms: £50B/£65B

HOLY CROSS
Bell & Cross *4 miles from M5 junction 4: A491 towards Stourbridge, then follow Clent signpost off on left; DY9 9QL*

With a classic unspoilt early 19th-c layout, the five small rooms and kitchen here open off a central corridor with a black and white tiled floor: they give a choice of carpet, bare boards, lino or nice old quarry tiles, a variety of moods from snug and chatty to bright and airy, and an individual décor in each – theatrical engravings on red walls here, nice sporting prints on pale green walls there, racing and gundog pictures above the black panelled dado in another room. Two of the rooms have small serving bars, with well

kept Banks's Bitter, Hook Norton, Timothy Taylors Landlord and maybe
a guest such as Hook Norton Hooky as on handpump. You'll find over 50
wines (with 14 sold by the glass), a variety of coffees, daily papers, coal fires
in most rooms, perhaps regulars playing cards in one of the two front ones,
and piped music; all dining areas are no smoking and food is delicious.
Pleasant views from the garden terrace and the pub cat is called Pumba.
*Enterprise ~ Lease Roger and Jo Narbett ~ Real ale ~ Bar food (12-2,
6.30-9.15(9.30 Fri-Sat); 12-2.30, 7-9 Sun) ~ Restaurant ~ (01562) 730319
~ Children welcome away from bar ~ Dogs allowed in bar ~ Open 12-3(3.30 Sat),
6-11; 12-4, 7-10.30 Sun*

KEMPSEY
Walter de Cantelupe *A38, handy for M5 junction 7 via A44 and A4440;
WR5 3NA*
The interesting choice of well kept real ales on handpump at this
welcoming pub includes Cannon Royall Kings Shilling, Hobsons Best,
Timothy Taylors Landlord and a guest such as Mayfields Naughty Nell. For
non-beer drinkers they have locally grown and pressed apple juices, wines
from a local vineyard, half a dozen wines by the glass, and in summer they
also have a farm cider. Boldly decorated in red and gold, the bar area has an
informal and well worn in mix of furniture, an old wind-up HMV
gramophone and a good big fireplace. The dining area has various plush or
yellow leather dining chairs, an old settle, a sonorous clock, and candles and
flowers on the tables; piped music and board games. The reasonably priced,
enjoyable bar food is cooked by the friendly landlord; you can buy jars of
home-made chutney and marmalade. The entire pub is no smoking on
Saturday nights – at other times just the dining area and counter are;
cribbage, dominoes and table skittles. There's a pretty suntrap walled
garden at the back; the sociable labrador is called Monti.
*Free house ~ Licensee Martin Lloyd Morris ~ Real ale ~ Bar food (12-2(3 Sun),
6-9.30; 12-2.30, 6.30-10 Fri, Sat; not Sun evening) ~ Restaurant ~ (01905)
820572 ~ Children in restaurant until 8.15 ~ Dogs welcome ~ Open 12-2.30(3
Sat), 6-11; 12-3, 7-10.30 Sun; closed Mon ~ Bedrooms: £44.50S(£49.50B)/
£55S(£77B)*

MALVERN
Nags Head *Bottom end of Bank Street, steep turn down off A449; WR14 2JG*
They keep an astonishing range of 16 real ales on handpump at this
welcoming old inn. Along with Banks's, Bathams, Greene King IPA,
Marstons Pedigree and Woods Shropshire Lad, you'll find changing guests
(last year they got through over 1000) from brewers such as Cairngorm,
Cottage, Dark Star, Fullers, Sharps and Three Rivers, to name but a few. If
you're having trouble making a choice they will happily give you a taste
first.They also keep a fine range of malt whiskies, belgian beers and decent
wines by the glass. The pub attracts a good mix of customers (with plenty
of locals), and the mood is chatty and easy-going, with friendly young staff.
There's a good variety of places to sit: a series of snug individually
decorated rooms with one or two steps between some, all sorts of chairs

including some leather armchairs, pews sometimes arranged as booths, a mix of tables with some sturdy ones stained different colours, bare boards here, flagstones there, carpet elsewhere, and plenty of interesting pictures and homely touches such as house plants and shelves of well thumbed books; there's a coal fire opposite the central servery; broadsheet newspapers and a good juke box; piped music, shove-ha'penny, cribbage and dominoes. Bar food plus evening meals in the extension barn dining room. Outside are picnic-sets and rustic tables and benches on the front terrace and in a garden, there are heaters, and umbrellas for wet weather. *Free house ~ Licensee Duncan Ironmonger ~ Real ale ~ Bar food (12-2, 6.30-8.30) ~ Restaurant ~ (01684) 574373 ~ Children welcome with restrictions ~ Dogs allowed in bar ~ Open 11-11.15(11.30 Sat); 12-11 Sun*

Dog Friendly Hotels, B&Bs and Farms

AB LENCH
Manor Farm House *Ab Lench, Evesham, Worcestershire WR11 4UP (01386) 462226 £80*; 2 rms. Comfortable 250-year-old house in a rural spot with a lovely fenced-in half-acre garden; relaxing reception rooms, a study with TV, some interesting objects collected from around the world, enjoyable evening meals, nice breakfasts, and charming, friendly owners; plenty of surrounding fields for walks; three resident dogs and one cat; children over 12; cl Dec-Jan; dogs in bedrooms, if small

BROADWAY
Broadway Hotel *The Green, Broadway, Worcestershire WR12 7AA (01386) 852401* (1 mile off A44 from B4632 roundabout; turn right on High St) *£135*; 20 well kept rms. Lovely 15th-c building, once a monastic guest house, with galleried and timbered no smoking lounge, cosy beamed bar, attractively presented food served by attentive staff in airy comfortable no smoking restaurant, and seats outside on terrace; plenty of walks nearby; dogs in some bedrooms

Lygon Arms *High St, Broadway, Worcestershire WR12 7DU (01386) 852255 £169*, plus special breaks; 69 lovely period rms (some more modern, too). Handsome hotel where Oliver Cromwell and King Charles I once stayed; interesting beamed rooms, oak panelling, antiques, log fires, fine traditional food in the Great Hall with minstrels' gallery and heraldic frieze, excellent service, and charming garden; health spa; disabled access; dogs in bedrooms and some public areas; doggie bags with treats; £15

Russells Restaurant *The Green, 20 High Street, Broadway, Worcestershire WR12 7DT (01386) 853555 £115*; 7 chic, spacious and comfortable rms. No smoking boutique restaurant-with-rooms with beams and inglenooks, stylish modern furnishings, a comfortable sitting area in the contemporary restaurant (there's also a new dining area), beautifully presented modern british cooking using the best local seasonal produce, an excellent wine list, very good breakfasts, and attentive, helpful staff; outside terrace seating in summer; dogs welcome in bedrooms

EVESHAM

Evesham Hotel *Coopers Lane, Off Waterside, Evesham, Worcestershire WR11 1DA (01386)* 765566 (off A44 via B4035 into centre; Coopers Lane, off Waterside) £126, plus special breaks; 40 spacious rms with games and jigsaws. Comfortably modernised and cheerful family-run hotel with a warmly friendly, relaxed and jokey atmosphere, popular restaurant with very good food (esp lunchtime buffet), huge wine and spirits list, and sitting room with games and toys; indoor swimming pool surrounded by table tennis and table football, and grounds with croquet, trampoline, swings and putting; can walk dogs in the garden or along the River Avon close by; cl 25-26 Dec; disabled access; dogs in bedrooms only

GREAT MALVERN

Cowleigh Park Farm *Cowleigh Park, Cradley, Malvern, Worcestershire WR13 5HJ (01684)* 566750 (0.8 miles off A449; A4219 NW) £75; 3 rms. Black and white timbered, no smoking 17th-c farmhouse in own grounds and surrounded by lovely countryside; carefully restored and furnished and serving good breakfasts with home-made bread and preserves; self-catering also; resident dog and cat; cl Christmas; children over 7; dogs in bedrooms; £2

HIMBLETON

Phepson Farm *Phepson, Droitwich, Worcestershire WR9 7JZ (01905)* 391205 £58, plus winter breaks; 6 rms, 4 in renovated farm buildings. Relaxed and friendly 17th-c farmhouse on small sheep farm with a fishing lake; a comfortable guests' lounge and good breakfasts in separate no smoking dining room; self-catering cottages; resident dogs and cats; walks on farm and nearby Wychavon Way; cl Christmas and New Year; dogs in ground floor bedrooms and must be well behaved

MALVERN WELLS

Cottage in the Wood *Holy Well Rd, Malvern, Worcestershire WR14 4LG (01684)* 575859 (just off A449; Holy Well Rd, which is off W, just N of B4209) £135, plus special breaks; 31 pretty rms, some in separate nearby cottages. Family-run Georgian dower house with quite splendid views across the Severn Valley and marvellous walks from the grounds; antiques, log fires, comfortable seats and magazines in public rooms, and modern english cooking and an extensive wine list in attractive no smoking restaurant; limited disabled access; dogs in ground-floor bedrooms; dog blanket and bonio offered; £5

Yorkshire

Dog Friendly Pubs

APPLETON-LE-MOORS
Moors *Village N of A170 just under 1½ miles E of Kirkby Moorside; YO62 6TF*
Now totally no smoking, this little stone-built pub is a very nice place to
stay with super breakfasts, well liked bar food, cosy bedrooms, and a
welcoming, helpful landlady. It's all strikingly neat and surprisingly bare of
the usual bric-a-brac. Sparse decorations include just a few copper pans and
earthenware mugs in a little alcove, a couple of plates, one or two pieces of
country ironwork, and a delft shelf with miniature whiskies; the whiteness
of walls and ceiling is underlined by the black beams and joists, and the
bristly grey carpet. Perfect for a cold winter evening, there's a nice built-in
high-backed stripped settle next to an old kitchen fireplace, and other
seating includes an unusual rustic seat for two cleverly made out of stripped
cartwheels; plenty of standing space. The games room has been converted
into an extra dining area. To the left of the bar, you'll probably find a few
regulars chatting on the backed padded stools: Black Sheep and Theakstons
Black Bull on handpump, and quite a few malt whiskies. Darts and board
games. There are tables in the walled garden with quiet moors views, and
moors walks straight from here to Rosedale Abbey or Hartoft End, as well
as paths to Hutton-le-Hole, Cropton and Sinnington.
*Free house ~ Licensee Janet Frank ~ Real ale ~ Bar food (see opening hours) ~
Restaurant ~ No credit cards ~ (01751) 417435 ~ Children welcome ~ Dogs
allowed in bar and bedrooms ~ Open 7-11; 12-2, 7-11 Fri, Sat and Sun; closed
all day Mon in winter; closed Mon, Tues, Weds, Thurs lunchtimes all year ~
Bedrooms: £35B/£56B*

ASENBY
Crab & Lobster *Village signposted off A168 – handy for A1; YO7 3QL*
This bustling and interesting place is handy for the A1. It's totally no
smoking, and the rambling, L-shaped bar has an interesting jumble of seats
from antique high-backed and other settles through settees and wing
armchairs heaped with cushions, to tall and rather theatrical corner seats;
the tables are almost as much of a mix, and the walls and available surfaces
are quite a jungle of bric-a-brac, with standard and table lamps and candles

keeping even the lighting pleasantly informal. There's also a dining pavilion with big tropical plants, nautical bits and pieces, and Edwardian sofas. Good bar food, Copper Dragon Golden Pippin and 1816 and John Smiths on handpump and quite a few wines by the glass; piped music. The gardens have bamboo and palm trees lining the paths, there's a gazebo at the end of the walkways, and seats on a mediterranean-style terrace. The opulent bedrooms (based on famous hotels around the world) are in the surrounding house which has seven acres of mature gardens, and 180-metre golf hole with full practice facilities.

Vimac Leisure ~ Licensee Mark Spenceley ~ Real ale ~ Bar food ~ Restaurant ~ (01845) 577286 ~ Children welcome ~ Dogs allowed in bar and bedrooms ~ Lunchtime jazz Sun ~ Open 11.30-midnight ~ Bedrooms: /£150B

BRADFIELD

Strines Inn *From A57 heading E of junction with A6013 (Ladybower Reservoir) take first left turn (signposted with Bradfield) then bear left; with a map can also be reached more circuitously from Strines signpost on A616 at head of Underbank Reservoir, W of Stocksbridge; S6 6JE*

In an area known as Little Switzerland, this isolated moorland inn was originally built as a manor house in 1275; superb scenery and surrounding walks. The main bar has a welcoming atmosphere and a good mix of customers, black beams liberally decked with copper kettles and so forth, quite a menagerie of stuffed animals, homely red-plush-cushioned traditional wooden wall benches and small chairs, and a coal fire in the rather grand stone fireplace. A room off on the right has another coal fire, hunting photographs and prints, and lots of brass and china, and on the left is another similarly furnished room; two rooms are no smoking. Good bar food, Adnams Broadside, Mansfield Bitter and Marstons Pedigree on handpump, and several malt whiskies; piped music. The bedrooms have four-poster beds (one has an open log fire) and a dining table, as breakfast is served in your room. Fine views from the picnic-sets, a safely fenced in children's playground, and wandering peacocks.

Free house ~ Licensee Bruce Howarth ~ Real ale ~ Bar food (12-2.30, 6-9 winter weekdays; all day weekends and summer weekdays) ~ (0114) 285 1247 ~ Children welcome ~ Dogs welcome ~ Open 10.30am-11pm; 10.30-3, 6-11 weekdays in winter; closed 25 Dec ~ Bedrooms: /£70B

BREARTON

Malt Shovel *Village signposted off A61 N of Harrogate; HG3 3BX*

To be sure of a seat, you must arrive at this 16th-c village pub promptly as they don't take reservations. Several heavily-beamed rooms radiate from the attractive linenfold oak bar counter with plush-cushioned seats and a mix of tables, an ancient oak partition wall, tankards and horsebrasses, an open fire, and paintings by local artists (for sale) and lively hunting prints on the walls. The dining area is no smoking. Bar food, Black Sheep Bitter, Daleside Bitter, Timothy Taylors Landlord and a couple of guests on handpump and 30 malt whiskies. You can eat outside on the small terrace where they have outdoor heaters.

Free house ~ Licensees Jamie and Hayley Stewart ~ Real ale ~ Bar food (not Sun evening or Mon) ~ (01423) 862929 ~ Children welcome ~ Dogs welcome ~ Open 11.45-3, 6.45(7 Sun)-11; closed Mon; first 2 weeks Jan

BURN
Wheatsheaf *A19 Selby—Doncaster; Main Road; YO8 8LJ*

There's masses to look at in this roadside mock-Tudor pub and it is all very nicely done up: gleaming copper kettles, black dagging shears, polished buffalo horns and the like around its good log and coal fire (and a drying rack with bunches of herbs above it), decorative mugs above one bow-window seat, and cases of model vans and lorries on the cream walls. The highly polished pub tables in the partly divided open-plan bar have comfortable seats around them, and the atmosphere is welcoming and chatty, with a friendly landlord and neat efficient young staff. Good value food and Brown Cow Bitter, Copper Dragon Golden Pippin, Ossett Pale Gold, John Smiths and Timothy Taylors Landlord on handpump at attractive prices, over 50 malt whiskies, and australian wines at exceptionally low mark-ups. A pool table is out of the way on the left, cribbage, dominoes, games machine, TV, and there may be unobtrusive piped music. A small garden behind has picnic-sets on a heated terrace.

Free house ~ Licensee Andrew Howdall ~ Real ale ~ Bar food (12-2 daily and 6.30-8.30 Thurs-Sat) ~ Restaurant ~ (01757) 270614 ~ Children welcome ~ Dogs welcome ~ Local live bands and theatre companies Weds or Sat evenings every two months ~ Open 12-11(midnight Sat and Sun)

CONSTABLE BURTON
Wyvill Arms *A684 E of Leyburn; DL8 5LH*

The emphasis in this popular, no smoking dining pub is on the very good food but they do have a small bar area with a mix of seating, a finely worked plaster ceiling with the Wyvill family's coat of arms, and an elaborate stone fireplace. The second bar, where food is served, has semicircled, upholstered alcoves, hunting prints and old oak tables; the reception area of this room includes a huge chesterfield which can seat up to eight people, another carved stone fireplace, and an old leaded church stained-glass window partition. Both rooms are hung with pictures of local scenes. Black Sheep, John Smiths Bitter, Theakstons Best, and a guest like Thwaites Lancaster Bomber on handpump, 10 wines by the glass, and friendly, efficient staff. Darts, chess and dominoes, board games, and piped music. Several large wooden benches under large white parasols for outdoor dining. Constable Burton Gardens are opposite and worth a visit.

Free house ~ Licensee Nigel Stevens ~ Real ale ~ Bar food ~ Restaurant ~ (01677) 450581 ~ Children welcome but with restrictions ~ Dogs allowed in bar and bedrooms ~ Open 11-3, 5.30-11 ~ Bedrooms: £50B/£75B

CRAYKE
Durham Ox *Off B1363 at Brandsby, towards Easingwold; West Way; YO61 4TE*

The tale is that this is the hill which the Grand Old Duke of York marched his men up; the view from the hill opposite is marvellous. The old-fashioned lounge bar has an enormous inglenook fireplace, pictures and photographs on the dark red walls, interesting satirical carvings in its panelling (Victorian copies of medievel pew ends), polished copper and brass, and venerable tables, antique seats and settles on the flagstones. In the bottom bar is a framed illustrated account of the local history (some of it gruesome) dating back to the 12th c, and a large framed print of the original famous Durham Ox which weighed 171 stones. Bar bites plus interesting meals and daily specials, and the main bar and restaurant are no smoking; piped music and board games. Theakstons Best, Coopers Butt and IPA on handpump and 12 wines by the glass. There are seats outside on a terrace and in the courtyard, and the comfortable bedrooms are in converted farm buildings.

Free house ~ Licensee Michael Ibbotson ~ Real ale ~ Bar food (12-2.30, 6-9.30(10 Sat; 8.30 Sun); not 25 Dec) ~ Restaurant ~ (01347) 821506 ~ Children welcome ~ Dogs allowed in bedrooms ~ Open 12-3, 6-11; 12-11 Sun and Sat ~ Bedrooms: £60B/£80B

EAST WITTON
Blue Lion *A6108 Leyburn—Ripon; DL8 4SN*
Not really the place for a casual drink, this dining pub is smart and rather civilised. The big squarish bar has high-backed antique settles and old windsor chairs on the turkey rugs and flagstones, ham-hooks in the high ceiling decorated with dried wheat, teazles and so forth, a delft shelf filled with appropriate bric-a-brac, several prints, sporting caricatures and other pictures on the walls, a log fire and daily papers; the friendly labrador is called Archie. The restaurant is no smoking. Black Sheep Bitter, Theakstons Best and Worthingtons on handpump, and an impressive wine list with quite a few by the glass. Picnic-sets on the gravel outside look beyond the stone houses on the far side of the village green to Witton Fell, and there's a big, pretty back garden.

Free house ~ Licensee Paul Klein ~ Real ale ~ Bar food ~ (01969) 624273 ~ Children welcome ~ Dogs allowed in bar and bedrooms ~ Open 11-11 ~ Bedrooms: £59.50S/£79S(£89B)

FERRENSBY
General Tarleton *A655 N of Knaresborough; HG5 0QB*
The good, interesting food remains the chief draw to this rather smart and comfortable old coaching inn – now totally no smoking. The beamed and carpeted bar has brick pillars dividing up the several different areas to create the occasional cosy alcove, some exposed stonework, and neatly framed pictures of staff on the red walls; there are new leather chairs around wooden tables, a big open fire and a door leading out to a pleasant tree-lined garden – which also has new furniture; seats in a covered courtyard, too. Black Sheep Best and Timothy Taylors Landlord on handpump, over 20 good wines by the glass, and quite a few coffees.

Free house ~ Licensee John Topham ~ Real ale ~ Bar food (12-2.15, 6-9.15(8.30 Sun)) ~ Restaurant ~ (01423) 340284 ~ Children welcome ~ Dogs allowed in bedrooms ~ Open 12-3, 6-11(10.30 Sun) ~ Bedrooms: £85B/£97B

GRINTON
Bridge Inn *B6270 W of Richmond; DL11 6HH*

As this pretty Swaledale village is surrounded by good walks, the sign here allowing dogs and muddy boots is very welcoming. The cheerful gently lit red-carpeted bar has bow window seats and a pair of stripped traditional settles among more usual pub seats, all well cushioned; a good log fire, Jennings Cumberland, Dark Mild, Cocker Hoop and a guest on handpump, nice wines by the glass, and a good collection of malt whiskies. On the right a few steps take you down into a dark red-walled room with darts, TV, board games, a well lit pool table and piped music. Well liked bar food and friendly, helpful service. On the left is an extensive, no smoking two-part dining room, past leather armchairs and a sofa by a second log fire (and a glass chess set); the décor is in mint green and shades of brown, with a modicum of fishing memorabilia. There are picnic-sets outside, and the inn is right opposite a lovely church known as the Cathedral of the Dales. The bedrooms are neat and simple, with a good breakfast.

Jennings (W & D) ~ Lease Andrew Atkin ~ Real ale ~ Bar food (all day) ~ Restaurant ~ (01748) 884224 ~ Children welcome ~ Dogs allowed in bar and bedrooms ~ Open 12-midnight(1am Sat) ~ Bedrooms: £42S/£64S

LITTON
Queens Arms *From B6160 N of Grassington, after Kilnsey take second left fork; can also be reached off B6479 at Stainforth N of Settle, via Halton Gill; BD23 5QJ*

'Unmissable' and 'a gem' are just two descriptions readers have used for this super little inn. It's got plenty of local charm, own-brewed beers, and a lovely setting. In fine weather you can make the most of the seats outside; the views over the fells are stunning, and there's a safe area for children in the two-level garden. The main bar on the right has a good coal fire, stripped rough stone walls, a brown beam-and-plank ceiling, stools around cast-iron-framed tables on the stone and concrete floor, a seat built into the stone-mullioned window, and signed cricket bats. The left-hand room is an eating area with old photographs of the Dales around the walls. You may smoke only in the bar. As well as Litton Ale, they also offer one other – Dark Star, Potts Beck Ale or Litton Light – on handpump from their own microbrewery; good, popular bar food. Darts, board games and piped music. Plenty of surrounding walks – a track behind the inn leads over Ackerley Moor to Buckden, and the quiet lane through the valley leads on to Pen-y-ghent. Walkers enjoy staying here very much – and there is a walkers' room (price on request).

Own brew ~ Licensees Tanya and Neil Thompson ~ Real ale ~ Bar food (not Mon or Jan) ~ (01756) 770208 ~ Children welcome away from bar ~ Dogs allowed in bar and bedrooms ~ Open 12-3, 6.30-11; closed Mon (except bank hols) and all Jan ~ Bedrooms: /£75S

LONG PRESTON
Maypole *A65 Settle—Skipton; BD23 4PH*

Handy for this busy road (and a good base for walking in the Dales), the

Maypole gets a warm-hearted feel not just from its log fires but also from its welcoming and obliging licensees – who have been the longest serving landlords here since 1700. The carpeted two-room bar has sporting prints and local photographs and a list of landlords dating back to 1695 on its butter-coloured walls, a delft shelf with whisky-water jugs and decorative plates, a couple of stags' heads, and good solid pub furnishings – heavy carved wall settles and the like, and heavy cast-iron framed pub tables with unusual inset leather tops. There's a good range of attractively priced and substantial food and a separate country dining room. They have Moorhouses Premier, Timothy Taylors Landlord and two changing ales such as Copper Dragon Scotts 1816 and Charles Wells Bombardier on handpump, and serve good strong coffee. Wines by the glass are reasonably priced. There's a piano in the room on the left, also darts, a games machine and dominoes; piped music only for major events. Out behind is a terrace with a couple of picnic-sets under an ornamental cherry tree, with another picnic-set on grass under a sycamore. If you're staying, they do a good breakfast.

Enterprise ~ Lease Robert Palmer ~ Real ale ~ Bar food (12-2, 6.30-9(9.30 Fri); 12-9.30 Sat; 12-9 Sun) ~ Restaurant ~ (01729) 840219 ~ Children welcome but not in bars after 9pm ~ Dogs allowed in bar and bedrooms ~ Open 12-2.30, 6-midnight; 12-midnight(11 Sun) Sat ~ Bedrooms: £29S/£55B

MIDDLEHAM

Black Swan *Market Place; DL8 4NP*

As this 17th-c stone inn is in the heart of racing country, it is popular with local trainers and stable staff. The immaculately kept heavy-beamed bar has high-backed settles built in by the big stone fireplace, racing memorabilia on the stripped stone walls, horsebrasses and pewter mugs, and Hambleton Fabulous Filly, John Smiths, Theakstons Best, Black Bull and Old Peculier, and Wensleydale Tony's Tipple on handpump; a decent little wine list with several by the glass, and piped music, TV, bar skittles, dominoes, cribbage and board games. Decent bar food and the dining rooms and area by the bar are no smoking. There are tables on the cobbles outside and in the sheltered back garden. Good walking country.

Free house ~ Licensees John and James Verbeken ~ Real ale ~ Bar food (12-2.30, 6.30-9) ~ Restaurant ~ (01969) 622221 ~ Children welcome ~ Dogs allowed in bar and bedrooms ~ Open 11-midnight; 11-1am Sat; 12-11 Sun; 11-3.30, 6-11 weekdays in winter ~ Bedrooms: £35S/£65S(£70B)

White Swan *Market Place; DL8 4PE*

There's a new dining room here (it was the old post office next door) which is light, spacious and modern with some popular window tables, a large fireplace, and in an area opposite the bar some contemporary leather chairs and sofa. Good food from a sensibly short menu and they also serve morning coffee and afternoon tea. The beamed and flagstoned entrance bar has a relaxed pubby atmosphere, a long dark pew built into a big window, a mix of chairs around a handful of biggish tables, Black Sheep Best Bitter and Emmerdale Ale, John Smiths and Theakstons Best on handpump from the curved counter, 17 wines by the glass and 20 malt whiskies; a good inglenook log fire. Another beamed room has a red oriental rug on its black boards, and like the first room, is candlelit. Piped music, cards and dominoes. *Free house ~ Licensees Andrew Holmes and Paul Klein ~ Real ale ~ Bar food (12-2.30, 6.30-9.30) ~ Restaurant ~ (01969) 622093 ~ Children allowed but not near bar area ~ Dogs allowed in bar ~ Open 11-midnight; 12-11.30 Sun ~ Bedrooms: £55B/£69B*

MILL BANK
Millbank *Mill Bank Road, off A58 SW of Sowerby Bridge; HX6 3DY*
From the outside, this dining pub is cottagey and traditionally Pennine but once inside, there's a clean-cut minimalist modern décor and local photographs for sale. The interior is divided into the tap room, bar and no smoking restaurant, with Tetleys and Timothy Taylors Landlord on handpump, and 20 wines by the glass including champagne, port and pudding wines; also, a specialised gin list. Daily changing, interesting food and discreet background music of a jazzy flavour. Outside, the terrace has a glass roof and fold-away windows that make the most of the glorious setting overlooking an old textile mill. Below this is a garden adorned with metal sculptures made from old farm equipment. The Calderdale Way is easily accessible from the pub.
Timothy Taylors ~ Licensee Joe McNally ~ Real ale ~ Bar food (12-2.30, 6-9.30(10 Sat); 12-4.30, 6-8 Sun; not Mon lunchtime) ~ Restaurant ~ (01422) 825588 ~ Children welcome ~ Dogs allowed in bar ~ Open 12-3, 5.30-11; 12-10.30 Sun; closed Mon lunchtime; 1st 2 wks Oct, 1st wk Jan

OSMOTHERLEY
Golden Lion *The Green, West End; off A19 N of Thirsk; DL6 3AA*
The roomy beamed bar on the left in this old stone-built pub is simply furnished with old pews and just a few decorations on its white walls, and has a pleasantly lively atmosphere, and candles on tables. Hambleton Bitter, Timothy Taylors Landlord and John Smiths or York Yorkshire Terrier on handpump and 45 malt whiskies; one side of the pub is no smoking. On the right, there's a similarly unpretentious and well worn eating area serving interesting, home-made food; you must book to be sure of a table and it does get pretty packed. There's also a separate dining room, mainly open at weekends; piped music. Benches out in front look across the village green to the market cross. As the inn is the start of the 44-mile Lyke Wakes Walk on the Cleveland Way, and quite handy for the Coast to Coast Walk, it is naturally popular with walkers.
Free house ~ Licensee Christie Connelly ~ Real ale ~ Bar food (12-3, 6-9) ~ Restaurant ~ (01609) 883526 ~ Children welcome if eating ~ Dogs allowed in bar ~ Open 12-3.30, 6-11; 12-midnight(11 Sun) Sat; closed 25 Dec ~ Bedrooms: /£70B

WATH IN NIDDERDALE
Sportsmans Arms *Nidderdale road off B6265 in Pateley Bridge; village and pub signposted over hump-back bridge on right after a couple of miles; HG3 5PP*
There is a welcoming bar in this very well run and civilised 17th-c

sandstone inn and locals do drop in for just a drink, but most customers are here to enjoy the particularly good food – and many stay overnight, too. It's been run by the charming Mr Carter for 29 years now and you can be sure of a genuinely warm welcome from both him and his courteous and friendly staff. The restaurant is no smoking. Black Sheep and a guest such as Wharfedale Folly Ale on handpump, a very sensible and extensive wine list with 15 by the glass (including champagne), over 30 malt whiskies and several russian vodkas; open fires and quiet piped music. Benches and tables outside. Seats outside in the pretty garden. As well as their own fishing on the River Nidd, this is an ideal spot for walkers, hikers and ornithologists, and there are plenty of country houses, gardens and cities to explore.
Free house ~ Licensee Ray Carter ~ Real ale ~ Bar food ~ Restaurant ~ (01423) 711306 ~ Children allowed with restrictions ~ Dogs allowed in bar ~ Open 12-2.30, 6.30-11; closed 25 Dec and evening 26 Dec ~ Bedrooms: £70B/£110B

Dog Friendly Hotels, B&Bs and Farms

BAINBRIDGE
Rose & Crown *Bainbridge, Leyburn, North Yorkshire DL8 3EE (01969) 650225* £**68**, plus special breaks; 12 comfortable rms. 15th-c coaching inn overlooking lovely green, with antique settles and other old furniture in beamed and panelled front bar, open log fires, cosy residents' lounge, big wine list and home-made traditional food in bar and restaurant; disabled access; dogs in some bedrooms

BOLTON ABBEY
Devonshire Arms *Bolton Abbey, Skipton, North Yorkshire BD23 6AJ (01756) 710441* (just off A59/B6160 roundabout) £**220**, plus special breaks; 40 individually furnished rms with thoughtful extras. Close to the priory itself and in lovely countryside with plenty of walks, this civilised, mainly no smoking former coaching inn owned by the Duke of Devonshire has been carefully furnished with fine antiques and paintings from Chatsworth; log fires, impeccable service, beautifully presented imaginative food and super breakfasts; health centre; two resident dogs; children over 12 in restaurant; disabled access; dogs in some bedrooms; bowls, dog bone, blankets

BRADFORD
Victoria Hotel *Bridge St, Bradford, West Yorkshire BD1 1JX (01274) 728706* £**85**, plus special breaks; 60 attractively refurbished rms. Carefully renovated Victorian station hotel with many original features and lots of stylish character, bustling bar, popular and informal brasserie serving good modern food, and marvellous breakfasts, small private gym and sauna; disabled access; dogs welcome in bedrooms

CRAY

White Lion *Cray, Skipton, North Yorkshire BD23 5JB (01756) 760262* £65, plus special breaks; 10 comfortable rms all with showers. Welcoming and no smoking little pub spectacularly isolated 335 metres (1,100 ft) up with super views, lots of walks, traditional feel with flagstones, beams and log fires, good bar food and decent wines; residents only 25 Dec; partial disabled access; dogs in bedrooms and other areas; £3

HALIFAX

Holdsworth House *Holmfield, Halifax, West Yorkshire HX2 9TG (01422) 240024* (1.2 miles off A629; heading N out of centre, fork right up Shay Lane) £120, plus wknd breaks; 40 traditional, individually decorated, quiet rms. Lovely, immaculately kept 17th-c house a few miles outside Halifax in its own neatly kept grounds; antiques, fresh flowers and fires in comfortable lounges, lots of sitting areas in the two bar rooms, friendly, particularly helpful staff, and three carefully furnished dining rooms with enjoyable food and very good wine list; disabled access; dogs in bedrooms and some public areas; £50 deposit

HAROME

Pheasant *Mill St, Harome, Helmsley, North Yorkshire YO62 5JG (01439) 771241* £111, plus special breaks; 12 rms. No smoking, family-run hotel with a relaxed homely lounge, and traditional bar with beams, inglenook fireplace and flagstones, good very popular food using their own eggs, vegetables and fruit, efficient service, and indoor heated swimming pool; walks along country lanes; cl mid-Dec-mid-Feb; children over 12; disabled access; dogs in bedrooms but must not be left unattended

HARROGATE

Alexa House *26 Ripon Rd, Harrogate, North Yorkshire HG1 2JJ (01423) 501988* (on A61 N of centre; 29 Ripon Rd) £80, plus winter breaks; 13 rms, some in former stable block. Attractive Georgian house with friendly staff, comfortable lounge, good home cooking in no smoking dining room and marvellous breakfasts; good disabled access; dogs welcome in bedrooms

HAWNBY

Laskill Grange *Easterside, Helmsley, York, North Yorkshire YO62 5NB (01439) 798268* £74, plus special breaks; 6 rms, some in beamy converted outside building. Attractive and welcoming no smoking, creeper-covered stone house on big sheep and cattle farm near Rievaulx Abbey and lots of nearby walks; open fire, antiques and books in comfortable lounge, conservatory overlooking the garden, good food using home-grown produce, and own natural spring water; self-catering also; cl 25 Dec; partial disabled access; dogs in bedrooms if well behaved

HELMSLEY

Black Swan *Market Place, Helmsley, North Yorkshire YO62 5BJ (01439) 770466* (on A170; Market Pl) £124, plus special breaks; 45 well equipped and comfortable rms. Striking Georgian house and adjoining Tudor rectory with beamed and panelled hotel bar, attractive carved oak settles and windsor armchairs, cosy and comfortable lounges with lots of character, and a charming sheltered garden; dogs in bedrooms and certain lounges; £10

KILBURN
Forresters Arms *Kilburn, York, North Yorkshire YO61 4AH (01347) 868386* **£62**, plus special breaks; 10 clean, bright rms. Friendly old coaching inn opposite the pretty village gardens; sturdy but elegant furnishings made next door at Thompson mouse furniture workshop, big log fire in cosy lower bar, interesting Henry Dee bar in what was a stable with manger and stalls still visible, and enjoyable food in no smoking restaurant and beamed bar; resident dog; cl 25 Dec; dogs welcome away from dining room

KNARESBOROUGH
Dower House *Bond End, Knaresborough, North Yorkshire HG5 9AL (01423) 863302* (on A59, just W of B6165; Bond End) **£136**, plus special breaks; 31 clean, comfortable rms. Creeper-clad 15th-c former dower house with attractively furnished public rooms of some character, good food in Terrace Restaurant, super breakfasts, helpful service, and leisure and health club; two resident cats; walks along the River Nidd; partial disabled access; dogs in annexe bedrooms only

Newton House Hotel *5-7 York Place, Knaresborough, Yorkshire HG5 0AD (01423) 863539* (A59 nr centre; York Pl) **£85**, plus special breaks; 11 very well equipped rms. Elegant family-run 18th-c house close to the river and market square, with a warm welcome for guests of all ages, comfortable sitting room with magazines, books, sweets and fresh fruit and good generous english breakfasts in no smoking dining room; no evening meals but plenty of places close by; they provide a list of local walks; resident dog; cl 1 wk Christmas; dogs welcome; bed, bowls, towels, toys and treats available

LEEDS
42 The Calls *Leeds, West Yorkshire LS2 7EW (0113) 244 0099* **£120**, plus special breaks; 41 attractive rms using original features. Stylish modern hotel in converted riverside grain mill in peaceful spot overlooking the River Aire, with genuinely friendly staff, marvellous food in restaurant and next-door chic but informal Brasserie Forty-Four, and super breakfasts; cl 4 days over Christmas; disabled access; dogs welcome in bedrooms

Malmaison *Sovereign Quay, Leeds, West Yorkshire LS1 1DQ (0113) 398 1000* **£167.90**, plus wknd breaks; 100 spacious rms with CDs and air conditioning. Stylish hotel, once a bus company office, with bold, modern furnishings, contemporary bar and brasserie, enjoyable food, decent breakfasts and popular Sunday brunch, and helpful friendly service; disabled access; dogs in bedrooms; £10

LONG PRESTON

Maypole *Main St, Long Preston, Skipton, North Yorkshire BD23 4PH* (01729) 840219 (on A65 towards NW end of village) £55, plus winter breaks; 6 comfortable rms. Neatly kept 17th-c pub with generous helpings of enjoyable traditional food (and nice breakfasts) in spacious beamed no smoking dining room, open fire in lounge bar, real ales and helpful service; walks on the moors close by; dogs in bedrooms and bar; £5

MALHAMDALE

Miresfield Farm *Malham, Skipton, North Yorkshire BD23 4DA* (01729) 830414 £60; 10 rms. Spacious old farmhouse with good freshly prepared food in beamed dining room, pleasant conservatory and two lounges (one with open log fire), and lovely garden by stream and village green; two resident dogs; walks along the Pennine Way; dogs welcome in bedrooms

MARKINGTON

Hob Green *Markington, Harrogate, North Yorkshire HG3 3PJ* (01423) 770031 (2 miles off A61 S of Ripon; keep on through village) £110, plus winter breaks; 12 pretty rms. Lovely gardens and over 800 acres of rolling countryside surround this charming 18th-c stone hotel; comfortable and pretty lounge and garden room, log fires, antique furniture, fresh flowers, relaxed atmosphere, good interesting food, decent choice of wines, and friendly service; dogs in bedrooms

MIDDLETON

Cottage Leas Country Hotel *Nova Lane, Middleton, Pickering, North Yorkshire YO18 8PN* (01751) 472129 (1.5 miles N off A170 just W of Pickering, via Middleton Lane/Nova Lane) £76, plus special breaks; 12 comfortable rms. Delightful, peaceful 18th-c farmhouse with extensive gardens, comfortable informal rooms, beamed ceilings, open log fire in cosy lounge, a well stocked bar, and enjoyable creative food; partial disabled access; dogs in some bedrooms

MONK FRYSTON

Monk Fryston Hall *Main St, Monk Fryston, Leeds, West Yorkshire LS25 5DU* (01977) 682369 (2.5 miles off A1 via A63 E (may be a little further when new section of A1(M) opens here)) £120, plus special breaks; 29 comfortable rms. Benedictine manor house in 30 acres of secluded gardens with lake and woodland, an oak-panelled lounge and bar with log fires, antiques, paintings and fresh flowers, interesting modern cooking in elegant no smoking restaurant, hearty breakfasts, and friendly helpful staff; limited disabled access; dogs in bedrooms and public areas (not restaurant) £5

OTLEY

Chevin Country Park Hotel *Yorkgate, Otley, West Yorkshire LS21 3NU* (01943) 467818 (1.8 miles off A660; up East Chevin Rd then 1st right on York Gate) £110 plus special breaks; 49 rms, some in log lodges deep in the woods. Built of finnish logs with walks through 50 acres of birchwood (lots of wildlife), this comfortable hotel has its own leisure club, good food in lakeside restaurant, and friendly service; tennis and fishing; disabled access; dogs in some bedrooms; £5

PICKERING

White Swan *Market Place, Pickering, North Yorkshire YO18 7AA (01751)* *472288* **£139**; 21 comfortable, well appointed rms inc 3 suites. Smart old coaching inn with a properly pubby bar, log fire and panelling, a charming country atmosphere, another fire in a handsome art nouveau iron fireplace, a big bow window and bare boards in lounge bar, particularly good imaginative food using the best local produce in stylish restaurant, well kept real ales, an impressive wine list, and a club room for residents with honesty bar, pool table and board games; dogs welcome away from restaurant; £12.50

REETH

Arkleside *Reeth, Richmond, North Yorkshire DL11 6SG (01748) 884200* **£96**; 9 cosy no smoking rms including a suite. Former row of 17th-c lead miners` cottages with lovely Swaledale views, this no smoking house has a friendly atmosphere, homely bar and a comfortable lounge, super, imaginative food in candlelit restaurant, nice breakfasts, and helpful, polite service; four resident dogs; cl Jan; no children; little garden and plenty of good walks; dogs welcome away from dining room

RICHMOND

Millgate House *Millgate, Richmond, North Yorkshire DL10 4JN (01748)* *823571* **£85**; 3 rms, 2 overlooking the garden. No smoking Georgian town house with lots of interesting antiques and lovely plants, a peaceful drawing room, warm friendly owners offering meticulous attention to detail, and good breakfasts in charming dining room which also overlooks the garden; it is this award-winning small garden with views over the River Swale and the Cleveland Hills beyond that is so special, filled with wonderful roses, ferns, clematis and hostas – they have a booklet listing the plants (no dogs here but riverside walks nearby); children over 10; dogs welcome in bedrooms

RIPLEY

Boars Head *Ripley, Harrogate, North Yorkshire HG3 3AY (01423) 771888* (just off A61 N of Harrogate) **£125**, plus special breaks; 25 charmingly decorated rms. In a delightful estate village, this fine old coaching inn has a relaxed, welcoming atmosphere, comfortable sofas in attractively decorated lounges (some of the furnishings come from the attic of next door Ripley Castle where the owners of this inn have lived for over 650 years), long flagstoned bar, notable wines by the glass, fine food in bar and restful dining room, and unobtrusive service; disabled access; dogs in some bedrooms (inc bed, bonio and bowls) and some public areas; £10

RIPON

Ripon Spa *Park St, Ripon, North Yorkshire HG4 2BU (01765) 602172* (1 mile off A61, via B6265, turning right into High Skellgate (A6108) in centre, then next left; Park St) **£108**, plus special breaks; 40 individually furnished rms, many overlooking the grounds. Neatly kept friendly and comfortable Edwardian hotel with seven acres of charming gardens, yet only a short walk from the centre; attractive public rooms, winter log fires, and good food in bar and restaurant; disabled access; dogs in bedrooms only

SEDBUSK

Stone House *Hawes, North Yorkshire DL8 3PT (01969) 667571* **£105**, plus special breaks; 23 rms, 5 with own conservatories. Small, warmly friendly no smoking Edwardian hotel in a stunning setting with magnificent views; country-house feel and appropriate furnishings, attractive oak-panelled drawing room, billiard room, log fires, and exemplary service offering good local information; pleasant extended dining room with excellent wholesome food (special needs catered for) inc super breakfasts, and reasonable choice of wines; wonderful walks; P. G. Wodehouse stayed here as a guest of the original owner who employed a butler called Jeeves – it was on him that Wodehouse based his famous character; cl Jan; disabled access; dogs welcome away from dining room; dog blankets offered

SKIPSEA

Village Farm *Back Street, Skipsea, E Yorkshire YO25 8SW (01262) 468479* **£65**; 3 quiet, attractively contemporary rms. Carefully renovated traditional no smoking farmhouse and outbuildings set around a central courtyard with good breakfasts in separate annexe; three resident dogs; walks along 40 miles of beach; self-catering, too; disabled access; dogs in bedrooms

STUDLEY ROGER

Lawrence House *Studley Roger, Ripon, North Yorkshire HG4 3AY (01765) 600947* (2.2 miles off A61; B6265 through Ripon) **£110**; 2 spacious, lovely rms with peaceful views. Attractive Georgian house with two acres of lovely garden on the edge of Studley Royal and Fountains Abbey; fine antiques and pictures, log fires, good breakfasts and delicious evening meals; two resident dogs; cl Christmas and New Year; children by arrangement; dogs in bedrooms

THORNTON WATLASS

Buck *Thornton Watlass, Ripon, North Yorkshire HG4 4AH (01677) 422461* **£75**, plus fishing, racing and special breaks; 7 rms, most with own bthrm. Cheerful country pub overlooking cricket green in very attractive village, with interesting beamed rooms, open fire, jazz Sun lunchtimes, enjoyable food in no smoking dining room, and lots of nearby walks; resident dog; cl 25 Dec; dogs in bedrooms and residents' lounge; £5

YORK

Dairy Guesthouse *3 Scarcroft Rd, York YO23 1ND (01904) 639367* £**75**; 5 attractive rms, most with own bthrm. Carefully restored no smoking Victorian house with lots of original features and attention to detail, enjoyable breakfasts (vegetarian and vegan choices offered) and plenty of nearby places to eat for evening meals, warmly hospitable atmosphere, and charming little flower-filled courtyard; cl Jan; disabled access; dogs welcome in bedrooms

Grange Hotel *1 Clifton, York YO30 6AA (01904) 644744* £**155**, plus special breaks; 30 individually decorated rms with antiques and chintz. Close to the Minster, this Regency town house has elegant public rooms, an open fire, newspapers, good breakfasts, excellent food in no smoking restaurant (there's also a brasserie), and warmly friendly staff; car park; disabled access; dogs welcome in bedrooms

London

Dog Friendly Pubs

Colton Arms *Greyhound Road; W14 9SD*
Readers visiting here invariably tell us first of all about the unprepossessing walk from the underground, and how it led them to expect disappointment, then go on to express astonishment that such an unspoilt little gem has survived intact. That it has is down to the friendly, dedicated landlord, who has kept it exactly the same for the last 40 years. Like an old-fashioned country pub in town, the main U-shaped front bar has a log fire blazing in winter, highly polished brasses, a fox's mask, hunting crops and plates decorated with hunting scenes on the walls, and a remarkable collection of handsomely carved 17th-c oak furniture. That room is small enough, but the two back rooms are tiny; each has its own little serving counter, with a bell to ring for service. Well kept Caledonian Deuchars IPA, Fullers London Pride and Greene King Old Speckled Hen on handpump (when you pay, note the old-fashioned brass-bound till); the food is limited to sandwiches (weekday lunchtimes only). Pull the curtain aside for the door out to a charming back terrace with a neat rose arbour. The pub is next to the Queens Club tennis courts and gardens.
Enterprise ~ Tenants N J and J A Nunn ~ Real ale ~ Bar food (12-2 weekday lunchtimes only) ~ No credit cards ~ (020) 7385 6956 ~ Children welcome lunchtimes only ~ Dogs welcome ~ Open 12-3, 5.30(6.30 Sat)-11; 12-4, 7-10.30 Sun; closed evening 25 Dec, all day 26 Dec and Easter Sat

Dove *Upper Mall; W6 9TA*
On good form at the moment, this famous old riverside pub has seen so many writers, actors and artists pass through its doors over the years that a framed list on the wall of the bar is the only way to keep up with all the names. Perhaps its best claim to fame is that *Rule Britannia* is said to have been composed in one of the upstairs room, but it was also a favourite with Turner, who painted the view of the Thames from the delightful back terrace. The main flagstoned area out here, down some steps, has a verandah and some highly prized tables looking over the low river wall to the Thames reach just above Hammersmith Bridge. There's a tiny exclusive area up a spiral staircase, a prime spot for watching the rowing crews out on

the water. By the entrance from the quiet alley, the front bar (said to be Britain's smallest) is cosy and traditional, with black panelling, and red leatherette cushioned built-in wall settles and stools around dimpled copper tables; it leads to a bigger, similarly furnished room, with old framed advertisements and photographs of the pub. They stock the full range of Fullers beers, with ESB, London Pride and seasonal beers on handpump, and maybe a guest like Gales HSB: no games machines or piped music. Well liked bar food includes traditional dishes and daily specials. The pub isn't quite so crowded at lunchtimes as it is in the evenings. A plaque marks the level of the highest-ever tide in 1928.

Fullers ~ Manager Nick Kiley ~ Real ale ~ Bar food (12-3, 5-9 weekdays; 12-9 Sat; 12-5 Sun) ~ (020) 8748 9474 ~ Dogs allowed in bar ~ Open 11-11; 12-10.30 Sun

Fox & Hounds *Latchmere Road; SW11 2JU*
It's the excellent very imaginative daily changing mediterranean cooking (though note they don't do food weekday lunchtimes) that makes this otherwise unremarkable big Victorian local worth a detour. The pub can fill quickly, so you may have to move fast to grab a table. The spacious, straightforward bar has bare boards, mismatched tables and chairs, two narrow pillars supporting the dark red ceiling, photographs on the walls, and big windows overlooking the street (the view partially obscured by colourful window boxes). There are fresh flowers and daily papers on the bar, and a view of the kitchen behind. Two rooms lead off, one more cosy with its two red leatherette sofas. Well kept Caledonian Deuchars IPA, Fullers London Pride and Harveys Sussex on handpump; the carefully chosen wine list (which includes a dozen by the glass) is written out on a blackboard. It's still very much the kind of place where locals happily come to drink – and they're a more varied bunch than you might expect here; the varied piped music fits in rather well. The garden has been extensively refurbished, with plenty of new planting and big parasols and heaters for winter.

Free house ~ Licensees Richard and George Manners ~ Real ale ~ Bar food (7-10.30(10 Sun), plus 12.30-2.30 Fri, and 12.30-3 Sat/Sun (no lunch Mon-Thurs)) ~ (020) 7924 5483 ~ Children welcome in eating area till 7 ~ Dogs welcome ~ Open 12-3 (not Mon), 5-11 Mon-Thurs; 12-11 Fri/Sat; 12-10.30 Sun; closed Mon lunchtime; 24 Dec-1 Jan; Easter Sat/Sun

Old Jail *Jail Lane, Biggin Hill (first turn E off A233 S of airport and industrial estate, towards Berry's Hill and Cudham); no station near; TN16 3AX*
Formerly a mainstay of RAF pilots based at nearby Biggin Hill, this interesting old pub feels so much in the heart of the countryside it's easy to forget you're only ten minutes or so away from the bustle of Croydon and Bromley. A highlight is the lovely big garden, with well spaced picnic-sets on the grass, several substantial trees, and a nicely maintained play area; it's a popular spot for families on fine weekends. Inside, several traditional beamed and low-ceilinged rooms ramble around a central servery, with the nicest parts the two cosy little areas to the right of the front entrance;

divided by dark timbers, one has a very big inglenook fireplace with lots of logs and brasses, and the other has a cabinet of Battle of Britain plates (it can be smoky in here at busy times). Other parts have wartime prints and plates too, especially around the edge of the dining room, up a step beyond a second, smaller fireplace. There's also a plainer, flagstoned room; discreet fruit machine, low piped music. Greene King IPA, Harveys and Shepherd Neame Spitfire on handpump; friendly, efficient service. Food runs from a standard menu to a wide choice of good, blackboard specials, and they do a choice of roasts on Sundays. With nice hanging baskets in front on the narrow leafy lane, the attractive building wasn't itself part of any jail, but was a beef shop until becoming a pub in 1869.

Punch ~ Lease Richard Hards ~ Real ale ~ Bar food (12-2.30(3 Sat/Sun), 7-9.30 (not Sun evening)) ~ (01959) 572979 ~ Children welcome ~ Dogs allowed in bar ~ Open 11.30-3, 6-11 (all day Fri in summer); 11.30-11 Sat; 12-10.30 Sun

Prospect of Whitby *Wapping Wall; E1W 3SH*

As we went to press this characterful place was about to reopen with a new manager after a short closure for refurbishment. But it's the kind of place where all that means is a sort of tidy-up rather than drastic changes; it claims to be the oldest pub on the Thames (dating back to 1543), so its whole appeal is based around its unspoilt old fittings and colourful history. For a long while it was better known as the Devil's Tavern, thanks to its popularity with smugglers and other ne'er-do-wells, and some of the capital's best-known figures were frequent callers: Pepys and Dickens both regularly popped in, Turner came for weeks at a time to study the scene, and in the 17th c the notorious Hanging Judge Jeffreys was able to combine two of his interests by enjoying a drink at the back while looking down over the grisly goings-on in Execution Dock. The tourists who flock here lap up the colourful tales of Merrie Olde London (it's an established favourite on evening coach tours), but only the most unromantic of visitors could fail to be carried along by the fun. Plenty of bare beams, bare boards, panelling and flagstones in the L-shaped bar (where the long pewter counter is over 400 years old), and an unbeatable river view towards Docklands from tables in the waterfront courtyard. They have had Charles Wells Bombardier, Fullers London Pride and Greene King Old Speckled Hen on handpump, and a wide range of standard dishes is usually available all day.

Spirit Group ~ Manager Chris Buckley ~ Real ale ~ Bar food (12-9.30) ~ Restaurant ~ (020) 7481 1095 ~ Children welcome ~ Dogs welcome ~ Open 12-11; 12-10.30 Sun

Spaniards Inn *Spaniards Lane; NW3 7JJ*

Famed for its tales of hauntings and highwaymen (some of which are best taken with a large dose of salt), this busy former toll house dates back to 1585, and the low-ceilinged oak-panelled rooms of the attractive main bar are full of character, with open fires, genuinely antique winged settles, candle-shaped lamps in shades, and snug little alcoves. But for many it's the charming garden that's the main draw, nicely arranged in a series of areas separated by judicious planting of shrubs. A crazy paved terrace with slatted wooden tables and chairs opens onto a flagstoned walk around a small raised area with roses, and a side arbour of wisteria, clematis and hops; you may need to move fast to bag a table. There's an outside bar, and regular barbecues out here in summer. The range of drinks is impressive, with between five and eight real ales at a time, typically including Adnams, Caledonian Deuchars IPA, Fullers London Pride, Marstons Old Empire and a guest like Roosters Leg Horn, some unusual continental draught lagers, and 22 wines by the glass – though in summer you might find the most popular drink is their big jug of Pimms. Popular bar food is served all day by friendly helpful staff. The food bar and the Georgian Turpin bar upstairs are no smoking. The pub is believed to have been named after the Spanish ambassador to the court of James I, who had a private residence here. It's fairly handy for Kenwood. The car park fills up fast, and other parking nearby is difficult.

Mitchells & Butlers ~ Manager David Nichol ~ Real ale ~ Bar food (11.30-10) ~ (020) 8731 6571 ~ Children welcome ~ Dogs welcome ~ Open 11-11(open from 10 at weekends)

Warrington *Warrington Crescent; W9 1EH*

The main bar of this striking late Victorian gin palace is well worth a look for its opulent art nouveau décor, with a highlight the splendid marble and mahogany bar counter, topped by an extraordinary structure that's rather like a cross between a carousel and a ship's hull, with cherubs thrown in for good measure. The drawings of nubile young women here and above a row of mirrors on the opposite wall are later additions, very much in keeping with the overall style, and hinting at the days when the building's trade was rather less respectable than it is today. Throughout are elaborately patterned tiles, ceilings and stained glass, and a remarkable number of big lamps and original light fittings; there's a small coal fire, two exquisitely tiled pillars, and high ceiling fans for summer. At the end a particularly comfortable area has tables around a long curved cushioned wall seat, and alcoves with elegant light fittings in the shape of dancers. It's very much a bustling local, with a real buzz of conversation from the broad mix of customers; some areas can get smoky at times. There's a similar but simpler public bar, with darts and a big-screen TV for sports. Caledonian Deuchars IPA, Fullers ESB and London Pride, Youngs Special and a changing guest on handpump; 24 wines are available by the glass, and the bottles are displayed around the top of the bar counter. Service is friendly and efficient. Though it looks thoroughly english, the upstairs evening restaurant is a very good value thai; it's no smoking in here. The same food is available in the bar at lunchtimes. No music, but quite a few games machines. There are plenty of picnic sets to the side of the pub, overlooking the street, with heaters for winter.

Free house ~ Licensee John Brandon ~ Real ale ~ Bar food (12-2.30 (1-3.30 Sat/Sun), 6-10.30) ~ Restaurant (6-10.30) ~ (020) 7286 2929 ~ Dogs allowed in bar ~ Open 11-11(midnight Fri/Sat); 12-10.30 Sun

White Cross *Water Lane; TW9 1TH*

At its best in summer when the busy paved garden in front is packed with people enjoying the river views, this perfectly-set Thameside pub can feel rather like a cosmopolitan seaside resort, and there's an outside bar to make the most of the sunshine (they may use plastic glasses for outside drinking). Inside, the two chatty main rooms have something of the air of the hotel this once was, with local prints and photographs, an old-fashioned wooden island servery, and a good mix of variously aged customers. Two of the three log fires have mirrors above them – unusually, the third is below a window. A bright and airy upstairs room has lots more tables, and a pretty cast-iron balcony opening off, with a splendid view down to the water, and a couple more tables and chairs. Available all day, bar food is fairly straightforward but there's a wide choice. Youngs Bitter, Special and seasonal beers on handpump, and a dozen or so carefully chosen wines by the glass; fruit machine, dominoes. It pays to check the tide times if you're leaving your car by the river; the water can rise rapidly, and you might return to find it marooned in a rapidly swelling pool of water; it's not unknown for the water to reach right up the steps into the bar. Boats leave from immediately outside for Kingston and Hampton Court.

Youngs ~ Managers Ian and Phyl Heggie ~ Real ale ~ Bar food (12-9.30) ~ (020) 8940 6844 ~ Children in garden area only ~ Dogs welcome ~ Open 11-12; 12-10.30 Sun; closed 25 Dec (exc 12-2)

Dog Friendly Hotels and B&Bs

22 Jermyn Street Hotel *22 Jermyn St SW1Y 6HP* (020) 7734 2353 £**258.50**; 5 rms and 13 suites – spacious with deeply comfortable seats and sofas, flowers, plants and antiques. Stylish little hotel owned by the same family for over 80 years and much loved by customers; no public rooms but wonderful 24-hr service, helpful notes and suggestions from the friendly owners, in-room light meals, and a warm welcome for children (with their own fact sheet listing shops, restaurants and sights geared towards them, free video library, old-fashioned and electronic games, and own bathrobes); walks in three nearby parks; disabled access; dogs if small and well behaved, in bedrooms by prior arrangement

Chesterfield *35 Charles St W1X 8LX* (020) 7491 2622 £**250**, plus special breaks; 110 well equipped, pretty rms. Charming hotel just off Berkeley Sq, with particularly courteous helpful staff, afternoon tea in panelled library, a relaxed club-style bar with resident pianist, and fine food in attractive restaurant or light and airy conservatory; Hyde Park for walks is close by; disabled access; dogs in bedrooms; bowls, treats, bed and menu

Conrad London *Chelsea Harbour SW10 0XG* (020) 7823 3000 £**209**; 160 luxury suites. Spacious hotel tucked away in the quiet modern enclave of the Chelsea Harbour development and overlooking its small marina; enjoyable mediterranean-asian cooking in Aquasia restaurant and bar, friendly service, and health club; disabled access; dogs in bedrooms; £10

Hazlitts *6 Frith St W1V 5TZ (020) 7434 1771* **£259.35**, plus special breaks; 23 rms with 18th- or 19th-c beds and free-standing Victorian baths with early brass shower mixer units. Behind a typically Soho façade of listed early Georgian houses, this is a well kept and comfortably laid-out little hotel that's very handy for the West End; good continental breakfasts served in your bedroom, snacks in the sitting room, lots of restaurants all around; kind, helpful service; cl Christmas; dogs in bedrooms if small and house-trained

L'Hotel *28 Basil St SW3 1AS (020) 7589 6286* **£155**; 12 well equipped rms. Small family-owned french-style city hotel, near Harrods, and set above the neatly kept, well run Metro wine bar where continental breakfasts are served – as well as good modern french café food; friendly staff; walks in nearby Hyde Park; disabled access; dogs in bedrooms

Malmaison *Charterhouse Square EC1 6AH (020) 7012 3700* **£175**, plus special breaks; 97 stylish, modern, very well equipped rms. Large, elegant red-brick Victorian hotel converted from a nurses' residence for St Bartholomew's hospital and set in the cobbled courtyard of leafy Charterhouse Sq; imaginative modern cooking in no smoking brasserie (exceptionally good steaks and popular Sunday brunch, too), chic bar set off the spacious lobby, with comfortable sofas, and helpful, attentive service; the Thames Path for walks is close by; cl Christmas; disabled access; dogs in bedrooms; dog basket; £15

Rubens *39-41 Buckingham Palace Rd SW1W 0PS (020) 7834 6600* **£198**, plus special breaks; 168 well equipped, individually furnished rms inc luxurious suites in the Royal Wing. Opposite Buckingham Palace and near Victoria Station, this attractive hotel has comfortable day rooms inc lounge with views of the Royal Mews, open fire in bar, and library restaurant with fine international food; disabled access; dogs in bedrooms; welcome hamper, pet concierge and lots of services offered

Scotland

Dog Friendly Pubs

ABOYNE
Boat *Charlestown Road (B968, just off A93); AB34 5EL*

As you step inside this pleasantly pubby waterside inn (with tables outside), you are greeted by a model train, often chugging around just below the ceiling, making appropriate noises. There are also scottish pictures and brasses and an openable woodburning stove in the two areas downstairs, a bar counter that runs down the narrower linking section, and games along in the public-bar end; piped music, TV. Spiral stairs take you up to a roomy additional dining area. Food is pleasantly served by prompt, friendly staff. They use plenty of fresh local produce, and are happy to accommodate special requests. Bass along with a couple of real ales from scottish brewers such as Caledonian, Harviestoun, Houston, Inveralmond and Isle of Skye; also 40 malt whiskies. The pub used to serve the ferry that it's named for; outside there are tables.

Free house ~ Licensee Wilson Forbes ~ Real ale ~ Bar food (12-2(2.30 Sat, Sun), 5.30-9(9.30 Fri, Sat)) ~ Restaurant ~ (01339) 886137 ~ Children welcome ~ Dogs allowed in bar ~ Open 11-2.30, 5-11(12 Fri); 11-midnight Sat; 11-11 Sun

GAIRLOCH
Old Inn *Just off A832/B8021; IV21 2BD*

Just a few steps away from a little fishing harbour and nicely tucked away from the main shoreside road, this 18th-c inn is well placed for strolls up Flowerdale valley to a waterfall. Picnic-sets are prettily placed outside by the trees that line the stream as it flows past under the old stone bridge; you might spot eagles over the crags above. The changing beers are a big draw, with usually around four or five on offer: a typical selection might be Adnams, Black Sheep, Cairngorms Tradewinds and Isle of Skye Red Cuillin and Blind Piper (a blend of Isle of Skye ales made for the pub and named after a famed 17th-c local piper). They have a lot of fairly priced wines by the glass, a decent collection of 30 malt whiskies, and you can get speciality coffees. The food is popular, and fresh locally landed fish is a speciality. The landlady makes her own chutneys and preserves – and grows many of the herbs they use (they also track down organic vegetables). Credit (but not debit) cards incur a surcharge of £1.75. It's nicely decorated with paintings and murals on exposed stone walls, and the cheerfully relaxed public bar has chatty locals; darts, TV, fruit machine, pool, darts and juke box.

Free house ~ Licensees Alastair and Ute Pearson ~ Real ale ~ Bar food (12-2.30(weekends), 5-8.30 in winter; 12-9.30 in summer) ~ Restaurant ~ 01445 712006 ~ Children allowed in some rooms ~ Dogs allowed in bar and bedrooms ~ Live music summer weekends ~ Open 11-1(12 Sat); 12.30-11.30 Sun ~ Bedrooms: £40B/£75B

GATEHOUSE OF FLEET
Masonic Arms *Ann Street, off B727; DG7 2HU*
A few years ago, when Chris and Sue Walker ran the Creebridge House Hotel over near Newton Stewart, they made it very popular with our readers for good food from Chris and his head chef, fine real ales, and the cheerful atmosphere fostered by Sue. They have now done the same trick here, this time in a pub which they have transformed through a careful refurbishment (and they have the same head chef). The comfortable two-room beamed bar is indeed a proper bar, with Masonic Boom (brewed for them by Sulwath) and a good changing guest like Black Sheep, Caledonian Deuchars IPA or Hook Norton Old Hooky on handpump, and a good choice of whiskies and wines by the glass, traditional seating, pictures on its lightly timbered walls, and blue and white plates on a delft shelf. Service is friendly and efficient, with everything kept spick and span, and there is a relaxed warm-hearted atmosphere. Good interesting food is generously served, and they also offer set evening menus. The bar opens into an attractive and spacious conservatory, with stylish and comfortable cane bucket chairs around good tables on its terracotta tiles, pot plants, and colourful pictures on one wall; it's airy even in bright sunlight (good blinds and ventilation). The conservatory also opens through into a smart contemporary restaurant, with high-backed thickly padded chairs around neat modern tables on bare boards. There are picnic-sets under cocktail parasols out in the neatly kept sheltered garden, and seats out in front of the flower-decked black and white building; this is an appealing small town, between the Solway Firth and the Galloway Forest Park.

Free house ~ Licensees Chris and Sue Walker ~ Real ale ~ Bar food (12-2 and 6-9) ~ Restaurant ~ (01557) 814335 ~ Children welcome ~ Dogs allowed in bar ~ Open 11.30-2.30, 5.30-11.30; closed Mon/Tues Nov-Mar

INVERARAY
George *Main Street E; PA32 8TT*
Pleasantly placed in the centre of this handsome little Georgian town, near Inveraray Castle and the shore of Loch Fyne, this comfortably modernised inn is a civilised place to stay. It is also well placed for walks and the great Argyll woodland gardens, best for their rhododendrons in May and early June. Run by the same family since 1860, the George has a bustling dark bar that oozes character from its bare stone walls, and shows plenty of age

in its exposed joists, old tiles and big flagstones. There are antique settles, cushioned stone slabs along the walls, carved wooden benches, nicely grained wooden-topped cast-iron tables, lots of curling club and ships' badges, and a cosy log fire in winter. Swiftly served by friendly staff (you order at the table), the generously served bar food is enjoyable. There's a conservatory restaurant, and tables in a very pleasant, well laid-out garden. Two beers include one from Fyne along with Caledonian Deuchars IPA on handpump, and they've over 60 malt whiskies; darts, board games, piped music and TV, but no bar games in summer. The individually decorated bedrooms (reached by a grand wooden staircase) have jacuzzis or four-poster beds. You may glimpse seals or even a basking shark or whale in the loch.

Free house ~ Licensee Donald Clark ~ Real ale ~ Bar food (12-9) ~ Restaurant ~ (01499) 302111 ~ Children welcome ~ Dogs welcome ~ Open 11(12 Sun)-12.30 ~ Bedrooms: £35B/£70B

ISLE OF WHITHORN
Steam Packet *Harbour Row; DG8 8LL*

This is an appealing place to stay or just pop in for a drink, and there's no piped music, fruit machines or other similar intrusions: from the big picture windows of this welcoming modernised inn you look out on to a restful scene of an attractive working harbour, with a crowd of yachts and fishing boats. The comfortable low-ceilinged bar is split into two: on the right, plush button-back banquettes and boat pictures, and on the left, green leatherette stools around cast-iron-framed tables on big stone tiles, and a woodburning stove in the bare stone wall. Bar food can be served in the lower-beamed dining room, which has excellent colour wildlife photographs, rugs on its wooden floor, and a solid fuel stove, and there's also a small eating area off the lounge bar, as well as a conservatory. Swiftly served by helpful but unfussy staff, the food is imaginative and very good. Theakstons XB is kept on handpump, along with a guest such as Houston Peters Well, and they've two dozen malt whiskies and a good wine list; TV. pool and board games. There are white tables and chairs in the garden. Several of the recently refurbished bedrooms have good views. Boat trips leave from the harbour; you can walk up to the remains of St Ninian's Kirk, on a headland behind the village.

Free house ~ Licensee John Scoular ~ Real ale ~ Bar food (12-2, 6.30-9) ~ Restaurant ~ (01988) 500334 ~ Children welcome except in bar ~ Dogs allowed in bar and bedrooms ~ Open 11-11(12 Sat); 12-11 Sun; closed 2.30-6 winter ~ Bedrooms: £30B/£60B

KILMAHOG
Lade *A84 just NW of Callander, by A821 junction; FK17 8HD*

An enthusiastic hands-on family run this lively pubby inn, which is a great place to visit at the weekend if you want to hear some traditional Scottish music. Another great feature is the organic beers brewed here – WayLade, LadeBack and LadeOut, which are well kept alongside a guest such as Broughton Clipper, eight wines by the glass and about 25 malts. By the time this *Guide* is published they hope to have opened a little shop selling a range of about 100 bottled Scottish real ales. Several small beamed areas are cosy with red walls, panelling and stripped stone, and decorated with Highland prints and a cigarette card collection; piped music. Bar food is fairly straightforward, but more ambitious dishes are served in a conservatory restaurant, which opens on to a terrace in a pleasant garden with three fish ponds.

Own brew ~ Licensees Frank and Rita Park ~ Real ale ~ Bar food (12(12.30 Sun)-9; 12-3, 5-9 winter wkdays) ~ Restaurant ~ (01877) 330152 ~ Children welcome till 8pm ~ Dogs allowed in bar ~ Ceilidhs Fri and Sat evenings ~ Open 12-11; 12-1 Sat; 12.30-10.30 Sun

KIPPEN

Cross Keys *Main Street; village signposted off A811 W of Stirling; FK8 3DN*
'Timeless and atmospheric' commented one reader on this cosy and unpretentious 18th-c village inn, which has dark panelling and subdued lighting; the friendly licensees really make an effort to make you feel at home. It has a strong local following, but extends a warm welcome to visitors. The straightforward lounge has a good log fire, and there's a coal fire in the attractive family dining room. Enjoyable bar food is generously served, making good use of fresh, local produce, and you can get smaller helpings. Harviestoun Bitter & Twisted on handpump, and they've more than 30 malt whiskies; cards, dominoes, TV, and maybe a radio in the separate public bar; they hold a quiz night on the last Sunday of the month. Tables in the garden have good views towards the Trossachs.

Free house ~ Licensees Mr and Mrs Scott ~ Real ale ~ Bar food (12-2, 6-9; 12.30-8.45 Sun; not 25 Dec, 1 Jan and some Mons in winter) ~ Restaurant ~ (01786) 870293 ~ Children welcome ~ Dogs allowed in bar and bedrooms ~ Open 12-2.30, 5.30-11(12 Fri); 12-12 Sat; 12.30-11 Sun ~ Bedrooms: /£70S

KIRK YETHOLM

Border *Village signposted off B6352/B6401 crossroads, SE of Kelso; The Green; TD5 8PQ*
Readers remark on the warm and friendly welcome as well as the imaginative use of carefully sourced fresh local ingredients at this comfortable hotel that makes a particularly cheering landmark for walkers at the end of the 256-mile Pennine Way National Trail. If you have done the full walk, and have with you a copy of the guide to the walk written and drawn by Alfred Wainwright, they will give you a free pint of beer. Originally Wainwright left some money at the inn, to pay for walkers claiming just a half-pint, but that's long gone, and the hotel now foots the bill itself. It's by no means just walkers who will enjoy the pub. Under its friendly chef/landlord and his wife, the food (including plenty of autumn game and summer fish) is careful and inventive without being at all pretentious. The public bar has been gently freshened up, but is still cheerfully unpretentious, with snug side rooms. It has beams, flagstones and a log fire, and a signed photograph of Wainwright and various souvenirs of

the Pennine Way, as well as appropriate borders scenery etchings and murals. They have Caledonian Deuchars IPA and a changing scottish guest beer on handpump, decent wines by the glass, a good range of malt whiskies, and a water bowl for dogs; service is warm and efficient. There's a roomy pink-walled dining room, a comfortably refurbished lounge with a second log fire and a neat conservatory; TV, darts, pool, board games, and children's games and books. A sheltered back terrace has more picnic-sets, and the colourful window boxes and floral tubs make a very attractive display outside. The pub experienced quite a bad fire just as we were going to press. The bar area was unaffected, but cooking is now being done from a contemporary kitchen, and they don't expect the bedrooms to be open again until Spring 2007.

Free house ~ Licensees Philip and Margaret Blackburn ~ Real ale ~ Bar food (12-2, 6-9, unless booked for weddings) ~ Restaurant ~ (01573) 420237 ~ Children welcome ~ Dogs allowed in bar and bedrooms ~ Open 11-11 ~ Bedrooms: £45B/£80B

PITLOCHRY

Moulin *Kirkmichael Road, Moulin; A924 NE of Pitlochry centre; PH16 5EH*

A strong attraction of this inviting flower-bedecked 17th-c inn is its excellent home-brewed beers, actually brewed in the little stables across the street, and it's an enjoyable place to stay, with an excellent range of walks close at hand. Ale of Atholl, Braveheart, Moulin Light and the stronger Old Remedial are superbly kept on handpump, and they also have around 40 malt whiskies, and a good choice of wines by the glass and carafes of house wine available by the litre and half litre. Although it has been much extended over the years, the bar, in the oldest part of the building, still seems an entity in itself, nicely pubby, with plenty of atmosphere. Above the fireplace in the smaller room is an interesting painting of the village before the road was built (Moulin used to be a bustling market town, far busier than upstart Pitlochry), while the bigger carpeted area has a good few tables and cushioned banquettes in little booths divided by stained-glass country scenes, another big fireplace, some exposed stonework, fresh flowers, and golf clubs and local and sporting prints around the walls; games include bar billiards and board games. The extensive bar menu includes lots of hearty traditional dishes, and in the evening, readers enjoy eating in the restaurant. Service is friendly; the landlord is a historic motor rallying fan. Surrounded by tubs of flowers, picnic-sets outside look across to the village kirk.

Own brew ~ Licensee Heather Reeves ~ Real ale ~ Bar food (12-9) ~ Restaurant ~ (01796) 472196 ~ Children welcome ~ Dogs allowed in bar ~ Open 12-11(11.45 Sat) ~ Bedrooms: £45B/£55B

STEIN

Stein Inn *End of B886 N of Dunvegan in Waternish, off A850 Dunvegan—Portree; OS Sheet 23 map reference 263564; IV55 8GA*

A comfortable spot to stay, this 18th-c inn has an extremely restful location by the water's edge on a far-flung northern corner of Skye. The tables outside are an ideal place to sit with a malt whisky (they've over 100 to choose from), and watch the sunset. Inside, the original public bar has great character, with its sturdy country furnishings, flagstone floor, beam and plank ceiling, partly panelled stripped-stone walls and peat fire. The atmosphere can be surprisingly buzzing, and there's a good welcome from the owners and the evening crowd of local regulars (where do they all appear from?) Good service from the smartly uniformed staff. There's a games area with pool table, dominoes and cribbage, and maybe piped music. Caledonian Deuchars IPA and Isle of Skye Reeling Deck (specially brewed for the pub) are kept on handpump, along with a guest like Isle of Skye Blaven or Orkney Northern Light; in summer they have several wines by the glass. The short choice of bar food makes good use of local fish and highland meat and includes good value sandwiches. There's a lively children's inside play area, and showers for yachtsmen. Some of the bedrooms have sea views, and breakfasts are good – readers tell us it's well worth pre-ordering the tasty smoked kippers if you stay here. Useful campsites nearby.

Free house ~ Licensees Angus and Teresa Mcghie ~ Real ale ~ Bar food (12(12.30 Sun)-4, 6-9.30(9 Sun)) ~ Restaurant ~ (01470) 592362 ~ Children welcome until 8pm if dining ~ Dogs allowed in bedrooms ~ Open 11-12(12.30 Sat); 11.30-11 Sun; 4-11weekdays, 12-12 Sat, 12.30-11 Sun winter; closed 25 Dec, 1 Jan ~ Bedrooms: £26S/£52S(£72B)

TAYVALLICH
Tayvallich Inn *B8025, off A816 1 mile S of Kilmartin; or take B841 turn-off from A816 2 miles N of Lochgilphead; PA31 8PL*
A pleasant place to make for on a sunny day, this dining pub has sliding glass doors opening onto a terrace with decking and awning, and getting lovely views over the yacht anchorage. Service is friendly, and people with children are made to feel welcome. Inside are exposed ceiling joists, pale pine chairs, benches and tables on the quarry-tiled floors, and local nautical charts on the cream walls; piped music. The good food focuses on the fresh seafood caught by the fishing boats out on Loch Sween, and the daily specials depend very much on what they've landed; they serve fresh milk shakes. Malt whiskies include a full range of Islay malts, and they have Loch Fyne Maverick and Pipers Gold on handpump. Until it was turned into a restaurant in the early 1970s, this was the village bus station.

Free house ~ Licensee Roddy Anderson ~ Real ale ~ Bar food (12-2, 6-9) ~ Restaurant ~ (01546) 870282 ~ Children welcome till 8pm ~ Dogs allowed in bar ~ Live music two Sats a month ~ Open 11-11(1 Sat); 12-12 Sun; 12-3, 5.30-11 in winter, when also closed Tues lunchtimes and all day Mon

WEEM
Ailean Chraggan *B846; PH15 2LD*
Small and friendly, this family-run hotel is a lovely place to stay, with well liked food (worth booking at busy times) and a couple of beers from the local Inveralmond Brewery, usually Lia Fail, Independence, Ossian or Thrappledouser on handpump. You're likely to find chatty locals in the

bar, and you can eat from the good changing menu in either the comfortably carpeted modern lounge or the dining room. There's also a very good wine list, with several wines by the glass, and you can choose from around 100 malt whiskies; winter darts and board games and the owners can arrange fishing nearby. From here you look to the mountains beyond the Tay from its two outside terraces, sweeping up to Ben Lawers (the highest peak in this part of Scotland).

Free house ~ Licensee Alastair Gillespie ~ Real ale ~ Bar food ~ Restaurant ~ (01887) 820346 ~ Children welcome ~ Dogs allowed in bar and bedrooms ~ Open 11-11; closed 1-2 Jan, 25-26 Dec ~ Bedrooms: £55B/£90B

Dog Friendly Hotels, B&Bs and Farms

ACHILTIBUIE
Summer Isles Hotel *Achiltibuie, Ullapool, Ross-shire IV26 2YQ (01854) 622282* £125; 13 comfortable rms. Beautifully placed above the sea towards the end of a very long and lonely road and with plenty of surrounding walks; warm, friendly, well furnished hotel with delicious set menus using fresh ingredients (in which it's largely self-sufficient), a choice of superb puddings and excellent array of uncommon cheeses; pretty watercolours and flowers; cl mid-Oct-Easter; children over 8; dogs in bedrooms but must not be left unattended

APPLECROSS
Applecross Inn *Shore St, Applecross, Strathcarron, Ross-shire IV54 8LR (01520) 744262* £80; 7 rms, all with breathtaking sea views over Sound of Raasay. Gloriously placed informal inn with tables out by shore, simple comfortable and friendly bar, log or peat fire in lounge, small restaurant with excellent fresh fish and seafood; plenty of walks; cl 25 Dec and 5 Jan; partial disabled access from summer 2007; dogs welcome

ARDEONAIG
Ardeonaig Hotel *Ardeonaig, Killin, Perthshire FK21 8SY (01567) 820400* £117, plus special breaks; 20 rms. Extended 17th-c farmhouse on South shore of Loch Tay, with log fire in snug and lounge, library with fine views, bistro or formal dining using fresh local produce; salmon fishing rights on the loch – as well as fishing for trout – a drying and rod room, and boats and outboards; shooting and stalking can be arranged, lots of surrounding walks; children over 12; partial disabled access; dogs in some bedrooms; £10

ARDUAINE
Loch Melfort Hotel *Arduaine, Oban, Argyll PA34 4XG (01852) 200233* £138, plus special breaks; 25 rms, gorgeous sea views. Comfortable hotel popular in summer with passing yachtsmen (hotel's own moorings),

nautical charts and marine glasses in airy modern bar, own lobster pots and nets so emphasis on seafood, pleasant foreshore walks, outstanding springtime woodland gardens; resident dog; cl Jan-mid-Feb; disabled access; dogs in cedar wing only; water bowls and food on request

AUCHENCAIRN

Balcary Bay *Auchencairn, Castle Douglas, Kirkcudbrightshire DG7 1QZ (01556) 640217* **£120**, plus special breaks; 20 rms with fine views. Once a smugglers' haunt, this charming and much liked hotel has wonderful views over the bay, neat grounds running down to the water, comfortable public rooms (one with log fire), a relaxed friendly atmosphere, good enjoyable food inc super breakfasts, and lots of walks; resident dog; cl 1 Dec-mid-Feb; disabled access; dogs in bedrooms only

BALLATER

Auld Kirk *31 Braemar Rd, Ballater, Aberdeenshire AB35 5RQ (01339) 755762* **£80**, plus special breaks; 6 attractive rms, inc 2 family rms. 19th-c church converted to a hotel in 1990 and still with bell tower, stained glass and exposed rafters; original pillared pine ceiling in refurbished restaurant, other public rooms with homely décor; two resident dogs; disabled access; dogs welcome in bedrooms

Balgonie Country House *Braemar Pl, Ballater, Aberdeenshire AB35 5NQ (01339) 755482* **£140**; plus special breaks, 9 pretty rms. Quietly set and spotless Edwardian house with fine views from four acres of mature gardens, particularly helpful friendly owners, fresh flowers, games and books in lounges, and most enjoyable food using the best local produce in charming dining room; cl 6 Jan-beg Feb; dogs in bedrooms by prior arrangement (not to be left unattended)

BRIDGE OF CALLY

Bridge of Cally Hotel *Bridge of Cally, Blairgowrie, Perthshire PH10 7JJ (01250) 886231* **£70**, plus winter breaks; 18 rms. Set on 1,500 acres of private moorland, this former drovers' inn is a friendly family-run place with good value home-made food using seasonal game in popular restaurant and a convivial, chatty comfortable bar; salmon fishing, deer stalking, shooting, golf and skiing can be provided or are within easy access; disabled access; dogs welcome in two rooms but must be well behaved

CALLANDER

Poppies *Leny Rd, Callander, Perthshire FK17 8AL (01877) 330329* (on A84 (Leny Rd)) **£70**, plus special breaks; 9 rms. Small private hotel with excellent food in popular and attractive candlelit dining room, comfortable lounge, a cosy bar with a good choice of malt whiskies, helpful friendly owners, and seats in the garden; children over 12; cl Jan; dogs welcome in bedrooms

CLACHAN SEIL

Willowburn *Clachan Seil, Isle of Seil PA34 4TJ (01852) 300276* £**168** inc dinner; 7 rms facing the water. Simple little white hotel on the shore of Clachan Sound, with enthusiastic, welcoming owners, open fire and local guidebooks in straightforward lounge and bar with lovely views, imaginative food using local and home-grown produce and delicious breakfasts in airy dining room overlooking water; guests` dogs get a letter from the hotel`s pets (two dogs and a cat); lots of wildlife and walks; cl Nov-mid-Mar; children over 8; dogs in bedrooms and residents' lounge; welcome pack, towels, bedding

CROMARTY

Royal *Marine Terrace, Cromarty, Ross-shire IV11 8YN (01381) 600217* £**70**, plus special breaks; 10 rms. Traditional waterfront hotel (you may see dolphins) with friendly owners and staff, attractive lounges, bars and sun lounge, garden and good home cooking with an emphasis on seafood; gets very busy in summer; good walks; dogs welcome away from eating areas

CULLEN

Seafield Hotel *Cullen, Buckie, Banffshire AB56 4SG (01542) 840791* £**85**; 22 attractively furnished, spacious rms. 19th-c former coaching inn with an easy-going, comfortable and friendly atmosphere, carefully reburbished residents` lounge and convivial bar, log fires, fresh flowers and antiques, good enjoyable food using plenty of local fresh fish (and of course the famous cullen skink soup) in informal restaurant, nice breakfasts, helpful staff, and fine sandy beach just 5 minutes away; lots to do nearby; partial disabled access; dogs in bedrooms; £5

DALCROSS

Easter Dalziel Farm *Dalcross, Inverness IV2 7JL (01667) 462213* (1.8 miles off A96 just E of Inverness, via B9039) £**54**; 3 rms with shared bthrm. Early Victorian farmhouse on 210 acres of family-run mixed farm (beef cattle and grain) with friendly helpful owners, log fire in lounge, and good scottish breakfasts in big dining room; two resident cats; self-catering cottages, too; cl Christmas and New Year; dogs in bedrooms (not to be left unattended)

DRUMNADROCHIT

Polmaily House *Drumnadrochit, Inverness IV63 6XT (01456) 450343* (2.5 miles off A82 via A831 W) £**130**, plus special breaks; 14 light, elegant rms. Very relaxing and comfortable hotel in 18 acres, with drawing room and library, open fire and excellent food in restaurant (wonderful packed lunches too); a happy place for families with well equipped indoor play area and lots of supervised activities, and plenty of ponies and pets; indoor heated swimming pool, tennis, croquet, fishing, boating and riding; lots of walks; partial disabled access; dogs in some bedrooms

DULNAIN BRIDGE

Auchendean Lodge *Dulnain Bridge, Grantown-on-Spey, Morayshire PH26 3LU (01479) 851347* £188 inc dinner, plus special breaks; 5 comfortable rms. Edwardian hunting lodge with wonderful views over the Spey Valley to the Cairngorm mountains; two homely lounges with plenty of pictures and knick-knacks, a piano for guests` use, and warm log fire; enthusiastic owners, good, interesting meals using home-grown and local produce, super breakfasts with home-made marmalade and jams, and lovely garden; Bess the owner`s dog loves taking other dog friends for walks in the nearby woods and moors; three cats; children must be well behaved; cl Nov-Easter; dogs in bedrooms and one lounge; £5

DUNBLANE

Cromlix House *Cromlix, Dunblane, Perthshire FK15 9JT (01786) 822125* £250, plus special breaks; 14 rms inc 8 spacious suites. Walking, loch and river fishing or shooting on 2,000 acres around this rather gracious country house; relaxing day rooms with fine antiques and family portraits, an informal atmosphere, very good food using local produce in two dining rooms, and courteous service; dogs in bedrooms only

EAST HAUGH

East Haugh House *East Haugh, Pitlochry, Tayside PH16 5TE (01796) 473121* (1 mile off A9 just S of Pitlochry, on Old Military Rd parallel to A9) £90, plus special breaks; 13 rms, 5 in converted bothy, some with four-posters and one with open fire. Turreted stone house with lots of character, delightful bar in cream and navy with a fishing theme, house-party atmosphere and particularly good food inc local seafood, game in season and home-grown vegetables cooked by chef/proprietor; excellent shooting, stalking and salmon and trout fishing on surrounding local estates; several resident dogs and lots of walks; cl Christmas week; disabled access to one room; dogs in ground floor bedrooms with direct access outside; £10

EDINBURGH

Malmaison *1 Tower Pl, Leith, Edinburgh EH6 7DB (0131) 468 5000* £162.90, plus special breaks; 100 stylish, well equipped rms, some with harbour views. Converted baronial-style seamen's mission in the fashionable docks area of Leith with very good food in the downstairs brasserie (wrought-iron work, leather banquettes and candlelight), cheerful light and airy café bar with terrace, and friendly service; gym; free parking; disabled access; dogs if small; £10

ERISKA

Isle of Eriska Hotel *Ledaig, Oban, Argyll PA37 1SD (01631) 720371* (2 miles off A828 N of Connel) £275; 24 rms. In a wonderful position on small island linked by bridge to mainland, impressive baronial hotel with very relaxed country house atmosphere, log fires and pretty drawing room, excellent food, exemplary service, and comprehensive wine list; leisure complex with indoor swimming pool, sauna, gym and so forth, lovely surrounding walks, and 9-hole golf course, clay pigeon shooting and golf – and plenty of wildlife inc tame badgers who come nightly to the library door for their bread and milk; three resident dogs; cl Jan; children over 5 in pool and evering restaurant (high tea provided); disabled access; dogs welcome in bedrooms

FINTRY

Culcreuch Castle *Fintry, Glasgow G63 0LW (01360) 860555* £116, plus special breaks; 14 individually decorated rms (inc 4 family rms) with lovely views. Central Scotland's oldest inhabited castle, nearly 700 years old, in beautiful 1,600-acre parkland and surrounding hills and moors (super walks), with log fires and antiques in the public rooms, good freshly prepared food in candlelit panelled dining room, and a friendly relaxed atmosphere, play area; 8 modern scandinavian-style holiday lodges, too; dogs in bedrooms and other areas by arrangement; £4

GATEHOUSE OF FLEET

Cally Palace *Gatehouse of Fleet, Castle Douglas, Kirkcudbrightshire DG7 2DL (01557) 814341* (2.5 miles off A75 via B727 or B796) £190 inc dinner, plus special breaks; 56 rms. 18th-c country mansion, a hotel since 1934, with marble fireplaces and ornate ceilings in the public rooms, relaxed cocktail bar and sunny conservatory, enjoyable food in elegant dining room (smart dress required), evening pianist, and helpful friendly staff; 18-hole golf course, croquet and tennis, indoor leisure complex with heated swimming pool, private fishing/boating loch, and plenty of walks; cl Jan, cl wkdys in Feb; disabled access; dogs in bedrooms but must not be left unattended; £5

GIFFORD

Tweeddale Arms *Gifford, Haddington, East Lothian EH41 4QU (01620) 810240* £80, plus special breaks; 14 rms. Civilised late 17th-c inn in quiet village, with comfortable sofas and chairs in tranquil lounge, gracious dining room, wide choice of good daily changing food, and charming service; walks nearby; disabled access; dogs in some bedrooms and must be well behaved

GIGHA

Gigha Hotel *Isle of Gigha PA41 7AA (01583) 505254* £79, plus special breaks; 13 rms, most with own bthrm. Traditional family-run hotel, small and attractive with lots of charm, bustling bar (popular with yachtsmen and locals), neatly kept comfortable residents' lounge, and local seafood in restaurant; self-contained cottages too; fields for dogs to walk in; cl Christmas; dogs in cottages; £15

GLASGOW

Malmaison *278 West George St, Glasgow G2 4LL (0141) 572 1000* £167.90; 72 very well equipped, individually decorated rms, some with french windows. Stylishly converted church with greek façade, striking central wrought-iron staircase, a well stocked bar in vaulted basement, relaxed contemporary atmosphere, friendly staff, and enjoyable modern food in attractive brasserie; gym; disabled access; dogs if small in bedrooms; £10

One Devonshire Gardens *Glasgow G12 0UX (0141) 339 2001* **£169**; 35 opulent rms. Elegant cosseting hotel a little way out from the centre, with luxurious Victorian furnishings, fresh flowers, exemplary staff, and fine modern cooking in the stylish restaurant; parks nearby for dogs to exercise; disabled access; dogs in bedrooms; £20

GLENELG

Glenelg Inn *Kirkton, Glenelg, Kyle, Ross-shire IV40 8JR (01599) 522273* **£178** inc dinner, plus special breaks; 7 individually decorated and comfortable rms, all with fine views. In extensive grounds and overlooking Skye across its own beach, this old coaching mews has a relaxed bar, comfortable sofas and blazing fires, friendly staff and locals, good food using local venison, local hill-bred lamb and lots of wonderfully fresh fish and seafood, and quite a few whiskies; the drive to the inn involves spectacular views from the steep road (and the pretty drive to Glen Beag broch is nice); resident dog; plenty of walks and climbs; cl end Oct-New Year; disabled access; dogs in bedrooms

GLENROTHES

Balbirnie House *Markinch, Glenrothes, Fife KY7 6NE (01592) 610066* (0.5 miles off A92 N of A911, via B9130) **£190**, plus special breaks; 30 rms. Fine Georgian country house in 400-acre park landscaped in Capability Brown style, with fresh flowers, open fires and antiques in gracious public rooms, extremely good inventive food, and a big wine list; disabled access; dogs in bedrooms; £20

GULLANE

Greywalls *Duncar Rd, Gullane, East Lothian EH31 2EG (01620) 842144* **£290**, plus special breaks; 23 individually decorated rms. Overlooking Muirfield golf course, this beautiful family-run Lutyens house has antiques, open fires and flowers in its comfortable lounges and panelled library, very good food and fine wines in the restaurant, impeccable service, and lovely Gertrude Jekyll garden, all of a piece with the perfect design of the house; several resident dogs; fields and beaches close by for walks; cl Jan and Feb; disabled access; dogs in bedrooms only

INNERLEITHEN

Traquair Arms *Innerleithen, Peebles-shire EH44 6PD (01896) 830229* **£80**; 14 comfortable rms. Very friendly hotel with interesting choice of good food in attractive dining room, cosy lounge bar, friendly service, superb local Traquair ale, nice breakfasts, and quiet garden; cl 25-26 Dec; dogs welcome away from restaurant

INVERNESS

Dunain Park *Inverness IV3 8JN (01463) 230512* (on A82 SW) **£198**; 13 rms inc 6 suites with own lounge. 18th-c italianate mansion in six acres of well tended gardens and woodland, a short walk from the River Ness and Caledonian Canal; charming owners, traditional homely décor with family photographs and china ornaments, log fires and fresh flowers, wonderful food using home-grown produce and local game, fish and aberdeen angus meat, generous breakfasts, and 200 whiskies; small warm swimming pool, sauna, lots of walks and golf courses nearby; cl1st 2 wks Jan; disabled access; dogs in bedrooms; £5

ISLE ORNSAY

Eilean Iarmain *Isle Ornsay, Isle of Skye IV43 8QR (01471) 833332* **£150**, plus winter breaks; 16 individual rms inc 4 suites (those in main hotel best), all with fine views. Sparkling white hotel with Gaelic-speaking staff and locals, big cheerfully busy bar, two pretty dining rooms with lovely sea views, and very good food; disabled access; well behaved dogs welcome

Kinloch Lodge *Isle Ornsay, Isle of Skye IV43 8QY (01471) 833214* **£100**, plus winter breaks; 14 rms. Surrounded by rugged mountain scenery at the head of Loch Na Dal, this charming white stone hotel has a relaxed atmosphere in its comfortable and attractive drawing rooms, antiques, portraits, flowers, log fires, and good imaginative food; cookery demonstrations; two resident dogs; plenty of surrounding walks; children by arrangement; cl Dec–Feb; dogs in bedrooms; £3

KELSO

Ednam House *Ednam, Kelso, Roxburghshire TD5 7HT (01573) 224168* **£101**; 32 rms (the original ones are the nicest) inc 2 suites. Large Georgian manor house by the River Tweed with three acres of gardens and owned by the same family since 1928; three distinctive lounges with antiques and plenty of comfortable seating, two bars (one with fishing theme), excellent food in large candlelit dining room that overlooks the river, a lovely informal atmosphere and particularly good, friendly service; shooting and fishing by arrangement; genuine welcome for children; two resident dogs; cl 2 wks over Christmas and New Year; disabled access; dogs welcome away from restaurant

KILBERRY

Kilberry Inn *Kilberry, Tarbert, Argyll PA29 6YD (01880) 770223* **£85**, plus special breaks; 3 ground-floor rms. Homely and warmly welcoming inn on west coast of Knapdale with fine sea views, old-fashioned character, very good traditional home cooking relying on fresh local ingredients; resident dog; cl Jan–Feb; children over 12; partial disabled access; dogs in bedrooms; bowls and treats; £10

KILCHRENAN

Ardanaiseig *Kilchrenan, Taynuilt, Argyll PA35 1HE (01866) 833333* £170, plus special breaks; 16 lovely big, themed rms with views of the loch or gardens. Scottish baronial mansion quietly set in its own natural gardens and woodland right on Loch Awe; antique-filled reception areas, comfortable squashy sofas, bold décor and colours, marvellous modern cooking, super afternoon tea, and very friendly young staff; open-air theatre, tennis and croquet, bathing, fishing and rowing boat; dogs in bedrooms; £10

Taychreggan Hotel *Kilchrenan, Taynuilt, Argyll PA35 1HQ (01866) 833211* £127, plus special breaks; 19 rms. Civilised hotel with fine garden running down to Loch Awe and 40 acres of grounds where dogs may walk; comfortable airy bar, attractively served lunchtime bar food, polite efficient staff, good freshly prepared food and a carefully chosen wine list in dining room, dozens of malt whiskies, and pretty inner courtyard; resident dog; cl Jan; no children; dogs in some bedrooms; £4

KILNINVER

Knipoch *Knipoch, Oban, Argyll PA34 4QT (01852) 316251* £166, plus winter breaks; 21 rms. Elegant very well kept Georgian hotel in lovely countryside overlooking Loch Feochan; fine family portraits, log fires, fresh flowers and polished furniture in comfortable lounges and bars, carefully chosen wines and malt whiskies, and marvellous food inc their own smoked salmon; three resident dogs; dogs welcome in bedrooms

KINCLAVEN BY STANLEY

Ballathie House *Stanley, Perth PH1 4QN (01250) 883268* £185, plus special breaks; 42 pretty rms, some luxurious and some in newer building with river views from balconies. On a vast estate with fine salmon fishing on the River Tay (lodges and facilities for fishermen) and plenty of sporting opportunities, this turreted mansion has a comfortable and relaxed drawing room, separate lounge and bar, good enjoyable modern scottish cooking, croquet and putting; resident dog; limited disabled access; dogs in some bedrooms; £10

KINNESSWOOD

Lomond Country Inn *Main St, Kinnesswood, Kinross KY13 9HN (01592) 840253* (3.7 miles off M90 junction 8 northbound; turn right off A90 on B919; a little further from junction 7 southbound, via A911) £70, plus special breaks; 12 comfortable rms, 8 in an extension. Attractive little inn in village centre with views across Loch Leven (nice sunsets), open fires, informal bustling bar, well kept real ales, and good reasonably priced bar and restaurant food using local produce; walks in grounds and elsewhere; disabled access; dogs welcome in bedrooms

KIRKTON OF GLENISLA

Glenisla Hotel *Glenisla, Blairgowrie, Perthshire PH11 8PH (01575) 582223* £70, plus special breaks; 6 cosy rms. Old coaching inn in lovely quiet countryside with lots of country pursuits all around; convivial, traditionally furnished beamed bar with open fire, drawing room with comfortable sofas, flowers and books, games room, enjoyable seasonal food and hearty scottish breakfasts in elegant dining room, and well kept real ales; cl Mon and Tues during Oct–April; dogs in bedrooms; £5

LOCKERBIE

Dryfesdale Hotel *Dryfebridge, Lockerbie, Dumfries-shire DG11 2SF (01576) 202427* (1 mile off A74 junction 17; B7076 N) £115, plus wknd breaks; 28 rms. Relaxed and comfortable former manse in five acres of grounds, open fire in homely lounge, good food in pleasant restaurant, garden and lovely surrounding countryside, putting and croquet; cl Christmas; good disabled access; dogs in some bedrooms; £5

MELROSE

Burts *Market Sq, Melrose, Roxburghshire TD6 9PN (01896) 822285* (2.9 miles off A7 via A6091 and B6374; Market Sq – handy for A68 too) £106, plus special breaks; 20 rms. Welcoming 18th-c family-run hotel close to abbey ruins in delightfully quiet village; coal fire in bustling bar, residents' lounge, consistently popular imaginative food, exceptional breakfasts; dogs can walk in park; cl 24–26 Dec; children over 12 in evening restaurant; partial disabled access; dogs in bedrooms

MINNIGAFF

Creebridge House *Creebridge, Newton Stewart, Wigtownshire DG8 6NP (01671) 402121* £100, plus special breaks; 18 rms inc 2 with four-posters. Attractive country-house hotel in three acres of gardens with relaxed friendly atmosphere, open fire in comfortable drawing room, cheerful bar, and big choice of delicious food inc fine local fish and seafood in garden restaurant; cl 3 wks Jan; dogs in bedrooms; bedding, bowls, chews

PITLOCHRY

Killiecrankie House Hotel *Killiecrankie, Pitlochry, Perthshire PH16 5LG (01796) 473220* (3 miles off A9 via B8019/B8079 Killiecrankie rd just N of Pitlochry) £130, plus special breaks; 10 spotless rms. Comfortable country hotel in spacious grounds with splendid mountain views, mahogany-panelled bar with stuffed animals and fine wildlife paintings, cosy sitting room with books and games, a relaxed atmosphere, friendly owners, and excellent well presented, locally sourced food and good wine list in elegant restaurant; two resident dogs; fine nearby walks; cl Jan–Mar; disabled access; dogs in some bedrooms but must not be left unattended; £10

PORT APPIN

Airds Hotel *Port Appin, Appin, Argyll PA38 4DF (01631) 730236* (2 miles off A828) £280 inc dinner, plus special breaks; 12 lovely rms. Instantly relaxing 18th-c inn with lovely views of Loch Linnhe and the island of Lismore, blissfully comfortable day rooms, professional courteous staff, and charming owners; the food is exceptional (as is the wine list), there are lots of surrounding walks, with more on Lismore (small boat every hour), clay pigeon shooting and riding; cl 8–28 Jan; children over 8 for dinner; dogs in some bedrooms; £10

PORTPATRICK
Knockinaam Lodge *Portpatrick, Stranraer, Wigtownshire DG9 9AD (01776) 810471* **£260** inc dinner; 9 individual rms. Lovely very neatly kept little hotel with comfortable pretty rooms, open fires, wonderful food, and friendly caring service; dramatic surroundings, with lots of fine cliff walks; children over 12 in evening restaurant (high tea at 6pm); cl Christmas; disabled access; dogs in some bedrooms; £15

PORTREE
Rosedale *Quay Brae, Portree, Isle of Skye IV51 9DB (01478) 613131* (0.4 miles off A87 via A855; on Bank St take sharp right down Quay Brae) **£80**, plus special breaks; 18 rms, many with harbour views. Built from three fishermen's cottages with lots of passages and stairs, this family-run waterfront hotel has two traditional lounges, small first-floor restaurant with freshly cooked popular food, lots of whiskies in the cocktail bar, helpful staff, marvellous views; walks along shore or in forest; cl Nov–Mar; dogs in some bedrooms and must be well behaved

RAASAY
Isle of Raasay Hotel *Isle of Raasay, Kyle, Ross-shire IV40 8PB (01478) 660222* **£80**, plus special breaks; 12 rms. Victorian hotel with marvellous views over the Sound of Raasay to Skye, popular with walkers and bird-watchers, home-made food with an emphasis on fresh fish; no petrol on the island; resident cats and chickens; disabled access; dogs in bedrooms; £5

SCARISTA
Scarista House *Scarista, Harris, Isle of Harris HS3 3HX (01859) 550238* **£180**, plus special breaks; 5 rms, some in annexe. Marvellously wild countryside and empty beaches surround this isolated small hotel with its antiques-furnished rooms, open fires, warm friendly atmosphere, and plenty of books and records (no radio or TV); an impressive wine list and good food in candlelit dining room using organic home-grown vegetables and herbs, hand-made cheeses, their own eggs, home-made bread, cakes, biscuits, yoghurt and marmalade, and lots of fish and shellfish; excellent for wildlife, walks and fishing; resident dog, guinea pig, two hamsters and three cats; cl Christmas and occasionally in winter; dogs in bedrooms only

SCONE
Murrayshall House *Perth PH2 7PH (01738) 551171* **£150**, plus special breaks; 41 rms inc 14 suites, plus lodge which sleeps 6. Handsome mansion in 300-acre park where dogs may walk, very popular with golfers (it has

two of its own courses); comfortable elegant public rooms, warm friendly
staff, relaxed atmosphere, imaginative food and good wines; resident cat;
disabled access; dogs in bedrooms

SCOURIE
Scourie Hotel *Scourie, Lairg, Sutherland IV27 4SX (01971) 502396* £**66**;
20 rms with views to Scourie Bay. A haven for anglers, with 36 exclusive
beats on 25,000-acre estate; snug bar and cocktail bar, two comfortable
lounges and good food using plenty of local game and fish in smart no
smoking dining room; fine walks on the doorstep; resident dog and two
cats; cl Oct-Apr; dogs in bedrooms, sitting rooms and cocktail bar; £1.50

SHIEL BRIDGE
Kintail Lodge *Glenshiel, Kyle, Ross-shire IV40 8HL (01599) 511275* (on
A87) £**98**, plus special breaks; 12 recently refurbished big rms. Pleasantly
informal and fairly simple former shooting lodge on Loch Duich, with
magnificent views, four acres of walled gardens, residents' lounge bar and
comfortable sitting room, good well prepared food inc local seafood in
conservatory restaurant, and fine collection of malt whiskies; cl Mon and
Tues in winter; dogs in bedrooms

SHIELDAIG
Tigh an Eilean *Shieldaig, Strathcarron, Ross-shire IV54 8XN (01520)
755251* £**144**, plus special breaks; 11 rms. Attractive hotel in outstanding
position with lovely view of pine-covered island and sea, kayaks, private
fishing and sea fishing arranged, within easy reach of NTS Torridon Estate,
Beinn Eighe nature reserve and Applecross peninsula; pretty woodburner
in one of two comfortable residents' lounges with well stocked honesty bar,
library, and modern dining room with delicious food inc home-baked
bread; two resident dogs; cl end Oct-Mar; dogs in bedrooms only;
bedding, bowls and meals on request

SPEAN BRIDGE
Letterfinlay Lodge *Letterfinlay, Spean Bridge, Inverness-shire PH34 4DZ
(01397) 712622* (on A82 7 miles N of Spean Bridge/A86 junction) £**75**,
plus special breaks; 13 rms, most with own bthrm. Secluded and genteel
family-run country house with picture window in extensive modern bar
overlooking loch; elegantly panelled small cocktail bar, good popular food,
friendly attentive service; grounds run down through rhododendrons to the
jetty and Loch Lochy – dogs may walk here; fishing can be arranged; cl
mid-Oct-Easter; dogs welcome away from dining room; £2

SPITTAL OF GLENSHEE
Dalmunzie House *Glenshee, Blairgowrie, Perthshire PH10 7QG (01250)
885224* £**120**, plus special breaks; 17 rms with fine views and named after
local families. Old-fashioned former Victorian shooting lodge peacefully set
in huge estate among spectacular mountains, plenty of walks within it, and
own golf course; comfortable drawing room, open fires in two other

lounges, cosy, informal bar and antiques-filled library, traditional country house cooking in candlelit restaurant using local produce, and good breakfasts; disabled access; dogs welcome in bedrooms

STRONTIAN
Kilcamb Lodge Hotel *Strontian, Acharacle, Argyll PH36 4HY (01967) 402257* £142, plus winter breaks; 12 rms. Warm friendly little hotel in 28 acres by Loch Sunart, with log fires in two lounges, carefully cooked food using fresh ingredients from organic kitchen garden, fine choice of malt whiskies in small bar, and a relaxed atmosphere; beach, fishing boat, four moorings and jetty; cl Nov, Jan–Mar; no children; dogs in some bedrooms; £5

TARBERT
Stonefield Castle *Stonefield, Tarbert, Argyll PA29 6YJ (01880) 820836* £100, plus special breaks; 33 rms. With wonderful views and 60 acres of surrounding wooded grounds where dogs may walk, this scottish baronial mansion has a panelled lounge bar and other comfortable sitting areas, a convivial bar, good food and super views in restaurant, and snooker room; disabled access; dogs in bedrooms; £10

Wales

Dog Friendly Pubs

CAPEL CURIG

Bryn Tyrch *A5 W of village; LL24 0EL*

This isolated and pleasantly informal inn is very much in the heart of Snowdonia; if you stay, you may even see other residents lighting the fire. Wholesome food, with an emphasis on vegetarian and vegan dishes, is generously served to meet the healthy appetite of anyone participating in the local outdoor attractions – very much what this place is about. Big picture windows run the length of one wall, with views across the road to picnic-sets on a floodlit patch of grass by a stream running down to a couple of lakes, and the peaks of the Carneddau, Tryfan and Glyders in close range. Comfortably relaxed, the bar has several easy chairs round low tables, some by a coal fire with magazines and outdoor equipment catalogues piled to one side, and a pool table in the plainer hikers' bar; the dining room and part of the main bar are no smoking. Camerons Castle Eden, Flowers IPA and Greene King Old Speckled Hen on handpump, and quite a few malt whiskies, including some local ones; lots of different coffee blends or Twinings teas. Pool, shove-ha'penny and dominoes. There are tables on a steep little garden at the side. Bedrooms are simple but clean, and some have views; £10 cleaning charge for dogs. You could hardly be closer to the high mountains of Snowdonia, with some choice and challenging walking right on the doorstep.

Free house ~ Licensee Rita Davis ~ Real ale ~ Bar food (12-3, 5-9.30 weekdays; 12-9.30 weekends) ~ Restaurant ~ (01690) 720223 ~ Children welcome ~ Dogs welcome ~ Open 12-11; closed lunchtime Mon-Thurs in winter ~ Bedrooms: £40(£45B)/£56(£65S)(£65B)

CRICKHOWELL

Bear *Brecon Road; A40; NP8 1BW*

A civilised old coaching inn in the centre of this delightful little town, the Bear manages to blend traditional charms with efficient service, and is a welcoming place to stay. The comfortably decorated, heavily beamed lounge has fresh flowers on tables, lots of little plush-seated bentwood armchairs and handsome cushioned antique settles, and a window seat looking down on the market square. Up by the great roaring log fire, a big sofa and leather easy chairs are spread among rugs on the oak parquet floor. Other good antiques include a fine oak dresser filled with pewter and brass, a longcase clock, and interesting prints. All areas except the main bar are now no smoking. Bass, Brains Rev James, Courage Directors and Greene King Ruddles Best on handpump, as well as 24 malt whiskies, vintage and late-bottled ports, unusual wines (with 10 by the glass) and liqueurs (with some hops tucked in among the bottles) and local apple juice. Good, honest bar food and a popular Sunday lunch. You can eat in the garden in summer; disabled lavatories.

Free house ~ Licensee Judy Hindmarsh ~ Real ale ~ Bar food (12-2, 6-10; 12-2, 7-9.30 Sun) ~ Restaurant ~ (01873) 810408 ~ Children in family lounge and over 8 in restaurant ~ Dogs allowed in bar and bedrooms ~ Open 11-3, 6-11; 12-3, 7-10.30 Sun ~ Bedrooms: £65S/£80S(£90B)

EAST ABERTHAW
Blue Anchor *B4265; CF62 3DD*

Back to normal and looking splendid after its enforced restoration in 2004, this charming medieval thatched pub is full of character. The warren of snug low-beamed rooms dates back to 1380, and has massive stone walls and tiny doorways, and open fires everywhere, including one in an inglenook with antique oak seats built into its stripped stonework. Other seats and tables are worked into a series of chatty little alcoves, and the more open front bar still has an ancient lime-ash floor. Friendly, helpful staff serve Brains Bitter, Theakstons Old Peculier, Wadworths 6X and Wye Valley Hereford Pale Ale on handpump, alongside a changing guest from a brewer such as Tomos Watkin; fruit machine, darts, trivia machine and dominoes. Enjoyable bar food, and a no smoking restaurant; piped music. Some of the fruit and vegetables come from the garden of the landlord's father. Rustic seats shelter peacefully among tubs and troughs of flowers outside, with more stone tables on a newer terrace. From here a path leads to the shingly flats of the estuary. The pub can get very full in the evenings and on summer weekends.

Free house ~ Licensee Jeremy Coleman ~ Real ale ~ Bar food (12-2, 6-8; not Sat evening, not Sun lunchtime) ~ Restaurant ~ (01446) 750329 ~ Children welcome away from bar ~ Dogs allowed in bar ~ Open 11-11; 12-10.30 Sun

FELINFACH
Griffin *A470 NE of Brecon; LD3 0UB*

Contempory and classy, but not at all pretentious, this restauranty dining pub is a delightfully civilised place for a good meal (and they grow many of the vegetables themsevles) – or even better, a relaxing break. The back bar is quite pubby in an up-to-date way, with three leather sofas around a low table on pitted quarry tiles, by a high slate hearth with a log fire, and behind them mixed stripped seats around scrubbed kitchen tables on bare boards, and a bright blue-and-ochre colour scheme. It has a few modern prints, and some nice photoprints of a livestock market by Victoria Upton. An upright piano stands against one wall – the acoustics are pretty lively, with so much bare flooring and uncurtained windows. The two smallish no smoking front dining rooms, linking through to the back bar, are attractive: on the left, mixed dining chairs around mainly stripped tables on flagstones, and white-painted rough stone walls, with a cream-coloured Aga in a big stripped-stone embrasure; on the right, similar furniture on bare boards, with big modern prints on terracotta walls, and good dark curtains. There may be piped radio in the bar. They have a good choice of wines including ten by the glass, welsh spirits, and Evan Evans, Tomos Watkins OSB and Tw Cwrw Braf on handpump. Wheelchair access is good, and there are tables outside. Though they generally close for the afternoon, they may stay open all day so it's worth checking. Bedrooms are comfortable and tastefully decorated, and the hearty breakfasts nicely informal: you make your own toast on the Aga and help yourself to home-made marmalade and jam.

Free house ~ Licensees Charles and Edmund Inkin ~ Real ale ~ Bar food (12.30-2.30, 6.30-9.30(9 Sun); not Mon lunch (exc bank hols)) ~ Restaurant ~ (01874) 620111 ~ Children welcome ~ Dogs allowed in bar and bedrooms ~ Open 12-3, 6-11 (10.30 Sun); closed Mon lunchtime except bank hols ~ Bedrooms: £67.50B/£97.50B

HAY-ON-WYE
Kilverts *Bullring; HR3 5AG*

A particularly friendly hotel in the centre of town, this comfortable place is now completely no smoking. Open all day, it has a pleasantly unrushed feel, and you can watch the world go by from tables in a small front flagstoned courtyard (with outdoor heaters) or while away the hours by the fountain in a pretty terraced back garden. Enjoyable bar food from a sensibly balanced menu and good service from genial staff. Calm and understated, the airy high-beamed bar has some stripped stone walls, *Vanity Fair* caricatures, a couple of standing timbers, candles on well spaced mixed old and new tables, and a pleasant variety of seating. They've an extensive wine list with about a dozen by the glass, as well as three well kept real ales such as Brains Rev James, Hancocks HB and Wye Valley Butty Bach on handpump, a decent choice of wines by the glass, a dozen malt whiskies, and good coffees; piped music. There's a £5.50 cleaning charge for dogs in the comfortable bedrooms.

Free house ~ Licensee Colin Thomson ~ Real ale ~ Bar food (12-2, 6.15(6.30 Fri/Sat)-9.30) ~ Restaurant ~ (01497) 821042 ~ Children welcome in eating area of bar until 9pm ~ Dogs welcome ~ Open 9am-11pm; closed 25 Dec ~ Bedrooms: £50S/£70S(£80B)

LLANARMON DYFFRYN CEIRIOG
Hand *On B4500 from Chirk; LL20 7LD*

The black-beamed carpeted bar on the left of the broad-flagstoned entrance hall has a good log fire in its inglenook fireplace, a mixture of comfortable armchairs and settees, and old prints on its cream walls, with bar stools along the modern bar counter, which has Weetwood Best on handpump from the modern bar counter, a dozen or so whiskies, and reasonably priced wines by the glass; happy and welcoming staff help towards the warm atmosphere. Round the corner, the largely stripped stone dining room, with a woodburning stove and parquet floor, has a seasonally changing menu, with an emphasis on local ingredients. If you are staying, they do a good country breakfast, and the residents' lounge on the right is comfortable and attractive. There are tables out on a crazy-paved front terrace, with more in the garden, which has flower beds around another sheltered terrace. Beyond the back lawn sheep pasture stretches up into the Berwyn Hills – it's a very quiet spot in this pretty valley, and the River Ceiriog runs through the village. Much of the building has been redecorated in the last year, and they have plans to revamp the bar – and even to open their own microbrewery.

Free house ~ Licensees Gaynor and Martin de Luchi ~ Bar food (12-2.30 (12.30-2.45 Sun), 6.30-9) ~ Restaurant ~ (01691) 600666 ~ Children welcome away from bar ~ Dogs allowed in bar and bedrooms ~ Open 11(12 Sun)-11(12.30 Sat) ~ Bedrooms: £45B/£70B

LLANFERRES
Druid *A494 Mold—Ruthin; CH7 5SN*

Originally a farmhouse, this extended 17th-c whitewashed inn in the Alyn valley has glorious views across to the Clwydian Range; you can enjoy the setting from tables outside at the front and from the broad bay window in the civilised, smallish plush lounge. You can also see the hills from the bigger beamed and characterful back bar, with its two handsome antique oak settles as well as a pleasant mix of more modern furnishings. There's a quarry-tiled area by the log fire, and a three-legged cat, Chu. Jennings Golden Host, Marstons Pedigree and a guest like Smiles April Fuel on handpump, and around two dozen malt whiskies.Welcoming staff serve a wide range of generously plated bar food and the attractive dining room is no smoking. A games room has darts and pool, along with dominoes, cribbage, shove-ha'penny, bagatelle, board games, also TV and perhaps piped music. The bedrooms have recently been refurbished.

Union Pub Company ~ Lease James Dolan ~ Real ale ~ Bar food (12-2.30, 6-9; 12-9 weekends and bank hols) ~ Restaurant ~ (01352) 810225 ~ Children welcome ~ Dogs allowed in bar and bedrooms ~ Open 12-3, 5.30-12; 12-12 weekends; closed evening 25 Dec ~ Bedrooms: £40S/£65S

MONKNASH
Plough & Harrow *Signposted Marcross, Broughton off B4265 St Brides Major—Llantwit Major – turn left at end of Water Street; OS Sheet 170 map reference 920706; CF71 7QQ*

Originally part of a monastic grange, and dating back almost nine centuries, this white-painted cottage is one of those pubs worth visiting just to see the building. Built with massively thick stone walls, its dimly lit unspoilt main bar used to be the scriptures room and mortuary; instantly welcoming and genuinely atmospheric, it seems hardly changed over the last 70 years. The heavily black-beamed ceiling has ancient ham hooks, an intriguing arched doorway to the back, and a comfortably informal mix of furnishings that includes three fine stripped pine settles on the broad flagstones. There's a log fire in a huge fireplace with a side bread oven large enough to feed a village. The room on the left has lots of Wick rugby club memorabilia (it's their club room); daily papers, piped music. Up to eight well kept real ales on handpump or tapped from the cask might include Archers Golden, Wye Valley Hereford Pale Ale, Worthington BB and thoughtfully sourced guest ales from brewers such as Black Isle, Kelham Island and RCH; helpful service from knowledgeable staff. The daily changing bar food is written up on blackboards. It can get crowded at weekends, when it's popular with families (they do children's helpings). There are picnic-sets in the front garden, which has a boules pitch, and they hold barbecues out here in summer. Dogs are welcome in the bar – but not while food is being served. In a peaceful spot not far from the coast near Nash Point, it's an enjoyable walk from here down to the sea, where you can pick up a fine stretch of the coastal path along the top of remarkable candy-striped cliffs full of blow holes and fissures.

Free house ~ Licensee Paula Jones ~ Real ale ~ Bar food (12-2.30, 6-9) ~ Restaurant ~ (01656) 890209 ~ Children welcome ~ Dogs allowed in bar ~ Live music Sun evening ~ Open 12-11(10.30 Sun)

RAGLAN

Clytha Arms *Clytha, off Abergavenny road – former A40, now declassified; NP7 9BW*

This fine old country inn stands in its own extensive well cared for grounds on the edge of Clytha Park – a mass of colour in spring. With long verandahs and diamond paned windows, it's comfortable, light and airy, with scrubbed wood floors, pine settles, big faux fur cushions on the window seats, a good mix of old country furniture and a couple of warming fires. Don't miss the murals in the lavatories. Run by charming licensees, it's the sort of relaxed place where everyone feels welcome, from locals who've walked here for a pint, to diners in the contemporary linen-set restaurant. There's a good bar menu and a more elaborate restaurant one. An impressive choice of drinks includes Bass, Felinfoel Double Dragon and Hook Norton Hooky, three swiftly changing guest beers from brewers such as Caledonian, Carters and Fullers, an extensive wine list with about a dozen or so by the glass, a good choice of spirits, farm cider and even home-made perry. They have occasional cider and beer festivals. The restaurant and lounge are no smoking; darts, shove-ha'penny, boules, table skittles, bar billiards, cribbage, dominoes, draughts and chess. The two friendly labradors are Beamish and Stowford and there's an english setter. The bedrooms are comfortable, with good welsh breakfasts.

Free house ~ Licensees Andrew and Beverley Canning ~ Real ale ~ Bar food (12.30-2.30, 7-9.30; not Sun evening or Mon lunch) ~ Restaurant ~ (01873) 840206 ~ Children welcome ~ Dogs allowed in bar ~ Open 12-12; 12-11 Sat; 12-11 Sun; closed Mon lunchtime; evening 25 Dec ~ Bedrooms: £60B/£80B

SHIRENEWTON
Carpenters Arms *Mynydd-bach; B4235 Chepstow—Usk, about ½ mile N; NP16 6BU*

Popular with locals (especially for Sunday lunch), this quaint stone-built pub was originally a smithy, and one of the unusual interconnecting rooms still has blacksmith's bellows hanging from the planked ceiling. Other interesting features include an array of chamber-pots, an attractive Victorian tiled fireplace, and a collection of chromolithographs of antique Royal occasions. Furnishings run the gamut too, from one very high-backed ancient settle to pews, kitchen chairs, a nice elm table, several sewing-machine trestle tables and so forth; shove-ha'penny, cribbage, dominoes, backgammon, and piped pop music. Bass, Fullers London Pride, Marstons Pedigree and Shepherd Neame Spitfire on handpump with an occasional seasonal guest. There's a wide choice of popular food written up on blackboards. Tables outside at the front under hanging baskets in summer.

Punch ~ Lease Gary and Sandra Hayes ~ Real ale ~ Bar food (12-9.30; 12-3, 6-9.30 in winter) ~ Restaurant ~ (01291) 641231 ~ Children welcome ~ Dogs welcome ~ Open 12-12; 11-10.30 Sun; 12-3.30, 5.30-12(10.30 Sun) in winter

SKENFRITH
Bell *Just off B5421, NE of Abergavenny and N of Monmouth; NP7 8UH*

Though they've grown their own herbs for a while, the licensees of this gently upmarket country inn are now developing a kitchen garden with organic fruit and vegetables, and the consistently good food is the place's main draw – though it's certainly not cheap. The owners are welcoming and enthusiastic, and service is cheerful and efficient. The big back bare-boards dining area is very neat, light and airy, with dark country-kitchen chairs and rush-seat dining chairs, church candles and flowers on the dark tables, canary walls and a cream ceiling, and brocaded curtains on sturdy big-ring rails. The flagstoned bar on the left has a rather similar décor, with old local and school photographs, and a couple of pews as well as tables and café chairs; Breconshire Golden Valley, Freeminer and Timothy Taylors Landlord on handpump from an attractive bleached oak bar counter. They have good wines by the glass and half-bottle, and make good coffee. The lounge bar on the right, opening into the dining area, has a nice Jacobean-style carved settle and a housekeeper's chair by a log fire in the big fireplace. The atmosphere is relaxed but smart (the lavatories are labelled Loos), and the pub is now entirely no smoking. There are good solid round picnic-sets as well as the usual rectangular ones out on the terrace, with steps up to a sloping lawn; it's a quiet spot. The bedrooms are comfortable, with thoughtful touches. Across the access road is a pretty bridge over the River Monnow.

Free house ~ Licensees William and Janet Hutchings ~ Real ale ~ Bar food (12-2.30, 7-9.30(9 Sun)) ~ Restaurant ~ (01600) 750235 ~ Children welcome in eating areas till 7, then over 8s only ~ Dogs allowed in bar and bedrooms ~ Open 11-11; 12-10.30 Sun; closed all day Mon in winter; last week Jan/first week Feb ~ Bedrooms: /£100B

TINTERN
Cherry Tree *Pub signed up narrow Raglan road off A466, beside Royal George; parking very limited; NP16 6TH*

The approach to this late-16th-c stone cottage is delightful, across a little stone slab bridge over a tiny stream. Not especially smart, it's a characterful place and very much at the heart of the local community – even more so now the building takes in the village shop and post office. It's been sympathetically extended in recent years, but not in a way that's altered its appeal: the well kept Hancocks HB and guests like Hereford Pale Ale, Sharps Doom Bar and Wye Valley Butty Bach are still tapped straight from the cask, and they also serve farm ciders from the barrel, along with a good few wines by the glass, and home-made country wines; warmly welcoming service. The original beamed and stone-built bar has a walnut serving counter in one area and a good open fire in another, and leads into the slate-floored extension; cribbage, darts, cards, dominoes and piped music. Good value food in big helpings made with fresh local ingredients. The pub is in a quiet and attractive spot, yet only half a mile or so from the honey-pot centre of Tintern, and there are tables out in a charming garden, and on a nicely refurbished patio; disabled access is difficult. They have two beer and cider festivals a year.

Free house ~ Licensees Jill and Steve Pocock ~ Real ale ~ Bar food (12-3, 6-9 (8.30 Sun); not winter Sun eves) ~ Restaurant ~ (01291) 689292 ~ Children in restaurant only ~ Dogs allowed in bar ~ Occasional live music ~ Open 12-11(10.30 Sun); 12-6 Sundays in winter ~ Bedrooms: /£60S(£60B)

TRELLECK
Lion *B4293 6 miles S of Monmouth; NP25 4PA*

Popular with a mix of locals, walkers and visitors, this stone-built pub has the feel of a chatty local – and an extraordinarily wide range of food. Unpretentious and traditional, the open-plan bar has one or two black beams in its low ochre ceiling, a mix of furnishings including some comfortable brocaded wall seats and tub chairs, a hop-hung window seat, varying-sized tables, and log fires in two fireplaces opposite each other. A small fish tank occupies a wall recess, and there's another bigger one in the lobby by the lavatories; piped music, cribbage, dominoes, shove-ha'penny and bar skittles. A colourful galaxy of pumpclips in the porch and on a wall show the range of rapidly changing guest beers such as Rhymney Bevans Bitter or Stonehenge Nine Lives that are kept alongside Wye Valley Butty Bach; they have an annual beer festival, as well as nearly two dozen malt whiskies, and traditional cider. Readers who've found the pub rather smoky will be pleased to hear that much of the public bar is now no smoking, as well as the restaurant.There are some picnic-sets and an aviary out on the grass, and a new side courtyard overlooking the church. Close by is a group of prehistoric standing stones.

Free house ~ Licensee Debbie Zsigo ~ Real ale ~ Bar food (12-2(2.30 weekends), 6(7Mon)-9.30; not Sun evening) ~ Restaurant ~ (01600) 860322 ~ Children welcome ~ Dogs allowed in bar ~ Live music on evening of bank hol Sats ~ Open weekdays 12-3, 6(7 Mon)-11(12 Thurs/Fri); 12-12 (12-3, 6.30-12 in winter)

Sat; 12-5 (4 in winter) Sun; closed Sun evening, all day 1 Jan, and evening 25
Dec ~ Bedrooms: £40S/£65S

TY'N-Y-GROES
Groes *B5106 N of village; LL32 8TN*
Elegantly romantic hotel with a marvellous relaxed atmosphere and very
good food. They make excellent use of local ingredients, such as lamb and
salmon from the Conwy Valley, and game birds from local shoots, and bake
their own bread and grow their own herbs. Said to have been the first
welsh pub to be properly licensed – in 1573 – it enjoys magnificent views
over the Vale of Conwy and the distant mountains. Past the hot stove in
the entrance area, the spotlessly kept series of rambling, low-beamed and
thick-walled rooms are nicely decorated with antique settles and an old
sofa, old clocks, portraits, hats and tins hanging from the walls, and fresh
flowers. A fine antique fireback is built into one wall, perhaps originally
from the formidable fireplace in the back bar, which houses a collection of
stone cats as well as cheerful winter log fires. The restaurant and family
room are no smoking, as is the airy and verdant conservatory. Ind Coope
Burton and Tetleys on handpump, and they've a good few malt whiskies,
kir, and a fruity Pimms in summer; light classical piped music at lunchtimes,
nostalgic light music at other times and a live harpist every now and then.
The neatly kept, well equipped bedroom suites (some have terraces or
balconies) have gorgeous views, and in summer it's a pleasure to sit outside
in the pretty back garden with its flower-filled hayricks; there are more
seats on the flower-decked roadside. They also rent out a well appointed
wooden cabin, idyllically placed nearby.
Free house ~ Licensee Dawn Humphreys ~ Real ale ~ Bar food (12-2.15, 6.30(6
Sat, Sun)-9) ~ Restaurant ~ (01492) 650545 ~ Children in family room till 7pm
~ Dogs welcome ~ Open 12-3, 6.30-11 (all day summer weekends); closed 25
Dec ~ Bedrooms: £79B/£95B

USK
Nags Head *The Square; NP15 1BH*
The family that runs this old coaching inn has been here almost 40 years
and there's always a good welcome. With its friendly chatty atmosphere,
the beautifully kept traditional main bar has lots of well polished tables and
chairs packed under its beams (some with farming tools), lanterns or
horsebrasses and harness attached, as well as leatherette wall benches, and
various sets of sporting prints and local pictures – look out for the original
deeds to the pub. Tucked away at the front is an intimate little corner with
some african masks, while on the other side of the room a passageway leads
to a new dining area converted from the old coffee bar. There may be
prints for sale, and perhaps a knot of sociable locals. Food is popular and
generously served. You can book tables, some of which may be candlelit at
night; nice proper linen napkins, and quiet piped classical music. They offer
15 wines by the glass, along with well kept Brains SA, Buckleys Best and
Rev James on handpump, 12 malt whiskies and Thatcher's Gold farm
cider. Two rooms are no smoking. The centre of Usk is full of pretty

hanging baskets and flowers in summer, and the church is well worth a look.

Free house ~ Licensee the Key family ~ Real ale ~ Bar food (12-2, 6-9.30) ~ Restaurant ~ (01291) 672820 ~ Children welcome ~ Dogs allowed in bar ~ Open 10.30-3, 5.30-11; closed 25 Dec

Dog Friendly Hotels, B&BS and Farms

ABERDOVEY

Penhelig Arms *Terrace Rd, Aberdovey, Gwynedd LL35 0LT* (01654) 767215 **£78**, plus special breaks; 16 comfortable rms, 4 in annexe impressively furnished, with fine harbour views. In a fine spot overlooking the sea, with cosy bar, open fires, delicious food with emphasis on daily-delivered fresh local fish in no smoking restaurant, extensive (and fairly priced) wine list with 30 by the glass (champagne, too), splendid breakfasts, and charming friendly service; lovely views of Dovey estuary and five miles of beach to walk on; cl 25-26 Dec; disabled access; dogs welcome away from restaurant; £3

ABERSOCH

Porth Tocyn Hotel *Bwlch Tocyn, Pwllheli, Gwynedd LL53 7BU* (01758) 713303 **£120**, plus special breaks; 17 cottagey and attractive rms, most with sea views. On a headland overlooking Cardigan Bay, this comfortable and homely place – converted from a row of lead miners` cottages – has been run by the same hard-working family for over 50 years; several cosy interconnecting sitting rooms with antiques, books and fresh flowers, a sunny conservatory, most enjoyable traditional cooking in no smoking restaurant (lots of options such as light lunches, high teas for children as they must be over 7 for dinner in the restaurant, and imaginative Sun lunches), and helpful young staff; lots of space in the pretty garden, heated swimming pool in summer, hard tennis court; they are kind to children; resident dog; cl Nov to mid-Mar; disabled access; dogs in bedrooms by prior arrangement.

BEDDGELERT

Sygun Fawr Country House *Beddgelert, Caernarfon, Gwynedd LL55 4NE* (01766) 890258 **£75**, plus special breaks; 11 rms. Spectacular scenery surrounds this secluded 17th-c hotel, with lots of surrounding walks; beams, stripped stone walls, inglenooks, and a restful atmosphere, a varied imaginative menu, antiques and an informal atmosphere in the no smoking restaurant and dining conservatory, and 20 acres of mountainside and gardens; cl Jan; dogs in bedrooms and bar; £4

BETWS-Y-COED

Ty Gwyn *Betwys-y-coed, Gwynedd LL24 0SG* (01690) 710383 (on A5 (and A470)) **£68**, plus special breaks; 12 pretty rms, most with own bthrm.

Welcoming and well run 17th-c coaching inn with interesting old prints, furniture and bric-a-brac, good food in no smoking restaurant and bar, and friendly service; pleasant setting overlooking river, plenty of surrounding walks, and a very good base for the area; children free if sharing parents' room; cl Mon-Weds in Jan; dogs in bedrooms; £5

BROAD HAVEN
Druidstone Hotel *Broad Haven, Haverfordwest, Dyfed SA62 3NE (01437) 781221* £120; 11 rms and 5 cottages, some with sea view, shared bthrms. Alone on the coast above a fine beach with exhilarating cliff walks, this roomy and informally friendly hotel, run by a very nice family, has something of a folk-club and Outward Bound feel at times; it's extremely winning and relaxing if you take to its unique combination of good wholesome and often memorably inventive food, slightly fend-for-yourself approach amid elderly furniture, and glorious seaside surroundings; resident dog and six cats; self-catering cottages; dogs welcome away from restaurant

CAERNARFON
Seiont Manor *Llanrug, Caernarfon, Gwynedd LL55 2AQ (01286) 673366* (2.7 miles off A487 via A4086 E) £190, plus special breaks; 28 luxurious rms. Fine hotel built from the original farmstead of a Georgian manor house, in 156 acres of mature parkland; open fires and comfortable sofas in lounge, restful atmosphere in library and drawing room, imaginative food in the no smoking restaurant's four interconnecting areas, and leisure suite with swimming pool, gym and sauna; disabled access; dogs in certain bedrooms

CONWY
Sychnant Pass House *Sychnant Pass Rd, Conwy, Gwynedd LL32 8BJ (01492) 596868* (2.5 miles off A55 junction 16 via Sychnant Pass Rd towards Conwy through Dwygyfylchi and Capelulo) £110; 10 rms. Victorian house in two acres among the foothills of the Snowdonia National Park; big comfortable sitting rooms (one is for smoking), log fires, a relaxing, friendly atmosphere, and enjoyable food (the restaurant is open to non-residents, too); four resident dogs and three cats; cl Christmas and Jan; disabled access; dogs welcome away from restaurant; dog beds and chews given

CRICCIETH
Mynydd Ednyfed Country House *Caernarfon Rd, Criccieth, Gwynedd LL52 0PH (01766) 523269* £85; 9 individually decorated rms, some with four-posters. Beautifully set 400-year-old house (totally no smoking) in 8 acres of garden, orchard, paddock and woods with lovely views overlooking Tremadog Bay, and once home to Lloyd George's family; traditional lounge bar, enjoyable food using local produce in comfortable dining room and airy conservatory, and friendly staff; all weather tennis court and new treatment room; cl 22 Dec-4 Jan; dogs if small and well behaved in bedrooms only; £7

EGLWYSFACH

Ynyshir Hall *Eglwysfach, Machynlleth, Dyfed SY20 8TA (01654) 781209*
(just off A487 SW of Machynlleth) £220, plus special breaks; 9
individually decorated, no smoking rms, two with four-posters. Carefully
run Georgian manor house in 14 acres of landscaped gardens adjoining the
Ynyshir coastal bird reserve; particularly good service, antiques, log fires
and paintings in the light and airy public rooms, extremely good food using
home-grown vegetables, and delicious breakfasts; resident dog; lots to do
nearby; cl 3 wks Jan; children over 9; disabled access to ground-floor rms;
dogs in two bedrooms; £3

GELLILYDAN

Tyddyn Du Farm *Gellilydan, Blaenau Ffestiniog, Gwynedd LL41 4RB
(01766) 590281* (just off A470 by A487 junction) £70, plus special breaks;
4 ground-floor, private stable and long barn suites with jacuzzi baths,
fridges and microwaves, one with airbath. 400-year-old farmhouse on
working farm in the heart of Snowdonia, with beams and exposed
stonework, and big inglenook fireplaces in lounge; children can help
bottle-feed the lambs, and look at goats, ducks, sheep and shetland ponies;
three dogs; fine walks, inc short one to their own Roman site; partial
disabled access; dogs welcome away from dining room

GILWERN

Wenallt Farm *Twyn-wenallt, Gilwern, Abergavenny, Gwent NP7 0HP
(01873) 830694* (0.6 miles off A465; turn off S just W of A4077 junction,
then bear left) £56; 5 rms. Friendly and relaxing 16th-c welsh longhouse
on 50 acres of farmland in the Brecon Beacons National Park, with oak
beams and inglenook fireplace in big drawing room, a TV room, good
food in dining room, packed lunches on request, and lots to do nearby;
partial disabled access; dogs in some bedrooms; £3

LLANABER

Llwyndu Farmhouse *Llanaber, Barmouth, Gwynedd LL42 1RR (01341)
280144* £80, plus special breaks; 6 charming rms, most with own bthrm,
some in a nicely converted 18th-c barn. Most attractive, no smoking
16th-c farmhouse just above Cardigan Bay, with a warm welcome from
friendly owners, big inglenook fireplaces, oak beams, mullioned windows,
relaxing lounge, enjoyable breakfasts, and good imaginative food in
candlelit dining room; two resident cats; plenty of walks; cl 25-26 Dec;
dogs welcome away from dining room

LLANARMON D C

West Arms *Llanarmon Dyffryn Ceiriog, Llangollen, Clwyd LL20 7LD
(01691) 600665* £125, plus special mid-week breaks; 15 rms. Charming
and civilised 16th-c inn with heavy beams and timbers, log fires in
inglenook fireplaces, lounge bar interestingly furnished with antique settles,
sofas in the old-fashioned entrance hall, comfortable locals' lounge bar,
good food, and friendly quiet atmosphere; large garden where dogs may

walk and the lawn runs down to the River Ceiriog (fishing for residents); disabled access; dogs in bedrooms; £6

LLANDELOY

Lochmeyler Farm *Llandeloy, Haverfordwest, Dyfed SA62 6LL (01348) 837724* £55, plus special winter breaks; 15 pretty rms. Attractive creeper-covered 16th-c farmhouse on 220-acre working dairy farm; two lounges (one no smoking), traditional farmhouse cooking in pleasant dining room, mature garden, and welsh cakes on arrival; can walk around the farm trails; cl Christmas and New Year; partial disabled access; dogs welcome in bedrooms

LLANDRILLO

Tyddyn Llan *Llandrillo, Corwen, Clwyd LL21 0ST (01490) 440264* £110; 13 pretty rms. Elegant and relaxed Georgian house with three acres of lovely gardens and surrounded by the Berwyn mountains (lots of walks); fresh flowers in comfortable public rooms, enjoyable food using the best ingredients, and an impressive wine list; fine forest walks (guides available), and watersports, fishing and horse riding can be arranged; three resident cats; cl 2 wks Jan; disabled access; dogs in bedrooms; £5

LLANDUDNO

St Tudno *15 North Parade, Llandudno, Gwynedd LL30 2LP (01492) 874411* £130, plus special breaks; 19 individually decorated rms, some with sea view. Opposite the pier, this well run, smart seaside hotel has genuinely helpful and friendly staff, Victorian-style décor in restful no smoking sitting room, a convivial bar lounge, relaxed coffee lounge for light lunches, and an attractive, no smoking italian-style restaurant; small indoor pool; dogs in bedrooms (but must not be left unattended); £10

LLANFAIR D C

Eyarth Station *Llanfair Dyffryn Clwyd, Ruthin, Clwyd LL15 2EE (01824) 703643* (0.6 miles off A494 S of Ruthin) £70, plus special breaks; 6 pretty rms. Carefully converted old railway station – totally no smoking – with quiet gardens and wonderful views; a friendly relaxed atmosphere, log fire in airy and comfortable beamed lounge, good breakfasts and enjoyable suppers in dining room (more lovely views), sun terrace and heated swimming pool, and lots of walks; resident cat; disabled access; dogs in bedrooms by arrangement and not to be left unattended; £6

LLANGAMMARCH WELLS

Lake *Llangammarch Wells, Powys LD4 4BS (01591) 620202* (2 miles off A483 via B4519, then 1st right) £160, plus special breaks; 30 charming, pretty rms with fruit and decanter of sherry. Particularly well run 1860s half-timbered hotel in 50 acres with plenty of wildlife, well stocked trout lake, tennis, riding or walking their two friendly labradors; deeply comfortable tranquil drawing room with antiques, paintings and log fire, wonderful afternoon teas (in summer under the chestnut tree overlooking the river), courteous service, fine wines and good modern british cooking in elegant candlelit dining room, and liberal breakfasts; children over 7 in evening dining room; disabled access; dogs in some bedrooms; £6

LLANSANFFRAID GLAN CONWY
Old Rectory Country House *Llanrwst Rd, Glan Conwy, Colwyn Bay, Clwyd LL28 5LF (01492) 580611* (1.7 miles off A55 junction 19 via A470 S) **£99**; 6 deeply comfortable rms. No smoking Georgian house in pleasant gardens with fine views over Conwy estuary, Conwy Castle and Snowdonia; delightful public rooms with flowers, antiques and family photos, good breakfasts (note that they no longer offer evening meals), and warmly friendly staff; cl 15 Dec-15 Jan; children under 9 months or over 5; dogs in coach house only

LLANWDDYN
Lake Vyrnwy Hotel *Llanwddyn, Oswestry, Powys SY10 0LY (01691) 870692* **£100**, plus special breaks; 52 individually furnished rms – some overlooking the lake. Large impressive Tudor-style mansion in a 26,000 acre estate – 16,000 acres are dedicated to the RSPB; conservatory looking over the water, log fires and sporting prints in the comfortable and elegant public rooms, convivial bar, a relaxed atmosphere, and good food using their own lamb and game from the estate, and home-made preserves, chutneys, mustards and vinegars; enjoyable teas too; disabled access; dogs in bedrooms; £10

LLANWRTYD WELLS
Carlton House *Dolycoed Rd, Llanwrtyd Wells, Powys LD5 4RA (01591) 610248* (just off A483, on Dolycoed Rd) **£60**, plus special breaks; 5 well equipped rms. Warmly friendly owners run this comfortable, no smoking Edwardian restaurant-with-rooms; relaxing little sitting room with plants and antiques, an attractive dining room with original panelling and log fire, exceptionally good modern british cooking using top-quality local produce (delicious puddings and home-made canapés and petits fours), super breakfasts with home-made bread and marmalade, and a thoughtful wine list; cl 10-31 Dec; dogs welcome in bedrooms

LLECHRYD
Castell Malgwyn *Llechryd, Cardigan, Dyfed SA43 2QA (01239) 682382* **£80**; 17 attractive rms. Handsome, creeper-covered 18th-c house with 7 acres of woodland, half-a-mile of river frontage (fishing and falconry), and lots of walks; homely comfortable lounge, convivial bar lounge, good, enjoyable food and nice breakfasts using local produce, friendly staff, and plenty of regular guests; one resident dog and one cat; dogs in bedrooms and library bar; £10

MONMOUTH
Riverside Hotel *Cinderhill St, Monmouth, Gwent NP25 5EY (01600) 715577* (1 mile off A40 via A466 and B4293, keeping left at Cinderhill St roundabout) **£64.95**, plus special breaks; 17 rms. Comfortable, warmly

welcoming bustling hotel overlooking River Monnow and the 13th-c fortified gatehouse, with good value bar meals, enjoyable food in no smoking restaurant, a bustling lounge bar, and conservatory; walks in nearby park; disabled access; dogs in some bedrooms

MONTGOMERY

Dragon *Market Sq, Montgomery, Powys SY15 6PA (01686) 668359* (3 miles off A483 via B4385; Market Sq) **£87.50**, plus special breaks; 20 rms. No smoking, 17th-c black and white timbered, family-run hotel with a pleasant grey-stone tiled hall, comfortable residents' lounge, beamed bar, and restaurant using local produce; indoor swimming pool, sauna; countryside walks; dogs welcome in bedrooms

NANTGWYNANT

Pen-y-Gwryd *Nantgwynant, Caernarfon, Gwynedd LL55 4NT (01286) 870211* **£80**, plus special breaks; 16 rms, some with own bthrm. In two acres, this cheery hotel is by the Llanberis Pass in Snowdonia National Park; warm log fire in simply furnished panelled residents' lounge, rugged slate-floored bar that doubles as mountain rescue post; lots of climbing mementoes and equipment, friendly, chatty games room (plenty of walkers, climbers and fishermen), hearty enjoyable food, big breakfasts, and packed lunches; sauna in the trees and outdoor swimming pool, table tennis; private chapel; cl Nov-Dec and mid-week Jan-Feb; disabled access; dogs in bedrooms and bar; £2

OXWICH

Oxwich Bay Hotel *Oxwich, Swansea, West Glamorgan SA3 1LS (01792) 390329* **£66**, plus special breaks; 26 rms. Comfortable, no smoking hotel on edge of beach in a lovely area, with dedicated friendly staff, food served all day, restaurant/lounge bar with panoramic views, summer outdoor dining area, and a welcome for families; cl 24-25 Dec; dogs in bedrooms; £7.50

PRESTEIGNE

Radnorshire Arms *High St, Presteigne, Powys LD8 2BE (01544) 267406* **£76**, plus special breaks; 19 rms. Rambling handsomely timbered 17th-c hotel with old-fashioned charm and an unchanging atmosphere, elegantly moulded beams and fine dark panelling in the lounge bar, latticed windows, enjoyable food (inc morning coffee and afternoon tea), separate no smoking restaurant, well kept real ales, and politely attentive service; walks nearby (or in the garden); disabled access; dogs in garden lodges; £5

PWLLHELI

Plas Bodegroes *Efailnewydd, Pwllheli, Gwynedd LL53 5TH (01758) 612363* **£150**; 11 rms. Lovely Georgian manor house, aptly described as a restaurant-with-rooms, in tree-filled grounds and fronted by a 200-year-old beech avenue; comfortably restful rooms, enjoyable modern cooking using superb fresh local produce and a good wine list in no smoking restaurant, very nice breakfasts, and genuinely friendly, helpful staff; cl 19 Nov–March; children over 10; disabled access; dogs in one bedroom

RHAYADER
Beili Neuadd *Rhayader, Powys LD6 5NS (01597) 810211* (2 miles off A470, via B4518 NE) **£50**; 3 rms with log fires, and converted stone barn with 3 bunkhouse rms. Charming, no smoking, partly 16th-c stone-built farmhouse with panoramic views and set in quiet countryside; beams, polished oak floorboards, log fires, and nice breakfasts in garden room; walks in paddocks and garden; self-catering also; two resident dogs and one cat; dogs welcome

ST BRIDES WENTLOOG
West Usk Lighthouse *St Brides Wentloog, Newport, Gwent NP10 8SF (01633) 810126* **£95**; 3 rms. Unusual ex-lighthouse – squat rather than tall – that was on an island in the Bristol Channel (the land has since been reclaimed); totally no smoking with modern stylish furnishings, lots of framed record sleeves (Mr Sheahan used to work for a record company), informal atmosphere, good big breakfasts, and a Rolls-Royce drive to good local restaurant; flotation tank, aromatherapy, reflexology and other complementary therapies, large roof terrace with palm and shrubs and a barbecue, and lots of nearby walks; dogs in bedrooms by arrangement; £5

ST DAVID'S
Warpool Court *St David's, Haverfordwest, Dyfed SA62 6BN (01437) 720300* **£190**, plus special breaks; 25 rms. Originally built as St David's cathedral school in the 1860s and bordering NT land, this popular – mainly no smoking – hotel has lovely views over St Bride's Bay; Ada Williams's collection of lovely hand-painted tiles can be seen in the public rooms, food in the elegant restaurant is imaginative (good for vegetarians too), and staff are helpful; quiet gardens (walks here and in surrounding fields), heated summer swimming pool, tennis, table tennis, pool and croquet; cl Jan; dogs in bedrooms; £6

TAL-Y-BONT
Lodge *Tal-y-bont, Conwy, Gwynedd LL32 8YX (01492) 660766* **£80**, plus special breaks; 14 rms. Friendly little modern hotel in over three acres on the edge of Snowdonia, with open fire, books and magazines in comfortable lounge, generous helpings of popular food using lots of home-grown produce in no smoking restaurant, and good service; lots of walks; good disabled access; dogs in bedrooms; £3

TINTERN PARVA
Parva Farmhouse Hotel *Tintern, Chepstow, Gwent NP16 6SQ (01291) 689411* **£78**, plus special breaks; 8 comfortable rms. Friendly, no smoking stone farmhouse built in 17th c, with leather chesterfields, woodburner and honesty bar in large beamed lounge, books (no TV downstairs), and very

good food and wine (inc wine using locally grown grapes) in cosy restaurant; 50 yds from River Wye and lovely surrounding countryside; resident dog; children over 12; dogs in bedrooms (must not be left unattended); £3

Channel Islands

Dog Friendly Pubs

ROZEL

Rozel *La Vallee De Rozel; JE3 6AJ*

Tucked away at the edge of a sleepy little fishing village and just out of sight of the sea, this friendly inn has a very pleasant steeply terraced and partly covered hillside garden. Inside, the bar counter (Bass, Charles Wells Bombardier and Courage Directors under light blanket pressure) and tables in the traditional-feeling and cosy little dark-beamed back bar are stripped to their original light wood finish, and there are dark plush wall seats and stools, an open granite fireplace, and old prints and local pictures on the cream walls. Leading off is a carpeted area with flowers on big solid square tables. Piped music, and TV, games machine, juke box, darts, pool, cribbage and dominoes in the games room; the lounge bar is no smoking. Food from a good value menu is served in generous helpings. The upstairs restaurant has a relaxed rustic french atmosphere, and a menu with up to ten fish dishes a day, and good value specials.

Free house ~ Licensee Trevor Amy ~ Real ale ~ Bar food (12-2.15, 6-8.45) ~ Restaurant (not Sun evening) ~ (01534) 869801 ~ Children welcome ~ Dogs allowed in bar ~ Open 11-11

ST BRELADE

Old Portelet Inn *Portelet Bay; JE3 8AJ*

You can get a very good value meal at this enjoyable 17th-c farmhouse, and as there's plenty to keep children occupied it's particularly good for families too. There's a supervised indoor play area (half an hour 60p), another one outside, board games in the wooden-floored loft bar, and even summer entertainments arranged by the pub; also TV, pool, cribbage, dominoes and piped music. From a short snack menu, generous helpings of food are served by neatly dressed attentive staff. The pub is well placed at the head of a long flight of granite steps, giving views across Portelet (Jersey's most southerly bay) as you walk down to a sheltered cove. There are picnic-sets on the partly covered flower-bower terrace by a wishing well, and seats in the sizeable landscaped garden, with lots of scented stocks and other flowers. The low-beamed downstairs bar has a stone bar counter (well kept Bass and a guest such as Flowers Original kept under light blanket pressure and reasonably priced house wine), a huge open fire, gas lamps, old pictures, etched glass panels from France, and a nice mixture of old wooden chairs on bare oak boards and quarry tiles. It opens into the big timber-ceilinged no smoking barn restaurant, with standing timbers and plenty of highchairs; disabled and baby-changing facilities. It can get very busy, but does have its quiet moments too.

Randalls ~ Manager Sarah Pye ~ Real ale ~ Bar food (12-2, 6-9 (snack menu 2.30-5.30)) ~ Restaurant ~ (01534) 741899 ~ Children in restaurant and family room ~ Dogs allowed in bar ~ Open 11-11

Old Smugglers *Ouaisne Bay; OS map reference 595476; JE3 8AW*
The welcoming bar at this straightforward pub has thick walls, black beams, log fires and cosy black built-in settles, with well kept Bass and two guests from brewers such as Charles Wells and Ringwood on handpump, and a farm cider; sensibly placed darts, cribbage and dominoes. A glassed porch running the width of the building takes in interesting views over one of the island's many defence towers. Bar food is fairly standard, and the entire restaurant is no smoking.

Free house ~ Licensee Nigel Godfrey ~ Real ale ~ Bar food (12-2, 6-9; not Sun evening Nov-Mar) ~ Restaurant ~ (01534) 741510 ~ Children welcome ~ Dogs allowed in bar ~ Open 11-11.30

ST JOHN
Les Fontaines *Le Grand Mourier, Route du Nord; JE3 4AJ*
The cheery bustle of happy families and locals livens up this enjoyable former farmhouse, which is in a pretty spot on the north coast, and a nice place for a pint after a walk (well kept Bass and Charles Wells Bombardier). As you go in, look out for a worn, unmarked door at the side of the building, or as you go down the main entry lobby towards the bigger main bar go through the tiny narrow door on your right. These entrances take you into the best part, the public bar, (where you might even hear the true Jersey patois), which has very heavy beams in the low dark ochre ceiling, massively thick irregular red granite walls, cushioned settles on the quarry-tiled floor and antique prints. The big granite-columned fireplace with a log fire warming its unusual inglenook seats may date back to the 16th c, and still sports its old smoking chains and side oven. The quarry tiled main bar is a marked contrast, with plenty of wheelback chairs around neat dark tables, and a spiral staircase leading up to a wooden gallery under the high pine-raftered plank ceiling; the dining area is no smoking; piped music and board games. A bonus for families is Pirate Pete's, a play area for children. Bar food runs from the quite straightforward to daily specials. Seats on a terrace outside have good views.

Randalls ~ Manager Hazel O'Gorman ~ Real ale ~ Bar food (12-2.15(2.45 Sun), 6-9(8.30 Sun)) ~ (01534) 862707 ~ Children welcome ~ Dogs allowed in bar ~ Open 11.30-11

Answers to Dog Quiz

1. Gunther IV
2. Sean Connery, in the film *Finding Forrester*
3. Emma, Linnet, Holly, Willow and Monty
4. Newfoundland (they were required equipment in 19th-c english lifeguard stations)
5. First dog in space, 1957
6. English mastiff
7. Chihuahua
8. More than 100,000 years
9. Stanley
10. Dogs can hear a sound up to four times as far away as humans
11. Milo
12. Cerberus
13. Aberdeen terrier, in Jonathan Jo's
14. Jellystone
15. Japanese
16. Dougal, in the *Magic Roundabout*
17. *Two Gentlemen of Verona*
18. Dartmoor
19. Flush
20. Stifle
21. Dolores
22. Bedlington – traditionally its tail has been undocked, the others docked
23. Boo
24. Minnie
25. Rob
26. Cat Stevens, now Yusuf Islam
27. 18th c; Jonathan Swift used it in *A Complete Collection of Polite and Ingenious Conversation*, 1738
28. Jess
29. 1987
30. Only the pharaoh hound, a rare breed
31. c, 150 million
32. 20 – the number can vary from 6 to 23
33. True
34. Sparky
35. Cumbria
36. Scamp and Angel
37. 350mm (14in) at the withers

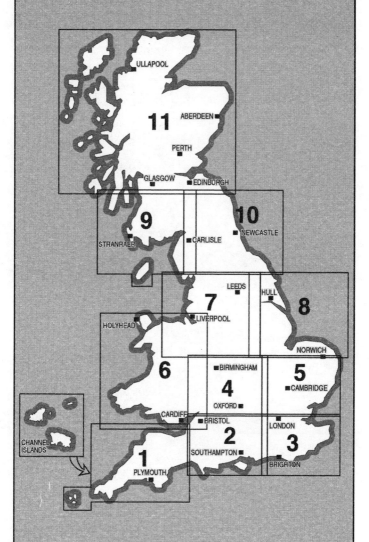

Key to map areas

ULLAPOOL

11 ABERDEEN

PERTH

GLASGOW EDINBURGH

9 **10** NEWCASTLE

STRANRAER CARLISLE

LEEDS HULL

7 **8**

HOLYHEAD LIVERPOOL

6 BIRMINGHAM

4 **5** CAMBRIDGE

OXFORD

CARDIFF

BRISTOL **2** LONDON

3

SOUTHAMPTON BRIGHTON

CHANNEL ISLANDS

1 PLYMOUTH

Reference to sectional maps

═══	Motorway	● **Totnes**	Dog friendly pub
───	Major road	◉ **Lynton**	Dog friendly accommodation
- - -	County boundary	■ **BODMIN**	Place name to assist location

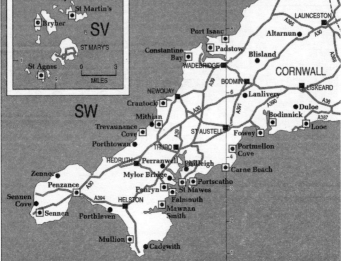

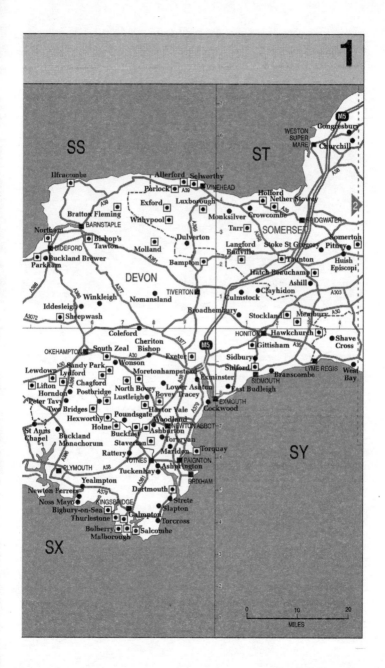

2

OXON

WANTAGE
Turville
Skirmett
Cholsey
Bovingdon Green
Marlow
Hedgerley
M40
Remenham
Taplow
East Ilsley
Streatley
Maidenhead
Aldworth
Shiplake
Dorney
M4
Ruscombe
M4
Ramsbury
Winterbourne
Stanford Dingley
READING
BERKSHIRE
A4
Hungerford
NEWBURY
A4
Shinfield
M3
Inkpen
Bagshot
Camberley
WOKING
Lower Chute
Hurstbourne Tarrant
SU
A339
Farnborough
SURREY
A342
ANDOVER
BASINGSTOKE
A30
M3
FARNHAM
GUILDFORD
Wherwell
Lower Wield
Bentworth
Charleshill
Easling
Longstock
HAMPSHIRE
Chawton
Haslemere
Stockbridge
Littleton
Ovington
Hawkley
Sparsholt
Easton
Tichborne
Winchester
Cheriton
Braishfield
A3090
Petersfield
Trotton
A272
Elsted
Petworth
Ower
M27
Chilgrove
WEST SUSSEX
M271
SOUTHAMPTON
Singleton
A31
Rowland's Castle
Charlton
LYNDHURST
A27
M27
East Ashling
Climping
Brockenhurst
FAREHAM
A3(M)
Chichester
M275
Lymington
GOSPORT
PORTSMOUTH
BOGNOR REGIS
COWES
Milford on Sea
Seaview
Shalfleet
NEWPORT
Yarmouth
A3054
Bembridge
Totland
Freshwater
ISLE OF WIGHT
Hulverstone
SANDOWN
SHANKLIN
A3055
Bonchurch
SZ
Ventnor

0   5   10
MILES

3

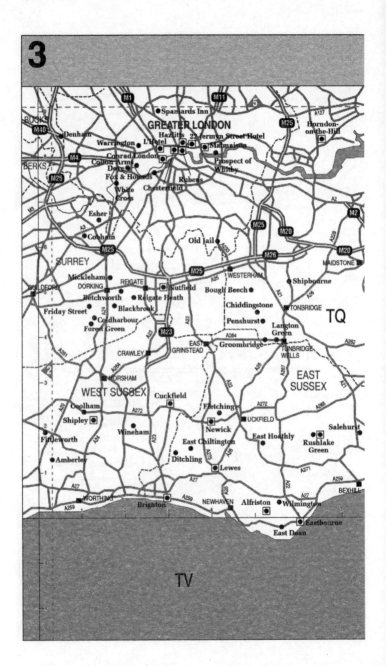

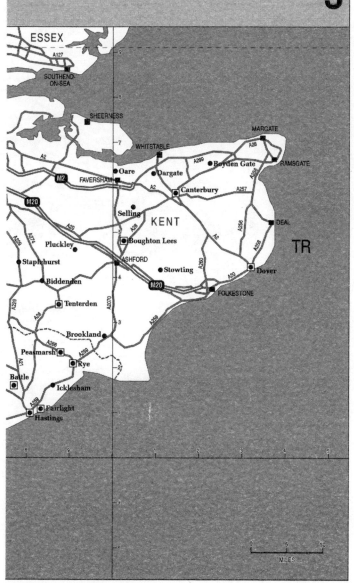

3

ESSEX

A127

SOUTHEND-ON-SEA

SHEERNESS

MARGATE

WHITSTABLE

A28

A2

A299 Boyden Gate

RAMSGATE

M2 FAVERSHAM ● Oare Dargate

A2

A256

● Canterbury

A257

M20

Selling

KENT

A20

A28

A2

A256

DEAL

A274

Pluckley

● Boughton Lees

TR

A229

● Staplehurst

ASHFORD

A20

A260

A256

● Biddenden

M20

● Stowting

A20

● Dover

A229

A28

□ Tenterden

A3070

M20

FOLKESTONE

3

A259

Brookland ●

A266

● Peasmarsh

A259

□ Rye

2

A21

● Battle

● Icklesham

1

A259

□ Fairlight

● Hastings

6   5   1   2   3   4   5

9

8

0   5   10
MILES

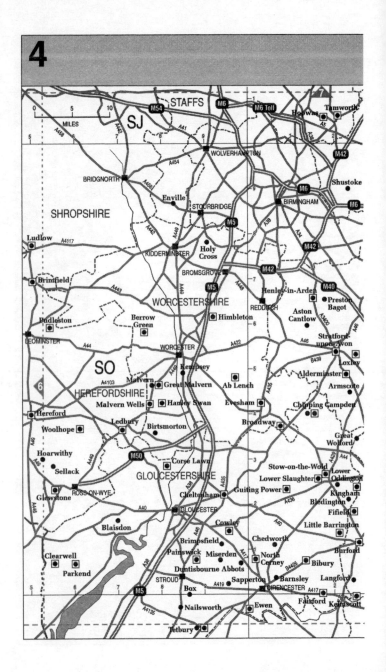

4

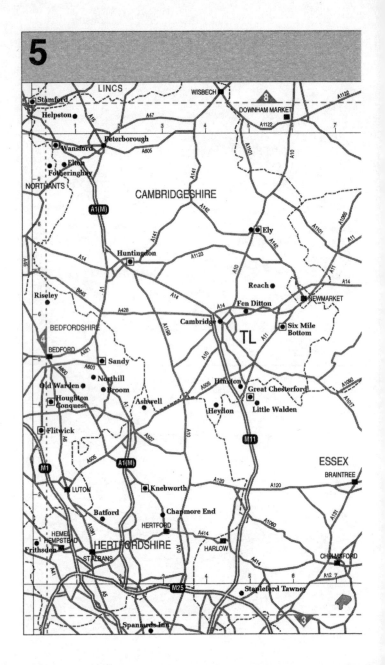

LINCS
WISBECH
A1122
Stamford
Helpston
DOWNHAM MARKET
A1122
A47
A605
Peterborough
A1101
A10
Wansford
Elton
Fotheringhay
CAMBRIDGESHIRE
A1(M)
NORTHANTS
A141
A142
Ely
A1101
A1065
A142
A11
A141
A14
Huntingdon
A1123
A10
Reach
A14
NEWMARKET
A14
A1
B645
Riseley
Fen Ditton
A428
A14
Cambridge
A11
Six Mile
Bottom
BEDFORDSHIRE
A1198
TL
A421
BEDFORD
A600
A10
Sandy
A603
Old Warden
Northill
Broom
A505
Hinxton
Great Chesterford
A1092
A1017
Houghton
Conquest
Ashwell
Heydon
Little Walden
A6
Flitwick
A505
A10
M11
A1(M)
M1
ESSEX
M25
BRAINTREE
LUTON
Knebworth
A120
A120
A151
Batford
Chapmore End
A1081
A1060
HERTFORD
A414
HEMEL
HEMPSTEAD
HERTFORDSHIRE
A10
HARLOW
CHELMSFORD
Frithsden
A414
A41
ST ALBANS
A12
A5
M25
Stapleford Tawney
Spaniards Inn

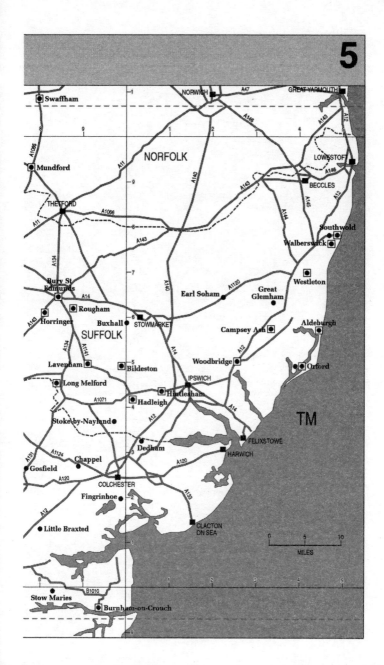

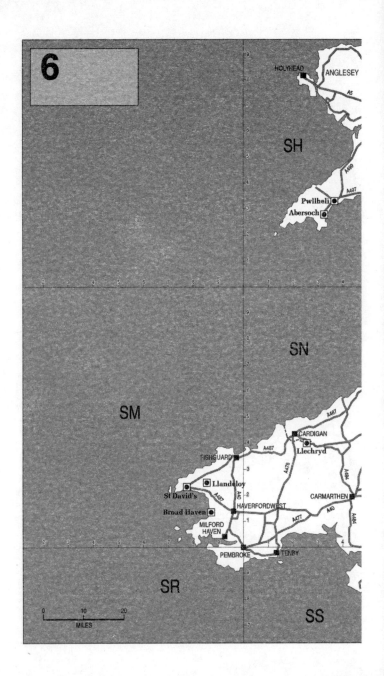

6

HOLYHEAD ANGLESEY
A5

SH

A499
A497
Pwllheli
Abersoch

SN

SM

A487
CARDIGAN
A487
Llechryd
FISHGUARD
A478
A487
Llandeloy
A484
St David's
CARMARTHEN
A40
Broad Haven
HAVERFORDWEST
A484
MILFORD
HAVEN
A477
A40

PEMBROKE
TENBY

SR

SS

0   10   20
MILES

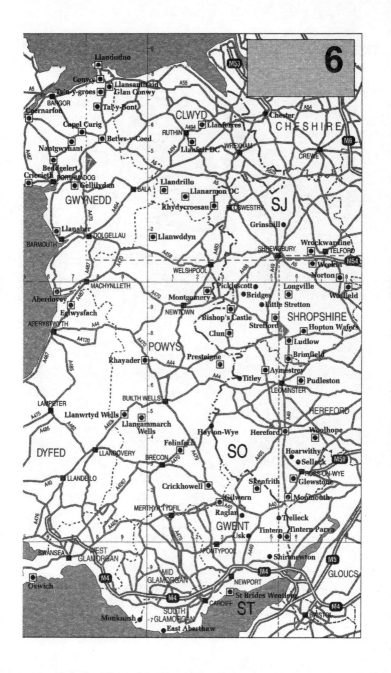

7

9
Cartmel
Ulverston
Cowan Bridge
A590
BARROW-IN-FURNESS
Yealand Conyers
A683
A65
M6
LANCASTER
SD
Long Preston
LANCASHIRE
0
10
20
MILES
Whitewell
Chipping
A6
A59
Great Mitton
Little Eccleston
Hurst Green
Blackpool
BLACKBURN
M55
Mellor
A584
PRESTON
M65
Whealton
A565
A581
SOUTHPORT
Bromley Cross
BURY
Bispham Green
M61
A5209
GREATER MANCHESTER
SKELMERSDALE
M58
M60
MERSEYSIDE
A580
LIVERPOOL
M62
BIRKENHEAD
M53
M56
Llandudno
Mobberley
Conwy
Llansanffraid Glan Conwy
A55
Knutsford
A537
CHESHIRE
A49
Ty'n-y-groes
Tal-y-Bont
A470
FLINTSHIRE
Hoole
A54
Peover Heath
Chester
A51
Tarporley
A525
Llanferres
A494
Beeston
A530
DENBIGHSHIRE
Aldford
Bunbury
A5
RUTHIN
Higher Burwardsley
Worleston
Betws-y-Coed
Llanfair DC
Fullers Moor
CREWE
Barthomley
WREXHAM
Wrenbury
A500
SJ
Bickley Moss
Betley
Aston
WHITCHURCH
Llandrillo
A41
A53
BALA
Llanarmon DC
OSWESTRY
A528
6
GWYNEDD
Rhydycroesau
Burlton
POWYS
Knockin
Grinshill
A494
Chetwynd Aston
A518
SHROPSHIRE
DOLGELLAU
Llanwddyn
A495
A483
Wrockwardine
SHREWSBURY
TELFORD

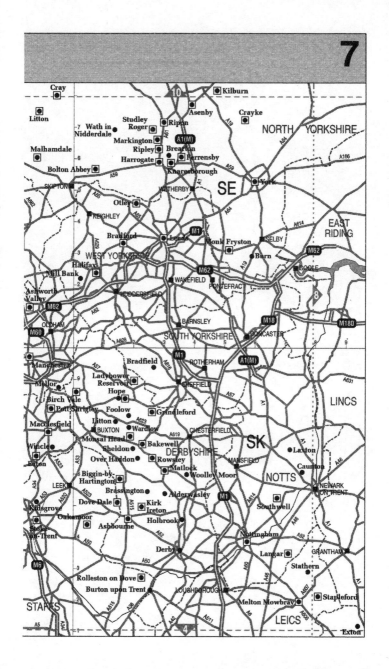

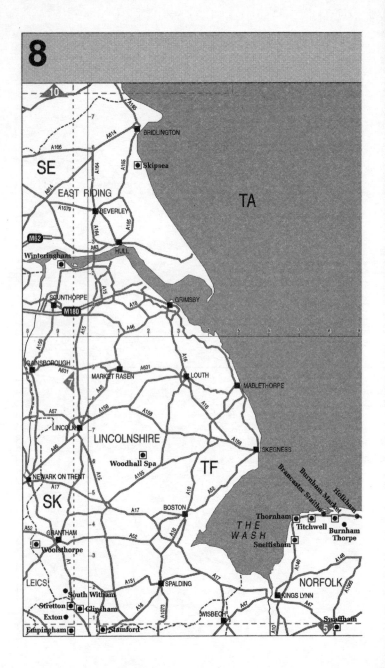

8

MILES

NORTH

SEA

TG

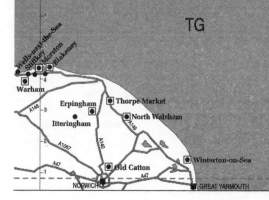

Wells-next-the-Sea
Stiffkey
Morston
Blakeney

Warham

Erpingham
Thorpe Market
North Walsham
Itteringham

Old Catton
Winterton-on-Sea

NORWICH
GREAT YARMOUTH

9

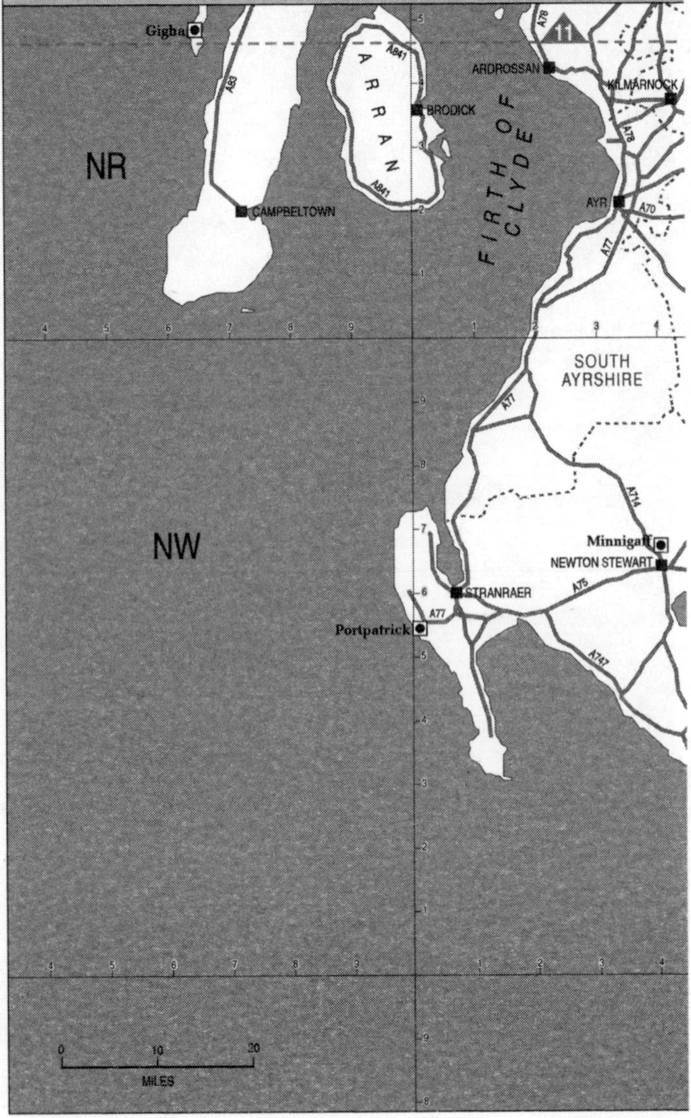

Gigha

ARRAN

A841

ARDROSSAN

KILMARNOCK

A78

A93

BRODICK

NR

A841

FIRTH OF CLYDE

AYR

A70

A77

CAMPBELTOWN

3

4

SOUTH
AYRSHIRE

A77

A714

NW

7

Minnigaff

NEWTON STEWART

6

STRANRAER

A75

Portpatrick

A77

5

A747

4

3

2

1

0   10   20
     MILES

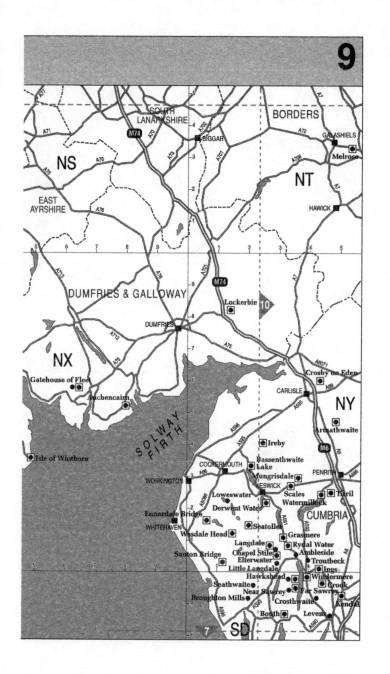

BERWICK-UPON-TWEED

COLDSTREAM
Cornhill-on-Tweed
Crookham

GALASHIELS
Innerleithen · Melrose · Kelso

Lucker

NT

Newton-by-the-Sea

BORDERS

JEDBURGH
Kirk Yetholm

HAWICK

Rothbury
Longframlington
Weldon Bridge

DUMFRIES
&
GALLOWAY

Longhorsley
MORPETH

NORTHUMBERLAND

M74

Wark

Crosby on
Eden

Newcastle
upon Tyne

CORBRIDGE

CARLISLE

HEXHAM

NY

Blanchland
Carterway Heads

M6

Armathwaite
Alston

DURHAM

Great Salkeld

A1(M)

Mungrisdale
Scales

DURHAM

PENRITH
Brampton

BISHOP AUCKLAND

KESWICK
Derwent Water

Yanwath
Watermillock

Romaldkirk

Headlam

Grasmere
Langdale
Rydal Water
Elterwater
Ambleside
Little Langdale

Appleby

BROUGH
Sandford

DARLINGTON

Greta Bridge

SCOTCH
CORNER

Chapel
Stile
Hawkshead
Far Sawrey
Near
Sawrey

Troutbeck
Ings
Windermere
Crook

CUMBRIA

M6

Reeth
Richmond

NORTH

Bowth
Levens

Crosthwaite
Kendal

Sedbusk
Grinton

Constable
Burton

Barbon

Bainbridge
Middleham
East Witton

SD

Thornton Watlass

10

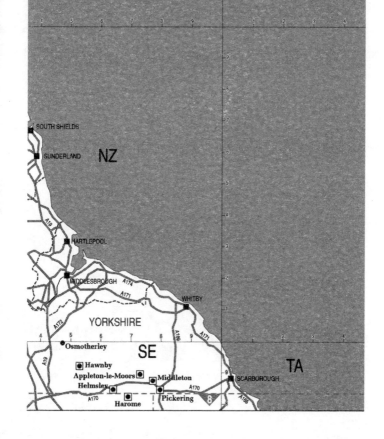

NU

N O R T H

S E A

NZ

SOUTH SHIELDS

SUNDERLAND

HARTLEPOOL

MIDDLESBROUGH   A174

A171

WHITBY

YORKSHIRE

A169   A171

SE

Osmotherley

TA

Hawnby

Appleton-le-Moors   Middleton

SCARBOROUGH

Helmsley

A170

A170

Harome   Pickering   **8**

A19

A172

A19

0   10   20
MILES

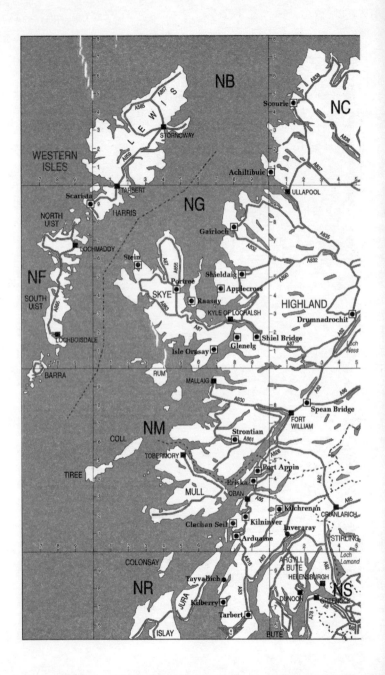

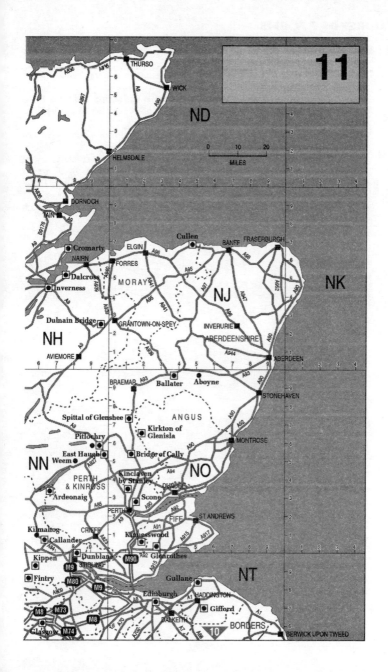

11

ND

NK

NJ

NH

NN

NO

NT

0   10   20
MILES

THURSO
WICK
HELMSDALE
DORNOCH
TAIN
Cromarty
ELGIN
Cullen
BANFF
FRASERBURGH
NAIRN
FORRES
Dalcross
Inverness
MORAY
Dulnain Bridge
GRANTOWN-ON-SPEY
INVERURIE
ABERDEENSHIRE
AVIEMORE
ABERDEEN
BRAEMAR
Ballater
Aboyne
STONEHAVEN
Spittal of Glenshee
ANGUS
Kirkton of
Glenisla
Pitlochry
MONTROSE
East Haugh
Weem
Bridge of Cally
Kinclaven
by Stanley
PERTH
& KINROSS
A94
DUNDEE
Scone
Ardeonaig
PERTH
ST ANDREWS
Kilmallog
CRIEFF
FIFE
Callander
Kinnesswood
Kippen
Dunblane
M90
Glenrothes
STIRLING
Fintry
M9
M80
Gullane
NT
M9
Edinburgh
HADDINGTON
M8
M73
Gifford
M8
DALKEITH
BORDERS
Glasgow
M74
10
BERWICK UPON TWEED

REPORT FORMS

Please report to us: you can use the tear-out forms in this book, or write on plain paper to our freepost address, The Good Pub Guide, FREEPOST TN1569, WADHURST, East Sussex TN5 7BR. Alternatively you can email us at dogs@goodguides.com.

We need to know what you think of the places in this edition, and we need to know about other places you think are worthy of inclusion. It would be helpful to know about ones that should not be included.

Please tell us how welcome you felt with your dog, and about any special facilities or welcoming touches that were provided for your dog.

The atmosphere and character are very important features – so please try to describe what is special about a place. And we need to know about any changes in décor and furnishings, too. Food and drinks are also important, and if you have stayed overnight, please tell us about the standard of accommodation.

It helps enormously if you can give the full address for anywhere new, though just its postcode is very helpful.

Though we try to answer all letters, please understand if there's a delay (particularly in summer, our busiest period).

I have been to the following places in *The Good Guide to Dog Friendly Pubs, Hotels and B&Bs*, and found them as described, and confirm that they deserve continued inclusion:

continued overleaf
PLEASE GIVE YOUR NAME AND ADDRESS ON THE BACK OF THIS FORM

Establishments visited continued..........

By returning this form, you consent to the collection, recording and use of the information you submit, by The Random House Group Ltd. Any personal details which you provide from which we can identify you are held and processed in accordance with the Data Protection Act 1998 and will not be passed on to any third parties.

The Random House Group Ltd may wish to send you further information on their associated products. Please tick box if you do not wish to receive any such information.

Your own name and address *(block capitals please)*

In returning this form I confirm my agreement that the information I provide may be used by The Random House Group Ltd, its assignees and/or licensees in any media or medium whatsoever.

Please return to
The Good Pub Guide,
FREEPOST TN1569,
WADHURST,
East Sussex
TN5 7BR

I have been to the following places in *The Good Guide to Dog Friendly Pubs, Hotels and B&Bs,* **and found them as described, and confirm that they deserve continued inclusion:**

continued overleaf
PLEASE GIVE YOUR NAME AND ADDRESS ON THE BACK OF THIS FORM

Establishments visited continued..........

....

By returning this form, you consent to the collection, recording and use of the information you submit, by The Random House Group Ltd. Any personal details which you provide from which we can identify you are held and processed in accordance with the Data Protection Act 1998 and will not be passed on to any third parties.

The Random House Group Ltd may wish to send you further information on their associated products. Please tick box if you do not wish to receive any such information. ☐

....

Your own name and address *(block capitals please)*

....

....

....

....

In returning this form I confirm my agreement that the information I provide may be used by The Random House Group Ltd, its assignees and/or licensees in any media or medium whatsoever.

....

Please return to
The Good Pub Guide,
FREEPOST TN1569,
WADHURST,
East Sussex
TN5 7BR

REPORT ON _(Establishment's name)_

Establishment's address

☐ **YES**, My dog was welcome   ☐ **NO**, My dog was not welcome
Please tick one of these boxes to show your verdict, and give reasons,
descriptive comments, prices and the date of your visit

PLEASE GIVE YOUR NAME AND ADDRESS ON THE BACK OF THIS FORM

REPORT ON _(Establishment's name)_

Establishment's address

☐ **YES**, My dog was welcome   ☐ **NO**, My dog was not welcome
Please tick one of these boxes to show your verdict, and give reasons,
descriptive comments, prices and the date of your visit

PLEASE GIVE YOUR NAME AND ADDRESS ON THE BACK OF THIS FORM

Your own name and address *(block capitals please)*
In returning this form I confirm my agreement that the information I provide
may be used by The Random House Group Ltd, its assignees and/or licensees
in any media or medium whatsoever.

DO NOT USE THIS SIDE OF THE PAGE FOR
WRITING ABOUT PUBS

By returning this form, you consent to the collection, recording and use
of the information you submit, by The Random House Group Ltd. Any
personal details which you provide from which we can identify you are held
and processed in accordance with the Data Protection Act 1998 and will not
be passed on to any third parties. The Random House Group Ltd may wish
to send you further information on their associated products. Please tick
box if you do not wish to receive any such information.

Your own name and address *(block capitals please)*
In returning this form I confirm my agreement that the information I provide
may be used by The Random House Group Ltd, its assignees and/or licensees
in any media or medium whatsoever.

DO NOT USE THIS SIDE OF THE PAGE FOR
WRITING ABOUT PUBS

By returning this form, you consent to the collection, recording and use
of the information you submit, by The Random House Group Ltd. Any
personal details which you provide from which we can identify you are held
and processed in accordance with the Data Protection Act 1998 and will not
be passed on to any third parties. The Random House Group Ltd may wish
to send you further information on their associated products. Please tick
box if you do not wish to receive any such information.

REPORT ON   *(Establishment's name)*

....

Establishment's address

....

☐ **YES**, My dog was welcome   ☐ **NO**, My dog was not welcome

Please tick one of these boxes to show your verdict, and give reasons,
descriptive comments, prices and the date of your visit

PLEASE GIVE YOUR NAME AND ADDRESS ON THE BACK OF THIS FORM

REPORT ON   *(Establishment's name)*

....

Establishment's address

....

☐ **YES**, My dog was welcome   ☐ **NO**, My dog was not welcome

Please tick one of these boxes to show your verdict, and give reasons,
descriptive comments, prices and the date of your visit

PLEASE GIVE YOUR NAME AND ADDRESS ON THE BACK OF THIS FORM

Your own name and address *(block capitals please)*
In returning this form I confirm my agreement that the information I provide
may be used by The Random House Group Ltd, its assignees and/or licensees
in any media or medium whatsoever.

DO NOT USE THIS SIDE OF THE PAGE FOR
WRITING ABOUT PUBS

By returning this form, you consent to the collection, recording and use
of the information you submit, by The Random House Group Ltd. Any
personal details which you provide from which we can identify you are held
and processed in accordance with the Data Protection Act 1998 and will not
be passed on to any third parties. The Random House Group Ltd may wish
to send you further information on their associated products. Please tick
box if you do not wish to receive any such information. ☐

Your own name and address *(block capitals please)*
In returning this form I confirm my agreement that the information I provide
may be used by The Random House Group Ltd, its assignees and/or licensees
in any media or medium whatsoever.

DO NOT USE THIS SIDE OF THE PAGE FOR
WRITING ABOUT PUBS

By returning this form, you consent to the collection, recording and use
of the information you submit, by The Random House Group Ltd. Any
personal details which you provide from which we can identify you are held
and processed in accordance with the Data Protection Act 1998 and will not
be passed on to any third parties. The Random House Group Ltd may wish
to send you further information on their associated products. Please tick
box if you do not wish to receive any such information. ☐

REPORT ON *(Establishment's name)*

....

Establishment's address

....

☐ **YES**, My dog was welcome ☐ **NO**, My dog was not welcome

Please tick one of these boxes to show your verdict, and give reasons, descriptive comments, prices and the date of your visit

PLEASE GIVE YOUR NAME AND ADDRESS ON THE BACK OF THIS FORM

REPORT ON *(Establishment's name)*

....

Establishment's address

....

☐ **YES**, My dog was welcome ☐ **NO**, My dog was not welcome

Please tick one of these boxes to show your verdict, and give reasons, descriptive comments, prices and the date of your visit

PLEASE GIVE YOUR NAME AND ADDRESS ON THE BACK OF THIS FORM

Your own name and address *(block capitals please)*
In returning this form I confirm my agreement that the information I provide
may be used by The Random House Group Ltd, its assignees and/or licensees
in any media or medium whatsoever.

DO NOT USE THIS SIDE OF THE PAGE FOR WRITING ABOUT PUBS

By returning this form, you consent to the collection, recording and use
of the information you submit, by The Random House Group Ltd. Any
personal details which you provide from which we can identify you are held
and processed in accordance with the Data Protection Act 1998 and will not
be passed on to any third parties. The Random House Group Ltd may wish
to send you further information on their associated products. Please tick
box if you do not wish to receive any such information. ☐

Your own name and address *(block capitals please)*
In returning this form I confirm my agreement that the information I provide
may be used by The Random House Group Ltd, its assignees and/or licensees
in any media or medium whatsoever.

DO NOT USE THIS SIDE OF THE PAGE FOR WRITING ABOUT PUBS

By returning this form, you consent to the collection, recording and use
of the information you submit, by The Random House Group Ltd. Any
personal details which you provide from which we can identify you are held
and processed in accordance with the Data Protection Act 1998 and will not
be passed on to any third parties. The Random House Group Ltd may wish
to send you further information on their associated products. Please tick
box if you do not wish to receive any such information. ☐

REPORT ON   *(Establishment's name)*

Establishment's address

☐ **YES**, My dog was welcome   ☐ **NO**, My dog was not welcome

Please tick one of these boxes to show your verdict, and give reasons,
descriptive comments, prices and the date of your visit

PLEASE GIVE YOUR NAME AND ADDRESS ON THE BACK OF THIS FORM

REPORT ON   *(Establishment's name)*

Establishment's address

☐ **YES**, My dog was welcome   ☐ **NO**, My dog was not welcome

Please tick one of these boxes to show your verdict, and give reasons,
descriptive comments, prices and the date of your visit

PLEASE GIVE YOUR NAME AND ADDRESS ON THE BACK OF THIS FORM

Your own name and address *(block capitals please)*

In returning this form I confirm my agreement that the information I provide may be used by The Random House Group Ltd, its assignees and/or licensees in any media or medium whatsoever.

DO NOT USE THIS SIDE OF THE PAGE FOR WRITING ABOUT PUBS

By returning this form, you consent to the collection, recording and use of the information you submit, by The Random House Group Ltd. Any personal details which you provide from which we can identify you are held and processed in accordance with the Data Protection Act 1998 and will not be passed on to any third parties. The Random House Group Ltd may wish to send you further information on their associated products. Please tick box if you do not wish to receive any such information. ☐

Your own name and address *(block capitals please)*

In returning this form I confirm my agreement that the information I provide may be used by The Random House Group Ltd, its assignees and/or licensees in any media or medium whatsoever.

DO NOT USE THIS SIDE OF THE PAGE FOR WRITING ABOUT PUBS

By returning this form, you consent to the collection, recording and use of the information you submit, by The Random House Group Ltd. Any personal details which you provide from which we can identify you are held and processed in accordance with the Data Protection Act 1998 and will not be passed on to any third parties. The Random House Group Ltd may wish to send you further information on their associated products. Please tick box if you do not wish to receive any such information. ☐